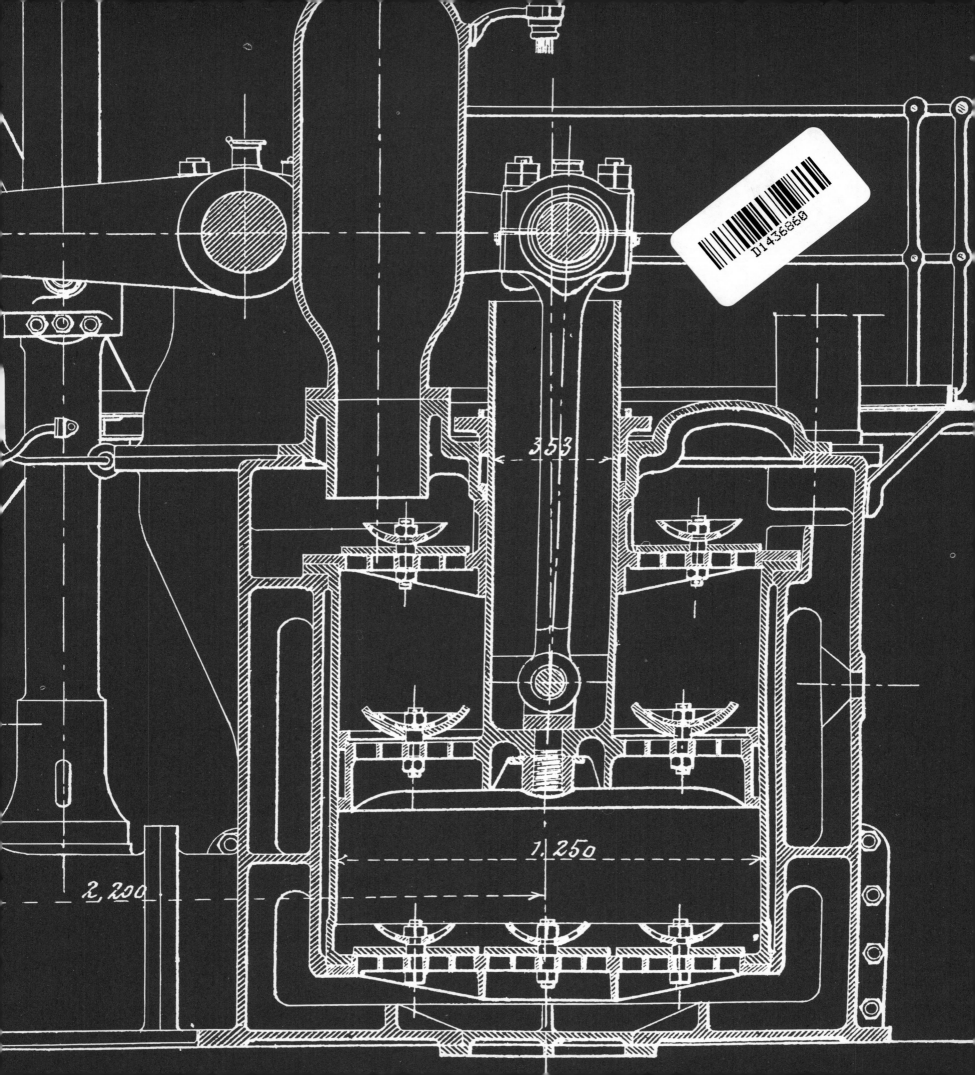

MACHINES
AN ILLUSTRATED HISTORY

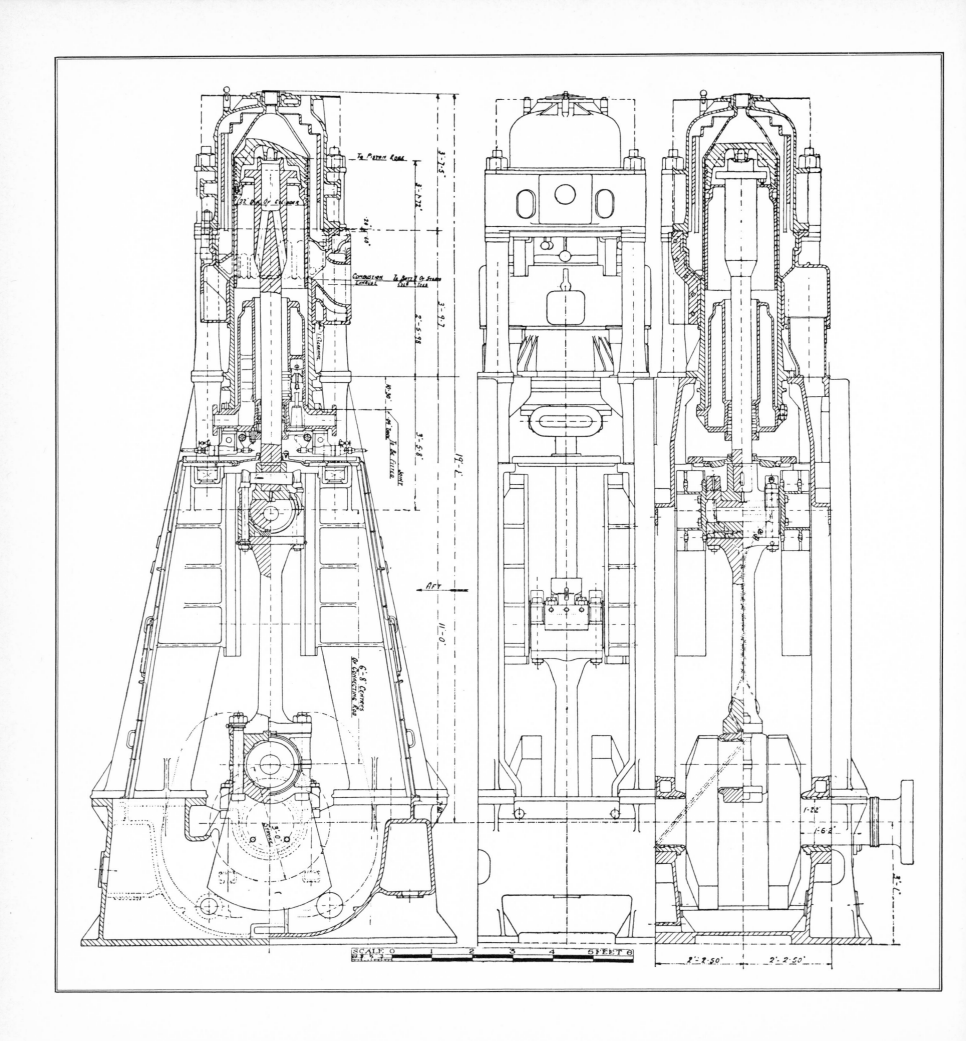

SCALE 0   1   2   3   4   5 FEET 6

MACHINES

AN ILLUSTRATED HISTORY

SIGVARD STRANDH

MITCHELL
ARTISTS
HOUSE
BEAZLEY

MACHINES has been designed and produced by AB Nordbok, Gothenburg, Sweden, under the supervision of Einar Engelbrektson and Turlough Johnston.

Graphical design and colour: Tommy Berglund.

Artwork: Syed Mumtaz Ahmad, Tommy Berglund, Inger Eriksson, Marie Falksten, Ferenc Flamm, Annette Johansson, Lars Jödahl, Hans Linder, Elise Lundqvist, Lennart Molin, Yusuke Nagano, Holger Rosenblad, Ulf Söderqvist, Roland Thorbjörnsson.

Translator: Ann Henning.

Lithographics: Nils Hermansson and Annette Johansson.

Editors: Turlough Johnston, Kerstin Stålbrand.

Assistant editors: Jeremy Franks, Donovan O'Malley.

Nordbok would like to express warm thanks to the following for their advice and assistance: Curt Falkemo, Jan Hult, William T. O'Dea, Holger Rosenblad, and Per Hedelin.

Further, Nordbok would like to thank the following for providing illustration research material or illustration material: Lars Harry Jenneborg, p. 8 ill. 2; Mary Evans Picture Library, p. 9 ill. 9, p. 131 B; P. Haase & Søns Forlag, p. 36 A–C, p. 37 A, B, p. 42 B–D; Derek de Solla Price, p. 46 A; Cambridge University Press, p. 47 C; Almqvist & Wiksell/Focus, p. 51 G; Denny Lorentzen, p. 88 ill. 1, 2; Ronan Picture Library, p. 141 C ill. 3, p. 231 C; Daimler Benz Museum, Stuttgart, p. 146–147 B; Marshall Cavendish, p. 146–147 B, p. 183 D, p. 196 B, p. 211 D, p. 223 D, E, p. 231 E; Teknisk Tidskrift, p. 166 B ill. 1, 2, p. 166 C ill. 1, 2; Chalmers Institution of Information Theory, p. 198; Motor, p. 201 B; P. A. Norstedts förlag, p. 208 A, B; Science Museum, p. 220 B, C, p. 220–221 E; Electrolux, p. 226 C; AEG, p. 232–233 A, C, D, E.

MACHINES
World copyright © 1979 AB Nordbok, Gothenburg, Sweden.

This edition published in the U.K. in 1979 by Artists House, Mitchell Beazley Marketing Ltd., Artists House, 14–15 Manette Street, London W1V 5 LB.

ISBN 0 86134 012 4

Typeset by Rotogravyr, Solna, Sweden.

Printed and bound in Italy.

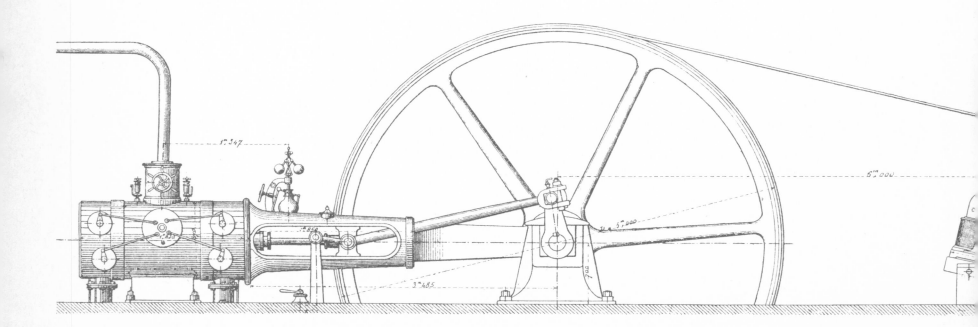

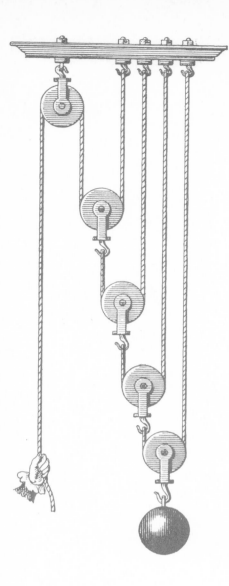

CONTENTS

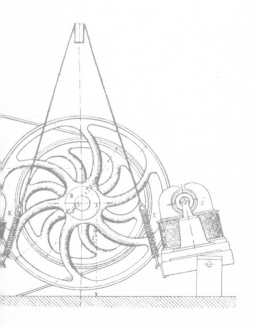

PREFACE

This book is about *machines*, and although this not-easily defined term has been generously interpreted, the machines discussed have been chosen subjectively and arbitrarily. The book is, then, not a comprehensive treatment of the whole field of study, a matter that has anyway become an impossibility. The French encyclopaedists of the latter part of the eighteenth century required thirty-five folio volumes to achieve an essentially complete description of the techniques of contemporary engineering, the natural sciences, and the arts. It is fruitless to speculate about the number of volumes that might be required in order to achieve the same result today.

The book does not, however, concern itself with the evaluation of technology, for all that this is currently in vogue throughout the western world. In my opinion, the writing of history should be clearly distinguished from polemics. Leopold von Ranke commented that the historical method should describe "how things actually occurred"; if this principle be applied in a history of machines, it is possible, by reading the text—and between its lines—to appreciate how technology has dominated the growth of both material well-being and non-material values. Technology has become more and more a carrier of culture and a powerfull instrument in fostering democracy—as it was even before the fall of the Bastille.

Is this to say, then, that the machine is to be regarded as wholly beneficial? Melvin Kranzberg, the American historian of technology, has hit the nail on the head in forming what he calls Kranzberg's First Law: "Technology is neither positive, negative, nor neutral". Professor Kranzberg may be interpreted as wishing to emphasize that while it is intrinsically neither good nor evil, technology is always present, in the midst of things. Since at least the eighteenth century, machine technology has attracted critics who have questioned its development—the first "fire and air" engines provoked reactions in many quarters that resemble the resistance to nuclear energy expressed two hundred years later. At the beginning of the nineteenth century, in England, the Luddites broke up machines that they feared would destroy their livelihood, and a little later, the railway met with scepsis of one sort and another, both in England and elsewhere.

In public debate over the past two centuries, criticism of machines has alternated with an optimistic faith in the machine's future. In the 1960s, the criticism became powerfully adverse, not only in alarm reports, such as Rachel Carson's *Silent Spring* (1961) and Ralph Nader's *Unsafe at Any Speed* (1966), but also in more general works, of which Jacques Ellul's *The Technological Society* is an example. Published in English translation in 1964, its original publication in French in 1954 had attracted practically no attention outside France. Ellul, a lawyer and social scientist, defines technology as not merely machines and techniques, but also all that they have entailed in the way of organization and methods. Having embraced so much in his definition, Ellul condemns this technology for losing control over itself, to the extent of being self-generating to the point where the means of technology have become an end in themselves. Ellul's thesis is that this leads to a condition that is inhuman, because moral values have been eradicated. But is not this appalling perspective already upon us? What if the roles were reversed, so that a technologist, as Ellul would call him, were to attack the judicial apparatus with definitions as all-embracing as Ellul's definition of technology? In countries with high income taxation many regard the politico-administrative rule-by-decree as self-generating and destructive of morals. Both the alarmist and the social philosopher in the spirit of Ellul ignore the fact that machines, in the wider meaning applied in this book, have raised the quality of life, making it easier for us to live in a style that could not have been dreamt of a hundred years ago, even by the most progress-enamoured optimist. This is not to say that I regard "Ellulian" and other criticism of machines as without interest: on the contrary, criticism in its different forms has a vital function in a democratic society, but it can, like the other elements that help to form democracy, lose control over itself. The remedy? One might be to meditate on the talmudic saying, that we do not see things as they are, but as we are.

What is particularly positive today are the powerful movements within the world of technology itself that are striving in a scientific manner towards the goal of "seeing things as they are". This is especially obvious in technology assessment and consequence evaluation of new techniques. The former implies, in fact, that a newly developed technique that is to be launched be first tested by adding to the previously dominating technical-economic parameters others that take account of, for example, repercussions on employment and society at large; in other words, technology is assessed for its effects on the lives of individual people. Consequence evaluation is much the same thing but takes a longer, broader view of inherent risks; much attention has been paid to the function of computer technology, for example in the employment market and in society as a whole, especially taking into account the current, explosive growth of the use of microprocessors. It has become apparent how vital it is to "look before one leaps" when introducing new technology.

Contemporary technology and the natural sciences provide methods and means of correcting development that has run amok. Many examples may be found in environmental engineering, where new processes and routines have rapidly been developed, since it became clear how industrial and urban growth have blighted the natural world. Recent years have seen marked improvements here, both within industry and in matters affecting its contamination of air and water. This book presents some of the techniques that have been used to protect the environment, perhaps primarily to exemplify that concern for the environment was not something brought about by the alarms of the 1960s. Environmental engineering has a history covering several hundred years.

While working on this book, I have greatly enjoyed the help and encouragement given me by many people, who have generously supported me by word and deed. I must thank first my colleagues at the National Museum of Science and Technology, particularly Inga-Britta Sandqvist, archivist. I am particularly grateful, too, to the staffs of the Deutsches Museum in Munich and the Science Museum in London, and to Dr. Brooke Hindle of the Smithsonian Institution in Washington. Dr. Wilhelm Odelberg, Principal Librarian of the Royal Academy of Science, Stockholm, has generously made his wide knowledge of scientific literature available to me. Professor C. G. Nilsson in Luleå has constantly assisted my work by stimulating discussions of problems both large and small. My gratitude extends, naturally, to the members of my family, who have made my work easier in every way. I owe a particular debt to my wife, Eivor, who has, in addition to taking care of the typing, never ceased to encourage me, and Christin and Ricky have helped by their discussion and criticism. Ricky's sketches and drawings—produced with great panache—have been a constant source of inspiration and pleasure, and a couple have inspired illustrations in the book.

Cooperation with Nordbok has been particularly inspiring and congenial during the whole period of production. My warm thanks to all at Nordbok—no one named, no one forgotten!

Sigvard Strandh

CHAPTER 1
WITHOUT TOOLS, NO MACHINES

I n one of his many essays the great American statesman-scientist Benjamin Franklin suggested that man is a tool-making animal. It is, he wrote, man's ability to manufacture tools that distinguishes him from the other animals. The study of human culture, both material and spiritual, is a fascinating subject, all the more so if we use as our starting-point the thought-provoking and dynamic combination of Franklin's manufacturing man, *Homo faber*, and Linnaeus's thinking man, *Homo sapiens*, and follow this from the time of man's first appearance, maybe a million years ago.

In the following chapters we shall examine some of the lines of development that have led from that time to the present day, with its host of machines of all kinds. These lines have never been straight and uncomplicated but have often wandered off on perplexing deviations. Our investigation will be further confused by the great number of ideas and inventions which, being born before their time, came to nought.

The origins of the vast multitude of today's machines can be found in the tools and implements fashioned in the dawn of history by *Homo sapiens faber*, our thinking, tool-making ancestor. Of course, it is a matter of definition whether or not the tools made by the early primates can be called machines. The only prime mover (a machine generating or, rather, converting energy) available to early man was his own muscle power. His tools and implements may be regarded as a reinforcement or extension of that power.

The German for "fist" is *Faust*, and in the sixteenth century, German miners used to call a sledge-hammer *Fäustling* (a "fister", as it might be called in English). This combination of arm and sledge-hammer has been called organ projection by the German scholar Ernst Kapp, who is often called the metaphysician of technology. In the hands of the miner, the "fister" was an extension of the muscle power he used to break ore from the bedrock. This combination of hand and "fister" might, perhaps, be regarded as a working machine, i.e., a machine which performs a special type of work.

What, then, is a machine? An oft-quoted definition is that formulated by a German engineer, Franz Reuleaux (1829–1905): "A machine is a combination of solid bodies, so arranged as to compel the mechanical forces of nature to perform work as a result of certain determinative movements."

This technically subtle definition does not really do very much towards clarifying the concept of a machine. It has recurred in many works of reference and has often aroused controversy. For instance, it has been asserted that the phrase "mechanical forces of nature" must exclude the large group of machines which are driven by human and animal muscle power, with the inevitable retort that these creatures must be regarded as part of nature! We, however, can set aside both the definition and the objections to it with an easy conscience and, instead, illustrate in more concrete terms what

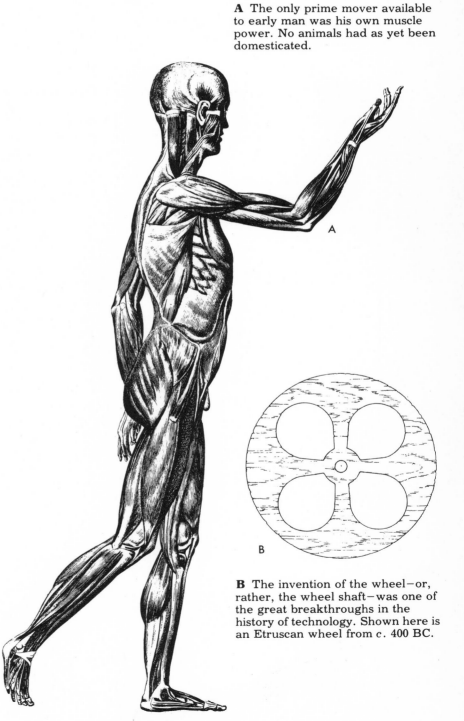

A The only prime mover available to early man was his own muscle power. No animals had as yet been domesticated.

B The invention of the wheel—or, rather, the wheel shaft—was one of the great breakthroughs in the history of technology. Shown here is an Etruscan wheel from *c.* 400 BC.

Today, it is generally believed that Earth as a planet has existed for about 4,500 million years. In order to gain perspective on this incomprehensibly long period of time, we can compare it to a flight from New York to London, a distance of almost 3,000 miles (5,000 km). Each mile will then represent a period of about 1.5 million years, while each kilometre will correspond to a period of about a million years.

As the aeroplane takes off from New York's Kennedy Airport, Earth has just come into existence and is still fluid. Only when the aeroplane has covered 900 miles (1,500 km) of its trip (1) has the crust solidified to a certain extent, and not until another 300 miles (500 km) have been covered do what are considered to be the first living creatures appear – blue-green algae, which feed on inorganic matter. After 2,400 miles (4,000 km), when

approximately one-fifth of the distance remains (2), the first green algae appear. Here, they are represented by *Diplopora phanerospora*; (*a*) section, seen from above, (*b*) side view. The outer lime cover has been removed from the upper part of the alga.

We are now rapidly approaching the destination of our journey, Heathrow Airport in London. When London is 300 miles (500 km) away (3), a multitude of invertebrates appears, including *Trilobites*, a large, now extinct group of crustaceans, represented here by *Triarthrus becki* (*a*) and *Acidaspis dufrenoyi* (*b*). At about the same time, cuttlefish (*c*) come into existence, and when a good 150 miles (250 km) remain (4), the first bony fishes appear, among them the coelacanth. One coelacanth species, *Latimeria chalumnae* (shown here), was long thought to have been

8

extinct for 65 million years. In 1938, however, the first of several such coelacanths was caught off the coast of southern Africa.

The first species of dinosaur, the order of reptiles which tends to fascinate modern man the most, show up (**5**) when only 140 miles (250 km) remain of our journey. For the next 60 miles (100 km) or so, more and more species of dinosaur emerge into view and then disappear, and the last of these giant lizards becomes extinct when we are about 40 miles (65 km) from Heathrow. One of the best-known of the herbivorous genera, *Diplodocus*, represents the period of the giant reptiles.

When the sign "FASTEN SEAT BELTS" is switched on (**6**), almost 2 miles (3 km) before landing, the first of the erect apes can be seen, and more than 1.5 miles (2 km) later (**7**), during the Pleistocene era,

is succeeded by another animal which has given rise to much interest, namely, the mammoth. Its pelt of russet wool and long, almost black bristles well suited it for its life in the cold climate of the Pleistocene era which, after all, we also call the Ice Age.

During the very last part of the flight, we must measure distances in yards or metres instead of miles or kilometres, with 1 yard or 1 metre corresponding to a thousand years. Less than 5 yards (**8**) before touchdown, we skim over the Egyptian pyramids, while the industrial revolution, here symbolized by the interior of a French steelworks, starts (**9**) when 6 in (0.2 m) remain of our trip. The passengers in this time-machine in the guise of a jumbo-jet certainly had better keep their eyes open during the last fractions of a second of the flight if they are to see all that went on!

The following names sometimes refer to different periods of time depending on the geographical area to which they are applied, but usually, they mean the following:

The Eolithic era (from the Greek *eos*, dawn, and *lithos*, stone). The dawn of the Stone Age.

The Paleolithic era (from the Greek *palaios*, old). Started *c.* 2 million years BC. Itinerant hunters and collectors.

The Mesolithic era (from the Greek **mesos**, middle, intermediate). Started 13000–10000 BC.

The Neolithic era (from the Greek *neos*, new). Started 6000–3000 BC. During this period, the "agrarian revolution" occurs—people once nomadic settle down, build dwellings, and begin to farm and to keep animals. The first cities appear (Jericho, *c.* 6000 BC).

The Aeneolithic era (from the Latin *aenus*, bronze or metal). The Bronze Age, which started 2500–1500 BC. Metals now occur more commonly.

During the Quaternary period, ice ages or glacial eras alternated with relatively warm periods or interglacial eras. In Europe, the main ice ages have been given the names of four Alpine rivers: Würm, Riss, Mindel, and Günz. Similar temperature variations occurred on the other continents as well. The diagram to the right shows the ice ages occurring during the past 600,000 years and gives the names of the glacial and interglacial eras.

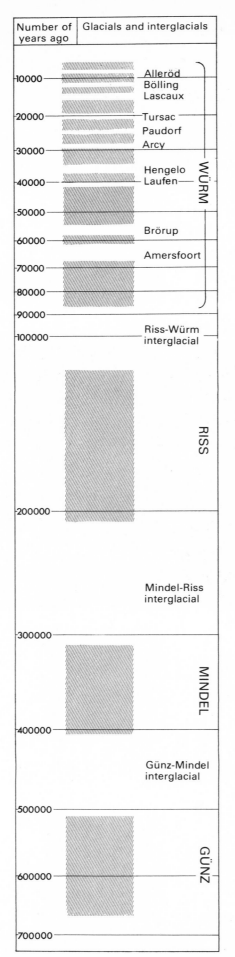

Number of years ago	Glacials and interglacials
10000	Alleröd / Bölling / Lascaux
20000	Tursac / Paudorf / Arcy
30000	
40000	Hengelo / Laufen — WÜRM
50000	
60000	Brörup
70000	Amersfoort
80000	
90000	
100000	Riss-Würm interglacial
200000	RISS
300000	Mindel-Riss interglacial
400000	MINDEL
500000	Günz-Mindel interglacial
600000	GÜNZ
700000	

machines are and what they could do even in their early, primitive forms.

This is by no means to disparage the work of Franz Reuleaux, which has been of very great significance to generations of engineers during the most expansive period of industrialism. His handbook of engineering was first published in 1861 and was reissued in new, revised editions and translated into many languages way into the twentieth century, becoming a standard work for engineers in every industrialized country in the world. Reuleaux was professor of mechanical engineering at the *Gewerbeakademie* ("Academy of Industry") and later became provost there. In 1875, he published a comprehensive work on the theory of mechanical engineering, *Theoretische Kinematik: Grundzüge einer Theorie des Maschinenwesens*, from which his definition is taken. Reuleaux's main purpose in this book is to determine the various species and types of machines. With genuine Teutonic thoroughness, he defines no less than fourteen species in this massive morphology of the machine.

But, first, let us return to the Palaeolithic period, the Early Stone Age, and consider the tools and implements which the early humans used to improve their lot. The primordial condition—wherever in time one locates it—was certainly no idyll. Without implements of various kinds, man, whatever his environment, was hopelessly inferior to the predatory animals that were once his competitors in the struggle for survival. They were swifter and, in many cases, stronger than him, to whom weapons were vital for defence and for hunting. He needed tools to make clothes for protection against the elements. Mere survival in the struggle to exist was literally a full-time occupation. Primeval man's incentive to improve his lot was, therefore, very strong. Modern man would have an extremely small chance of coping under such conditions.

Archaeological finds during the past thirty or forty years have cast a great deal of light on early primeval cultures and have enabled scientists to date the appearance of man the tool-maker further and further back. The first finds were exciting. During excavations in Sicily, the British palaeontologist Weyland found a number of stone chippings of various sizes among remnants of bones and other traces of human activity. At first, this was thought to be a coincidence, but more stone chippings from the same cultural stratum were soon found on other sites. All these chippings were on some points similar and on others dissimilar. But the important thing about them was that they had been *manufactured*. They had been made by the direct percussion of a stone striker against a stone nodule which was supported on a solid underlay, or anvil. These tools had a sharp cutting edge, but the other edge was comparatively flat and smooth, thus allowing the tool to fit neatly in the hand. The cutting edge was set at different angles on different-sized chippings, although not in a random fashion. This has been interpreted as an indication that tool-making man had discovered that different materials, such as the various woods, bone, horn, etc., call for different cutting angles in order to achieve the best result. Thousands or tens of thousands of years may have been required to establish this. But early man had plenty of time. The position of the cultural stratum, together with various other factors, enabled Weyland to date finds from various sites to between 100,000 and 250,000 years before our time. Early cultures of this type are known as anvil cultures. Since Weyland's Sicilian excavations, remnants of several such cultures have been unearthed. What they all have in common is the use of an anvil—and a stone striker—in the manufacture of their tools.

The people of the anvil cultures had cutting tools which they used when making other useful implements. For example, they used their "axes" and "knives" to fashion spear shafts, and then they fitted these with pointed heads and used them to kill animals and to cut

A In the earliest cultures, manufactured stone chippings were used for scraping and cutting. These chippings, which modern archaeologists call flakes, are usually two or three times as long as they are wide. Attempts have been made to establish how they were made. It seems likely that the most primitive method was simply to strike a stone nodule (**1**) with a chunk of some hard type of rock. Another early method was pressure-flaking (**2**) of the stone nodule. The next step in human progress was to work the material against a solid underlay, an anvil (**3**).

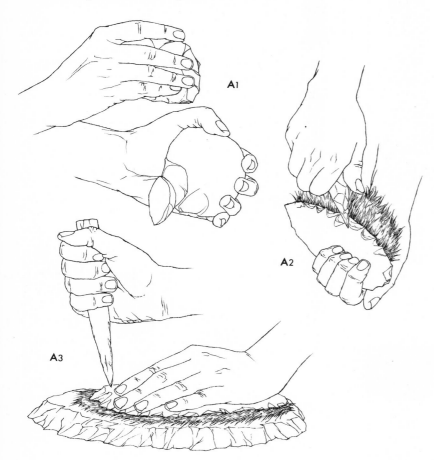

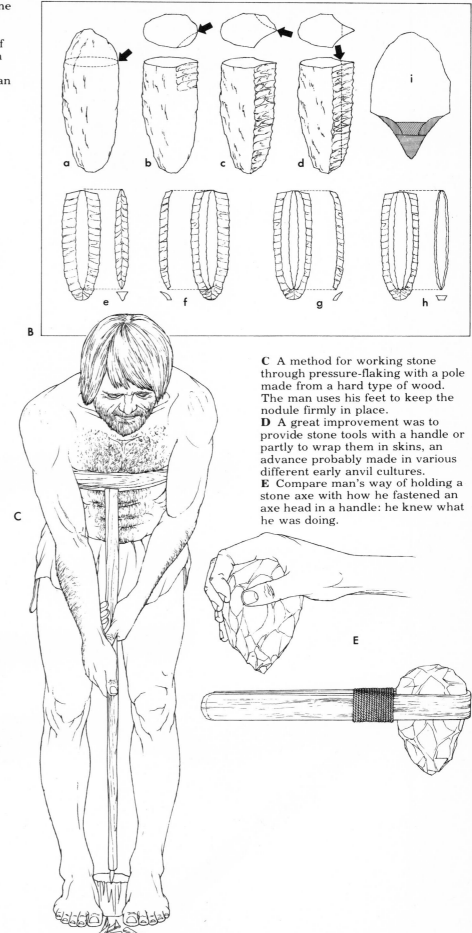

B How flakes with different cutting angles were produced by indirect percussion, i.e., by holding a "chisel" against a stone nodule and striking the "chisel". Firstly, the top of a suitably shaped flint nodule was detached (*a*). Then chips were struck off, first along one (*b*) and then along the other (*c*) "long side" of the flint nodule – the small illustrations above the main ones show the flint nodule as seen from above. Thereupon, the flakes were detached (*d*–*h*; the same flake is shown in *d* and *e*), and their sections are shown by the small illustrations below each flake. At *i*, the flint nodule is shown as seen from above. The preliminary chipping has been made, and the parts used for the flakes are indicated.

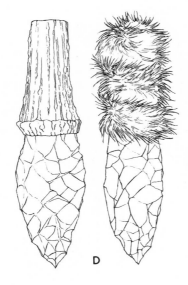

C A method for working stone through pressure-flaking with a pole made from a hard type of wood. The man uses his feet to keep the nodule firmly in place.

D A great improvement was to provide stone tools with a handle or partly to wrap them in skins, an advance probably made in various different early anvil cultures.

E Compare man's way of holding a stone axe with how he fastened an axe head in a handle: he knew what he was doing.

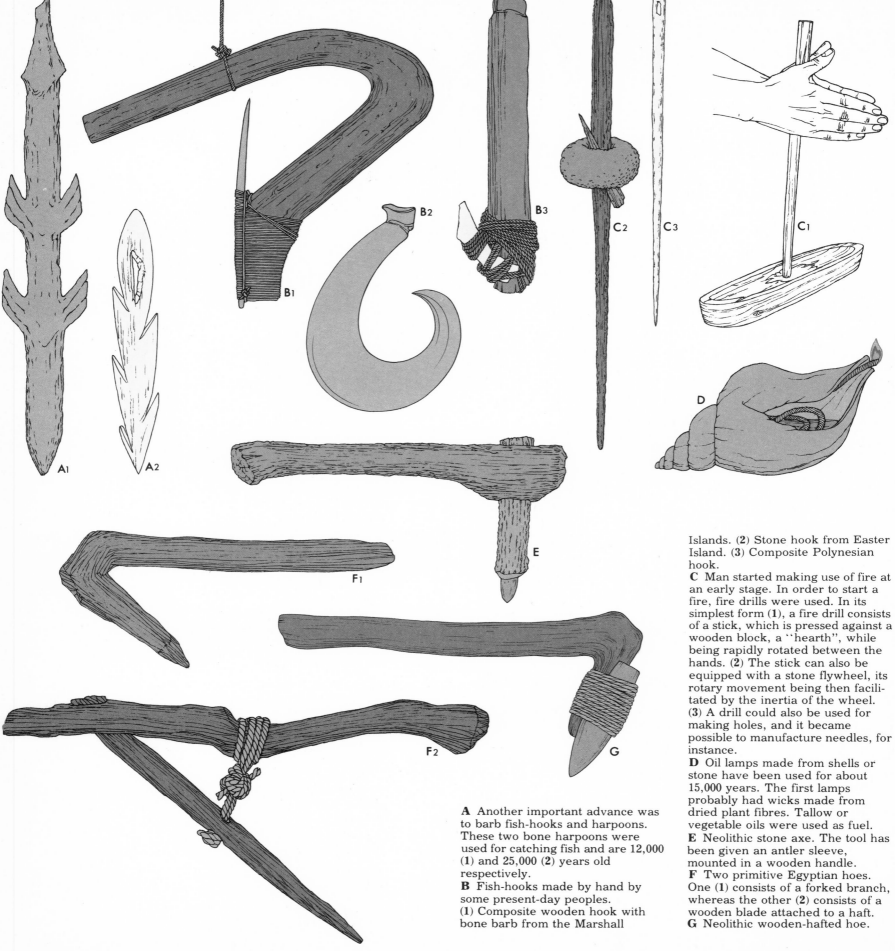

A Another important advance was to barb fish-hooks and harpoons. These two bone harpoons were used for catching fish and are 12,000 (**1**) and 25,000 (**2**) years old respectively.

B Fish-hooks made by hand by some present-day peoples. (**1**) Composite wooden hook with bone barb from the Marshall Islands. (**2**) Stone hook from Easter Island. (**3**) Composite Polynesian hook.

C Man started making use of fire at an early stage. In order to start a fire, fire drills were used. In its simplest form (**1**), a fire drill consists of a stick, which is pressed against a wooden block, a ''hearth'', while being rapidly rotated between the hands. (**2**) The stick can also be equipped with a stone flywheel, its rotary movement being then facilitated by the inertia of the wheel. (**3**) A drill could also be used for making holes, and it became possible to manufacture needles, for instance.

D Oil lamps made from shells or stone have been used for about 15,000 years. The first lamps probably had wicks made from dried plant fibres. Tallow or vegetable oils were used as fuel.

E Neolithic stone axe. The tool has been given an antler sleeve, mounted in a wooden handle.

F Two primitive Egyptian hoes. One (**1**) consists of a forked branch, whereas the other (**2**) consists of a wooden blade attached to a haft.

G Neolithic wooden-hafted hoe.

them up. The hides could then be scraped and used as protection against the wind, for covering huts, and for making clothes. The people of these early cultures knew also how to make fish-hooks and crochet needles.

It is possible that some resourceful primate of an anvil culture may have invented the animal trap, a device which, to some extent at least, fulfils the conditions of Reuleaux's definition of a machine. The pitfall, which can be made with the simplest and most primitive techniques, probably comes from this time, too. The making of a snare or gin trap, both of which have releasing mechanisms, would, however, call for more than a little skill and an even greater measure of constructive thought. If the gin trap was made during Palaeolithic times, and it is highly likely that it was, then it represents the first automatic mechanism. It performs its job—to catch or kill game— without human intervention. At a pinch, the gin may be regarded as the nucleus of the most advanced automatic mechanism of our time, the computer.

Perspective on Our Existence

Despite the creditable efforts of, among others, Reuleaux, it is strange that no one has succeeded in finding a crystal-clear, unambiguous definition of the concept "machine". To try to pinpoint the appearance of the first machine is just as difficult a task, partly due to the vagueness of the definition and partly because this primeval machine—whatever we may understand by the expression—in all probability was invented before the creation of writing, so that no written sources are available. But no matter how primitive this first machine was, it could not have sprung forth, complete, from the brain of its inventor. It had to be manufactured, and the prerequisite for this is, quite simply, our tool-making man; for without tools, there can be no machines.

To attempt to establish when and where the first tool-making man appeared is beyond the scope of this book. But it may not be amiss to try to present a perspective to man's existence on the planet we call Earth, which, it is generally believed, has existed for about 4.5 thousand million years—an inconceivable length of time on man's own time-scale. It is both instructive and entertaining to "translate" this vast expanse of time into the twenty-four hours of the day. The first signs of life appear some time during the afternoon, whereas the first man-like creatures, the hominids, came on stage only a few minutes before midnight. That must, undeniably, give food for thought! Even more drastic results are obtained if we compare the earth's life-span with a flight from New York to London. The hominids entry takes place just before the aeroplane lands at Heathrow!

No certain knowledge of what happened here on earth during its first three or four thousand million years is as yet available, but the considerable progress being made in research in this field makes it probable that the present theories will shortly be replaced by hard facts. Consider, for instance, the recent discovery of the planar structure of the earth's crust. This caused a breakthrough in its field as sensational as the discovery of DNA did in the field of molecular biology.

During the past hundred years or so, archaeologists have been able to form a fairly clear picture of the development that has taken place during the last ten million years, when the prelude to human civilization was first slowly struck up. Interesting climatic changes which have taken place since the arrival of man are shown on the time-scale on page 10. It has been possible to trace about a dozen ice ages during the last 600,000 years. Further, there is reliable evidence to indicate that, even since the last ice age, considerable climatic changes, for better or worse, have taken place. Many scientists maintain that a favourable climate was one of the reasons for the

blossoming of the advanced cultures during antiquity. For instance, they believe that a "pleasant zone" existed in Mesopotamia during the fourth millennium BC, when Ur, Babylon, and Nineveh flourished. A deterioration in the climate, resulting in hotter, drier conditions of the type prevailing in present-day Iran may have contributed to the decline and fall of these cultures. We know for certain that even earlier cultures were swept away by natural disasters. The Bible's Deluge appears in the chronicles of several cultures, with variations in detail but agreement about an all-destroying flood. The Gilgamesh epic gives an exhaustive account of a global cataclysm, as do the Eddic sagas.

During recent years, new finds have been made which originate from cultures existing before the Flood, or whatever one chooses to call the major disaster which befell the earth at the dawn of history. New information is continuously coming to light, and what has just been said of our knowledge of the geological genesis of the earth can also be said about the eras before the appearance of man—the "scientific guesses" we have made so far about these cultures will, in all probability, soon be replaced by well-founded facts. Among other projects that are being worked on is that of the Leakeys in East Africa.

A lot of valuable results were produced by Mary and Louis S. B. Leakey, whose work there started at the beginning of the 1930s. In recent years, their sons Richard and Jonathan have also been working there. The Leakeys' research has brought many fascinating finds to light. For instance, in northern Kenya the remains of human skeletons over two million years old have been found. A partly preserved skull, found by Richard Leakey and numbered 1470, has been identified as belonging to the genus *homo*, and its age has been established at about 2.5 million years. "Tools"—mainly stone chippings—which were used by these ancestors of the human race have also been discovered. Similar finds have been made in other parts of the world, and scientists are now busy tracing the development of these early human beings throughout the past twenty million years.

During the past century, the perspective which we have had on our own existence here on earth has been considerably extended. Even as late as the middle of the nineteenth century, it was the teachings of James Ussher which dominated the ecclesiastical and scientific worlds. Ussher (1581—1656) was Archbishop of Armagh in Ireland. Two years before his death, he published a comprehensive work on biblical chronology, *Annales Veteris et Novi Testamenti*, which created a stir throughout all Christendom. With the help of the genealogical tables in the Old Testament and of datings in the New Testament, Ussher could date the Creation to 4004 BC. His book led to a flood of learned works which went even further in pinpointing the date of the story of creation as recorded in Genesis. A calendar published by St. John's College, Oxford, at the start of the eighteenth century, was able to state that, "In the beginning God created the heaven and the earth" at 9.00 am on March 23, 4004 BC.

Today, we may well smile at this strict dogmatic approach and at the fact that its results were accepted for so long and through centuries which could, after all, boast of considerable progress, not least in the fields of natural science and technology. But then, we must remember that the Church maintained an iron grip on both theological orthodoxy and the secular sciences.

This cocksure dating of the Creation was, however, soon called into question by some remarkable archaeological finds. In the seventeenth century, the remains of long-extinct animals—among them, mammoths—were found in several places in Europe. These remains were discovered in deep earth layers which can only have been formed by deposits left by the Flood or by an even earlier and greater inundation. Supporters of the Bible's chronology countered by explaining that there must have been more than one period of creation!

Several interesting finds of early flint tools were made in the seventeenth and eighteenth centuries. Scientists were perplexed by a well-tooled stone axe, found in *c.* 1690 during work in a gravel-pit near Gray's Inn Lane in London. It was found in the remains of an elephant's skeleton by an apothecary. Again, the traditionalists had an answer: "It was a weapon used by the courageous Britons in their battles against the elephants of the Roman army during Claudius's invasion of Britain in the fifth decade of our era." Similar finds of tools and weapons were made during the eighteenth and early nineteenth centuries but, with a few exceptions, their origins were explained away and dated in a similar way to that used for the axe found in Gray's Inn Lane.

Today, we know beyond doubt that this axe dates from the Early Stone Age, as do several other tools and implements found during the long period when the scientific world adhered to Archbishop Ussher's dating of the Creation. The breakthrough occurred on the publication, in 1859, of Charles Darwin's theory of evolution in his book *On the Origin of Species . . .*, which immediately caused a violent controversy. While feelings ran at their highest, in 1868, the Cro-Magnon cave was discovered in south-western France, and this discovery was followed, a few years later, by that of the Altamira cave in the Pyrenees. Excavations brought to light skulls, parts of skeletons, and a great number of tools of various kinds, and the famous murals were found in the latter cave. The datings of these finds have long been a matter of dispute, but it was realized from the first that these humans had lived long before the year of Ussher's Creation, 4004 BC. Nowadays, scientists more or less agree that the Cro-Magnon culture goes back to the latest ice age, *c.* 20,000 years ago, while the Altamira culture is older, being generally considered, at present, to date back to 30,000–40,000 years before our time.

The giant Altamira murals have attracted much attention, and so have the similar paintings in the Lascaux and La Madelaine caves, discovered later. In the present context, we can leave to one side the art experts' interpretation of the significance of the paintings, because of greater interest is the fact that the inhabitants of these cultures could create *the technical prerequisites* of painting—the tools with which to prepare paint and to apply it to the cave wall. The pigments were derived from naturally occurring minerals, for instance, the warm red of iron ochre (the colour of life, probably first used for cult ceremonies), the yellow of manganese oxides, and the blue of cobalt salts. Nature offers a bountiful palette, but most of these minerals are hard and must be pulverized by crushing and grinding, before they can be mixed with a binder and used for painting. The implements used in the preparation of these paints were found in the caves (tools for crushing, grinding, and mixing—processes which are still used in the chemical industry, in the so-called basic unit operations).

A replica of part of the Altamira cave has been built at the Deutsches Museum in Munich. This permanent exhibit, entitled "The Earliest History of Chemical Technology", shows among other things how the paint used in the murals was prepared. The machines now used for these basic unit operations have, without a doubt, a long prehistory!

We can say to sum up that, in a relatively short period of time, our perspective on the existence of our own species on earth has been extended further and further back in history. The arsenal of technical aids at the disposal of the modern archaeologist has helped enormously towards increasing our knowledge of the long prehistory of our time.

The scholars of classical antiquity and the history of art used to be those who worked closely with the archaeologist. Nowadays, his colleagues are more often physicists and technologists, specialists in the Carbon-14 method, pollen analysis, the determination of the age of ceramics by thermoluminescence, and so on. In many cases the archaeologist relies on the computer engineer to process the finds he has made.

A half a million years or so ago, some primate, one of man's precursors, learnt how to master fire. During excavations in China in the 1920s, two Swedish scientists, J. G. Andersson and B. Bohlin, established that the so-called Peking Man, or *Sinanthropus pekingensis* (from *Sin*, "China", and *anthropus*, "human being"), had been acquainted with fire. The dating, three to four hundred thousand years before our time, is a matter of controversy. However, Peking Man was by no means the first to use fire.

In recent years, finds have been made in Central and South Africa of remnants of human skeletons which can be definitely dated earlier than the Peking Man. The scientific names for these hominids (man-like creatures) have since had the element *pithecus* added to them, and this is sometimes combined with *anthropus*. The South African finds showed manifest traces of fire, the earliest yet to have been found – about half a million years old. These primeval masters of fire now go under the name of *Australopithecus prometeus*, *australis* meaning "southern" and the latter part of the name coming from the Titan of Greek mythology, Prometheus, who stole fire from Zeus and gave it to mankind.

And indeed, fire *was* a god-sent gift. It afforded protection against the dark and the cold, and, to a certain extent, against wild animals. But it was also a tool, which could be used to hollow out tree trunks and to shape them into log canoes. Even solid rock was not impervious to the onslaught of fire; alternate heating and drenching will, in the end, crack most rocks. The job can then be finished off with sledge-hammers and pick-axes.

Man also discovered, although much later than the period under discussion, that certain kinds of rock, when heated, start to "bleed" a fluid which rapidly solidifies, and it was thus that metals were discovered. Copper is considered to have been known in Egypt at least 4,500 years before Christ and in the other great river cultures of classical antiquity a millennium or so later. Many finds show that the art of working meteoric iron was known in these cultures, but this, obviously, had no influence on the general development of the art of iron working. The supply of "raw material" was fortuitous and, to say the least, minimal. Its origin was enshrouded in mystery, and anything made from meteoric iron usually became a cult object in religious or magic rites.

The discovery of metal, a new raw material for tools, was not only an important breakthrough in the field of tool development, which was then in its infancy, but also a great step forward for human culture as a whole. Man's ability to shape metals and alloys through casting and forging opened up whole new vistas and led to a wide assortment of new and more effective tools; these, in their turn, made possible the production of many useful everyday articles, as well as – and this is often overlooked – the development of new forms of art. The visual arts are simply inconceivable without the artist's tools and other technical paraphernalia.

Metal Tools

At this very early stage of tool technology, one of the most practical tools to be developed was the scissors. Indeed, the invention of the scissors was a definite step forward, as the technology of the earlier anvil cultures had not been capable of making such a tool. They could make cutting tools, such as knives, axes, and saws, from various types of hard stone, and there still exist some marvellous examples of these well-produced and highly finished tools. However, the introduction of metals made it possible to introduce a new way of working a material—by cutting with scissors. Apart from the purely trivial applications of this new technique—it is hard to imagine how a modern household could function without at least one pair of scissors—the ancient Egyptians began to create works of art with scissors, cutting silhouettes which portrayed their dear ones. This became a high art form, developed to perfection by a much-respected guild of artists and, later, influential in painting, which could begin only when man had mastered the technique of mixing colour pigments with a binding medium and of applying the resulting paint to a surface with a tool, a brush. For thousands of years, the traditional profile view used in the highly developed art of silhouette making came to be used also in portrait painting in that part of the world. During this period, the head was hardly ever painted full face, but in profile, like in a silhouette, but with the almond eyes exquisitely coloured and the lines of forehead, nose, and chin delightfully classic.

But what are almond eyes and portraits in profile doing in a book on the history of the machine? Well, part of the answer is that there is a more concrete connection between pure technical development and the cultivation of the mind—in this case, painting—than is generally supposed. The development of the arts goes hand in hand with advances made in technology. This applies not only to the visual arts, but also to literature—writing materials, the art of printing—and to music, where the instruments can be seen as technical creations.

But let us return to the scissors, which in all their simplicity and functional beauty as the first clipping tool were the first, and thus decisive, application in tool technology of what is called the "simple machine". In classic mechanics, the term "simple machine" covers a handful of fundamental innovations which have contributed in an exceptionally high degree to the progress of human culture. The first of these, the lever, goes back to the earliest anvil cultures. With a lever, it is possible to move heavy objects which could not otherwise be moved by hand. It is, of course, completely futile to speculate on exactly when this technique became manifest to prehistoric man, but it is fairly safe to conjecture that it happened during the Early Stone Age. The same goes for both the inclined plane and the wedge, which are based on the same theory.

The Tools of the Pyramid Builders

The simple machines and the art of working stone are our foremost heritage from prehistoric times, i.e., those before we have access to written sources. In the Nile culture, the art of shaping stone developed very rapidly during the fourth millennium BC. Striking tools were used on chisels of different kinds to form beautifully shaped stone vessels, urns, and vases. The raw material was granite and porphyry, but even rock crystal was used in making ornaments. The Egyptians also developed a special technique for quarrying boulders of considerable size from the bedrock.

It was with this advanced technology, based on purpose-built tools, and with the help of the simple machines known at the time, that the pyramids of Egypt could be built. The first of these, the pyramid of Pharaoh Neter-khet (commonly known as Djoser or Zoser) at Sakkara, rises to a height of about 203 ft (62 m) and was originally covered with polished limestone—a truly remarkable construction, completed around 2,800 BC. Other cultures of very early times had also mastered the technique of erecting monumental structures. Striking examples of this are, for instance, the impressive cult centre at Stonehenge, and the pyramid-like constructions erected by the early mound-building cultures of Mexico and Central America.

In ancient Egypt, shears were used to cut silhouettes (*above*), an art form which was developed to exquisite perfection by an esteemed guild of artists. This tradition later also left its mark on the pictorial art in these parts of the world. For thousands of years, portraits were practically always executed in profile (*below*), as in a silhouette.

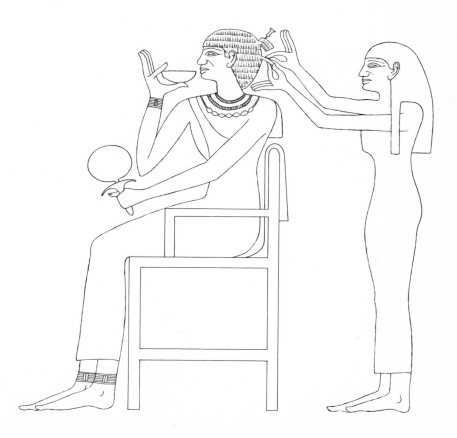

A Many scientists nowadays hold the opinion that a "machine tool", a fiddle borer, of the type shown here (1) was used during the Stone Age for drilling holes in stone tools. The object to be worked (a) was securely anchored beneath a drill (b), which was a bone of circular cross-section, perhaps a thigh-bone of some large animal. A flywheel (c) facilitated the drill's rotation, which was imparted by a bowed string (d). To bring pressure to bear on the drill, a lever (e), equipped with a weight (f), was employed. (2) Sectional view of how the drill penetrated the stone. Naturally, as the drill material alone—bone—was not hard enough to have any effect on stone, some sort of abrasive (g), such as finely ground flintstone, must have been used.

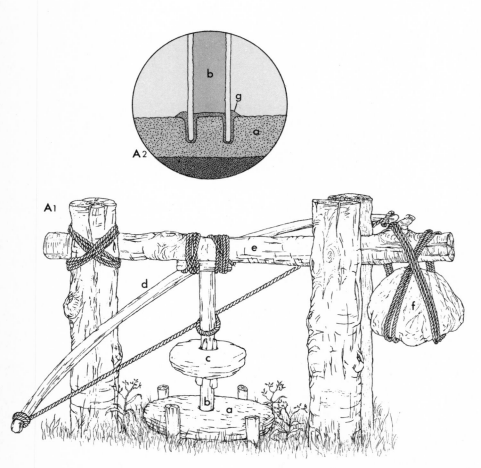

Several scholars who have described the mound cultures of the Neolithic era point out that the archaeological excavations undertaken have given very little information on the tools and implements used when the great structures of classical antiquity, for instance, the pyramids of Egypt, were erected. The Swede Henry Kjellson looks for, among other things, drawing blocks and machines for drawing precious metals and iron into thin, even wires. (Wire was used for a variety of utilitarian and ornamentative purposes by the ancient cultures of Sumeria and Egypt.) Axes, chisels, and saws made from hard types of stone can be used to work softer types, but this explains only part of the mystery of how early man in the dawn of history, from the Eolithicum to the Neolithicum, could produce magnificent results in stone, as the many finds from the period testify. The German Albert Neuburger exclaims in his classic *Technik des Altertums* ("The Technology of Antiquity"), "Without mining, no technology!" We can add, "Without metals, no tools to build machines."

As we have said already, man's discovery of metal brought about a definite breakthrough in the art of making tools. In all probability, copper is the earliest known of the metals. From at least 5000 BC, copper ore was mined from opencast and pit mines on Mount Sinai, and we know that rich deposits were being mined in Cyprus a couple of thousand years later. (The Latin for the metal, *cuprum*, is derived from the name of the island.) But copper is a soft metal, and even if the art of alloying it with other metals was known at an early stage—copper alloyed with tin gives bronze, and with zinc gives brass—the tools made from these alloys had little chance of producing good results with hard types of rock, such as granite and porphyry. But these were the very materials used for the artefacts we have mentioned already to demonstrate the advanced stone-working techniques of the Neolithic era.

How, then, was it possible to produce these technically advanced artefacts? There have been no significant finds of any of the tools used. One of the reasons for this may be that, until very recently, archaeologists have concentrated on quite different aspects of the earliest cultures, especially on their religion and art. However, there has been a lot of speculation about the tool technology which made possible these impressive artefacts of hard stone, which we can still examine and admire in museums all over the world. Several scientists have suggested that tools of copper or copper alloy could have been fitted with diamond chips, cast or forged into the metal. This would apply to such stone-working tools as chisels, saws, and drills. On different types of building stones and in quarries, clear indications have been found that show that the tools used penetrated quite deeply into the stone for every revolution or stroke. This further indicates that the tool—a drill or a saw—was the active element in a "machine tool", in which the tool had been exposed by mechanical means to very high pressure. The simple machines, which are our technical heritage from the Palaeolithic era, include the lever and the wedge, and although no finds have been made to verify it, there are good grounds for assuming that both the lever and the wedge were used as construction elements in these early machines.

Numerous artefacts of hard stone, with polished, lustrous surfaces, are known from the earliest of the ancient mound cultures. Also, there is, from the Eolithic and Palaeolithic eras, a multitude of stone striking tools—axes, sledge-hammers, and hammers—in which holes have been drilled to take a shaft. The archaeologists of the nineteenth century and earlier found it almost impossible to explain how these neat holes were made. This is easily understandable, bearing in mind the pitifully poor technical education available to the profession at the time. The reason that these poor humanists were so mystified was that they thought that all of the material in the holes was removed by drilling, an operation which would have taken an unrealistically long time. A drill was, indeed, used, but it was not a solid drill. Many believe that a bone was used as a hollow drill, and a string and bow—a fiddle borer—with a lever and load, converted and increased the power. Naturally, bone is far too soft a material for it alone to have any effect on stone, but with the help of an abrasive material, for instance a powder of a hard rock type, one can work wonders with this simple tool. Many abrasives are naturally available, and the basic unit operations of crushing and grinding were well known. Finely ground flintstone ought to have been effective—and maybe some privileged culture had thought of using crushed diamond chips. In recent times, several attempts have been made to drill holes in stone using these methods. The experiments show that, with a drill of circular section and an abrasive, it is possible to make a tube-shaped cutting in the material, without having to tackle the core of the cutting at all. Several unfinished holes of this sort have been found and dated to the Palaeolithic era. These consist of cylindrical cores left in holes which have been partly drilled with tubular drills; abrasives have clearly been used during the operation.

The sophisticated technique and the highly developed skill used by craftsmen in producing from stone such utility articles as beakers, urns, pots, and vases presuppose the use of specialized tools and some sort of sanding machine and abrasive. Possibly, pulverized flintstone was used as an abrasive, although quartz and basalt could also have been used. But the abrasive which immediately springs to mind is that which occurs so abundantly in that part of the world, namely, the desert sand.

When compared to iron and steel, copper is a soft metal. But when the Mount Sinai copper deposits began to be worked, probably at the beginning of the fifth millennium BC, copper was immediately used to make edged tools, such as axes, chisels, knives, and scissors. Within a millennium, metallurgy had made such purely empirical progress that copper could be made considerably harder by cold-hammering.

In the Brinell scale (B), red copper has a hardness of *c*. 80−90 B, but cold-hammered copper reaches a degree of 135−145 B. This means that a skilled craftsman could make the edge of a copper stone-cutting chisel as hard as good-quality wrought iron. At the beginning of the third millennium BC, copper mining began in Oman, on the Persian Gulf; the ore there was not as pure as that in the Mount Sinai mines, for it contained nickel, tin, and some other metals. However, these "contaminants" produced an alloy, ready-made by Nature, which was vastly superior to red copper; it had a natural hardness of 140−160 B, and this could be improved to 275 B and over if the metal was skilfully cold-hammered. Thus, an alloy was available that had properties comparable with those of reasonable tool steels in the early 1900s.

At the beginning of the third millennium BC, therefore, everything was poised for a breakthrough in stone-working techniques, above and beyond the technology that had produced the beautiful utility articles already mentioned, for now, man had tools which were capable of working even hard rock. The breakthrough was imminent.

It was at this time that the first *qanaat*s were built. These were conduits for carrying the drinking-water supply to the cities and towns which were springing up during this period; a pre-condition for the formation of any society is the availability of water. When the first *qanaat* was built is not known for sure. In the beginning, *qanaat*s were built of fairly short water pipes with relatively small cross-sections. Later, however, as the Assyrians developed the system, the dimensions of the pipes increased dramatically, and *qanaat*s were

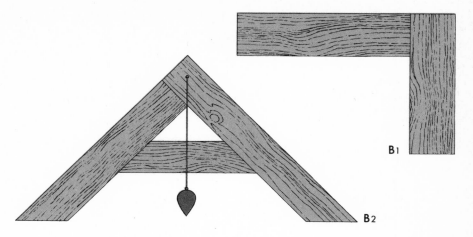

B Levelling instrument used in ancient Egypt. (**1**) Set-square of 90°. (**2**) Instrument used to establish whether a surface was horizontal or not. If it was, the plumb line would hang straight in front of a groove in the middle of the cross-bar. (**3**) Instrument used to establish whether a surface was vertical or not. All these instruments have been found at Thebes and have been dated to *c*. 1100 BC.

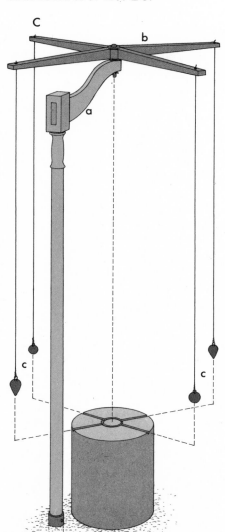

C A *groma*, an instrument used during classical antiquity to set out right angles. It consisted of an arm (*a*), which carried a pivoted, horizontal cross (*b*). A plumb bob (*c*) was suspended from each arm of the cross. One opposing pair of plumb lines was used to align the instrument with a given line, and the other pair was used to lay out a line at right angles to the first. For the instrument to work, it was necessary that the cross was absolutely horizontal, and the weather absolutely calm!

built throughout the countries of classical antiquity—north-east Africa, Iran, and India. In Iran alone, there are today over twenty thousand conduit systems, with an accumulated length of over 168,000 miles (c. 270,000 km), and most of these are still in use, although the majority were built in the third millennium BC.

In order to direct these water tunnels successfully, the difficult art of surveying had been learnt, and the tools necessary for this had been created. The crux was to calculate, and then to drive the tunnels to give, the best inclination for the most effective water-flow. The theory and the technique used in such calculations are fundamentally the same as those used today in laying out safe foundations for large buildings.

The time is a century or so into the third millennium BC. The necessary skills now seem to be well enough developed to explain that great and truly remarkable breakthrough in structural engineering, the building of the pyramids. Posterity has been highly puzzled by the lack of a significant link between the relatively primitive building forms previously in common use and the gigantic pyramids.

True, the earliest Neolithic cultures in various parts of the world had already developed the more relevant constructional principles of structural engineering, but in ancient Egypt, the main building material was *terre pisé*, i.e., clay mixed with straw and baked to form bricks. Simple huts as well as splendid palaces can be built with this material, but it is not very lasting and calls for substantial maintenance. Only fragments of such buildings from this period are still extant.

In any case, a major advance in construction techniques took place, from building in *terre pisé* to building in stone, and the results of this new technique have not been surpassed until very recent times, in terms of volume of material, work effort, precision, and permanence.

How was all this possible five thousand years ago?

The fundamental reasons are three. Firstly, the new tool material, copper alloy, and the metallurgic knowledge of how this material could be tempered by cold-hammering. Secondly, the long tradition of skilled craftsmanship in working hard stone into beautiful utility articles. This tradition also comprises the knowledge, gained by long experience, of tool design and of how it is varied to suit different working materials. Thirdly, a not insignificant knowledge of the mathematical rudiments of engineering, plus the necessary tools, instruments, and implements for surveying and for taking all the measurements required in structural engineering.

A fourth and very significant factor in the construction of the pyramids must be mentioned. This is the ancient Egyptian conception of life after death. If ever there was a state religion, it was the Egyptian during this period. The head of state, the Pharaoh, was the god's representative on earth. As such he was immortal and was an absolute authority, both religious and political, over his subjects. When corporeal death inevitably occurred, the Pharaoh was embalmed—along with his family and servants—so as to be able to live and work in eternity. The art of embalming reached a high level of perfection in this culture and, later, it became a nursery for the young sciences of chemistry and anatomy.

Naturally, the master-builders of the time were fully aware that a palace intended to last forever could not be built of *terre pisé*. The Pharaoh's eternal abode obviously had to be constructed of an everlasting material. The answer to this problem lay in the near-at-hand bedrock, which consisted of granite. If ever there was a lasting material, it was primary rock!

The first engineer whose name is known now enters the arena of history. His name was Imhotep; a polymath, as gifted as he was versatile, and the counsellor of Pharaoh Neter-khet.

The many small Neolithic countries in the Nile valley had been united in the third millennium BC by the legendary Pharaoh Menes, who also founded Memphis, the capital of the Old Kingdom. Memphis had developed into an important cultural centre under several colourful rulers when Pharaoh Neter-khet came into power some time around 2800 BC. His assumption of power, as it happened, took place in extremely unhappy circumstances, which may well have been the decisive factor in triggering off the development of the tooling and machining techniques described below. It was these techniques which made it possible to take the great step of building the pyramids.

When Pharaoh Neter-khet assumed power, the entire Nile valley was stricken by famine, because the otherwise regular flooding of the river had not occurred for several years running. When faced with what he took to be a sinister omen, Neter-khet consulted Imhotep, and they concluded that the divinity of the Nile cataracts—with the African-sounding name of Khnuma—had become incensed with the new Pharaoh. By way of punishment, he had kept back the floods. Imhotep advised Neter-khet to build Khnuma a temple, the like of which the world had never before beheld. This was done under Imhotep's supervision, and the floods returned with their former regularity.

Order was re-established in the country, and Neter-khet could devote himself to planning his eternal abode. The earlier graves in the Old Kingdom consisted of a rectangular sepulchral chamber, sunk into the ground and covered by a couple of more or less crude boulders. Such a grave was called a *mastaba* after the bench which usually stood outside the hut of every Egyptian farmer. Around or on top of the boulders, a wall of mud-brick was built, broad at the base and tapered upwards to counteract the tendency of the material to moulder. It is generally considered that this is the origin of the pyramid shape.

At Sakkara, outside Memphis, Neter-khet ordered a bench grave to be built. However, Imhotep made it square and of stone only. The grave was 230 ft (70 m) square by 29.5 ft (9 m) high—even this was an impressive construction. Obviously, it must have whetted Neter-khet's appetite. Stage by stage, the project assumed gigantic proportions. Firstly, the dimensions of the original mastaba were considerably increased, and then, Imhotep went on building, in several stages, until the first step pyramid, with six steps, was completed in c. 2760 BC. This pyramid was only the start of an even more gigantic structure, with palaces, temples, and other buildings, covering a space of 1,756 × 886 ft (535×270 m), and all surrounded by a 33-ft (10 m) high wall with a total length of 1 mile (1.6 km)—to protect the regal corpse for the course of eternity.

This first edifice of masterfully worked stone was soon followed by several others. Less than a hundred years after this remarkable breakthrough in constructional engineering, the Cheops pyramid, which ranks among the seven wonders of the world, was built. Its foundation is 754.9 ft (230 m) square, and its peak rises almost 490 ft (c. 150 m) above the ground. The Cheops pyramid consists of 2.3 million stone blocks, each weighing around 2.5 tons. These giant blocks were quarried at several places near Aswan, from where they were shipped down the Nile to the building site at Gizeh. They were then hoisted into place after being finely worked with such precision that it is all but impossible to fit a hair between the joints.

Some seventy pyramids of various sizes were built by the Egyptian rulers principally during the Old Kingdom, that is, during the four-hundred-year long period from 2800 BC (a controversial date).

Other Building Aids

We have already mentioned the tools and techniques available to the pyramid builders. But what other aids were at their disposal? Many of those who have speculated over this have started from the Greek historian Herodotus' vivid description of building the pyramids. He mentions, among other things, various mysterious "mechanisms" and cranes which lifted the stone blocks from ledge to ledge. Herodotus also makes several statements about the number of workers employed in the quarries and on the sites; he also tells how long it took to build the pyramids. But we must remember that the erection of the pyramids was as distant in time from Herodotus, the "father of history", as he is from us. When he studied the pyramids on the spot, in the fourth century BC, there were already "tourist guides", who were certainly as accomplished in spinning a yarn as their modern colleagues.

Many riddles concerning the building of the pyramids are as yet unsolved. However, it is generally accepted that working machines for several operations were used at the quarries. This was suggested by Sir W. M. Flinders Petrie (1853–1942), who, in his work *The Pyramid and Temples of Gizeh*, gives detailed descriptions of grooves found in the quarries, on the stone blocks, and on a number of other objects. Unusually enough, this archaeologist had a good enough general technical education to realize that these grooves were marks made by tools with cutting edges of a very hard material, possibly diamond chips embedded in cold-hammered bronze. The great stone sarcophagus found in the sepulchral chamber of the Cheops pyramid has sawn grooves, which suggest not only saws of considerable length (the long side of the groove is 8.2 ft, or 2.5 m), but also the fact that they could stand up to very high loads, judging by the penetration per cut. In theory, such a saw—with a power stroke of at least 10 ft (c. 3 m)—might, of course, have been handled like a modern two-man felling saw—if a dozen men worked each end. Neuburger mentions a quarry in south Germany, worked by the Romans, where monoliths have been found. These obviously have been sawn out of the rock with stone saws, which according to Neuburger must have had a power stroke of at least 15 ft (4.5 m). The same technique, but two thousand years later.

It is, however, also conceivable that some sort of machine tool for sawing stone had been developed, possibly according to the principles illustrated on pages 20–21. The fact that this machine is hypothetical should be stressed, even if it definitely could have been constructed, given the technology of the time. In 1914, an archaeologist in Finland found a saw-toothed knife while excavating a site on the Karelian Isthmus. The find has been dated to about 6000 BC and is made from the shin-bone of a moose. Sharp points of flint have been hammered along the edge of the blade. The knife may have been intended for use as a stabbing weapon, but it could have been used also for sawing wood or similar material.

In Flinders Petrie's opinion, there is proof that the people of the Old Kingdom were familiar with the unsurpassed hardness of diamonds, since he considers it likely that this material was used for engraving hieroglyphics in very hard basalt. On beautifully carved bowls from the fourth dynasty (c. 2700 BC), there are gracefully made inscriptions which, without any doubt, are made "in one stroke", not chiselled or scraped. Several lines lie only about a tenth of a millimetre apart. The engraver must indeed have had splendid eye-sight—the author points out while adjusting his indispensable spectacles—or did he have access to magnifying glasses as well?

Undeniably, it would be tempting to follow that trail, too—so-called reading stones, transparent minerals cut to a planoconvex form, are known since way back in time—but let us return to the quarries of the pyramids!

Through the ages, many theories have been put forward on the methods used to quarry the great monoliths. One explanation com-

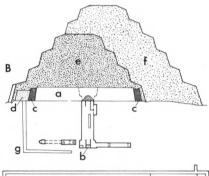

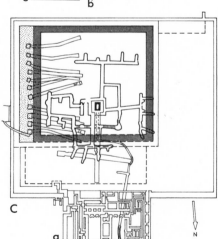

A King Neter-khet's step pyramid, the first monumental structure to be built of stone.
B Longitudinal-section of the pyramid, which was originally built as a mastaba (a). The burial chamber (b) was situated at the foot of a 91-ft (29 m) shaft. However, Imhotep caused the dimensions of the structure to be increased, and the building was given an extra layer of stone all around (c). After that, the eastern wall was increased (d), and, later, the entire structure was incorporated into the pyramid (e). Later still, Imhotep caused further additions (f) to be made. (g) Tombs for members of the royal family.
C Underneath the pyramid is a maze of galleries and shafts. Certain galleries were intended for use as tombs for members of Neter-khet's family, whereas others were to connect the burial chambers with one another as the pyramid was built. Some of the shafts and galleries may, however, have been made only in order to lead grave-robbers astray. (a) The funeral temple.

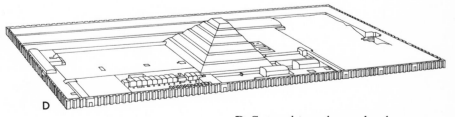

D Several temples and palaces were erected around the pyramid, and the whole area was surrounded by a high wall.

A

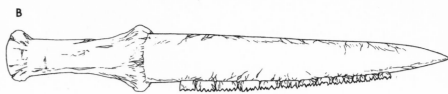

B

A Cracks in the granite were the reason why work on this monolith in one of the Aswan quarries was never completed. It is accepted that dolerite balls were used in cutting the narrow trenches around the block, but how they were used is still a matter of controversy.

B A reconstruction of the almost 8,000-year-old tool found on the Karelian Isthmus. The "knife-blade" is made from the tibia of a moose, and sharp flint chips have been driven into its edge.

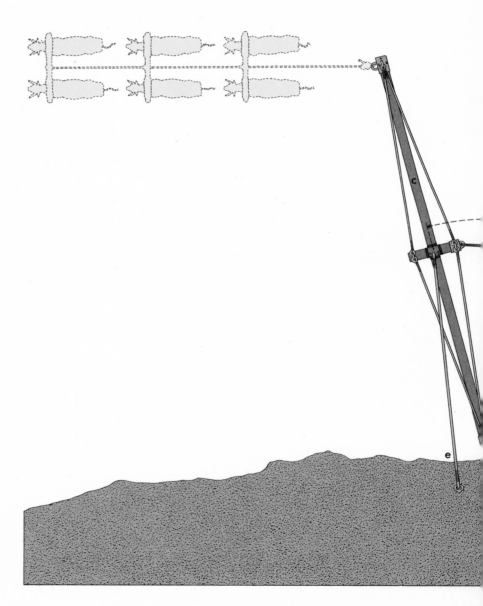

monly given is that the pyramids' great stone blocks were broken loose from the bedrock by means of sun-dried wooden plugs, which were driven into bored-out holes in the rock. The force necessary to split the rock was obtained by making the plugs expand by drenching them with water. One would be tempted to accept this explanation, were it not for the fact that drenching a fibrous material such as wood causes it to expand in a way that completely differs from the expansion of metal when heated. When a wooden plug is inserted in a bored hole, a counter-pressure arises, and water poured on it would penetrate into the cavities of the fibres. Several scholars, among them Kjellson, have made experiments which prove that this alleged bursting effect is minute, or even non-existent.

There are many indications that, instead, copper or bronze wedges were used. Neuburger and several other scholars have suggested that the bursting effect of such wedges would have been reinforced by heating after they had been driven in, either by means of boiling water or by covering them with red-hot charcoal.

In one of the Aswan quarries, there is an incompletely quarried monolith, intended as an obelisk which was abandoned apparently because of cracks in the stone. The monolith is *c.* 135 ft (41 m) long, and it has a cross-section of 14.1 ft (4.3 m) at the base and 9.2 ft (2.8 m) at the top. For centuries, the monolith was almost completely covered with sand, but in the early 1920s, the Englishman R. Engelbach dug it out. A narrow trench (*c.* 30 in, or 70 cm) had been cut into the rock on both sides of the monolith. On the sides of these trenches can be seen grooves which are about 10 in (25 cm) wide with rounded cross-sections. Many theories have been put forward about the tools used to make these grooves. Engelbach believes that dolerite balls about 12 in (30 cm) in diameter were struck so hard with sledge-hammers that the granite underneath was ground asunder. When the balls had been worked down a bit into the rock, the stone cutters probably used sturdy wooden poles as links between sledge-hammer and ball.

Others doubt that this was the method employed, although they

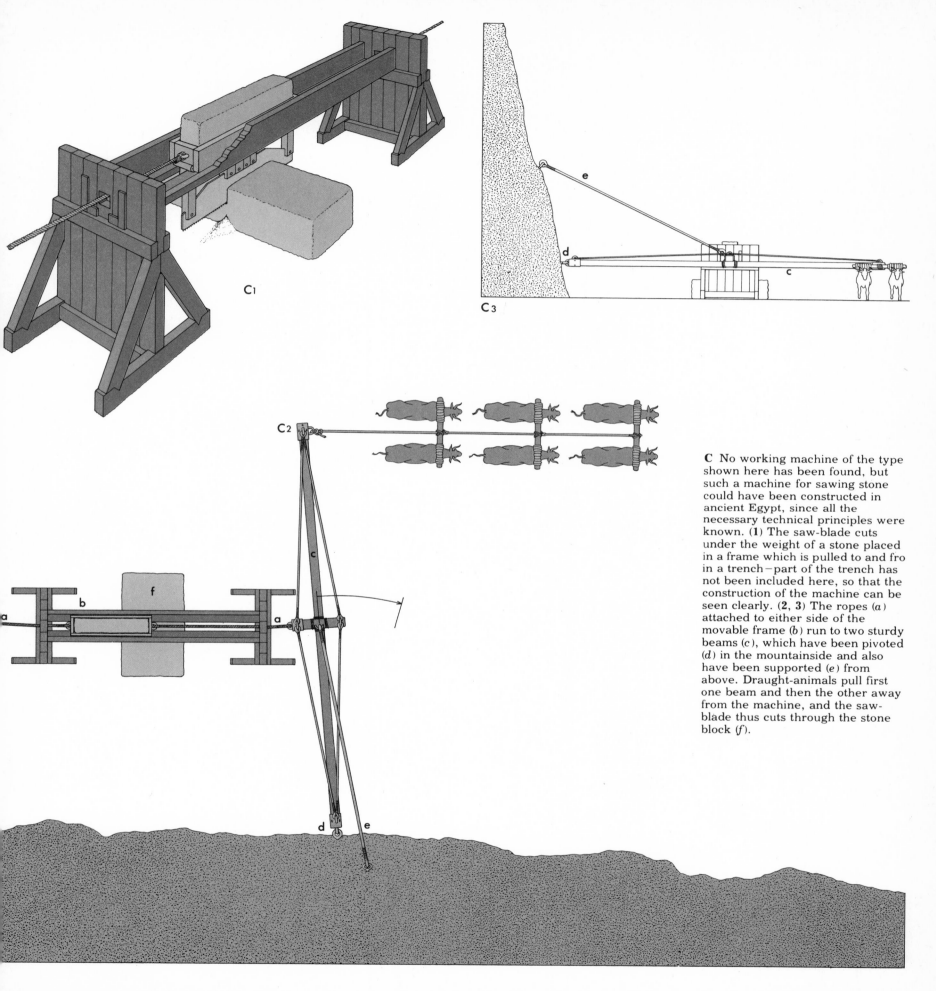

C No working machine of the type shown here has been found, but such a machine for sawing stone could have been constructed in ancient Egypt, since all the necessary technical principles were known. (**1**) The saw-blade cuts under the weight of a stone placed in a frame which is pulled to and fro in a trench – part of the trench has not been included here, so that the construction of the machine can be seen clearly. (**2, 3**) The ropes (*a*) attached to either side of the movable frame (*b*) run to two sturdy beams (*c*), which have been pivoted (*d*) in the mountainside and also have been supported (*e*) from above. Draught-animals pull first one beam and then the other away from the machine, and the saw-blade thus cuts through the stone block (*f*).

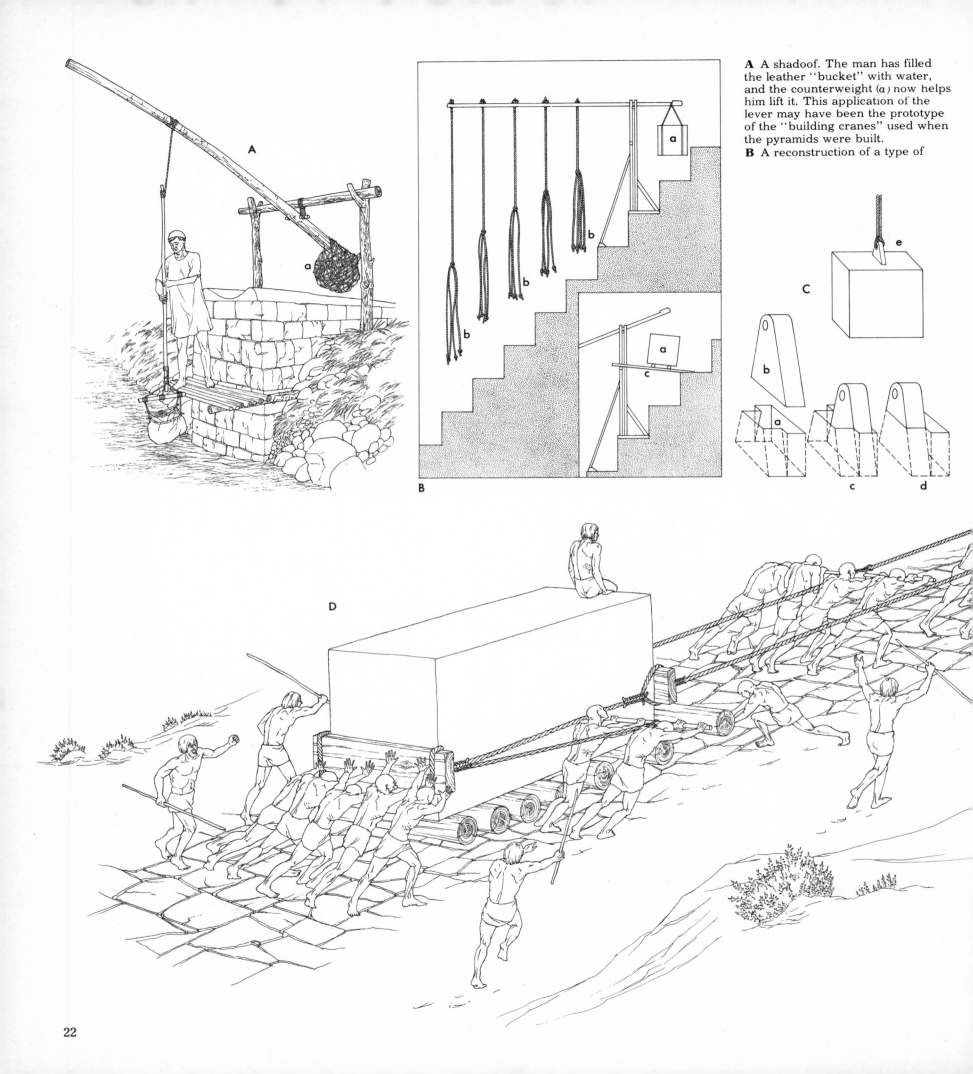

A A shadoof. The man has filled the leather "bucket" with water, and the counterweight (a) now helps him lift it. This application of the lever may have been the prototype of the "building cranes" used when the pyramids were built.
B A reconstruction of a type of

building crane which may have been used by the Egyptians. The stone block (a) was lifted when a number of workmen pulled the ends of the ropes (b).The block was then slid into place by means of a ramp (c) and rollers.

C A method for lifting blocks that eliminates the placing of ropes under them. This was described by Hero in his *Mechanica*. A partly wedge-shaped cavity (a) was cut into the top of the block, and a metal wedge (b), a "hanger", with a hole in it, was inserted (c) into the cavity. When the hanger had been fitted into the wedge-shaped part of the cavity (d), a wooden block was inserted in front of it, so that the hanger would be safely secured in the block as it was lifted.

D The muscle power of well-organized masses of workers was used to shift the heavy granite

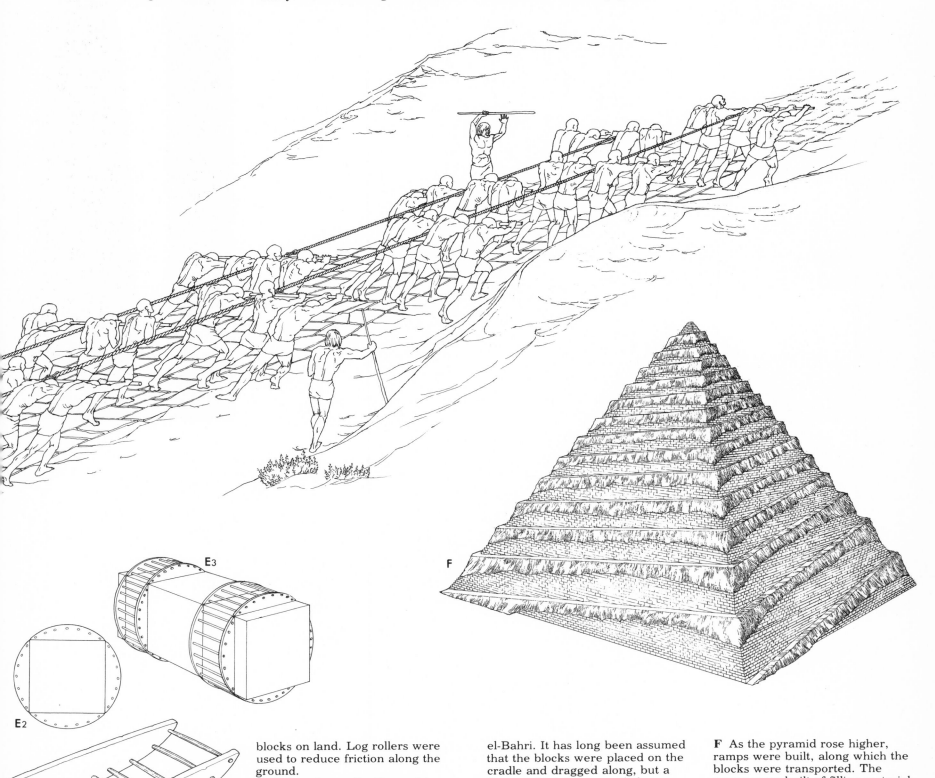

blocks on land. Log rollers were used to reduce friction along the ground.

E A draught cradle (**1**), used in ancient Egypt for transporting stone blocks. After a model from the fifteenth century BC, found in Queen Hatshepsut's grave at Deir el-Bahri. It has long been assumed that the blocks were placed on the cradle and dragged along, but a theory which has recently been published suggests instead that cradles might have been fastened round the blocks (**2**, **3**), which were then rolled to their destination.

F As the pyramid rose higher, ramps were built, along which the blocks were transported. The ramps were built of filling material and had a top layer of logs, which prevented the runners of the sledges from digging themselves in.

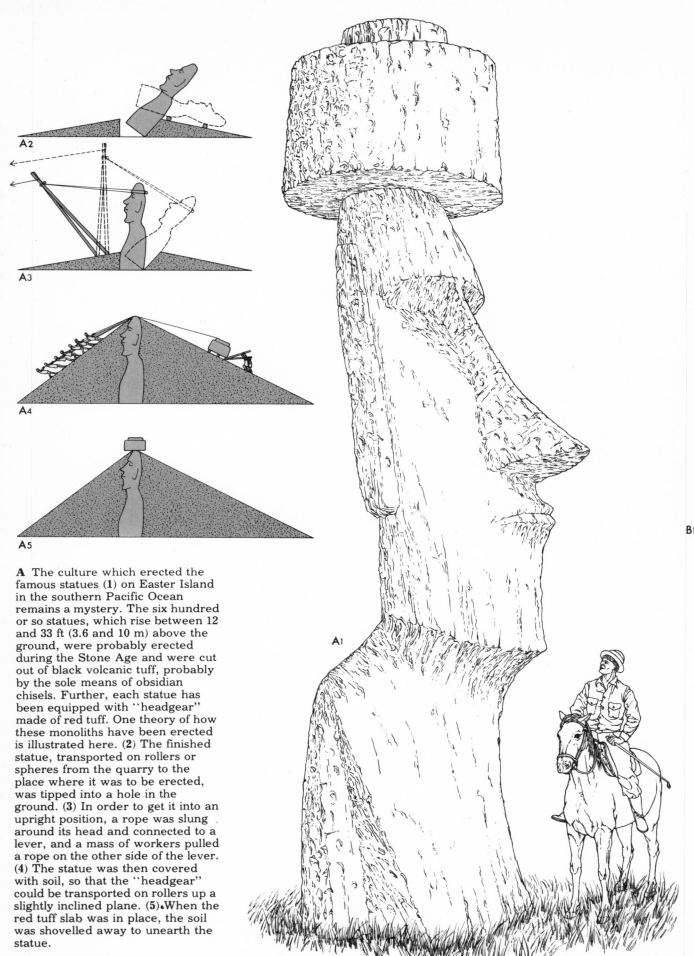

A The culture which erected the famous statues (1) on Easter Island in the southern Pacific Ocean remains a mystery. The six hundred or so statues, which rise between 12 and 33 ft (3.6 and 10 m) above the ground, were probably erected during the Stone Age and were cut out of black volcanic tuff, probably by the sole means of obsidian chisels. Further, each statue has been equipped with "headgear" made of red tuff. One theory of how these monoliths have been erected is illustrated here. (2) The finished statue, transported on rollers or spheres from the quarry to the place where it was to be erected, was tipped into a hole in the ground. (3) In order to get it into an upright position, a rope was slung around its head and connected to a lever, and a mass of workers pulled a rope on the other side of the lever. (4) The statue was then covered with soil, so that the "headgear" could be transported on rollers up a slightly inclined plane. (5) When the red tuff slab was in place, the soil was shovelled away to unearth the statue.

B Wooden poles carved with totem symbols have been erected in various ancient cultures and might perhaps be regarded as counterparts to the Easter Island statues. These two totem poles come from North America (1) and New Zealand (2).

C El Tajin, 6 miles (10 km) west of the Mexican city of Papantla, is the site of the remains of this pyramid-shaped, terraced temple. Its sculptural ornamentation is strangely rich, and 365 square niches line the terraces. The building was erected in the late sixth century AD by the Totonacs, whose Classic Veracruz civilization flourished during the first millennium AD. In this nineteenth-century reconstruction, however, the proportions are completely wrong, for the temple was considerably lower and wider than in this illustration.

D Approximately 3,500 years ago, Stonehenge was erected on a Neolithic graveyard on Salisbury Plain. The theories underlying the monument may derive from the Helladic culture, and the monument is nowadays considered to have had astronomical functions.

agree that dolerite balls were used, as these have been found on the site. Dolerite is definitely hard enough to crush granite, but as a tool, it could be made more effective if some form of working machine were fitted to it. If the ball was continuously struck and rotated, and if an abrasive powder was used, then the results would have been better. So far, however, no sign of any such machine has been found.

The stones were shipped 620 miles (c. 1,000 km) down the Nile from the Aswan quarries to the construction site at Gizeh. The most difficult part of the operation was moving them to and from the quays. The stone blocks were first placed on rollers and then dragged up slightly inclined ramps by well-organized work gangs. Loading the blocks onto large, specially built barges was quite a story in itself. The barges had a fairly deep draught when fully loaded, so they had to be ballasted with sand to bring their gunwales level with the quay. As loading progressed, the sand was unloaded, so that the barges had safe freeboards.

The first phase in building a pyramid involved levelling the bedrock to an absolutely horizontal square, orientated exactly in the direction of the four cardinal points. As we have already said, the Egyptians had mastered the art of measuring position in relation to a horizontal line or level, and the tools and instruments for such surveying had been developed and refined by the *qanaat* builders.

In the 1920s, an accurate survey using modern geodetic instruments was made of the Cheops pyramid. The results showed that the divergence from the absolute level plane was at its least 0.08 in (2 mm) and at its most 0.43 in (11 mm). Few, if any, great constructions today call for such high precision.

When the foundation had been laid, two methods were used for lifting the stone blocks into place, from the second step upwards. A ramp was built—an inclined plane of soil and sand with an inclination of 1:10 or less. Then the stone blocks were dragged up to their final position, again with organized muscle power.

The second method involved lifting the stone blocks to their correct positions with a "building crane". It is likely that such a crane was also used with a ramp to lift the stone blocks over the last bit. The friction between two even granite surfaces and the weight of the stone block would call for enormous power to move it horizontally. The crane's main constructional element may have been a lever, and its prototype was almost certainly the shadoof, a pole with bucket and counterpoise used mainly in Egypt for raising water and which exists or has existed in many other parts of the world.

The wheel was not known in the Old Kingdom, nor was the pulley, so we can eliminate the possibility of a crane construction which involved a pulley wheel and rope. But cranes of some kind must have been used for hoisting, and the proof of this lies in the longitudinal flanges found on the stone blocks in some of the great pyramids, and in the slits, obviously intended for hoisting-loops, found on other blocks. (The latter arrangement was also used by the builders of the great monuments of Greece and Rome, erected two millennia later.)

The Mighty Five

"The mighty five" is what the philosophers of ancient times called the five simple machines: the inclined plane, the wedge, the screw, the lever, and the wheel. The first three of these are closely interrelated, and so are the wheel and the lever. At least "the mighty four"—the exception being the wheel—were in all probability known by the Palaeolithic age. The lever may well have been one of the very first tools employed by tool-making man. But the wheel has its very special history, which we shall touch upon first.

The wheel can be regarded both as an appliance (for instance, the

C

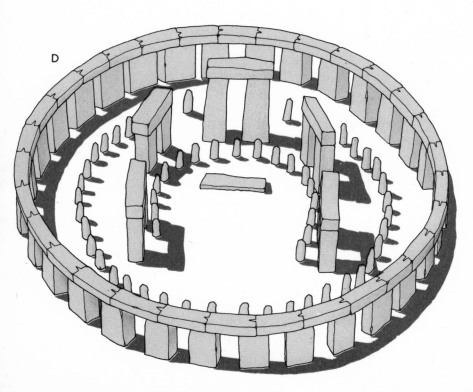

D

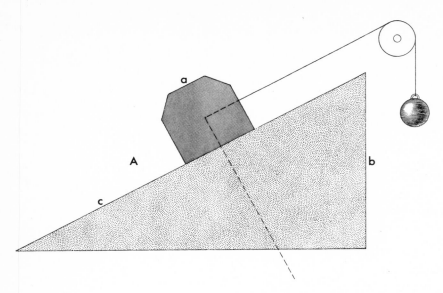

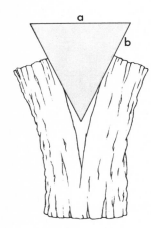

A An inclined plane is a flat surface at an angle to the horizontal. To keep an object (a) in place on an inclined plane, a force is required that is equivalent to the proportion of the object's total weight that the inclined plane's height (b) bears to its length (c), if the force is parallel to the inclined plane and directed towards its top, and if friction is ignored. The weight of an object resting on an inclined plane may be divided into two components, one acting at right angles to, and the other acting parallel to the inclined plane; the force needed to move the object up the inclined plane must exceed that of the parallel component, which gets smaller as the length (c) of the inclined plane exceeds its height (b)—with the simple machines, any decrease in force is accompanied by a reciprocal increase in distance.

B The wedge is based on the same principle as the inclined plane. When a wedge of regular section is driven into a piece of wood, for instance by a force acting at right angles to the wedge's base (a), a force acts at right angles to each of the wedge's sides (b). These forces are together greater than the force acting on the wedge's base in the same proportion as the side of the wedge bears to its base.

C Archimedes regarded the screw as the circular analogy of the inclined plane, and his reason for so doing is illustrated here. If a right-angled paper triangle is wound round a cylindrical pencil, starting with one (a) of the two smaller sides running parallel with the pencil, the pitch of the screw's threads will be marked by the hypotenuse (b).

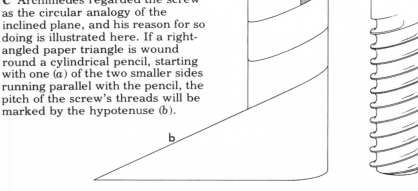

wagon wheel, a means of transportation) and as a mechanical component (at that period, mainly in the form of the cog-wheel). To say that modern civilization would fall apart if these two forms of the wheel did not exist is almost trite. The wheel is what keeps our entire society rolling—literally. True, the wheel can be replaced by other machine elements and components, but the wheel is the life-blood of the machine age, which is certainly not drawing to a close but will continue for many years yet.

The discovery of a practical use for the wheel was, of course, an enormous step forward for mankind—technically, economically, and socially. But exactly when and where this occurred is unknown. Most historians leave the question more or less open. To date the advent of the wheel from the dating of the first picture of a wagon is, obviously, very questionable. After all, the art of making illustrations in durable materials was not very widespread during the period under discussion, i.e., some time between the fourth and third millennia BC. But as far as is now known, the wheel first appeared in the kingdom of the Sumerians in Mesopotamia. Its several predecessors—the dray, the sledge, and the log roller—can be traced with certainty back to the Palaeolithic era. These are still in use in many developing countries. Charles Singer, the English historian, has pointed out drawings of both a sledge and a four-wheeled wagon which occur in a Sumerian pictograph, found during excavations at Erech, Mesopotamia. This find is generally dated at about 3500 BC. But even if this does not pinpoint the birth of the wheel, it is quite clear that it was in these parts that the first wheel appeared. As further proof, Singer cites an artefact from a grave in Tepe Gawra in the Old Assyrian kingdom. This was a little toy, a covered four-wheeled wagon, from the third millenium BC.

So far, we have been discussing the wagon wheel. But the wheel as a machine element is probably older. Many scholars believe that the throwing wheel, used in pottery, antedates the wheel by about a thousand years. The potter's wheel was in all probability made from wood, and this is why none have survived down the ages. However, Sumerian pottery, obviously made on a throwing wheel, has been found, and Singer dates the oldest example to 3250 BC, give or take 250 years. As is the case with the illustrations, the earliest finds cannot be dated with any certainty. The first use of the throwing wheel may have occurred much earlier; and in all probability, *before* the first practical application of the wagon wheel. One fact which must be considered to be most remarkable is that the Old Kingdom in Egypt, the nearest neighbour to the Sumerian river culture, had no knowledge of the wheel. Only in about 2500 BC did it become known there, probably in the form of a two-wheeled chariot used in battle. During the technologically important era when the great pyramids were built, the wheel was unknown. Instead, the technique of using the sled and log rollers for the transport of heavy loads was developed to near-perfection. Here, one may naturally reflect that it is really rather embarrassing that we have no more exact knowledge of the first appearance of one of the most important constructional elements used by mankind.

Archimedes

The first to systematize the simple machines and propound the theory of their functions was Archimedes of Syracuse (287–212 BC), who was undoubtedly the principal figure in Hellenic cultural circles of his time. It was probably he who invented the compound pulley, a device for increasing traction or lifting power, and it was he who propounded the theory of the lever, both one- and two-armed. Archimedes regarded the wheel as the circular figure described by the rotating one-armed lever, and the screw as the circular analogy of the inclined plane. (The latter is not as difficult as it sounds. Cut a right-angled triangle from a piece of paper and wind it round a cylindrical pencil, so that one arm of the right angle is parallel to the axis. The pitch of the threads will then be marked by the hypotenuse.)

Archimedes was a remarkable man who deserves a somewhat better introduction. He was one of the most distinguished mathematicians and engineers ever. Sarton notes ironically, but rightly, that great engineers of every period have been compared to Archimedes, and considers it foolhardy to compare the achievements of any person to those of the greatest genius of antiquity.

Archimedes was born in Syracuse, Sicily, one of the more important cities in the Hellenistic world, Magna Graecia, as the Romans came to call it. Syracuse had a vast harbour and a highly developed shipbuilding industry, as the economy was based on the export of grain, for which big ships were necessary. Archimedes worked there as technical adviser to his cousin, King Hiero II (and to the latter's son and successor, Gelon II), and he was responsible for the defence of the city. Hiero's great passion was shipbuilding, and he had the *Syrakosia*, the biggest ship of its day, built. Unfortunately, when it was about to be launched, it got stuck and could not be budged. Now Archimedes had become fascinated by the power-amplifying qualities of the simple machines—one of his famous sayings is, "Give me a place to stand, and I will move the earth". Hiero challenged him now not to move the earth, but only the ship.

With the help of compound pulleys coupled to levers at strategic points under the hull, Archimedes was able to give a practical demonstration of the validity of his theories. With an elegant gesture, he offered the end of the main connecting rope to Hiero, who could pull the *Syrakosia* free using only one hand.

But the most interesting of Archimedes' many engineering feats is the construction of the different war engines which he devised to defend his city against the Romans, who had designs on the riches of Syracuse. Tragically, Archimedes himself fell a victim of the Romans during the Second Punic War, in 212 BC, when he was slain by a Roman soldier whom he rebuked for stepping on a diagram he had drawn in the sand while working out a problem.

For a long time, however, Syracuse had been able to withstand the Roman siege, thanks to the monstrous war engines devised by Archimedes. A simply enormous catapult, the construction elements of which were levers and pulleys, hurled giant boulders at the attacking Roman ships. According to the Danish historian A. G. Drachmann, these boulders weighed 550 lb (*c*. 250 kg), and he quotes Plutarch, who tells that the Romans panicked and fled as soon as a beam of wood or a rope's end became visible on the walls of Syracuse, in the belief that Archimedes had some new diabolical device with which to attack them.

The most gruesome of all the war engines was, however, that intended as the last line of defence in the inner basin of Syracuse's harbour. It was a giant claw, which lay hidden under the water. If an enemy ship succeeded in getting that far, the claw was to grab the vessel, lift it high up in the air, turn it over, and shake it until the crew fell out! The existence of such a machine has been doubted, not surprisingly. However, the historian Polybius describes a different version, in which an iron claw, mounted on a tall crane, was to grab the ship, hoist it into the air, and then let go of it, so that it smashed into the water or was dashed against the breakwater.

Of course, it is quite possible that the whole story was pure terror propaganda, invented in order to strike fear into the rank and file of the enemy. There are many examples of this in the history of warfare. Real or not, such a construction is definitely possible, if the principles of the simple machines are applied. This remarkable construction has, apparently, never been depicted, but we have amused

D The characteristics of a lever are that it pivots round a fulcrum and that it moves under the influence of an applied force, or effort, and a load. Two applications of the two-armed lever are shown here: the oar (**1**), whose fulcrum is the rowlock, and the common balance (**2**). The amount of amplification of the effort applied to a lever is known as the mechanical advantage; the effort is increased in the same proportion as the distance between the effort and the fulcrum exceeds the distance between the fulcrum and the weight. The balance here is in a state of equilibrium because although the objects in the scale (*a*) weigh more than the weight on the hook (*c*),

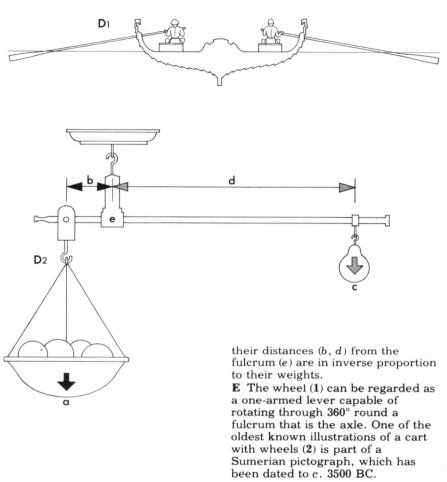

their distances (*b*, *d*) from the fulcrum (*e*) are in inverse proportion to their weights.

E The wheel (**1**) can be regarded as a one-armed lever capable of rotating through 360° round a fulcrum that is the axle. One of the oldest known illustrations of a cart with wheels (**2**) is part of a Sumerian pictograph, which has been dated to *c*. 3500 BC.

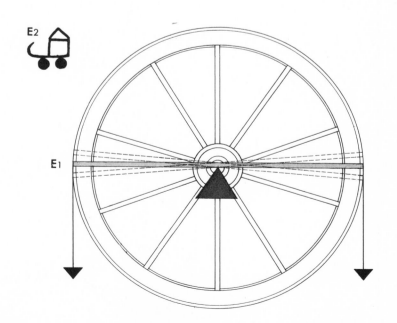

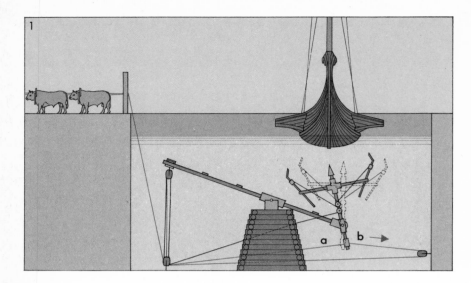

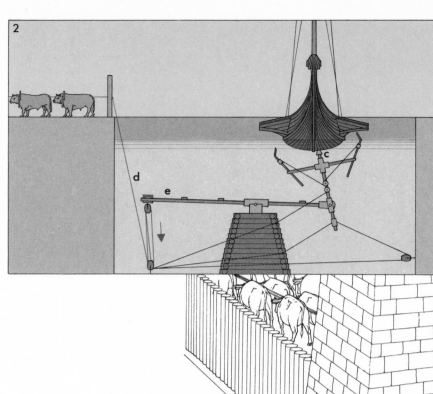

ourselves by illustrating a possible design. Naturally, this reconstruction is based on mere assumption, and it excludes Polybius's version. After all, a tolerably prudent commander would hardly take his ship near such a crane, which, with its giant claw, would be easier to detect than an underwater construction. Even if the latter were visible—for we may assume that the water there was clearer than it is nowadays—it would not have been too difficult to stir up enough mud to cover it, thus allowing its sudden appearance to cause a most horrible shock.

There has been much interest in the burning-mirrors invented by Archimedes to burn the rigs of the attacking Roman vessels. The construction is said to be similar to that of modern sun reflectors, that is to say, it consisted of numerous small, polished metal mirrors on a lattice-work structure of parabolic cross-section, rather like the one at the United States Army Research Station at Matick, Massachusetts. The story of Archimedes' burning-mirror fascinated Leonardo da Vinci (1452–1519), but he doubted if the construction was practicable. True, Archimedes was familiar with mirrors and with geometrical optics, but Leonardo believed that it was impossible to build a great burning-mirror which could be aimed with reasonable accuracy. Leonardo had scrutinized the writings of Archimedes, and he credits him with the much-discussed steam-gun, *architronito*. This consisted of a cylindrical barrel of copper, sealed at one end, that shot a well-fitting, iron cannon-ball. If a little water was poured in between the sealed end and the ball and heated rapidly, enough steam pressure would be created to fire the ball. According to Leonardo's notes, a cannon-ball weighing one talent (17.6 lb or 8 kg) could have been fired a length of six stadia (4,102 ft or c. 1,250 m)—no mean achievement. However, Hart, who is perhaps the foremost of Leonardo's biographers, is of the opinion that the steam-gun was never built. Leonardo is sometimes mentioned as one of the pioneers of steam power, but we must remember that the idea of a steam-gun can, in fact, be traced back to Archimedes.

One of the monstrous engines said to have been constructed by Archimedes was a "ship-shaker" in the form of a giant claw, hidden at the bottom of Syracuse's harbour. It is quite possible to construct such a machine by applying only the principles of the simple machines. It might, for instance, look like the machine to the right—a sturdy platform, carrying a system of levers—which would work as illustrated above. (1) When the enemy ship has managed to enter the harbour, the claws are directed towards it by oxen pulling ropes *a* or *b*, to give the

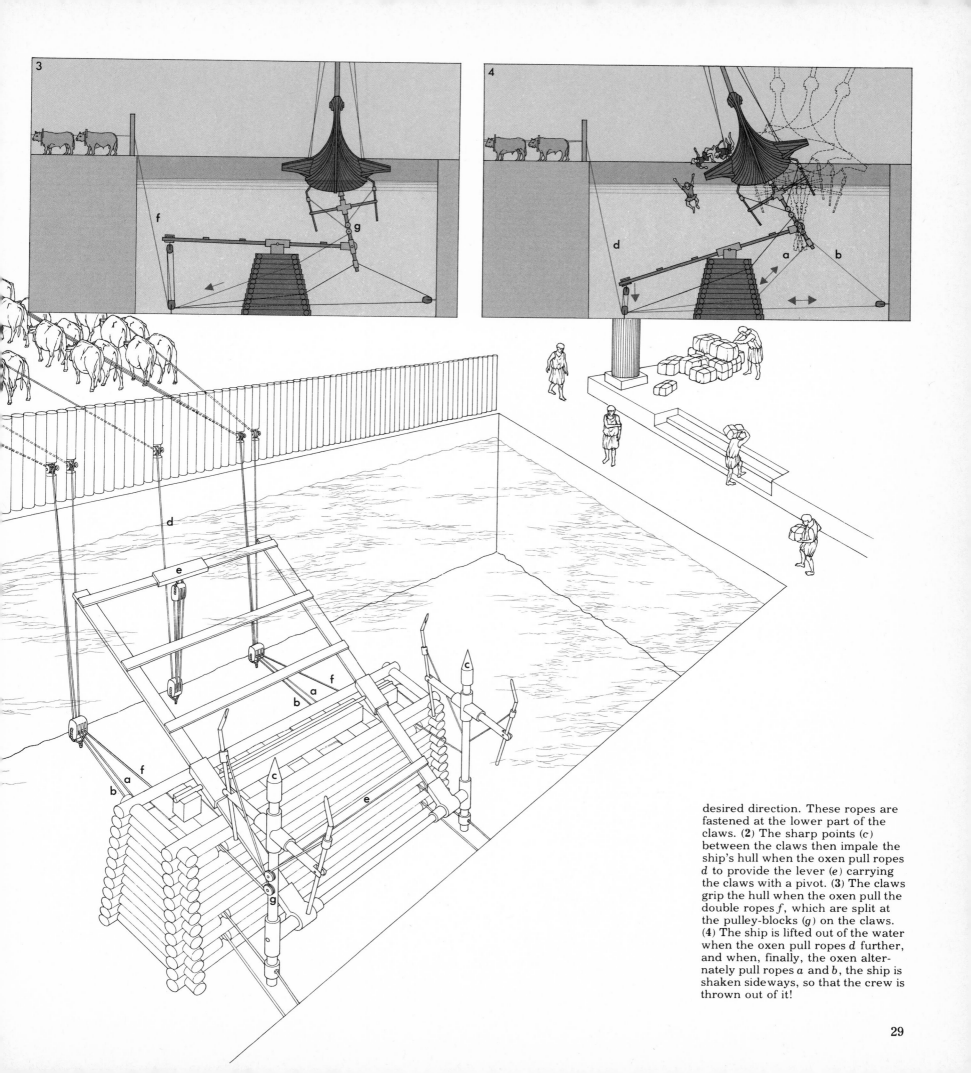

desired direction. These ropes are fastened at the lower part of the claws. (**2**) The sharp points (*c*) between the claws then impale the ship's hull when the oxen pull ropes *d* to provide the lever (*e*) carrying the claws with a pivot. (**3**) The claws grip the hull when the oxen pull the double ropes *f*, which are split at the pulley-blocks (*g*) on the claws. (**4**) The ship is lifted out of the water when the oxen pull ropes *d* further, and when, finally, the oxen alternately pull ropes *a* and *b*, the ship is shaken sideways, so that the crew is thrown out of it!

A A cutler displaying a variety of knives in his shop. The illustration is based on an original found on a Roman tombstone from the time of the birth of Christ.

B From illustrations in the grave of an Egyptian vizier, Rekhmire, in Thebes in the fifteenth century BC. The three men on the left are considered to be goldsmiths, and the one furthest left is hammering gold on an anvil. The man furthest right is using a blowpipe to smelt metal.

C Roman granite mould for embossing gold and silver ornaments.
D Soldering-copper (**1**) and blow-pipe (**2**) from ancient Rome, found at Chatelet, France.

E Roman dies, used to punch decorations in metals.
F A blacksmith's workshop. Above the workers, various products from the smithy are shown. From a painting on an Attic vase from the sixth century BC.
G Metal tools forged by the ancient Romans.

Archimedes' achievements as a theorist are in no way overshadowed by his exploits. We will not discuss his extremely subtle and, indeed, brilliant mathematical theories here, although mathematics is one of the more important "tools" of engineering, but we shall give just one example. During his technical calculations, Archimedes was irritated by the prevailing Greek numerical system, in which the numbers 1–9 were simply the first nine letters of the alphabet (alpha to iota), the multiples of ten between 10 and 90 were the following nine letters, and so on. But the alphabet was not long enough to express more than thousands, up to but not including ten thousand. Thus, it was possible to count to 9,999—but that was all. For the number 10,000, the concept of *myria* was introduced, but a word instead of the alphabetical numerals was not very handy when, say, adding. Things were a bit better after the abbreviation M for myriad had been invented; it was then possible to multiply this M with the alphabetical numerals and count all the way to 99,999,999, a number which, nowadays, we can represent, simply, as 10^8-1. Archimedes called the numerical system up to this numeral an octad, i.e., having eight numerals. Here, he must have been fully aware of the mathematical system's tenth power—or, the power series—but he was so

deeply rooted in the Hellenistic way of writing numbers with nine letters that he did not come to think of the decimal system.

Nevertheless, the great mathematician Carl Friedrich Gauss (1777–1855), who was a devotee of Archimedes, could never forgive him for not having taken the radical step of introducing the power series!

Archimedes presented his ideas on high numbers and how to express them in *Arenarius* ("The Sand Counter"), in which he attempted to estimate the number of grains of sand the universe could hold. (It was then the custom, as it was later on, too, to present a theory in the form of a philosophical problem.)

Archimedes continued his numerical system so that it formed finally a myriad octads, that is, a one followed by eight hundred million noughts! His goal had been to expand the Hellenic numerical system so that it could express high numbers. We must agree that he undoubtedly succeeded! Archimedes the sand-counter is still remembered in our language by the word *myriad*, even if its original meaning, "10,000", has been almost lost, and the word now stands for "a very great number".

However, such subtle philosophical problems as this did not occ-

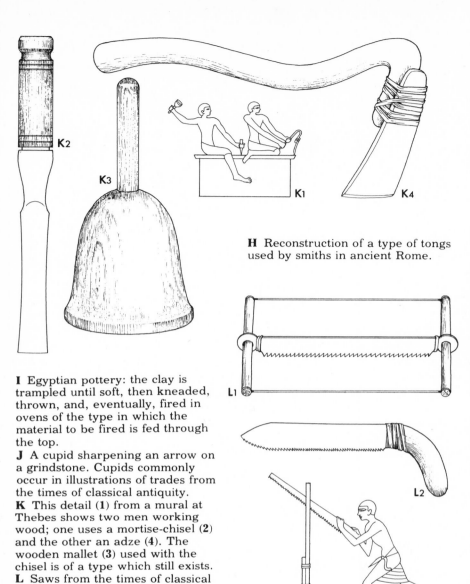

H Reconstruction of a type of tongs used by smiths in ancient Rome.

I Egyptian pottery: the clay is trampled until soft, then kneaded, thrown, and, eventually, fired in ovens of the type in which the material to be fired is fed through the top.
J A cupid sharpening an arrow on a grindstone. Cupids commonly occur in illustrations of trades from the times of classical antiquity.
K This detail (**1**) from a mural at Thebes shows two men working wood; one uses a mortise-chisel (**2**) and the other an adze (**4**). The wooden mallet (**3**) used with the chisel is of a type which still exists.
L Saws from the times of classical antiquity. (**1**) Roman saw.
(**2**) Egyptian compass saw.
(**3**) A man sawing.

History, alas, does not record the outcome of the case, but the principle which Archimedes propounded is still with us and forms the basic theory behind, for instance, the calculation of a ship's stability.

The amplifying power of another of Archimedes' inventions, the compound pulley, fascinated Leonardo da Vinci, who sketched several suggestions for machines in which the compound pulley could be used. In fact, many of Leonardo's ideas for simple machines were based upon the solid theoretical and practical foundation which Archimedes had laid down. Of course, Leonardo's achievements in this and other areas did not benefit technology, as his scientific papers were not published in his time, but lay hidden and forgotten in the archives of several princely houses, and were not scientifically studied or published until the end of the nineteenth century.

The writings of Archimedes, above all those which describe the mighty five, may be regarded as the Genesis of engineering. This statement contains neither blasphemy nor an idolization of the machine, for his writings, and above all the oral tradition of his achievements, became widespread in the classical cultures. The man who contributed the most to spreading the works of Archimedes was the Roman engineer Vitruvius Pollio, who, in his famous book *De architectura*—completed in 37 AD—exhaustively described the simple machines and their technical applications.

Tools and Implements in the Time of Archimedes

What tools and implements did Archimedes and his engineers use to build the great throwing machine or the "ship shaker" in Syracuse harbour? Tools for working iron and wood, and some kind of lifting system, would have been necessary to assemble the various parts. All we know of these tools is that tools and implements used by different trades have changed little from the time of their first recorded appearance. We have already covered the long chain of development that resulted in the tools, implements, and methods used by the pyramid builders. At the time of Christ, tools such as the carpenter's and the mason's were almost identical in form and material to those used fifteen hundred years previously, at the time of the transition from the Old to the New Kingdom in Egypt, and most of them were to remain unchanged for at least another fifteen hundred years.

Naturally, this does not mean that there was no development during this time. New trades came into being as new needs arose. The new methods demanded new tools. Pliny the Elder (23?—79), in his *Naturalis historia*, has covered in detail the methods used by various trades—among them the smith's, the painter's, the carpenter's, and the sculptor's. He leaves the reader with a strong feeling that specialization is an ancient phenomenon, even if seen from Pliny's time perspective!

But even if we do not have very much information about the actual tools used at the time of Archimedes, we do have comprehensive descriptions of the results produced by the skilled craftsmen of the time. In the second century AD, the Greek author Athenaeus of Naucratis wrote an extensive account of the great ship *Syrakosia*, the flagship of Hiero's fleet. This ship is a magnificent example of what could be accomplished with contemporary tools. At the same time, *Syrakosia* is a graphic presentation of a technologically advanced culture.

Athenaeus' account gives no exact dimensions of the ship, but from the freight capacity and all the equipment described, it is clear that they were considerable, even by modern standards. The ship was planned as the first and largest of sixty (!) quadriremes—a ship with four banks of oars—which were to be built for Hiero's fleet. The

upy Archimedes full-time. His great pioneering contributions to mathematics lie in his elucidation of the mighty five and, above all, in the easily comprehended constructions he created in order to make clear to the engineer the concept of the simple machines as construction elements. Archimedes was both theoretical and practical in his approach.

"Eureka" is a well-known expression all over the world, and for this, too, we can thank Archimedes. He is believed to have shouted this, meaning "I have found it!", when he chanced upon the solution to a problem posed by King Hiero, namely to establish whether or not a crown made for the king by a goldsmith, was of pure gold. Hiero suspected that silver or some other metal had been alloyed with the gold. How could this be proved? Archimedes came upon the answer one day when he was taking a bath, and in his joy, he ran naked through the streets of Syracuse, shouting "Eureka!". He had just discovered what has been known since as Archimedes' principle: that, when a body is immersed in a liquid, its apparent loss of weight is equal to the weight of the liquid it displaces. By working out the specific weights of gold and silver, Archimedes was able to say whether or not the crown was genuine and the goldsmith honest.

A An Archimedean screw. As the handle (a) is turned, a certain amount of water (b) is brought into the helical screw, which then brings the water up to a reservoir or trough.

B Hero's *aelopile*. The lower container (a) was partly filled with water and was heated. The steam that was then produced was led via pipes (b) to a metal sphere (c), which could turn on its axle and had exhaust pipes (d), whose openings were directed at right angles to the axle. As steam escaped into the air, the sphere rotated because of the steam's reaction.

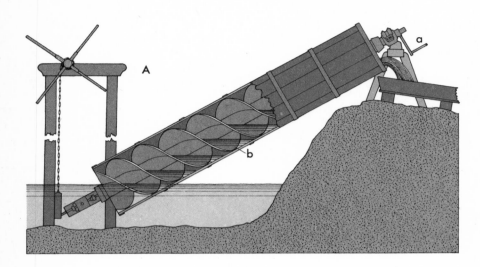

normal warships and merchant ships used by Hiero were triremes or biremes which he caused to be built by his shipbuilder, Archias. For the *Syrakosia*, Archias had to buy timber from the Italian mainland, hemp for the cordage from Spain, and tar from the Rhône valley; he attracted skilled tradesmen from wherever he could get his hands on them. He succeeded in rounding up three hundred specialist tradesmen, "not counting their helpers", to equip and fit out the ship. The hull, which took a year to build, was first covered in canvas saturated with tar. Then it was fitted with lead sheeting, soldered together. Apparently, the shipbuilders had had plenty of experience of the damage that the ship-worm and other marine organisms can cause to wooden hulls.

The ship was heavily armed, as its costly freight would certainly have been an attractive prize for the pirates who roamed the Mediterranean at that time. Sturdy iron bars formed a lattice-work along the bulwarks, and sixty fully armed marines mounted guard there at times of peril. *Syrakosia* was a three-master with eight towers, two each at stern and bow, and four amidships. The towers were equipped with rock-throwing engines, and hoists were installed for raising the projectiles from the deck up to the tower. Deep in the hull was a fresh-water tank, a sea-water well for fish, and space for provision stores, mills for grinding grain, fuel for the galley stoves, and so on. A stable for twenty horses was built on the lower deck, together with quarters for the horsemen (despatch riders on land), their slaves, and the marines. On the middle deck, there were cabins for passengers and the ship's officers. Athenaeus measured these cabins in *clines*, or couches, which at night served as beds. (The Japanese still measure a room by the number of straw mats, also used as beds, which can be fitted into it.) On each side of the ship were thirty cabins, each with four *clines*. The commander's quarters had an area of fifteen *clines*.

Throughout the ship the floor was decorated with mosaics depicting the entire Iliad. The wall and ceiling decorations illustrated the same theme. On the upper deck there was a gymnasium and a garden filled with all kinds of magnificent plants. Vines and ivy were planted along the bulwarks, forming a shaded promenade around the ship. The plants were watered by an ingenious system of pumps and pipes. Also on this deck was a temple to the goddess of fertility, Aphrodite. The floor of the temple was of polished gemstones, the walls were of cypress and cedar, and the doors were inlaid with ivory. The interior was extravagantly decorated with statues, paintings, and magnificent urns. Alongside the temple lay a library filled with books of all kinds, from philosophy to light reading. The interior decoration was of the same high standard as that in the rest of the ship. The roof was vaulted, and in the centre of the library stood a magnificent sun-dial.

The library, too, had a bathroom with three bronze baths and hand-basins of beautiful marble.

Thus far Athenaeus and his description of the *Syrakosia*. We do not need to quote any more to demonstrate that the like of the standard on board Hiero's flagship did not return to the surface of the ocean before the great era of the Atlantic liners in the early twentieth century. A list of all the tradesmen required to build and decorate the *Syrakosia* would make fascinating reading. It would include a strange mixture of types—everything from gardeners and mosaic layers to the builders of war machines. One wonders if the modern shipyards which built the great, but now vanished, Atlantic liners had as many specialized tradesmen!

The Engineers, Machines, and Tools of the Alexandrian School
Alexandria, situated in the western part of the Nile delta, was found-

ed by Alexander the Great (356–323 BC) in 332 BC and quickly grew into a large metropolis, becoming one of the more important scientific and cultural centres of the world. One of the main reasons for this pre-eminence was the excellence of the university, known as the Museum, which was dedicated to the nine muses, the protectresses of science and the fine arts.

Archimedes received his education at the university of Alexandria, where, during the centuries before the birth of Christ, groups of mathematicians and scientists worked, devoting themselves to the construction of numerous fascinating machines, the functions of which were impressive and which were clearly the result of a fine understanding of the principles involved. Best known among the mathematicians is Euclid (*fl.c.* 300 BC), who, with his *Elements of Geometry*, has been the great master of logic to many generations of students of all kinds from the Middle Ages to the present time.

But the greatest and most colourful of what is known as the Alexandrian school of engineers is undoubtedly Hero, who lived sometime during the second century BC–the exact dates of his life are a matter of dispute. Hero was of a playful turn of mind; therein lay his strength as well as his weakness. His best-known invention is the *aelopile*, the first reaction turbine, which converted heat into mechanical energy through the medium of steam. It never became anything more than an amusing plaything, as it could not be made to function as a working machine, that is, it could not perform useful work. The power which it developed was sufficient to make the ball revolve at a reasonable speed, but in order to produce a power surplus, the speed would have had to be increased to at least a few thousand rpm, and this would have required a very high head of steam, which would have meant a very efficient transfer of heat from the fire to the rotating ball. Another problem was that the centrifugal force, together with the slightest imbalance in the ball, would, at the speed necessary to produce a reasonable effect, have produced great strains on the material. Hero and his assistants probably tried to get the *aelopile* to perform useful work, but they must have been disappointed at the results.

In the 1780s, James Watt had occasion (see page 131) to work out the theoretical operating conditions of a reaction turbine, and his conclusion was that such a turbine could not be built, given the state of contemporary technology.

However, Hero had several other strings to his technical bow. His playful attitude is demonstrated best, perhaps, by the automata he invented. One of the best known and most ingenious of his automatic devices is the one by which the doors of the inner sanctum of a temple were opened by the lighting of a sacrificial fire on a nearby altar. This must have seemed miraculous to the uneducated and illiterate members of the congregation, who undoubtedly believed that this was tangible proof of the almighty power of the gods.

Hero himself would certainly have objected to anyone calling his temple machine ''playful'' and would have pointed out sharply that very serious thought lay behind both the construction and the function. However, in those of his works that have been preserved, Hero describes many other amusing automatic devices that certainly were designed for amusement and entertainment. Examples of these are the toy birds which were made to sing by a mechanism powered by a water-wheel, and the crown of dancing figurines, rather like a modern angel chimes, which was driven by a heat turbine. These should not be dismissed out of hand just because they were built for pleasure. After all, those principles of natural law that Hero and the other engineers of the Alexandrian school were demonstrating with their automata came to play a significant role in the future development of science and engineering.

The first great engineer of the Alexandrian school was, however, not Hero but Ctesibius, who also lived sometime during the second century BC. He was a most talented mathematician and had certainly become acquainted with Euclid's *Elements* at the Museum. It is a matter of controversy whether he knew the works on the mighty five that had been written by Archimedes and Aristotle. Also a matter of controversy are the exact dates of his life.

Ctesibius, the son of a barber, had in his youth followed his father's footsteps, and it was in the barber's shop that he made his first technical device. It may seem simple to us, but then, of course, it attracted an enormous amount of attention. By suspending a mirror from a rope which ran over concealed rollers, he could raise and lower the mirror due to the fact that it was counterbalanced by a lead cylinder which moved inside a copper tube, built into the wall. Such magic had never been seen before, and it is easy to imagine the astonishment of the clients. This simple device soon had, however, a totally unforeseen technical spin-off.

The counterweight filled the tube so closely that the mirror was difficult to move. Ctesibius must have pondered a great deal on the mystical power that hampered the movement of the counterweight. At length, he concluded quite rightly that the air in the tube was compressed and, consequently, worked as an elastic substance. So he bored a little hole at the bottom of the tube, and this allowed him to raise and lower the mirror without any difficulty, but to the accompaniment of a strange whistling sound. Ctesibius detected the cause of this, too, and this led him to construct the world's first organ.

At this time, very little was known about the properties of air, so we can assume that Ctesibius devoted his time to numerous experiments with pumps and other devices for producing compressed air. He must also have spent time speculating about the fundamental laws of acoustics, for just as little was known about these. He was treading unbroken ground, and the organ he designed had a number of components which can be regarded as basic inventions. Sarton remarks that, if the patent system had existed at the time, there is no doubt that Ctesibius would have been granted a large number of fundamental patents for his organ and his many other inventions.

The literature of the subject quite rightly attributes the water clock to Ctesibius. This device, also called the clepsydra, had certainly been used to measure time in ancient Egypt as early as the second millennium BC, and perhaps even earlier in the Far East. But the early types were not at all accurate. From his work on the pressure of air and of various liquids, Ctesibius realized that the principle of the water clock must be the flow of water at a constant pressure through an unchanging nozzle. Ctesibius made a nozzle out of precious stone and constructed a basin with a spillway which gave a constant pressure, provided that the water flow was constant and slightly excessive.

The works written by Ctesibius himself have been lost, but they were known to some of his successors, and some of their writings have been preserved. Only fragments, sometimes in Arabic translations, remain of many of these original works. Tragically, many priceless and irreplaceable scientific works were lost in 47 BC during Julius Caesar's Egyptian campaign, when he plundered Alexandria and burnt down the Museum. The richly comprehensive library, with its estimated half a million works, was destroyed–a dreadful loss to science, literature, and art.

Ctesibius had many disciples at the Museum, and it is mainly from their writings that we have been able to learn something about the master's work. The more important of these engineers were Philo of Byzantium and Hero of Alexandria.

Philo was active in Alexandria in the latter part of the second century BC. Later, he became a military engineer in the service of

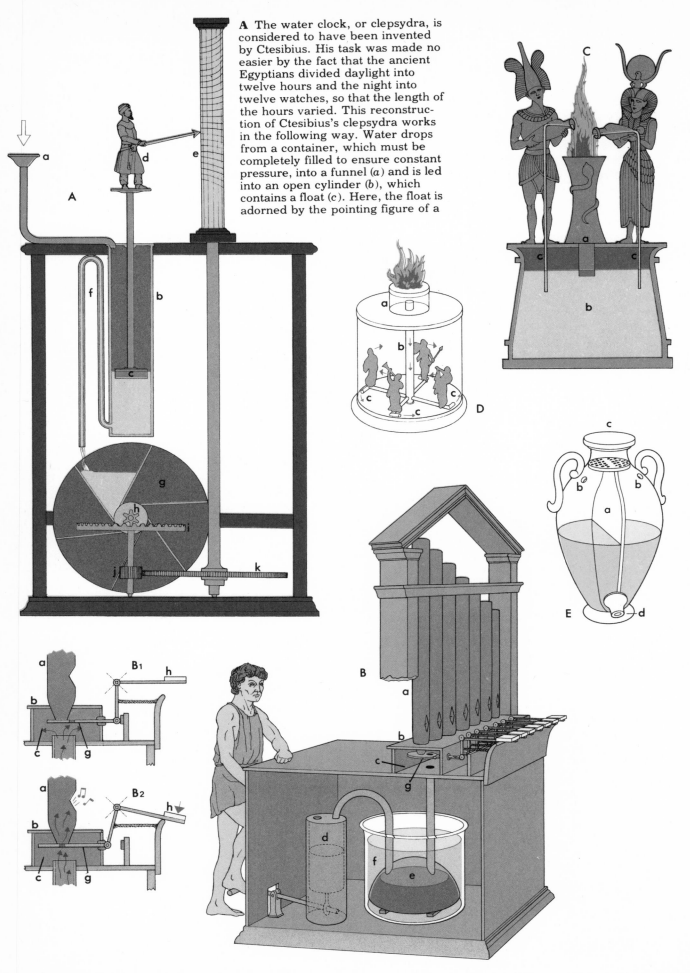

A The water clock, or clepsydra, is considered to have been invented by Ctesibius. His task was made no easier by the fact that the ancient Egyptians divided daylight into twelve hours and the night into twelve watches, so that the length of the hours varied. This reconstruction of Ctesibius's clepsydra works in the following way. Water drops from a container, which must be completely filled to ensure constant pressure, into a funnel (a) and is led into an open cylinder (b), which contains a float (c). Here, the float is adorned by the pointing figure of a man (d). As the water in the cylinder rises, so does the float, and the figure points to the time on the pillar (e). At the same time, the water level in the siphon (f) rises, and when the shorter leg of f is completely filled, the external air pressure forces the water out of the cylinder and into a drum (g) which is divided into compartments. As each compartment becomes full, the drum turns a little. A cog-wheel (h) on the drum shaft then drives three other cog-wheels (i, j, k); k is mounted on the shaft carrying e. The lines showing the time on the pillar are not horizontal, so the length of the hours is varied as the pillar is turned.

B The organ has also been attributed to Ctesibius and has been described by both Hero and Vitruvius. A row of pipes (a) were mounted on a board (b), under which ran a duct (c) for air compressed by a pedal-driven pump (d). To keep the air pressure constant, Ctesibius used a pressure-equalizing tank (e). When air was pumped into the tank, the water inside was forced into the container (f) around it. (1) Under each pipe was a perforated wooden board (g). (2) When one of the sprung keys (h) was pressed, the board protruded, so that its hole connected the pipe to the compressed-air duct; the pipe then emitted a tone.

C This altar has been attributed to Ctesibius's disciple Hero; the fire on it was automatically extinguished when it had burnt for long enough to heat and expand the air inside the metal cylinder (a) enough to force part of the water in the basin (b) up through the pipes (c) inside the statuettes.

D A hot-air version of Hero's aelopile. When the fire is lit, the air inside the altar (a) is heated, expands, and travels through a piping system (b). The figurines are driven round by the heated air, which spurts out through the bent pipe ends (c).

E A jug, designed by Hero, in which a wall (a) separates wine and water. In the upper part of the jug are two holes (b); its top (c) is well sealed. A narrow opening (d) at the bottom is connected to both inner sections of the jug. As long as a finger is held over each of the holes b, nothing can be poured from the jug. When either finger is removed, air can enter into the relevant section(s), and because of the equalization of the pressure, wine, water, or mixture of both pours through d.

F Hero's ingenious device which opened the doors of the temple's inner sanctum. When the sacrificial fire is lighted, the air inside the altar (a) expands, causing the pressure to increase in the sphere (b), which is

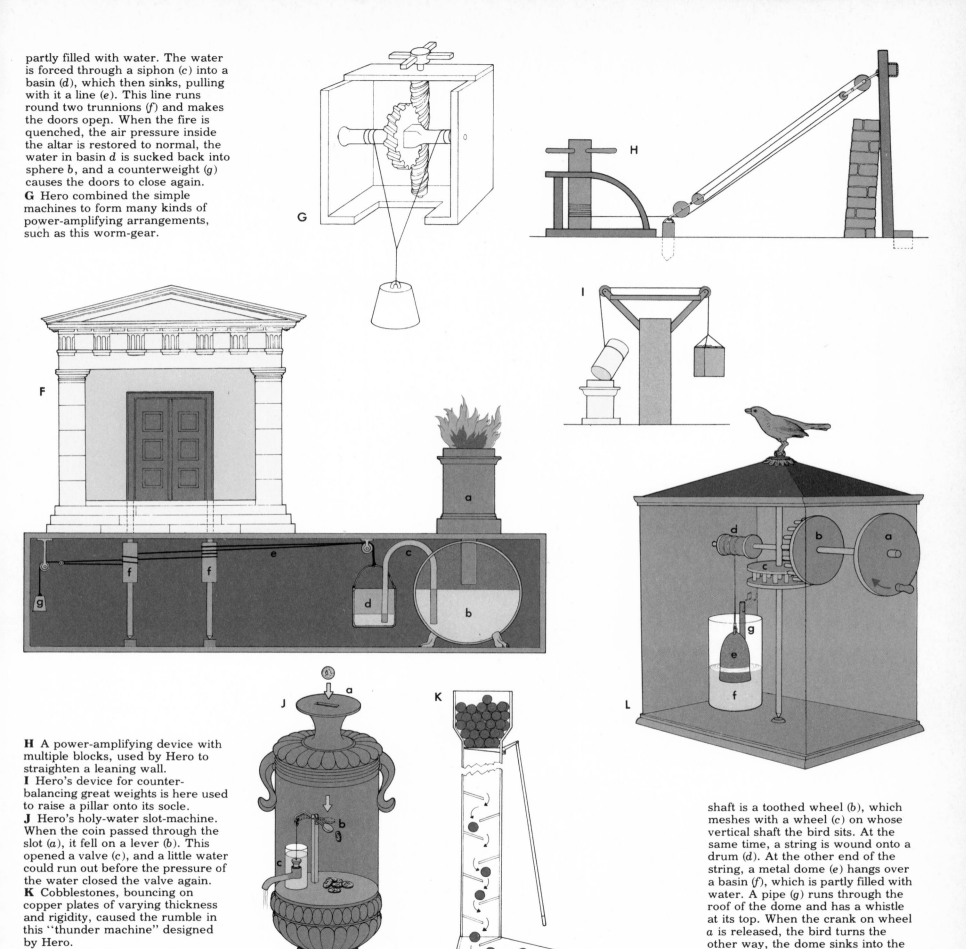

partly filled with water. The water is forced through a siphon (c) into a basin (d), which then sinks, pulling with it a line (e). This line runs round two trunnions (f) and makes the doors open. When the fire is quenched, the air pressure inside the altar is restored to normal, the water in basin d is sucked back into sphere b, and a counterweight (g) causes the doors to close again.
G Hero combined the simple machines to form many kinds of power-amplifying arrangements, such as this worm-gear.

H A power-amplifying device with multiple blocks, used by Hero to straighten a leaning wall.
I Hero's device for counter-balancing great weights is here used to raise a pillar onto its socle.
J Hero's holy-water slot-machine. When the coin passed through the slot (a), it fell on a lever (b). This opened a valve (c), and a little water could run out before the pressure of the water closed the valve again.
K Cobblestones, bouncing on copper plates of varying thickness and rigidity, caused the rumble in this "thunder machine" designed by Hero.
L Hero's "divine box". When wheel a has been cranked, the bird turns and whistles! On the wheel

shaft is a toothed wheel (b), which meshes with a wheel (c) on whose vertical shaft the bird sits. At the same time, a string is wound onto a drum (d). At the other end of the string, a metal dome (e) hangs over a basin (f), which is partly filled with water. A pipe (g) runs through the roof of the dome and has a whistle at its top. When the crank on wheel a is released, the bird turns the other way, the dome sinks into the water, and the air then forced out of the dome through the pipe causes the whistle to sound.

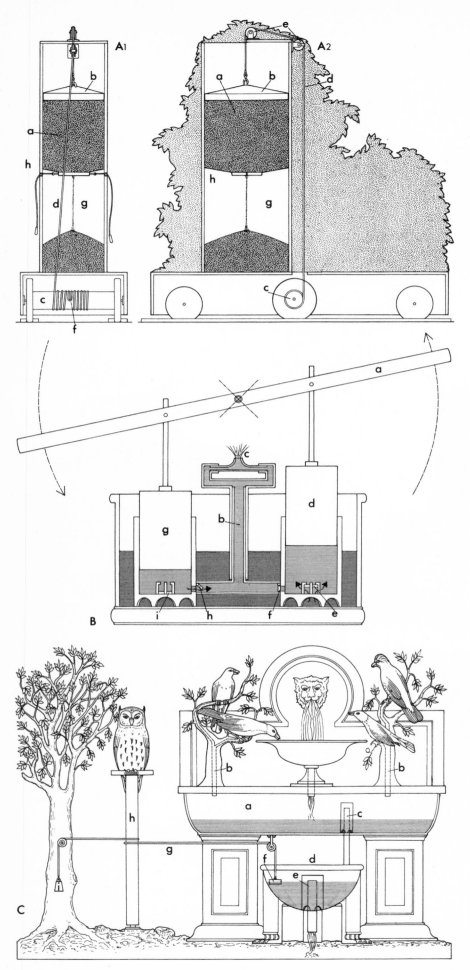

the rulers of Rhodes, designing all kinds of weapons for attack and defence—ballistas, battering rams, and suchlike. Philo is considered to be the first to have collected and described the age's military engineering technology and its applications. Only a couple of chapters of his comprehensive work, *Mechanice syntaxis*, survive, but one of them, ''Pneumatica'', on air pumps and compressed air, derives in part from Ctesibius.

The most brilliant engineer of the Alexandrian school was, however, Hero, whom we have already mentioned. His books on mathematics, mechanics, and automata contain descriptions of about seventy mechanical devices, ranging from compound elements, such as gearwheels, to highly complicated automatic devices. Drachmann believes that Hero was aided in his very extensive work by pupils and collaborators. It is probable that he provided the inspiration and ideas for a number of engineers, and that these, in their turn, had skilful craftsmen available to assist them to put their ideas into practice.

A Hero's sand motor for automata theatres, here shown in section from the side (**1**) and from the front (**2**). The tall box contained two compartments, of which the upper was filled with sand, millet, mustard-seed, or something of the same sort. On top of the sand was a weight (*b*), which was connected to the wheel axle (*c*) by a rope (*d*) running over pulleys (*e*). If the theatre was to roll forward onto the stage and then return the way it came, the rope was wound round the axle first in one and then in the other direction; the length of the coil (*f*) then decided for how long the theatre would remain standing on the stage. When the sand was allowed to run out through a small opening in the dividing wall (*h*) into the lower compartment (*g*) of the box, the weight sank and thus pulled the rope, so that the wheel axle was turned and the theatre started to move.

B This combined suction- and force-pump has been described by Hero and was intended for fire-fighting. The contrivance consists of two cylinders with pistons, which are moved up and down by one and the same handle (*a*). The cylinders are connected to each other and to an ascending pipe (*b*), from whose top water is pumped out through an opening (*c*), which can be directed upwards or to either side. When one piston (*d*) is moved upwards, the change in pressure causes a valve (*e*) in the bottom of the cylinder to open, and water comes pouring in. The valve (*f*) which connects the cylinder to the ascending pipe is then closed, for when piston *d* is moved upwards, the other piston (*g*) is lowered, and the water contained in its cylinder is forced through a valve (*h*) into the ascending pipe. The increased pressure of the water then keeps valves *f* and *i* closed.

C Hero's singing birds. Water flows from the lion's head into a covered container (*a*). Air is then forced out of the container through pipes (*b*), leading to whistles inside the birds. When the water level rises above the top of a pipe (*c*) covered by a cope—which lets in water at its lower end and is mounted with its top slightly above the top of the pipe—the pipe and cope together work as a siphon, and the water is emptied from container *a* into another container (*d*). A similar siphon arrangement (*e*) is built into this container, which also contains a float (*f*) to which a rope (*g*) is tied. The rope is wound once round a rotating pillar (*h*) and carries a weight (*i*) at its other end. When the water level—and, thus, the float—rises in container *d*, the pillar with its owl rotates until the water level has risen so high that the siphon starts working, and the container is emptied of water. The float then sinks, and the owl rotates back to its original position.

CHAPTER 2

MACHINE ELEMENTS AND ELEMENTARY MACHINES

Archimedes and, somewhat later, the engineers of the Alexandrian school showed what could be achieved, both in theory and in practice, by the simple machines, "the mighty five". As technical aids in saving power, the balanced lever, the gradient plane, the wedge, the screw, and the wheel added enormously to most areas of human achievement. Each one of the mighty five can rightly be called invaluable, but their combined value is truly infinite. The engineers of the Alexandrian school joined connected levers to cog-wheels, screws, and wedges and thus constructed the first real machines, in the modern sense of the word. Among the first full-scale applications of the newly-defined principles of mechanical engineering were the ingenious stage devices which were used to amaze the audiences in the Greek and Roman amphitheatres. The expression *deus ex machina*, "the god from the machine", derives from these devices. In the ancient theatre, which was often associated with religious festivals, levers, blocks, and ropes would enable, for example, the corpulent Bacchus to be suspended "magically" above the stage. However, the reverse, *machina ex deo*, would be just as appropriate, suggesting that the first real machines originated from the suspended god or similar full-scale applications of the many devices designed in "toy"-scale by Hero and his assistants. This implies that the engineers of the Alexandrian school had fully realized the applicability of the simple machines as machine elements.

The term "machine element" was not introduced until the nineteenth century, when mechanical engineering was first studied seriously from mathematical and kinematic viewpoints by, among others, Reuleaux, who will be dealt with in detail later. However, there is no doubt that, when designing their machines, Hero and his assistants were to a large extent inspired by the immense possibilities that arose when they tried systematically to combine the simple machines in different ways. The first machine elements consisted mainly of combinations of cog-wheels and endless screws, both of which are used in worm gears.

The Gear

The origin of the wheel has been suggested above, where we mentioned the multitude of contradictory and more or less unfounded suppositions that is all we know of the first appearance of this extremely important human invention. We know just as little of its development into a cog-wheel. Very likely, these two phenomena are related—the wheel may have been in use for perhaps a thousand years before it was depicted or mentioned in writing, and this may well be the case with the cog-wheel, too. Very few surviving written sources deal with this branch of engineering. It is probable that there were many early descriptions, but these have since been lost. Moreover, many documents were compiled by disciples of the great men

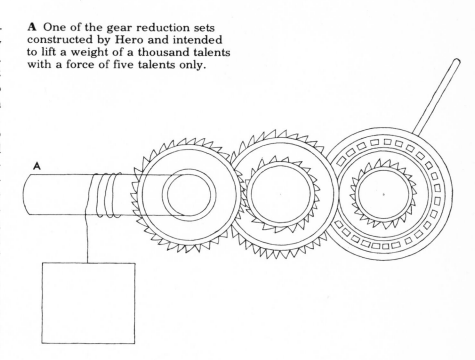

A One of the gear reduction sets constructed by Hero and intended to lift a weight of a thousand talents with a force of five talents only.

B Hero's *barulkos*, or weight-puller, was a developed version of the gear reduction set shown in illustration **A**. Among other things, an endless screw has been coupled to the last of the cog-wheels.

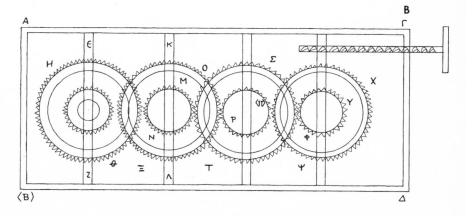

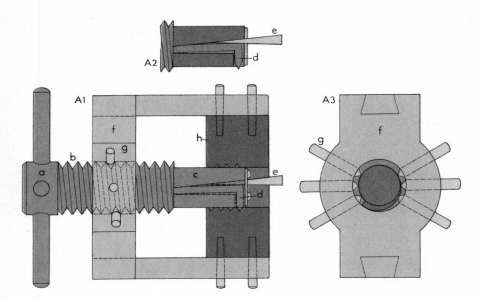

A A reconstruction of Hero's device for cutting female screw threads. (**1**) A round wooden stick, slightly more than twice as long as the screw thread about to be cut, was equipped with a handle (*a*) at one end. A male screw thread (*b*) of the same dimensions as those of the desired female screw thread was cut in the stick. The remaining part (*c*) of the stick was turned on a lathe until its diameter corresponded to that of the male screw's core. This part of the stick was then split lengthwise (**2**), and one lengthwise and one crosswise groove were hollowed out in the part still attached to the stick. An iron cutter (*d*), whose sharp end corresponded to the profile of the desired female screw thread, was fitted into the grooves, and the cut-off part of the stick was replaced. A wedge (*e*) was then forced into the lengthwise groove, so that the cutter was firmly kept in place. A hole, big enough for the male screw to pass through, was drilled in a piece of wood (*f*;

illustration **3** shows a cross-section), and smaller holes were drilled radially against this hole. Small dowels (*g*) of a hard wood were then hammered into the smaller holes, so that the piece of wood worked as a provisional nut when the sharp ends of the dowels guided the female screw thread. Finally, a hole with a diameter corresponding to that of the core of the male screw was drilled in the workpiece (*h*) about to be equipped with a female screw thread, and the piece of wood with the male screw was attached to the workpiece. When the handle (*a*) was then turned, the cutter (*d*) cut female screw threads of the desired dimensions in the workpiece.

of early times; for example, a comprehensive work, *Mechanical Problems*, formerly attributed to Aristotle (384–322 BC), is nowadays generally considered to have been written between 290 and 280 BC. During the years after Aristotle's death, important details may have been lost or neglected. The descriptions of different gear devices in *Mechanical Problems* are considered to be the earliest proof of the existence of cog-wheels and gears, but Drachmann is not convinced that Aristotle actually used cog-wheels, since the text does not mention anything about making them. Aristotle may instead have had plain wheels touching each other, transmitting motion by friction. Still, we shall never know whether the disciple had lost some part of his master's message, when he came to write it down, some forty years after Aristotle's death.

Derek de Solla Price, an American science historian, thinks it probable that Archimedes used the worm gear in one or other of the many war machines he built. It is also possible that the "endless screw" worm was used by Archimedes in the "planetarium" he is believed to have built. We have already mentioned Archimedes' work as well known by Ctesibius and by the other engineers of the Alexandrian school.

Around 60 AD, Hero described several cog-wheels for various uses. One of these he calls *barulkos*, "weight puller", and it is depicted both in Hero's *Mechanics* and in his *Dioptra*, although in slightly different versions. Hero also calculated the number of cogs on the various wheels, that is, the gear ratio of the weight puller, and gives it as 1:200. With a force of five talents, the weight puller should have been able to lift a weight of one thousand talents (about twenty-five tons). The calculation is, of course, purely theoretical—and even somewhat naive, since Hero did not consider the friction, which would be considerable in a case like this—not only between the cogs, but also in the shaft bearings. The cog-wheels are depicted with sawtooth-shaped cogs, and how they meshed is not shown clearly. Drachmann observes that cogs were not shaped like that at the time; but that, usually, they were either shaped as equilateral triangles or given a slightly trapezoid form ("pin-wheels"). The sawtooth shape may have been invented by Hero's draughtsman!

It is quite obvious that the illustrations accompanying Hero's original text have been misunderstood frequently by translators or copyists, both during his lifetime and later. The learned Italian poet Bernardino Baldi (1553–1617) thus mentions in the preface of his translation from the Greek of Hero's *On Automata* that, "ever since ancient times, the illustrations have been distorted by ignorant copiers", and that, for this reason, he has had the illustrations completely redrawn in this Italian edition, which was published in 1589.

One of Hero's illustrations of the weight puller shows a worm working against the last cog-wheel of the gear. The worm, especially the version used for drawing water, is believed to have been invented by Archimedes. The worm gear, that is, a machine element containing an endless screw, should be attributed to Hero, however, for he gave a fairly extensive description of designs for cutting external and internal threads for worm gears. The drawings of worm gears in Hero's book are, however, not easily interpreted, but Drachmann, Beck, and others have made reconstructions based on the text. It is, in other words, a question of the screw in its functions as a fastening (a metal bolt with a nut) and as a machine element. A number of "elementary machines" will be discussed in order to illuminate the development of machine elements over the years.

Hero's Worm Gears and Screw Constructions

Hero designed a great number of machines with the screw as the major machine element. Many of these designs were to remain relatively unchanged up to the days of industrialism.

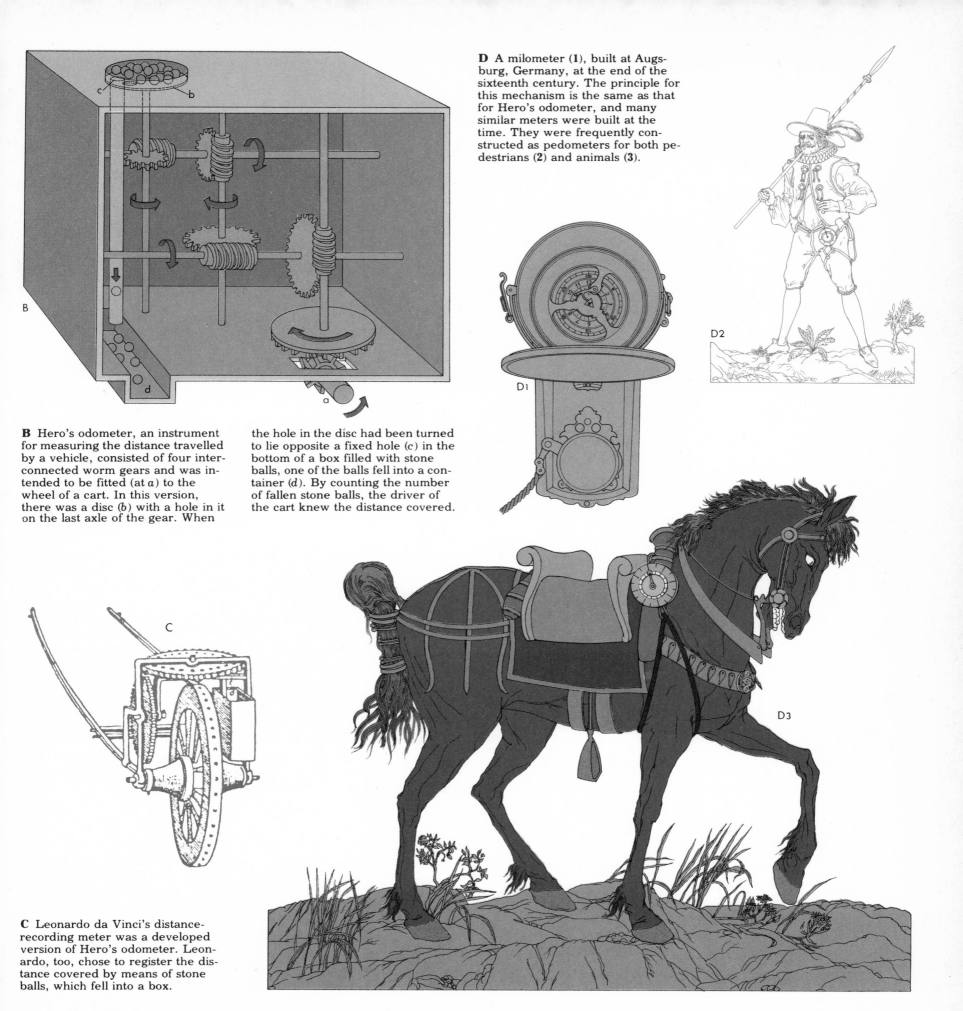

D A milometer (**1**), built at Augsburg, Germany, at the end of the sixteenth century. The principle for this mechanism is the same as that for Hero's odometer, and many similar meters were built at the time. They were frequently constructed as pedometers for both pedestrians (**2**) and animals (**3**).

B Hero's odometer, an instrument for measuring the distance travelled by a vehicle, consisted of four interconnected worm gears and was intended to be fitted (at *a*) to the wheel of a cart. In this version, there was a disc (*b*) with a hole in it on the last axle of the gear. When the hole in the disc had been turned to lie opposite a fixed hole (*c*) in the bottom of a box filled with stone balls, one of the balls fell into a container (*d*). By counting the number of fallen stone balls, the driver of the cart knew the distance covered.

C Leonardo da Vinci's distance-recording meter was a developed version of Hero's odometer. Leonardo, too, chose to register the distance covered by means of stone balls, which fell into a box.

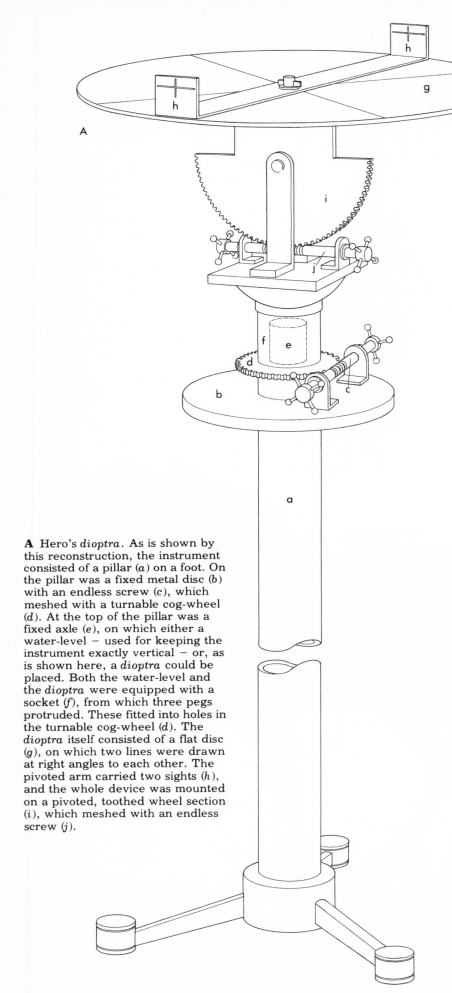

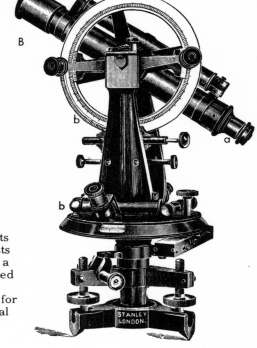

A Hero's *dioptra*. As is shown by this reconstruction, the instrument consisted of a pillar (*a*) on a foot. On the pillar was a fixed metal disc (*b*) with an endless screw (*c*), which meshed with a turnable cog-wheel (*d*). At the top of the pillar was a fixed axle (*e*), on which either a water-level — used for keeping the instrument exactly vertical — or, as is shown here, a *dioptra* could be placed. Both the water-level and the *dioptra* were equipped with a socket (*f*), from which three pegs protruded. These fitted into holes in the turnable cog-wheel (*d*). The *dioptra* itself consisted of a flat disc (*g*), on which two lines were drawn at right angles to each other. The pivoted arm carried two sights (*h*), and the whole device was mounted on a pivoted, toothed wheel section (*i*), which meshed with an endless screw (*j*).

B The modern equivalent of the *dioptra* is called a theodolite. In its simplest form, a theodolite consists of a telescope (*a*), equipped with a hairline cross, which can be turned round a horizontal and a vertical axle. Graded circles (*b*) are used for measuring angles in the horizontal and vertical planes.

The odometer, an instrument for measuring the distance travelled by a vehicle, consisted of four worm gears following on each other. It was to be attached to one of the wheels of a cart to measure the distance travelled. Several different versions of the odometer are described in Hero's works. One version was fitted with a disc with holes, similar to a modern telephone dial. This disc was attached to the last axle of the gear, and when the disc had been turned so that one of its holes lay opposite a fixed hole in the bottom of a box filled with stone balls, one of the balls would fall into a container. This version was probably used as a "taximeter" in cabs. Counting a few stone balls was certainly less difficult for a poorly educated driver than reading an instrument. Burstall has called this odometer the first recording instrument. Another version was meant to be a ship's log and had its first gear axle connected to a little paddle-wheel; but it is unlikely that this instrument for measuring the distance sailed would have had a very wide application. Leonardo da Vinci developed Hero's idea of a distance-recording meter, and he drew a design for an instrument which is not unlike those used by surveyors at the end of the nineteenth century.

Milometers first came into use in the sixteenth and seventeenth centuries, when the need for drawn maps was making itself felt in Europe. In the 1640s, the versatile German monk and natural scientist Athanasius Kircher (1602–80) designed milometers for carriages—these instruments were based on Hero's odometer—and pedometers for both horses and pedestrians.

In the previous chapter, we mentioned that the art of surveying by measuring angles and establishing levels in a scientific fashion was well mastered in ancient times. Hero gives a detailed description of a geodetic instrument which he calls *dioptra* (in a paper bearing this

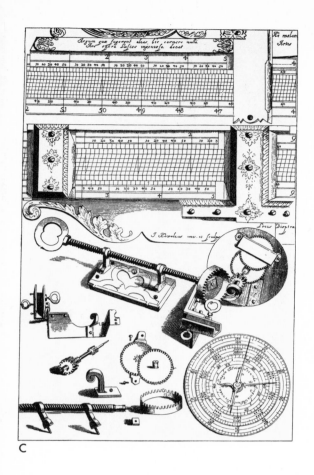

C

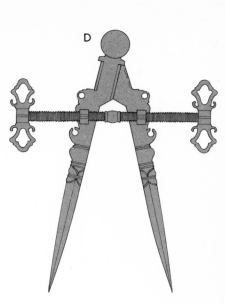

D

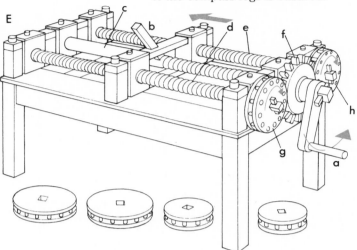

E

C The German astronomer Johann Hevelius (1611–87) built several instruments for making observations and determining positions with the naked eye. His instruments are characterized by their extreme precision. Shown here are a setting device and dividing scales from Hevelius's *Machina cælestis.*

D A pair of compasses of *c.* 1620, with adjusting screws with right-hand and left-hand threads respectively, so that a uniform motion of the compass legs is ensured.

E Leonardo's screw-cutting machine. When the crank (*a*) was turned, the tool (*b*) cut threads on the workpiece (*c*). The tool was advanced by two lead-screws (*d, e*), which were rotated by the gear (*f*) on the crank axle. By varying the ratios of gears *g* and *h*, the pitch of the thread cut on the workpiece could be varied.

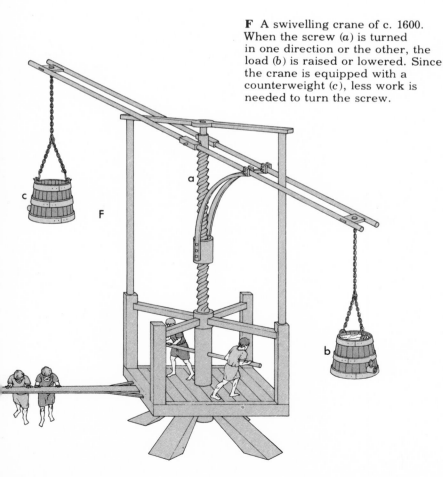

F A swivelling crane of c. 1600. When the screw (*a*) is turned in one direction or the other, the load (*b*) is raised or lowered. Since the crane is equipped with a counterweight (*c*), less work is needed to turn the screw.

title); it was intended for measuring angles both vertically and horizontally and was, in other words, based on the same principle as the modern theodolite. Hero here uses the worm to adjust the sight rule in both directions.

When Hero's work was rediscovered during the Renaissance, engineers were inspired to find new applications for the worm gear as well as for the worm. Leonardo da Vinci, among others, used the worm gear for various designs, including a machine for cutting screw threads.

In the ancient cultures, different kinds of presses were used for, among other things, pressing the juice out of grapes and the oil out of olives. In the Old Kingdom of Egypt a version of the press was already known; it can best be described as a wringing machine, in which olives or grapes were placed in a cloth bag, which was then wrung by means of levers and muscle power. The ancient Greeks generally used a press-beam, that is, a single-shank lever, which was pressed against a leather container by weights and muscle power. Wine and olive presses played an important part in the national and domestic economy at that time, and every big household had some such kind of press. Aristotle tells us—with, perhaps, a certain critical irony—a story about the great philosopher and natural scientist Thales of Miletos, who lived in the fifth century BC. One winter, Thales anticipated that the olive harvest would be unusually bountiful and, consequently, bought all the olive presses he could find in the area. When the harvest time approached, he hired them out at prices set by himself. Obviously, neither leasing nor monopoly coups are modern inventions.

Hero built various types of presses, all with the screw as a machine element, and in a couple he also combined the screw with the lever.

A A beam-press, used for olives and grapes. The right-hand end of the beam (*a*) was placed in a recess in the wall. The fruit was put between planks or in bags, and the whole thing (*b*) was bound with a rope and placed under the beam, which was loaded with weights (*c*). The juice was allowed to flow into a vessel (*d*). Athenian vase decoration, sixth century BC.

B A screw press described by Hero. A sturdy screw (*a*) was fastened to the beam. A stone weight (*b*) was attached to a nut (*c*), which was turned by means of a handle (*d*). (*e*) Fruit to be pressed.

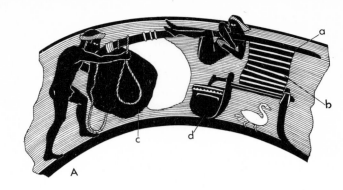

A

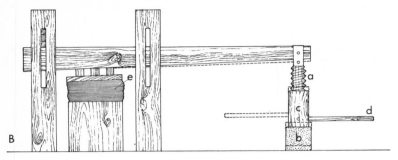

B

C Hero's direct screw press. The screw worked directly on the press lid (*a*), and the fruit was placed in a box (*b*) made from interlocked planks between which the juice seeped out.

D A direct double-screw press described by Hero; (**1**) front view, (**2**) cross-section. As the screws (*a*) were turned, the beam (*b*) bore down on a wooden block (*c*) on the lid (*d*) of the press. (*e*) Fruit container. (*f*) Box for collecting the juice.

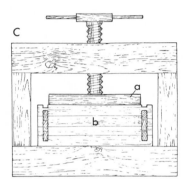

C

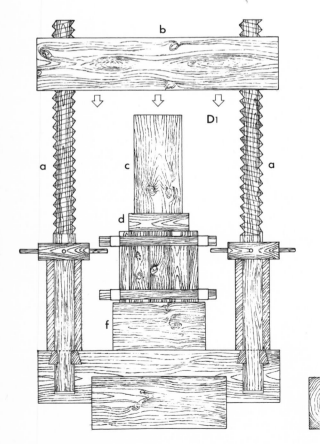

D1

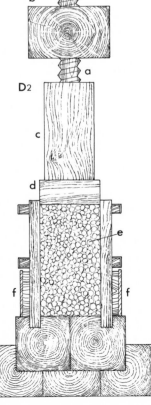

D2

E

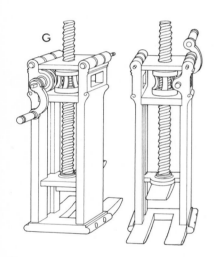

E The first printing presses were simple, wooden screw presses.
F Screw presses were also used for minting, as shown by this copperplate from 1771.

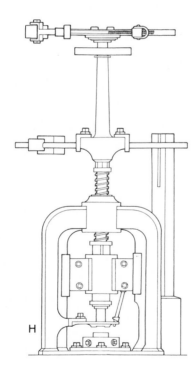

G A sixteenth-century elbow-joint press is shown here from two sides. It was used to lift and hang large, heavy doors, such as church doors. Usually, two or three presses like this were needed, together with a stable scaffold for horizontal steering, if a heavy door was to be hung on its hinges.
H A press used for minting, from *Encyclopédie Moderne, ou Dictionnaire Abrégé des Sciences, des Lettres, des Arts, etc.*,(Paris, 1863).

In his historical survey of the press, given in *Naturalis historia*, Pliny the Elder regards Hero's designs as new inventions in the development of the press.

Hero's press constructions spread rapidly all over the Mediterranean area, speeded by Pliny's extensive descriptions. These presses can also be said to have become prototypes for later press designs, from the Middle Ages up to modern times. Johann Gutenberg's first printing press, built in the 1430s, was more or less a direct copy of the Hero press with its screw design. The Hero screw was also used in coin-minting machines, where considerable pressure is required. The screw used in Hero's devices, with its pressure and thrust-generating properties, has also been the model for a great number of mechanical devices which came into being around the end of the Middle Ages. One example is the jack.

The Differential

An interesting application of the cog-wheel and the differential is found in what is known as the south-pointing carriage, designed in the third century AD in China. The dating has long been disputed; some sources would date it more than a thousand years earlier, but by relying on archaeological finds as well as on original texts, the English scientist Joseph Needham has been able to clarify the issue.

The carriage had two wheels and carried a wooden sculpture in the shape of a man whose extended arm was supposed to point south, whatever direction the carriage took. During the latter part of the nineteenth century, the first literary evidence of the carriage's actual existence was found. Some fragmentary finds were also made. These were taken as proof that the magnetic compass originated in China. Many writers, including the German historian of technology Franz M. Feldhaus, have depicted the south-pointing carriage with the sculpture mounted on top of a ''magic box'' between the shafts. The box supposedly contained the magnetic needle, which ensured the constant southerly direction of the pointing arm. This erroneous reconstruction caused some people to speculate that the magnetic compass—in the shape of the south-pointing carriage—had been invented as a result of the competition in the transport of silk and other goods from China to the Mediterranean countries. The caravans crossed the high plateaux of Tibet en route first to Samarkand and then to the commercial towns of the eastern Mediterranean. When the caravans travelled across the plateaux—an obvious short cut—they risked losing their sense of direction, especially in fogs or sand storms, so for safety, they usually skirted the bordering mountains. But time was money, then as now, and there was time to be gained. The solution presented itself in the shape of the south-pointing carriage!

A magnetic compass would certainly have led caravans safely across the high plateaux, a task now considered indisputably beyond the capacity of the south-pointing carriage; in fact, the pointing arm was moved, not by a magnet, but by connected differentials that compensated for the difference of the angle of rotation between the two carriage wheels, that occurred as the carriage turned. The statue was mounted on the outgoing axle of this device and thus pointed constantly south, whatever the direction of the carriage.

This device basically compensated for differences in the angles of rotation; this is quite impressive, for its construction required not only a thorough knowledge of the properties of the differential (which, for example, the almost contemporary Alexandrian school lacked), but also a considerable skill in the art of estimating the gear ratios of composite cog-wheels. The differential mechanism of the south-pointing carriage can hardly have been the result of experiments but must have been based on theoretical calculations.

The American Otto Mayr and several other historians of technology claim that the famous carriage was used as a "mechanical compass" by caravans and by travellers, but this appears impossible. Each imperfection in the mechanism and each bump to its wheels due to uneven ground would distort its indication of the direction. Simple mathematics show that a difference of only 1 per cent between the diameters of the two carriage wheels would shift the indicated south by 180° after only about 3 miles (5 km). South and north would then have changed on the compass! The designer was probably quite aware of these deficiencies, and it is likely that the south-pointing carriage was only used by those in power to show the people that their rulers had supernatural powers. One might, therefore, compare its use to Hero's ingenious device, mentioned earlier, which was used to open the doors of the temple's inner sanctum.

A Two-Thousand-Year-Old Calculator

The Antikythera device is a remarkable astronomical calculator dating from the first century BC. Some sponge fishermen found it in 1900 in a wrecked ship near the island of Antikythera, between Crete and the Peloponnesus. The ship lay in more than 130 ft (c. 40 m) of water. On board, there were art treasures and some inconspicuous verdigrised bronze objects, which were later fitted together to form a box of about 12×7×4 in (30×17×10 cm). The art treasures of this first, major marine-archaeological find were immediately examined by experts from the Athens National Museum, but it was not until a couple of years later that someone took an interest in the little box. It turned out that it contained some relatively well preserved cog-wheels and fragments of several others, bearing inscriptions which indicated that they could have been part of an astronomical instrument. The first guess was that the Antikythera device, as the object was soon called, was an astrolabe, but this was immediately contradicted. Over the years, many theories have been aired about the device and its application. Someone even suggested that it had been left behind by astronauts from an alien, advanced civilization visiting Earth, a notion obviously inspired by von Däniken, even if motivated by the very high level of scientific thinking and advanced technology represented in the device; it is unique in the cultural area where it was found and, indeed, elsewhere. Derek de Solla Price comments that the motivation as such may be justified, but that astronauts as a source must be ruled out; instead, we ought to upgrade our estimation of the Hellenic culture's abilities in natural science and technology.

In the early 1950s, Price started to interest himself in the Antikythera device, and in the following two decades, he was given several opportunities to examine its construction. Price is a professor in the history of ideas at Yale University and an internationally acclaimed expert on scientific instruments. Using X-ray, radiography, and other methods, Price succeeded in reconstructing the entire device and in clarifying its function and application. It is an advanced aid for calender calculations, based on such phenomena as the sun's passage through the zodiac and the phases of the moon.

Although the enigma of the function of the Antikythera device has now been largely answered, some questions still remain. Who, for instance, designed and built the instrument? It can hardly have been wholly exceptional, constructed by some Greek Leonardo da Vinci, who had mastered both the necessary theory and the technical problems of construction. The strange mechanism should rather be seen as the unexceptional result of a marriage between a wide-ranging scientific culture and sound craftsmanship in precision mechanics.

Price also suggests that the school of Posidonius (135?–51? BC) in Rhodes may have produced this wonder of science and technology, implying that Posidonius had gathered round him natural scientists, technicians, and craftsmen, just as Hero did in Alexandria. Indeed,

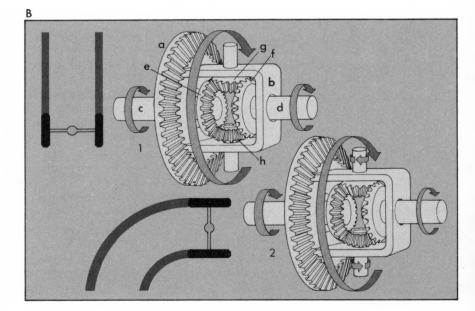

A The design of the south-pointing carriage is based on an ingenious use of the properties of the differential. The carriage shown here (**1**) is a reconstruction made at the National Museum of Science and Technology in Stockholm. It was built with standard parts from a mechanical building kit. Illustration **2** is a skeleton drawing of the carriage's construction, whereas illustration **3** shows the carriage as seen in a cutaway view from behind. The rotation of the carriage wheels (a, b) is transferred by gearwheels (c, d) to the differential. This consists of two other gearwheels (e, f) which pivot on the axle g and rotate in opposite directions, meshing with the gears h and i, which pivot on the axle j. This axle is, however, journalled in fixed bearings in the axle g. As long

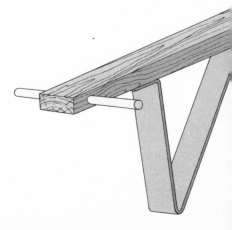

as the carriage wheels rotate at the same speed, axle *g* does not rotate, since the gears *e* and *f* have the same speed and thus rotate the gears *h* and *i* round the axle *j* without the latter (and, consequently, axle *g*) being rotated. When the carriage turns, however, one of its wheels will rotate slower than the other, and gears *e* and *f*, too, will then rotate at different speeds. In order to compensate for this difference in speed, *i* and *h* start to rotate about the axle *g* as well. When the carriage turns in relation to the ground, the south-pointing figure (*k*) attached to the axle *g* will turn in relation to the carriage and will stubbornly point towards the south, no matter in which direction the carriage is driven (**4**).

B The differential is included in most modern cars; fundamentally, it works as is shown here. Engine power is transmitted to the crown wheel (*a*) by a bevel pinion (not shown here). Bolted to the crown wheel is a differential cage (*b*), through which the axle shafts (*c*, *d*) pass; *e* and *f* are axle-shaft gears. As long as the car is driven straight ahead (**1**), the two axle shafts rotate at the same speed, and the differential gears (*g*, *h*) rotate together with the crown wheel (*a*) and the differential cage (*b*) − without rotating about their own axes. When the car turns (**2**), one axle shaft (*c*) rotates faster than the other (*d*), and the differential gears (*g*, *h*) will then compensate for the difference in speed by rotating about their own axes.

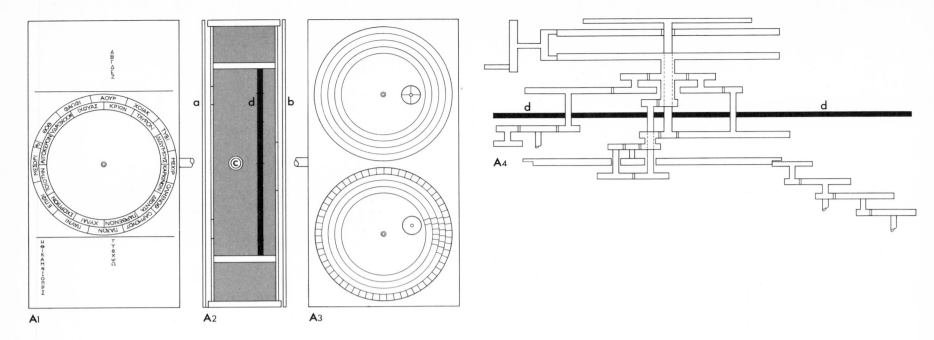

A1

A2

A3

A4

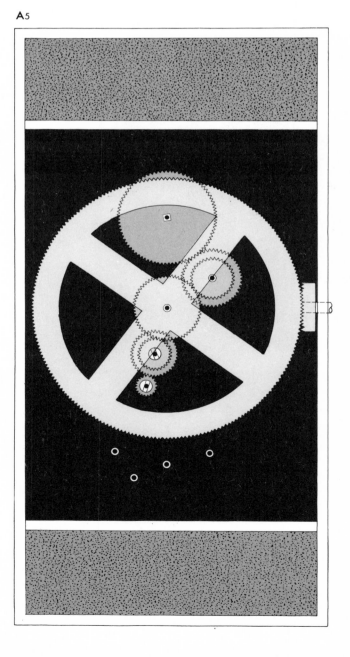

A5

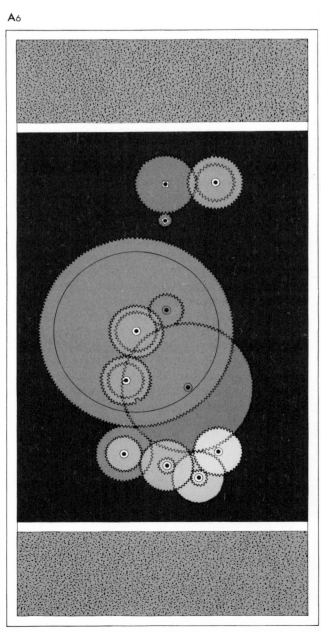

A6

A Four fragments are all that remain of the Antikythera mechanism. It is possible that these were joined when the find was made, but nobody realized then how much wood can distort and split if it is allowed to dry out after being immersed in water for so long. Unfortunately, no photographs were taken of the mechanism when it was retrieved from the almost two-thousand-year-old wreck. Illustrated here is Derek de Solla Price's reconstruction. On the front (**1**) of the mechanism were two circular scales, the outer containing the names of the months, the inner the names of the zodiac. (**2**) A side view of the mechanism: (*a*) front door, (*b*) back door, (*c*) drive axle. (**3**) The back of the mechanism had two sets of circular scales. Both front and back carried inscriptions (**4**). The mechanism itself, here in cross-section, consists of over thirty cogwheels; (*d*) base plate. (**5**) Cogwheels for the scales on the front. (**6**) Cogwheels for the scales on the back of the base plate. Of especial interest is the differential which was used to show how the movements of the sun and moon coincided with the phases of the moon.

the two schools may well have been connected. As mentioned above, Philo of Byzantium found his way from the Alexandrian school to Rhodes, where he designed war machines. But as few texts mention Posidonius of Apamia, as he is usually called, little is known about him, even if some writers, Pliny among them, do refer to him. Sarton remarks that our estimation of Posidonius necessarily must be vague because of this, but that his position could well have been as highly esteemed as that of Aristotle. Perhaps future finds will tell us more about Posidonius and his school.

Water Clocks

Another question in connection with the Antikythera device is whether or not it formed part of another, larger instrument, perhaps something like the famous astronomical clock in the Tower of Winds in Athens. This tower was built in the first century BC and included a water clock, showing by means of cog-wheel mechanisms such astronomical data as the motion of the planets and the moon. Similar water clocks with mechanical "clockworks" existed elsewhere in the ancient cultures, and it is possible that Posidonius's school also designed such a clock, using the Antikythera device as a piece of additional equipment. This, too, can be answered only by new finds.

The Tower of Winds at the Roman *agora* (square) in Athens was built during the Roman period in Greece as a monument to time and space. It is an octagonal marble tower, almost 43 ft (13 m) high, with graceful sundials on the top frieze and a stately weathercock at its very top. The tower is still more or less intact, but the astronomical water clock has not survived. The Romans built many such water-driven ornamental clocks in their huge empire, and the art spread from there to other cultures.

In the fifth century AD, a magnificent ornamental clock was built in Ghaza. This clock was very similar to the mechanical astronomical clocks which became almost status symbols in European cathedrals and town halls from the fourteenth century onwards. Neither the Ghaza clock nor its housing still exist, but the German linguist Hermann Diels has managed to reconstruct them from a comprehensive contemporary description. The works were almost 13 ft (4 m) high and were housed in an open, stylish building with pillars, vaults, and a dome. A statuette depicting the sun god proceeded past twelve doors and pointed to the one corresponding to the hour of the day. Each hour was divided into twelfths, marked by a figure of Hercules successively showing illustrations of his twelve labours. An eagle attached a coronet to Hercules' head for each labour. At night, the doors showing the hours were lit. This ornamental clock not only showed, but also struck, the time: a large statue of Hercules struck a metal cylinder with a hammer on the hour and the half hour.

One can easily see the connection here with the Alexandrian school and its stage devices and theatrical *deus ex machina* effects.

The components of the Ghaza clock were the same as those used by Hero and the unknown designer of the Antikythera device.

The Ghaza clock became very famous and, for centuries, inspired other designers to similar achievements. It was the obvious model for an ornamental clock built in the Large Mosque of Damascus, and which was described in the twelfth century by the oriental explorer al-Kinani. The Damascus clock featured two brass falcons, which dropped brass balls from their beaks into bronze dishes to mark the hours. Above the falcons were twelve doors, which closed automatically along with the passing of the hours, as the brass balls "struck". Eleven men were required to keep this ornamental clock going; apparently, it had not been possible automatically to light and dowse the lanterns which lit the doors that closed automatically at night. Al-Kinani's account spread to China; but Needham says that similar automata had been built there since the eighth century.

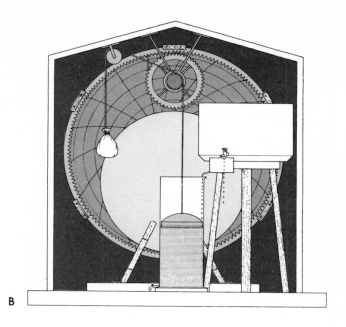

B

B A reconstruction of a 6-ft (2 m) high Roman clock.
C A reconstruction of an approximately 40-ft (13 m) high astronomical clocktower, which was built in c. 1090 AD in the Chinese city of Honan by one Su-Sung. The clockwork was driven by a water-wheel (*a*), whose ladles were filled with water from a tub (*b*). An ingenious device prevented the water-wheel from turning while each ladle was being filled. The water-wheel also rotated a bronze planetarium (*c*) and a celestial globe (*d*). A series of automata (*e*) indicated the passage of time by appearing in niches (*f*) and striking bells and gongs.

The water clocks designed in the Middle Ages were not only astronomical. For example, Leonardo da Vinci made a sketch of an alarm clock, but this design was probably more of a joke than a serious proposal. The round dish is held up by a tube which works like a two-armed lever. At the other end of the tube is a flat dish containing water; a rope from this end is fastened by a noose to the sleeper's feet. When the round dish is half filled, it becomes heavier than the flat dish, which swings up, pouring its water through the tube down into the round dish and brutally jerking the rope round the sleeper's ankles.

The Mechanical Clock

It is yet to be established when the first mechanical clock was designed. One of the difficulties in fixing the date is purely linguistic, since the most relevant western languages—Latin, Italian, French, English, and German—use the same word to denote both mechanical and water clocks. In his *Divine Comedy*, Dante Alighieri (1265–1321) mentions (in "Paradiso") a clock, and it has long been disputed whether this was water- or mechanically powered. A. P. Usher, the American historian of technology, feels that Dante's stanzas can be interpreted as describing a mechanical clock, calling upon the Englishman G. H. Baille's work to support this theory. If this is correct, the first "machine of machines" can be dated to the beginning of the fourteenth century.

The distinguishing component of the mechanical clock is the escapement, which controls the constant motion of the hand; the other components, such as cog-wheels with axles and the weight driving the machine, have been known since ancient times. The first escapement is usually attributed to the French architect Villard de Honnecourt, who, in a book of drawings called *Album*, shows one, even if it is rather difficult to interpret. *Album* dates from the late thirteenth century and describes various devices noted by Honnecourt during his travels. It is hardly likely that Honnecourt himself originated this component, but very probably he did see a mechanical clock, for his drawings include a picture of a clock tower, and perhaps the clock he saw may even have been the one mentioned by Dante!

Usher has compiled a list of twenty "clocks" mentioned in literature, inscriptions, and other sources from the period between 1286 and 1335; all of these, according to him, are to be regarded as water clocks. The tower clock of Dover Castle in England was long considered the oldest mechanical clock, being said to have been built in 1348. It was discovered in 1851 in the castle attic, having probably lain there for centuries. It was claimed at the time that "1348" was engraved on its framework, and this date has been given since then. Recently, however, the clock has been restored, but no such inscription has been found. Singer believes that the tower clock was probably made around 1650, whereas Usher dates it at around 1500. The reason the clock was put away seems to be simple enough: it was a very bad timekeeper.

The first sure evidence for the existence of a mechanical clock dates from 1335. It refers to a clock built by Guglielmo Zelandino and mounted in a tower on the San Gottardo chapel in Milan. Similar clocks were made in Modena in 1343, in Padua the following year, and in Monza in 1347. The designer of the Padua clock was Jacopo di Dondi, whose son, Giovanni, made an ingenious astronomical clock which showed the motion of the sun, the moon, and five planets. It also included an eternal calendar of the movable feasts. This clock was completed in 1364, after sixteen years of work, and was placed in the tower of the castle at Pavia. Dondi had obviously looked to the earlier, water-driven, astronomical clocks for several of the design elements of his clock.

At this time, tower clocks, ornamental clocks, and astronomical

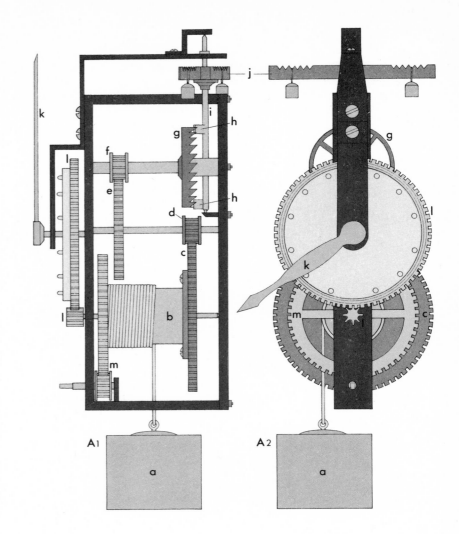

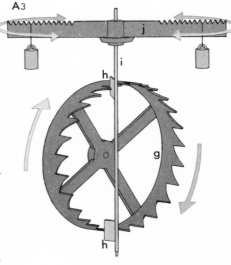

A Heinrich von Wiek's ornamental clock of 1354 was a weight-driven clock with a verge escapement. A side view (**1**) and a front view (**2**) of the clockwork are shown here, with an enlarged illustration of the verge escapement (**3**). The weight (*a*) drives a barrel (*b*) with a great wheel (*c*), which meshes with a pinion (*d*) on a spindle. On this spindle is a second wheel (*e*), which transmits the rotary motion by way of a pinion (*f*) to the escape wheel (*g*). This wheel has an odd number of ratchet-shaped teeth, and its rotary motion is constantly impeded by two pallets (*h*), arranged to form an angle with each other on a verge (*i*). When the escape wheel is turned, one of the pallets is pushed aside, causing the verge to turn, and the foliot balance (*j*), a cross-bar with weights, begins turning with increasing velocity until its movement is abruptly checked when the other pallet engages with a tooth on the escape wheel. The verge, and thus the foliot balance, are then turned in the opposite direction until the first pallet again engages with a tooth. The rotary motions are regulated all the time by the foliot balance's inertia, which may be adjusted to some extent by moving the weights. The hand (k) is driven by the weight's (a) influence on the barrel by way of a pinion-and-wheel system (l). (m) Winding pinion and wheel.

B A reconstruction of Giovanni di Dondi's astronomical clock, which was mounted in the castle at Pavia in 1364. Not only the passage of time but also the movements of the planets were indicated by the clock.

C The ornamental clock in the cathedral at Lund, Sweden, in its present state. The clock is surmounted by two knights, and below them is a dial whose hands show local and astronomical time, the sun's passage through the zodiac, and the phases of the moon. At the base of the clock is a calendarium, which completes a 360° clockwise turn per year — every midnight, it moves one step forward. In the middle of the clock, an image of the Virgin Mary is situated; the three wise men and their servants enter through the door on her left.

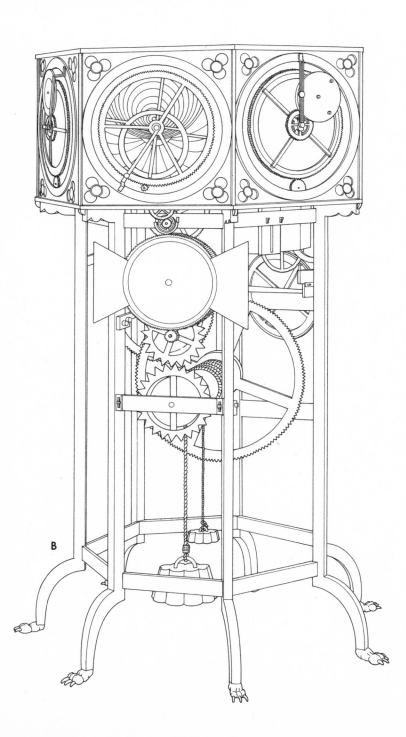

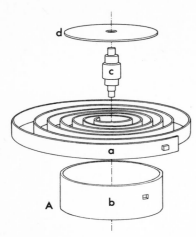

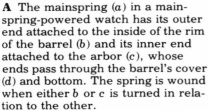

A The mainspring (*a*) in a main-spring-powered watch has its outer end attached to the inside of the rim of the barrel (*b*) and its inner end attached to the arbor (*c*), whose ends pass through the barrel's cover (*d*) and bottom. The spring is wound when either *b* or *c* is turned in relation to the other.

B In order to compensate for the irregularity of the force transmitted by the mainspring — the force is at its greatest when the spring is fully wound and at its least when the spring has almost completely run down — the mainspring barrel can be combined with a fusee. The mainspring arbor (*a*) is then fixed, and the mechanism is wound by turning the fusee's arbor (*b*). A cord (*c*), one end of which is attached to the barrel (*d*), will then be wound onto the fusee's spiral groove (*e*); simultaneously, the barrel will be turned. As the mainspring runs

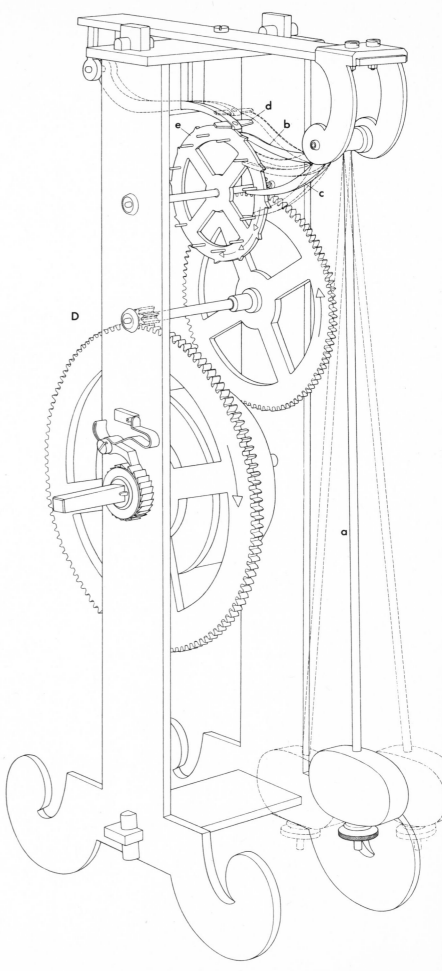

clocks were built to adorn public buildings and royal palaces all over Europe. In 1354, Strasbourg cathedral was given an ornamental clock with a mechanical cock which crowed and flapped its wings at twelve noon. The German clockmaker Heinrich von Wiek designed several ornamental clocks, the most famous being the one attached to Charles V's palace (now the Palais de Justice) in Paris in 1354.

The astronomical clock in the cathedral at Lund in Sweden – *Horologium Mirabile Lundense* – is considered to date back to the 1380s, but an exact date and information concerning its design, builder, etc., cannot be given. A comparison between the ornamentation and technology of the Lund clock and those of similar ornamental clocks in central Europe confirms this approximate date, although the existence of the clock is not documented in any original text older than 1424. In the 1580s, a comprehensive description of the clock was written by the cathedral's chaplain, Mogens Madsen. Notes from the mid-sixteenth century indicate that, at that time, the clock no longer worked but had fallen into decay. The clockwork was taken out and scrapped in the 1830s, but the front with the faces was kept and set up in the interior wall of the north aisle of the cathedral. Around 1910, a Danish tower clockmaker, Julius Bertram-Larsen, became interested in trying to restore the mediaeval clock. In due course, his work led to a reconstruction of the "wonderful clock in Lund" in all its mediaeval splendour, and it was reinstated in 1923, on the 800th anniversary of the cathedral. During reconstruction, a replica of the clock had been made on a scale of 1:3. This was

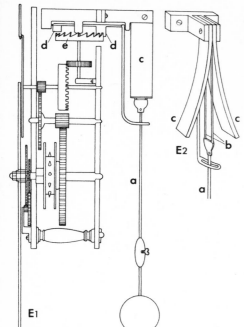

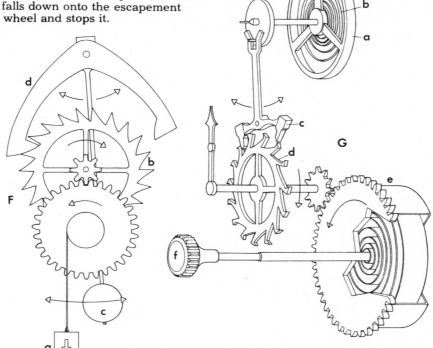

rotary motion of the escapement wheel (*e*). One of the twelve pins projecting from the side of the escapement wheel then pushes arm *c* downwards, so that the pendulum swings outwards. Arm *b* is then withdrawn from the pallet, which falls down onto the escapement wheel and stops it.

E Huygens's pendulum clock (1), a weight-driven clock with a verge escapement. Through his investigations of the theory of the pendulum, Huygens discovered that the pendulum swings with perfect homogeneity of period only if its path is cycloid. A cycloid is a curve which corresponds to the movement of a fixed point on a circle which rolls along a straight line. (2) Huygens solved the problem of how to get the pendulum to swing in this manner by making the top part of the pendulum rod from two silk cords (*b*), which were suspended from between two cycloid-shaped metal plates (*c*). (*d*) Pallets. (*e*) Crown wheel.

F The anchor escapement was invented in the middle of the eighteenth century. The weight (*a*) drives the escapement wheel (*b*) by means of a wheel and pinion. As the pendulum (*c*) swings to the right, the left-hand pallet of the anchor, which is attached to the pendulum rod, catches a tooth on the escapement wheel and receives an impulse, which makes the pendulum swing to the left. The anchor's right-hand pallet then gets an impulse from the escapement wheel so that the pendulum swings to the right, and so on.

G Mainspring-powered clock with a balance wheel and an anchor escapement. The balance (*a*) has taken over the pendulum's regulating role. Its movements are limited by the length of the coil-spring (*b*). (*c*) Anchor. (*d*) Escapement wheel. (*e*) Mainspring barrel. (*f*) Winder.

down, the cord is rewound onto the barrel. Thus, when the spring is fully wound, the cord pulls against the smallest part of the fusee, whereas it pulls against the largest spiral when the spring has almost run down. (*f*) Great wheel.

C The first portable timekeepers usually had a hinged cover over the dial.

D A pendulum clock, constructed according to Galileo's suggestions by his son Vincenzio in 1649. On the pendulum rod (*a*) are two arms (*b*, *c*). As the pendulum swings inwards, arm *b* lifts a pallet (*d*), which will then no longer constrain the

given by a patron of the arts to the Stockholm Town Hall, which was opened in 1923, on the 400th anniversary of King Gustavus Vasa's entry into Stockholm. The replica of the Lund clock was displayed in the Town Hall, but for various reasons, it was sold a few years later. After a varied career, it was acquired by the National Museum of Science and Technology in Stockholm in 1966. It is now displayed there after extensive restoration. The clock shows local and astronomical time, the phases of the moon, and the sun's passage through the zodiac. Moreover, it has a calendarium which shows the date and the day of the week. By means of this calendarium, it is also possible to find the day of the week of a given date in any year between 1923 and 2123. It is, however, the automata of the clock that most fascinate onlookers. Two mediaeval knights on the dome of the clock hourly exchange blows to the number of the hour. At twelve o'clock, after the twelfth blow, a hymn resounds from a mechanical trombone, a little door beside an image of the madonna opens, and the three wise kings from the East come out, followed by their servants, and file, bowing, past the Virgin Mary.

The mechanical clock derives technically from the ancient machine elements; but its spiritual roots lie in the regular life led within the walls of the monasteries. The Cistercian monastic rules of about 1260 describe in detail the responsibilities of the bell-minder. When the water clock showed the hour, the bell-minder was to mark this by ringing the monastery bell—hence the synonym "bell" for the word "clock" in some languages. Lewis Mumford comments:

It would not be an exaggeration to say that the monasteries helped to give human enterprises the regular, collective pulse and rhythm of a machine. A clock not only helps to keep track of the hours, but also synchronises the actions of man. . . . The instrument rapidly spread beyond the monastery, and the regular striking gave new regularity to the craftsman's and merchant's lives. The measuring of time turned into time slavery, time estimating and time rationing. When this happened, eternity gradually stopped to be the yardstick and the aim of people's actions. The clock, not the steam engine, is the key machine of the modern industrial age.

Precision Engineering

Up to the middle of the sixteenth century, the progress being made in the development of the clock strongly stimulated the crafts. Many new tools and working methods were developed, and this in turn led to the invention of new machine elements. The escapement was successively refined, and new methods to drive it were invented. The first spring-driven clocks appeared in the early sixteenth century. This invention, and thereby the first pocket-watch, is usually attributed to a Nuremberg locksmith, Peter Henlein (1480–1542), who is believed to have made, around 1510, the first of his *Nürnberger Eierlein*, "Nuremberg eggs", as these clocks came to be called due to their elliptical shape. Usher, however, points out that at least two older spring-driven clocks are known from literature.

The appearance of the pocket-watch challenged craftsmen working in precision mechanics to develop even more precise and still smaller machine elements. The new prime mover, the spring-driven clockwork of the watch, was soon used to power automata of various kinds. For example, mechanical toys of all kinds were spring-driven from the mid-nineteenth century and up to the arrival of the miniature electric motor in the 1950s.

From the late Middle Ages up to the early nineteenth century, the development of the mechanical clock was distinguished by the interaction between science–mainly mathematics and technology–and practical application. Over the years, this process has had a great influence in both directions. The most revolutionary contributions to the techniques of clockmaking were made by the Italian Galileo Galilei (1564–1642) and the Dutchman Christiaen Huygens (1629–95). Even as a student in Pisa in the 1580s, Galileo is believed to have come upon the laws determining the movement of the pendulum. Legend has it that this occurred when he was at mass and saw a chandelier suspended from the ceiling slowly swing back and forth. By counting the beats of his pulse to time the pendulum, Galileo established that all the swings took an equal time. He used a pendulum to measure short intervals of time, but his was a free-swinging pendulum with a manually maintained movement. The problem of mechanically maintaining the swings of the pendulum was solved by Huygens, who, in 1657, patented the first pendulum clock. It was driven by a weight, and the escapement was made up of an escape wheel with sawtooth-shaped cogs, which, with each regular impulse, gave the pendulum a push, making it swing continuously.

Inspired by his success, Huygens tackled the mathematics of time-measuring technology and, in 1673, he published the results of his studies in *Horologium oscillatorium*, which can be considered the first fundamental work on both scientific and practical mechanics. Huygens introduced a great many machine elements, but we shall mention only one here: the coil spring, or fly, which, up to the present, has been the fundamental mechanism in all watches and most clocks.

For obvious reasons, clocks with swinging pendulums are not very suitable for use at sea. In the seventeenth century, the great seafaring nations–England, Holland, and France–tried frantically to produce a precise timepiece so that longitude could be determined at sea. For years, Huygens strove to develop a mechanism as constant as the swinging pendulum but less sensitive to external influence. The breakthrough came in Paris on January 20, 1675, when he could write "Eureka" in his diary next to a sketch of the torsion pendulum. Whether, like Archimedes, he ran naked through the streets on this occasion, crying out his "eureka", is not recorded. Huygens immediately contacted the French Academy of Science and demonstrated his invention. A few days later, he was granted the sole manufacturing rights for it, becoming in due course a rich man. Huygen's contributions to timekeeping technology illustrate one of the many fruitful results of the above-mentioned interaction between theory and practice.

We have touched upon the increased demand for tools and more refined methods of precision working that followed the appearance of the mechanical clock. The demand for high-quality materials also increased sharply, and one of the results of this was crucible steel. The crucible process was discovered by an English clockmaker of German extraction, Benjamin Huntsman, who manufactured clock springs, wheel axles, and other steel parts for his clocks. He had been encountering great difficulty in finding raw material of sufficiently high and uniform quality for his needs, for the commercial steel of the time was, above all, not homogenous, and the clock springs made of it were often of poor quality. In the 1730s, Huntsman began to consider whether melted steel would blend better if it were heated slightly above its melting point. The problem was to achieve the high temperature required. Foundries had never been able to do this. Huntsman, however, managed to build a well-insulated furnace with a high chimney which gave a strong draught. His raw material was powdered blister steel (preferably of Swedish Dannemora iron), which he mixed with crushed glass in a relatively small crucible (about 10 in, or 25 cm, high). The crucible had a stone lid and was embedded in crushed coke. The melting process took three to four hours, and when the steel was sufficiently fluid, it was stirred vigorously before the crucible was taken out of the furnace. Huntsman's crucible steel process, which was successively refined, remained for more than a century the chief method of producing top-quality steel for use in many more areas than the one originally intended. In his search for better material for clock springs, Huntsman thus found a new kind of steel, and this resulted not only in great progress in precision mechanics, but also in new designs in practically all areas of mechanical engineering.

The Machine of Machines

Lewis Mumford calls the mechanical clock "the machine of machines". Nowadays, it is ubiquitous; most of us wear a wrist-watch and have several clocks around us, both at home and at work. The clock made industrialism possible, and more so than the steam-engine and other prime movers, Mumford says, and adds that the clock is the typical symbol of all the development stages of the machine, a statement which holds a great deal of truth–not least from a prophetic point of view, as it was made in the 1930s. Today, in the age of computers, we can observe the marked symbolism of the fact that the mechanics of the clock have given way to electronics, because the electronic oscillating circuit gives far greater accuracy than could be achieved economically by mechanics.

Mumford's symbol of a machine in the form of an innocent watch also plays a key role in a much-reprinted controversial book, first published in 1872, about the machine age. The title of the book is *Erewhon, or Over the Range*, and it was written by Samuel Butler (1835–1902); it has appeared again and again in debates on social matters. It has been interpreted and misinterpreted, and today it is quoted more than ever. In brief, the book is about a sheep-farmer (as a young man, Butler emigrated to New Zealand and for some years had a sheep farm there, before returning to England), who gets lost on unmarked tracks, walks across a mountain range and, to his astonishment, finds an entirely new civilization, called Erewhon, on the other side. Quite inexplicably, he is arrested and put into prison. The language of this country is totally incomprehensible to him, but he eventually learns that the terrible crime he has committed is the possession of a watch. There had been a civil war in Erewhon some five hundred years earlier between the machinists and the anti-machinists, that is, between those who were for and those who were against machines. The anti-machinists had won, and everything in the nature of a machine had been destroyed. Owning a machine in Erewhon was, from that time on, treason of the highest order.

Butler's hero–and *alter ego*–is pardoned in due course, after having learnt the Erewhonian language, and he is taken care of by Mr. Nosnibor (Robinson!), who is a leading merchant in the metropolis. Later on, the sheep-farmer meets venerable professors of the Colleges of Unreason, which is the very telling name of the Erewhonian universities. Butler's sharp satire is positively scathing when he describes these unscientists and their activities. They have long been engaged in, among other things, a careful study of the historical development of mechanical engineering, not with the aim of using such machinery again, but "with the feelings of an English antiquar-

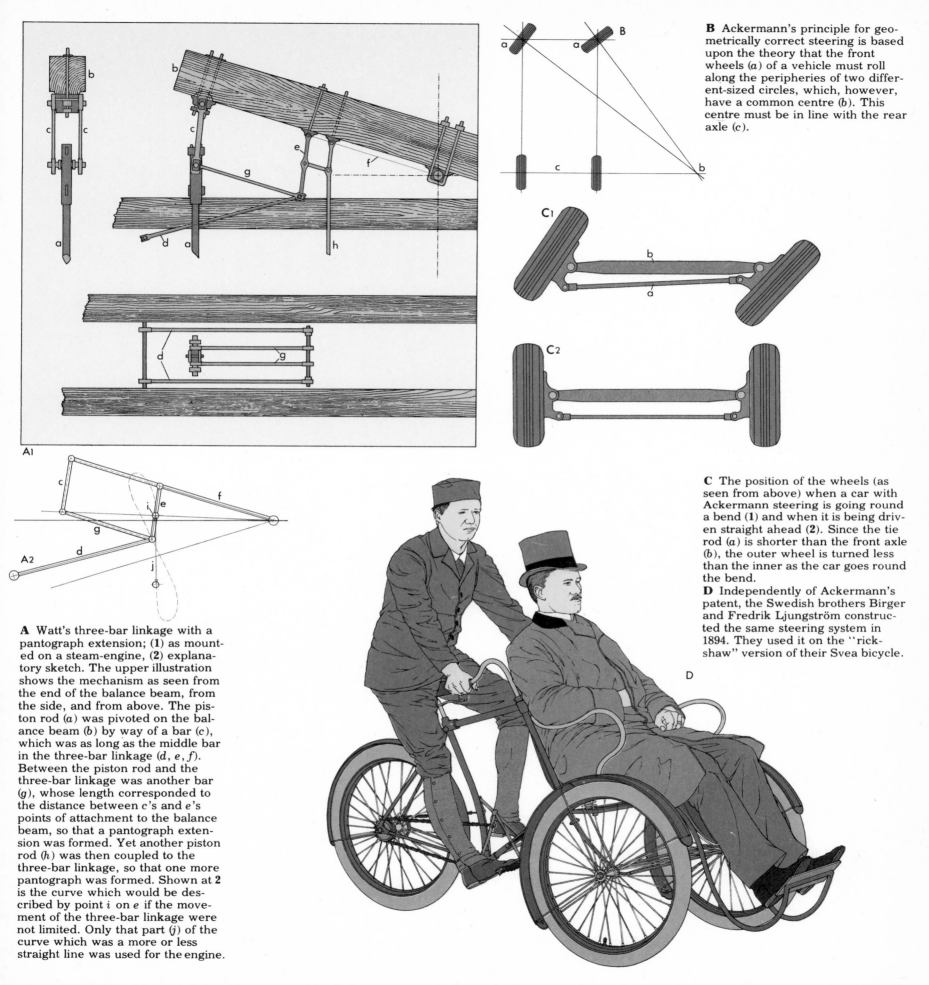

A1

A2

B Ackermann's principle for geometrically correct steering is based upon the theory that the front wheels (a) of a vehicle must roll along the peripheries of two different-sized circles, which, however, have a common centre (b). This centre must be in line with the rear axle (c).

C1

C2

A Watt's three-bar linkage with a pantograph extension; (**1**) as mounted on a steam-engine, (**2**) explanatory sketch. The upper illustration shows the mechanism as seen from the end of the balance beam, from the side, and from above. The piston rod (a) was pivoted on the balance beam (b) by way of a bar (c), which was as long as the middle bar in the three-bar linkage (d, e, f). Between the piston rod and the three-bar linkage was another bar (g), whose length corresponded to the distance between c's and e's points of attachment to the balance beam, so that a pantograph extension was formed. Yet another piston rod (h) was then coupled to the three-bar linkage, so that one more pantograph was formed. Shown at **2** is the curve which would be described by point i on e if the movement of the three-bar linkage were not limited. Only that part (j) of the curve which was a more or less straight line was used for the engine.

C The position of the wheels (as seen from above) when a car with Ackermann steering is going round a bend (**1**) and when it is being driven straight ahead (**2**). Since the tie rod (a) is shorter than the front axle (b), the outer wheel is turned less than the inner as the car goes round the bend.

D Independently of Ackermann's patent, the Swedish brothers Birger and Fredrik Ljungström constructed the same steering system in 1894. They used it on the "rickshaw" version of their Svea bicycle.

D

53

ian concerning Druidical monuments or flint arrow-heads". Butler lets a machinist and an anti-machinist explain their views and argue their cases. The standpoint of the machinist is mainly a mixture of the philosophies topical at the time when *Erewhon* was written; in particular, the machinist is impressed by the theories regarding machines as extensions and reinforcements of the human limbs. This idea of "organ projection" had appeared in both Germany and England in the 1860s and was developed with scientific brilliance and thoroughness ten years later by the German Ernst Kapp in his great work, *Grundlinien einer Philosophie der Technik*, which was then very much debated. The idea that a hammer, a spade, or a crowbar externally reinforces the function of the hand and arm needs no further explanation, but Butler's machinist takes the notion even further when he says that a train is "a seven-leagued foot that five hundred people may own at once". The machinist, in other words, has a basically positive attitude to technology. However, the ruling party in Erewhon, the anti-machinists, fear that machines would compensate the weak, thus making equal everybody's ability, so that even those of inferior physique would be able to survive. According to Erewhonian law, illness and weakness are also crimes against the state, and during the centuries of the anti-machinist regime, the rulers had striven to create a physical élite, favouring the strong and tall; all physical frailties were to be abolished. Machines, even of the simplest kind, would enable the weak to assert themselves, and this, according to the anti-machinists, had to be prevented.

For their time, Butler's ideas were not quite so original as is claimed by those who use isolated, out-of-context quotations in today's debate. The key role played by the "machine of machines" at the beginning of the book seems rather anachronistic. The anti-machinists, after many years of fighting and various compromises, had decided to accept any machine older than 271 years, so either Butler or his Erewhonian professors made a mistake over the clock, for the mechanical clock was then far older than that. Still, the ban may have been created according to the rules of the Colleges of Unreason.

Machine Elements of the Steam Era

During the long era when power was produced by harnessing wind and water, wood was the main material used in building machines, and even the machine elements of this era—such as the gearwheel in the power transmission of a windmill—were no exception. Iron fittings were used sparsely up to the beginning of the nineteenth century. Then, when steam power and its associated techniques began their progress, iron became, for various reasons, the predominant building material. Steam generated not only power but also new machine elements, many of which have found additional applications in different technical fields. One example is parallelogram steering, and another is the sun-and-planet drive; both were invented by James Watt.

When designing his steam-engine, Watt encountered the problem of making the piston rod move vertically in a straight line without breaking, although it was connected with the balance beam, the outer end of which oscillated, or moved in a curve. He solved the problem by using two jointed levers to steer the piston rod. His double-acting steam-engine (see also Chapter Five) had a smaller piston pump for the condenser, and this, too, required rectilinear steering of the piston rod. Watt connected the levers of the working piston with the pump piston rod. The connected levers formed a parallelogram, and the levers moved gracefully when the steam-engine was working.

Ever since it was invented, Watt's parallelogram has inspired engineers to many similar designs. A versatile German by the name of Rudolph Ackermann, who lived most of his life in London, took out a patent for the system in 1818, although it had been invented some years earlier by Georg Lankensperger, coachmaker to the king of Bavaria. The system has been used on cars since about 1900. The most common application of the principle today must surely be the tie rod in Ackermann's steering system for cars. The tie rod has an effect, however, contrary to the rectilinear effect intended by Watt; as a car goes round a bend, the inside front wheel, which has a smaller turning circle, gives a larger torsional angle than the outside wheel. The Swedish brothers Birger and Fredrik Ljungström, not being aware of the existence of Ackermann's system, developed the same design for use on the "rickshaw" version of their Svea bicycle, to be described in Chapter Nine.

The sun-and-planet drive is an interesting piece of machinery, which was developed by Watt when he modified his steam-engine to achieve a rotary motion. The background of the design is curious. The obvious way to transform the reciprocating motion of the piston to a rotary motion was to use a crankshaft and connecting rod, for this machine element had been known since the Middle Ages and generally applied in the spinning-wheel, the lathe, and so on. But in 1780, the crank motion with a crank wheel had cleverly been patented by James Pickard, who was apparently tipped off by one of Watt's assistants. Watt, however, never disputed this but decided to get around Pickard's patent. Watt tried a number of designs, but his solution was to attach a cog-wheel to the "connecting rod" and then to marry it to another, usually smaller, cog-wheel, joined to the flywheel. This planetary drive—or sun-and-planet drive, as Watt himself called it—was patented in 1781 and was used extensively in Watt's own steam-engines as well as in several later versions of the steam-engine.

Watt's sun-and-planet drive is a machine element which has been used in widely different contexts and in many forms, for example as a gear box in machine tools. In about 1890, a metal-turning lathe was equipped with such a drive, which made it possible to vary the speed of the lathe spindle over a very large range. Somewhat later, a sun-and-planet motion was introduced on the spindle itself of a different kind of machine tool, in this case, a grinding machine. At the same time as the grinding machine rotated, its centre would move on a circular path. The machine in question was specially developed to make it possible to grind internal holes in workpieces of such a shape that they could not be rotated when they were being machined. Another example of the application of Watt's invention can be found in scales for fine adjustment of measuring instruments, where a sun-and-planet drive—usually made as a friction gear—can give a good gear ratio and great accuracy. These sun-and-planet drives are also common in radio technology, where they are used for fine tuning of tuned circuits in transmitters and receivers.

Machine-made Machine Elements

The machine elements for the clockmaking industry were first made by hand, that is, by manufacture. The clockmaker used simple tools to hand file the teeth of cog-wheels, axles, and other details. One of the first attempts at machine manufacture was made by Christopher Polhem (1661–1751) at the Stjernsund Works in Sweden in the early eighteenth century. The works were founded in 1699 and were mainly intended for the mechanized production of such everyday utility objects as tin mugs, plates, nails, hammer heads, etc. Polhem understood fully the advantages of machines over hands. "Nothing increases the demand as much as a considerable lowering of the price of a product", Polhem wrote, and continued, "That is why we need machines to take over the heavy and time-consuming labour by hand. The result will be a saving of 100–1,000 per cent in costs."

Polhem's machine tools to produce cog-wheels are first mentioned in documents dating from 1708. Very likely, the successful sales of the everyday objects made at the works encouraged Polhem to provide the clockmakers of Sweden with cog-wheel "kits". He believed that it was economically indefensible for craftsmen to waste their skill on so time-consuming a process as making cog-wheels by hand. Therefore, he standardized a number of wheel kits for clocks of different sizes, from wall and table clocks to tower clocks. They were made with the aid of water-wheel-driven machines of different sizes. Six to eight of these machines must have been designed by Polhem and were used at the Stjernsund Works. The largest and probably most automatized was, unfortunately, destroyed in a devastating fire in 1737. Polhem's grandson, Reinhold Rückersköld, who later took over the management of the works, described how:

a machine, driven by water and operated by just one man, simultaneously filed out the teeth in all wheels, both large and small, after the same machine had cut them out of brass to a circular shape with spokes and a centre hub. The machine also cut out the teeth of all gears, which were also provided with axles. These were produced by smoothing and round filing between parallel files.

This machine, so skilfully made and consisting of unlimited connected movements, in eight days produced gearwheels with the accuracy required for clocks, on a scale large enough to supply several clockmakers for a whole year.

The machine described was probably made in 1729. It was not damaged in the fire and was still in use in the 1760s. Today, it is on display in the National Museum of Science and Technology in Stockholm, and it can no doubt be regarded as one of the first automatic machine tools. Another two of Polhem's cutting machines for cogwheels are preserved at the same museum. One is a robust machine for making cog-wheels for tower clocks, and the other is a model of a manually operated cutting machine.

For various reasons, the mechanized production of cog-wheels at the Stjernsund Works did not turn out to be the success Polhelm had anticipated. One contributory factor was the professional pride of the clockmakers; they felt that a first-class clock should be made completely by hand, and semi-finished products did not appeal to them. Another reason was the difficulty in distributing the goods; Sweden was a sparsely populated country with bad roads and very poor communications. Generally, one could say, with Usher, that the main reason why Polhem's ideas and designs for cog-wheel production were so unappreciated was the fact that here, as in many other areas, Polhem was far ahead of his time.

Mechanized Manufacture of Blocks

The multiple block with the pulley was mentioned above as a machine element in the group of the "mighty five". The block was used at an early stage in the rigging of sailing vessels, and in the great era of sailing, up to 1,000 blocks could be needed to fit out one large ship. In the early nineteenth century, the annual need of the British navy was 130,000 blocks of different sizes. These were manufactured by hand at the Portsmouth Dockyard, where 110 craftsmen were kept busy.

However, the French-born engineer Marc Isambard Brunel (1769–1849) suggested in 1801 that the manufacture of blocks ought to be mechanized. He presented models of a series of block-making machines to the Inspector General of Naval Works, Sir Samuel Bentham, who, a couple of years earlier, had had milling machines installed at the yard, along with saws and other mechanical aids for working wood. Some of these he had designed himself. At this time, a block was almost entirely made of wood; the shell was of oak and

Watt's "sun-and-planet" drive shown here from the front (1) and in cross-section (2). The reciprocating movement of the steam-engine's balance beam (a) was transmitted to a fixed gearwheel (b), the "planet", which meshed with a gearwheel (c), the "sun", on the flywheel axle, making it rotate. An annular guide (d) kept the "planet" in its track round the "sun".

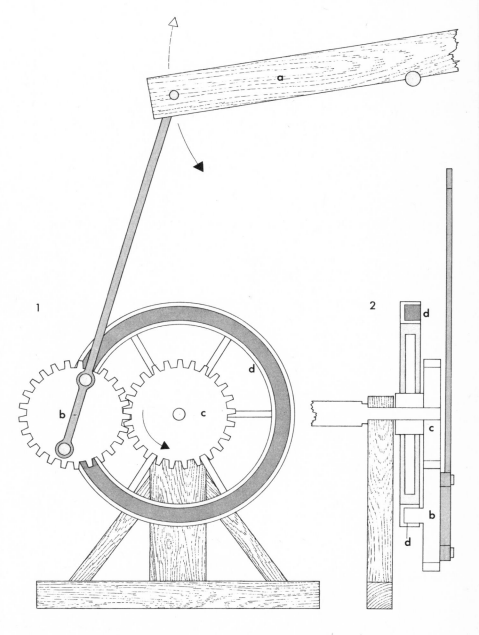

the sheave of lignum vitae, a very hard South American wood. Only the sheave pin was of steel.

At first, Brunel's suggestion met with strong opposition, within the Dockyard as well as from the main supplier of blocks to the navy, but in due course, full-scale machines based on the models were built, and the mechanized production of blocks started in 1803. A total of forty-five machines, driven by two 30-hp steam-engines were in production two years later, and produced blocks of four different size ranges. By adjusting the machines, the dimensions of the blocks could be varied within each size range; in the largest range, for example, the dimensions of the blocks could be varied between 10 and 18 in (25.4 and 45.7 cm). From 1808 on, 10 unskilled workers using Brunel's machines produced as many blocks per unit of time as were previously produced by 110 skilled workers. As a result, the annual production costs were lowered by £17,000 ($85,000).

Brunel's machines contained a number of new construction elements, such as a circular saw, which was used to cut off the material for the block shells. It had a pendulum movement and an interesting type of power transmission by ropes. One machine for mortising the shells employed a cone clutch, a machine part which may have been used for the first time here. Nowadays, the cone clutch is used in all cars which have not been fitted with automatic gear boxes.

Marc Isambard Brunel was born in Normandy and received a technical education at the French marine academy. Among his teachers was the famous mathematician Gaspard Monge (1746–1818). During the French revolution, Brunel fled to the United States, where he continued his technical education, studying civil and mechanical engineering. Eventually, he was appointed chief engineer for the city of New York. In 1798, he went to England to marry Sophia Kingdom, and he then settled in London. An important reason for this was the influential post his brother-in-law held in the navy. From his first years in the United States, Brunel had taken an interest in the mechanical production of blocks and how this could be improved.

The mechanization of block production for the British navy meant a great success for Brunel. Among his later achievements, the greatest was the first tunnel under the Thames in London, a project dramatically begun in 1824 and completed only in 1843. (Non-British literature often confuses Marc Brunel with his son, Isambard Kingdom Brunel (1806–59), who became a celebrated railway engineer who also designed ships and bridges.)

A few decades after Brunel and Bentham had introduced their

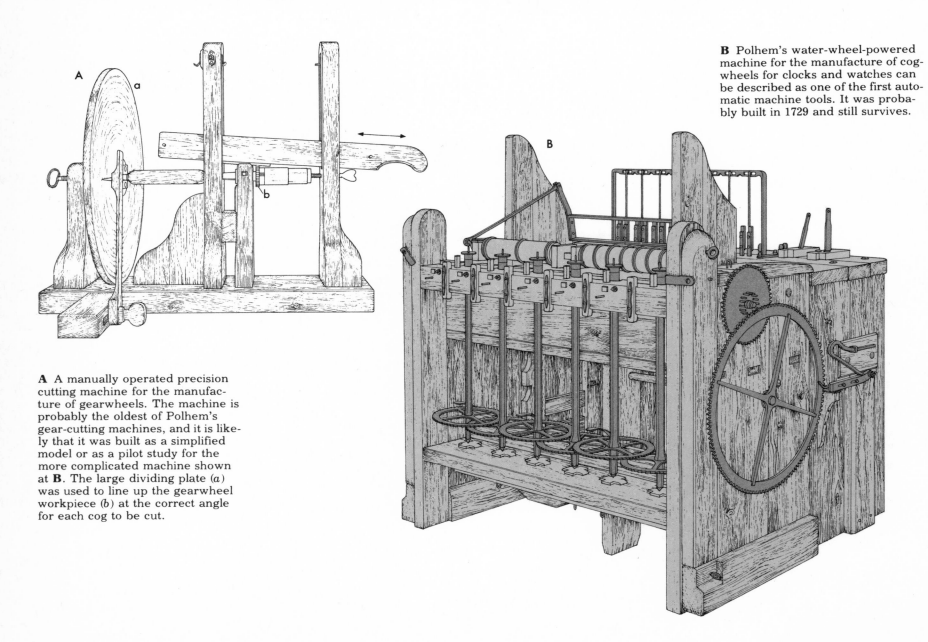

B Polhem's water-wheel-powered machine for the manufacture of cogwheels for clocks and watches can be described as one of the first automatic machine tools. It was probably built in 1729 and still survives.

A A manually operated precision cutting machine for the manufacture of gearwheels. The machine is probably the oldest of Polhem's gear-cutting machines, and it is likely that it was built as a simplified model or as a pilot study for the more complicated machine shown at **B**. The large dividing plate (*a*) was used to line up the gearwheel workpiece (*b*) at the correct angle for each cog to be cut.

mechanized methods of block-production, the Royal Navy began to go over to steam, and the demand for blocks consequently diminished. At the same time, new block designs were introduced; first, the pulley and the mountings were made of metal, and then the wood was completely replaced by other materials. Nowadays, small blocks are usually made of stainless steel or malleable iron (cast iron processed to a tougher and more ductile form by removing part of the carbon in the material). The pulleys are now usually made of nylon.

Machine Elements in Motion

Leonardo da Vinci was the first to show components separately when he was making drawings of machines. Such drawings are called exploded views and were used by several Renaissance authors; two of these were Agricola and Ramelli, but they did not have access to Leonardo's books as direct examples. Agricola, for example, often described machines by showing detailed drawings of the machine elements which were in reality concealed inside the machine. Christopher Polhem learnt this method during a tour of England and Central Europe in 1694–96. Although very impressed, he could not practise it himself, for the very simple reason that he was totally

unable to draw even the easiest of diagrams! His talent was the ability to think in three dimensions and make simple models to express his ideas for designs. After his return from abroad, Polhem designed a number of models of machine elements which he must have seen during his tour or been inspired to invent by the sight of some mechanical device. He often made prototypes of his models himself, and then some skilfull craftsman would take over the final construction.

Polhem considered these working models to be more instructive than illustrations in books, and therefore suitable for teaching mechanical engineering. In an account of his travels, which he gave to the Mines Authority in Stockholm, he suggested that a *laboratorium mechanicum* be established to serve both as a college and as an experimental workshop developing new machinery. What Polhem had in mind was an equivalent of the *laboratorium chymicum* which the great Swedish doctor and natural scientist Urban Hjärne (1641–1724) had opened in 1685 for the production of medicines, for testing medicinal herbs, etc.

In his proposal, Polhem eloquently pleaded the advantages of such a mechanical laboratory, especially when it came to encouraging young, talented people and giving them a thorough education in

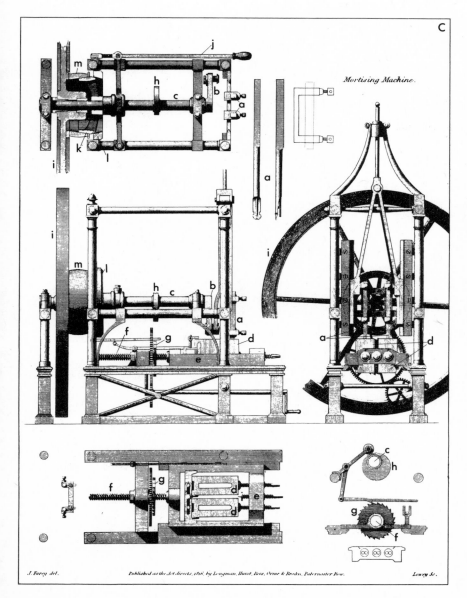

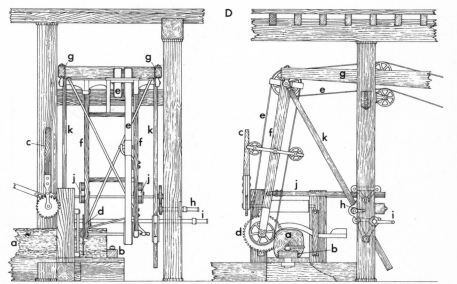

C Brunel's mortising machine for medium-sized blocks. The machine could mortise either two blocks or one two-sheaved block at a time. The two chisels (*a*) were given a working speed of up to 400 strokes a minute by a crank (*b*) on a rotating shaft (*c*). Scantlings (*d*) – cut pieces of wood for the blocks – were placed in a carriage (*e*), which was slowly brought forwards by a screw (*f*) as a ratchet-wheel (*g*) on the screw was turned by one tooth for each revolution of a cam (*h*) on the shaft. The rotation of the shaft could be interrupted without the flywheel (*i*) being brought to a halt, since the machine was equipped with a cone clutch (a section of it is shown top left). By means of a lever (*j*), the

conical wheel (*k*) on the shaft (*c*) could be brought into contact with either a brake drum (*l*) or with the driving pulley (*m*) on the flywheel (*i*).

D This pendulum saw for cutting logs into scantlings was also constructed by Brunel. The log (*a*) was drawn forwards to a stop (*b*) when a handle (*c*) was rocked. For the transmission of power to the saw , blade (*d*), belts (*e*) were used. The saw blade could be moved horizontally and vertically since it was mounted on pivoted frames (*f*, *g*) which could be adjusted by means of cranks (*h*, *i*). When these were turned, the rods *j* and *k* were moved by rack-and-pinion devices.

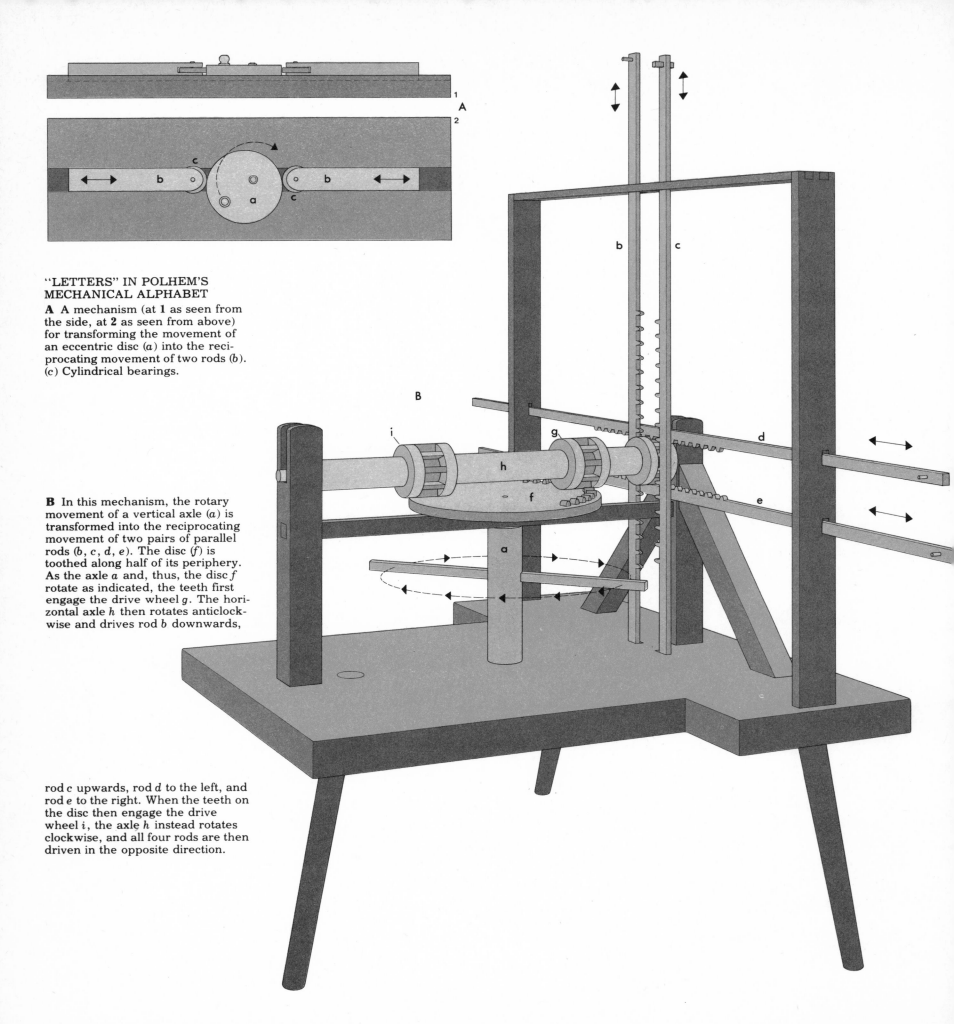

"LETTERS" IN POLHEM'S
MECHANICAL ALPHABET

A A mechanism (at **1** as seen from
the side, at **2** as seen from above)
for transforming the movement of
an eccentric disc (*a*) into the reciprocating movement of two rods (*b*).
(*c*) Cylindrical bearings.

B In this mechanism, the rotary
movement of a vertical axle (*a*) is
transformed into the reciprocating
movement of two pairs of parallel
rods (*b*, *c*, *d*, *e*). The disc (*f*) is
toothed along half of its periphery.
As the axle *a* and, thus, the disc *f*
rotate as indicated, the teeth first
engage the drive wheel *g*. The horizontal axle *h* then rotates anticlock-
wise and drives rod *b* downwards,

rod *c* upwards, rod *d* to the left, and
rod *e* to the right. When the teeth on
the disc then engage the drive
wheel *i*, the axle *h* instead rotates
clockwise, and all four rods are then
driven in the opposite direction.

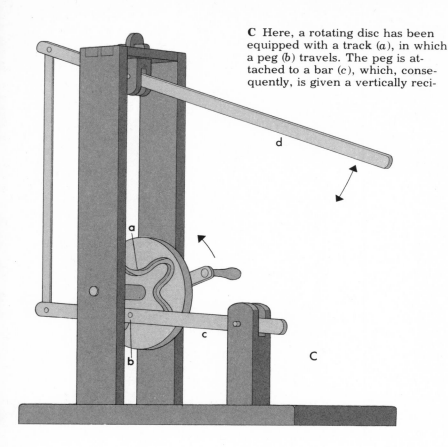

C Here, a rotating disc has been equipped with a track (*a*), in which a peg (*b*) travels. The peg is attached to a bar (*c*), which, consequently, is given a vertically reci-

engineering, using visual aids. He also drew up a magnificent plan for his institution, where some ten instructors and model designers were to be active under his management. The suggestion was submitted in the autumn of 1696, and by the beginning of the following year, a royal decree allowed him to carry out the plans. The Gripenhielm house in Stockholm was bought for the purpose, and the activities of the mechanical laboratory were able to commence the same year. The staff, however, turned out to be not as numerous as Polhem had planned. He had at his disposal two skilled craftsman—a carpenter and a smith—who, aided by two apprentices, made models after his directions. The series of models to be used for teaching was systematized and complemented by Polhem to include all the machine elements known at the time, eighty in all. Several of these had been invented by himself. He called this systematized collection of machine elements "the mechanical alphabet". Polhem believed that, if a poet can produce the finest poetry from simple letters, an engineer, by mastering the mechanical alphabet, should be able to design useful machines. "The mighty five" were the vowels of this alphabet, whereas the other elements were the consonants.

However, Polhem could devote only less than a year to the initial stages of his mechanical laboratory. In the early 1690s, before his travels, he had gained great fame as a designer of remarkable machines, including the *Machina Nova*, an ore-whim installed at the Falu copper mine. On his return from abroad, while he was so preoccupied with his plans for the mechanical laboratory, he was in great demand with several mining companies, who wanted to employ his services. Most of the models of the mechanical alphabet

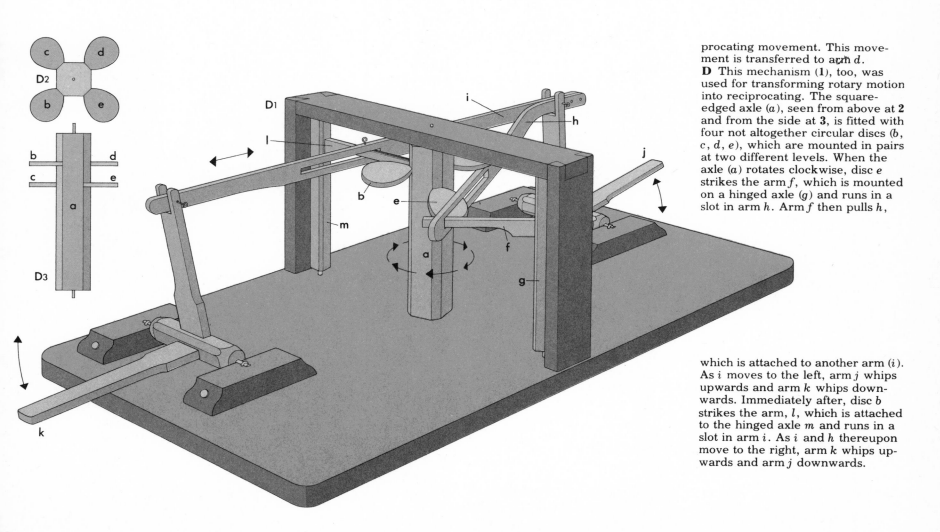

procating movement. This movement is transferred to arm *d*.

D This mechanism (**1**), too, was used for transforming rotary motion into reciprocating. The square-edged axle (*a*), seen from above at **2** and from the side at **3**, is fitted with four not altogether circular discs (*b*, *c*, *d*, *e*), which are mounted in pairs at two different levels. When the axle (*a*) rotates clockwise, disc *e* strikes the arm *f*, which is mounted on a hinged axle (*g*) and runs in a slot in arm *h*. Arm *f* then pulls *h*,

which is attached to another arm (*i*). As *i* moves to the left, arm *j* whips upwards and arm *k* whips downwards. Immediately after, disc *b* strikes the arm, *l*, which is attached to the hinged axle *m* and runs in a slot in arm *i*. As *i* and *h* thereupon move to the right, arm *k* whips upwards and arm *j* downwards.

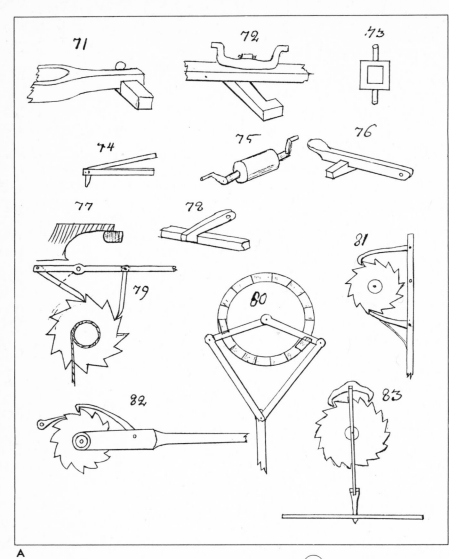

A

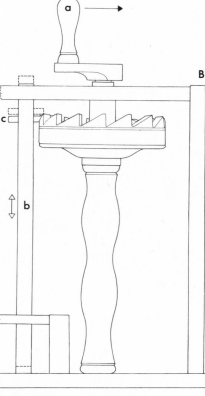

a

B

c

b

A A page from Carl Johan Cronstedt's sketchbook, in which he systematized and summarized Polhem's mechanical alphabet in 1729. **B** Yet another "letter" in the mechanical alphabet. When the crank (a) is rotated in a clockwise direction, the rod (b) receives a reciprocating motion, due to its being equipped with a cross-bar (c).

were probably built during the year when Polhem directly supervised the work, but, in the summer of 1698, he left the management to his assistant, Fredrik Buschenfelt, who had been with him on his tour abroad and was conversant with his ideas and objectives.

The main reason, however, why Polhem left his mechanical laboratory to others was the fact that his stay in England had inspired him to set up his own manufacturing company. Preparations for this now claimed all his time, and, in 1699, he founded the Stjernsund Works and equipped it with a large number of newly designed machines which showed in practice how "poetry" could be written with the mechanical alphabet.

Still, Polhem did not completely abandon his mechanical laboratory. In 1706, Buschenfelt died, and the activities of the laboratory ceased for a few years; but in the early 1710s, the institution was reestablished at Falun. The various projects Polhem took on during this period included the technical directorship of the Stora Kopparberg mine. His title was *konstmästare*, "art master". King Charles XII of Sweden, whose headquarters were then at Bender in Turkey—where, during his Russian campaign, he had temporarily retired—had received a report of the activities of the laboratory and summoned Polhem to him to discuss the future of the institution. The king had extensive plans for both the Stjernsund Works and the mechanical laboratory. The latter was to be extended into what we would call a research and development laboratory for the works and to be used, at the same time, for education. New products were to be developed there to make Sweden self-sufficient in all kinds of metal goods.

Polhem, however, did not think himself able to undertake the time-consuming and dangerous journey through a turbulent Europe to Turkey, and Charles XII had to be satisfied with providing funds through the Mines Authority to enable Polhem to operate his mechanical laboratory at Stjernsund. How far Polhem followed the wishes of the king is not known, but many young students came to Stjernsund from the German mines, and in return for a handsome fee—Polhem was also a very good businessman—they were boarded there and taught mechanics. In the 1720s, several Swedes also went to Stjernsund as Polhem's pupils and assistants; one of these was Carl Johan Cronstedt (1709–79), who studied mechanics and mechanical engineering with some other young noblemen from 1729 to 1731. Cronstedt later studied architecture under the famous palace architect Carl Hårleman and was to build palaces and machine plants himself; he turned out to be an excellent administrator, however, and crowned his career by becoming the president of the Swedish Crown Lands Judiciary Board.

Cronstedt is of interest here because, in 1729, he systematized and summarized Polhem's mechanical alphabet. His illustrations of these machine elements are preserved in a sketchbook listing no less than 103 "letters"; some twenty elements had been added since Christopher Polhem launched the idea of a mechanical laboratory in 1696, although the basic notion was still the same. Cronstedt wrote in his sketchbook:

It is necessary for a lettered man to keep in mind all the words needed to compose a sentence or an article. In the same way, it is necessary for an engineer to be familiar with all the simple movements. If a writer, when putting the words together, had to find one letter here and one there in hidden or remote places, his writing would become unreadable, full of the most awful trash. In the same way, if an engineer, when compiling machines and inventions, did not know all the simple movements of the *Mechanicus Alphabet* but had to produce them from distant nooks and crannies, that is, in notes, articles, and books, then the work would obviously proceed very slowly. . . . New machines are nothing more than words or bodies compiled of letters or limbs, applied to their appropriate places depending on the application of the machine, so that, when finished, they achieve the desired effect.

Cronstedt's neat sketches and drawings of the mechanical alphabet were unfortunately not published. They are now kept in the archives of the National Museum of Science and Technology in Stockholm. Nor did Polhem, incidentally, describe his alphabet in print, and only a few of the designs included in it are mentioned by contemporary text-books, such as *Föreläsningar öfver naturkunnigheten* ("Lectures in Natural Science") by Mårten Triewald, published in two volumes in 1735–36.

The mechanical laboratory operated at Stjernsund with a varying number of pupils up to 1735, when Polhem's wife died. He then moved to his son-in-law, Carl Gripenstierna, of the Kersö estate on the island of Ekerö on Lake Mälar. He brought with him at least a part of his collection of models and went on designing machines. In 1739, he received a special grant to employ three skilled craftsmen, who were to build his "useful" machines, which were intended for use in agriculture and were made both as models and in full scale.

When the old sluice in Stockholm was to be rebuilt in 1746, Polhem was asked to manage and supervise the work on site. He was then eighty-five but just as restlessly active as in previous years. The government now commissioned him to collect all his models, and they were put on public display in a wing of the Royal Palace, called the Royal Model Chamber, where those who were interested could learn a lot about elementary mechanics, even if there was no actual teaching. After Polhem died in 1751, his son Gabriel tried to reorganize a mechanical laboratory along the lines his father had first planned, but engineering was not as popular with the authorities then as it had been in Christopher Polhem's heyday. Gabriel's efforts went unnoticed. Efter varying fortunes, the model collection was taken over by the Technological Institute (later the Royal Institute of Technology) when this was founded in 1827, and, at first, the models were used educationally. In the late 1920s, the model collection was found in the attic of the old Institute building. What had once been national treasures in the Royal Model Chamber were then in a lamentable state; most of the models were simply falling to pieces. The collection was handed over to the National Museum of Science and Technology, where a painstaking job of identifying and restoring it was undertaken by Dr. Torsten Althin; the result was, eventually, a reconstruction of the Royal Model Chamber as a department within the museum.

Kinematics

In his sketchbook, Cronstedt described about a third of the machine elements in Polhem's mechanical alphabet. This description is entitled *De simpla mekaniska rörelser som kunna tjena som ett mechaniskt alphabet* ("The Simple Mechanical Movements which can Serve as a Mechanical Alphabet"). What most fascinated Cronstedt was the fact that relatively simple combinations of "the mighty five" could achieve very advanced—and useful—movements. In his study of the simple machines, Archimedes concentrated mainly on clarifying their power-amplifying properties, which were very important in the development of the first prime movers, the water-wheel and the windmill, and also of the working machines invented in the Middle Ages, during the technical revolution of the Renaissance—whims, ore crushers, forge hammers, and frame-saws. From the beginning of industrialization, in the eighteenth century, these properties became increasingly important in the design of machines. What man had previously done by hand was now executed by machines, of which different elements somehow imitated human movements, as in, for example, the spinning-machine and the mechanical loom.

The designers of these machines (and many other designers during the same era) were talented but pragmatic inventors, who certainly gave little thought to the machines, their laws of motion, and their internal relations. But there were others who did, and they caused mechanics and mechanical engineering to be included in the syllabuses of the technical colleges, both military and civil, which started to emerge at the end of the eighteenth century in the Old World and the New alike, keeping burning, as it were, the light which Polhem first lit.

In 1806, the professor of geometry at the Ecole Polytechnique in Paris, Jean Nicolas Pierre Hachette (1769–1834), gave a course on machine elements while teaching descriptive geometry. Five years later, Hachette published the first text-book on the systematized functions of machine elements. This book set the pattern for at least a hundred years. In it, Hachette defined six "orders" of machine elements, functionally different from each other: *récepteurs*—receiving the motion of a prime mover; *communicateurs*—passing on the motion; *modificateurs*—transforming the motion, for example, from reciprocating to rotary; *supports*—bearings, guides, and so on; *régulateurs*—connecting and disconnecting, speed regulation; and, finally, *opérateurs*—machine elements giving the final effect. It was fashionable to systematize and to clarify, and to introduce definitions tying up conceptions and nomenclature. Hachette's definitions were the beginning of a systematization of mechanical engineering, which can be compared to Carolus Linnaeus's works on flora and fauna, and to Jac Berzelius's work on the standardization of chemical nomenclature.

Among his compatriots, Hachette acquired many followers. The leading name here is André Marie Ampère (1775–1836), a talented mathematician and physicist from Lyons, whose name is best remembered as the unit of electric current. Ampère was professor of theoretical and experimental physics at the Collège de France in Paris, and to equip himself for the task of preparing a syllabus, he took upon himself the enormous job of compiling a survey of all human knowledge! The result was a comprehensive study in two volumes, published in 1829, and in the tradition of the great French encyclopaedists. Unlike d'Alambert and Diderot, however, Ampère devoted plenty of space to the philosophy of natural science, which he regarded as the basis of rational classification. Ampère's classification of mechanics into statics (bodies at rest) and into a new branch, which he called kinematics (bodies in motion), shows the amount of consideration he had given the matter. And his definition of the new science is still valid:

The movements are to be studied as movements, independent of the power creating them, in the same way as we observe the movements of static bodies around us, especially in such combinations as we call machines.

Ampère's definition is just as abstract as is fitting in a philosophical-scientific work. Fundamentally, it implies that the most important thing when designing a machine—say, a mechanical loom—is to establish what movements are required and by what machine elements these can be achieved. Once that is clear, one should calculate the stresses to which the machine elements are to be exposed and adjust their dimensions accordingly.

At this time, two of Ampère's compatriots were particularly active in kinematics—the mathematicians Gustave Gaspard de Coriolis and Charles-Nicolas Peaucellier. Coriolis is mainly known for his discovery of the acceleration power (the Coriolis force), which causes, among other things, the currents of the oceans to move in curved paths. But he also studied machine elements in motion and *en passant* defined the physical notion "work" as the product of the force and the distance.

After Ampère died, the bulk of kinematic study was done in England, which was then very much the homeland of mechanical engineering, where steam power was rapidly developing on land and at sea. In the late 1830s, Robert Willis (1800–75) lectured in Cambridge on the kinematics of machine elements, and in 1841, these lectures were published in book form as *Principles of Mechanism*. Willis was professor of natural and experimental philosophy, a discipline which, today, would hardly be associated with the design of machines. But in England, natural philosophy was the classical name for what would today be called physics and, as such, had been part of the academic world at least since 1662, when the Royal Society was founded. So Willis's subject was theoretical and experimental physics, that is, the subject on which Ampère, too, had lectured.

Willis developed kinematics into a practical science, and his descriptions of machine elements and their functions resulted in mathematical formulae which could be applied directly by a machine designer. Willis's book became one of the first mechanical engineering handbooks and circulated widely.

Willis also introduced the word "kinematics" into the English language. The most important of his pioneering contributions to the subject were his methods of analyzing moving systems, or *pure mechanisms*, as he called them.

Among those who took up Willis's ideas was Ferdinand Redtenbacher, professor of applied mathematics at the Karlsruhe Polytechnic. He made creditable attempts to simplify Willis's methods and to find a practicable system for classifying machine designs, but he was not particularly successful. Instead, it was to be as a talented and inspiring teacher that he was to play an important, albeit indirect, rôle in the development of kinematics. In the early 1850s, Redtenbacher had a young student by the name of Franz Reuleaux, who, guided by his professor, became fascinated by kinematics, realizing their importance to the further progress of mechanical engineering.

Franz Reuleaux, whom we have already met, is worthy of fuller introduction, as he was a leading light not only in the field of kinematics, but also in contemporary cultural circles. His family were Walloons, and he was related in a direct line to the builder who, in the days of Louis XIV, erected the great pumping station at Marly, on the Seine–a gigantic construction which aroused great interest throughout Europe (see page 102). His grandfather was a noted "art master" in Liège, and his father had settled in Eischweiler in the Rhineland, where he had had great success designing and building steam-engines. After leaving school, Franz spent a few years as an apprentice in his father's workshop. In 1850, he began more advanced studies in Karlsruhe. He graduated as an engineer and then continued his schooling at the universities of Berlin and Bonn, studying natural sciences and arts. In 1856, when Reuleaux had just set up an engineering consultancy in Cologne, he was nominated professor of applied mechanics at the Eidgenössische Technische Hochschule in Zürich. He remained there until 1864, when he became a professor at the Gewerbeakademie in Berlin. The following year, he was appointed head of this institution, which later (in 1879) merged with the Berliner Bauakademie, forming the large Technische Hochschule, which was located at Charlottenburg, outside Berlin. Reuleaux was to be head of this school, and a professor there, until he retired in 1896.

For his classes in mechanical engineering, Reuleaux compiled a "mechanical alphabet" of models of different mechanical devices, which eventually numbered almost eight hundred. Just at that time, there was an enormous increase in the number of mechanical devices available for various purposes, so Reuleaux became wholeheartedly involved in systematizing and classifying these. His aim was to achieve the same uncompromisingly logical order in the field of engineering that Linnaeus had established for flora and fauna. In his lectures and papers, Reuleaux referred often to Linnaeus and emphasized the importance of his work in the development of botany and zoology. He and his assistants followed Linnaeus's way of working and attempted to trace every conceivable mechanical construction–no easy task, and the model collection grew and grew.

Reuleaux presented the results of his endeavours to create a "sexual system" of mechanical engineering in a series of elegantly lucid lectures, which soon attained general renown. The audience was treated to practical demonstrations of models from the ever-growing collection, and to theoretical speculation on a high, scientific level of abstraction. In 1875, he published his findings in the great work already mentioned in Chapter One and entitled *Theoretische Kinematik: Grundzüge einer Theorie des Maschinwesens* ("Theoretical Kinematics: Principles of a Theory of Machine Technology"). The book aroused keen interest, not only among engineers and technicians, but also in wider circles. At last, some method and order was to be established also in the ever more complex field of mechanical engineering. The desire to systematize and classify was one of the hall-marks of the optimistic and progressive spirit of the age.

Reuleaux planned this book as the first part of a trilogy, and the other two parts were to follow shortly afterwards. In the event, this was not the case. Twenty-five years were to pass before the second part was published, and the third never got beyond the stage of an incomplete draft.

One of Reuleaux's contemporaries, Alexander B.W. Kennedy, professor of applied mathematics at University College, London, soon translated the book into English, and it was published in England as early as 1876. It was an almost greater success in England, the "workshop of the world", than it was in the Germany of the Second Reich. The Science Museum in London quickly took advantage of this and arranged an exhibition of some of Reuleaux's teaching models. The exhibition, the book, and Reuleaux's scientific work as a whole became the object of great interest and were reviewed and discussed in both the technical and daily press. Technical circles caught something of a "Reuleaux fever", which then spread to other countries.

Reuleaux was not an unknown name internationally. As early as 1861, he had published a handbook on engineering, *Der Konstrukteur* ("The Designer"). This was one of the first books of its kind and was translated into one language after another. Never before 1876, however, had Reuleaux been the object of such enormous interest. His work on kinematics had been translated at just the right psychological moment in the Anglo-Saxon world. In the year that the translation was published, the great Centennial Exposition was opened in Fairmount Park in Philadelphia. This was an international exhibition to commemorate the hundredth anniversary of the signing of the American Declaration of Independence. The exhibition became a monumental manifestation of "pure mechanisms" (in Willis's words) and was an almost stunning expression of confidence in the potential of steam power to solve all the energy and power problems of both society and industry. President Ulysses S. Grant opened the exhibition by starting the huge Corliss steam-engine and, metaphorically speaking, thus released a burning enthusiasm for pure, applied mechanics, a branch of science which would save mankind from the hard, often humiliating, struggle for survival.

Reuleaux was present in Philadelphia as leader of the German delegation, and he gave an account of his impressions in *Briefe aus Philadelphia* ("Letters from Philadelphia"), which was widely read and appreciated in Germany. In it, he eloquently describes the numerous technical wonders demonstrated in Fairmount Park, and he writes that they exceeded everything he had experienced previously. And his statements carried some authority, for he had been on the jury of two earlier world exhibitions, one in Paris in 1867 and another held six years later in Vienna. (Reuleaux also led the German delegations to the world exhibitions in Sydney in 1879 and Melbourne in 1881.) But at Philadelphia there were exhibited not only machines, but also all sorts of products of craft and industry, besides works of art and much else from the whole world. The overall picture of human civilization thus presented made a very strong impression on Reuleaux. He felt that all of it—even the works of art—was, ultimately, the result of technical progress.

In the years following the Philadelphia exhibition, Reuleaux began to develop the relation between technology, culture, and social development. In 1882, he expanded his views of technology as a carrier of culture in a lecture given to an industrial association in Vienna. This lecture, first published in Vienna and in a couple of German journals, was entitled *Kultur und Technik* ("Culture and Technology") and aroused a lively debate which raged for many years. When published in French, Italian, and English journals, it also became the subject of discussion in these countries. As late as 1890, the lecture was printed in the annual report of the Smithsonian Institution, that admirable research institute in Washington, which runs, among other things, the American central museums of technology, natural history, and art.

In his lecture, Reuleaux first gives a brief survey of the world distribution of the civilized peoples, in which he attacks the fairly widespread idea of the time that the races of the world can be divided into active and passive. He then goes on directly to his beloved kinematic fundamentals, ratchet gears, rack gears, and so on. These he generalized and extended to include various other phenomena in technology as well as in society as a whole. For example, he regarded a fire—be it under a steam boiler or a conflagration—as a chemical ratchet, released at the moment the fire started. He also intimated that socio-political events could be seen in a similar manner. This automatically makes one think of the American Norbert Wiener (1894–1964), the man who, seventy-five years later, developed cybernetics, that is, the science of the control and regulation of animals and machines by feed-back circuits—of which more later.

In the 1880s and 1890s, Reuleaux was highly prolific in various fields. The following are a selection of the many articles and books he wrote during this time: *The Machine and the Capacity for Work: Social Contemporary Questions, German Achievements and Future Prospects in Technology and Industry, Indian Miniature Works of Art, On the Importance of Water to Human Welfare, Interpretation of Folk Legends, Oriental Chessmen,* and *Hiawatha,* a German translation of Longfellow's famous poem. From the mid-1870s onwards, Reuleaux became rather unpopular in certain German industrial circles, due to his lectures and articles unceasingly criticizing the low standards and the poor designs of various companies' products. He believed that German goods ran the risk of being considered abroad as *billig und schlecht* ("cheap and bad"). This, too, gave rise to a debate, which in its own way probably had a positive effect on German industrial development.

It is obvious that, in the wide range of interests cultivated by Reuleaux at the height of his powers, kinematics took rather a back seat. His prolific writings and his assumption of the rôle of opinion builder made Reuleaux one of the foremost German cultural figures for at least twenty years.

Reuleaux's pioneering work on theoretical kinematics gave a totally new picture of mechanical engineering in general and of the function of machine elements in particular. The principles he introduced, simplified almost as far as could be, made those designers,

Reuleaux also took an interest in human anatomy. To him, man's limbs and joints were coupled levers, and he tried to apply the methods of kinematics to them in order to find the best possible positions for the human body when it performed different operations. In the illustration of the man at the grindstone (*below*), there is also an indication of how Reuleaux linked one human and one technical system of coupled levers.

Reuleaux's epoch-making studies of composite machine elements and their reciprocal movements turned kinematics into a science.

A Various types of gear-reduction sets were among the machine elements studied by Reuleaux from a kinematic point of view. Shown here is a reduction set with hyperbolic gearwheels. The dashed prolongation line of the smaller cogwheel indicates the shape of the hyperbola.

B This "kinematic linkage with four joints" was used by Reuleaux

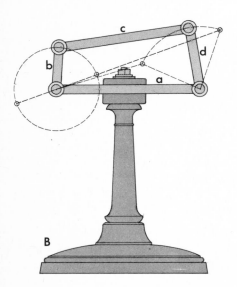

to illustrate the thesis that a closed kinematic linkage can be made to move in as many ways as the linkage has bars. The dashed lines show the movements of bars b, c, and d if a is fixed.

C Reciprocally movable machine elements with a continuous engagement between complicated geometric shapes usually led to theoretical calculations of great complexity. Examples of such machine elements are those included in this air-pump.

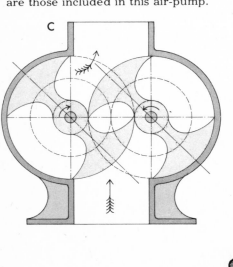

D This composite machine element was used by Reuleaux as a basis for exercises in which the reciprocal movements of cog-wheels with varying numbers of cogs were calculated.

E Reuleaux considered even the universal joint to be a kinematic chain and stated its theory.

F A kinematic linkage with a cam. The machine elements transformed a rotary to a reciprocating movement.

who were engaged on practical work, stop and think. They now began to strive after the simple rather than the complicated in their designs, for the latter often resulted in poorly functioning machines.

In his analysis of the function of machine elements, Reuleaux distinguished in his first principles between, among other things, "elementary pairs" and "kinematic chains". The first group contained, for example, the nut and bolt, the axle journal and bearing, and a cog-wheel engaging with a rack (rack gearing). The second group included connected and jointed levers, such as the crank, but also combinations, such as Watt's parallel motion linkage, which achieved rectilinear motion. When Reuleaux wrote his book in the 1870s, the kinematics of parallel motion was somewhat in vogue among the great theoreticians, and we shall soon return to that. Reuleaux, however, was totally unconcerned by the sophistry of the great minds and concentrated on the technical realities involved. When analyzing complex constructions, he simplified them quite considerably. For example, he described a number of different designs for rotary steam-engines and stated with obvious delight that they were fundamentally identical; in many cases, he added, the designers had quite needlessly complicated their creations!

In 1900, when at last Reuleaux published the second part of his *Theoretical Kinematics*, his star had started to dwindle. This volume, which deals with the relationship between kinematics and geometry and mechanics, does not have the brilliance and vigour which had distinguished the first, and on the whole it seems to have been little appreciated by those engaged in practical engineering, while the theoreticians gave it scant attention. During the following decades, kinematics and Reuleaux's contributions came to be less esteemed. The principles were certainly considered to be of theoretical interest, but in practice they gave rise to extremely complicated mathematical problems. Reuleaux's *Theoretical Kinematics* was rarely found on the engineer's bookshelf after 1900, although his engineering handbook, *The Designer*, was. However, the latter, too, became the subject of severe criticism when the author's fame was at its lowest. In a commemorative article in 1929, the great mathematician Rudolf von Miese called it a "simple cookery book for engineers". But it was only some ten years later that the tide turned in favour of Reuleaux and kinematics.

"Rectilinear Motion" Leads Kinematics Astray

When James Watt designed his parallel motion linkage, he probably did not realize that he was releasing a flood of solutions—some more imaginative than others—to the problem of achieving rectilinear motion. Watt's linkage solved the particular concrete problem which he had faced in getting his steam-engine to function, and he was very proud of his brilliant invention. He confided to his son, "Though I am not over anxious after fame, yet I am more proud of the parallel motion than of any other mechanical invention I have ever made." But during the next hundred years, a number of geniuses, mainly mathematicians, were to spend their time inventing a number of highly curious devices to give rectilinear motion, despite the fact that Watt had already provided a practicable and satisfactory solution to the problem. And the number of these devices far exceeded the actual need. One of the first came from the English clergyman Edmund Cartwright (1743–1823), to whom the invention of the mechanical loom is usually attributed. In 1800, he took out a patent for a device, as simple as it was ingenious, which converted the reciprocating motion of the steam-engine piston to rotary motion. It consisted of two crank webs, each working on its own cog-wheel, one of which also drove the balance wheel. That which distinguished the device was that the cranks also ensured the rectilinear motion of the piston. However, this invention found very few applications.

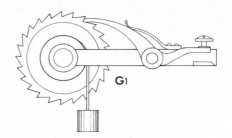

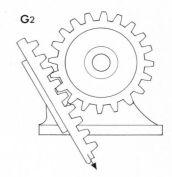

G In his essay *Kultur und Technik*, Reuleaux tried to generalize his kinematical theories in order to apply them to phenomena in society. A ratchet gear (**1**), which could be released by pressing the key, would then symbolize, for example, a conflagration or an act of God, whereas a running gear (**2**) symbolized things like international commerce. Since the movement of a ratchet gear was not constant and, further, was different when running forwards and when running backwards, a ratchet gear, according to Reuleaux, differed completely from a running gear.

At about the same time, another Englishman, James White, discovered that the mathematical properties of the hypocycloid (a curve traced by a point on the circumference of a circle rolling along the interior of a larger circle) could be exploited. If the diameter of the inner circle is half that of the outer, a point on the circumference of the inner circle will move back and forth in a straight line. This, White suggested, could be applied to the cog-wheel. He described his device as "pretty" but added that it was not considered generally to be especially good. The motion of this mechanism is certainly pretty—and amusing (it is usually included in most of the mechanical alphabets used in teaching engineering)—but deficiencies in the art of gear cutting at the time caused a number of practical complications, and the invention was, like Cartwright's, little used.

During the following decade, one of the most interesting devices for achieving rectilinear motion was, perhaps, that constructed by the pioneer American steam engineer, Oliver Evans (1755–1819), for his "Columbian Engine", a beam engine with a single-shaft bar. (This type of engine became very popular in England, where it was known as "the grasshopper".) Evans's device produced an almost rectilinear motion. Curiously enough, the design later returned to its country of origin, in a somewhat modified version, on the "Stourbridge Lion", the steam locomotive built by George Stephenson, and the first ever to be used in the United States. The design was used in the coupled levers connecting the driving wheels.

One of the few devices for rectilinear motion which was, like Evans's invention, designed for a definite technical purpose, is usually attributed to the Englishman Richard Roberts (1789–1864). In 1816, he founded a mechanical workshop in Manchester. Some years later, he designed a smooth-planing machine for metal working, in which this "Roberts device" was a machine element. But Eugene Ferguson, the noted American historian of technology who has made a study of kinematics, claims that this device originated in France, where it had been described as early as 1769. Its rectilinear motion was then used for a completely different purpose, namely, to saw off piles under water. But the principle of the device's construction was identical to that of Roberts's.

Various more or less (often more!) bizarre devices for rectilinear motion appeared in the following decades, but these can easily be excluded from this account, as they were of no real importance. However, in the 1860s, things became more interesting in this field. In 1864, the previously mentioned French military engineer Charles-Nicholas Peaucellier wrote a letter to the editor of a mathematical journal, in which he briefly pointed out the possibility of constructing a mechanism with coupled and jointed levers, which could both produce a rectilinear motion and describe a circle of arbitrary radius. But no one, mathematician or otherwise, responded to his suggestion, and the letter was forgotten. In the 1870s, when interest in kinematics began to grow, Peaucellier made a model of such a mechanism, which he called a *compas composé* ("compound compass"). With this he showed that the path followed by a point on, say, a joint can be expressed as an algebraic equation, and that the reverse also applies, that is to say, any curve which can be described in an equation can also be achieved by a kinematic chain. It was "simply" a question of finding the right combination.

The reaction of the experts to Peaucellier's model was immediate. Among them was the Russian mathematician Pafnuti Chebysev (1821–94), who was, at that time, interested in rectilinear motion and had improved upon Watt's design. Chebysev's version achieved considerably greater accuracy but was more complicated. It was used on a steam-engine shown at the world exhibition in Vienna in 1873, but the reaction of the technical press was very negative. The English journal *The Engineer*, for example, pointed out that the design had too many joints and couplings to grease, and too many pins which could break. Reuleaux might have given his Russian colleague a lesson in the complicated art of simplification!

Chebysev is said to have been very impressed by Peaucellier's mechanism, which, according to its originator, gave an exactly straight line. But what Chebysev tried to do was to prove the opposite; he even tried to produce evidence that a kinematic chain, no matter how many links it contains, can never give a mathematically straight line. Throughout the rest of his life, Chebysev attacked this problem with "an interest bordering on obsession", to quote Ferguson, but he never found the solution. The mathematical analysis of kinematic chains leads to extremely complicated equations, which not even a great mathematician like Chebysev could solve.

Chebysev corresponded regularly with the British-American professor of mathematics James Sylvester (1814–97), and in 1873 wrote to urge him to take up kinematics as rewarding and more fruitful than geometry for it would add a fourth dimension to space. Sylvester followed this advice and became almost as obsessed by the subject as his correspondent. Only a year later, he gave a much publicized lecture at the Royal Institution in London, in which he demonstrated Peaucellier's mechanism and developed his own theories on kinematic chains for producing rectilinear motion. The lecture, which was later published, turned out to be an ardent song of praise of Peaucellier's "*compas composé*", which he extolled for its mathematical beauty. Why, Sylvester asked rhetorically, had not

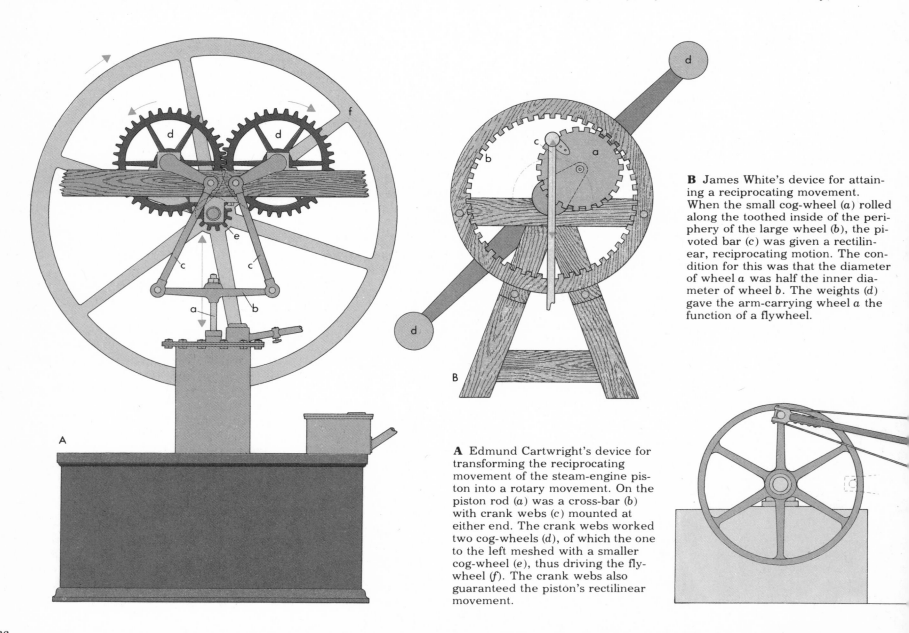

B James White's device for attaining a reciprocating movement. When the small cog-wheel (*a*) rolled along the toothed inside of the periphery of the large wheel (*b*), the pivoted bar (*c*) was given a rectilinear, reciprocating motion. The condition for this was that the diameter of wheel *a* was half the inner diameter of wheel *b*. The weights (*d*) gave the arm-carrying wheel *a* the function of a flywheel.

A Edmund Cartwright's device for transforming the reciprocating movement of the steam-engine piston into a rotary movement. On the piston rod (*a*) was a cross-bar (*b*) with crank webs (*c*) mounted at either end. The crank webs worked two cog-wheels (*d*), of which the one to the left meshed with a smaller cog-wheel (*e*), thus driving the flywheel (*f*). The crank webs also guaranteed the piston's rectilinear movement.

such an apparently simple mechanism been invented much earlier? His answer was that the mechanism, from the mathematical point of view, was so very complicated that it would have been more natural if it had first appeared a good hundred years later!

But the practical use of this simply wonderful mechanism was another of Silvester's questions. One answer lay in the story he told of a well-known London architect who, to a plumber's infinite astonishment, had used the mechanism to guide the piston in a water pump. In the same breath, Sylvester added that this brilliant design ought to be tried out in water closets, where it could replace the flimsy chain!

Today, we may well laugh at such desperate attempts to find practical applications for the *compas composé*, but we must remember that Sylvester was a theoretician and was not particularly interested in the practical uses of the mechanism. It was the mathematical properties of kinematic chains which attracted him, and he designed a number of devices which made it possible to calculate, among other things, square and cube roots and the angle trisector. Sylvester believed that, in this way, the possibilities of constructing mathematical aids were endless.

The chief engineer of the Houses of Parliament, a Mr. Pim, found Sylvester's lectures a source of inspiration, and he installed a "blow-ing engine" in the House of Commons to improve the ventilation there. It was, in actual fact, a large air pump, and Peaucellier's *compas composé* was used to guide the pump rod. The device is said to have worked perfectly, and almost noiselessly.

Sylvester was indefatigable in lecturing on and demonstrating the complex problems of rectilinear motion. This intense and temperamental scientist was also a man of wit and very much enjoyed the society of his fellows. Wherever he came with his message, he was made welcome, even in literary and political circles, where normally the members would not be considered to have too profound an interest in advanced mathematics and engineering. But it was, naturally, in scientific circles that Sylvester had his greatest successes. He has given his own account of his appearance before the Athenaeum Club in London. After the meeting, supper was served, and as they ate their dessert, he passed Peaucellier's *compas composé* around the table. Among the many famous scientists present was the great physicist Sir William Thomson (later Lord Kelvin), who studied the mechanism with great interest. As Sylvester reached out his hand to take back the model, Sir William sharply reproved him and said that he was far from finished with it, stating that it was by far the most beautiful thing he had ever seen!

In the summer of 1876, after spending three years in London as the

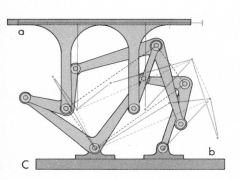

C Sylvester's and Kempe's kinematical, translating linkage. The plates (*a*, *b*) can be moved sideways but will remain constantly parallel and equidistant.

D Mr Prim's air-pump, in which he used Peaucellier's *compas composé* to steer the piston (*a*) rectilinearly. The mechanism consisted of four bars (*a*) of uniform length, which were linked together to form a parallelogram. From its opposite corners ran two equally long bars, which were pivoted to a common point of attachment (*d*). When point *e* on the parallelogram was given a circular movement, point *f* moved in a straight line, since the distance between the point of attachment of the bars *c* and the point of attachment of the bar *g*, which ran to a third corner of the parallelogram, was equal to the length of bar *g*.

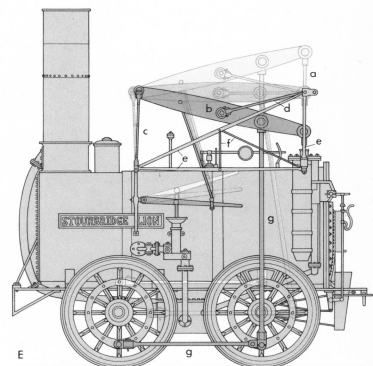

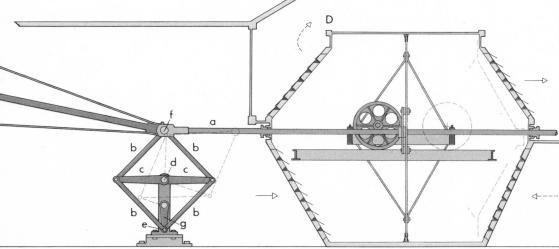

E A modified version of Evans's mechanism was used for the *Stourbridge Lion*. The piston (*a*) was steered rectilinearly by its being mounted on one end of a beam (*b*), whose other end was attached to a pivoted bar (*c*), and whose movement was limited by a strut (*d*). The other end of the strut was attached to a triangular scaffold (*e*), which was reinforced by rods (*f*). Coupled levers (*g*) connected the driving wheels with one another and with *b*.

great prophet of kinematics, Sylvester left the city to take up the position of professor of mathematics at the highly esteemed John Hopkins University in Baltimore, Maryland. This was the year in which Franz Reuleaux's great work *Theoretical Kinematics* was published in English; it was also the year in which the huge Centennial Exposition took place at Philadelphia. Back in England the cause of kinematics received a new champion in Alfred Kempe, a young lawyer for whom mathematics had long been a hobby. Kempe had closely followed Sylvester's activities. They had become close friends and had started to collaborate; Kempe was obviously as fascinated as Sylvester by the kinematics of rectilinear motion. When Reuleaux's mechanical alphabet was put on display at the Science Museum in London, Kempe gave a series of lectures entitled "How to Draw a Straight Line", which to a large extent contributed to raising the temperature of the Reuleaux and kinematics fever which was then raging in London. Kempe began these lectures, which were published as a book of the same name the following year, 1877, with some almost childishly simple assumptions: a circle can be drawn with a pair of compasses, a straight line can be drawn with a ruler. But why should a ruler give a mathematically defined straight line? Kempe's further thoughts on this are as amusing to read as the title of his book is provocative. However, Kempe was, if possible, even further removed from technical reality than his teacher and mentor, Sylvester. But together they managed to construct some kinematic chains which caught the public eye; one of these was a chain for translatory (reciprocating) rectilinear motion. As far as is known, no practical application has been found for this device, which is one of several models in existence, and it is rather fun to watch it in operation.

"La Belle Epoque" of the Machine

We have already mentioned that Reuleaux and his kinematics went out of fashion during the first decades of the twentieth century. There is indeed a considerable contrast between the enthusiasm for kinematics which in London reached its climax in the events surrounding the exhibition at the Science Museum, and Rudolf von Miese's criticism of *The Designer*, quoted above. There were several reasons for this undeniably remarkable about-face. The last decades of the nineteenth century saw a rapid acceleration in the growth of technology in the industrialized countries and marked a watershed between what was established and what was new in the technical field. Steam power was established; electricity was new and was making great headway. The Centennial Exposition in Philadelphia, in 1876, was one of the last great manifestations of the steam era and of pure mechanics. It was also the beginning of the end both for steam and for machine elements. However, the beautiful designs of both prime movers and working machines still pleased the eye, and the graceful movements of their parts were still a joy to behold. No wonder that young people of today spend so much of their spare time working on the restoration of steam-engines, traction engines, locomotives, and other machines of this period!

What followed were the machines of the electrotechnical age. The first generators and engines were open, exciting constructions, but soon they became enclosed, partly for technical reasons—closed magnetic fields, protection from the dangers of high voltage, etc.—and partly because of new trends in design. And all of a sudden, every single machine was enclosed, and the era of the "grey box" had begun. The colour may have changed, but we are still there.

Another aspect of this development was the increased speed at which machine elements and moving parts generally could be driven. The designer had to consider the dynamic properties of the parts rather than their kinematics, which, according to Ampère's

definition, took into account only the motion as such; forces and strains were disregarded. Thereupon, kinematics had to give way to dynamics.

One lasting effect of the teaching of Reuleaux, Kennedy, and their successors up to the turn of the century, however, was the strong preference which designers were to show for simplicity and efficiency in machine design. It is interesting to follow the development of this trend in the design handbooks which were published from the beginning of the nineteenth century onwards, beginning for instance with the one published by Hachette in 1811. In these books, machine elements for different movements and functions are listed in tabular form. Many of the later books in this genre tried to outdo the others by listing more and more intricate, and often over-complicated, devices. Technical journals, which had begun to come out during the first part of the nineteenth century, had as a rule a regular feature on new machine elements, including material from newly granted patents as well as articles which were quite simply copied from other journals. *The Scientific American*, first published in 1845 by Rufus Porter, a patent lawyer, had such a feature from its first number onwards. So had *The American Artisan*, the chief editor of which, Henry T. Brown, gathered the most important articles in a book first published in 1867 and entitled *Five Hundred and Seven Mechanical Movements*. It has been reissued many times since then, most recently as late as 1970, when an American machine manufacturer brought out an edition especially for use as a gift book. The heyday of this genre was the period of about twenty years after 1850; in the twentieth century, the number of design handbooks published has diminished considerably. One exception is an American work published in four parts, each containing more than five hundred pages, entitled *Ingenious Mechanisms for Designers and Inventors*. Volume I, published in 1930, and Volume II, published in 1936, were edited by Franklin D. Jones; Volume III, published in 1951, was edited by Holbrook L. Horton; and Volume IV, published in 1967, was edited by Horton and John A. Newell. In this work, each device is described in great detail, and its function, choice of material, and so on are commented on.

There is no doubt that mechanical engineering has been greatly influenced by Reuleaux's wholehearted advocacy of simplicity in the design of machine elements. This applies not only to large machines, such as steam-engines (where the theoretician Chebysev was taught a lesson by the practical engineers), but also to many of the smaller machines which were then appearing on the market and which were intended for daily use in the home, in agriculture, etc. The sewing-machine, the first "domestic appliance", had met with initial resistance when the first types appeared around 1850—their designs were obviously over-complicated, and breakdowns were frequent. When the various components had been simplified and better material introduced, the sewing-machine gradually gained the confidence of housewives. In most industrialized countries, therefore, the sewing-machine did not make its breakthrough until the 1880s or later. The mowing-machine, first mass-produced in 1848, went through a similar process of development. Cyrus McCormick's (1809—84) invention, the "finger-knife", goes back to 1834 but had to be modified considerably before the machine could be mass-produced and marketed. But the mowing-machine, too, had a reputation for needing frequent repairs, and it was simplified further after McCormick's patent had expired. The result of these improvements was that the mowing-machine came to be accepted universally and that designers were encouraged to continue developing agricultural machines. There then followed in rapid succession the reaper, the binder, and the combine harvester—all based on a practically functioning finger knife. The first combines were introduced in the United States in the

1890s. They were impressive machines, pulled by eighteen pairs of horses and operated by a team of twelve to fifteen men.

In March, 1876, the first telephone was patented by the American scientist and inventor Alexander Graham Bell (1847–1922). At the Centennial Exposition in Philadelphia in the same year, Bell was able to demonstrate a working model, which attracted great interest. A speaking telegraph! However, the new invention had not yet found its technical form, but in spite of this, *The Scientific American* published an enthusiastic article (October, 1877) on Bell's telephone, predicting a splendid future for it. A month or so later, the article was read by a Swedish instrument maker, Lars Magnus Ericsson, who became fascinated by the new apparatus. A year previously, he had established a workshop where he and some others repaired telegraphic equipment, fire telegraphs, and other signalling devices used at the time. He had been considering designing and manufacturing telegraphic equipment himself, since working with repairs had given him a good idea of the weaknesses of existing models. He now devoted himself completely to the task of designing a telephone. It was ready by the following year, and the telephone built to that design is considered to be the world's first table telephone. In that year, Ericsson produced twenty telephones, and when the Stockholm Telephone Company was founded some years later, production really got going. The Bell Telephone Company, which Alexander Graham Bell had founded in 1877 and which had opened an office in Stockholm in 1880, was soon ousted from the market by the Stockholm Telephone Company, and by 1885, Stockholm had more telephones than any other capital city in Europe.

Today, we take it for granted that the telephone works properly, but in the early days, it was a highly unreliable appliance. The faults were mainly due to poor design. Lars Magnus Ericsson was determined to produce a telephone in which all the parts exposed to wear and tear would be as robust as possible—and where every single detail had a function. The result was a "telephone that did not look like a telephone", and it later became the company symbol and figured in the trademark for many years. The first model built to this design appeared in 1884 and was soon nicknamed "the dachshund". The magnets in the magneto generator were bent outwards and served also as a stand for the instrument. This version had a fixed microphone and a separate receiver, but as early as 1892, Ericsson launched a model which set the style for future telephones. The "dachshund" was given a hand microphone combined with the receiver—the first of its kind—resting in a cradle. It was both practical and comfortable to use.

Ericsson had studied Reuleaux's work, both *The Designer* and *Theoretical Kinematics*. When designing his table telephone of 1882, he had followed in detail his master's theses on the simplicity and functions of design. The apparatus is a fine example of *la belle époque* of the classical machine.

The Renaissance of Kinematics

By the turn of the century, the great wave of enthusiasm for kinematics, which had been at its height in the latter part of the nineteenth century, had gone into a considerable decline. The exception to this was in Germany, where, all along, kinematics remained on the syllabus of courses in mechanical engineering. Between 1900 and the late 1930s, nothing exciting was written on the subject. Then, however, things began to happen; a German engineer, Robert Kraus, wrote an article on the double-crank mechanism. This was published in the engineering journal *Maschinenbau*. Kraus's article came in for severe criticism from a Russian, Z.S. Bloch, and the ensuing polemics, like most other academic rows, were closely followed by other engineering journals. It is possible that the Second

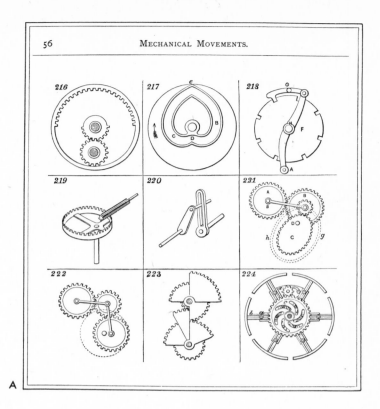

A A page in *Five Hundred and Seven Mechanical Movements*, the book in which Henry T. Brown compiled articles which had earlier been published in *The American Artisan* and dealt with new machine elements.

B This model of L. M. Ericsson's telephone – popularly known as "the dachshund" – was introduced in 1892. Every single part has a function, and the telephone is a good example of *la belle époque* of mechanical engineering – not only with regard to its construction but also to its design.

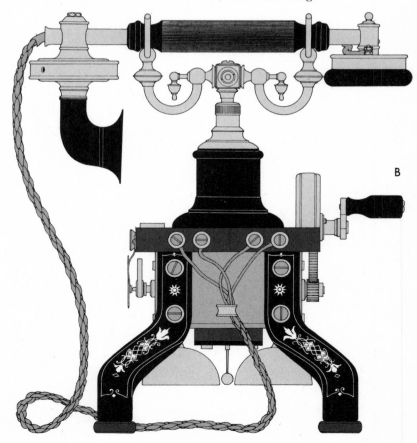

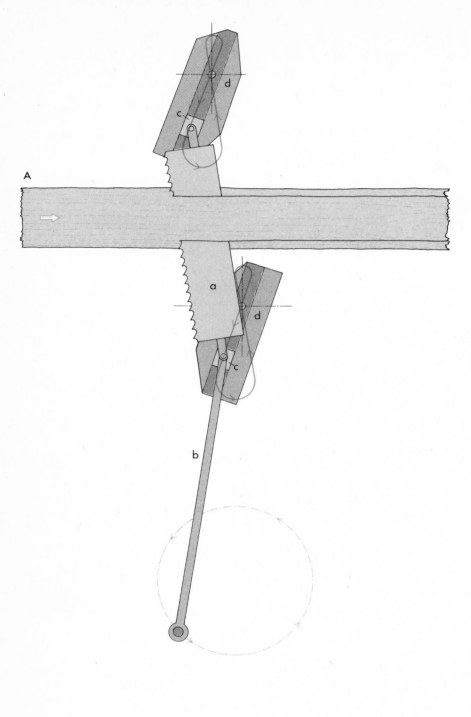

World War, by then in full progress, was also inspiring machine designers to take up and re-examine long-neglected ideas. Anyhow, the number of publications on kinematics increased considerably at this time. After the War, many important works on kinematics were published both in Europe and in the United States. These dealt with and furthered the thoughts of Reuleaux, Kennedy, and the other great kinematicians and used their terminology and definitions of principles. The old classical kinematical problems were once again the subject of examination and discussion. One work among many in this field deserves special attention, that by the Americans J.A. Hrones and G.L. Nelson, entitled *Analysis of the Four Bar Linkage*. It was published in 1951 and gives a very comprehensive and graphic description of the properties of such mechanisms as Watt's parallel motion . . .

There were several reasons why kinematic chains of this kind—jointed and coupled levers—became topical again. First and foremost is the quite simple fact that, today, we are surrounded by kinematic chains in such profusion that no one in Reuleaux's time could have dreamed of. We use kinematic chains everywhere; normally, of course, we have no reason to reflect on this. The male adult's most popular toy, the motor-car, has, for instance, a great number of kinematic chains. They are found in the mechanisms governing the catching and locking devices of the doors, in the crank mechanisms of the side windows, in the track rod, and in the combination of crankshaft, connecting rod, and piston. Continuing from the car, we find an applied kinematic chain in the upwards-tilting garage door. Coupled levers can be found in most of our domestic appliances, especially in the sewing-machine. No matter how much such an appliance can be controlled electronically, the fact remains that both the needle and the under-thread are moved by combinations of mechanical levers—kinematics of the best kind. Typewriters with type bars are fitted with several coupled levers which perform a number of different functions. Calculators have, or rather, used to have, a number of advanced machine parts with jointed and coupled levers. (Today, the mechanical calculator is almost obsolete, and the electronic calculator is taking over.) Outdoors we can find kinematic chains in such construction machines as bulldozers, excavators, rock drills, and so on; and also in all sorts of means of transport—aeroplanes, locomotives, ships, and not least, the bicycle, which is one of the most highly developed applications of mechanical engineering.

We can also look at our own reflection in a mirror. Man's anatomy and skeletal structure comprise kinematic chains which have been tried and tested over millions of years. Reuleaux had pointed this out and even illustrated it with his models. Today, this is a highly topical subject in ergonomics and the sciences related to work.

So kinematics is well represented in our surroundings. In itself that should be enough to explain why interest in this important branch of mechanical engineering has risen so sharply again, especially in the past few decades. Another factor that has contributed greatly is that, since the 1950s, designers have had access to advanced aids in solving the often extremely difficult mathematical problems that a kinematic analysis can entail. Today, a computer can, easily and elegantly, solve the problems which not even Chebysev and the other great mathematicians of the previous great era of kinematics could get to grips with. Of course, the problem still has to be stated, and this provides the greatest difficulty nowadays, requiring immense theoretical insight before it can be overcome. However, once the problem has been stated, the computer can do the rest in no time at all.

The Eight Saw

There are many examples of problems in technology where inter-

A In the eight saw, a sash of the same type as that of an ordinary frame saw is used. The main difference concerns the suspension and bearing of the sash. In principle, the eight-saw is designed as is shown here. The saw blades (a) are braced in a sash which is given a reciprocating movement by a connecting rod (b). Blocks (c), which are mounted on the frame by spherical bearings, here slide in guides (d), which are rotatable round their shafts. The guides are constructed so that the sash describes a curve similar to a figure-of-eight when it is in operation. Thus, "reverse sawing" can be eliminated, and the saw blades are exposed to considerably less wear than were the old frame saw's blades on their way up, fitted, as they were, with fixed guides.

esting and, sometimes, surprising solutions have been arrived at due to the fact that kinematics benefitted from the help of the computer. Most of these problems are very intricate, both from the engineering and the mathematical points of view, but let us look at one example, not only because it is easy to understand, but also because it casts some light on an aspect of the history of technology. From the Middle Ages onwards, the frame-saw was used to saw logs into planks and boards. As such, it played an important rôle in the forestry industry of many countries. The first picture of a frame-saw is considered to be the one found in Villard de Honnecourt's *Album*, which dates back to the late thirteenth century. In Sweden the frame-saw was in common use in the sixteenth century, but in the eighteenth century, it was replaced here and there by the circular saw. Sawn timber was produced mainly for export to England, and it was found that the circular saw gave a smoother surface to the wood. However, the British refused to accept such new-fangled products as smooth-sawn timber. "The surface should be as rough as the fur of a bear", wrote an English importer to his Swedish supplier!

Here we have in a nutshell the main drawback of the frame-saw. The sawn surface of the wood was rough, because the frame-saw's blade saws only when moving downwards. When it moves upwards, however, the timber is still fed forwards, and the saw teeth abrade the surface of the wood. This "back-sawing" was something that, for centuries, just had to be accepted. In the 1950s, however, the band-saw began to replace the frame-saw, and this resulted in an immediate and sharp increase in production at the sawmills. The log could now be fed through more quickly, and the sawing was done continuously. The old frame-saw, with its back sawing and rough planks, was now relegated to the collections in museums of technology.

However, even the band-saw had its drawbacks, for when its speed was increased above a certain limit, the band began to flutter. This resulted in a sawn surface that was corrugated. In the beginning of the 1970s, therefore, a group of engineers at the Convexa laboratory in Stockholm began to analyze the problem of back-sawing from a kinematic point of view. They had access to a computer, which they fed with a number of variations of possible devices. The computer then gave them the solution, which was quite simply to let the blade move in a figure-of-eight. The blade then works continuously, and there is no back-sawing. The older type of frame-saw had, however, another disadvantage, namely that large mass forces were created when the saw frame moved up and down. The base was made very stable, but the vibrations were still considerable. The Convexa team found the solution to this problem as well; they found that the vibrations could be completely eliminated by erecting a pendulum suspension for the frame and by counter-weighting the balance wheels. This rather intricate system was simulated in the computer, which also gave the correct dimensions of the system's components. After extensive prototype tests, the "eight saw" was ready for production in 1977.

New Machine Elements?

In this chapter we have had to go back quite far in time to find the first machine element, and some of the earliest have remained basically unchanged for thousands of years. This may lead one to ask whether or not the field is exhausted. Can we expect new machine elements to be created in the future? This is, naturally, a question of definition, but even if we are fairly restrictive in calling something new, it is clear that new ideas for machines are constantly appearing. One example is the wheel hub without an axle, designed for motor-cars and developed by the SKF European Research Centre in Holland. The idea for this new machine element was introduced in 1972, and the design has now been tested in the field.

B The advantage of the shaftless wheel hub is, among other things, that fewer movable parts are needed for the wheel suspension and that the assembly becomes simpler. Here, we show the inner construction of such a hub (1) as well as a cross-section of the hub as mounted on a car (2). The brake and the wheel are mounted on the flange of the inner ring (a), whereas the suspension is mounted on the outer ring (b). The rings are coupled to each other by a double-row, maintenance-free bearing (c).

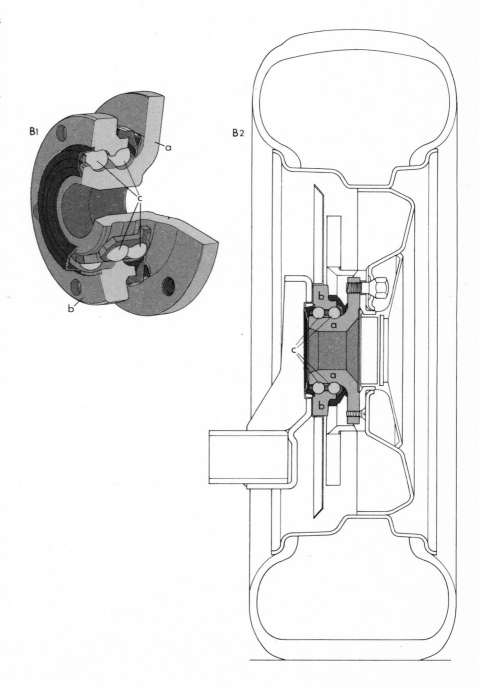

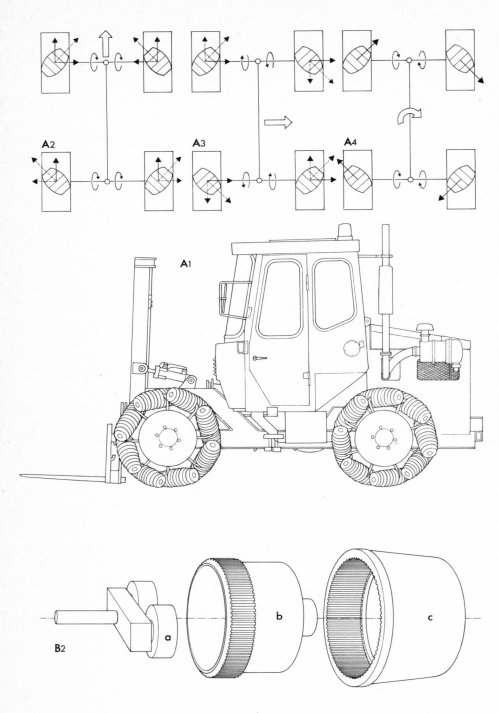

A The four non-turnable wheels of a vehicle (**1**) with the ilonator steering system are each equipped with eight slightly spool-shaped rolls, which are mounted at an angle of 45° on a hydraulic-engine-powered rim. Since the rolls run freely, no force can be received in the direction of rolling. In the direction of the shaft, however, a force can be received, and this force can be divided into two components, one which is parallel to the longitudinal axis of the vehicle and one which is perpendicular to it. When the vehicle is driven straight forward (**2**), all the wheels are driven at the same speed and in the same direction. Those force components which are perpendicular to the longitudinal axis of the vehicle then balance each other, and the remaining components drive the vehicle forwards. If the vehicle is to be driven towards one side, for instance to the right (**3**), the two right-hand wheels are driven towards each other at the same speed as the two left-hand wheels are driven away from each other. The force components which are parallel to the vehicle's longitudinal axis then balance each other, and the remaining components drive the vehicle to the right. When the vehicle is to rotate round its own vertical axis (**4**), all four wheels are driven at the same speed in the direction in which the vehicle is to rotate. These three fundamental movements (**2–4**) can be combined with each other in every conceivable way.

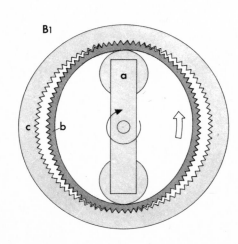

B One of the disadvantages of the conventional planetary gearing is its limited gear ratio. During the 1970s, however, several new planetary-gearing constructions have appeared, and these give a very high gear ratio. One example is the American Harmonic Drive (**1**), which consists of three basic components (**2**): an elliptic "wave generator" (*a*), which has an eccentric ball race, a thin, flexible steel cylinder (*b*), which has cogs on the outside, and a non-flexible steel cylinder (*c*) with internal cogs. When the wave generator rotates, *b* is deformed, and the cogs on those parts of *b* which then protrude mesh with the cogs on the outer steel cylinder. Since the number of cogs on *c* exceeds that of *b* by two, *a*'s rotation causes a relative movement between *b* and *c*. The gear ratio can be from 78:1 to 320:1. If several Harmonic Drive units are coupled to each other, a considerably higher gear ratio is obtained.

CHAPTER 3
FROM HAND TOOL
TO INDUSTRIAL ROBOT

After the gradual decline of the Roman Empire and its fall in the fifth century AD, the spiritual development of the West was engulfed in a listless darkness. There was naturally more than one reason for this mental stagnation. Active trade, both within the Empire and with the surrounding countries, collapsed, and this eliminated the economic basis for the growth of science and the arts. The crafts deteriorated, too. The Christian church, growing in strength as fast as the Roman Empire fell apart, more and more dominated intellectual life with its dogmatic message. Charles Singer holds the apostolic father Augustine (354–430) responsible for the stifling effect of this dogmatism on spiritual life. Augustine's leading doctrine was that the individual should turn his gaze in on himself to resist worldly temptations, expressing this metaphorically by saying: "Do not go outside the door, for truth dwells in the heart of Man." Singer adds that, for a thousand years, the thinking man in the Christian West did not venture outside.

Outside Christendom, however, an entirely new cultural sphere was emerging, rapidly and unexpectedly. The Arab world was set in motion in 622, when, on the Mountain of Light, the Prophet Mohammed (570?–632) was called by Allah to preach Islam, the doctrine of submission. Islam then issued forth with irresistible power from the Land of the Twin Rivers over all of North Africa. Within a single century, a spiritual growth blossomed within the borders of Islam, which, in extent and vitality, can be compared to that of ancient Rome.

The Moslems returned to the classics of the ancient Hellenic culture and based their work on the experience of the engineers of the Alexandrian school and of other great engineers and scientists. As mentioned above, many of the classical works in this area are known to us only in Arabic translations and revisions.

Tools, implements, and working methods from the stone construction technology of antiquity were revived by the Arabs, and new masterpieces were built, from Alhambra and Cordoba in the West to Samarkand and Bagdhad in the East—royal palaces, mosques, and minarets. The Moorish palace in Alhambra, with its famous Lion Court, to take only one example, must have needed for its erection and decoration at least those three hundred skilled crafts which King Hiero needed to build his flagship about a thousand years earlier.

The Craft Guilds

Continued specialization by craftsmen in the late Middle Ages resulted in the creation of craft guilds, or more correctly, the re-creation of craft guilds. During the Roman Empire, tradesmen had organized themselves in corporations, which protected their rights, and came to be reckoned as a strong political force. The mediaeval equivalent of these corporations, the guilds, soon became very powerful, both by right of their economical strength and by the effective control exercized by the elders and masters on their colleagues and their work. The guild system naturally had both positive and negative aspects. The strictly prescribed course of training no doubt favoured high standards of work. To learn a craft, a young man had to be accepted as an apprentice of a guild, and a precondition for this was

that the rulers of the guild felt that there was room for a new master once the apprentice had completed his training; in other words, an efficient control of new establishment. After the apprentice had passed his first tests, he had to go out as a journeyman and work with his colleagues, both at home and in foreign countries. In this way, new ideas and methods were spread to an extent which would otherwise have been impossible. The long journey, which often lasted for four or five years, was crowned by a guild entrance test, executed under the strict and critical supervision of the elders.

Technical news could be spread relatively effectively thanks to this journeyman system, but even so, the guild and the strong position of the elders still had a markedly conservative effect on the technical development of the different crafts. How should the journeyman construct the tools for his guild entrance test, and what working methods and practices should he use? This question had mostly a single answer—everything must be precisely as the elders prescribed.

What is known as the Mendel book, from the fifteenth century, is an invaluable source of knowledge of the late mediaeval crafts and tools. The original is in the city library of Nuremberg, but in 1965, this extensive work was published in a magnificent edition of two volumes, in which most illustrations are reproduced full-sized. The Mendel book has an interesting background. The mercantile house of Mendel was active in Nuremberg for several generations, and it flourished in the late 1300s, when three Mendel brothers (Marquart, died 1385, Conrad, died 1414, and Peter, died 1423) ran it. They traded handicrafts from Nuremberg and had agents in places like Rome, Venice, Cologne, and Prague. The city of Nuremberg was, above all, famous for its textiles and leather work, but there were also prominent goldsmiths, pewterers, coppersmiths, and workers in brass. In Nuremberg, however, the guild system lacked the power that it had elsewhere. Merchants dominated the community, which was, very likely, one reason why, in 1388, Conrad Mendel donated money to establish the famous "house of the twelve brethren" to honour the Holy Trinity. In this house, twelve honest craftsmen—the number was in honour of the apostles—were to be given accommodation and a place to work, so far as possible. This "protected workshop" was intended mainly for craftsmen who had been prevented by illness from working or had been worn out prematurely. The house of the twelve brethren existed until the early 1800s.

The rules laid down by Conrad Mendel for his foundation include the stipulation that a "book of thoughts" should be kept, in which both the governors and the brethren should be depicted at work. This stipulation was not given effect, however, until his grandson Marquart became the governor of the Mendel foundation in 1425. He retained this position until his death in 1438. That part of the Mendel book which has been published covers the period to 1539, during which time no less than 355 craftsmen brethren were depicted. Frans M. Feldhaus and many others have wanted to date these frequently reproduced pictures to the late 1300s, but it has now been verified that the paper of the manuscript was made between 1423 and 1429. The paper has water marks which have been identified as coming from the long famous Italian papermill in Fabriano.

New Tools for Precision Mechanics and Heavy Engineering

The appearance of the mechanical clock (see Chapter Two), in the first half of the fourteenth century, opened a new era in tool technology and caused a new branch of technology to be developed—precision mechanics. The clock quickly became a status symbol, and the prominent men of the time were soon vying with each other in installing this novelty on their houses and public buildings. Only half a century after the first mechanical clocks had appeared, very complicated clocks were being built, which testified to both sound craftmanship and a good understanding of astronomical mathematics. Still, the development was not quite as sudden as it seems. At this time—about 1400—there was already a long-established clockmaking tradition, a tradition that had begun with the water clock and which had asserted itself mainly in the cultural circles of Islam. We know very little of the details of the clockmaker's tools. Since ancient times, for example, different types of files had been used to shape and work metals. The ancient Greek word for file, *rine*, also denotes a type of shark, which implies that fish skin with sharp spines had once been used, for example, to smooth a rough surface, but this was probably before tools were commonly made of metal.

Many files have been found from Roman times or later. It has been proved that the files used in the fourteenth and fifteenth centuries were more or less the same types as those used today. They were flat, round, semi-circular, or multi-edged, made in all different sizes, from small tapered files to the large types used for heavy engineering. File cutting at this time was a skilled craft and had certainly been in existence for some time. In the Mendel book, the file cutter is depicted in several illustrations, which also show the methods used to make the file teeth. A hammer shaped like a chisel was employed, and also a separate chisel, which was struck with a mallet. It was natural to mechanize file cutting, if for nothing else than to make the teeth of the files more regular. Leonardo da Vinci made a drawing for such a machine, in which the file being worked was automatically moved forward between each blow. During the following centuries, many file-cutting machines of different designs were built by, among others, Polhem. Various devices to keep the workpiece in place, such as the hand vice, the screw vice, and the carpenter's bench mechanism, all with precedents in ancient cultures, acquired their form in the late Middle Ages.

In precision mechanics, and particularly in the work of the clockmaker and the goldsmith, different methods of joining metals were developed to near perfection at this time. Pliny the Elder describes several different ways to soft- and hard-solder with different fluxes, among them green spar, a basic copper acetate. The Romans also knew how to use a soldering iron, and also, they most probably used a blast pipe to direct a flame at the joint. In the fourteenth and fifteenth centuries, however, the blast pipe was developed into a flexible, all-round tool for joining metals. During this time, the art of the smith was on the upswing. With all the building in the early days of the Renaissance, growing demands were made on blacksmiths to produce both light and heavy products, for example, tools for various purposes, and fittings, cramps, and other objects for churches and other monumental buildings. Increased trade led to a need for forged iron for diverse applications in transport, from iron fittings on barrels and other casks to detailed work and fittings for ships and wagons. The manufacture of arms and armour devoured ever increasing quantities of forged iron and metals, and state controls saw to it that the available metals were directed towards these requirements. At this time, the common man in most European countries, who tilled the land or worked at a craft, was short of iron and copper. Edward III of England (1327–77) introduced a law under which the export, and even the re-export, of iron was prohibited under pain of heavy punishment.

The Technical Revolution of the Renaissance

During the last century of the later Middle Ages, the situation changed radically. The use of water and wind power for purposes other than flour-milling, such as in mining, spread rapidly, reciprocating the emergence of new methods, tools, and implements in heavy engineering. One can with good reason talk about the techni-

A1

A Two illustrations from the Mendel book. Both represent file cutters, but the men use different methods to produce the file teeth. The man in the left-hand picture (**1**) uses a sharp-edged hammer to cut files directly, whereas the man in the right-hand picture (**2**) uses a separate chisel, which he strikes with a mallet. Both men use anvils, which have been spiked to large wooden blocks, as underlays for their work. When the files had been cut, they were tempered by heating and quenching.

A2

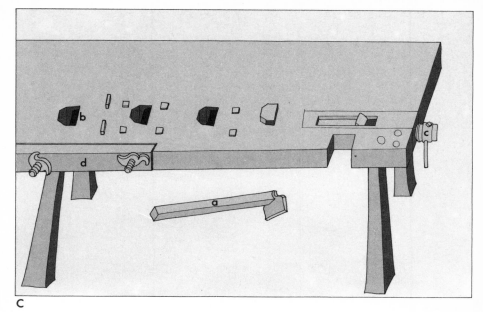

C

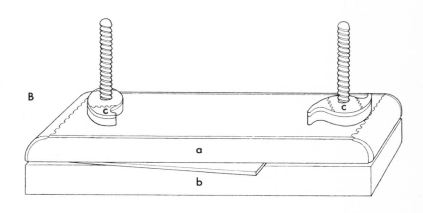

B

B A mediaeval vice, in which the upper, movable part (*a*) was brought closer to the lower, fixed part (*b*) when two "nuts" (*c*) were turned. This type of nut was very common until the advent of the hexagonal nut at the beginning of the nineteenth century.

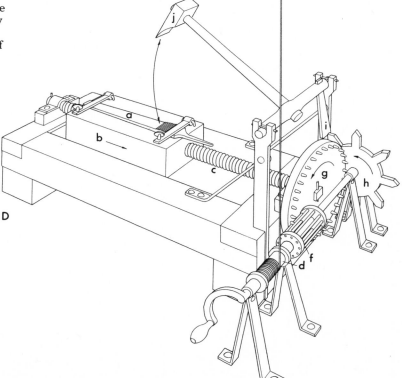

D

C The carpenter's bench, too, attained its form during the late Middle Ages. Just as on a present-day carpenter's bench, the work-piece was braced between a bench clamp (*a*), which was inserted through one of the holes (*b*) in the bench, and a screw (*c*). (*d*) Vice.

D A sketch by Leonardo da Vinci is the basis of this drawing, which shows a file-cutting machine. The file blank (*a*) was braced on a board (*b*), through which a screw (*c*) ran. Before the cutting could start, a rope had to be wound onto a drum (*d*). At the other end of the rope, a weight (*e*) hung, and on the drum shaft, there was a cog-wheel, which meshed with a larger cog-wheel (*g*) mounted on the screw. When the weight was allowed to fall, *g* was rotated, and the board with the file blank was brought towards *g* at an even speed. Another wheel (*h*) on *d*'s shaft was turned at the same time, and its large, sparse teeth in turn brought a lever (*i*) downwards. A sharp-edged hammer (*j*), mount-ed on the same shaft as *i*, was then lifted, and every time a tooth let go of the lever, the hammer fell against the slowly forward-moving blank.

A One of the oldest known woodcuts. It bears the date 1423 and depicts St. Christopher carrying the Infant Christ on his shoulders. The woodcut was found in a manuscript of 1417 in the middle of the eighteenth century.
B Early woodcuts were made using knives of this type (1). The blade consisted of a piece of clock-spring steel. Later, other special tools, such as this graver (2), were used to hollow out those parts of a block which were to remain white during printing.
C The composing room (1) of an eighteenth-century printer's workshop as depicted by Diderot. The typesetter (*left*) has the copy in front of him. He picks out letters (2) from the typecase and places them in a

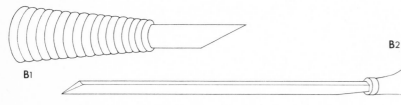

composing stick (3). The man in the middle of the picture then puts the completed lines in the galley, a long, narrow tray in which typeset text is stored. When the whole copy has been typeset, the page-maker (*right*) steps in and puts the typeset lines in forms which have the exact width and height of the book's pages. He then sees to it that all types are at the same level by hammering against a flat, wooden board, which is placed over them.

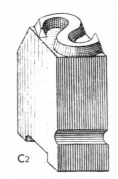

cal revolution of the Renaissance, one that affected almost all ways of life. In many parts of Europe it meant an economic upswing, which stimulated ideas in art, literature, and science. This boom was also one of the reasons why interest was aroused in what lay beyond the horizon; the era of the great geographical discoveries began.

Neither the industrial revolution of the eighteenth century nor this technical revolution was marked by any sudden technical or social upheaval, and in both periods it is more appropiate to talk of an evolution of new practices, tools, implements, and products through internal interaction. The effect of improvements in clockmaking on manufacturing technology during the Renaissance has already been described, as has the way in which a demand for metals affected mining, which in turn stimulated the growth of heavy engineering. Wind and water power were more and more exploited during the fifteenth century, whereas, in the eighteenth century, it was steam power that really got things going. Many useful objects, such as needles, nails, and knives, were manufactured on a "pre-industrial" scale during the fifteenth century. Leonardo da Vinci had many ideas on how needles could be produced in large quantities. He described a machine evidently capable of producing four hundred needles an hour, and he worked out even the profits of such manufacture, provided that prices were the same as those for manually made needles!

In the early sixteenth century, a Dutchman, Walter Vollmar, founded a company for the manufacture of needles on an industrial scale in the Germany city of Aachen. The Mendel book depicts a needle maker who died in 1533. The eye of the needle was then made by hand. The needle was split at one end, and the two parts were then shaped as a loop. The manufacture of needles and pins entirely by machine came relatively late. Pin manufacture was automated first. The so-called rocking machine, which cut off pieces of steel or brass wire and then crushed one end of the piece of wire to form a flat "knob", was invented in Nuremberg in the mid-1680s. The design of the machine was improved in both England and the United States at the beginning of the nineteenth century. In Italy the manufacture of pins with heads of glass in different colours began in 1825.

Even in ancient times, nails were manufactured on a large scale. When some Roman fortifications were excavated in England in the 1950s, the remains of a Roman nail factory were discovered. Packages of nails in "standard" sizes were also found, from nails fit for solid timber to tacks. During the Renaissance, nailsmiths were already recognized as such and established tradesmen, and several nailsmiths are represented in the Mendel book. Nails were formed in moulds, and in the Mendel book one can see how nails of three different sizes could be formed in the same mould. Due to the great demand for nails during the Renaissance, there was a specialization of labour. Apprentices wrought iron into square sections of different sizes, and their masters finished them off. Production could thus be reasonably high.

Knives began to be produced, in principle, in the same way as nails. Apprentices prepared the material for the knife blades, and the master then forged and shaped them. The Mendel book has a picture of a number of knife blades with hafts. It is likely that the hafts were "mass produced" as well.

Art and Literature in Mass Quantities

The tools of precision mechanics were, without doubt, the technical pre-conditions for making wood cuts and for the development of printing. The oldest dated wood engraving is from 1418. It shows fine lines throughout and a richness of detail, which imply that the tools used, the knives, burins, and so on, must have been eminently suitable. At this time, it was only the precision mechanics of clock-making which could achieve the technique required for such tools. A woodcut was produced by transferring a drawing, reversed from left to right, onto a carefully surface-ground "block" of wood, after which the surface wood on either side of each line in the drawing was cut away with a burin of forged steel. The remaining wood on all surfaces which were to be white in the drawing were then cut away with gravers and gouges, so that the lines of the drawing became raised. They were then inked and pressed against paper. The wood-cut method spread rapidly in the late Middle Ages, when pictures were a rarity. At first, skilful craftsmen made the woodcuts, but before long, eminent artists were themselves cutting their own draw-ings in wood. One of the first was the German Albrecht Dürer (1479–1528) who, in 1498, published the famous pictorial series of the Reve-lations of St. John. Graphics had become an independent art form—based on the progress of precision mechanics!

The 1440s saw the first book printed with movable die-cast type. The letter-press printing method used by Johann Gutenberg (1399?–1468) was basically the same as the one used for printing woodcuts, but Gutenberg used cast, movable type instead of cut blocks. The production of dies for the type was made possible by the tools of precision mechanics, too. It does not detract from Gutenberg's con-tribution that printing with movable type had been practised in the Far East, or more specifically Korea, two thousand years prior to this. Several of the techniques described here, which developed so quickly during the technical revolution of the Renaissance, had had predecessors in other parts of the world.

The Art Books of Technology

The technical revolution during the early Renaissance paved the way for the accelerating development which took place during the High Renaissance, when there was progress made in all spheres of human life; in retrospect, this progress must be seen as a sharp contrast to the so-called darkness of the Middle Ages. Enlightened contemporaries were also acutely aware of this. In the sixteenth century, the German humanist Ulrich von Hutten uttered the famous words: " The spirits awaken, and it is a joy to be alive."

During and after the technical revolution of the Renaissance, a whole arsenal of new tools came into being, as well as methods and techniques for using them. The spirits of technology could truly awaken and find joy in designing machines. What are called "art books" first appeared, and they flourished from the sixteenth cen-tury to the middle of the eighteenth. These were magnificent pictor-ial books that contained descriptions of ingenious machines, both real and imaginary. In general, art books were extremely important for the spread of technology in the West, especially for mining, for they illustrated machinery for raising water, and other devices de-scribed by Agricola and Biringuccio, among others. The chief engin-eers, or art masters, of the mines took ideas from the art books, copying the designs or modifying them to suit themselves. This meant that heavy mechanical equipment and the tools used were largely similar in the different European mines, and in the same way, the tools and equipment of all the other crafts soon acquired similar forms all over Europe. Any kind of technical novelty quickly spread via the art books; one example of this is the mangle. The Italian Vittorio Zonca (1580?– ?) gave one of the first descriptions of such a machine in his art book *Novo teatro di machine et edificii*, (Padua, 1607). He even presented two versions of it, one an impres-sive mangle, over 30 ft (c. 9 m) long and driven by two men in a treadmill; the other was driven by a horse capstan. The mangle, one of the first domestic machines, was invented in northern Italy at the end of the sixteenth century, and it was intended for the huge linen-

D1

MANGANO PER MANGANAR ZAMBELOTTI TELE ET ALTRE GOSE

D2

D One of the earliest known descriptions of a mangle has been found in Vittorio Zonca's art book, from which these illustrations of two such machines have been taken. The upper picture (**1**) depicts a horse-whim-driven mangle, where-as the lower one (**2**) represents a model driven by two men in a treadmill.

In the mid-1650s, Carl Gustaf Wrangel (1613–76), a Swedish military commander in the Thirty Years' War who was exceedingly fond of splendour, decided to have the baroque-style castle of Skokloster erected in the Swedish province of Uppland. Some fifteen years later, the castle was complete, with the exception of a large baronial hall. According to plans, this hall was to be decorated with extravagant architectonic splendour, but the castle had already cost vast sums, and Wrangel had no money left. All the craftsmen who had been engaged to perform the decorative work simply walked out when they were no longer paid for their work. They left their tools and implements behind, and these remained intact until the middle of the 1970s, when restoration of this part of the castle started.

A Some of the master glazier's tools. (**1**) A roller bench, where bars of lead were shaped to profiles of U-section. These were used for leaded window-panes. The rolling machine itself was hand-cranked. (**2**) An anvil used for finishing the U-

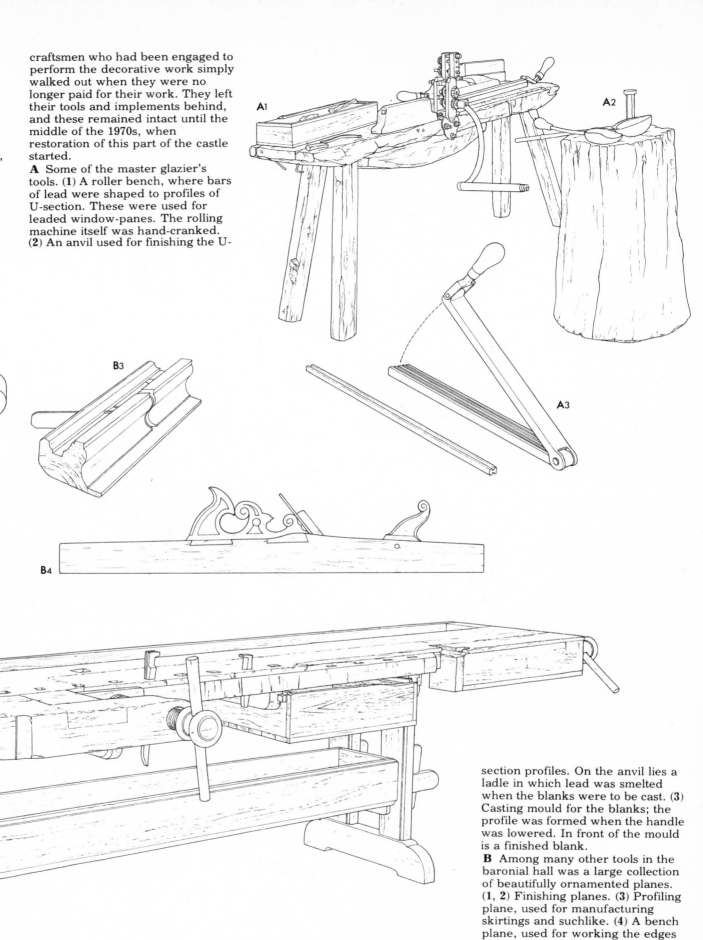

section profiles. On the anvil lies a ladle in which lead was smelted when the blanks were to be cast. (**3**) Casting mould for the blanks; the profile was formed when the handle was lowered. In front of the mould is a finished blank.

B Among many other tools in the baronial hall was a large collection of beautifully ornamented planes. (**1, 2**) Finishing planes. (**3**) Profiling plane, used for manufacturing skirtings and suchlike. (**4**) A bench plane, used for working the edges of boards which were to be joined.

C A carpenter's bench, probably built at the beginning of the seventeenth century.

stores of the principal ducal courts. The original meaning of the word "mangle" is "a large machine" and is derived from the Greek word *magganon*, first used to designate large military machines, such as ballistas, but later to cover large, intricate machines in general. Once the mangle had been reduced to easier-to-handle proportions, it spread rapidly all over Europe, and a century later, it formed part of the equipment in almost every large household.

The Tools and Implements of Industrialism

It has already been stressed that the most common hand tools had been realized and had acquired a stable form at a very early stage. Such changes as occurred over the centuries were due to better materials and new occupations that required tools other than those already in existence. From the Middle Ages until the era of industrialism, however, the tools of the carpenter, joiner, and smith remained more or less the same.

The great French encyclopaedia, *"Encyclopédie, ou dictionnaire raisonné des sciences, des arts et des métiers"*, edited by Denis Diderot (1713–84) and Jean Lerond d'Alembert (1717–83), and published between 1751 and 1780, is a priceless source of knowledge of the tools, implements, and machines in existence on what was the threshold of industrialism. This bulky work of thirty-five folio-sized volumes describes comprehensively more than eighty trades and illustrates them in a masterly fashion. All tools and implements are depicted in detail, the intention being that any person who was interested and practically inclined could use the encyclopaedia so as to be able to establish himself in one of the trades described. With few exceptions, the tools shown were produced manually, often according to mediaeval principles. (Industrial manufacture of hand tools on anything like a large scale did not occur until the mid-1800s.)

When the last volumes of the encyclopaedia were published at the end of the eighteenth century, an new era—the beginning of industrialism—had started with the appearance of James Watt's steam-engine. Several engineers before Watt had had feasible ideas about exploiting steam power, but the tools and methods to realize their intentions simply did not exist. What we have called heavy engineering was too clumsy, and precision mechanics could be applied only to small items.

Many of the parts and components needed for the exploitation of steam power required new methods and tools, mainly to make pipes, taps, and valves. Even in ancient times, pipes of different materials had been used. In mining, ever since the Middle Ages, pipes had been used for conducting water, but these pipes were hollowed tree-trunks. In the eighteenth century, there was a well-developed technique for the manufacture of such pipes, and in some places it was used even into the nineteenth century. But wooden pipes were not good enough for steam power, which required pipes which were resistant to heat and high pressure.

During the first decades of the steam era, pipes were made manually of iron, copper, and bronze. The process started with sheet metal, which was bent round a steel bar, and the joint or "seam" was then brazed or soldered. The first seamless pipes were cast. In 1790, the Englishman John Wilkinson (1728–1808) patented a method of casting lead pipes in a mould with a steel bar in the middle. Not until the mid-1830s was the same method used for producing pipes of bronze and copper. Steel pipes were not in common use until the 1880s, when the Mannesmann brothers in Germany developed a method of rolling pipes with a mandrel. Similar ideas had cropped up on several previous occasions, for instance, in a British patent granted to G.W. Dyson and H.A. Hall in 1870. In the 1860s, the Mannesmanns' father, Reinhard (1814–94), had already experimented with rolled pipes in his tool factory in Remscheid, which had been

D This water-wheel-driven boring machine was reproduced by Salomon de Caus in his art book, *Les raisons des forces mouvantes*, and was used for boring holes in tree trunks, which were then used as water-pipes. In the foreground, some of the different-sized augers used in the machine can be seen.
E The Mannesmann method for the manufacture of iron tubes was demonstrated at the international exhibition held in Chicago in 1893, and Thomas A. Edison is said to

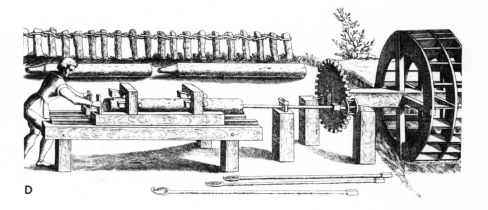

D

have remarked that this impressed him more than anything else at the whole exhibition. By exposing the surface of a red-hot iron bar to a powerful, stretching machining while the internal parts of the bar were not allowed to partake of the elongation stress, cupping occurred inside the bar. The machining was brought about by two rollers (*a*) which were mounted at an angle to the bar (*b*) and rotated, thus forcing the bar towards a mandrel (*c*).
F Among many other trades described in Diderot's encyclopaedia is that of the goldsmith. The type of lathe shown here was used in the eighteenth century for engraving plates of precious metal. The plate blank (*a*) was attached to a detachable template (*b*) on the lathe's turntable (*c*). The template's edge

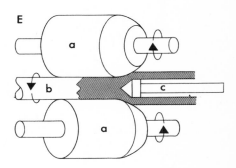

E

was followed by a roller (*d*) which guided the graver (*e*) laterally. The plate to which the roller and graver were attached was moved longitudinally along the work table by means of an inner screw device operated by a crank (*f*).

F

A One of Wilkinson's water-wheel-powered boring mills for producing cylinders. This was erected at the Bersham Ironworks in 1775; (**1**) outline diagram, (**2**) a model of the construction, in which two cylinder blanks (one is here shown in section) could be bored simultaneously. The tubular boring bars (*a*) were supported in sturdy bearings and had longitudinal slots. Inside the boring bars were rods which were attached to the cutter heads by lugs running through the slots. The cutter heads could move freely along the boring bars and were automatically moved forwards through the cylinder blanks because the outer ends of the rods (*b*) were jointed to racks (*e*), which meshed with pinions (*f*). On the pinion shafts were weight-loaded levers (*g*), which slowly sank, thus turning the pinions. Cross-bars (*h*) stopped the racks from rotating. (*i*) Water-wheel. (*j*) A lathe, probably used for facing and turning large, disc-shaped objects. (*k*) A simpler lathe.

B When the Soho Foundry was to be closed down at the end of the nineteenth century, a London magazine, *The Engineer*, sent some members of its staff to the foundry. Their task was to depict and describe the foundry's machines before they were dismantled. Among the illustrations later published in *The Engineer* was this one, which shows a large face-plate lathe, built in c. 1850.

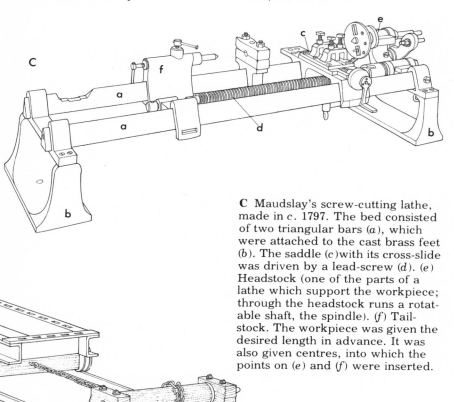

C Maudslay's screw-cutting lathe, made in c. 1797. The bed consisted of two triangular bars (a), which were attached to the cast brass feet (b). The saddle (c)with its cross-slide was driven by a lead-screw (d). (e) Headstock (one of the parts of a lathe which support the workpiece; through the headstock runs a rotatable shaft, the spindle). (f) Tailstock. The workpiece was given the desired length in advance. It was also given centres, into which the points on (e) and (f) were inserted.

in the family for generations, but it was his sons, Reinhard (1856–1922) and Max (1857–1915), who managed to arrive at a method that was very much in advance of its time, and they patented it in 1885. A few years later, pipes were being made on an industrial scale. The Mannesmann method was shown at the world exhibition in Chicago in 1893. Thomas A. Edison is reputed to have said that this method impressed him more than anything else at the exhibition. The demand for steel pipes increased rapidly and was one reason why the Mannesmann concern developed into one of the largest industrial companies in Germany.

Machine Tools Take Over

A large number of factors contributed to the development of industrialism in the nineteenth century. From the technical point of view, the basic conditions were the constantly improved versions of the old hand tools. These hand tools made it possible to manufacture the new tools required by technical progress, particularly in power engines. Some of these tools and parts have already been mentioned.

"Industrialization" means that manual methods of manufacture are mechanized, that is, taken over by machines. The machine tool is a logical outcome of this process. We have already dealt with many machine tools, such as the potter's wheel and the machines we have suggested were used by the pyramid builders for sawing stone. What we today call machine tools, however, are mainly metal-working machines.

The large French encyclopaedia of the mid-eighteenth century describes a number of lathes for turning wood as well as metal; at that time, the art of turning was quite advanced. One thing shown in the encyclopaedia is an engine lathe, where the material could be formed to a pattern of regularly repeated contours, so-called rose-engine turning (the same name is used for the method of producing on bank-notes and documents, patterns that are hard to forge). Engine turning was a very popular hobby even among princes and statesmen, from the Holy Roman Emperor Maximilian I to Gustavus Adolphus IV of Sweden; wood was the material they worked in, for attempts to use metals were not made until about 1700. The first detailed description of a lathe for turning iron appears in a book by Charles Plumier, *L'art de tourner* ("The Art of Turning"), published in 1701. The lathe must be solidly constructed, Plumier points out, and also must be stiff enough to resist the great forces arising between the tool and the material. Christopher Polhem had at least one iron lathe in operation at the Stjernsund Works at the beginning of the eighteenth century. This lathe was driven by a water wheel, and the tool holder was fed by a lead screw, driven by a gearwheel. In 1760, the Frenchman Jacques de Vaucanson (1709–82), a masterly designer and a man of many talents, built a metal lathe on an iron bed. The whole constructions was braced by a framework, which made it very stable. Vaucanson's lathe is representative of the basic type from which machine tools rapidly developed over the following decades. By the 1830s, machine tools had already assumed the shapes which they have retained up to the present.

We have already pointed out that steam power required a lot of tools and parts (see also Chapter Five). One problem with the manufacture of the earliest steam-engines was to produce good enough cylinders. Attempts were made to cast them, but there was the difficulty of finishing them by chiselling and filing, which left the inside still very rough. In 1774, however, John Wilkinson, a friend and colleague of Matthew Boulton and James Watt, designed a machine intended for machining cylinders that, being very robust, was very accurate. The cylinder material was held firmly in place in a solid bed mounted on a cradle of thick oak beams (Wilkinson was certainly taking Plumier's recommendations seriously!). A strong,

A A lathe of a type common during the latter half of the nineteenth century. (*a*) Bed. (*b*) Headstock in which the cone pulley, gears, and spindle were included. A cone pulley is a belt pulley with several different pulley diameters. Since the lathe was equipped with a cone pulley, various gear ratios could be attained. The spindle was carried in two cradles and was often tubular on this type of lathe. It was then easier to work rod-shaped material, since the blank could simply be inserted into the spindle. (*c*) Movable tailstock. (*d*) Hand wheel for moving *c*. The tailstock was locked in position by means of a lever (*e*). (*f*) Saddle. (*g*) Cross-slide. (*h*) Apron, in which the feed attachments were mounted. (*i*) The lead-screw, a carefully threaded spindle which was used to move the lathe tool when threads were to be cut. Behind the lead-screw was a rack, which meshed with a pinion. This device was used when one wanted to do other types of turning than threading. When a hand-crank (*j*) was manually rotated, the saddle was rapidly moved sideways without being influenced by the lead-screw.

B In Whitworth's planing machine of 1835, the workpiece was fixed while the slide rest was movable. Shown here is the drawing which accompanied Whitworth's patent application; the machine is seen from its long (**1**) and short (**2**) sides as well as from above (**3**). (*a*) Foot. (*b*) Bed, to which the workpiece was clamped. Two uprights (*c*), each equipped with two wheels (*d*) which were guided along V-slideways (*e*), together carried a cross-slide (*f*), on

patent lock, a delicate construction that required extremely accurate components. Around 1800, Maudslay constructed a lathe primarily intended for cutting threads. The lathe was made entirely of metal and included several new features. The support for the lathe tool, the so-called tool-holder, was carried on a slide-rest driven by a lead-screw along the lathe, while the tool was moved towards the work-piece in a V-slide, by means of a screw fitted with a winch handle. Thanks to the V-slide, the tool could be moved very accurately, and with a considerable saving of labour. The Scots engineer James Nasmyth (1808–90) illustrated this in a drawing showing a lathe of Maudslay's design and an older lathe, in each of which identical workpieces were being turned. The operator of the older lathe was shown using the weight of his whole body to press the tool against the material, while the operator of the Maudslay lathe was keeping it in place by resting one hand on the knob of the support; his other hand rested nonchalantly in his pocket.

Maudslay designed his first machines in 1794, while still working for Bramah, and patented them in 1797, when he opened his own workshop, where he made further improvements to his machines. It was here, about three years later, that the metal lathe found the form it has retained ever since.

Maudslay's work appeared at the right time. The British workshop industry was then beginning to expand rapidly, not least because the patent on Watt's steam-engine expired in 1800. As a result, many engineers introduced new designs exploiting steam power. Maudslay was inundated with orders for his precision lathe, and the first mass production of machine tools started in his workshop during the first decades of the nineteenth century. To be sure, many lathe units were built to order, but they always contained the components patented by Maudslay.

Maudslay's principle, where design was concerned, was precision and more precision. Precision mechanics now started to intrude on areas traditionally occupied by heavy engineering and consequently brought about the technical pre-conditions for both more efficient power engines and an industrial production of machine tools. In England a machine-tool industry came into being and rapidly won world fame.

That striving after precision that was sought and fruitfully attained by Maudslay also influenced the work of Sir Joseph Whitworth (1803–87). In 1835, he patented a face-plate lathe that was so well adapted to its purpose that its success laid the foundations of a machine-tool industry, Whitworth & Company, which was one of the foremost of the time, with an impressively wide range of machines for different purposes. The account of the company's programme which was presented at the world exhibition in London in 1851 became one of the most discussed features of this general demonstration of contemporary technical progress. Accuracy in all kinds of processing became Whitworth's consuming passion and formed the foundation for many of his pioneering contributions. He introduced, for example, a system for indicating measurements in drawings, and he designed an instrument which could measure length to an accuracy of a millionth part of an inch. He also standardized the thread profile and the pitch per unit length, of metal screws and nuts at a time when both wood and metal screws had long been made on an industrial scale, but with threads that varied from factory to factory. Whitworth's system was later named BSW (British Standard Whitworth) and was used alongside threading based on the metric system in most industrial countries, until the Anglo-Saxon countries in the 1970s gradually went over to the metric system.

Great Britain was the leader where machine tools were concerned, but important contributions were made also in other countries. The first milling machine, in the modern sense of the word,

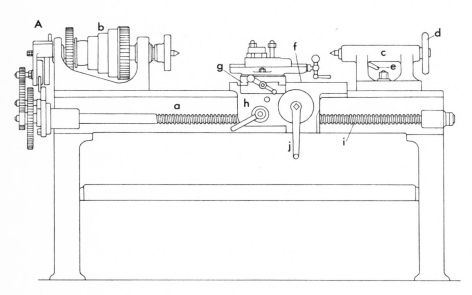

tubular boring bar rotated round the centre-line of the cylinder material and machined the required hole. When Boulton & Watt's workshop had taken delivery of a trial order of Wilkinson's cylinders, they found that the internal diameter of a 50-in (c. 175 cm) cylinder deviated from its proper dimensions by no more than the "thickness of a worn shilling-piece" in any place – a degree of precision that they never had dreamt possible. Wilkinson's machine attracted a great deal of attention, and it set the pattern for at least the next seventy-five years. The design, with slight modifications, was used as late as 1851 to bore cylinders for locomotives! Wilkinson's boring machine is rightly considered the first real machine tool, in the modern sense of the word.

Mainly on the basis of their experience of Wilkinson's machine, Boulton and Watt constructed an improved cylinder-boring machine and a face-plate lathe in the early 1790s. Both machines were pioneering, and similar machines were installed in many mechanical workshops in England and other countries during the following fifty years.

The first modern metal lathe was designed by an Englishman, Henry Maudslay (1771–1831). As a young man, Maudslay had worked for Joseph Bramah (1748–1814), who had invented the first

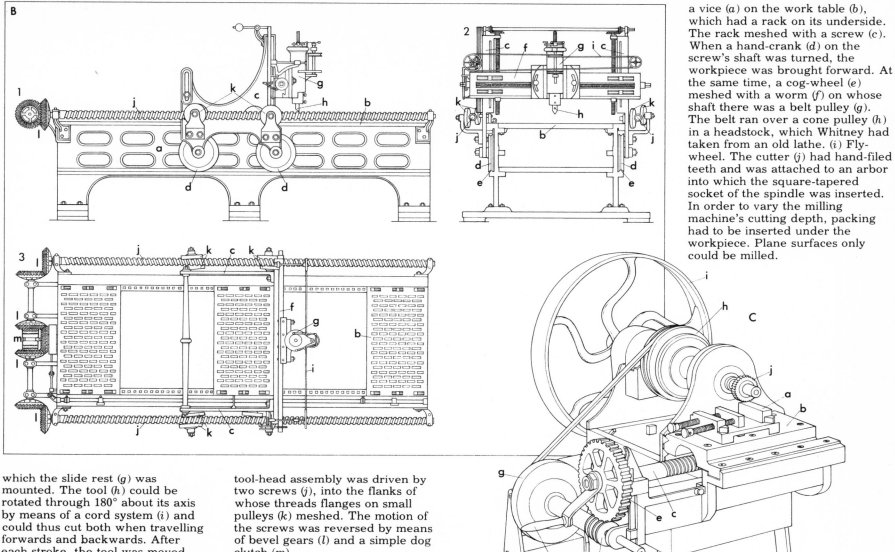

B

a vice (*a*) on the work table (*b*), which had a rack on its underside. The rack meshed with a screw (*c*). When a hand-crank (*d*) on the screw's shaft was turned, the workpiece was brought forward. At the same time, a cog-wheel (*e*) meshed with a worm (*f*) on whose shaft there was a belt pulley (*g*). The belt ran over a cone pulley (*h*) in a headstock, which Whitney had taken from an old lathe. (*i*) Fly-wheel. The cutter (*j*) had hand-filed teeth and was attached to an arbor into which the square-tapered socket of the spindle was inserted. In order to vary the milling machine's cutting depth, packing had to be inserted under the workpiece. Plane surfaces only could be milled.

C

which the slide rest (*g*) was mounted. The tool (*h*) could be rotated through 180° about its axis by means of a cord system (*i*) and could thus cut both when travelling forwards and backwards. After each stroke, the tool was moved sideways, so that a new shaving was cut next to the previous one. The tool-head assembly was driven by two screws (*j*), into the flanks of whose threads flanges on small pulleys (*k*) meshed. The motion of the screws was reversed by means of bevel gears (*l*) and a simple dog clutch (*m*).

C Eli Whitney's milling machine of 1818. The workpiece was placed in

was constructed in 1818 by the American Eli Whitney (1765–1825). Whitney was most famous for his cotton *gin*, the cotton-separating machine he had patented in 1794, which made it possible for the Southern states to increase their cotton production considerably. Elisha K. Root (1808–65) also made some pioneering new constructions. He was the chief engineer of the Colt Armory in Hartford, Connecticut, which mass produced the revolver patented in 1835 by Samuel Colt (1814–62). Mass production really is the word, for over 300,000 units of the most popular models were made. Root concentrated on machine tools for precision manufacture. He wanted to use labour-saving machines to eliminate the human factor and to make all the units of a long series identical. He introduced what was later called the American system of interchangeable parts. Appropriately, he and Colt designed the first turret lathe, in the mid-1850s. When metal-working requires several different tools to be used one after the other, much labour is saved when they are mounted on to a revolving drum, called a turret head, and brought into place, step by step, by a spider.

Root and Colt's lathe first appeared in Europe in the mid-1870s, in an improved form that came to be the model on which all further development of this machine tool was based. However, it was not Root who first came upon the idea of feeding forward tools on a lathe. As early as the 1840s, several companies, among them Silver & Gray, were thinking on these lines, but it was Root and Colt's construction that was to be the model for all further turret-lathe development.

Root's clever system of interchangeable parts soon spread to England and the rest of Europe, although it should be added that this "American system" actually originated in Europe in the late eighteenth century, where hand firearms with interchangeable parts were being manufactured in several countries. From the middle of the nineteenth century, when mass-produced domestic machines began to make their appearance–sewing-machines, typewriters, bicycles, harvesters, etc.–the system of interchangeable parts played a major role.

The Industry of Industry

Mass production of machine tools has been called "the industry of industry", and it became widespread in the 1870s. Industrial manufacture of machine tools had certainly existed in Great Britain since the beginning of the nineteenth century and in the United States since the 1840s, but these machines had been built on only a relatively small scale. The increasing demands for precision in mass production of interchangeable parts called for more and more specialized machine tools, but even so, as late as the latter part of the nineteenth century, it was still quite common for companies to build their own machine tools, at least in smaller factories in the engineering industry. At the world exhibition in Philadelphia in 1876, there was displayed the greatest collection of American and European machine tools that had been seen to date, the many different varieties and novelties making an enormous impression on engineers from both sides of the Atlantic.

The Automats Arrive

In the 1870s, an new kind of machine tool appeared that, fully automatically, made smaller parts according to an adjustable program. After several years' hard work, Christopher M. Spe

(1833–1922), an American, could present the first of these in 1873; in essence it was a turret lathe, in which a camshaft and a camshaft pulley moved levers that fed the workpiece forward and changed the tools.

Spencer built his automat to mass produce parts for a sewing-machine, but it was not long before "Hartford automats" also appeared, Spencer being one of the founders of the Hartford Machine Screw Company. These automats produced screws, nuts, cogwheels, and other things en masse, a fact having an impact on the whole of the engineering workshop industry that can hardly be overrated. Demand was immediately great, and within only some years of Spencer's pioneering contribution, automats had given the "industry of industry" a great boost that would create better resources for the development of new and improved manually operated machine tools.

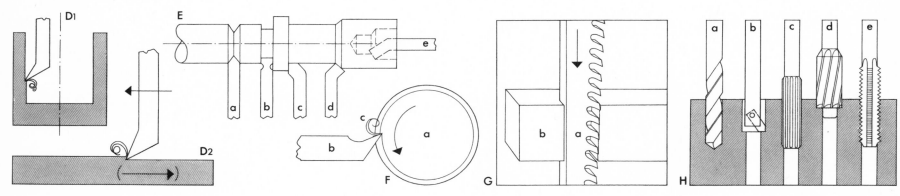

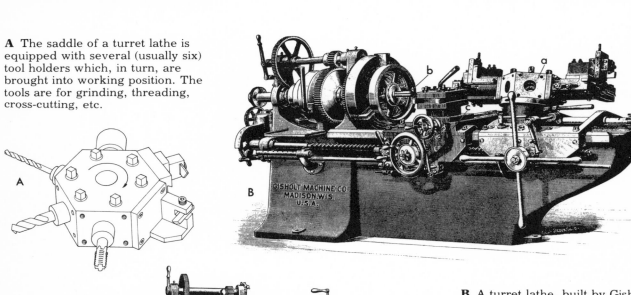

A The saddle of a turret lathe is equipped with several (usually six) tool holders which, in turn, are brought into working position. The tools are for grinding, threading, cross-cutting, etc.

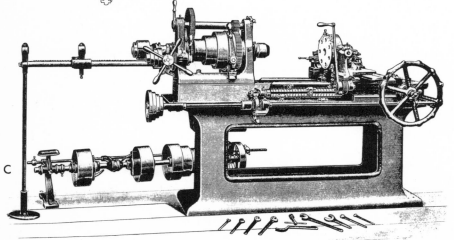

B A turret lathe, built by Gisholt Machine Co. in the United States. On this machine, the turret head (*a*) was set at an angle, so the tools would not upset the moving of the machine when large workpieces were being turned. During machining, the workpiece was fitted to a steel mandrel (*b*). The machine was also equipped with a cross-slide (*c*), which had holders for lathe tools and could be moved along or across the lathe by means of screws.
C A turret lathe with a vertical turret for six tools. Both this machine and that at **B** were manufactured during the second half of the nineteenth century.

In other words, Spencer's contribution meant an important breakthrough in the development of machine tools. A pioneer in the processing of metals, he had several predecessors in the processing of wood. One was a colourful Englishman, Thomas Blanchard (1788–1864), who, in 1820, designed a lathe to make rifle butts. These had been carved manually ever since hand-held firearms first appeared in the Middle Ages, and the butt makers formed, in due course, a highly esteemed craft guild, taking great pride in making skilfully ornamented rifle butts, a pride reflected, naturally, in high prices. Blanchard's first design could make two rifle butts in an hour, and when this reproducing lathe had been improved, it could make nearly a dozen in the same time. Blanchard built various reproducing lathes to make different objects, including axe handles and shoe lasts. This technology was developed and just about perfected by Holtzappfel & Co., of London, whose reproducing lathes made

D The shaping machine and the slotting machine are both chip-cutting and have short cutter strokes. The slotting machine's cutter (**1**) makes vertical cuts and the shaping machine's (**2**) makes horizontal cuts.
E Some simple types of lathe-tool: (*a*) V-groove steel, (*b*) groove steel, (*c*) left-hand corner steel, (*d*) right-hand roughing steel, (*e*) internal roughing steel.
F During turning, the workpiece (*a*) rotates while a lathe tool (*b*) is fed against it and removes chips (*c*).
G The purpose of broaching is to enlarge drilled holes. The broach (*a*) moves downwards while the workpiece (*b*) is fixed.
H Various methods of machining holes: (*a*) drilling, (*b*) broaching, (*c*) reaming (making the cylindrical surface of the hole even), (*d*) counter-sinking (bevelling the top of the hole to make room for a screw-head), (*e*) threading.
I When ordinary milling is performed in a horizontal milling machine, the workpiece (*a*) is fed in the direction opposite to the rotation of the milling tool (*b*).
J Three common types of milling tool: (**1**) face cutter, (**2**) milling cutter, (**3**) V-groove cutter.
K In a vertical milling machine, the spindle (*a*) is mounted vertically. (*b*) Workpiece.
L Gigantic belt transmissions char-

acterized the mechanical workshops of the early twentieth century.
M Spencer's automatic lathe for screw manufacture; (**1**) from above (**2**) from the side. On the bed (*a*), there were two opposed, belt-driven headstocks (*b*, *c*) and the metal rods to be machined were fed through *b*'s spindle. A slowly rotating shaft (*d*) supported two drums (*e*, *f*) with cams in the form of guide rails. These guided the feeding and chucking of the work-pieces as well as their transfer from *b* to *c* for the final machining. Cams on *f* also guided the axial movement of one of the turrets (*g*), which was attached to a shaft (*h*) which continuously tried to rotate since a chain (*i*) connected it to a wheel (*j*) with a sliding clutch. Shaft *h* as well as *g* could, however, not turn when one of the stops (*k*) on *g* bore on a fixed abutment (*l*). Only when a work operation had been concluded had *g* been pushed far enough sideways to free the stop, so that the next tool could be turned into the working position. When the work-piece had been transferred to *c*'s spindle, the second turret (*m*) came into use. It was fixed axially but could partake of *g*'s gradual rotation. Mounted on *m* was, among other tools, a milling cutter (*n*) for nicking the screw-heads. (*o*) Cam-shaft pulley, guiding a cross-bar (*p*) with cross-cutting and other tools.

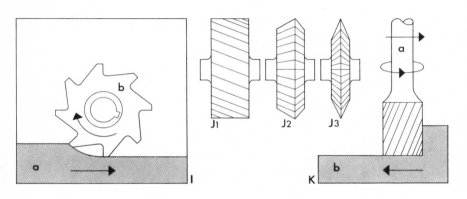

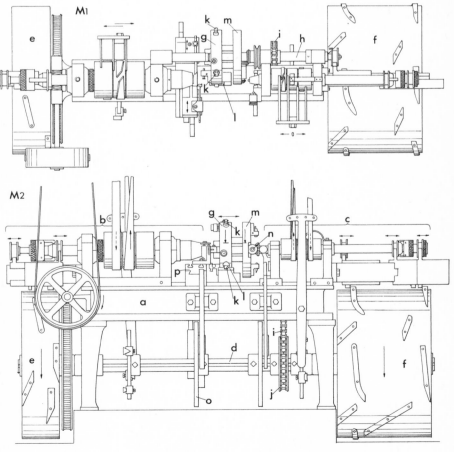

many different products, mainly mass-produced decorative parts for furniture and other wooden ornaments for interior decoration.

The Machine Tools of the Twentieth Century

Thanks to the rapid expansion of the "industry of industry", engineering workshops at the turn of the century had an abundant supply of both machine tools and automats. There were lathes, drilling machines with multiple spindles, milling machines, shaping machines, and even grinding machines, both for production and for grinding the tools of the machine tools. A typical feature of the engineering workshops of the early twentieth century was the overhead line shafts from which power was transferred to each machine tool by a belt. The shafts were driven by large steam-engines. By the 1890s, small, compact steam-engines had been designed in many parts of the world, and these generated sufficient power to drive individual lathes, drilling machines, and so on. The idea was to distribute steam from a central boiler via pipelines to each machine in the workshop. The advocates of this system maintained that the total efficiency of the system would far exceed that of one employing belt transmission, as the latter suffered a loss of power due to friction. However, at the turn of the twentieth century, steam power was in crisis, as electrical energy was becoming more easily available and offered the possibility of a technically superior method of replacing the old power-consuming belt-transmission system. Machine tools driven individually by electricity began to appear at the end of the 1890s and made their breakthrough in the following decade.

The Development of Cutting Materials

It is obvious that the material of the tools in a machine tool must be harder than the material of the workpiece. In the early machine tools, crucible steel was used to manufacture lathe steel, drills, and so on. Crucible steel for chip removal contained 1−1.4 per cent carbon and was called carbon steel. In the mid-1860s, Robert F. Mushet (1811−91), an Englishman, found that the addition of relatively small amounts of tungsten and manganese to carbon steel gave a tool steel with very good cutting properties. This low alloy steel, Mushet steel, appeared at a time when the machine-tool industry was entering a stage of rapid expansion, and it soon found a wide application.

In 1898, after many years of metallurgical development work, the two Americans Frederick W. Taylor and Mansel White presented a hardening process for low-alloy carbon steel, which made it possible to produce a tool steel with much improved properties. The carbon steel was alloyed with tungsten, chrome, vanadium, and molybdenum, which gave it very high resistance to wear. Taylor steel, which has also been called high-speed steel, initiated a development which became extremely important to the production economy of the workshop industry. The high-speed steel led to an increase of production speed, since workpieces could now be machined many times faster than before.

At a stroke, the new tool steel outdated all the existing machine tools. These were simply too delicate and lacked the dynamic properties required. The driving motors were too weak for the forces and counter forces set up by the tools of the new material. In many places this damaged the reputation of the high-speed steel tools, since they contributed to a premature wearing down of drilling machines and lathes.

The machine-tool manufacturers had to think again. They realized that new designs were necessary, and that these had to be based on the actual performance of the tools. A feature of the continued development was the introduction of new cutting materials which made constantly increasing demands on the machine tools. It be-

came necessary to design motors with more power and constructions with greater stability.

In 1926, this development took an important step forward with the introduction of the first hard metal for cutting material; produced in Germany, it was marketed under the name of Widia. Hard metal is an alloy of chrome, tungsten, and titanium or molybdenum with their carbides (carbon compounds). The alloys can be either cast or sintered, which means that metallic or mineral elements in powder form are heated to the temperature at which one or more of them melt and cement the remainder together. During the next few years, a series of hard metals were introduced, with trade names including, for cast alloys, Celsit, Akrit, Miramant, and Stellit and, for sintered alloys, Carboloy, the name used in the United States for Widia, Ramet, Seco, and Titanit. During the 1970s, the cutting properties and the durability of the hard metals were improved further by new metallurgic processes. Tools made of these metals were also coated with a layer, often no more than a thousandth of a millimetre thick, of titanium carbide and aluminium oxide. This development of cutting materials in the twentieth century has meant a revolution in metal-working technology: machining a 500-mm long steel axle with a diameter of 100 mm required 100 minutes with carbon-steel tools, while the same work can be done in less than a minute by a tool coated with, for example, the hard metal known as Coromant, which was introduced in 1976.

The Automat Becomes an NC-machine

Numerically controlled machine tools (NC-machines) are now making rapid progress in the machine-tool industry, and while it is easy to get the impression that they are quite a new invention that has emerged from computer technology, this is not so. Their development can be traced, logically, from Spencer's pioneering machine-tool automat of the 1870s.

A textbook on machine tools from 1955, for example, describes an automatic lathe from the late nineteenth century as still basically "quite modern". Along with the general technical development in the twentieth century, new components were added to change the position of tools and workpieces—electrical, pneumatic, and hydraulic servo motors—while camshaft pulleys and camshafts were still used to carry out the work program. During the first decades of the twentieth century, the cam gear was added, where the "giving of orders" for the various work stages was released by movable cams on a cylinder. When the new cutting materials started to come into use towards the end of the 1920s, it was possible to increase the speed of the different work operations considerably. A common fault of the machine-tool automats of that time was the omission of one of the work operations. In due course, however, sequence control was introduced, which meant that a new work operation could not be commenced until the preceding operation had finished.

In the 1930s and 1940s, copying control of machine-tool automats was also developed. This type of control was in principle the same as that applied by Blanchard in his first copying lathe, in which a pin followed the contours of a rifle butt, while the pin's vertical and horizontal movements controlled the lathe slide and the tools, enabling the shape of any kind of object to be reproduced.

Copying control had a renaissance with the advent of new methods for sensing, principally the electro-optical methods, in which the sensing system operates by means of a luminous ray and photoelectric cells. These methods were rapidly developed during the Second World War, mainly in the United States. An important step was to develop electro-optical devices capable of reading drawings and using this information to control signals for work operations. A further, decisive step was numerically to transform the data of a drawing into a system of three-dimensional coordinates, the principle being developed at the Massachusetts Institute of Technology, where the first NC-machine was taken into operation in 1952.

NC-machines employ one of two basically different methods: general contour control, and positioning, an intermediate form being called limited contour control. With general contour control, numerical information is fed into the machine to control the tool along a two- or three-dimensional curve; the latter requires numerical data–coordinates–in quantities proportionate to the precision to be achieved and, for this reason, computers were used early on to compute the data needed for a specific level of precision. The data was stored on magnetic tape which could be used as input to the NC-machines.

Positioning is used mainly in drilling machines where the tool is to be brought to a predetermined position. Limited contour control is basically related to positioning and is applied on machines which are controlled in rectilinear movements only. The predominant part of the work operations in the average workshop industry is, however, of this type, and consequently, numerically controlled machine tools with limited contour control have found a wide application.

The first NC-machine from the Massachusetts Institute of Technology was a standard three-geared milling machine with a separate numerical control attachment. By the mid-1950s, when a number of different numerical control attachments had been introduced for standard versions of machine tools, it was becoming obvious that the control devices would have to be fully integrated with the machines, and the first such machine to be mass produced appeared on the market in 1955. It was a milling machine with general contour control, manufactured by an American machine-tool company, Giddings & Lewis. By 1960, however, only about 100 general contour control and about 350 positioning or limited contour control machine tools had found a place in American industry, for their introduction required the routines of an industry to be changed or adjusted, from designs and drawings up to programming. In 1967, within only seven years, half of all newly manufactured machine tools were numerically controlled, and by 1977, more than 30,000 such machines were in operation in the United States, almost 5,000 in West Germany, and over 2,000 in Sweden.

Since the early 1970s, numerical control technology has also been applied to devices other than machine tools, mainly for function tests of different types of electrical and electronic products. In the future, numerical control technology will quite likely be applied in other fields where intricate processes have to be controlled.

The Industrial Robot

No internationally accepted definition yet exists of the somewhat indeterminate concept "industrial robot". At one extreme is the pick-and-place unit intended for moving objects from one place to another, a product derived from automation in the 1950s, while at the other is the radio-controlled robot which, among other things, takes inhuman risks in nuclear industry. We shall, however, mainly take note of production aids marketed as industrial robots.

The Game Becomes Serious

The first industrial robot, the Unimat, was developed in the United States in the early 1960s and stumbled onto the market in 1963. Its design team was less likely to have thought of either Karel Čapek and his robots (see page 202) or the walking tin monsters and other fanciful engineers' toys which were common in the 1930s, than of the numerical control technology that had inspired other designers to automate the industrial handling of materials. Despite all mechanization, workpieces had then, and are still, frequently to be merely

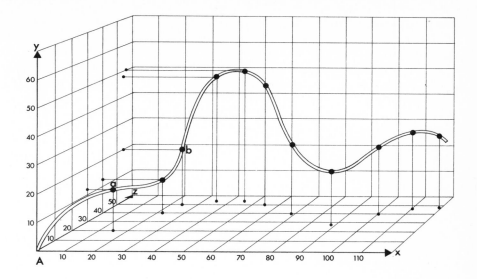

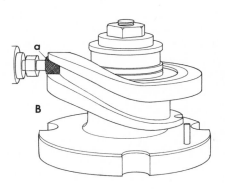

A A three-dimensional curved line can be numerically defined by means of a system of coordinates with three planes which are perpendicular to each other and which cut each other along three axes. The point where the axes x, y, and z meet is called the origin of coordinates. The higher the demanded precision, the shorter must be the distance between those points on the curved line which are defined by coordinates–three for each point (the x, y, and z coordinates. The length of a coordinate is the distance between the origin and the point on one of the planes where an imaginary line drawn at right angles from the point on the curved line crosses the plane. In the curve shown here, the x coordinate of point a is 16 mm, its y coordinate is 13 mm, and its z coordinate 30 mm. The corresponding coordinates for point b are 25, 20, and 55 mm respectively.

B If a detail like this one is to be produced automatically by a turret lathe, the tool (a) must be equipped with general contouring.

C A modern turret lathe, TNC Combi, with general contouring control of twelve tools. The control unit with its operation board is to the left of the illustration. Since the work program can be rapidly changed in numerically controlled machines, these are especially well suited to the manufacture of details in short series.

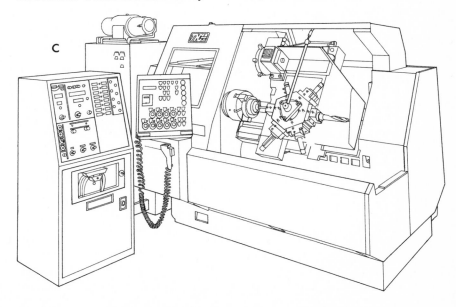

moved, turned, or twisted by hand between two work operations.

The first industrial robot to appear in Europe was installed in 1964 in a Swedish foundry, being employed to lift castings from moulds and place them on a cooling bed. This was in itself quite a simple operation, but the castings were very hot and of an alloy that gave off a foul, acrid smoke that, despite effective ventilation, was very unpleasant. The company had difficulty finding people willing to work in this section, so the industrial robot was very welcome to the work team! Lifting and moving things is, primarily, the sort of work that has occupied industrial robots, but they are also used for spray painting, arc welding, and other things.

The Anatomy of the Industrial Robot

An industrial robot consists of an arm equipped with a gripping device, a power unit, and a control system. The pattern of movements which a robot can carry out depends on its degrees of freedom, that is, what vertical and horizontal and turning movements it can make. The human hand has 22 degrees of freedom, far more than any industrial robot has yet been equipped with; six degrees of freedom are enough for a robot to move an object from one place to another.

The arm to which the gripping device of the robot is attached is usually made of a set of telescopic steel tubes, so that a driving device can change the length of the arm. It is usually mounted on a column, from which it gets its degrees of freedom in a vertical or horizontal direction. Smaller industrial robots are usually pneumatically driven, whereas the larger ones are hydraulically or electrically driven.

The shape of the gripping device usually attempts to resemble the human hand and it is often "tailored" for specific tasks. The first gripping devices to appear had only two unhinged fingers, but since then, development has been rapid, and modern gripping devices

have several hinged fingers. In recent years, workshop engineers and medical technicians who design artificial hands have cooperated in some very fruitful research in this area. Among other things, they have succeeded in developing a sense of touch in the gripping devices. Although at first there were difficulties because the robots were much too hard-handed—they could handle only robust objects—the matter is now nearly resolved through the use of what are called extension transmitters, applied to the fingers of the gripping device. These feel the objects gripped by the fingers and also register even the minute deformations caused by the force of the grip. These deformations are naturally proportional to the force of the grip, and signals from the extension transmitters then control the servo motor which supplies the force. A demonstration number for this artificial sense of touch is when the robot "eats" a boiled egg, by taking the egg in its "fingers", making a hole in the shell and spooning out the contents without crushing the rest of the shell, a performance possible only if the force of the grip can be moderated within very strict limits. Attempts are also being made to provide the gripping device with "eyesight", or at least an indicator of presence, by equipping it with a mouthpiece, through which air is blown in a fine jet. The pressure of the air is measured in the mouthpiece, and when the pressure changes to indicate an obstacle obstructing the gripping device, the robot receives the information. The gripping device can also be magnetic, for such things as handling steel plate, or pneumatic for handling sheets of metal plate, plastic sheets, plate glass, and so on.

The control system of the industrial robot usually consists of transmitters, which indicate the position, and a programme device. To enable the robot to be controlled in its various degrees of freedom, the position of the gripping device must be known from moment to moment, a job performed by electric potentiometers on the robot.

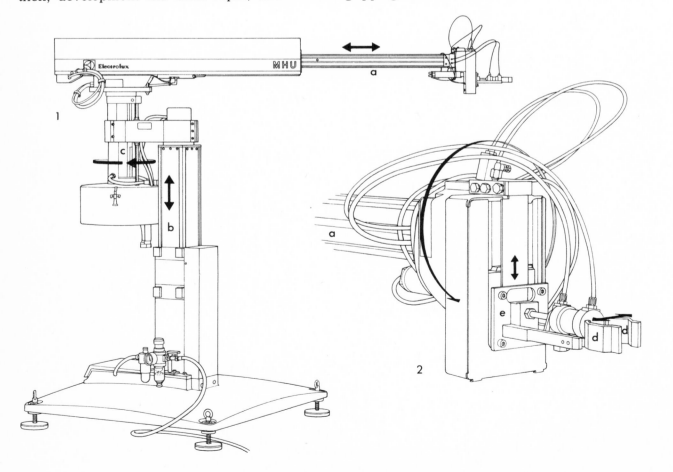

This pneumatically powered industrial robot (1) with six freedom degrees is manufactured by Electrolux in Sweden and is able to move an object to any point within its working area. The robot arm (a) can be moved to and fro horizontally and is mounted on a pillar (b), by means of which it can be raised and lowered. The arm can also rotate round its shaft (c). The grab device (2) has two fingers (d), which can be moved against, and away from, each other and are mounted on a plate (e), which can be moved vertically. The whole grab device can also be rotated round the robot arm.

CHAPTER 4
PRIME MOVERS I
Muscle, Water, Wind

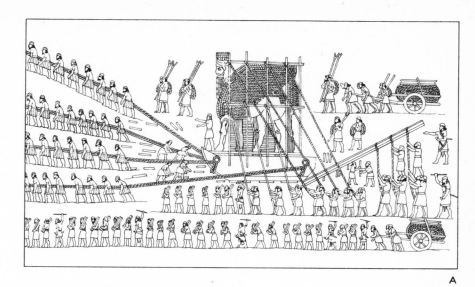

The techniques involved in moving the large blocks of stone which were used to build the first pyramids have already been touched upon. The necessary forces were supplied by a well-organized combination of human and animal muscle power. Similar methods were to be used for almost four thousand years, until the invention of other sources of power and means of transport, such as steam, railways, and so on.

In 41 AD, Roman engineers transported an ancient obelisk from Egypt to Rome, where it was erected in Circo di Nero, with the aid of muscle power boosted by levers, blocks, and capstans. Some fifteen hundred years later, in 1586, the obelisk was moved once again, this time merely across Rome to Piazza di San Pietro, under the direction of the military engineer Domenico Fontana: but the means he used were essentially no different from those of his Roman predecessors.

The average man can only develop a power of one seventh of a horsepower, or about one hundred watts. For a short time, he can develop perhaps twice as much. The form of the early European harness prevented the draught animals of ancient times from developing more than perhaps two hundred to four hundred watts; in those days, both horses and oxen were harnessed by a fork-shaped yoke, which was fitted by straps under the animal's neck. If the animal pulled too hard, it choked itself. At the end of the eighth century, the oval horse-collar, which had been in use in China since the third century BC, appeared in the Mediterranean countries and, in the following centuries, spread all over Europe. This collar enables the horse to pull with its shoulders, thus boosting its output at least fourfold. While the horse-collar was spreading across Europe, the iron horseshoe came into use and further increased the horse's output, by giving it a better grip on the ground. Improvements in agriculture and transport were consequences of these developments.

There were very few technical aids which exploited human muscle power in a rational way. Those that did exist were mainly intended to allow as many people as possible to pull or lift simultaneously. The most common aids were rope clusters or ropes with loops for lifting or pulling, and long beams to spread the weight of a heavy object more evenly when it had to be lifted. The combined muscle power could then be boosted by levers or multiple blocks.

"The human use of human beings!", proclaims the mathematician Norbert Wiener (1894–1964) in the title of his book on cybernetics and society (first published in 1951). The diametrical opposite of this would be to use gangs of slaves as prime movers of large ships. Rowing is, of course, almost as old as man himself; the first primates probably paddled themselves along sitting astride a log or in a hol-

A A stone image being moved on a sledge, pulled by a large number of people. Assyrian relief, ninth century BC.
B A simple crane. Several men could lift a heavy load jointly if each pulled at one of the rope ends.

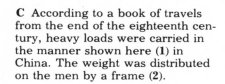

C According to a book of travels from the end of the eighteenth century, heavy loads were carried in the manner shown here (1) in China. The weight was distributed on the men by a frame (2).

C2

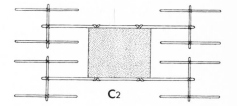

C1

A3

A In 1586, a 312-ton Egyptian obelisk was moved from Circo di Nero to Piazza di San Pietro in Rome under the direction of Domenico Fontana. Later, Fontana published a detailed account of the work, and it is from this book that the illustrations shown here derive. The obelisk was surrounded by a stout scaffold before it was lifted from its socle (**1**). For this critical phase of work, Fontana employed 900 men and 75 horses at 37 windlasses (**2**). Trumpet blasts and bell peals indicated when the windlasses were to be started and stopped. To utter a single word while work was in progress was forbidden on pain of death. In spite of this, a man is reputed to have risked his life by crying "Water on the ropes!" when these threatened to break. He was imprisoned but, later, was rewarded amply. The obelisk was placed on a bed of rollers and transported along a timber-reinforced road to the new site, where it was erected (**3**). This last phase took thirteen hours and was accomplished by means of blocks.

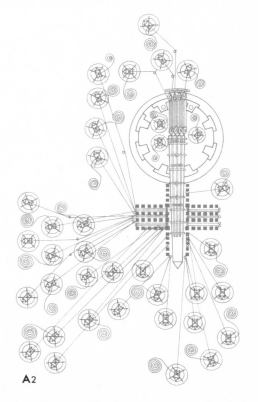

A2

A1

lowed-out tree-trunk. But it is a long way from that to the vast amount of muscle power which galley-slaves had to produce. Some ancient civilizations—for instance, the Sumerian, the Phoenician, and the Egyptian—had fairly large oar-propelled ships, but it was not until the fourth and third centuries BC that the Hellenic civilization produced the first great galleys. The shipbuilding techniques then used by the Greeks were later adopted by the Romans. Sarton tells of a contemporary description of the flagship of the famous fleet of Ptolemy IV Philopator (244?–203? BC), a ship considered to have been the most magnificent of antiquity, and that is saying a lot when one thinks of the *Syrakosia*, which has been described in Chapter One. Ptolemy's ship was claimed to have been 394 ft (*c*.120 m) long and 63 ft (*c*. 19 m) wide and was manned by 4,000 oarsmen and 400 relief oarsmen, together with 2,850 soldiers for the heavy armament on board. The account omits to say how many banks of oars there were (probably four, which would have made the ship a quadrireme), but it does say that the oars of the upper bank were almost 66 ft (*c*. 20 m) long. "However", the account continues, "these oars had lead counterweights and thus were very easy to handle." One feels tempted to remark that everything is relative, while recalling Sancho Panza's complaint, when he and Don Quixote ended up in a gallery, that "if this is not hell on earth, then it must be at least purgatory". Sarton doubts the size given for the crew, although all the primary sources give the same figures. But what if the numbers of oarsmen and soldiers are exaggerated?. A tenth of those figures would be impressive enough! (At this time, the Greeks did not use the position system when writing numbers, but used letters instead, and these could be misread easily, especially during translation.)

The Romans developed the galley to as near technical perfection as possible. The trireme, that is, a vessel with three banks of oars, one above the other, was the standard type of the Roman navy. The oars, of considerable length in the upper row, were usually equipped with counterweights, which naturally made rowing less backbreaking, although Sancho Panza's comment still comes to mind. This inhuman exploitation of labour decreased in the Middle Ages, when sail-rigging techniques gradually improved, but a modified form of these ancient galleys survived until steam took over in the nineteenth century. In many countries, the navy used galley slaves to row its ships, although sometimes regular soldiers were told off for this task.

The Capstan and the Treadmill

The simplest and probably the earliest capstan is the vertical winder of the kind used by Fontana in Rome in 1586, but this prime mover, is, very likely, of ancient origin. From the late Middle Ages onwards, there appeared an abundance of imaginative designs for animal-driven capstans and treadmills; many were purely theoretical. For example, Olaus Magnus (1490–1557) mentions in his *History of the Nordic People*, published in 1555, that, in the fifteenth century, a treadmill driven by Nordic brown bears was in use at the Falu copper mine in Sweden, and although the Stora Kopparberg company, which still owns the mine, used advanced techniques even in the Middle Ages, it is probable that Olaus Magnus did not recognize that the story was a joke.

A remarkable warship, propelled by ox-driven paddle-wheels, is described by the author known as Anonymus Byzantinus ("the unknown from Byzantinum"!) in his work *De re bellicis*, which dates from the middle of the sixth century. Byzantinus was a military engineer in the employ of the Byzantine emperor Justinian I (482?–565), who is probably best known as the builder of Hagia Sophia, "the church of divine wisdom", in Constantinople (antiquity's Byzantium). The vessel described was driven by three pairs of paddle-wheels, each being turned by a capstan driven by a pair of oxen.

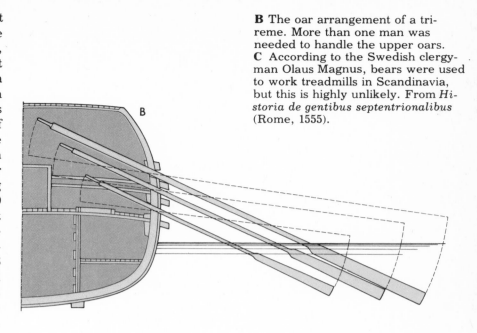

B The oar arrangement of a trireme. More than one man was needed to handle the upper oars.
C According to the Swedish clergyman Olaus Magnus, bears were used to work treadmills in Scandinavia, but this is highly unlikely. From *Historia de gentibus septentrionalibus* (Rome, 1555).

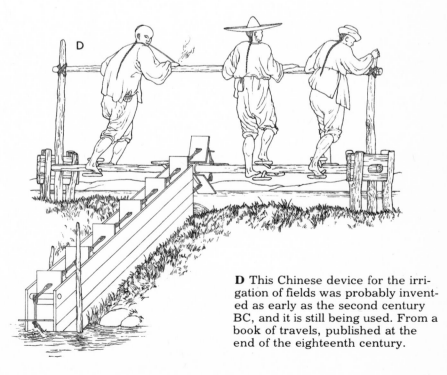

D This Chinese device for the irrigation of fields was probably invented as early as the second century BC, and it is still being used. From a book of travels, published at the end of the eighteenth century.

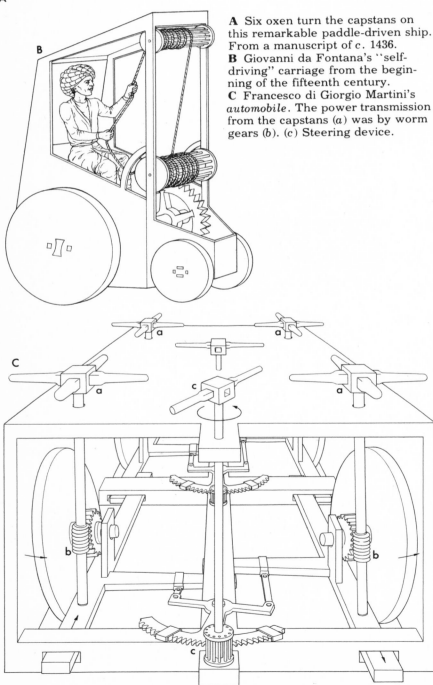

A Six oxen turn the capstans on this remarkable paddle-driven ship. From a manuscript of *c.* 1436.
B Giovanni da Fontana's "self-driving" carriage from the beginning of the fifteenth century.
C Francesco di Giorgio Martini's *automobile*. The power transmission from the capstans (*a*) was by worm gears (*b*). (*c*) Steering device.

Byzantinus claims that the mere din of this ox-machine was enough to scare the enemy away! The ship was probably never built, although technically it could have been. Byzantinus really gives free rein to his imagination in *De re bellicis* and suggests other incredible constructions, such as a temporary wartime bridge, which consisted of a gigantic sack of hide. The sack was to be filled with air from two bellows, and the troops were then to march dry-shod across the river!

What is interesting here is that the paddle-wheel was being discussed as a technical possibility in the sixth century AD, although Byzantinus may have based his design on an even older one. This kind of propulsion, in more or less unrealistic designs, also appears here and there in mediaeval literature. A German manuscript from the early fifteenth century illustrates a hand-driven device for powering paddle-wheels on a boat. However, the poor man in the boat looks slightly nonplussed by the impressive cog-wheel! Good advice for him would be to throw the machinery overboard and get himself a pair of oars.

The potential of muscle power boosted by capstans and windlasses inspired many designers to produce curious inventions. From the Middle Ages onwards, many suggestions for self-propelled carriages were put forward. Around 1410, the Italian architect Giovanni Fontana illustrated a hand-driven carriage with an intricate gearing in which the machine elements are very interesting examples of contemporary technology. The driving wheel and the upper "roller" are similar to those used then in windmills, and their configuration is usually known as the "lantern" design, which was used throughout the era of water and wind power. The carriage's large cog-wheel has teeth of a shape similar to those in Hero's writings and in the Antikythera device.

Another remarkable carriage was that designed by the Italian engineer Francesco di Giorgio Martini (1439–1502) in the late fifteenth century. Again, this design probably never left the drawing-board. All four wheels have individual drives powered by winch-type capstans, and power transmission is by worm gears. Unlike most similar designs, this has a steering device. Giorgio Martini called his creation *automobile*, i.e., self-moving, and as far as we know, this is the word's earliest appearance in literature.

The capstan is an example of how a great length of time can elapse between the first and the last applications of an invention. Another example is the treadmill; it was used in the building-crane described by Vitruvius, as well as in the port-and-derrick cranes which were in use in Central Europe as late as the nineteenth century. Many of the latter have been preserved as monuments of the history of technology.

In the latter part of the eighteenth century, many horse-wheels which had been used to power industrial machines, such as machine tools and machines in the textile industry, were replaced. Horse-wheels powered the first spinning-machines in England, among them Sir Richard Arkwright's pioneer machine of 1769, which, in 1771, was adapted to take power from a water-wheel; later, it was converted to steam. The use of the horse-wheel in agriculture, on the other hand, increased in the nineteenth century, and such machines as chaff-cutters, threshing-machines, and hay-hoists were all driven by horse-wheels. From the latter part of the nineteenth century on, horse-wheels were used also to drive milk separators.

Water Power

The origins of the water-wheel and its earliest forms are not yet clear. The first reference to it in Roman literature was around the time of the birth of Christ, but we know that the power of falling water had been exploited in the Far East about six hundred years

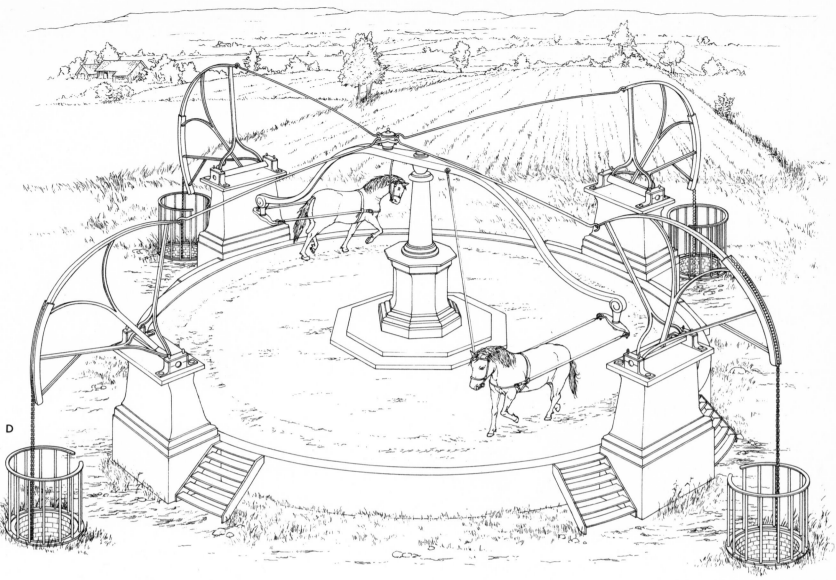

D

E

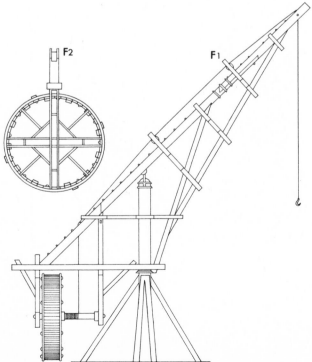

F2

F1

D A two-horse-whim, used for raising water from four wells. The illustration is based on an eighteenth-century model in the Museo di Storia della Scienza, Florence.
E A mediaeval, treadmill-powered port crane in the Belgian city of Bruges. The sledge in the foreground was probably used for transporting the casks on land. After a Flemish calendar from the beginning of the sixteenth century.
F A treadmill-powered crane (1) from the eighteenth century. Cranes of this type were used for hundreds of years; a similar device was described by Vitruvius. (2) The treadmill.

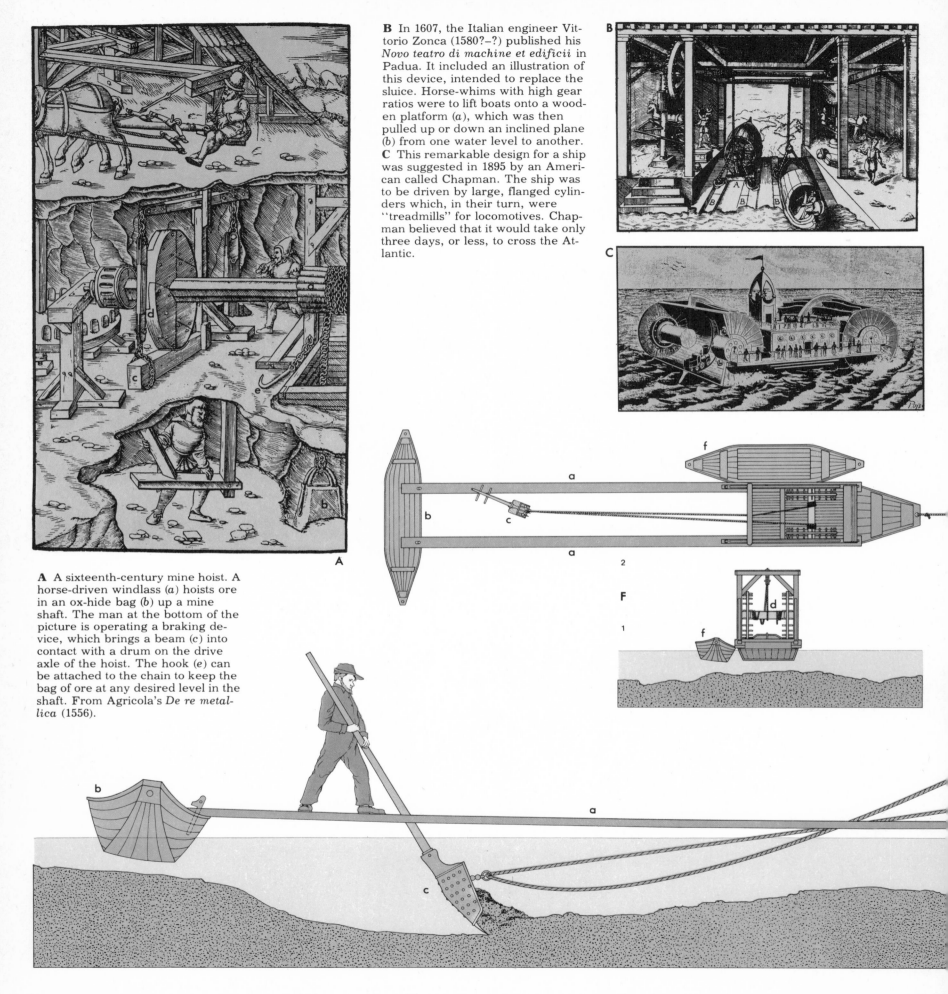

B In 1607, the Italian engineer Vittorio Zonca (1580?–?) published his *Novo teatro di machine et edificii* in Padua. It included an illustration of this device, intended to replace the sluice. Horse-whims with high gear ratios were to lift boats onto a wooden platform (*a*), which was then pulled up or down an inclined plane (*b*) from one water level to another.

C This remarkable design for a ship was suggested in 1895 by an American called Chapman. The ship was to be driven by large, flanged cylinders which, in their turn, were "treadmills" for locomotives. Chapman believed that it would take only three days, or less, to cross the Atlantic.

A A sixteenth-century mine hoist. A horse-driven windlass (*a*) hoists ore in an ox-hide bag (*b*) up a mine shaft. The man at the bottom of the picture is operating a braking device, which brings a beam (*c*) into contact with a drum on the drive axle of the hoist. The hook (*e*) can be attached to the chain to keep the bag of ore at any desired level in the shaft. From Agricola's *De re metallica* (1556).

D In 1878, when the Swedish engineer de Laval launched his milk separator, he had also designed a horse-whim to drive it. As can be seen from the illustration, the gear ratio was considerable. The separator worked best at speeds exceeding 7,000 rpm.

E This monumental horse treadmill was intended to power a mine pump and was designed in the early eighteenth century by an Englishman, Walter Churchman. However, it is most unlikely that it ever got beyond the drawing-board.

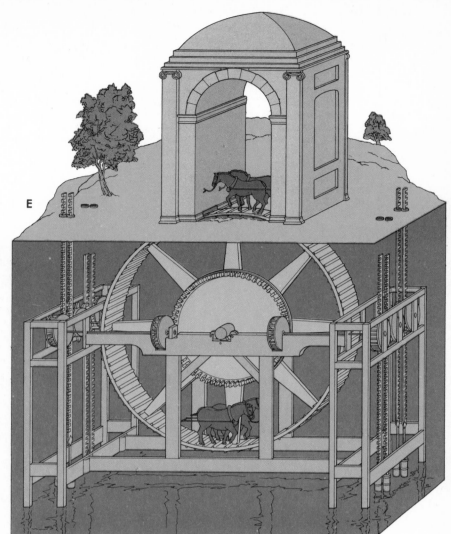

F An early dredger; (**1**) from the front, (**2**) from above, (**3**) in operation. During the first half of the eighteenth century, many dredgers on pontoons, with outriggers (*a*), were built in France. The construction remained in use until well into the twentieth century. The outriggers were often double and fastened to a small boat (*b*). The dredger shovel (*c*), which was of iron and had a sturdy wooden handle, was hauled in by a windlass (*d*), driven by one or more treadmills (*e*). A barge (*f*) was often moored alongside to take the dredged material.

A The noria, with its jars and paddles, is considered to be the oldest type of water-wheel. Before it came into use, only jars had been mounted on the wheels, which were rotated by muscle power.

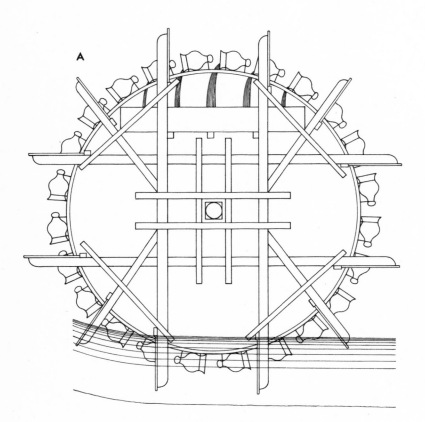

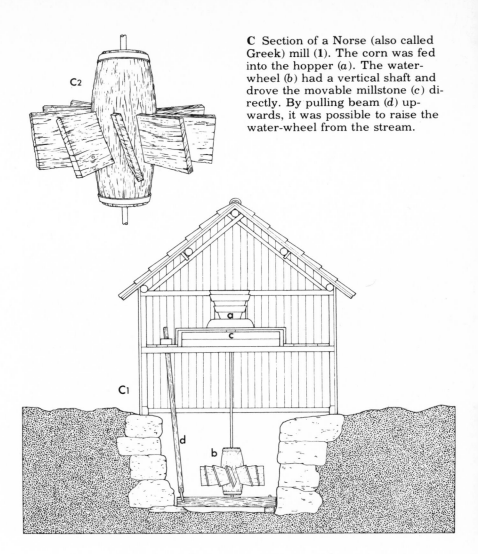

C Section of a Norse (also called Greek) mill (**1**). The corn was fed into the hopper (*a*). The water-wheel (*b*) had a vertical shaft and drove the movable millstone (*c*) directly. By pulling beam (*d*) upwards, it was possible to raise the water-wheel from the stream.

B This more developed type of noria is usually attributed to Philo. The rotary movement of the water-driven paddle-wheel (*a*) is transmitted by means of a chain (*b*) to an upper shaft (*c*) on which a triangular drum (*d*) is mounted. When *d* rotates, the water-filled jars are brought up to be emptied in a pipe (*e*).

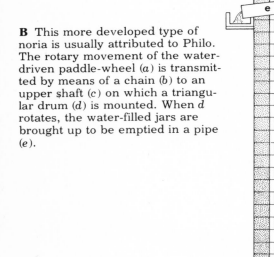

previously. A. P. Usher believes that three different devices developed independently in different geographical locations. The simplest, and probably the earliest, is thought to have been the paddle-wheel, driven by the current of a river and used to raise water from it. A further extension of the noria, as this device was called in the Mediterranean countries, has been described by Philo of Byzantium, but Drachmann considers that it is likely that, at a later stage, these details were added to Philo's original text during translation. Usher's second device is the horizontal, or Norse, water-wheel, which achieved the first "automation" in household work. The third is the water-wheel often attributed to Vitruvius, which dates back to the first decades after the birth of Christ.

We have already mentioned Hero's use of falling water to drive one of his automata. But the dramatic début of the water-wheel as a prime mover took place in ancient Rome where, within only a few decades, it had quickly become widespread. The first account of a water-wheel in the West is attributed to the Roman engineer Vitruvius, who describes in detail the design and application of this innovation in his book *De architectura*. The first form of this wheel had a vertical shaft and inclined blades, and was used to drive grinding mills. Long previously, grain had been ground in hand-mills; this was a task for the womenfolk that, in large households, often took up most of their day. The water-mill caused, therefore, something of a revolution, and, while poets were loud in praise of this new wonder, they also raised a moral finger of warning at the

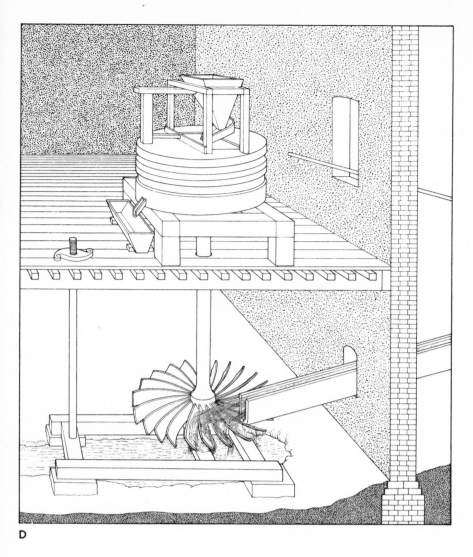

D

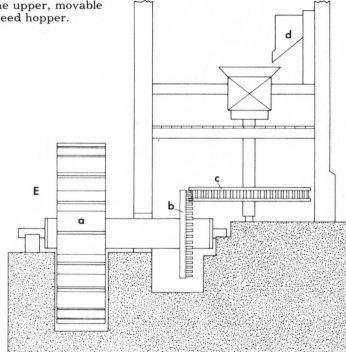

D This type of mill was once common in the French districts of Provence and Dauphine. The water was led into a chute and drove a vertical-shafted wheel. The lever in the mill window was used to close off the chute.
E This mill with its gearwheels has been described by Vitruvius. On the shaft of the water-wheel (*a*), a toothed wheel (*b*) is mounted. It meshes with another wheel (*c*) which drives the upper, movable millstone. (*d*) Feed hopper.

same time. What, they asked, will the women do now?

This labour-saving device soon spread to other parts of Europe. The Greek poet Antipater of Thessalonica praised the mill in the following lines:

Stop grinding, ye women who toil at the mill,
Sleep on, though the crowing cocks announce the break of day.
Demeter has commanded the water nymphs
to do the work of your hands.
Jumping onto the wheel, they turn the axle
Which drives the gears and the heavy millstones.

In his book *Moving Forward*, Henry Ford writes that the main importance of the machine in the evolution of mankind has been that it has lifted the heavy toil off man's back and placed it on its own shoulders. The same thoughts as Antipater had had two thousand years previously, but now expressed in prose.

Philo's description of the noria dates from the third century BC, the horizontal water-wheel appeared in the first century BC, and the actual water-wheel came some fifty years later. The sharp typological distinction made by Usher between these three designs has a certain appeal nowadays, but in reality these distinctions may not have been so clear-cut. The noria was, apparently, not very widespread in the Mediterranean countries, probably because it requires an abundant supply of swiftly running water. It is rather difficult to dismiss completely the notion that the noria may have belonged to

the same category as the frivolous designs of the Alexandrian school, as Philo's inventions included a whistling water-wheel. This consisted of a paddle-wheel with a horizontal shaft and sealed cavities between the blades. Each cavity had a whistle, which sounded when the water forced the air out. It is not completely unlikely that some practical technician took the joke seriously, eliminated the whistling cavities, and connected the wheel to, say, a mill! After all, the gearing necessary in such a construction was already quite well known.

Between the noria and Vitruvius's water-wheel, there is another form, in which pails are suspended from the blades of a paddle-wheel. This method of drawing water was used in India and Mesopotamia. It was quite a short step for a practical-minded engineer to remove the pails and enlarge the blades. A simple water-wheel of this kind was used to provide motive power for the water-drawing version of the Archimedean screw, which was especially common in Egypt and is still used in many parts of Africa.

The water-mill spread so quickly because its design was simple, and because it afforded relief from the heavy, monotonous toil of grinding grain. As modern advertising would put it, it was "simply indispensable in every household". Still, the water-mill had its limitations. Its output would not now be thought impressive, being only about half a horsepower, or three to four hundred watts; besides, it could not be regulated easily. A horizontal shaft and a reduction gear between the mill and the millstone were obvious steps to take to

A Different types of water-wheels with horizontal shafts. (**1**) Undershot water-wheel. (**2**) Breast-wheel. The flow of water was regulated with a sluice-gate (*a*). (**3**) Overshot water-wheel.

B A reconstruction of a lock system, here seen from the side (**1**) and from above (**2**), which was built during the first half of the nineteenth century in the United States. The arrangement was intended for the transport of barges between two different water levels, and the transport took place on carriages running on rails. The two parallel locks (*a*, *b*) are here shown during the drained phase of the cycle. A carriage (*c*) with a barge (*d*) has just been pulled up the rails (*e*) in lock *a*, while lock *b* is not being used at the moment. If it were used, the barge using it would reach the lower water level at the same time as *d* reached the upper. (**3**) The carriages in the locks were pulled by a chain (*f*), which was arranged in an M-shaped loop over a sprocket (*g*) and two wheels (*h*), one on each carriage (seen here in one carriage in **1** and **2**). (**4**) The sprocket was driven by a water-wheel (*i*) by way of two gearwheels (*j*, *k*) and a mitre gearing (*l*), whose direction of rotation could be reversed. When the carriages had reached their respective turning-points, the water-wheel (*i*) was stopped, the fore lock gate (*m*) was raised by hand, and, at the same time, a sash gate (*n*) was slid over the lock's drainage opening (*o*). A smaller water-wheel (*p*) was then started; by way of a gear arrangement (*q*; shown at **5**), *p* opened the rear lock gate (*r*; shown in detail at **6**) by lowering it into a shaft (*s*). Water then rushed into the lock and lifted the barge from its carriage at the same time as the water pressure provided an adequate sealing of *m* and *n*. When the barge had been towed out of the lock chamber and another barge had taken its place, *r* was closed again by the gear arrangement *q*, whose direction of rotation had now been reversed. When *r* had almost reached its topmost position, it automatically slid *n* away by means of a chain (*t*), and the water in the lock chamber ran out through *o*. Lock gate *m* was opened, and the new barge, now placed on carriage *c*, was pulled down the rails. When the barge going upwards weighed (*Continued below, left*)

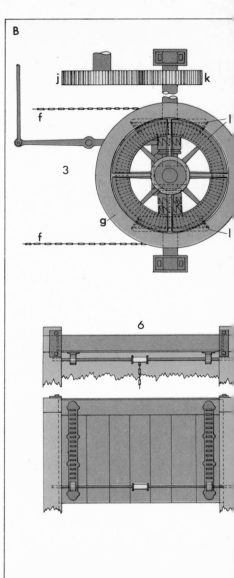

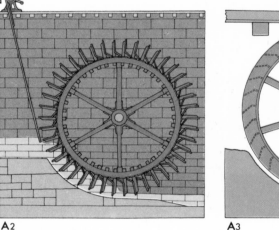

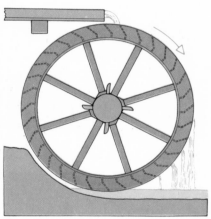

A1

A2

A3

less than the one going downwards. or when only a downward-going barge was being transported, the water-wheel (*i*) was braked by the arrangement shown at **7**.

C The Roman mill plant (**1**) at Barbegal was erected in the early fourth century AD and no longer exists. It may possibly have looked as shown here. (**2**) Plan of the structure. Water from the aqueduct (*a*) was gathered in a basin (*b*) and directed into two chutes (*c*) over the water-wheels.

C1

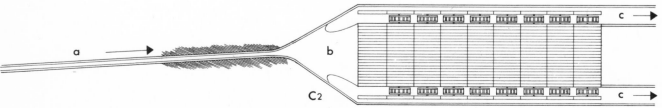

C2

D In this seventeenth-century smithy, the same water-wheel is employed to drive the hammer-forge and two bellows. From J. de Strada's *Kunstliche Abriss allerhand Wasser- Wind- Ross- und Hand Mühlen* (Frankfurt-on-Main, 1617).
E Agricola included this mine-ventilation device in his *De re metallica*, published in 1556. An overshot water-wheel (*a*) rotates a fan (*b*) whose four blades are equipped with long feathers. The fan is enclosed in a drum (*c*), and the air is pumped into the mine through a hollow log (*d*).
F Water-wheel-powered bellows. Protrusions on the shaft of an overshot wheel press first one and then the other of the bellows together. After a manuscript from the fifteenth century.

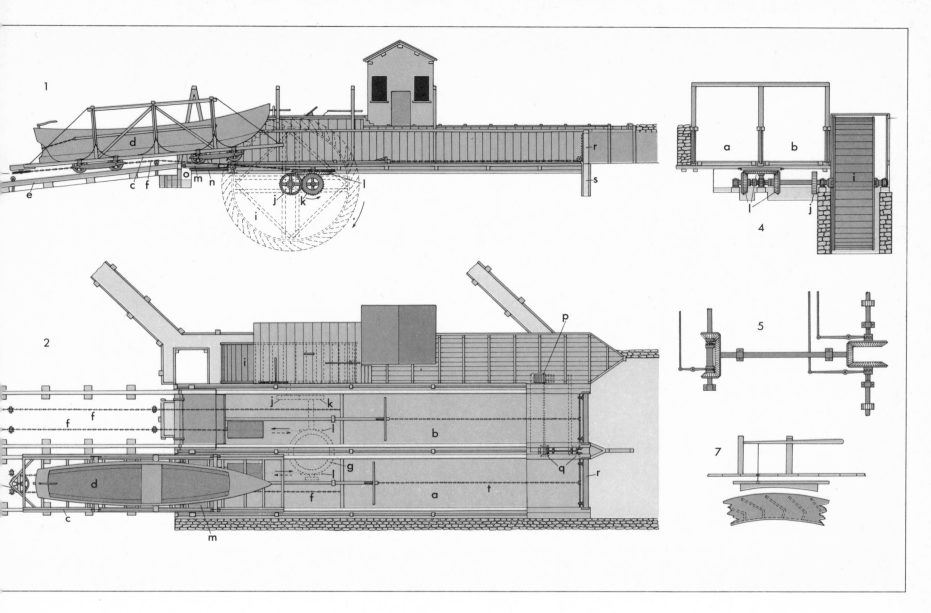

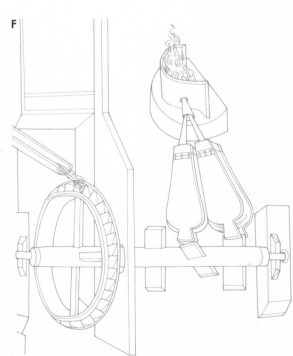

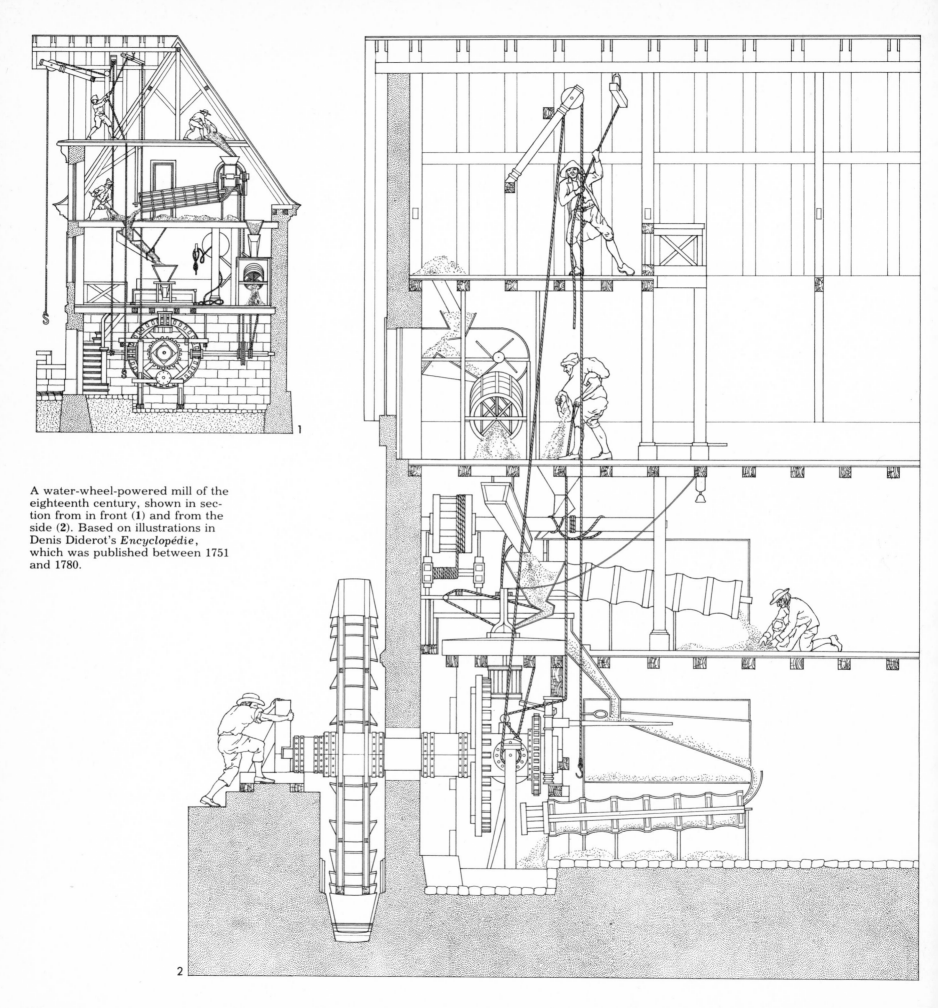

A water-wheel-powered mill of the eighteenth century, shown in section from in front (1) and from the side (2). Based on illustrations in Denis Diderot's *Encyclopédie*, which was published between 1751 and 1780.

improve the design. Quite early on, it must have been necessary to adjust the speed of the wheel, which was largely determined by the speed of the current, to produce optimal milling output.

It should be clear from what has just been said that there does not exist any clear, intrinsic distinction between the different types of water-wheel described above. It is quite likely that they are versions of one and the same phenomenon, the origin of which is still difficult to trace.

During the first centuries AD, the water-mill spread relatively slowly beyond the boundaries of the Roman empire into the north of Europe. However, according to the Danish archaeologist A. Steenberg, the water-mill was known in Denmark at the time of the birth of Christ. In the fourth century AD, the Romans erected a large mill at Barbegal, near Arles, France. Water was supplied from a spring and, via an aqueduct, from the river Arcoule. The aqueduct, which has impressive dimensions—6 ft 7in (2 m) wide and 18 ft 5 in (5.6 m) deep—slopes at an angle of 30° at Barbegal. The eight pairs of overshot wheels have each a diameter of 7 ft 3 in (2.2 m) and a width of 2 ft 4 in (0.7 m), and each wheel drives a pair of millstones. The flour production of the mill, estimated at 2.8 tons a day, would have greatly exceeded the local needs, and most of it was shipped to Rome via the port of Arles. Water-mills are mentioned in an eighth-century Irish law, ''Senchus Mor'' and are known also to have existed in Central Europe. Further, a document of the period mentions a sawmill driven by a water-wheel.

After the disintegration of the Roman empire, most of the products of its advanced engineering technology fell into disuse—its aqueducts, baths, arenas, and so on—while water-mills actually seem to have been employed more widely and further improved in design. In 1086 in England, the great land census recorded in the Domesday Book that there were more than 5,600 water-mills in the country, which was then relatively sparsely populated. Lewis Mumford has pointed out that this equals one mill per four hundred inhabitants—and this in a country situated "on the outskirts of European civilization".

Already at the time of the Domesday Book, water-wheels drove not only flour-mills, but also ore crushers and forge hammers, and by the end of the Middle Ages, they were used generally in mining to raise ore and to power bellows. Water-wheels drove machines in other processes, too—wire-drawing, leather tanning, cloth fulling, rag-pounding (in paper-making), sawing, crushing minerals for dye-stuffs, to name only some of them.

Floating Mills

An interesting application of the water-wheel occurs in the floating water-mill. Equally interesting is the story of its invention. In 537, when Rome was besieged by the Goths, the eternal city was defended by the Byzantine general Belisarius, who had occupied most of the Roman provinces on the Italian peninsula a year or so earlier. At that time, most of the water-mills in Rome were driven by water from the aqueducts (in actual fact, this is a token of the decline of Roman technology). In an attempt to starve the Romans out, the besieging army cut off the water supply. However, Belisarius found a way out of this dilemma. Possibly inspired by Byzantinus's ox-driven vessel, he caused flour-mills driven by paddle-wheels to be installed in boats that were then moored in the Tiber; Rome's flour supply was thus ensured.

News of this achievement spread far and wide, and within a few centuries, there were floating mills both in Venice and Baghdad. In the twelfth century, three were built under the arches of the Grand Pont in Paris. Towards the end of the Middle Ages, there were many such mills in use on the great rivers of Europe, pumping water or grinding grain; several on the Rhine at Cologne, built in the fifteenth century, were still in use three hundred years later.

The most spectacular installation of this kind was, without a doubt, the pumping station at Marly. Built in the 1680s to supply water to the many fountains of Versailles, the pumping station had 235 pumps, which were driven by thirteen great water-wheels and which pumped water from the river to the reservoirs 525 ft (c.160 m) above. The pumping was carried out in three stages, and the power was transmitted by two rows of oscillating rods and levers. A builder from Liège, Rennequin Sualem, supervised the construction of this enormous plant, which took 1,800 men eight years to complete. The original output was about 125 horsepower, and the capacity was 1.1 million gallons (5 million litres) per day. The plant was difficult to maintain, especially the energy-consuming rod-and-lever transmission. In 1725, the Marly machine was entirely rebuilt, and in the early nineteenth century, a steam-engine of 150 horsepower was installed.

The Ballet-dancing Machine

The Marly pumping station was severely criticized by contemporary engineers, who maintained that the ideas behind the design were erroneous. Undershot water-wheels were very inefficient, and so was the rod-and-lever transmission. The designer defended himself by claiming that there was nothing else available. Maybe he did not know that, more than a century previously, Juanelo Turriano, a talented Spanish engineer of Italian origin in the employ of the emperor, Charles V, had faced the same sort of problem, in Toledo, and solved it successfully. Little is known about his background, but he was over eighty when he died in 1585. He was first employed by the emperor when, as a youth, he managed to repair an ornamental water-clock, which the foremost clockmakers of the day had failed to mend. It is considered to have been of the complicated type described in Chapter Two. Turriano later built a number of other clocks, including a very advanced, mechanical ornamental clock for the emperor. Many of the difficult technical problems of the day were solved by Turriano, one of them being how to provide the city of Toledo with water.

Toledo lies in the centre of a rich mining area and had already grown into a major city, with over 200,000 inhabitants. Its water was carted from the river Tajo, some 1,970 ft (600 m) below the city, in leather bags borne by mules. As the city grew, this means of supplying it with water became inadequate, and German mining engineers were called in to build a pumping station. At first, everything worked satisfactorily; but later the pipes burst.

Some years earlier, the emperor had been residing in the Alcázar in Toledo, and in his entourage was Turriano. When the Germans' installation failed, Turriano was commissioned to do the job, and he could soon demonstrate his solution with a perfect working model, which did not include a single pipe! In the early 1540s, after six years of work, Turriano had the full-scale plant ready.

A combined water-wheel and noria continuously filled a container with water. This was then poured into one end of a "cradle", which was the central element of the whole design. The water-wheel also drove a reciprocating rod-and-lever transmission, which rocked a whole chain of cradles so that each cradle poured its contents into the one above it. The result was a mechanized bucket brigade.

The Toledo waterworks received a great deal of attention all over Europe, and the graceful movements of the transmission system and the cradles, from which not a drop of water spilled, inspired an enthusiastic spectator to describe the plant as "the ballet-dancing machine". In 1645, a ballet, "El Mago", was performed in Madrid, the dancers imitating the movements of Turriano's waterworks,

A The giant Marly machine, which was built on the River Seine in the 1680s. Thirteen water-wheels powered 235 force pumps, which pumped up to 1 million gallons (5,000 m³) of river water into the reservoirs daily. The reservoirs were situated 525 ft (160 m) above the river.

B (**1**) One of the enormous wheels of the Marly machine. On the shaft of the water-wheel was a crank (*a*), whose rotary movement was transformed into a reciprocating movement by a connecting rod (*b*). At the other end of the connecting rod was a rocking arm (*c*), which reciprocated round a fixed shaft (*d*) and was connected to the rocking arm (*e*), which drove the pumps (*f*). (*g*) A device for raising and lowering a sluice (*h*). (*i*) A gate which prevented floating objects from being brought towards the water-wheel by the river water. (**2**) The water-wheels also drove the rows of rocking levers and rods (*j*), which were used to drive the pumps (*m*) in the basins (*n*) at the pumping stations by means of rocking arms (*k*, *l*). (*o*) Detail, showing how the pumps were connected to the water-pipe.

C An eighteenth-century tug, shown here from above (**1**), in cross-section (**2**), and in longitudinal-section (**3**). When the paddle-wheels were rotated by the stream, the tug was pulled upstream by a chain (*a*), one end of which was attached to the

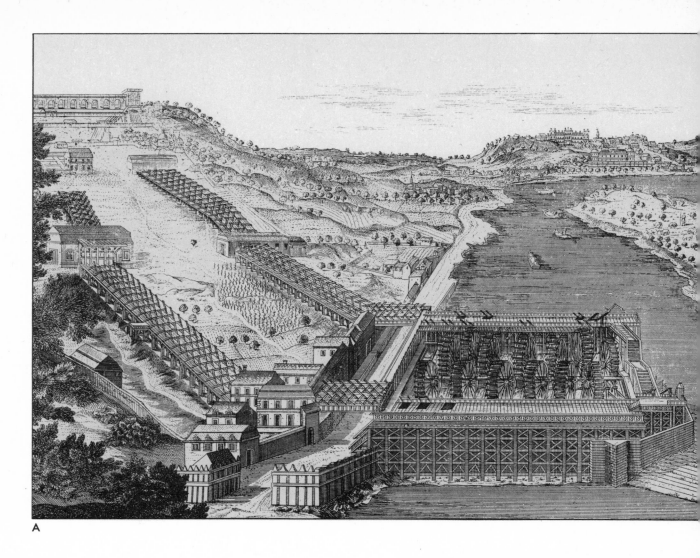

A

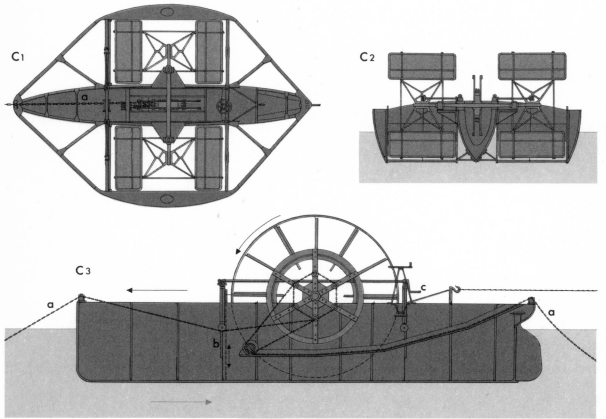

C₁

C₂

C₃

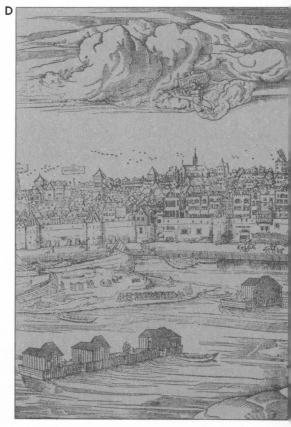

D

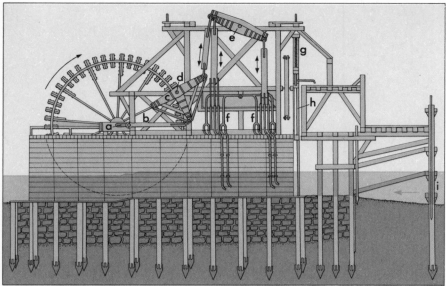

B1

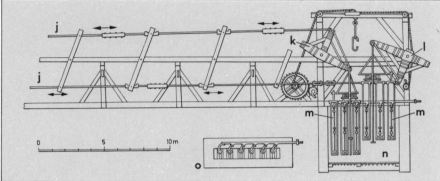

B2

mooring-place upstream whereas the other end ran round a block at the mooring-place downstream and was attached to the tug. When the tug was to go downstream, gates (b) were lowered in front of the paddle-wheels by means of a crank (c).
D A woodcut of 1531 showing floating mills in the Rhine at Cologne, Germany.
E Section of a floating mill. (a) Water-wheel.(b) The enclosed mill-stones. (c) Feed hopper.

E

moving with arms crossed as if to transfer water from one to the other in a chain.

Agostino Ramelli, who described the Toledo waterworks in his book *Le diverse et artificiose machine*, published in 1588, states that the capacity of the works equalled that of three hundred mules working day and night, tended by almost as many mule drivers. That capacity is about a fifth of what Louis XIV of France, the Sun King, needed for his fountains in Versailles. Technically, however, it would not have been difficult for Turriano to have built his works on a larger scale or to have doubled or even trebled the number of cradles by using parallel chains.

When the Sun King had his magnificent baroque palace designed, the architects made a serious mistake in not ensuring that the water supply in the area was sufficient. There was, in fact, no water, so enormous sums of money had to be spent building the Marly pumping station, in order that Versailles could be supplied with water.

Tidal Power-stations

The term "lunar power-station", which is sometimes used instead of "tidal power-station", originates in today's France, where a power-station driven by the tide has been built in the tidal estuary of the river Rance in Brittany. The idea of exploiting the tide (and, indirectly, the moon) to produce energy is far from new. As far back as the 1130s, a mill was built near the mouth of the river Adour in France, and a century later, several tide-mills were in operation near Venice. The first tide-mill, however, is believed to have been built in the third century AD in the port of Dover in England. A tide-driven pump was installed on the Thames in 1582 by Peter Morice. This pumped almost 4 million gallons (18 million litres) of water per day up to a tank more than 130 ft (c. 40 m) higher up. However, the design was unsuccessful, and the scheme was soon abandoned.

The Golden Age of Water Power

From the late sixteenth to the late eighteenth century, machines were built to exploit the fall of water with ever-increasing efficiency. Some impressive installations are described by the German Georg Bauer (1494–1555), also called Agricola, in his great work *De re metallica*, published the year after his death. (An English translation was made in the early 1900s by the young mining engineer Herbert C. Hoover, later president of the United States, and his wife.) A clear picture of the progress made during these years in machine construction is provided by the great books on what is now called technology; the best known of these are *Le diverse et artificiose machine* by Agostino Ramelli (Paris, 1588), *Les Raisons des Forces Mouvantes* by Salomon de Caus (Paris, 1615), and *Theatrum machinarum* by Jacob Leupold (Leipzig, 1725). Such books were originally called "art" books, in the sense of human skill rather than nature, while the term "fine arts" was used to designate painting, sculpture, and so on. The word "technology" in its present meaning was not in general use until the early nineteenth century. Until then, for example, the chief engineer of a mine was called the "art master".

Water Turbines

The first turbine is one of the few phenomena in the history of technology that can be dated accurately, as both the machine and its name resulted from a competition held in France, in 1826. La Société d'Encouragement pour l'Industrie Nationale had offered a prize of six thousand francs for the design of a water-wheel for use in industry; one of the conditions was that the water-wheel must work under water without any loss of efficiency. One of the competitors, Claude Burdin (1790–1873), suggested that such a wheel should be called "turbine", from the Latin word *turbo*, a top. Burdin's own

A

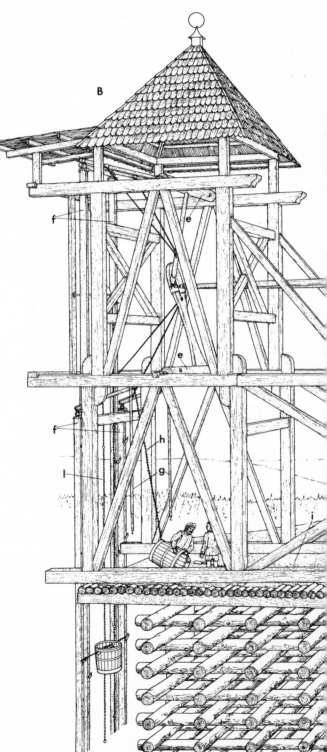

B

A Juanelo Turriano's *Artificio*, which provided Toledo with water from the river Tajo. The water-wheel (*a*) continually filled a container (*b*) with water and, at the same time, drove two rows of oscillating rods and levers (*c*) so that ladles (*d*) kept rocking to and fro. The water was thus poured from ladle to ladle all the time. After an illustration in Ramelli's *Le diverse et artificiose machine*, 1588.

B Despite the fact that Christopher Polhem's plans for a new ore-hoisting mechanism at the Swedish Falu mine had been met with the utmost distrust by the "art master" there, Olof Henriksson Trygg, this *Machina Nova* was erected at Blankstöten in 1694. Trygg, however, insisted upon building an ordinary hoisting mechanism beside Polhem's machine, so that the two devices could be compared when hoisting ore from the same depth. It turned out that more than twenty-two barrels of ore could be hoisted in one hour with Polhem's new construction, whereas it was possible to hoist only sixteen with the ordinary mechanism.
The *Machina Nova* was powered by an overshot water-wheel (*a*), on whose shaft a gearwheel (*b*) was mounted. It meshed with another gearwheel (*c*), which had one end of a row of oscillating rods and levers (*d*) attached to its periphery. The

other end of *d* was attached to two opposed cross-levers (*e*), to which two pairs of 195-ft (59.4 m) long rods (*f*) were fastened. Each pair was equipped with fifteen pairs of hooks. Each barrel was fastened to a bar which was laid on the pair of hooks at the bottom of the shaft. As the rods were alternately brought upwards and downwards, the bar with its barrel was brought from hook-pair to hook-pair, so that the barrel was hoisted. At ground level, two suspended hooks (*g*) were fastened to the rim of the barrel, and an iron chain (*h*) was hooked to its bottom. The chain was suspended from one of the arms of the cross-lever (*e*), and when it was raised by *d*, the ore was emptied onto the pithead frame (*i*), where it was loaded onto carts. These were driven onto a bridge (*j*), which, too, was raised and lowered by another cross-lever (*k*) on the row of oscillating rods and levers. The ore was then brought into the so-called bucking-house, where it was separated from the barren rock. The empty barrels were attached to an endless chain (*l*) to be brought down again into the mine shaft. The chain was equipped with thirty small, equidistant balls, and its speed was checked by two iron forks, so that the barrels were kept from too rapid a descent.

104

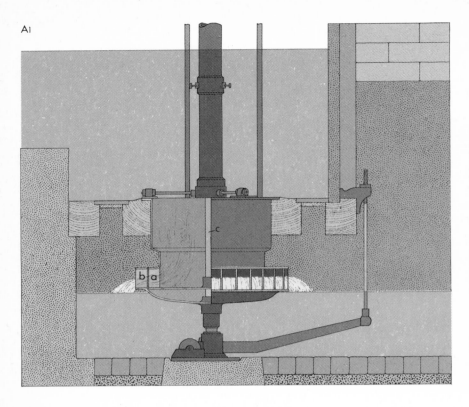

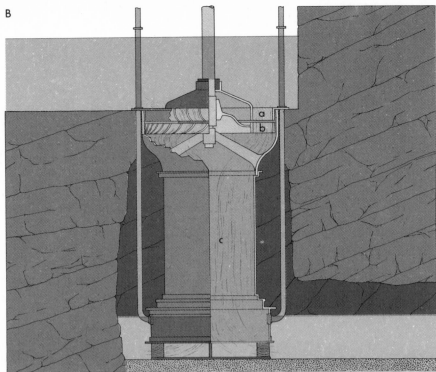

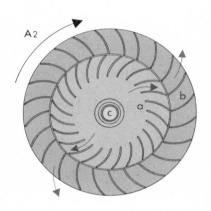

A Like all the early turbines, Fourneyron's (**1**) was a reaction turbine. Water passes under pressure through such a turbine and transmits its energy to the runner by pressure against its blades. Fourneyron's turbine had two concentric, horizontal wheels (**2**); the fixed, inner wheel (a) had guide vanes which directed the water through blades set at an angle on the runner (b). The shaft (c) was vertical. The amount of water passing through the turbine could be regulated by the lowering or raising of a ring which was mounted between the guide vanes and the runner.

entry was not successful, however, as it did not fulfil the necessary conditions; the young engineer Bénoit Fourneyron (1802–67) won with an interesting design featuring two concentric horizontal wheels. The fixed inner wheel had curved guide vanes which directed the water against runner blades on the outer wheel, which is known as the rotor. The efficiency of this outward-flow radial turbine, as the type is called, was as high as eighty to eighty-five per cent, but it had a disadvantage in that turbulence occurred at certain speeds when the water left the guide vanes. However, Fourneyron's technically elegant design set the style for a number of new water turbines which were built during the remainder of the nineteenth century. Later, guide vanes came to be used also in steam turbines. The first Fourneyron turbine was installed between 1835 and 1837 at Saint-Blaise in the Black Forest. This type of turbine spread rapidly all over Europe, often replacing the undershot wheels which were then used where the head of water was small, and which had a very low efficiency—twenty per cent or less.

One of the variations which lay very near Fourneyron's design was a turbine in which the guide vanes were installed above the rotor. This was Karl Anton Henschel's idea, and in 1841, he installed such a turbine in a stone-polishing works in Brunswick, Germany, where a

Frenchman called Jonval saw it and, in 1843, took out a patent for the design.

Another variation of Fourneyron's turbine was arranged with the rotor within the guide vanes, so that the water flowed against the central rotor through an outer circle of fixed guide vanes. First suggested by the Frenchman Jean V. Poncelet in the late 1820s, this idea was patented as the inward-flow radial turbine in the United States by Samuel B. Howd in 1838. Two years later, James B. Francis (1815–92) built such a turbine, under licence from Howd, and achieved very good results with it. Francis later carried out a series of experiments in which he compared the performance of a Fourneyron-type turbine with that of his own, both turbines being installed in a factory in Lowell, north of Boston. The results of these experiments, carried out in the 1850s, were to determine the essential features of the type of turbine which was to become known as the Francis turbine. Considerable improvements, however, were made to this design by the Briton James Thomson (the elder brother of Lord Kelvin), who introduced adjustable guide vanes and curved blades on the rotor. These are still the characteristic features of this type of turbine. Thomson based the shape of the blades on the results of his theoretical studies of the vortices appearing in a centrifugal pump. The rotor is usually called a vortex wheel (from the Latin *vortex*, a whirlpool). In the 1860s, the Francis turbine began to replace the water-wheel and, by the turn of the century, had become the most commonly used turbine in hydroelectric power-stations.

A new type of turbine, whose invention was due to sheer chance, was the Pelton wheel. During the gold rush in California in the 1860s, the most common method of washing for gold was to flush the sand and gravel away with a jet of water under very high pressure. The water was usually led in pipes or hoses to the site from reservoirs higher up the river. About 1870, when the gold ran out, this piped water was often used to drive water-wheels. A mining engineer, Lester A. Pelton (1829–1908), who worked in these parts, had built a water-wheel with curved blades. One day, the water jet happened to strike the outer edges of the blades, and the speed of the wheel increased so much that it flew into pieces.

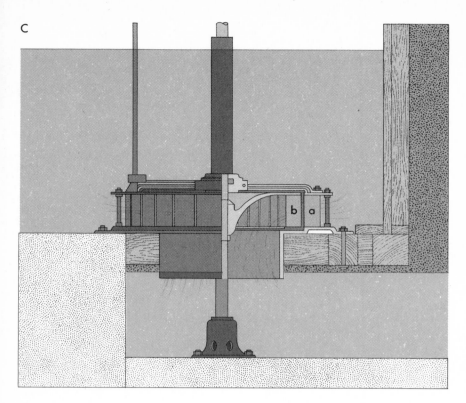

C

B In Jonval's axial-flow turbine, the guide-vane wheel (*a*) was placed above the runner (*b*), and both wheels had the same diameter. Since the turbine's outlet (*c*) was in the form of a cylindrical draft tube in which suction arose, it was possible to set the turbine wheels well above tail-race level and still make use of the head below the runner.
C An early Francis turbine. Turbines of this type can be mounted both vertically and horizontally and today are usually equipped with a helical flume casing which opens inwards, and with a draft tube. In the turbine shown here, water entered freely through the whole circumference and through the outer ring of guide vanes (*a*), which could be adjusted so that the amount of incoming water could be controlled. The inner runner (*b*) had curved blades, which increased the efficiency of the turbine.
D The Pelton turbine (**1**), an action turbine whose blades consisted of two ladles which were joined to an edge towards which a jet of water

was aimed. The jet thus completely changes its direction, as is shown by the explanatory sketch at **2**, and this meant that the force of the water jet was utilized to the full. The nozzle (*a*), through which the water was forced, was improved considerably by a Californian, Abner Doble, who equipped it with a needle (*b*).

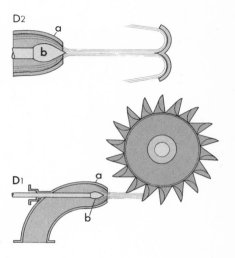

D2

D1

E In a tidal power plant, the turbines must have a high efficiency whether the tide is on its way out or in. Consequently, tubular turbine units are used for such power plants. In a tubular turbine unit, a Kaplan turbine (*a*) has its generator enclosed in a streamlined bulb (*b*), which is placed in the waterway. The power plant building (*c*) is erected above the turbine. (*d*) Water storage side. (*e*) Ocean side.

F The Kaplan turbine, a propeller turbine with a — usually — vertical shaft. In the Kaplan turbine, unlike all other propeller turbines, the runner's blades (*a*) were movable. The guide vanes (*b*) could also be turned and were automatically adjusted to an angle suitable to that of the blades by a "combiner", so that the turbine was efficient at different work-loads. A circular stay collar (*c*) absorbed the compressive forces acting on the flume casing (*d*). (*e*) Flume tube. All low-head, high-discharge propeller turbines had to be

E

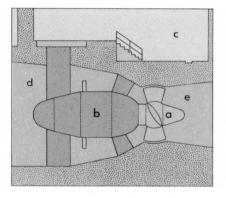

given amply dimensioned draft tubes (*f*), since the efficiency of the turbines depended on a strong pressure. However, if the height of the draft tube was too great, the water pressure around the runner became so low that cavitation posed a serious problem, and it was therefore sometimes necessary to mount the runner below tail-race level.

This intrigued Pelton. After long consideration, he realized that the power of the jet was best exploited when its direction was completely reversed by the blade. He changed the blade design to incorporate two buckets, whose edges were joined to form the middle of the blade. This split the jet of water in two, and the shape of the buckets caused both jets to reverse direction. One or more nozzles could be used to supply water to the wheel, which became known as the Pelton wheel or the jet-splitting double-bucket turbine. This type of turbine is especially suitable for large heads of water with a moderate or low rate of flow. Manufacture of the Pelton wheel began on an industrial scale in the 1880s.

A completely new idea in turbine design was put forward in the 1910s by an Austrian, Victor Kaplan (1876–1934). He had been trying to improve the Francis turbine, which, if the head of water is low, has a low effect, when he came upon a better idea and designed a turbine which had a vertical axle and a propeller-like rotor with variable-pitch blades. Kaplan patented his design in 1912 and 1913, and a number of the foremost turbine manufacturers began to produce the turbine under licence. In 1919, the first Kaplan turbine was installed, in a textile mill at Velm in Austria. It had an effect of 25.8 horsepower and a head of 7 ft 6 in (2.3 m). Several others of this size

F

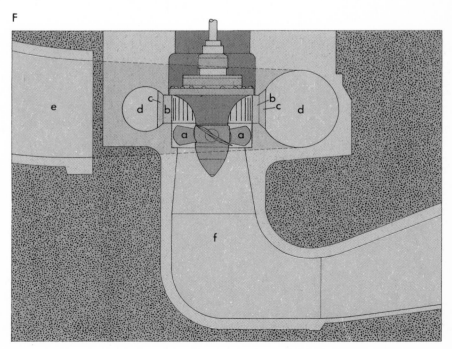

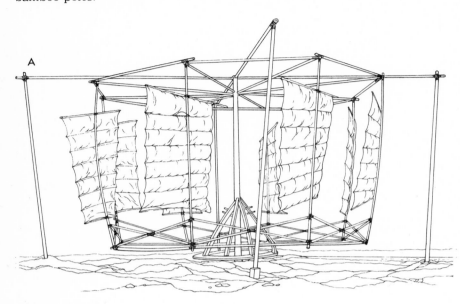

A In China, this type of vertical-shaft mill is still used in combination with a chain-pump for irrigation and for pumping brine into salines. The sails look very much like the sails on a junk, and it seems probable that the construction used to be built of bamboo poles.

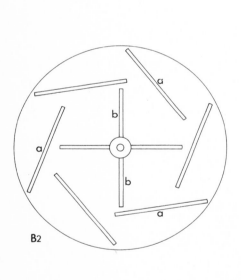

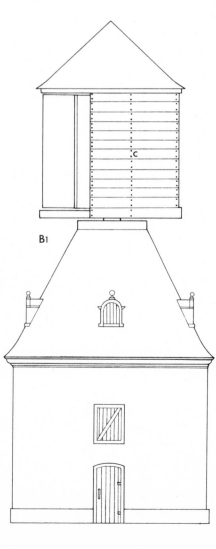

B A type of windmill (**1**) occurring in Poland and, possibly, Portugal in the eighteenth century. The mill had six guide vanes (*a*) and four sails (*b*) which were mounted round a vertical shaft; at **2**, the arrangement is shown as seen from above. A movable screen (*c*) was mounted round part of the circumference of the sails. It was used to adjust the action of the wind on the sails.

were taken into service elsewhere in the following year, and the future seemed bright for the Kaplan turbine. Just then, however, it was discovered that the rotor blades of the Velm turbine had become badly pitted. No reason could be found for this at first, but then Kaplan himself found the cause—cavitation, a phenomenon that occurs when a propeller turns at high speed under water; the flow of water around the propeller creates an area of low pressure on the suction side of the blade, and if the pressure falls enough, bubbles of steam are created. (Water can boil at temperatures way below 100°C—even at 0°C if the pressure is low enough.) When the steam bubbles condense on the blade, they corrode the surface.

This problem caused the manufacturers to have doubts about the Kaplan turbine, and they turned to other designs. At this time, 1920, the Swedish State Power Board was developing the hydroelectric possibilities of the Göta river. A power-station equipped with a Kaplan turbine was planned for Lilla Edet, and the Power Board asked the turbine manufacturer Ignaz Storek, of Kaplan's home town, Brünn, to build it. However, due to the cavitation problem, the project never got beyond the drawing board, so the State Board turned for help to a Swedish company, Karlstads Mekaniska Werkstad, which had built an experimental Kaplan turbine in 1914 and was now working on the cavitation problem. An order for a Kaplan turbine was placed, while a Francis turbine was ordered from another company, in case the Kaplan turbine should fail.

A hectic period of research and development now followed. The company's chief engineer, Olov Englesson (1884–1953), was in almost constant contact with Victor Kaplan. Among other things, the company developed a completely new steering system, in the form of a hydraulic servosystem, for turning the rotor blades. Against all the odds, the turbine was completed and taken into service in 1926, within the contracted time. It had an effect of 10,000 horsepower and a head of 20 ft (6.5 m). The diameter of the rotor was 19 ft (5.8 m). The Francis turbine was never needed, and the company eventually sold it.

Now that the ice was broken, many countries bought Kaplan turbines. Among Karlstads Mekaniska Werkstad's customers was the Soviet Union, which took delivery of eight 28-megawatt Kaplan turbines in 1929 and installed them at a power-station on the river Svir at Lake Ladoga. The Kaplan turbine is specially suited to low heads and large flows, and dominates the market in this field.

During the 1940s, an interesting variation of the Kaplan turbine was developed in Germany. Known as the bulb turbine, it consisted of a Kaplan turbine in which the electric generators were placed in a streamlined case and installed horizontally in the power-station's tunnel. After further development in France, twenty-four 10-megawatt reversible bulb turbines were installed at the Rance tidal power-station. In the Soviet Union in 1968, a small experimental tidal power-station with a bulb turbine was built at Kislogub on the Kola peninsula. The intention is to use the experience gained from this project to design and build very large tidal power-stations elsewhere.

Wind Power

It seems likely that Palaeolithic man used the power of the wind to propel his simple vessels through the water. The sail he used was possibly made of interwoven branches, or even a leafy branch on the tree trunk which formed the actual vessel! The art of cloth-making is ancient, and cloth sails were known to the Sumerians as early as 3,500 BC.

During the last few centuries BC, the art of rigging sails on fairly large ships was well developed in the Mediterranean. Some of the "toy-scale" machines built by the engineers of the Alexandrian school were powered by the wind, and it springs to mind that the sail could have inspired this choice of a power source. An even more direct connection between the sail and the wind motor is the type of windmill which can still be seen on the Greek island of Mykonos in the Cycladic archipelago. During Hellenic times, the inhabitants of this island were great seafarers, who had perfected the art of sailing. It can hardly be a coincidence that the sails on the Mykonos windmills are not made of wood but of sailcloth, which is stretched from a nearly-horizontal "mast" in the hub along wooden "spokes" whose ends are connected by ropes, so that the whole construction forms a wheel. At the beginning of the Christian era, there may have flourished a technically advanced civilization in this area, with Rhodes as its centre. While we know very little about this civilization, Derek de Solla Price believes that it probably produced the Antikythera device. We must hope that new finds will teach us more about this civilization, and thus also cast some light on the earliest uses of wind power in the West.

However, the first windmill is generally considered to have originated in Persia (today's Iran), in the seventh century AD. The exact place of origin is said to be the province of Seistan, which is described as "a country of wind and sand" by an Arabian geographer of the tenth century. He continues: "A characteristic of the area is that the power of the wind is used to drive pumps for watering gardens." It is also generally accepted that the prototype of the Seistan windmill was the wind-driven prayer-wheel, which was common in Central Asia at the time and had been described by Chinese travellers as early as the fifth century. The drive mechanism consisted of a paddle-wheel which rotated round a vertical shaft, not unlike a modern anemometer with cupped or hemispherical blades.

The Seistan windmills also had vertical shafts, which drove the millstones directly, without any form of intermediate gearing. One peculiarity of these windmills was that they were built in two storeys, with the sails on the ground floor and the millstones, one of them fixed, on the upper floor. This design is reminiscent of that of the first water-mills, but it is unlikely that there was any direct connection between the blades of the water-mill and those of the Seistan windmill, even if it is possible that the construction of the millstones in the water-mill may have influenced the design of those of the windmill. Besides, the two constructions appeared in entirely different types of landscape.

Opinions differ about how knowledge of the windmill reached Europe, but it is generally accepted that it travelled along two routes: one followed the spread of Islam through Morocco and Spain, and the other comprised the trade routes from Persia, across the Caspian Sea and along the Russian rivers, to the Baltic countries and northern Europe. Vikings who travelled east may also have contributed to the spread of this knowledge.

The first mention of a windmill in Europe occurs in a Papal Bull of 1105, in which the Abbot of Savigny is granted a concession to build windmills in the dioceses of Bayeux, Coutances, and Evreux. By the early thirteenth century, the windmill had spread throughout most of Europe. It was most popular in Holland, where, from the late thirteenth century, it was used for pumping water and draining land. In 1341, the bishop of Utrecht tried to get a monopoly of all the wind which blew in his diocese! As Lewis Mumford points out, this alone should underline the enormous importance of the windmill at this time in Holland.

Windmills are classified by the way in which their sails are kept constantly facing the wind. One of the two main types is the post-mill, the mill house of which rests on bearings mounted in a fixed foundation of wood or stone. The larger and heavier the mill, the more difficult it is to turn. As a consequence, the second main type,

C Tower-mills with eight to twelve lateen-type sails are still a typical feature of the Aegean landscape. The origins of this type of mill are not known, but it is thought that it was inspired by the tower-mill which came into use in western Europe in the fourteenth century.

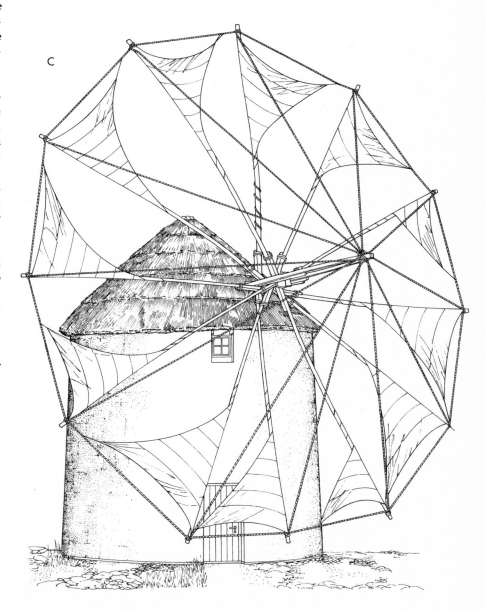

C

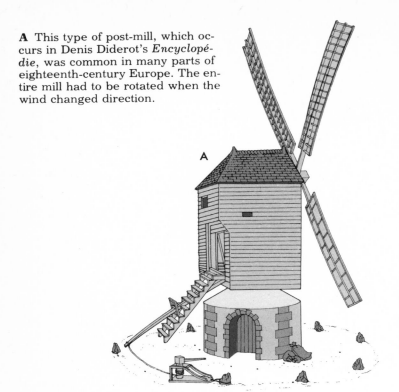

A This type of post-mill, which occurs in Denis Diderot's *Encyclopédie*, was common in many parts of eighteenth-century Europe. The entire mill had to be rotated when the wind changed direction.

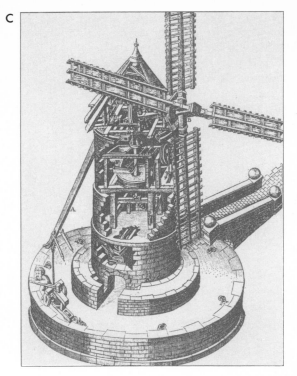

B The interior of a mill as shown in Diderot's *Encyclopédie*. The miller could control the speed of the millstone by means of a brake (*a*).

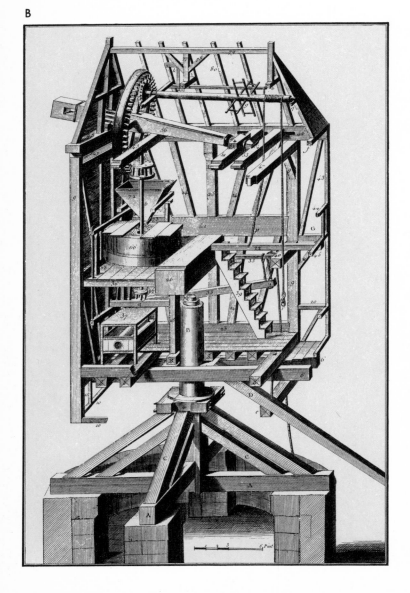

C Ramelli was the first to depict windmill interiors. This tower-mill is one of several mill types found in his book of 1588, *Le diverse et artificiose machine*. The system used for rotating the top cap can be clearly seen.

D A Dutch tower-mill of the early eighteenth century. From Peter Linperch's *Architecture mechanica of Moole-Boek van eenige opstallen van Moolens nevens hare Gronden*, published in Amsterdam in 1727.

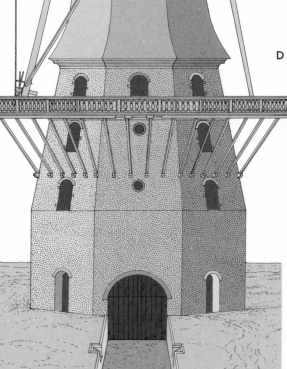

the tower-mill, was developed. In this, the windshaft of the sails is mounted on bearings in the top cap, the rotatable upper part of the mill house. This type came into use as early as the late fourteenth century.

In the following centuries, wind power was harnessed to perform many other tasks besides grinding grain. In the fifteenth century, wind-driven sawmills were in use, and wind-powered machines were raising and crushing ore at mines.

Just as the water-wheel had done, the windmill fired the imaginations of inventors. An illustrated manuscript of the 1320s, compiled by the monk Walter de Milimete, shows many remarkable uses to which the windmill could be put, one of them being to hurl beehives into besieged castles! (The same manuscript, by the way, contains the first known picture of a cannon.) At the end of the fifteenth century, it was the ambition of several Renaissance engineers, among them Taccola, to build a wind-driven carriage.

An unusual application of wind power was to be found in London of the mid-eighteenth century. A wind engine was erected over the impressive portal of Newgate prison to drive a ventilation system, which had been designed by Dr. Stephen Hale, a biologist. Sanitary conditions, especially ventilation, were then generally very poor in England, due partly to the extraordinary window tax that was levied on residences and prisons alike and charged according to the size of the windows in a building. Hale's ventilation system was installed at Newgate in 1752 and, later, at several other prisons. It was said to have benefited the health of the inmates.

The introduction of windmills and water-mills had a great effect on the science of mechanical engineering and resulted in a number of new trades, from mill building to maintenance, the latter normally being carried out by the miller and his apprentices. These tradesmen were the predecessors of today's mechanical engineers.

For centuries, the work carried out by engineers, *mechanici*, "art masters", or whatever they were called, had been governed by rule of thumb and common sense. It was not until the eighteenth century that attention began to be directed towards the theoretical background of the increasingly impressive machines which were appearing. The works of Isaac Newton (1642–1727) on classical mechanics were by then widespread and contributed to this awakening interest. In the 1690s, Christopher Polhem had built a machine to compare the performances of various types of water-wheels with different blade constructions, etc. He applied his conclusions in practice at the Falu mine and when building the Stjernsund works in 1700. In his descriptions of the results of these experiments, Polhem came very close to defining the unit of power. However, it was James Watt who eventually, in 1783, introduced this unit, the horsepower, which he defined as the work needed to lift 33,000 lb one foot in one minute.

In the 1750s, the Englishman John Smeaton (1724–92) carried out detailed comparative studies of power obtained from water and wind. He tested the results in practice before presenting them to the Royal Society in London in 1759. Smeaton's *Experimental Enquiry Concerning the Natural Power of Water and Wind* came on the eve of the appearance of steam power. Widely read in Europe, it certainly contributed to the fact that wind and water power were used in many places alongside steam until well into the twentieth century.

The role of wind and water power in the early stages of industrialization has often been underrated, for until steam took over, these natural forces provided the power in most factories. Mention has already been made of the fact that Sir Richard Arkwright's famous spinning-machine was driven by a water-wheel; another important machine of this era was driven by a dog-wheel!

E Through the ages, many attempts have been made to use wind power for different purposes. In ancient China, for example, wheelbarrows (**1**) equipped with sails occurred, and as late as the nineteenth century, a sail-powered cart (**2**) on rails was constructed. The latter vehicle had, however, little or no success.

F This wind-powered vehicle was constructed during the Renaissance by an Italian engineer called Roberto Valturio (?–1484).

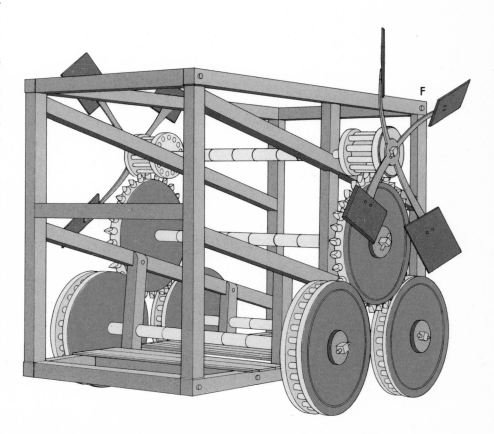

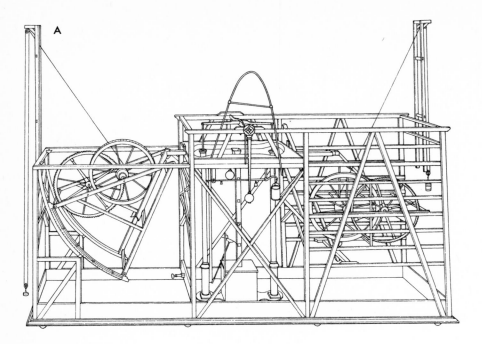

A

A This device was used by Christopher Polhem at the beginning of the eighteenth century to test the efficiency of, for example, different types of water-wheels. The results of Polhem's experiments were, however, not very reliable, since he failed to realize that the relationship between his results and the results which would be obtained from experiments with full-scale water-wheels and machinery is more complicated than one might be led to believe. The first reliable investigation into the efficiency of different types of water-wheels was carried out by John Smeaton, who published his results in 1757.

B A cross-section of John Smeaton's model of a device with which the power of an undershot water-wheel could be measured. Water was raised into a cistern (a) by means of a plunger-pump (b). The cistern also contained a float with a rod (c) marked in inches. When a sluice (d) was opened, water ran towards the water-wheel (e), round whose shaft a rope (f) was wound. The rope ran over two pulleys (g) and was attached to a beam (h). In one of the pulleys hung a pan loaded with weights. If slightly modified, this device could also be used for experiments with overshot water-wheels.

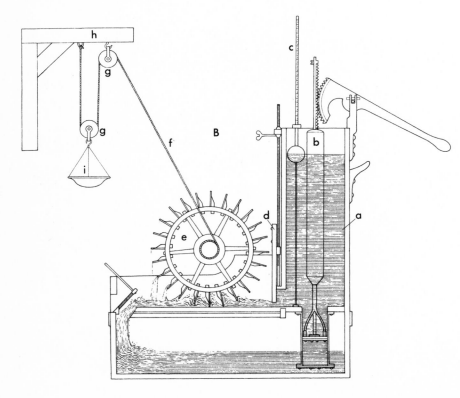

CHAPTER 5
PRIME MOVERS II:
Steam and Combustion Engines

We have already come across the early attempts to exploit the power of steam—for instance, Hero's *aelopile* and Archimedes' thoughts on a steam cannon, later taken up by Leonardo da Vinci. But what stopped the development? And why did no one take over where Hero and Archimedes left off? (We must disregard Leonardo, as his sketches and notes were hidden in archives until they had lost their novelty.) Some have attempted to answer these questions by saying that there was no need of steam power during antiquity and the Middle Ages, as there was such a good supply of cheap manpower available. If that were the case, could they not just as well have done without wind and water power? Of course not. The powerful princes and feudal lords would have become even more powerful, had they had access to steam-driven prime movers. Their engineers would certainly have designed warships with paddle-wheels driven by steam-power instead of capstans turned by oxen, and assault vehicles driven by steam instead of the wind.

It is nearer the truth to say that, before steam power could be put to use, a knowledge of certain scientific principles was needed, principles which are now considered basic but which were quite obscure until the mid-eighteenth century. For example, well into that century, it was generally believed that water was an element, and what happened when matter burnt was, chemically and physically, a mystery. Did a magical substance, phlogiston, leave a burning object? Fire gave heat, but what was heat, and what happened when water was heated and converted to steam? These questions were first answered in the seventeenth and eighteenth centuries, and it was also then that steam power was born, developed, and attained its majority.

From the days of Leonardo onwards, many people, both scientists and engineers, had been fascinated by the properties of steam. Their imaginations were probably fired by the works of Hero and Archimedes, which had been translated, adapted, and disseminated during the Renaissance. One can discern Hero's *aelopile* behind the imaginative "prime movers" suggested by the Italians Giovanni Battista della Porta (1538–1615), Vannocio Biringuccio (1480–1538?), and Giovanni Branca (1571–1640). In the seventeenth century, the great French engineer Salomon de Caus (1576–1626) experimented with steam pressure in spherical containers and found that, via a pipe into such a container, he could produce a magnificent water jet for his fountains with their dancing and playing statuettes. Caus built full-scale versions of what Hero probably built only on a toy scale.

However, the man who laid the foundations for the breakthrough of steam technology was the versatile mayor of Magdeburg, Otto von Guericke (1602–86). He, too, had been influenced by the engineers of the Alexandrian school and, among other things, considerably improved Ctesibius's air pump, which he later used when experi-

Giovanni Branca's somewhat naive proposal for a steam-turbine-powered stamp-mill, a device which was used to crush ore before it was put into the smelting furnace.

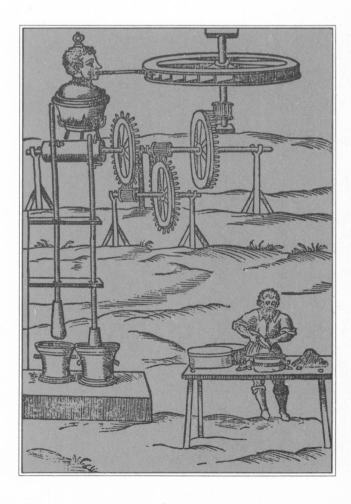

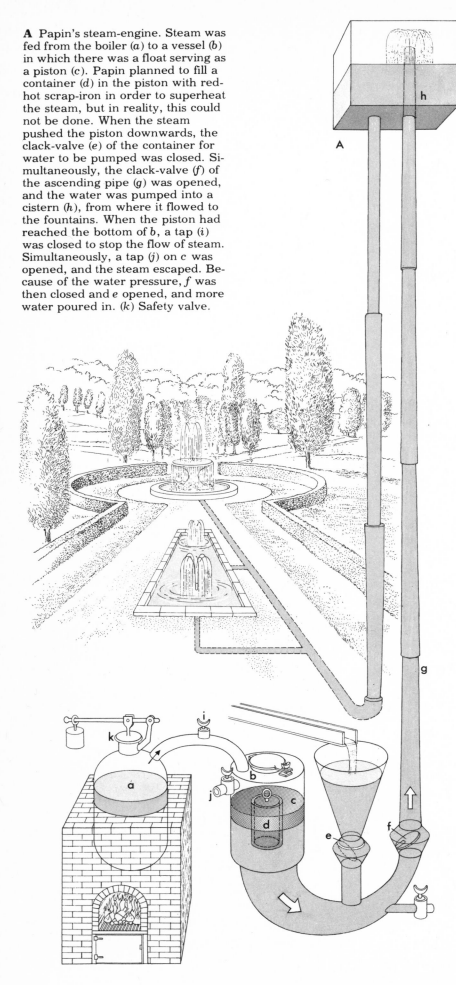

A Papin's steam-engine. Steam was fed from the boiler (a) to a vessel (b) in which there was a float serving as a piston (c). Papin planned to fill a container (d) in the piston with red-hot scrap-iron in order to superheat the steam, but in reality, this could not be done. When the steam pushed the piston downwards, the clack-valve (e) of the container for water to be pumped was closed. Simultaneously, the clack-valve (f) of the ascending pipe (g) was opened, and the water was pumped into a cistern (h), from where it flowed to the fountains. When the piston had reached the bottom of b, a tap (i) was closed to stop the flow of steam. Simultaneously, a tap (j) on c was opened, and the steam escaped. Because of the water pressure, f was then closed and e opened, and more water poured in. (k) Safety valve.

menting with vacuums, or the "space devoid of air", his most famous experiment being that with the Magdeburg hemispheres, two large hemispheres of copper; not even four pairs of horses could pull them apart once, having been joined together to form an air-tight sphere, the air had been evacuated from them. Another experiment provided Guericke with dramatic evidence of the pressure of air: his air pump had been connected to a spherical container made of copper plate, and two strong men were working the pump with all their might. A deafening bang—and the sphere crumpled as if made of paper! This, the first known implosion (the opposite of explosion) inspired Guericke to use the vacuum to produce power. He realized immediately that *die Kraft aus dem Nichts* ("power from nothing") could do useful work.

Today, the vacuum and the pressure of air are obvious phenomena, but to the seventeenth-century scholar they were matters for profound philosophical discussion. The philosophers of antiquity designated air as one of the four elements. But what was air? Was it anything at all? In the 1660s, when the English king Charles II and his court visited the Royal Society, they were shown an experiment which attempted to weigh air. The courtiers laughed themselves silly; how could anyone ever think of weighing air? There is nothing in air, anyone can see that!

It is said that Guericke solved one of the mysteries of air by following his nose. One day when he was holding a rose, he noticed that, when he held it a little away from himself, the scent was not so strong. The air diluted the scent, he thought, just as water dilutes a drop of red wine dropped into it. In other words, air must consist of matter! This may be a later rationalization or a poetic improvement of what actually happened, but as the old Italian proverb puts it, *se non è vèro, è ben trovato*, "it may not be true, but it is a good story". In the first experiment with the copper sphere, the sphere was filled with water, so it could be seen that matter was being pumped out. But after learning from the rose, Guericke pumped out only air. That was when the bang came, the starting signal, as it were, for the work which eventually led to the utilization of the "power from nothing".

Guericke has been called the "father of the power machine", and rightly so, although such a sweeping statement should only be accepted with a certain reservation. In the mid-1650s, he published accounts of his experiments with vacuums, and all over Europe the hemisphere experiments were repeated, with spheres both large and small.

Some years later, the pioneering Dutch scientist Christiaen Huygens (1629–95) was living in Paris, where he was assisted by a young French doctor, Denis Papin (1647–1714), in his experiments with high and low pressures. Papin had worked earlier with pressure; in 1681, he published his most famous invention, the "digester", or pressure cooker, for which he had invented the safety valve. Later in the decade, he and Huygens spent some time trying to evacuate the air from a cylinder by igniting gunpowder in it. They soon realized that the pressure in the cylinder did not fall, but rose considerably. They then designed what could be called an internal combustion engine, borrowing the idea of a piston inside a cylinder from Guericke; they intended to use this gunpowder engine to raise water. They offered Louis XIV an improved version of the engine to pump water for the Versailles fountains, but Colbert, the pragmatic minister of finance, declined the offer.

Papin continued his experiments with the vacuum, from 1687 as a professor in Marburg, Germany. He designed a very efficient, double-acting air pump and, according to the German philosopher and mathematician Gottfried Wilhelm von Leibniz (1646–1716), became the first man really to understand what a gas is. Papin now began to study the properties of steam and discovered that what he had been seeking ensued when steam was cooled and condensed. The "power from nothing" had been captured! Papin realized the importance of his discovery, writing triumphantly that what he had tried to achieve with gunpowder could be obtained simply and cheaply by heating water and cooling the steam. With this method, he continued, it would be easy to build machines to drive mills, propel ships against the wind, drive self-propelling carriages . . . In a visionary moment in a letter to the great Leibniz, he enlarged on the blessings the new machines would bring to mankind, when they took over all the heavy work.

Papin was now in the service of the Duke of Hesse, to whom he showed a model of his machine, describing with enthusiasm how it would function as a full-scale machine. There were, however, no ironworks that could produce the large cylinders necessary, nor craftsmen capable of building such a machine. Papin suggested that the duke should finance a factory to manufacture machines, where craftsmen could be trained to assemble and operate them. Despite Papin's assurances of its commercial viability, the duke did not have the money for such an enterprise. Besides, the good duke knew little of natural science and had difficulty in following the scholarly professor's enthusiastic explanations. What he wanted was to improve his gardens in Kassel by installing fountains, like the French king had done at Versailles. Could not Papin design a machine to power fountains?

Of course he could. And that was when his real problems started. After many attempts, he completed a model of a steam pump and delighted the duke with it. He then built it as a full-scale machine and installed it at Kassel in one of the palace towers. Papin had decided to use steam at over atmospheric pressure to drive a piston in a cylinder. The steam boiler was based on Papin's digester with a safety valve, and the plant took a year to build. When the steam pump was tried out, everything went according to plan: the fountains played, the duke was delighted. Then, the ascending pipe to the water tank burst. Another was made—pipes were not kept in stock in those days—but that burst, too. At the height of Papin's troubles, Leibniz wrote to Papin that an Englishman, Thomas Savery, had manufactured a steam pump powered by steam at over atmospheric pressure and by the vacuum obtained when steam condensed.

This was too much for Papin, whose relations with the duke had become somewhat strained. He decided to leave Marburg and settle in London where, in his youth, he had been active in the Royal Society. He planned a memorable return, heading up the Thames in his own paddle-wheeler, which would be driven by steam! Plenty of myths have been woven about this "steamboat", and a statue in Marburg represents Papin holding a model of the boat in his hands. Like so many others in the history of technology, this myth was probably created in retrospect. He certainly arrived in London around 1704 and, in the following year, modified Savery's pump. The only recognition this got, however, was when Jacob Leupold (1674–1727) included it as an interesting machine in his art book *Theatrum machinarum*. Papin lived his final years in poverty and died in 1714.

Thomas Savery (1650–1715) had patented his steam pump in 1698, calling it the "miner's friend", as it was to be used for pumping water from mines. However, it suffered in part from the same deficiencies as had Papin's, for while the demonstration model in his workshop in London worked very well, in practice the ascending pipe caused problems. The steam pressure rose to as much as ten atmospheres, and joints and pipes often burst, or the steam boiler exploded, as there was no safety valve. But Savery must have been a clever businessman, and a number of steam pumps of this design were in use during the first years of the eighteenth century—one of them for powering fountains!

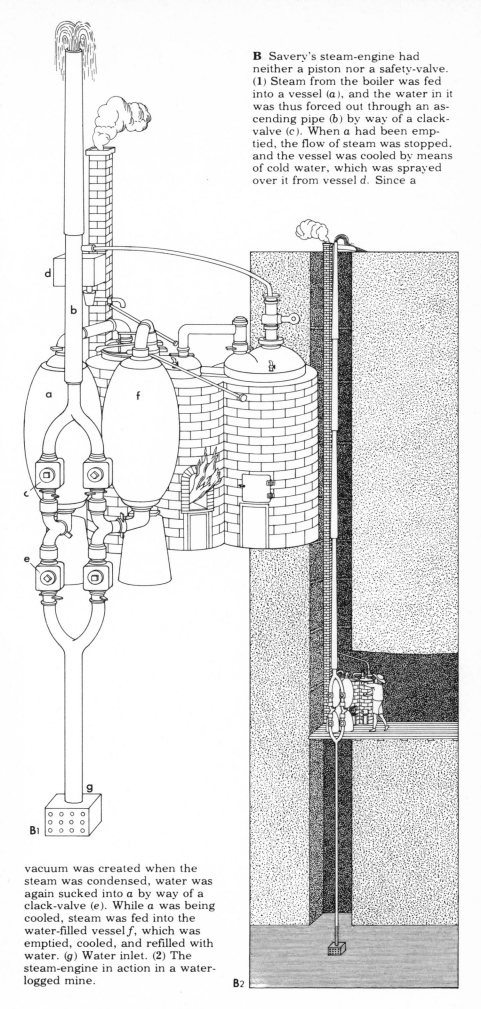

B Savery's steam-engine had neither a piston nor a safety-valve. (1) Steam from the boiler was fed into a vessel (*a*), and the water in it was thus forced out through an ascending pipe (*b*) by way of a clack-valve (*c*). When *a* had been emptied, the flow of steam was stopped, and the vessel was cooled by means of cold water, which was sprayed over it from vessel *d*. Since a

vacuum was created when the steam was condensed, water was again sucked into *a* by way of a clack-valve (*e*). While *a* was being cooled, steam was fed into the water-filled vessel *f*, which was emptied, cooled, and refilled with water. (*g*) Water inlet. (2) The steam-engine in action in a water-logged mine.

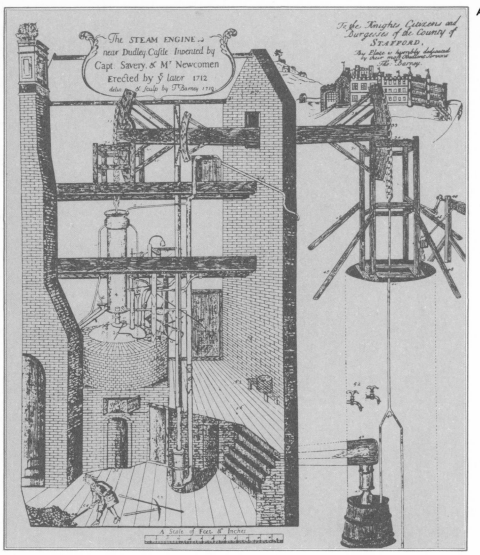

B Newcomen's atmospheric steam-engine worked in the following way.
(**1**) Steam was admitted into the cylinder (*a*) by a tap (*b*); the piston (*c*) was then supposed to be forced up by the pressure of the steam, which was not, however, very great, and the piston was drawn up mainly by the weight of the pump rod (*d*). The power stroke began when the tap (*b*) was closed. (**2**) At the same time, another tap (*e*) was opened, spurting cold water into the cylinder, thus condensing the steam, turning it into a very small amount of water. The external air pressure then forced the piston down.

If the piston had fitted tightly against the cylinder wall, the cylinder would have been practically

A In 1712, Thomas Newcomen's first atmospheric steam-engine was built at Dudley Castle, near Wolverhampton. This print, published in 1719, was accompanied by a description of the engine. It is interesting to note that, here, the design is called a "steam engine", a name not previously found in print. Newcomen, like Triewald, always used the name "fire and air machine", sometimes abbreviated to "fire machine". This atmospheric steam-engine is estimated to have developed a power just over 5 horsepower, with twelve strokes per minute. About 38.5 gallons (175 l) were pumped up per stroke.

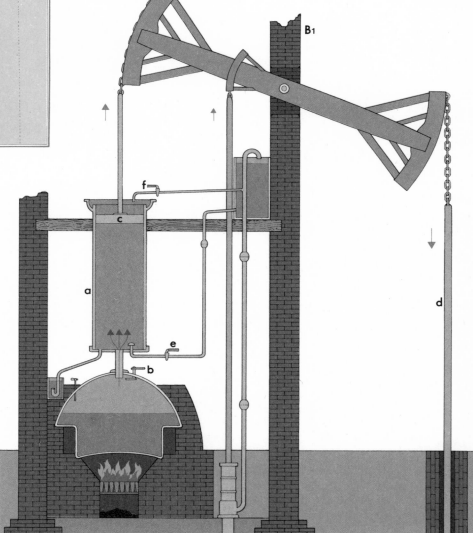

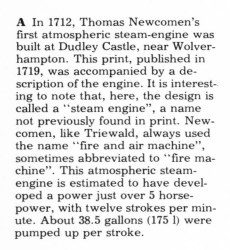

empty of air when the steam condensed. But one of the difficulties with this engine was the roughness of the cylinder wall. The cylinder was cast, since there were then no machines for cutting workpieces internally. The piston was sealed as well as possible by a gasket of leather or rope. To improve the seal, what is known as a water seal was added; water was poured–or dripped, if that was all that was necessary–onto the top of the piston by a tap (*f*). Due to these imperfections, only about half of the theoretically potential negative pressure in the cylinder is estimated to have been exploited during each power stroke.

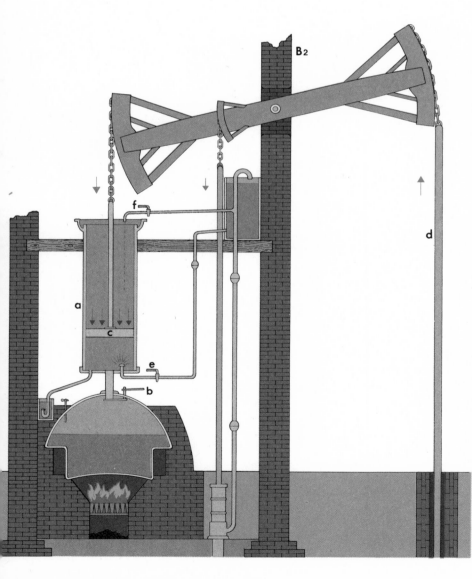

"Power from Nothing" Returns

Thomas Newcomen (1663–1729) was a merchant from Dartmouth, England, who traded in mining equipment. In the course of his business, he often visited the mines in Staffordshire, which had great problems with water. Newcomen became interested in the mechanization of mine pumps. This was in the 1690s, at about the same time as Savery was working on his invention. Nevertheless, Newcomen's work was totally independent of Savery's "miner's friend", although he was aware of Papin's ideas for a prime mover based on the creation of a vacuum by the condensation of steam. In 1702, Newcomen wrote for advice to the scientist Robert Hooke (1635–1703) at the Royal Society. Hooke was a man held in high esteem at the time; he confirmed that the principle of Papin's prime mover was correct, but he doubted if it would be possible to produce a piston which could fit tightly in a cylinder. Newcomen, aided by a mechanic called John Calley, continued his experiments, in spite of Hooke's discouragement. In 1712, after many years of experiments, the first "atmospheric" steam-engine was built at Dudley Castle, near Wolverhampton, in Staffordshire.

Thus did Newcomen and Calley become the first to build a practical prime mover in which "power from nothing" performed the work delivered by the machine. Here, the steam was only an intermediary agent, being condensed to create a vacuum. The air pressure was the source of power. The Newcomen engine is, therefore, called the atmospheric steam-engine or, to give it its contemporary name, the fire and air engine, which is a vivid description–the fire gave heat to transform the water to steam, but it was the air which acted.

Newcomen was not a scientist, he was an addicted amateur, and typical of his age. But he knew enough to seek the advice of people with more insight than himself, and he surrounded himself with those who had practical or theoretical qualifications. John Calley was one of the former; Mårten Triewald one of the latter. Triewald (1691–1747) was a very talented Swedish scientist and engineer who, in 1716, left a Sweden badly hit by Charles XII's wars and moved to England, where he received a sound education in natural science at the Royal Society, working as the assistant of John T. Desaguliers. He made friends with the aged Newton and, for some time, worked as Thomas Newcomen's assistant. Triewald helped to build at least one atmospheric steam-engine, and he was the first to give a physically correct description of its *modus operandi*. After his return to Sweden in 1726, Triewald tried to persuade Swedish mining companies to build a Newcomen engine, and the Dannemora mines commissioned one. This engine, to which Triewald had made several useful modifications, was completed in 1728, but it was only six years later that he wrote a comprehensive description of it. His account, "A Description of a Fire and Air Engine at the Dannemora Mines", was, unfortunately, not made available in any internationally useful language until 1928, when an English translation was published by the Newcomen Society, then celebrating the 200th anniversary of the engine. (The Newcomen Society, founded in 1920, is one of the oldest associations of people interested in the history of technology.)

Since Savery's 1698 patent for his steam pump, the "miner's friend", was so comprehensive, Newcomen was unable to patent his atmospheric steam-engine. Into the bargain, Savery had managed to prolong his patent until 1733, so that it greatly exceeded the normal fourteen years. However, Triewald states that, early on, Newcomen bought part of Savery's patent rights from the consortium which administered them after Savery's death in 1715.

After the first atmospheric steam-engine was taken into service in 1712, a few more were built, but the Newcomen design was not made fully practicable until the mid-1720s. Newcomen met the same problems as Denis Papin had before him: a technology much more advanced than that used in the construction of wind and water-mills was required to produce the various parts of his engine, especially its valves, pipes, taps, and joints. The crafts had not yet caught up with theoretical developments. Triewald also had great problems with the Dannemora engine, which started work in June, 1728. Its pump rods and bearings were too weak to stand its characteristically violent jerks, and to start with, the engine was in action for only a couple of days at a time between repairs. One reason the pump rods broke so easily was that the cylinder had a higher effect than was normal with a Newcomen engine. Triewald had achieved this by finishing the inside of the cylinder so well that a tight seal between cylinder and piston resulted. It took two years to pump the mine reasonably dry, and by then, the engine was on its last legs. In 1731, the enraged mine owners sued Triewald, who had to pay heavy damages. This trial, which dragged on in various stages for over ten years, also started a debate about the atmospheric steam-engine. General opinion held the design to be worthless. In his own defence, in 1734, Triewald published the account we have mentioned. This account contained an illustration of the engine.

Triewald was convicted by court of law, and his engine by miners and public opinion. Not until 1768 were the Swedes to try another atmospheric steam-engine, this time at the Persberg mines in Värmland.

Despite the heavy strain of the lengthy court case, Triewald continued his work on the steam-engine. In 1976, some of his papers were discovered, and among them were his drawings for an ingenious arrangement that would change the engine's reciprocating movement to a rotary movement. He intended that the engine be used also for raising ore. For understandable reasons, he never managed to find a backer for this idea.

Newcomen had had great difficulty in sealing the piston in the cylinder. In those days, cylinders with diameters greater than 20−30 in (c. 50−75 cm) could be neither cast nor produced in any other way. The insides of cylinders had to be finished by hand with chisels and files. The top of the piston was usually fitted with a leather washer covered with a thin layer of water to form what was known as a water seal. Due to the inevitably poor fit of the piston, the air pressure on the piston could not be used to its full potential.

The taps and valves on the earliest engines were probably operated by hand, but they were soon mechanized. There are many nice little stories about how this came about, all most probably unfounded. A favourite tells of a shepherd-boy who was given the job of looking after the engine. He got bored with this after a while, so he attached some pieces of string and metal here and there, and the engine functioned automatically. No doubt heart-warming, but very likely just another of the myths we have come across so far.

After Savery's patent had expired in 1733 (Newcomen had died four years earlier), several atmospheric steam-engines were built in England. By the 1760s, more than a hundred were in use, most of them in coal-mines. The engines became bigger and bigger but were still built according to the original design, with few modifications. The atmospheric steam-engine was severely criticized, mainly because of its high fuel consumption and the heavy wear and tear of the material. It was said that an iron-mine was needed to build and maintain one, and a coal-mine to keep one running!

Newcomen's successors in this field were no more than craftsman-mechanics and, as machine designers, had little vision. Oddly enough, none of the great natural scientists, either in England or anywhere else, took any interest in the physical principles of the atmospheric steam-engine. It was left to an engineer whom we have met already, John Smeaton, to do this, and he did it just as meticu-

lously as he had conducted his pioneering experiments with prime movers driven by wind and water.

In his youth, Smeaton, who had grown up in a coal-mining area in Yorkshire, had become interested in the Newcomen engine. Later on in life, when several great engineering achievements had brought him fame, he took up this interest again and, in 1767, designed an atmospheric steam-engine for the pumps at the New River waterworks in London, which had previously been powered by a horse-wheel. Although Smeaton's engine probably worked better than the horse-wheel, its efficiency was poor. He therefore built an experimental atmospheric steam-engine in his workshop and tested many different designs and machine elements. He also collected all the information available about the construction and use of more than a hundred Newcomen engines which were active in England at the time. Smeaton then used this information to try to find a connection between different construction data, such as cylinder diameter and length of piston stroke, and the efficiency of the engines. The experience gained by this research he then applied to the experimental engine.

The greatest fault in the machines studied by Smeaton was the one of which Hooke had warned Newcomen and which Papin had also pointed out about a hundred years before, namely, the impossibility of sealing the piston tightly against the wall of the cylinder. As we have pointed out, there was neither the technology nor the craftsmen available to build tightly fitting pistons and cylinders. The craftsmen usually employed to make cylinders were founders of ornaments or bells, used to working in bronze or brass and able to handle the large charges necessary for casting such objects as an equestrian statue or a large church bell. The cylinder for Triewald's Dannemora engine, for example, was cast by the bell-founder Ad. Meijer of Stockholm. But what the founders of the time had no experience of was finishing the surface; indeed, many bell-founders considered a rough surface inside the bell very good for its tone!

The need for a satisfactory internal finish of the cast cylinder led Smeaton to design a machine in which a steel cutting-edge was attached to a rotating axle which was introduced into the centre of the cylinder. The machine worked on the same principle as a modern boring mill, but the idea it embodied appeared in the sixteenth century, when Biringuccio suggested a similar device for boring cannon barrels. Smeaton's design was later improved by the famous machine-tool maker John Wilkinson.

Once Smeaton had produced a cylinder with a really smooth inner surface, he could achieve a better seal than hitherto between the piston and the wall of the cylinder. This meant that his engine could exploit fifty per cent more of the atmospheric pressure than the majority of the engines which he had studied. Further modifications enabled the efficiency to be increased even more, and the engine which Smeaton built in 1772 for the Long Benton coal-mine was two or three times more efficient than the Newcomen engines. But powering even Smeaton's atmospheric steam-engine still required the coal-mine of which Newcomen's critics had spoken; the thermal efficiency of the most successful version was only about one per cent.

Russian Interlude

At about the same time that Smeaton was busy trying to improve Newcomen's engine, a remarkable design was invented in Russia. This was the first continuously operating atmospheric steam-engine, and it was invented by Ivan Polsunov (1728−66). His early death unhappily prevented his technically interesting creation from becoming known, either in Russia or in western Europe, until a hundred years later.

Polsunov, the son of a low-ranking officer, grew up in simple circumstances in Yekaterinburg (now Sverdlovsk). At an early age, he showed signs of great technical talent and, by the age of nineteen, was employed as an engineer at the Altai silver-mines, which were owned by the czar's family and were expanding in the 1740s and 1750s. Polsunov distinguished himself by the great inventiveness of the improvements he introduced to the smelting and mining plants which were then being built. It is probable that he occasionally visited the mines' administrative headquarters at St. Petersburg (now Leningrad), which were situated beside the czar's Summer Gardens, a park built in the French style and based on Louis XIV's gardens at Versailles. With his burning interest in machines, Polsunov would have seized the opportunity of studying the atmospheric steam-engine built there in 1717 by John T. Desaguliers, the friend and teacher of Mårten Triewald. This machine drove the pumps which provided the many fountains in the Gardens with water. Whatever can be said about the Sun King—and a lot has been said—he has certainly had a considerable influence on technical development!

In early 1763, Polsunov had worked out a detailed suggestion for a double-cylindered atmospheric steam-engine, in which the counter-acting pistons achieved a direct rotary motion. The purpose of the design was to create an engine capable of driving any kind of machine found in a mine. While the Altai and other mines in the Urals, unlike those of many parts of England, Sweden, and Central Europe had no problems with water, they still needed power to drive machines for raising and crushing ore and for powering the bellows of the smelting works. As many silver and gold mines can be worked only for a year or so, Polsunov designed his engine so that it could easily be dismantled and moved to another site.

Prospects for Polsunov's engine were, therefore, exceptionally promising. The mines' administration thought so, too, and disregarding all red tape, gave Polsunov a completely free hand to put his ideas into practice. However, when he set to work on his magnificent engine late in 1763, he had the bitter experience of not being able to find craftsmen who were able to build it: the same fate which had befallen Papin, Newcomen, and Smeaton. Assisted only by some apprentice smiths, Polsunov had to build the engine with his own hands. The work must have made great physical demands on Polsunov, for it broke his health. He contracted a deficiency disease, and, in May, 1766, just as his engine was ready to be tested, he died, only thirty-eight years of age. A week after his death, the engine, an impressive structure about 43 ft (13 m) high, was put to work driving four pairs of bellows in the smelting works at the Kolivano-Voskresensky silver-mine. The air was blasted to three smelting furnaces, but the engine was built to supply air to another nine furnaces, which were to be built when the smelting works was expanded; the surplus air was now allowed to escape. The engine was in use until November, 1766, and the fault which then occurred could probably have been repaired easily if the designer had been there. But neither the mining engineers nor the craftsmen who had helped build the engine could get it going again. It was as difficult for them, with the general technical education of the time, to understand the physical principles of the *modus operandi* of the atmospheric steam-engine as it would be for a modern audience of laymen to understand how a nuclear power-station works.

Polsunov's contribution to the development of the atmospheric steam-engine must be seen as a definite breakthrough, mainly due to the fact that rotary motion was produced by the two cylinders, an idea totally unknown to Newcomen, Triewald, and Smeaton. It is unfortunate that death prevented Polsunov from publishing his invention. It remained unknown both in Russia and the rest of the world, despite the great reward given to Polsunov's family by the

Smeaton's first atmospheric steam-engine was put into service in 1772 and worked in essentially the same way as Newcomen's engine. Considerable construction improvements had, however, been made. Smeaton's engine, shown here in section, had a cylinder (*a*) of considerably greater diameter than that common in Newcomen's engines, and the length of the piston (*b*) stroke was great — 7 ft (2.13 m). The two boilers, only one of which (*c*) can be seen here, were built of rivetted iron plates. Newcomen's boilers were usually manufactured of copper plates combined with lead plates, a construction which was not very durable. In order to lessen the exchange of heat between the piston and the steam, Smeaton provided the under-side of the piston with a layer of wood.

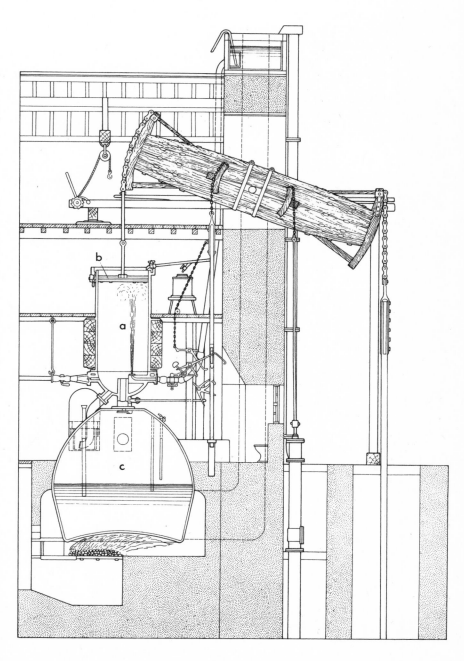

A The first continuously working atmospheric steam-engine was built by Ivan Polsunov and was completed in 1766 in the city of Barnaul. The boiler, which was made from forged copper, had two safety valves (only one of them, *b*, can be seen here) and could be emptied by means of a cock (*c*). Further, there were two pipes with cocks (*d*), with which the water level in the boiler could be checked; if the upper cock was opened, only steam should escape, whereas water should run out when the other cock was opened. Steam from the boiler was admitted through a pipe system (*e*) to the two copper cylinders (*f*). The valves at the bottoms of the cylinders were opened and closed to alternately admit steam in one and cooling water in the other cylinder by a rack-and-pinion device (*g*), powered by a chain (*h*), and two bars (*i*) which were connected by a chain (*j*). These chains ran over a wheel (*k*) which also carried the chain (*l*) connecting the two piston rods (*m*). The wheel (*k*) was thus rocked to and fro, and this motion was transmitted by way of an endless chain (*n*) to another wheel (*o*), which also carried the chain (*p*) working the two bellows (*q*). These were equipped with weights which squeezed them together after they had been filled with air. A water tank (*r*) supplied cooling water to condense the steam, for use as a water seal, and for the boiler. Condensate and heated cooling water collected in a tank (*t*) and was pumped to *r*.

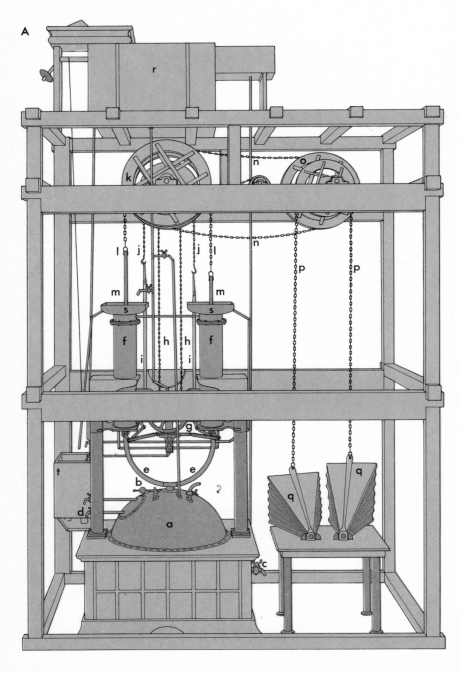

James Watt

In the 1760s, a young man who was greatly to influence the development of the "fire and air engine" made his entrance on the stage of technology. This was James Watt, who began his career as "Mathematical Instrument Maker to the University" in Glasgow. A model of Newcomen's engine which had been used in the physics department had broken down, and a clockmaker summoned all the way from London could not get it going again. Watt succeeded, but the engine ran out of steam after only five strokes, and it had to "catch its breath" before it could be started again. Watt wondered why the engine needed so much steam. After all, it was the atmospheric pressure which did the work!

He came to the conclusion that the steam kept losing heat when cold water was injected to make the steam condense; this cooled the cylinder, too, which did not improve matters: without actually defining the concept, Watt had discovered latent heat. The potential heat of the steam was wasted by cooling, and this was the main reason for the high fuel consumption.

Watt's remedy was to condense the steam in a separate cylinder, a condenser, which he placed next to the working cylinder. To improve thermal efficiency still more, he fitted a steam jacket round the working cylinder, to keep it as hot as the steam which entered it. Watt made a model of his engine; it worked perfectly. In 1769, he was granted a patent for "A New Method of Lessening the Consumption of Steam and Fuel in Fire Engines"; this is one of the more important patents in the history of technology.

Watt shared his patent with an industrialist, John Roebuck, who financed the construction of a full-scale experimental engine. But Roebuck ran into financial difficulties before the engine could be tested. Watt then got in touch with the great industrialist Matthew Boulton (1728–1809), whose factory lay in Soho, near Birmingham, and who had previously expressed interest in Watt's engine, recognizing its great advantages over Newcomen's engine. Watt then secured an extension of his patent until 1800 (it should have expired in 1783), and in 1775, he and Boulton formed a company, Boulton & Watt, whose factory was the first in the world to manufacture prime movers on an industrial scale.

Matthew Boulton, the son of an art-loving iron merchant, was an experienced man of the world, at his ease in the company of artists and writers. In the 1760s, when Benjamin Franklin spent a few years in London, Boulton contacted him in order to discuss the issues of the day. Franklin had been sent to London by the American colonists to represent them in negotiations with the British government on such issues as the hated stamp duty. The infrequent negotiations gave him plenty of time to devote to his passion, natural science. He and Boulton became good friends and often discussed how they could improve Newcomen's engine. Boulton was worried by a serious problem. He wanted to extend his factory, but the water-wheels which provided the power in it were not able to drive any more machines. On Franklin's advice, Boulton built a model of an improved "fire engine". But Franklin was recalled to his own country, and his place as Boulton's companion in science was taken by James Watt.

Both Boulton and Watt took a great interest in contemporary ideas and were involved with the humanities as well as with the natural sciences. They were founder-members of the famous Lunar Society, a club of artists, writers, scientists, and industrialists which met to discuss the issues of the day. The society met at the home of one of its members every month, on an evening when the moon was full—to allow the members "to enjoy the advantage of a moonlit path homewards". This was before the advent of street lighting, although gas lighting was on the way.

As soon as they were put into commission, the first two engines made by Boulton & Watt aroused great public interest. One had a cylinder diameter of 50 in (127 cm) and was installed at a coal-mine in Staffordshire. The other was used to work the bellows of a blastfurnace owned by the John Wilkinson mentioned previously. The fame of these "fire engines", which had a fuel consumption of a third of that of the old coal-eating Newcomen engines, spread rapidly among industrialists in England. The two partners were inundated with orders, especially from the owners of tin-mines in Cornwall, where coal was more expensive than in any other part of the country. Business flourished, and the Soho factories were extended and equipped with the very latest machinery. How Denis Papin would have loved those workshops! His dreams, in which he had tried to interest the Duke of Hesse a hundred years earlier, had been fulfilled by these two men. The Soho workshops attracted many technically talented young men and became a forcing ground for generations of mechanical engineers.

An important factor in Boulton & Watt's success was a clever business idea they had: a form of "leasing". Their engines were not sold outright but were made available to customers on condition that they agreed to pay a fee that equalled the savings they made in fuel cost by using a Boulton & Watt engine instead of a Newcomen engine of similar size.

The instrument maker turned factory-owner was not satisfied with this success but worked tirelessly to improve his engine. In 1781, as we have mentioned, he invented the sun-and-planet drive to solve the problem of converting the piston's reciprocating motion to rotary motion. In the following year, he doubled the engine's output by making it double-acting. As the piston in Watt's double-acting steam-engine worked in both directions, the chains connecting the piston rod and the pump rod to the main beam had to be replaced by rods. That is how parallelogram steering, which Watt later called his masterpiece, was invented. In 1787, the centrifugal governor, which permitted automatic speed regulation, was introduced, and seven years later, a crankshaft came to be used to replace the sun-and-planet drive.

The Century of Steam

The nineteenth century was the great, resplendent era of steam. The effects of steam power were felt not only in the field of technology, but also in most areas of human civilization. During this century, steam was used to power the machines of the rapidly growing industrial sector and to drive the engines of the various means of land and sea transport. All this technical progress caused a great wave of optimism and faith in the future, something which we may find rather difficult to understand today. After centuries in which society more or less stood still, these technical breakthroughs, coming one after the other in quick succession, created an atmosphere in which it was believed that machine technology, aided by steam, was on the brink of rescuing mankind from at least some of the worst of the hard struggle for survival. The Swedish author Harry Martinson (1904–1978), a Nobel laureate in literature, described the railway as the first truly democratic invention and indeed, before the era of steam, travel was not accessible to everyone.

When King George II of England once paid a visit to the Boulton & Watt factory in Soho, near Birmingham, Matthew Boulton assured him: "Your Majesty, I have at my disposal what the whole world demands; something which will uplift civilization more than ever by relieving man of all undignified drudgery. I have *steam power*."

Those words, filled as they are with intimations of power—political as well as industrial—were uttered by a man who knew what he was talking about. More than five hundred of Watt's steam-engines had

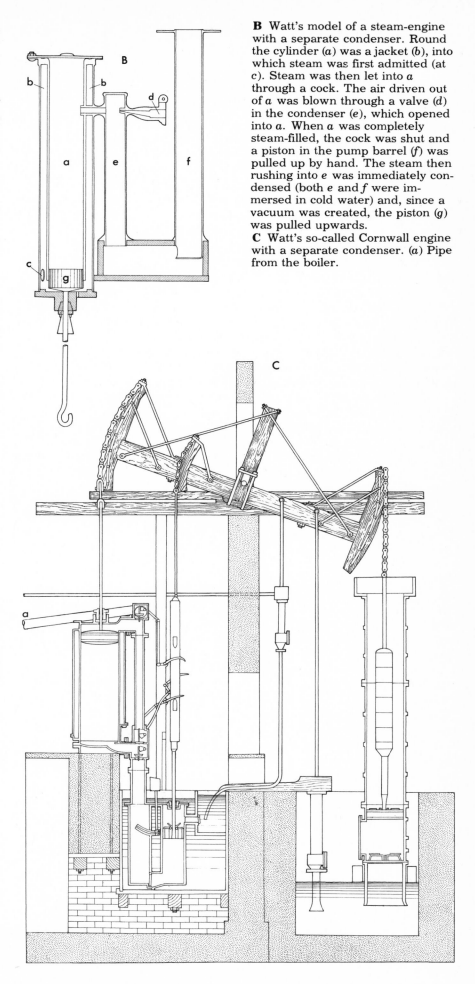

B Watt's model of a steam-engine with a separate condenser. Round the cylinder (a) was a jacket (b), into which steam was first admitted (at c). Steam was then let into a through a cock. The air driven out of a was blown through a valve (d) in the condenser (e), which opened into a. When a was completely steam-filled, the cock was shut and a piston in the pump barrel (f) was pulled up by hand. The steam then rushing into e was immediately condensed (both e and f were immersed in cold water) and, since a vacuum was created, the piston (g) was pulled upwards.
C Watt's so-called Cornwall engine with a separate condenser. (a) Pipe from the boiler.

been delivered by Boulton & Watt by the time the patent expired in 1800. The two partners then left the company in the hands of their sons. Watt retired to his country estate and devoted himself to his many other interests. He died in 1819 at the age of eighty-three, one of the great standard-bearers in the history of technology, being not only a pioneer in the field, but also a true humanist. The inscription on his memorial stone in Westminster Abbey is a sublime ode to technology, humanism, and James Watt, benefactor of mankind.

By the time James Watt died, steam had shown that it was a source of energy to be reckoned with. There were, however, negative reactions. One example of these was the riots which broke out in England in the second decade of the nineteenth century, when the Luddites, led by a man who went by the name of Ned Ludd, attacked and destroyed steam-driven spinning machines. They feared that these new machines would cause unemployment. There were similar reactions in most countries. When the designer of the first high-speed press, the German Friedrich König (1774–1833), wanted to install a steam-driven press in the Cotta printing works in Stuttgart, one of the editors declared that he would rather write without a roof over his head than work in the same building as a steam-engine. Modern anxiety about nuclear power springs immediately to mind.

When Boulton & Watt's monopoly of steam-engine construction ended in 1800, the market was open for new designs. Watt's engine had not really been improved since 1785. The company produced a standardized version, and every effort was concentrated on increasing production to meet the growing demand.

Watt's engine was still "atmospheric", that is, the air pressure (the "power from nothing") did all the work. Only a minor improvement was needed to increase the pressure to several atmospheres and thus improve performance. Watt's assistants wanted to make it but Watt refused to listen to them—as a young man, he had seen one of Savery's pumps explode at a London waterworks. He was certainly wise to be so careful; at that time, no one had any experience of designs or materials suitable for the construction of high-pressure steam boilers.

Steam-engines after Watt
During the first half of the nineteenth century, the steam-engine developed along three main lines: higher steam pressure, improved utilization of steam expansion, and new mechanical designs. About the year 1850, however, these trends in development changed course, mainly due to the fact that the theory of heat and how it worked in the steam-engine became better understood.

Two interesting pioneers, one on either side of the Atlantic, Richard Trevithick (1771–1833) in Great Britain and Oliver Evans in the United States, separately improved the steam-engine by increasing the steam pressure, and by trying to develop new design ideas for it.

When Trevithick was growing up in Cornwall, Watt's engines were beginning to appear in the local mining districts. It was only natural that the technically gifted boy should take an interest in these engines and discover their potential—and their weaknesses. Watt's engine, just like Newcomen's, was more or less integrated with a building, its heavy balance beam being supported by a solid pillar, usually of brick. One English mill-owner in the 1790s considered that the steam-engine would never spread if it did not become "as movable as a piece of furniture". Even before Watt's patent expired, Trevithick was experimenting with steam at high pressure. His idea was to build a very compact engine which was to be extremely "movable"—it was intended to propel a vehicle! On Christmas Eve, 1801, he was ready to test his steam-driven carriage. The trial took place outside Camborne, Trevithick's home town, on an uphill (!) slope towards Beacon Hill, a little village on a hilltop. It was not

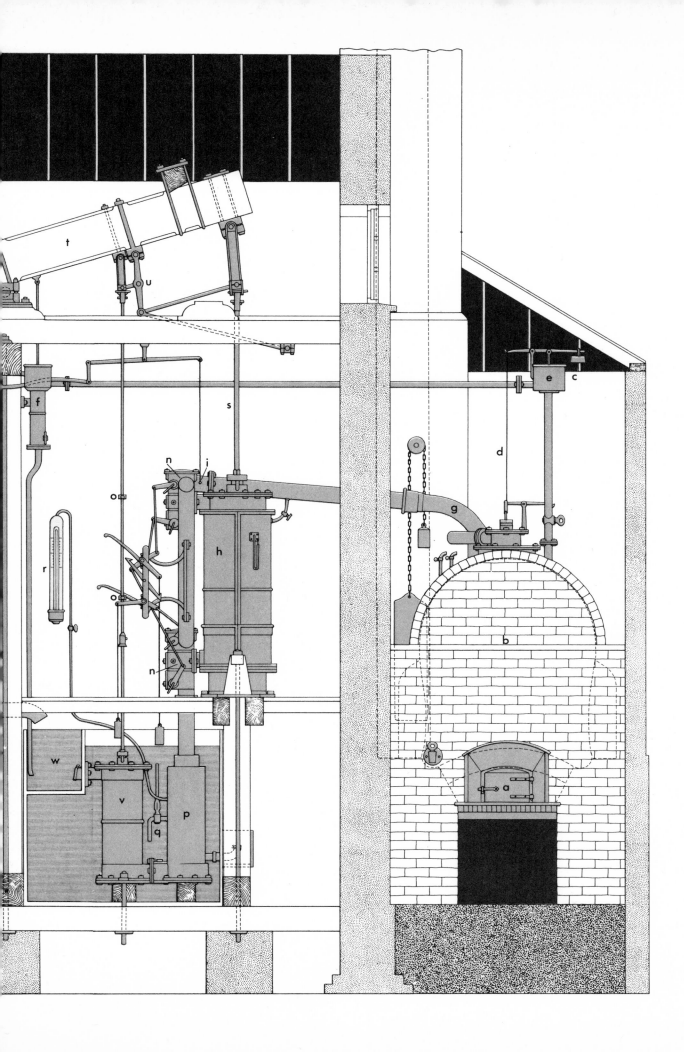

Between the years 1787 and 1800, quite a large number of double-acting steam-engines of this type were manufactured at the Boulton & Watt workshops. The engine's effect was 10 horsepower, and it worked with twenty-five double strokes a minute. (*a*) Furnace door. (*b*) Boiler. (*c*) A device by means of which the water level in the boiler was controlled. At the bottom end of a string (*d*), a float was attached. When the float sank too much inside the boiler, a valve (*e*) was opened and water, hoisted by a feed water pump (*f*), poured in. When the float had returned to its correct level, the valve was closed again. Steam from the boiler was admitted through a pipe (*g*) to the cylinder (*h*) by way of a throttle valve (*i*), the size of whose aperture was determined by a centrifugal governor (*j*). By way of a gear train (*k*) and a belt (*l*), the governor was powered by the sun (*m*) of the sun-and-planet drive. The cylinder (*h*) was closed at both ends, and steam alternately entered it above and below the piston through two valve chests (*n*), in which the valves were opened and closed by projections (*o*) on a pump rod. (*p*) Condenser. (*q*) Pipe for spraying cold water into the condenser. (*r*) Manometer. The piston rod's (*s*) motion was transmitted to the balance (*t*) by a parallel linkage (*u*), which was also linked to a pump (*v*), by means of which condensation water and air were pumped into a cistern (*w*). (*x*) Pump, driven by the balance and used to pump cooling water to the cistern in which the condenser and pump *v* were immersed. The balance's oscillating movement was transformed into a rotary movement by a non-rotating cog-wheel, the planet (*z*), which meshed with the sun (*m*) on the flywheel's (*y*) shaft.

A A reconstruction of Trevithick's steam carriage of 1801 as seen from above (**1**) and from the side (**2**). (*a*) Boiler. (*b*) Furnace with a double right-angled flue duct. This allowed as much heat as possible from the stack gas to be utilized. (*c*) Smoke stack. (*d*) Cocks for control of the water level in *a*. (*e*) Water filler funnel with tap. (*f*) Safety valve. (*g*) Double-acting cylinder. (*h*) Steam distributing cock; a 2×2 plug cock. (*i*) Feed pipe from *a*. (*j*) Exhaust

steam pipe. Leads to *c*, where the steam by its blasting action forces the draught. (*k*) Piston. The piston rod's (*l*) extension (*m*) was fork-shaped, in order to give room for the crank web (*n*), and had vertical openings, to give room for the crankshaft (*o*). Because of this arrangement, *o* could be set very close to *g*. (*p*) Connecting rod. (*q*) Guides controlling the fore end of *m*. (*r*) An actuating rod, which was connected to *h* and which, from the driver's

seat, could be made to engage with *l* for an automatic reversal of the distribution of steam to the turning-points of the piston. When disengaged, *r* could probably be used for manual control of *h*. (*s*) Flywheel. (*t*, *u*) Gearwheels for the transmission of power to the wheels. (*v*) Coupling gear, used to disengage either of the wheels when cornering a sharp bend. The front axle (*w*) was turned round a central pivot by means of the handle bar (*x*).

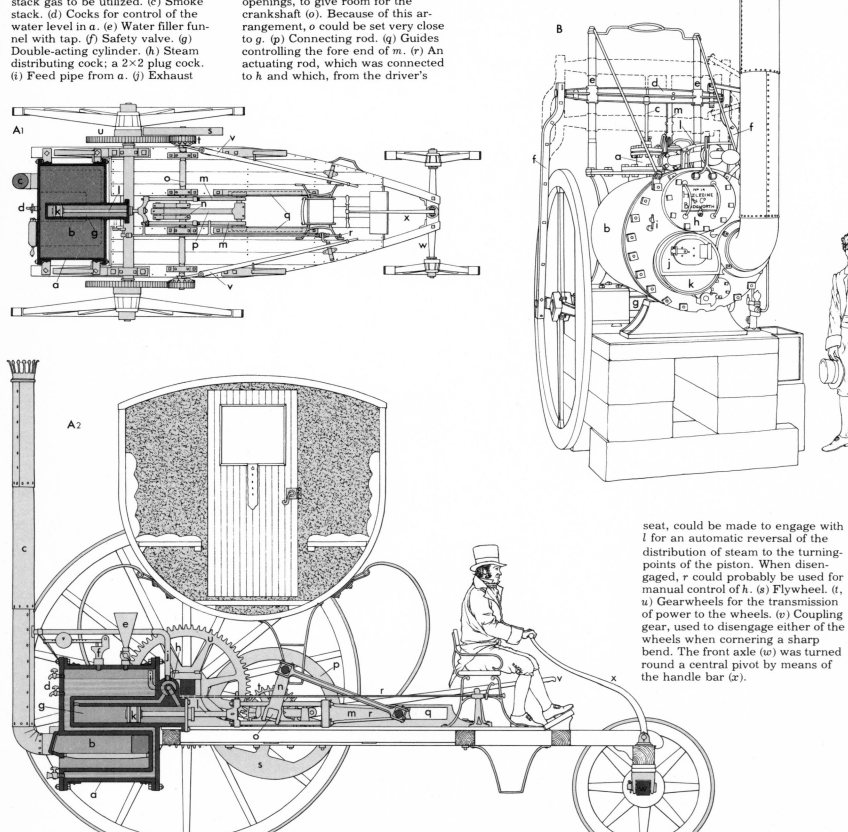

successful. The boiler could not produce enough steam, and the carriage failed to puff up the hill. Three days later, Trevithick tried again, now in the company of some merry friends. This time, the hill was conquered, and they actually reached Beacon Hill, despite damage to the carriage on the frozen, rutted road. Their triumph was celebrated with mulled drinks and stuffed goose at the local inn. The carriage had been parked in a shed—but they had forgotten the fire under the boiler, so when they returned from their hearty repast, all they found was a heap of twisted scrap iron.

This, however, did not daunt Trevithick. By March of the following year, he took out patents for his high-pressure steam-engine and for its use in powering a carriage. These patents represent an essential breakthrough in the history of steam technology. The engine had a cylindrical boiler in which the cylinder was encased, thus avoiding loss of heat. Steam was led to the cylinder via a multiple cock which allowed it to act on either side of the piston in turn. The thought in itself was not new; as early as 1725, Leupold had suggested it in his *Theatrum machinarum.*

Back in the 1780s, the American millwright and engineer Oliver Evans had begun to take an interest in steam as a source of power. He realized its great potential, although in those days in the United States the steam-engine was very rare—in 1800, there were only six in the entire country. Completely independently of Trevithick, Evans built a high-pressure steam-engine. It had a horizontal, cylindrical steam boiler with a three-way cock—driven by the balance wheel—which led steam to a separate vertical cylinder. The steam pressure was about three atmospheres. The engine was built on a wooden base and, like Trevithick's, was movable. In 1804, the engine was ready and was used for various tasks, including driving a marble saw in Philadelphia. Evans's engine was the first movable prime mover.

The multiple cock used by Evans and Trevithick as a valve gear had certain drawbacks. For one thing, it wore out very quickly. In 1799, one of Watt's assistants, the Scotsman William Murdock (1754–1839), took out a patent for what is known as the D-slide valve, which was driven by an excentric disc on the axle of the balance wheel. But Watt was sceptical, and his engines retained the old type of valve gear with levers. Some years later, the slide found its perfect form in the simple flat valve, or valve slide, invented in 1802 by yet another Scotsman, Matthew Murray (1765–1826). This slide, or versions of it, remained in use throughout the steam era.

In a high-pressure steam-engine the steam expands while it works. One of Watt's ideas was to allow the steam to expand in a series of connected cylinders. He had experimented with this idea in 1782, but the steam pressure was too low, and Watt abandoned the scheme. An Englishman, Arthur Woolf, was more successful. He used steam pressure at about four atmospheres and let the steam expand in two cylinders in series, the second cylinder having a larger diameter than the first. Woolf's compound machine, as the invention was called, was made in 1804 and was the first of its kind.

Within only a couple of years of the start of the nineteenth century, the steam-engine had radically changed its appearance. The moment Watt's patent expired, the flood-gates opened, and new ideas flowed out. (This is an example of how the patent system can impede technological development.) But there were other factors contributing to this rapid progress. New machining methods and machines were appearing all the time, and, as the first technical colleges were founded, the engineer who was qualified in both theory and practice came on the scene. These colleges were often military institutions, but later, civilians were admitted to them.

In the following decades, the steam-engine developed at an increasing pace, mainly along the lines indicated above. New designs aimed at raising steam pressure still further and at a better use of the

B Trevithick himself here stands next to his steam-engine of c. 1805. The cylinder (a) was submerged in the boiler (b). The piston rod (c) ended in a cross-bar (d) with two casings which slid along two guides (e). (f) Connecting rods. (g) Crank axle. (h) Inspection cover. (i) Cock for control of the water level in b. (j) Furnace front. (k) Fresh-air intake and ash bin. (l) Safety valve. (m) Connecting link between d and the steam distribution cock.

C Evans's steam-engine of 1813. The fumes from the furnace (a) first flowed round the outside of the boiler (b), then travelled by way of a pipe inside b to the smoke stack (c). (d) Cylinder. (e) Piston rod. (f) Connecting rod. For the power transmission from e to f, a "grasshopper" (g) was used, whose fulcrum (h) was attached in a "floating" fashion to the engine's foundation (i) by two struts (j). A stay (k) between i and g compensated g's tendency to move its free end along an arc.

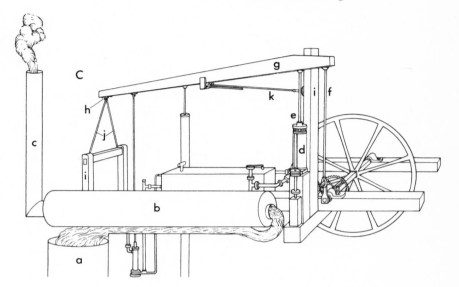

expansion of steam. One interesting example is the high-pressure steam-engine designed by the German Ernst Alban (1791–1856). This operated in a textile mill in Plau, Mecklenburg (now in East Germany). Alban, originally an oculist, first experimented with pressures of up to fifty atmospheres but decided for practical reasons to settle for about ten atmospheres. The engine had an oscillating cylinder which worked directly on the connecting rod of the balance wheel. It had a centrifugal governor, and the entire engine was built according to a monumental design, with cast-iron pillars in Grecian style supporting a lovely classical pediment. Another of Alban's achievements, produced after much hard work, was a safe and efficient steam boiler suitable for high pressures. He is considered to be the first to design a usable tubular boiler.

As has been mentioned above, new types of steam-engine began to appear about 1850, the main reason being that steam technology was now beginning to get a firmer theoretical ground on which to stand. In the early stages, the exploitation of steam power had been severely hampered by a complete lack of theoretical insight into the real nature of such basic phenomena as air, fire, and water. In 1824, the French engineer and physicist Sadi Carnot (1796–1832) presented the first basic theory of the steam-engine in a pamphlet entitled *Réflexions sur la Puissance Motrice du Feu* ("Reflections on the Driving Power of Fire"). Its subject was all kinds of heat engines, and it was written on a very high level of abstraction, containing a very advanced mathematical presentation of the problems involved. In other words, it was almost completely unintelligible to contemporary practitioners of steam technology and therefore attracted little attention in the engineering journals then beginning to appear. It was not until 1834 that Carnot's compatriot Benoît Clapeyron (1799–1864), a works engineer and a designer of steam-engines, tried to enlarge upon these theories and explain them to those who were working practically in the field. However, he did not have much success either. In 1842, the German scientist J. Robert Mayer (1814–78) introduced his theory of applied thermodynamics, which clarified many concepts. The Englishman James Prescott Joule (1818–89) developed Mayer's ideas in a work published in 1847, and the German Rudolf Clausius (1812–88) did the same in his *Ueber die bewegende Kraft der Wärme)* ("On the Driving Power of Heat"). In the late 1840s, Carnot's book of 1824 found its way into the hands of the great natural scientist William Thomson (later Lord Kelvin), who read it and exclaimed, "Never before in the history of natural science has such a great book been written!"

This may have been a slight exaggeration, but Thomson was the one who was later to sum up all these theories in his formulation of the main laws of thermodynamics, which was first published in 1851. Today, his clearly articulated interpretations of natural laws still form the basis for our attempts to solve the present world energy supply problems.

Pre-eminent among the engineers who broke new ground in steam-engine technology is the American George Henry Corliss

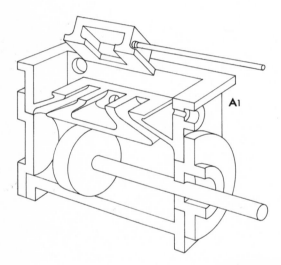

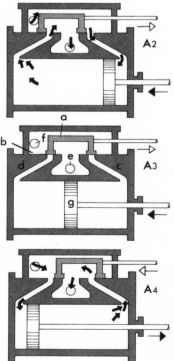

A A steam-engine cylinder with a valve slide. (**1**) The slide (*a*) consisted of a hollowed-out plate. It was moved to and fro on the valve face (*b*), which had two steam passages (*c, d*) leading to the ends of the cylinder, and an outlet (*e*) through which steam left the cylinder. High-pressure steam was let in through an opening (*f*) in the valve chest. (**2**) When *a* was situated in its left-hand position, steam entered from *f* through *c*. The steam which had filled the space to the left of the piston (*g*) simultaneously left the cylinder through *d* and *e*, and the piston was pushed to the left by the pressure of the incoming steam. (**3**) When *a* was positioned in the middle of the valve face, both of the steam passages were blocked. The steam in the cylinder worked through expansion. (**4**) Just before the piston had reached its turning-point, *d* was opened, and steam entered to the left of the piston. At the same time, the steam on the other side of *g* escaped by way of *c* and *e*.

(1817–88). In his twenties, Corliss determined to build a steam-engine in which the vital parts would consist of completely new elements, superior to those already in existence. In 1846, he and two partners founded a mechanical workshop in Providence, Rhode Island, where they manufactured steam-engines. At first, the engines were relatively conventional, but they were successively improved. Corliss first concentrated on the slide mechanism, and he took out a patent for an entirely new idea in 1849–the gear with cylindrical rocking valves, later known internationally as the Corliss slide. Among the foremost of its many advantages was the fact that the slide valve was indirectly controlled by the centrifugal governor so that the amount of steam it admitted depended on the work load of the engine. If the load were heavy, the intake increased, and vice versa. This saved steam and thus improved fuel economy. However, the Corliss slide and Corliss's other important inventions differed so much from those that were established that he could not find customers for them. He solved this problem, however, by lending the engine free of charge–as long as he had his share of the money saved by its lower fuel consumption. His engines came up to expectations, and Corliss was soon the most celebrated engineer in the United States. He reached the zenith of his career as a mechanical engineer when he built the huge engine for the Centennial Exposition in Philadelphia in 1876. This engine became almost a symbol of the Exposition and, indeed, of the whole era of steam. A beam engine with vertical cylinders, Corliss's steam-engine had an effect of 2,500 horsepower and was the largest steam-engine hitherto constructed.

In 1870, when the American Academy of Arts and Sciences awarded Henry Corliss its prestigious Rumford medal, it was tacitly stating that no other inventor since James Watt had meant so much to steam technology. This judgement is indisputable. Corliss's work was of great importance both to steam technology and to the engineering industry in his native country. When his patent expired, his ideas were developed by the principal steam-engine manufacturers in both the United States and Europe.

Several European engineers were inspired by William Thomson's theories of thermodynamics to enter what was to prove a fruitful field of research. In the 1870s, Gustav Adolf Hirn (1815–90), the owner of a textile mill in Alsace, now a part of France, made a comprehensive survey of the steam-engines which drove the spinning-machines in his mill. He wanted to find ways of improving their operating efficiency, and he concentrated especially on the exchange of heat between the steam and the cylinder wall, a phenomenon which is known in steam technology as cylinder condensation, one of the greatest sources of heat loss in the steam-engine. Hirn came to the conclusion that heat loss would be reduced considerably if the steam were superheated. The results of his research were taken up by the Swiss company Gebrüder Sulzer in Winterthur, especially by its chief designer Charles Brown (1827–1905). Brown collaborated with Heinrich Sulzer, the son of one of the brothers who owned the firm, in building the first engine for superheated steam, which was ready in 1866. Both engineers had been very impressed by Corliss's ideas, and among other things, a modified Corliss slide was incorporated in their design. The engine had an effect of 56 horsepower and worked with a steam pressure of five atmospheres. It was shown at the world exhibition in Paris in 1867, together with several engines built by Corliss. The new designs aroused a lot of interest, both at the exhibition itself and in the technical press, and stimulated engineers all over the world to try out new ideas and concepts which would improve the steam-engine. During the following decades, many attempts were made to increase the pressure of the steam in steam-engines. Also the idea of letting steam expand successively in

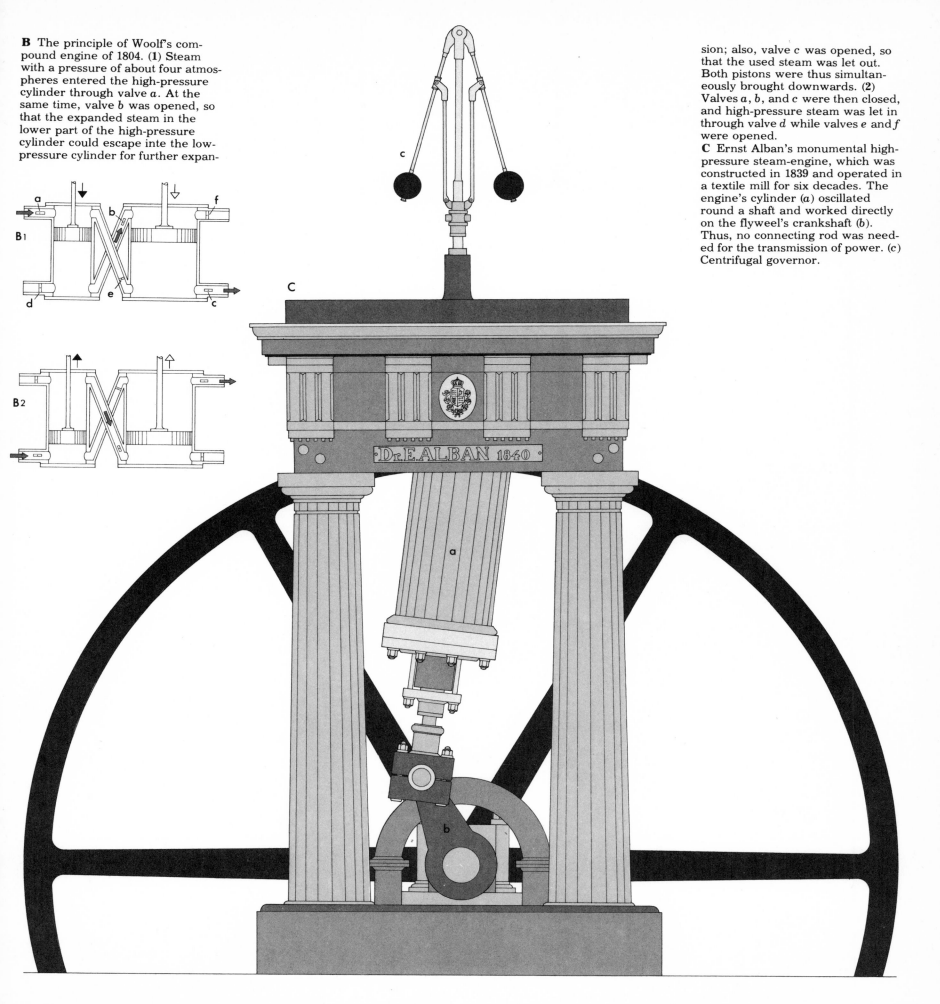

B The principle of Woolf's compound engine of 1804. (1) Steam with a pressure of about four atmospheres entered the high-pressure cylinder through valve *a*. At the same time, valve *b* was opened, so that the expanded steam in the lower part of the high-pressure cylinder could escape inte the low-pressure cylinder for further expansion; also, valve *c* was opened, so that the used steam was let out. Both pistons were thus simultaneously brought downwards. (2) Valves *a*, *b*, and *c* were then closed, and high-pressure steam was let in through valve *d* while valves *e* and *f* were opened.

C Ernst Alban's monumental high-pressure steam-engine, which was constructed in 1839 and operated in a textile mill for six decades. The engine's cylinder (*a*) oscillated round a shaft and worked directly on the flyweel's crankshaft (*b*). Thus, no connecting rod was needed for the transmission of power. (*c*) Centrifugal governor.

B1

B2

C

Dr.E.ALBAN 1840

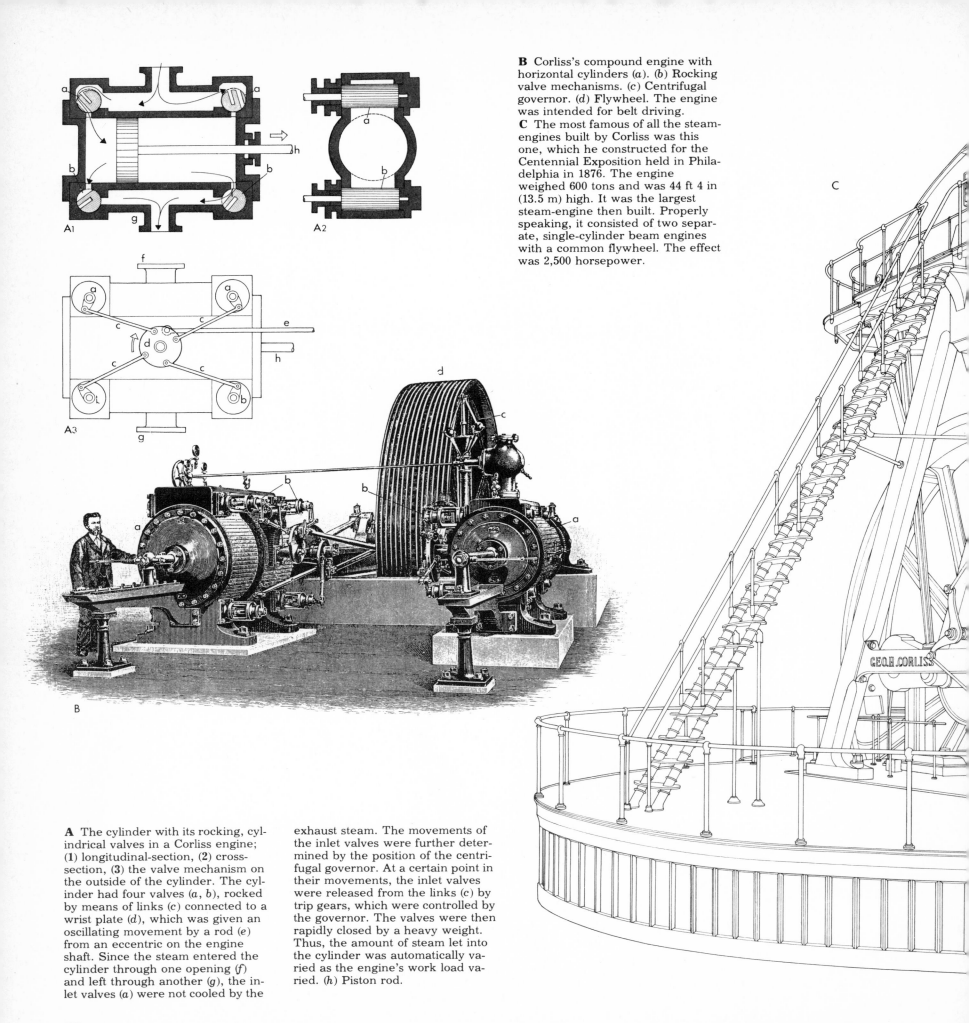

C

B Corliss's compound engine with horizontal cylinders (a). (b) Rocking valve mechanisms. (c) Centrifugal governor. (d) Flywheel. The engine was intended for belt driving.
C The most famous of all the steam-engines built by Corliss was this one, which he constructed for the Centennial Exposition held in Philadelphia in 1876. The engine weighed 600 tons and was 44 ft 4 in (13.5 m) high. It was the largest steam-engine then built. Properly speaking, it consisted of two separate, single-cylinder beam engines with a common flywheel. The effect was 2,500 horsepower.

A The cylinder with its rocking, cylindrical valves in a Corliss engine; (**1**) longitudinal-section, (**2**) cross-section, (**3**) the valve mechanism on the outside of the cylinder. The cylinder had four valves (a, b), rocked by means of links (c) connected to a wrist plate (d), which was given an oscillating movement by a rod (e) from an eccentric on the engine shaft. Since the steam entered the cylinder through one opening (f) and left through another (g), the inlet valves (a) were not cooled by the exhaust steam. The movements of the inlet valves were further determined by the position of the centrifugal governor. At a certain point in their movements, the inlet valves were released from the links (c) by trip gears, which were controlled by the governor. The valves were then rapidly closed by a heavy weight. Thus, the amount of steam let into the cylinder was automatically varied as the engine's work load varied. (h) Piston rod.

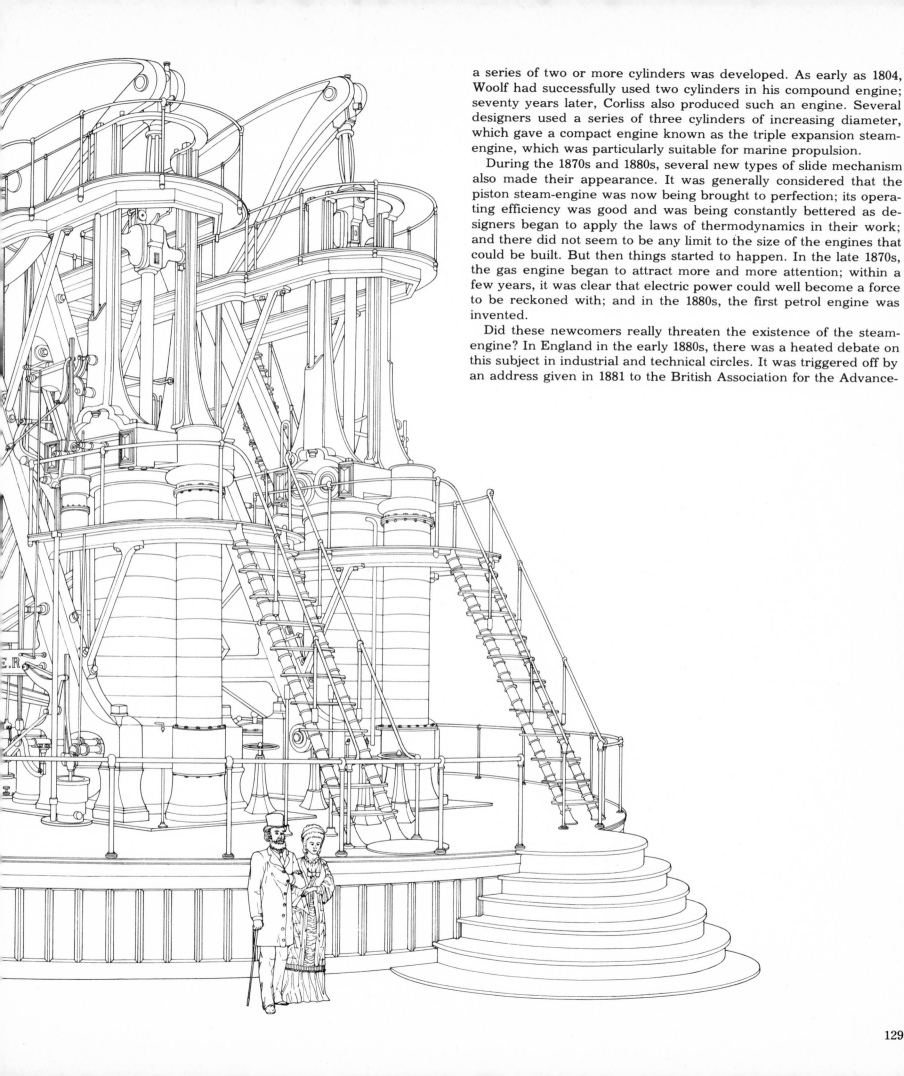

a series of two or more cylinders was developed. As early as 1804, Woolf had successfully used two cylinders in his compound engine; seventy years later, Corliss also produced such an engine. Several designers used a series of three cylinders of increasing diameter, which gave a compact engine known as the triple expansion steam-engine, which was particularly suitable for marine propulsion.

During the 1870s and 1880s, several new types of slide mechanism also made their appearance. It was generally considered that the piston steam-engine was now being brought to perfection; its operating efficiency was good and was being constantly bettered as designers began to apply the laws of thermodynamics in their work; and there did not seem to be any limit to the size of the engines that could be built. But then things started to happen. In the late 1870s, the gas engine began to attract more and more attention; within a few years, it was clear that electric power could well become a force to be reckoned with; and in the 1880s, the first petrol engine was invented.

Did these newcomers really threaten the existence of the steam-engine? In England in the early 1880s, there was a heated debate on this subject in industrial and technical circles. It was triggered off by an address given in 1881 to the British Association for the Advancement of Science by Sir W. George Armstrong, a well-known industrialist who was later made a peer. In his speech, which attracted considerable notice, Armstrong severely criticized the piston steam-engine, mainly for its poor operational efficiency. He maintained that entirely new avenues had to be explored in the search for a new prime mover. Sir Frederic Bramwell, who was an authority in the field of technology, agreed with him and added provocatively that there would be no steam-engines in operation fifty years hence—in 1931—they would be museum pieces! In 1888, Sir Frederic repeated this prophecy and also donated a sum of money to the British Association, to be given to anyone who could develop these ideas in an authoritative lecture. Sir Alfred Ewing gave just such a lecture three years later. In the meantime, however, a new prime mover, the steam turbine, had appeared and was showing great promise. Sir Alfred was able to maintain that steam was neither dead nor dying, and that the steam turbine would, very likely, show the world both larger and more efficient machines than Bramwell had ever dreamt of. Today, we know that Sir Alfred Ewing was right.

However, the designers of the steam-engine did not give up so easily. Both in England and on the Continent admirable attempts were made to improve the piston steam-engine. In the early 1890s, the German Wilhelm Schmidt, working along the lines of the Sulzer engine for superheated steam, developed an engine for steam at a temperature of no less than 350°C. In the following decade, another German, Johann Stumpf, developed a simplified piston steam-engine which he called the "uniflow" engine because the steam flowed in one direction only through the cylinder. The uniflow engine enjoyed a certain popularity, especially in Germany, where one of its uses was in locomobiles.

At first, the steam turbine did not appear to be the serious rival to the piston steam-engine that Sir Alfred Ewing had predicted it would be. But around the year 1910, the situation changed, and the turbine gained a great deal of ground. The fate which befell Henry Corliss's engine from the Centennial Exposition in Philadelphia serves to illustrate this. When the engine had been returned to the factory in Providence, George Mortimer Pullman visited Corliss there and bought the engine on the spot. He then used it to drive the machines used in the manufacture of sleeping-cars for the Pullman Palace Car Company until 1910, when it was replaced by a stationary steam turbine.

The Steam Turbine

In the 1770s and 1780s, when Watt's steam-engines were coming into service, the eyes of many engineers were opened to the potential of steam power. But these early engines could only produce a reciprocating motion. If steam could also produce a rotary motion, would it not be of much more general use? Watt himself had raised this question several times. The first occasion was in 1769—the year in which he took out his condenser patent—when he experimented with a ring-shaped "cylinder" in which a piston was to be driven round by steam. However, the device did not work, and he abandoned the scheme. But fifteen years later, he was compelled to reconsider the idea, since the Hungarian Baron Wolfgang von Kempelen (1734–1804) had taken out a patent on a steam turbine. This attracted a great deal of attention in England, not least because von Kempelen claimed that his engine was superior to Watt's and could easily push it off the market. Well, if the good baron was an indefatigable inventor, he was also a great joker. In the history of technology he is best remembered for his chess-playing Turk (see page 178).

The design of von Kempelen's turbine is not unlike that suggested by the Italian Giovanni Branca in 1629. It was known as an action turbine, that is, one in which a jet of steam exerts pressure—"acts"—

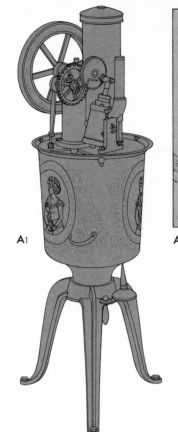
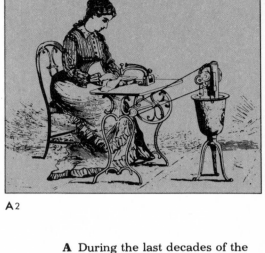

A During the last decades of the nineteenth century, tiny steam-engines (1) for household use were marketed. This example was manufactured by Tyson and was considered to be especially well suited for powering sewing-machines (2). In order to regulate the speed of the sewing-machine, a braking device could be attached to the belt pulley. The brake would then be connected to a spring-loaded pedal and a counterweight.

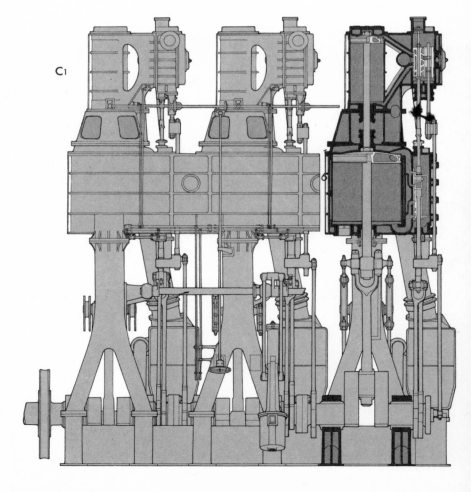

C1

B Steam ploughing in the mid-nineteenth century. A rope was stretched over pulleys round the field. The plough was attached to the rope and was pulled across the field between two of the pulleys when one end of the rope was wound onto a drum and the other end was unwound at the same speed from another drum. The steam-engine alternately drove the drums forwards and backwards, and the pulleys were moved by hand closer and closer to the steam-engine for each furrow to be ploughed.

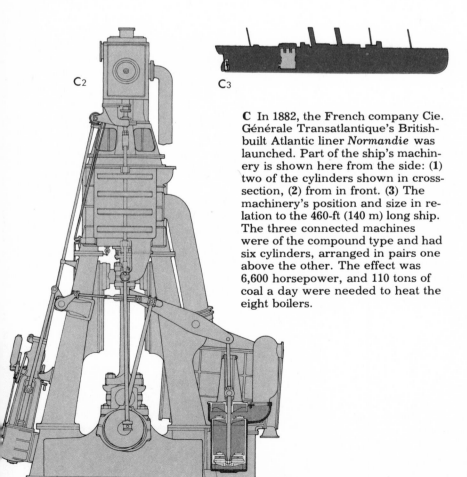

C In 1882, the French company Cie. Générale Transatlantique's British-built Atlantic liner *Normandie* was launched. Part of the ship's machinery is shown here from the side: (**1**) two of the cylinders shown in cross-section, (**2**) from in front. (**3**) The machinery's position and size in relation to the 460-ft (140 m) long ship. The three connected machines were of the compound type and had six cylinders, arranged in pairs one above the other. The effect was 6,600 horsepower, and 110 tons of coal a day were needed to heat the eight boilers.

on the blades of the turbine wheel. But after a thorough examination of such facts as the steam consumption, the speed of rotation, and the output of von Kempelen's engine, Watt concluded that the design was technically impossible. To make the output in any way reasonable, the speed of the turbine wheel would have to be enormous—so enormous that its own centrifugal force would cause it to burst into pieces! At a more normal speed, its steam consumption would be disproportionately high in relation to its output. These calculations were all that Watt needed to calm his partner, Matthew Boulton, who had been quite distressed by the rumours that their steam monopoly was in danger.

During the following decades, several engineers concentrated their efforts on finding a way of producing rotary motion from steam power. In 1797, the versatile English clergyman Edmund Cartwright presented an idea not unlike Watt's but it, too, did not work in practice. In 1799, Watt's assistant William Murdock took out a patent on an interesting device in which two engaged cog-wheels were rotated by a steam jet. The idea was a good one—the same design is still used for things like oil pumps—but in Murdock's day, the necessary precision in manufacturing could not be achieved.

The first person to use steam power to produce rotary motion was Carl Gustaf Patrik de Laval (1845–1913), who developed his first invention, the milk separator, in the 1870s. To achieve the desired result, the container had to be rotated at a very high frequency, 6,000–10,000 rpm. The small hand-cranked units for domestic use employed a gearing to achieve this speed, whereas the larger units were driven by horse-wheels. However, de Laval wanted a prime mover which could be connected directly to the separator without a gear mechanism. He first tried out a simple reaction turbine with an S-shaped rotor; this worked on the same principle as Hero's ball. Twenty years later, de Laval described these experiments:

> Fully convinced that speed is a gift from the gods, I dared, in 1876, to believe in the direct exploitation of steam on a power-generating wheel. It was a bold venture. At that time, only low speeds were employed. The speeds which were considered normal in later separators were never used. In contemporary handbooks they wrote about steam: "Unfortunately, the density of steam is too low to permit any thought of exploiting it in a power-generating wheel." In spite of this I succeeded.

The reason de Laval succeeded was partly his experience of the technical problems which occurred at high speeds, and partly the fact that the turbine gave exactly what he was looking for, namely, high-speed rotation. At the same time that he was working to perfect the separator, which he patented in 1878, de Laval was developing several versions of the S-turbine. He had reached the same conclusion as Watt, that the efficiency of the steam turbine is not satisfactory until it attains 30,000–40,000 rpm. He spent a great amount of time and much effort in trying to solve the very difficult technical problems that occurred at these speeds, for example, how to balance the axle and the S-rotor. The slightest imbalance generated such great forces that they broke even heavy steel axles. It was not until 1883 that de Laval considered that he had mastered these problems, when he took out a patent for his engine for driving milk separators, which was the first steam turbine with a practical application.

Nevertheless, de Laval was not satisfied. He abandoned the reaction turbine and concentrated instead on the action turbine, that is, Branca's model. He tried everything to increase its output while keeping its speed within reasonable limits. "Reasonable" in this context has to be seen from de Laval's point of view. *Gustaf de Laval—Man of High Speeds* is the title of a biography written by Torsten Althin. One version of de Laval's S-turbine was designed for a speed of 42,000 rpm!

While working on his action turbine, de Laval discovered an interesting method of letting the steam jet expand in the nozzle before "acting", thus increasing the exploitation of kinetic energy. The first draft of his design for these nozzles shows that they had "widening outlets" which enabled the steam jet to expand before hitting the blades of the turbine wheel. In 1888, de Laval patented an action turbine with just such a nozzle. Later, the nozzle found many other applications in the field of technology, one being in the rocket engines of spacecraft, where the driving jet of gas expands in Laval nozzles, as they are nowadays called.

De Laval also solved the problem of mass forces. Instead of increasing the diameter and thus the strength of the axle, he made it slimmer and resilient. The turbine-wheel/axle system was so dimensioned that the practically inevitable imbalance produced a resonance in the vibrations at a relatively low speed of rotation (when the turbine was being started or stopped). At the resonance point, the axle could vibrate with an amplitude of about 0.4 in (10 mm) or more. A resilient axle can take this, if it is fitted with bearings which can stand up to such a "whipping" rotary movement. He solved this by fitting the bearing in a spherical segment in which it could follow the motion of the axle. When the resonance point had been passed and the turbine had assumed its running speed, the turbine-wheel/axle system adjusted itself automatically, whereupon the vibrations ceased.

The patent for the nozzle of de Laval's action turbine was taken out in 1888. The combination of expansion nozzle and turbine wheel proved very effective in exploiting steam energy. But the speed was too high and had to be reduced to a level where the turbine could be applied practically.

A lot of dogged research was required to solve this problem. Once de Laval had designed an efficient, slim axle, he tested different gear mechanisms in an effort to find one which could transmit large forces at high speeds. The solution he found was a double helical gear, the so-called fish-bone gear, which was to characterize the de Laval turbines for a long time.

De Laval had many ideas on how his "steam-motor", as he called it, could be put to practical use. For a while, he considered using it to propel ships and, in 1892, had drawings ready for a small turbine-powered vessel. But in the end, he decided to concentrate on producing units for generating electrical energy. These units were built with a capacity ranging from 5 to 500 horsepower.

The turbine had an extremely high operating efficiency. A comparative test made in 1890 between a 6-horsepower steam-engine and a 5-horsepower de Laval steam turbine showed that the steam-engine consumed seventy-five per cent more steam! An important contributory factor to this was a steam boiler with relatively small helical pipes, yet another of de Laval's designs. In this boiler the coils were strongly heated by forced combustion in the furnace, created by automatically controlled electric fans. This produced a huge amount of steam at very high pressure. However, the amount of steam in the helical pipes at any given time was relatively small, so a bursting pipe would cause little damage.

Gustaf de Laval must be considered one of the pioneers of high-pressure steam. At the craft and industry exhibition in Stockholm in 1897, the electric power was supplied by two de Laval units. On one occasion when the Swedish king, Oscar II, the patron of the exhibition, was shown these units, de Laval mentioned that the boiler could produce a pressure of 110 atmospheres; the king instinctively took a step backwards. When they got to the other unit, de Laval informed him that it worked at a pressure of 220 atmospheres; Oscar II rapidly left the exhibition.

By the early 1880s, the idea of a steam turbine was very much in the air. The year after de Laval had taken out a patent for his S-turbine, the Englishman Sir Charles Parsons (1854–1931) set about developing a turbine specifically for driving an electric generator. The year was 1884, and Parsons had to grapple with the technical problems that arose at extremely high speeds, as well as with the problems of bearings and strength—that is to say, with the same problems that were troubling de Laval. Parsons, a brilliant designer and an ingenious inventor, soon overcame these stumbling-blocks. He did not take the usual path via laboratory models and production prototypes but implemented his ideas in a full-scale machine, ready for industrial use. The unit was in operation in the Forth Bank in London until 1900, when it was donated to the Science Museum in the same city.

The basic idea for Parsons's steam turbine was taken from the water turbine as designed by, among others, Fourneyron. Parsons let the steam flow between fixed guide vanes, so that it met the blades of the wheel at right angles. The turbine had fourteen fixed rims with guide vanes, and fourteen rotating blade wheels on a common axle. The steam was admitted at the middle of the axle and flowed parallel to it in both directions, while working and expanding to atmospheric pressure. The steam pressure was 6.5 atmospheres, and the speed of rotation was as high as 18,000 rpm. The electric generator was directly connected to the turbine axle. It must be considered a brilliant achievement of Parsons to have designed a generator that could function at such a high velocity. The electric generators of the time were usually made for 800–1,200 rpm. Parsons's generator gave a voltage of 100V with a maximum load of 75A. The turbine developed about 10 horsepower.

Parsons's axial-flow turbine (with steam working in the direction of the axle) represents an important breakthrough in the history of technology, and it introduced the era of the turbine's spectacular development. While that restless inventor Gustaf de Laval soon left his successful turbine company in other hands and devoted himself to a mass of different projects, Charles Parsons spent the whole of his active life, from 1884 onwards, working on turbines.

By 1889, almost three hundred axial-flow turbines had been produced by the Gateshead-on-Tyne firm of Clarke, Chapman & Co., of which Parsons was a partner. However, due to differences of opinion with his fellow owners, Parsons had to terminate the partnership and give up his turbine and generator patents. This forced him to find fundamentally new designs, if he was to continue in the field. So he formed C. A. Parsons & Co. Ltd., Newcastle-upon-Tyne, later of worldwide renown, and designed a turbine in which steam worked radially, that is, from the centre out towards the periphery. The first Parsons-designed radial turbine was delivered in 1891 to the Cambridge Electric Lighting Co. and was remarkable for the fact that it had an inbuilt condenser in which the steam, after doing its work, was condensed at atmospheric pressure. The spent steam had so far always been exhausted to the outside, but now the condensate could be pumped away. The unit was of 100-kW single-phase alternating current with a frequency of 80 periods per second and a voltage of 2,000 V. The frequency of rotation was only 4,800 rpm, and the operating efficiency was very high.

The Cambridge turbine created a sensation among electrical engineers, both in England and elsewhere. Similar units, but of ever increasing capacity, were soon delivered to different parts of Britain. In 1898, Parsons & Co. built the then largest turbine unit in the world for an electric power-station being built in Elberfeld, Germany. The capacity was 1,000 kW, so high that contemporary engineers felt it to be somewhat risky.

In the 1890s and the early years of the twentieth century, engineers all over the world contributed towards opening up new ground in the field, and by about 1910, the piston steam-engine was totally surpassed by the steam turbine.

In 1895, the American Charles Gordon Curtis (1860–1953) took out a patent for a combination of the principles of the action and reaction turbines. In the Curtis design the steam impinged upon a rotor with fixed guide vanes, like the one used by Parsons in his axial-flow turbine. The guide vanes changed the direction of the steam jet; at the same time, the steam expanded, just as it did in the Laval steam nozzle. Curtis ran a small factory in Brooklyn, New York, in which electrical appliances were manufactured. He contacted the General Electric Co. in Schenectady, in New York State, and offered them the right to develop his invention further. General Electric hesitated for some time before trying out the design in a 500-kW plant which supplied their Schenectady factory with electricity. They were positively surprised by the results, and plans were immediately drawn up for a Curtis turbine of 5,000 kW, which was completed in 1903. It had an interesting design, with a vertical turbine axle necessitating a specially designed axle bearing, which was lubricated with oil under very high pressure. The Curtis GE turbine was later developed under licence by AEG in Germany and by British Thomson-Houston in England.

In France Auguste Rateau (1863–1930) developed what is known as the multi-stage turbine, which he patented in 1896. Rateau divided the expansion of the steam into a number of successive stages, which meant that the fall in steam pressure at each stage was successively smaller. This enabled the turbine wheel to rotate more slowly, yet without any loss of output. As a rule, an electric generator could be connected directly to the turbine axle without the use of an intermediate reduction gear. The first multi-stage turbine designed by Rateau was built in 1898 by Sauter, Harlé & Cie. This type of turbine had its commercial breakthrough at the world exhibition in Paris in 1900. Auguste Rateau was a professor at the Ecole Polytechnique in Paris and was highly thought of both as a research scientist and a designer. Among the companies which manufactured his multi-stage turbine under licence were the well-known engineering company Oerlikon in Switzerland and the Skoda works in Czechoslovakia. The licensees often found ways of improving and developing the turbine.

During the first years of the twentieth century, the Swedish inventors Birger Ljungström (1872–1948) and his brother Fredrik (1875–1964) set about developing a very compact boiler for high pressure steam. Some of the work had been done in England, where, during a visit to Charles Parsons's factory in Newcastle-upon-Tyne, Birger had become fascinated by the potential of the turbine. At the same time as they were working on other projects, the Ljungström brothers began looking for new design principles for turbines. By 1906, after some years' work, they had found a solution that was as original as it was simple, and in which nobody else in Sweden or England believed. They then contacted the leading turbine authority at the time, Professor Aurel Stodola of the Eidgenössische Technische Hochschule in Zürich, Switzerland. Stodola was most positive about their design, but in spite of this, it was very difficult for the brothers to find investors willing to risk their capital in the manufacture of the new turbine. At last, in 1908, a company was founded, and Ljungströms Steam Turbine Co. began its activities.

The principle of the new turbine design was based on making the steam flow radially, from the centre to the periphery, and at the same time, allowing it to expand, while the guide vanes rotated in the opposite direction to the turbine wheel. Actually, the design consisted of two turbine wheels rotating in opposite directions, a blade rim on one wheel acting as a guide vane for a blade rim on the other, and vice versa. In 1910, a full-scale prototype was ready. With

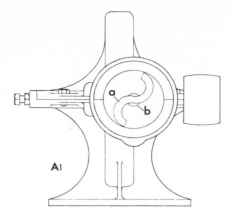 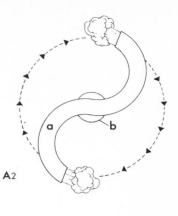

A The simple reaction turbine (1) constructed by de Laval in 1876. The turbine was intended to be connected directly to a separator, and its principle was the same as for Hero's ball. The S-shaped rotor (2, *a*) was set in motion by the reaction pressure occurring when steam escaped through the bent arms of the rotor. The steam was supplied through a pipe (*b*) in the middle of the turbine.

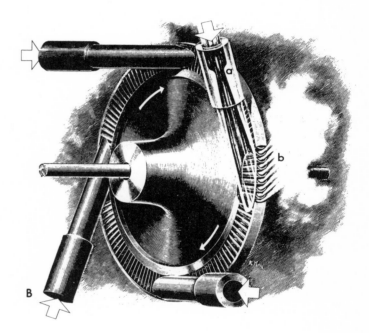

B The principle of de Laval's action turbine. High-pressure steam was blown through nozzles whose inner shape (*a*) allowed the steam to expand to low pressure. Its velocity was then greatly increased, and when the steam jets hit the turbine wheel's bent vanes (*b*), the wheel was set in motion.

C The slim, resilient turbine axle (1) developed by de Laval. The axle bearings were fixed in spherical segments (2) so that the axle could stand up to the "whipping" resonance vibrations. (3) A graphic representation of the size of the resonance vibrations (*f*) in relation to the turbine's speed of rotation (*n*). (*a*) Resonance point. (*b*) The turbine's normal running speed.

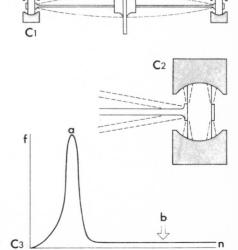

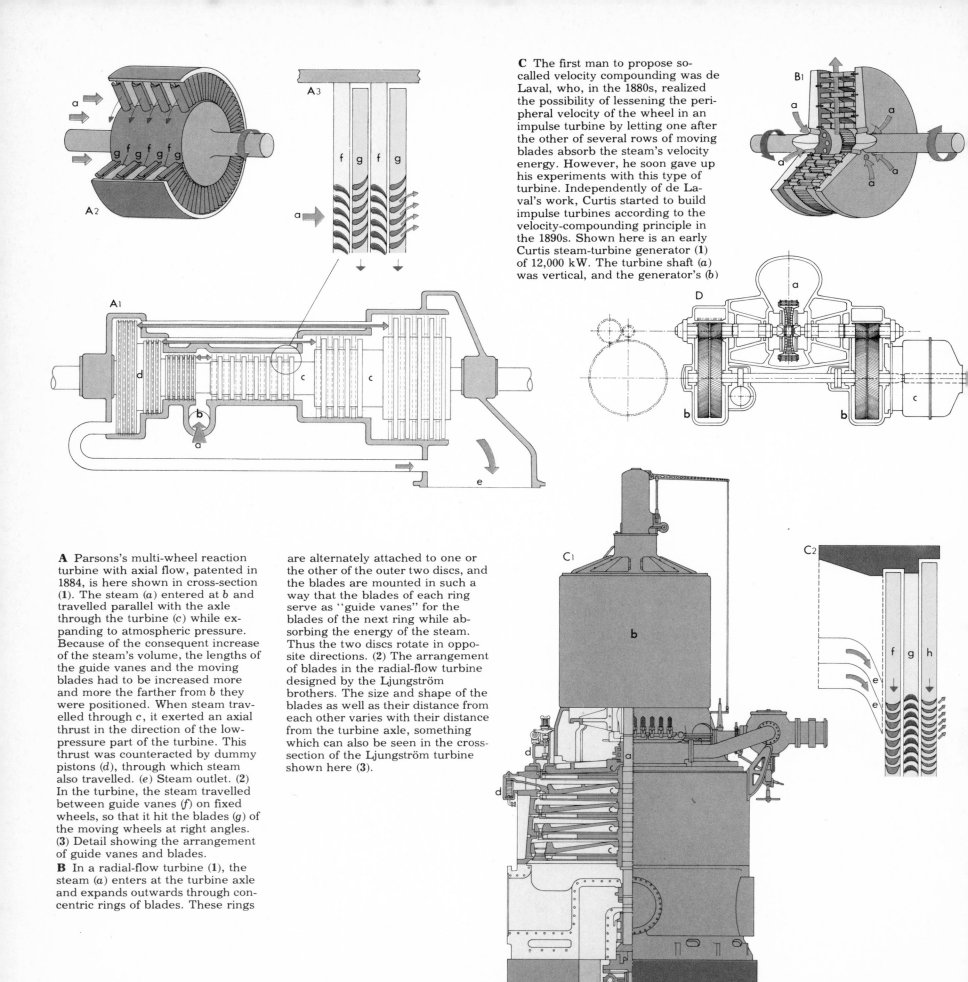

A₃

f g f g

A₂

a

g f g f g

A₁

d

c c

b

a

e

C The first man to propose so-called velocity compounding was de Laval, who, in the 1880s, realized the possibility of lessening the peripheral velocity of the wheel in an impulse turbine by letting one after the other of several rows of moving blades absorb the steam's velocity energy. However, he soon gave up his experiments with this type of turbine. Independently of de Laval's work, Curtis started to build impulse turbines according to the velocity-compounding principle in the 1890s. Shown here is an early Curtis steam-turbine generator (1) of 12,000 kW. The turbine shaft (a) was vertical, and the generator's (b)

B₁

a a

a

a a

D

a

b b c

A Parsons's multi-wheel reaction turbine with axial flow, patented in 1884, is here shown in cross-section (1). The steam (a) entered at b and travelled parallel with the axle through the turbine (c) while expanding to atmospheric pressure. Because of the consequent increase of the steam's volume, the lengths of the guide vanes and the moving blades had to be increased more and more the farther from b they were positioned. When steam travelled through c, it exerted an axial thrust in the direction of the low-pressure part of the turbine. This thrust was counteracted by dummy pistons (d), through which steam also travelled. (e) Steam outlet. (2) In the turbine, the steam travelled between guide vanes (f) on fixed wheels, so that it hit the blades (g) of the moving wheels at right angles. (3) Detail showing the arrangement of guide vanes and blades.
B In a radial-flow turbine (1), the steam (a) enters at the turbine axle and expands outwards through concentric rings of blades. These rings

are alternately attached to one or the other of the outer two discs, and the blades are mounted in such a way that the blades of each ring serve as "guide vanes" for the blades of the next ring while absorbing the energy of the steam. Thus the two discs rotate in opposite directions. (2) The arrangement of blades in the radial-flow turbine designed by the Ljungström brothers. The size and shape of the blades as well as their distance from each other varies with their distance from the turbine axle, something which can also be seen in the cross-section of the Ljungström turbine shown here (3).

C₁

b

a

a

d

d

C₂

f g h

e

e

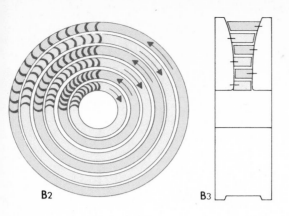

B2   B3

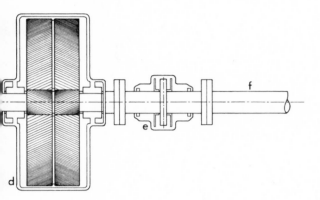

d   e   f

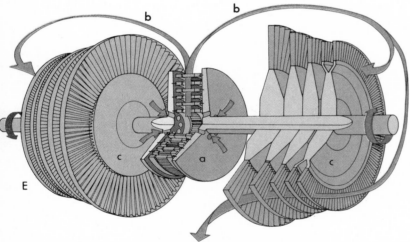

b   b

E   c   a   c

rotor was mounted on the shaft extension. The turbine consisted of five wheels (c), each with two rows of moving blades. The steam entered through nozzles (d) that could be closed automatically and travelled (2) through guide vanes (e), where it expanded, completely or partly, and through moving blades (f), where it parted with velocity energy. It then passed reversing guide vanes (g), where its direction was changed and a possible further expansion took place. The steam's remaining velocity energy was finally absorbed to a large extent by a second row of moving blades (h).
D A Stal turbine from the 1920s with toothed wheel gearing and reversing gear. The machinery was

intended for marine propulsion. Since a steam turbine must revolve very rapidly and a propeller shaft must not be allowed to rotate very fast, some sort of gearing must be employed to connect the two. (a) Turbine. (b) Turbine gear. (c) Reversing gear. (d) Propeller gear. (e) Thrust bearing. (f) Propeller shaft.
E In the 1930s, this type of Stal turbine with both radial and axial flow was developed. The steam first expanded through a radial-flow turbine (a). When the steam's volume was so large that its velocity had almost reached its maximum, the steam jet was split (b) and led to axial-flow turbines (c), where it was allowed to expand further.

a capacity of 500 horsepower, it was designed for a one hundred per cent overload. Its rate of revolution was 3,000 rpm, and its thermal efficiency about thirty per cent.

The first big order the company received came from Willesden, England. It was for a 1,000-kW unit which was to supply electricity to the town's trams. The unit was delivered in 1912 and remained in operation until 1924. The Ljungström brothers' company was reformed in 1913 to become Svenska Turbinfabriks Aktiebolaget Ljungström (Stal), and from that year onwards, the Ljungström turbines, or the Stal turbines, as they were soon called, were manufactured under licence by the British firm Brush Electrical Engineering Co. in Loughborough.

From the second decade of the twentieth century onwards, the steam turbine became the main source of power used in generating electrical energy, and the demands for greater power per unit kept growing. Designers all over the world searched for new principles upon which they could base further development, but the variations had been more or less exhausted by the work of the above-mentioned pioneers. The 50,000-kW Stal turbine built in 1932 for the Swedish National Power Administration is typical of the development that has taken place since 1930. To enable the unit to achieve the high output required, the turbine was designed for both radial and axial steam flow. The Ljungström brothers had discussed this combination with Stodola as early as 1910, but he had advised them to concentrate on a purely radial turbine—probably a sound piece of advice at that stage. Combining radial with axial flow would, without doubt, have been considered a patent infringement by both Curtis and Parsons.

External Combustion Engines

We have already described the wave of new ideas and designs which appeared when Watt's steam-engine patent expired. At about the same time, people started to speculate about new methods of exploiting heat to produce motion. One possible way was suggested by the colourful and highly talented aviation pioneer, the Englishman Sir George Cayley (1773–1857). He was only twenty when he first began to take an interest in aviation, and in 1799, he outlined the principles of aircraft design, with stiff wings and body, and a stabilizing tail unit with control surfaces. This seems very obvious to us today, but Sir George's contemporaries did not even take him seriously. In 1783, the first balloon ascents had taken place in France (by the Montgolfier brothers in a hot-air balloon and by Professor Jacques Charles in a hydrogen balloon), and these stimulated a lot of ideas about conquering the air with other kinds of craft. Most of these ideas aimed at imitating the flight of birds. At that time, it was more or less axiomatic that this would be the answer. The "flapping-wing flier", or ornithopter, was the aircraft of the future. And from the time of Sir George Cayley until the end of the next century, many inventors tried to design such a machine, but it was not until our own time that a functioning ornithopter has been actually produced—on a toy scale.

Cayley carried out extensive practical experiments, both with scaled-down and full-scale models. His "aeroplanes" (the term had yet to be invented) were based on the principles that he had established. But he needed a prime mover. He discussed this problem in an article in *Nicholson's Journal* in October, 1807, stating that a steam-engine was out of the question, as it was too bulky and heavy. But, he continued, air increases its volume when heated and reduces it when cooled, and these properties can surely be exploited for kinetic energy. He also touched upon the possibility of using a "gunpowder engine", but he went no further than to suggest that a heat engine with air as its medium must be the best means of powering an aircraft. Sir George also made a sketch of this engine, which he

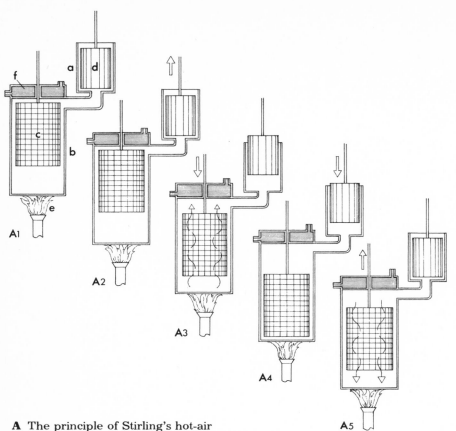

A1 A2 A3 A4 A5

called the caloric engine, and of its mode of operation. Although the design never left the drawing-board, we must see Sir George Cayley as the originator of the caloric, or hot-air, engine.

The first practical attempts to realize Sir George's idea were made by the Scottish clergyman Robert Stirling (1790–1879) who began work on his engine in 1816. After extensive experiments in which his brother James helped, Stirling's engine was ready to be patented in 1827. In order to exploit the properties of air, as Cayley had suggested, the Stirling brothers used two cylinders. In one of them, air was heated and cooled alternately. When the air expanded, it effected the power stroke in the other cylinder. The machine is reported to have worked well and efficiently, by the standards of the time. The Stirling brothers built several engines but never mass-produced them. The largest Stirling engine ever built had a power of 21 horsepower; the diameter of the working cylinder was 15.7 in (40 cm), and the piston stroke was 47.2 in (120 cm).

The versatile Swedish inventor John Ericsson (1803–89) was only nineteen when he first took an interest in the ideas that would later lead to the first mass-produced hot-air engine. He reasoned that the heat flow in the steam-engine was an unnecessary detour via water and steam, stating that:

> If the flame itself was alternately admitted to and barred from a chamber corresponding to the cylinder of a steam engine, a kinetic power would result, which would be as useful as that of

A The principle of Stirling's hot-air engine. (1) The engine consisted of a cylinder (*a*) which was closed only at its lower end and was connected by way of a pipe to another cylinder (*b*), which was closed at both ends. The piston (*c*) in cylinder *b* was of the usual type. Both pistons were connected to a crank axle. (*e*) Heat source. (*f*) Cooling water. Piston *c* is here in its uppermost and piston *d* in its lowest position. (2) As the bottom of cylinder *b* was heated, *c* remained where it was while *d* moved upwards due to the expansion of the air in *b*. (3) Piston *d* then remained at its topmost position while piston *c* was lowered. The heated air at the bottom of *b* then travelled through *c* and up to the top of the cylinder, where it was cooled by the water (*f*). While travelling through *c*, the air had also lost a lot of its heat to the iron plates. (4) As the air's temperature sank, its pressure fell too, and piston *d* consequently moved downwards. Piston *c* thereupon moved upwards again while piston *d* remained at its lower position. When the cooled air again travelled downwards, it absorbed heat from piston *c* and was further partly heated by *e*.

B Ericsson's first caloric engine employed the same principle as Stirling's engine. The regenerator consisted of a cylindrical vessel (*a*), closed at both ends, through which thin pipes (*b*) ran. These opened towards two domes (*c*, *d*). Metal sheets (*e*) were fitted across the regenerator's inside; they were alternately cut off at the top and at the

bottom, so that air could circulate. Similar metal sheets were fitted inside the thin pipes (*b*) and in pipe *f*, which was surrounded by cooling water. (*g*) Hot-air cylinder. (*h*) Cold-air cylinder. (*i*) Valve chest. (*j*) Furnace.

C Ericsson's caloric engine in its final form. The engine is shown here in longitudinal-section; the drawing was made by the inventor himself.

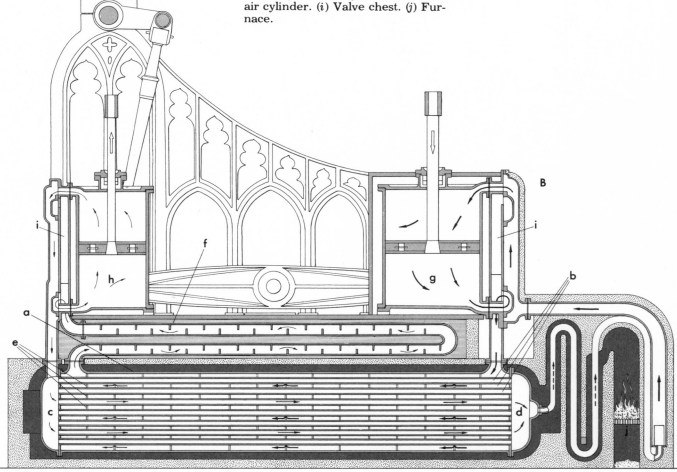

steam, but would have the advantage of being produced in less time and with less fuel.

Model-scale attempts with this "fire-machine", as Ericsson called it, had encouraging results. Unfortunately, he could not find a partner to help develop his ideas—Sweden at that time was very much of an industrial backwater—so he left for England where, in 1826, he settled. In 1833, after a lot of struggle—both with his "fire-machine" and in the fight to survive—Ericsson completed his caloric engine, which generated 5 horsepower. The engine attracted a lot of attention from industrialists as well as from academics. The principle of the engine was the same as that of the Stirling engine, but the two inventors had arrived independently at their solutions from different starting points. Ericsson, however, had provided his engine with a "regenerator", which he imagined would enable the heat from the furnace to work "over and over again", as he said in his enthusiastic description of the engine in his *The Caloric Engine*, published in London in 1833. The great physicist Michael Faraday (1791–1867) warmly admired Ericsson but had reservations about Ericsson's explanation of the function of the regenerator. It would, he said, almost be a *perpetuum mobile*, if it really worked as Ericsson claimed. The two gentlemen were, however, ignorant of an important detail in the theory of heat—the law of the mechanical equivalence of heat, formulated in 1842 by Robert Mayer.

But John Ericsson had plenty of other interests, one of them being

D How Ericsson's ultimate caloric engine worked. The working piston (a) and the feed piston (b) worked in the same cylinder. (c) Furnace. A crank mechanism (d) was necessary in order to make a and b move in a suitable way. (e) Valve regulated by a disc cam on the crank axle and connecting the cylinder space f with the outside air. (g) Air-pressure-regulated valves. (h) Holes connecting cylinder spaces f and i: uncovered when b moved to the right; e is closed, holes h are uncovered. Since a moves faster than b, g open, and cold air enters the cylinder. (2) Piston b turns, h are covered, and e is opened, so that the air in f can escape. (3, 4) Piston a turns but moves at a slower speed than b, so valves g remain open. (5) Piston b turns and e is closed. The holes (h) are uncovered, and when the air enclosed in i and f is now heated, its pressure increases, and valves g close. (6–7) The increasing pressure of the air, which becomes hotter and hotter, forces a to the right.

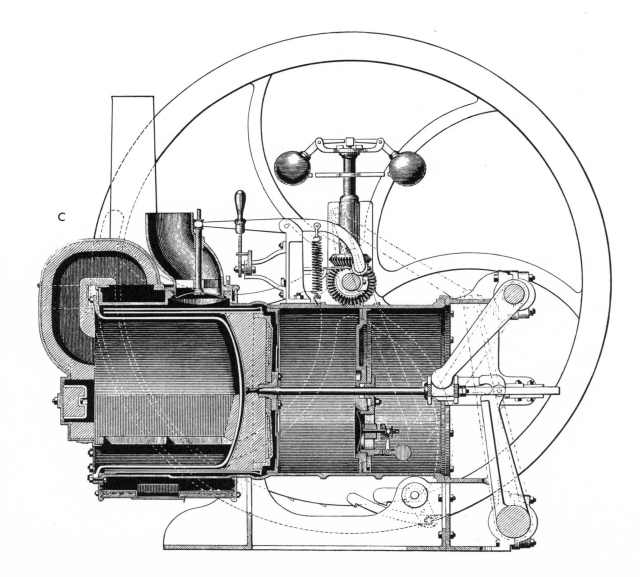

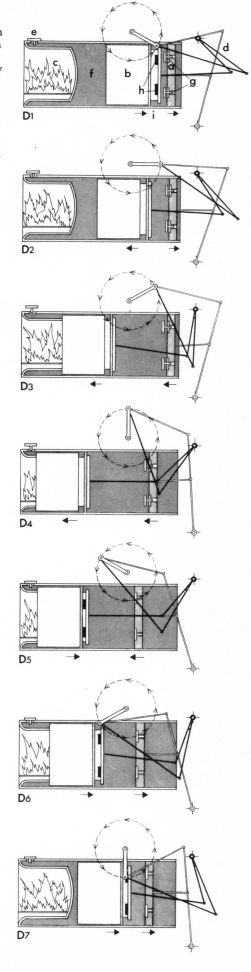

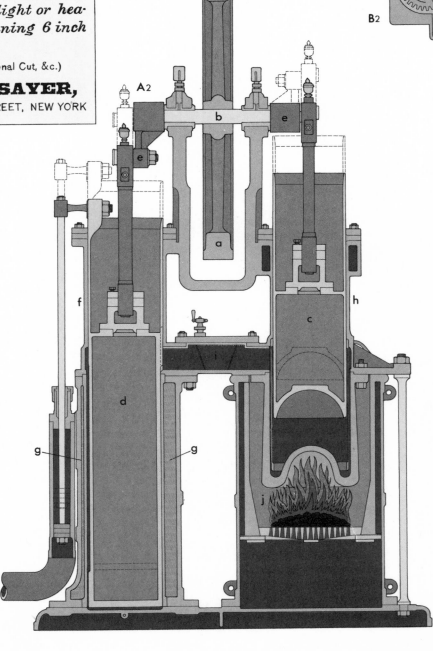

A1

A Rider's closed hot-air engine, which, according to the ads (**1**), was "UNRIVALLED for light or heavy pumping", had an effect of $0.25-1$ horsepower. (**2**) Cross-section of the engine. The flywheel (*a*) on the crank axle (*b*) was driven by both plunger pistons (*c*, *d*) by means of cranks (*e*), which were set almost perpendicularly to each other. The cold-air cylinder (*f*) was surrounded by a jacket (*g*), through which cooling water continually flowed. The engine worked in the following way: first of all, piston *d* compressed the air in *f* to about one-third its normal volume. Simultaneously, piston *c* moved upwards. When *d* had almost completed its down-stroke, the air was transferred − without changing its volume very much − from cylinder *f* to the hot-air cylinder (*h*) by way of a passage (*i*) containing the regenerator. This consisted of small, thin iron plates which gave up their heat to the air as it passed. The air was then further heated since *h* was sunk in the furnace (*j*). The air pressure thus increased considerably and impelled piston *c* upwards. The pressure increase further caused piston *d* to travel upwards and the air rapidly returned to cylinder *f*, giving up its heat to the regenerator when

passing it. In *f*, the air was further cooled by *g*; the air pressure sank to its minimum, and the piston *d* returned downwards.

B In the closed Stirling engine, an inert gas, helium, is used as a working agent. (**1**) The gas in the hot space (*a*) of the cylinder is heated by an external burner (*b*) and expands. The two pistons (*c*, *d*), which are both connected to a rhombic drive linkage (*e*), are then pushed downwards because of the pressure increase. (**2**) When the gas is almost fully expanded, piston *c* turns, and the hot air starts travelling by way of the regenerator (*f*) and pipes surrounded by cooling water (*g*) down to the cold space (*h*) of the cylinder. During this part of the working cycle, piston *d* is still on its down-stroke. (**3**) As piston *c* approaches the top of its stroke, most of the gas has been transferred to *h*, and, since its pressure is sinking, piston *d* is drawn upwards. The gas is then returned to *a* by way of the regenerator, and the cycle starts anew.

developing the marine propeller. In 1839, he moved to New York, where he continued working on his hot-air engine. In 1851, he had a new and different version ready, and it was shown at the Great Exhibition in London the same year. Initially, Ericsson had imagined that the caloric engine would be most suitable for propelling ships, and, in 1852, he managed to get a couple of investors to finance his project for building a ship in which his engine could demonstrate its real value. A paddle-wheeler was built with a displacement of 2,200 tons; it was almost 295 ft (90 m) long and 46 ft (14 m) wide. The maiden voyage took place at New Year, 1853, and was a complete fiasco. The hot-air engine took up most of the hull space and gave only half the power estimated by Ericsson; the speed was proportionately low. Moreover, the ship was not very seaworthy, and capsized and sank in a storm in the entrance to New York harbour.

John Ericsson, undaunted, set about finding new areas of use for his engine. Only a year or so after the ship failure, he presented yet another version of his engine, this time intended to satisfy the increasing demand for medium-sized sources of power in industry. This engine turned out to be a great success and, in the late 1850s, was manufactured under licence by some ten companies in the United States and in Europe.

In 1862, the American Academy of Arts and Sciences awarded the Rumford medal to Ericsson for his caloric engine. In the same year, Ericsson built a ship—this time with a steam-engine to propel it—which brought him immediate fame. The ship was the *Monitor*, which not only brought about a turning-point in the American Civil War to the advantage of the Northern states, but also introduced a new element into marine warfare.

The caloric engine was enormously popular because it was easy to run and used any kind of fuel. Its successes inspired many inventors to try to produce technically better versions. A weak point in Ericsson's machine was its relatively small furnace, which made constant supervision necessary if it was fired with a quick-burning fuel, such as wood. One inventor who succeeded in improving the hot-air engine was a German, Wilhelm Lehmann, who presented his version in 1868. It worked with a closed system, which further increased fuel economy; it spread not insignificantly in Germany and parts of Central Europe. Among the engineers who produced variations of the hot-air engine in the 1870s and 1880s was the American Alexander K. Rider, who introduced a regenerator in the closed system. Unlike the regenerator tried out by John Ericsson in the 1830s, Rider's design was theoretically sound, due to progress that had been made in thermodynamics since then. Ericsson's caloric engine was manufactured by several companies, among them the DeLamater Iron Works, New York, which employed Rider in 1887. The company had a long-standing connection with Ericsson and had built *Monitor*. Rider and Ericsson soon became partners and formed the Rider-Ericsson Engine Co., which, after Ericsson's death in 1889, bought up the DeLamater Iron Works. Caloric engines of both Rider's and Ericsson's design were produced, and the Rider-Ericsson Engine Co. soon dominated the American market, continuing to produce caloric engines until that type of prime mover was superceded by newer and better types, and the company ceased to operate in the beginning of the 1930s.

Cayley's ideas were, however, tried again in the late 1930s by Philips in Holland. The company was trying to establish new export markets in developing countries for their radio receivers but, in places without electricity, the operating costs of battery-powered radio receivers with current-absorbing electronic tubes became too great. A search began for a power source that would drive a small generator, the hot-air engine was recalled, and engineers led by Dr. Roelof Meijer set about rejuvenating the old ideas. The Second World War intervened, and when, by the early 1950s, results began to be promising, the original application had been rendered technically redundant by the more economic transistor. Meijer and his research team then sought new applications for what had become known as the Stirling engine. At first, various military applications were suggested, where the silent running of the engine would be an advantage. Another interesting possibility was also tried by running the heat process in the engine backwards, thus creating a cold engine, suitable for powering deep-freezes. Continued development during the 1960s pointed in an entirely different direction, however, for it suggested that the Stirling engine could be used in vehicles, primarily in buses and lorries.

The working medium of the Stirling engine is helium in a closed system, which gives, among other things, minimum mechanical and chemical wear and tear. As a result, lubricating oil consumption is negligible. The external combustion also makes it possible to deliver fuel continuously and to let it mix with air in the proportions that give optimal efficiency and the purest exhaust fumes possible. All this makes the Stirling engine much quieter than other vehicle engines, which "puff" their exhaust fumes out of the cylinders with each exhaust stroke. With suitable fuel, the Stirling engine can be made practically free of harmful exhaust fumes. The connecting rod of the ordinary engine has been replaced in the Stirling engine by what is called rhomboid drive linkage, which all but eliminates vibration. Its efficiency is high, too; in larger units of 300 to 400 horsepower it is nearly twice that of conventional vehicle engines. Even if its power-to-weight ratio cannot yet compete with that of the petrol engine, it certainly can with that of the diesel engine.

Internal Combustion Engines

Time and again, the history of technology records suggestions for burning a high-energy fuel inside a cylinder and for using the combustion gases to do useful work as they expand. We have already mentioned the unsuccessful attempts of Huygens and Papin to build gunpowder engines in the 1680s. In 1684, a French monk, Jean de Hautefeuille, fared no better with various suggestions for a gunpowder-driven fountain.

When different forms of steam-engine started to appear in the eighteenth century, suggestions of how to build "explosion" engines were conspicuously absent, but from about 1800, they were plentiful, and we shall mention a few of them. In 1794, an Englishman, Robert Street, tried to build a cylinder engine in which the piston was to be driven by the combustion of gasified tar or turpentine oil. In 1801, the Frenchman Philippe Lebon came up with a similar idea and tried out a kind of double-acting steam-engine driven by the internal combustion of a mixture of lighting gas and air, ignited electrically. During the 1790s, Lebon had experimented with the preparation from coal and wood of gas for lighting, and, by 1799, he had an apparatus ready for demonstration. Boulton & Watt in England had been thinking along the same lines, and James Watt's son Gregory visited Lebon in Paris. This brought about Boulton & Watt's development, under the supervision of William Murdock, of a commercially viable lighting gas. Lebon, however, took no further part in the development of the engine, for he was assaulted and killed in the Champs Elysées in Paris in 1804.

A report of Lebon's internal combustion engine came to the notice of Sir George Cayley, who was searching indefatigably for a new, compact engine which could help him power a flying machine. In 1809, Sir George described with admirable lucidity how a gas engine ought to work, but, as with the hot-air engine, he did not himself attempt any experiments, although his compatriots William Cecil and Samuel Brown did. In 1817, Cecil, a parson, had made an experimental model of an atmospheric gas engine, which he tried to improve by systematic experiments. The engine is said to have worked very well, but it consumed vast amounts of gas, and Cecil eventually abandoned his efforts. Brown was more successful. He took out a patent for his engine—also of the atmospheric type—in 1823 and subsequently built several engines that were practicable. He attempted to use a two-cylinder version of his design to drive a carriage. It worked well in principle, but he could not possibly think of a way of carrying the gas along with the engine! In 1833, Lemuel Wellman Wright, an Englishman, built an interesting gas engine—the first in which the gas pressure worked directly on the piston. It was much like the high-pressure steam-engines which were then enjoying increasing popularity. Wright's engine, which had a double action and a water-cooled cylinder, was the first to really show the shape of things to come. In 1854, two Italians, Eugène Barsanti and Felix Matteucci, built a gas engine with electrical ignition and a "freely flying" piston. Both of these concepts were to reappear—the latter quite soon.

A remarkable gas engine was invented by a Munich clockmaker called Christian Reithmann (1818–1909). He started his experiments in 1852, and six years later, he was able to demonstrate a gas engine

which, today, we would call a two-stroke engine. Reithmann used his engine to drive various machine tools in his workshop. In 1860, he was given a royal Bavarian charter to manufacture his engine, and in due course he founded an engine factory. In 1872 and 1873, he developed the engine into a four-stroke. Later, however, he became involved in serious patent disputes, since several other inventors had thought of the same possibilities.

Etienne Lenoir (1822–1900) was a Frenchman born in Luxemburg. In 1860, he patented a brilliantly thought-out design for a gas engine. He was extremely talented and even as a young man had made some important inventions, including a method of enamelling plate, which had made him financially independent. His first engine employed a horizontal, water-cooled cylinder and generated 4 horsepower. The fuel was lighting gas mixed with air, and the engine had a slide mechanism on either side of the piston. The ignition was electric, current being delivered by two Bunsen elements, and the voltage was stepped up in an induction coil of the Ruhmkorff roll-type with hammer interrupters.

The engine was very well received—at last, an alternative to the steam-engine! Mass production was soon under way, undertaken partly by Marioni & Lefevre (later Société Lenoir) in Paris and

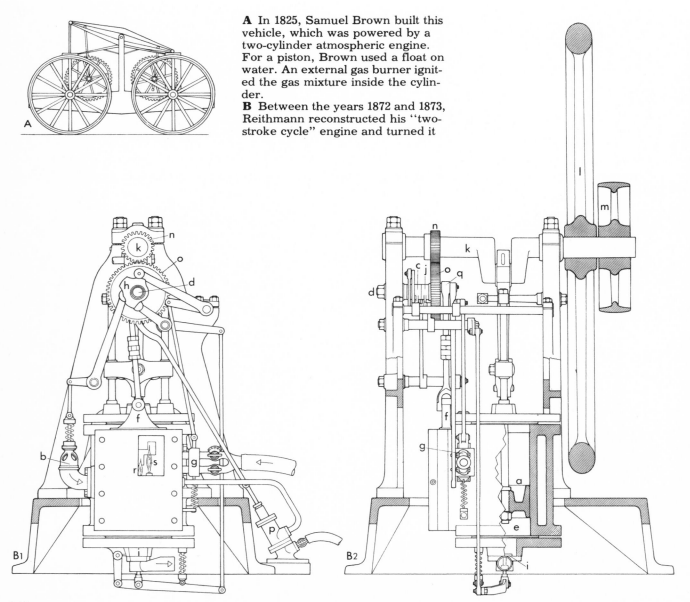

A In 1825, Samuel Brown built this vehicle, which was powered by a two-cylinder atmospheric engine. For a piston, Brown used a float on water. An external gas burner ignited the gas mixture inside the cylinder.

B Between the years 1872 and 1873, Reithmann reconstructed his "two-stroke cycle" engine and turned it

into a four-stroke one, shown here as seen from the side (**1**) and front (**2**). Only a single engine was built. The piston (*a*) moved upwards and sucked in air through a valve (*b*), which was regulated by a cam (*c*) on the steering shaft (*d*). The air travelled from the valve to the compression chamber (*e*) by way of the main slide valve (*f*). When two-thirds of the piston stroke remained, a distributor slide valve (*g*), regulated by a cam (*h*) on *d*, was opened. The air sucked into *e* was then mixed with gas. As the piston (*a*) changed its direction, *b* as well as the upper gas pipe in the slide valve (*g*) were closed. Since the piston was now travelling downwards, the gas mixture in *e* was compressed. It was then ignited and burnt, considerably increasing the pressure. The piston was forced upwards again, and when it had reached its topmost position, a valve (*i*) regulated by a cam (*j*) was opened. The exhaust gas escaped from the compression chamber through *i*, and the piston sank. The lower gas pipe in slide valve *g* was closed as soon as ignition had started. The piston's movement was transmitted to the crankshaft (*k*), on which a flywheel (*l*) and a belt pulley (*m*) were mounted. A cog-wheel (*n*) on the crankshaft meshed with another, larger cogwheel (*o*) on the steering shaft (*d*), which was thus rotating half as fast as *k*. A small pump (*p*), which like the slide valve *f* was powered by a crank (*q*) on *d*, supplied pilot flame *r* with a mixture of gas and air. Pilot flame *s* in the lid of slide valve *f* was connected directly to the gas conduit.

partly by Reading Iron Works Ltd. in England. Lenoir had an eye for publicity and devoted himself to an intense campaign on behalf of his engine, for which he predicted a splendid future. Stationary gas engines of up to 100 horsepower would soon eclipse the steam-engine, he claimed, while others could be used also for locomotives, which would carry gas generators instead of steam boilers. The steam-engine manufacturers gave as good as they got (they had plenty to say about Lenoir's claims), but the Lenoir engine, in spite of—or perhaps because of—the polemics, gained ground in the 1860s. One incontestable point was the fact that its thermal efficiency was higher than that of smaller steam-engines. But there is no evidence that gas engines with a higher output than about 12 horsepower were ever built.

Lenoir's publicity campaign had one effect that he probably had not envisaged: the German merchant Nikolaus August Otto (1832–91) became so interested in the engine that he had a couple of gas engines made under licence by a workshop in Cologne. They did not work very well, however, so Otto, who was convinced of the engine's great potential, sat down and redesigned the whole thing. The new gas engine was patented in England in 1863 and later in France and various other countries. Otto teamed up with an inventive engin-

eer, Eugen Langen (1833–95) and, in 1864, founded N. A. Otto & Co. in Cologne.

The first gas engine built by Otto had several interesting design features. It had a "freely flying" piston, that is, a piston which was driven up quickly, as the gas mixture exploded in the lower part of the cylinder. The piston was fitted with a rack, which, via a ratchet, engaged a cog-wheel on the axle of the balance wheel. As the piston moved up, the rack was disengaged from the balance-wheel axle. After the piston in its extreme top position had been slowed down by a rubber bumper (!), the pressure in the cylinder dropped drastically, the piston was driven down by atmospheric pressure, and at the same time, the ratchet engaged the cog-wheel. During this power stroke, the balance wheel was, in other words, given additional energy. In one of his many books, Franz M. Feldhaus gives a hilarious description of an Otto-Langen engine in operation. He grew up in a German health resort named Godesberg where his father was a director of the company that bottled the spa's mineral water, which an Otto-Langen engine pumped up. Feldhaus describes how, as a little boy, he was scared out of his wits whenever he had to pass the pump house.

The engine was placed in a dark corner, and the piston rose up

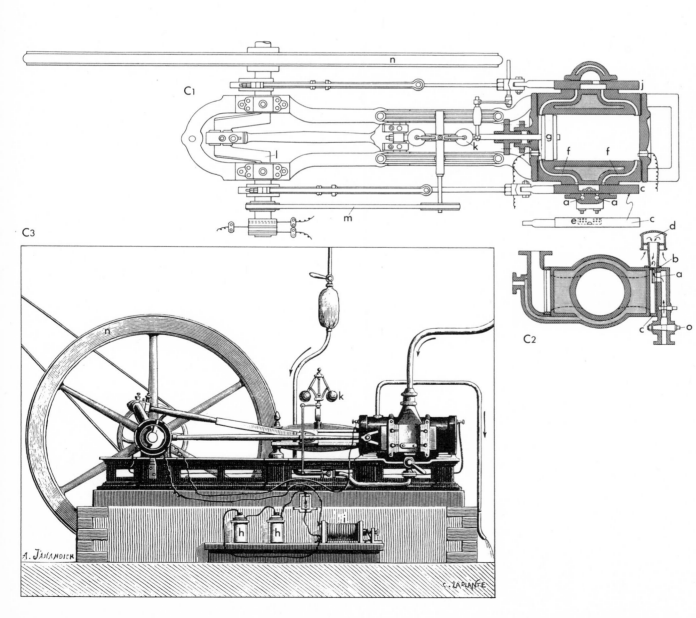

C Lenoir's gas engine; (1) the construction as seen from above, (2) cross-section through the engine, (3) an early Lenoir engine as seen from the side. The coal gas entered through two flues (a) which were alternately connected to the slide valve flue. From there, the gas was directed through another flue in the slide valve (c) and to a mixing chamber (d). Air from outside the engine entered d, which was connected to the slide valve by a number of small holes (e). The gas and air mixture was sucked through these holes and into either end of the cylinder by way of the slide valve (c) and one of the cylinder flues (f). When the piston (g) had travelled less than halfway through the water-cooled cylinder, the gas and air inlets were closed by the slide valve (c), and the coal-gas mixture in the cylinder was ignited by an electric spark. The current was delivered by two Bunsen elements (h), and the low voltage was transformed into high in an induction coil (i). While the combustion gases expanded and forced the piston in front of them, the combustion gases on the other side of the piston left the cylinder through an exhaust slide valve (j). (k) Centrifugal governor, driven by the crank axle (l) by way of a belt (m). (n) Flywheel. The coal-gas feed could be regulated with taps (o).

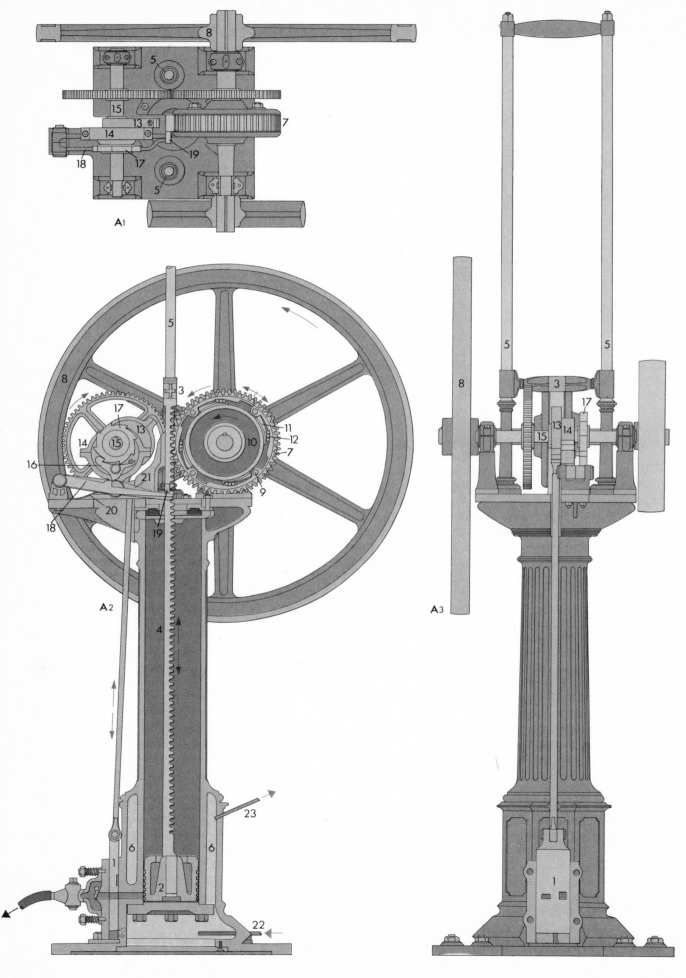

A₁

A₂

A₃

A Otto's and Langen's gas engine of 1867; (1) from above, (2) front view, (3) side view. Coal gas and air entered the cylinder through a slide valve (1) when the piston (2) started its upward stroke. The piston was guided by a cross-bar (3), fitted on the piston rod (4) and glid along two rods (5). When the piston had moved a little, the gas and air supplies were closed by the slide valve, and the gas mixture combusted, forcing the piston up until it hit a rubber bumper. Since the gases expanded and transferred heat to the cooling water (6), the pressure in the cylinder sank below atmospheric. The piston was forced down, and the piston rod (4) with its cogs then drove a cog ring (7) on the shaft of the flywheel (8). Since the flywheel rotated to the left, the engine had a friction clutch, so that the flywheel shaft was released from the cog ring when the latter was turned to the right (and also when it was turned to the left but ran slower than the flywheel shaft). The clutch is shown here in section. The cog ring (7) was attached by four bolts (9) to two loose discs, one on either side of a disc (10) which was secured to the flywheel axle. The inside of the cog ring was shaped to hold four wedges (11) whose wide ends bore against the bolt joints and whose narrow ends had noses. Three small cylinders (12) were fitted between each wedge and 7. When the cog ring rotated to the right and 10 to the left, the wedges stayed in this position and glid against the periphery of the disc. However, when 7 rotated to the left and went faster than 10, the wedges moved forwards until the cylinders had been clamped against 7, so that 7 and 10 were engaged. During the last part of the piston's downward stroke, a valve was opened by slide valve 1, and the combustion gases left the cylinder. The slide valve was controlled by two joined eccentrics (13, 14), set at right angles to each other and mounted on shaft 15 without being attached to it. The slide valve was connected by an eccentric rod to the ring on 13. On 14, a pawl (16) was mounted, which engaged a ratchet wheel (17), fixed to shaft 15, when a lever (18) was pushed downwards by a knob (19) on 4. When this happened, the eccentrics rotated with the ratchet wheel. When the piston started upwards again, 18 was lifted by a spring (20), 16 was released, and the eccentrics stopped. While the gas mixture entered the cylinder, the piston was raised by a second lever (21), whose one end was situated beneath 19 while the other bore against the eccentric band of 14. When 14 was turned, 21 brought the piston rod upwards. (22) Cooling-water inlet. (23) Outlet.

B In 1876, "Silent Otto" was developed. Here, its construction can be seen from above (**1**) and from the side (**2**); the steering gear (**3**), the exhaust valve (**4**), and the slide valve in longitudinal- (**5**) and cross-section (**6**) are shown in greater detail. The engine worked according to the four-stroke principle – sucking in of the charge, compression, combustion and expansion, and exhaust of combustion gases took place during four consecutive piston strokes. (**1**) Piston. (**2**) Compression chamber. (**3**) Cooling-water jacket. (**4**) Cooling-water outlet. (**5**) Lubricating cup. (**6**) Exhaust valve for the combustion gases. (**7**) Cock for control of gas supply. A cog-wheel (**8**) on the crankshaft meshed with another cog-wheel (**9**), which had twice as many cogs and was mounted on the camshaft (**10**). (**11**) A centrifugal governor which, by way of a gearing, was driven by the camshaft and used a double lever (**12**) to control the gas supply. When the machine's work load was reduced so that its rpm increased too much, the weights in the governor swung outwards. The governor's casing then rose, and **12** displaced a cam (**13**) along the camshaft so that another double lever (**14**) no longer bore against it. This lever opened and closed the gas valve (**15**) only when it bore against **13**. When this was not the case, air only was sucked into the cylinder until the machine's rpm had been reduced. Another cam (**16**) on **10** controlled the exhaust valve (**6**) by way of a spring-loaded lever (**17**). The slide valve (**18**) was given a reciprocating movement by a crank (**19**) on **10**. (**20**) Gas pipe for the ignition flame. From the position the slide valve has at **5**, it moves left and then back to its original position. Meanwhile, air and gas are sucked into the cylinder; the air enters through duct **21**, which is connected to the air outside the engine, travels through the slide-valve duct (**22**), where it is mixed with gas from duct **23**, and eventually enters the cylinder through duct **24**. The slide valve also contained a chamber (**25**) which was connected to a separate gas duct (**26**) just before ignition was to take place. The chamber was then filled with gas mixed with air, which entered through duct **27**. In the slide-valve lid was a continually burning flame which ignited the gas mixture in **25**, whereupon the connection between the flame and the chamber was closed; instead, a very narrow duct which connected the chamber with the cylinder's inlet duct (**24**) was opened. When the pressure in **25** had risen to equal the pressure inside the cylinder, the chamber was connected directly to **24**, and the gas combusted.

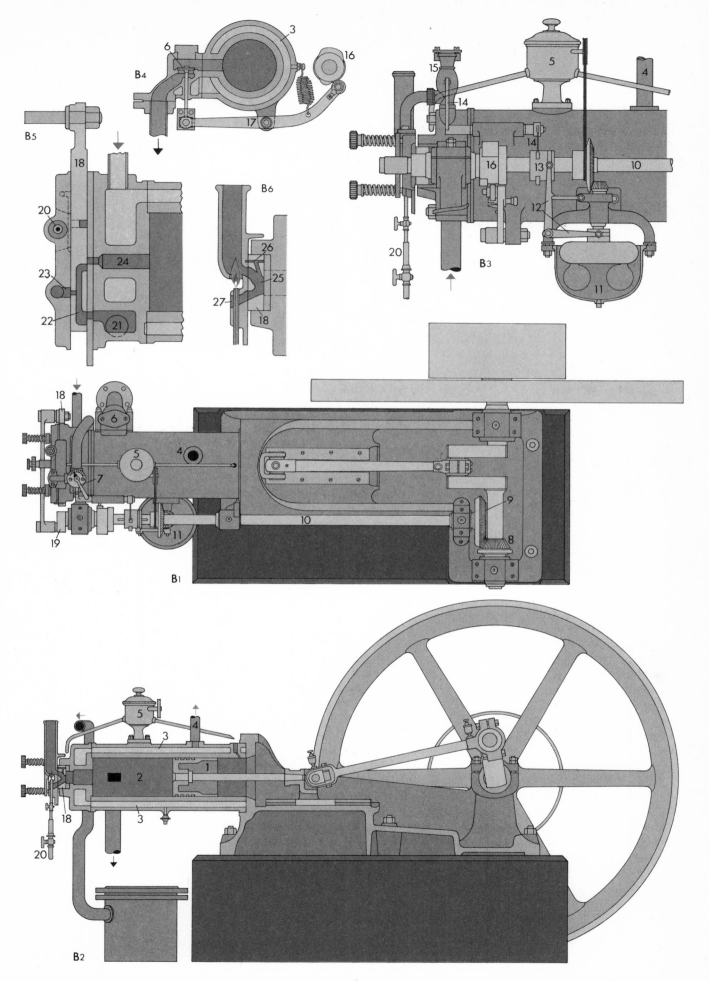

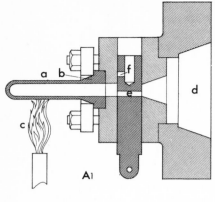

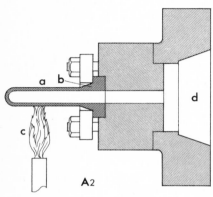

A The ignition device in combustion engines with a pilot flame was sensitive and not very reliable, and the invention of the controlled hot-tube ignition (**1**) was a great improvement. The tube (*a*) was made of china or nickel and was closed at one end. It was fitted with a flange (*b*), so that it could be attached to the engine. The tube was heated by a gas burner (*c*), and when the gas mixture in the compression chamber (*d*) was to be ignited, a small portion of it was let into the hot tube through a slide-valve flue (*e*) or a valve. In between, the tube was in contact with the outside air, which entered through another flue (*f*). The open hot-tube ignition (**2**) was a later invention used by Daimler and Maybach in the engine they began to construct in 1882. The tube was connected to the compression chamber, and by placing the burner at different distances from the open end of the tube, it was possible to cause earlier or later ignition.

B Daimler's combustion-engine-powered bicycle of 1885 was first tested in November, 1886.

B

with a terrible crash; with a rattling sound it engaged with the balance wheel, and then descended with an anxious whine. . . . The explosions seemed quite arbitrary, and in between there was only sinister silence. The convulsions of this engine inspired real fear.

The little boy's reaction was quite natural. If an Otto-Langen engine were to be taken into service somewhere in industry today, the union security officer would undoubtedly take immediate action!

At the world exhibition in Paris in 1867, the Otto-Langen engine competed for attention with no less than fourteen Lenoir engines. At first it was marked down, not least because of the awful noise it made, but after Franz Reuleaux, the German representative on the jury, had intervened, the engine was thoroughly tested. It transpired that the operating efficiency of the Otto-Langen engine was much better than that of Lenoir's gas engine, and the gold medal was awarded to Otto and Langen.

This success was incontestable; however, Otto and Langen were aware of the shortcomings of their creation and carried on experimenting. The outcome, in 1876, was a great breakthrough for gas engines: the first four-stroke engine. It was immediately nicknamed "Silent Otto"—a self-explanatory name. The four-stroke engine became a great success. In the first ten years, more than thirty thousand engines were manufactured at the Gasmotorenfabrik Deutz AG, which was the name of Otto and Langen's company after it was reorganized in 1872.

"Silent Otto's" celebrated début on the international market took place at the world exhibition in Paris in 1878. Franz Reuleaux had followed Otto's development work since his first engine had been displayed in 1867, and they had become good friends. Reuleaux now praised "Silent Otto" abundantly. He considered it the greatest step forward in the field of engine technology since James Watt, and this at a time when he had just attacked German industry, accusing it of producing inferior goods—*billig und schlecht*—so this praise was made much of in the papers.

In the following decade, a storm blew up regarding the patent rights of the gas engine. This development could have been anticipated, since several designers had been thinking along the same lines as Nikolaus Otto. In France it was claimed that the principle of the four-stroke engine had been stated as early as 1862 by Alphonse Beau de Rochas (1815–91), although his ideas had never got beyond the drawing-board. The Gasmotorenfabrik Deutz sued Reithmann for patent infringement—his engine worked in the same way as "Silent Otto"—but the case was dismissed, since Reithmann could easily prove that his engine had been in operation since 1873. The clockmaker must have been very bitter to see the Deutz factory expand as rapidly as it did even as early as the 1880s. One might add that this company, which has merged with others and is today called Klöckner-Humboldt-Deutz, has a splendid works museum, containing a fine collection of many of the earliest internal combustion engines, including even Reithmann's engine.

When the great demand for gas engines started in the early 1870s, the Deutz factory took on two engineers, who were later to become very famous. One was Gottlieb Daimler (1834–1900) and the other Wilhelm Maybach (1847–1929). Daimler realized the development potential of the Otto engine and, a few years later, went his own way in order to develop a compact engine capable of a high number of revolutions. In 1882, Daimler set up a little workshop in conjunction with Maybach in Cannstatt outside Stuttgart, where he could try out his ideas in practice. In 1883, he invented hot-tube ignition. He planned to use volatile petroleum derivatives as fuel, and, in the same year, he and Maybach gave their first engine a trial run. The third experimental model was used to drive a bicycle with iron-shod wheels, the engine turning at 900 rpm—the normal rpm of the Otto engine was around 200—and developing 0.5 horsepower. In 1886, this motor vehicle began to roll along the roads, driven by *Benzin*—an almost unknown liquid that, in those days, could be bought in any chemist's shop.

Daimler built his first four-wheel motor vehicle in 1887, but the honour of having designed the first real "motorcar" does not belong to him. The previous year, Karl Benz (1844–1929) had jeopardized the safety of the roads in Mannheim with his three-wheel carriage, driven by an 0.75-horsepower engine. Quite independently of Daimler, Benz had developed an engine with a design almost identical to that of the Daimler engine. In 1871, Benz had started a factory for manufacturing gas engines, Rheinischen Gasmotorenfabrik AG, which he managed successfully. Even as a student at the Polytechnikum in Karlsruhe, he had been toying with the idea of designing an engine-driven vehicle. He worked on the development of this idea parallel with the manufacture of gas engines, and in 1886, his efforts were crowned with success.

The Two-Stroke Engine

Despite the enormous success of the four-stroke engine, it came to be criticized. It was suggested that it was inefficient for the same cylinder to function as a pump on one revolution and as a working cylinder on the next, for its dimensions were adequate for its working function but unneccessarily large for its pumping function. Several designers attacked this problem, and the first to find a successful solution was the Scotsman Sir Dugald Clerk (1854–1932). In 1878, he built a two-stroke engine, in which the fuel was fed in by a special pump cylinder (which Clerk called a "displacer") next to the working cylinder.

Both the four-stroke and the two-stroke engine turned out to be very hard-wearing, and their basic designs have survived until the present day. A number of essential improvements have been added over the years, but in both engines the mode of operation has remained unaltered.

The fascinating story of the development of the automobile has been told in many books. But, here, we shall concentrate on the engine as a prime mover.

Rudolf Diesel and his "Rational Heat Engine"

In December, 1892, Rudolf Diesel (1858–1913) was granted a German patent for the engine which has borne his name ever since. The following year saw the publication of his pioneering work *The Theory and Construction of a Rational Heat Engine*. It attracted a great deal of attention—and considerable criticism. Diesel considered that the cylinder compression should be greatly increased to attain an internal temperature high enough to ignite the fuel that would be injected during the last part of the compression stroke. Diesel based his theory on the fire-piston, which had already been launched in several versions in the early 1800s and was, in a way, a forerunner of the match.

The fuel which Diesel first intended to use in his engine was finely powdered coal, a fuel that many designers were then thinking of using for various kinds of engine. Diesel, however, soon abandoned this idea and instead started to experiment with crude oil. In 1897, after intensive development work which took its toll of his health, Diesel had achieved an engine with an efficiency wholly superior to that of other combustion engines. Before long, the diesel engine had become a concept and had begun its victorious progress round the world. At an early stage, two German companies, Maschinenfabrik Augsburg-Nuremberg (MAN) and the Krupp concern, and the Swiss firm Gebrüder Sulzer had begun to make diesel engines on licence

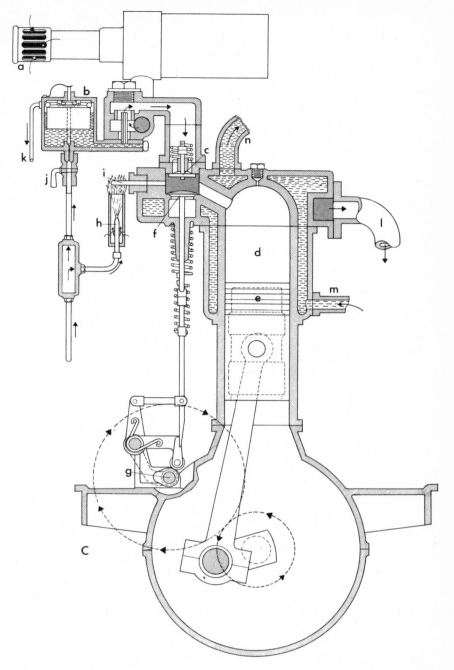

C A four-stroke Daimler engine of 1897. (a) Adjustable air intake. The carburettor (b) worked by transforming the fuel into a mist. Maybach's carburettor was less sensitive to the degree of volatility than earlier carburettors, and it suppled more fuel in proportion to the amount of air, since the fuel took up less volume when in drop-form than when in gaseous form. The engine lacked a throttle. A certain adjustment could, however, be obtained by varying the amount of air in the fuel/air mixture. The spring-loaded suction valve (c) opened because of the vacuum created in the cylinder (d) at the start of the suction stroke, and it closed again when the piston (e) approached its lowest position. The disadvantage of this was that c always opened too late and closed too early. The exhaust valve (f) was governed by a camshaft (g), which rotated at half the number of engine revolutions. A burner (h) with an "eternal" flame kept the ignition tube (i) glowing. The reason ignition did not take place arbitrarily during the suction and compression strokes was that i's length had been adjusted so that the residue of combusted gases which always remained in the ignition tube stopped the fuel mixture from reaching the glowing part. Only at the very end of the compression stroke had the fuel mixture been pressed far enough into i to be ignited. The engine was switched off when a tap (j) was turned, so that the fuel supply was cut off. (k) The float chamber's overflow. (l) Exhaust pipe. (m) Cooling water inlet. (n) Outlet.

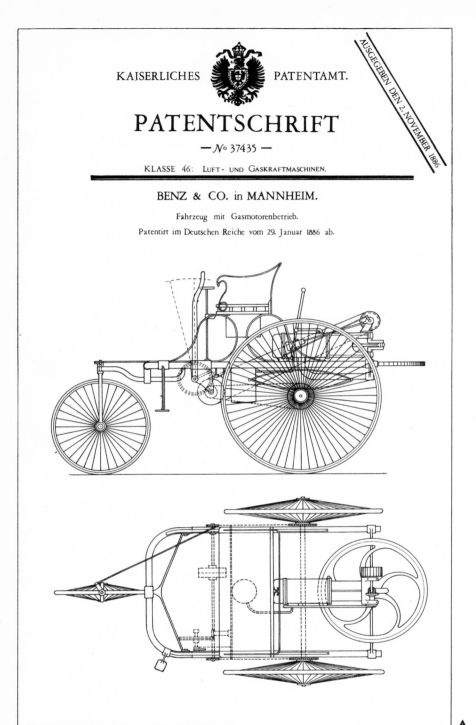

KAISERLICHES PATENTAMT.

AUSGEGEBEN DEN 2. NOVEMBER 1886

PATENTSCHRIFT
— № 37435 —

KLASSE 46: LUFT- UND GASKRAFTMASCHINEN.

BENZ & CO. in MANNHEIM.

Fahrzeug mit Gasmotorenbetrieb.

Patentirt im Deutschen Reiche vom 29. Januar 1886 ab.

A

B

A The front page of Benz & Co.'s 1886 patent for the gas-engine-powered car.

B A motor-car built by Karl Benz in 1888. The carriage (*a*) was carried by the "chassis" (*b*) by means of three fully elliptical springs (*c*), the foremost of which was mounted cross-wise. The rear wheel had iron rims, whereas the front wheel had a massive rubber tyre. On its vertically cradled crankshaft, the one-cylinder, four-stroke engine (*d*) had a flywheel (*e*), which ran horizontally, since it was feared that a vertical flywheel would impair manoeuvra-

bility (practical tests, however, allayed these fears). In the evaporation-type carburettor (f) the sucked-in air passed over the fuel and became saturated by its vapour. The fuel, petrol, was float-regulated and was kept in a tank underneath the driver's seat. The high-voltage electrical ignition was fed by batteries. The lubricating oil was poured into glass containers (g), from which it flowed under its own pressure to the various oiling points. The engine was cooled by simply letting water from a container (h) boil away. The power transmission from engine to wheels took place by means of bevel gears (i), a belt pulley (j), and a belt (k), whose forward end ran over one of two parallel belt pulleys, which were situated beneath the driver's seat. One of these belt pulleys ran freely on its shaft, whereas the other was connected to a differential of more or less modern construction. The two separate shafts of the differential (the left-hand one can partly be seen at l) drove the rear wheels via sprocket wheels and chains. The chain drive gave a flexible transmission which remained unaffected by the swaying movements of the car; further, the shaft pivots were free from torsion. A crank handle on a lever (m) to the left of the driver was used to engage or disengage the gear; when the crank was turned, belt k was moved between the above-named parallel belt pulleys. The brakes (n) were activated by pulling lever m backwards. When a handle (o) was reset, a device was actuated which shifted the car's neutral into a crawling forward gear which could be used for climbing steep hills (with an maximum inclination of 1:10). This gear worked by way of an intermediate shaft with chains and sprocket wheels (p). However, the car was always set in motion in normal gear; it was only possible to switch from crawling to neutral via normal. The engine's number of revolutions per minute could be varied within certain limits by adjusting the air intake to the carburettor by means of a valve. However, the low cruising speed, about 6 mph (10 km/h)—the maximum speed was about 9 mph (15 km/h)—made engaging, disengaging, and braking unwarranted. (Compare, for instance, how you use the clutch and a constant pressure on the throttle when you reverse a modern car.) The car was steered by means of a lever (q) mounted on a vertical shaft which affected the front wheel by way of a pair of racks (r). The front end of the steering lever was shaped like an arrow, which indicated the position of the front wheel (not visible from the driver's seat) on a fixed "direction indicator disc" (s).

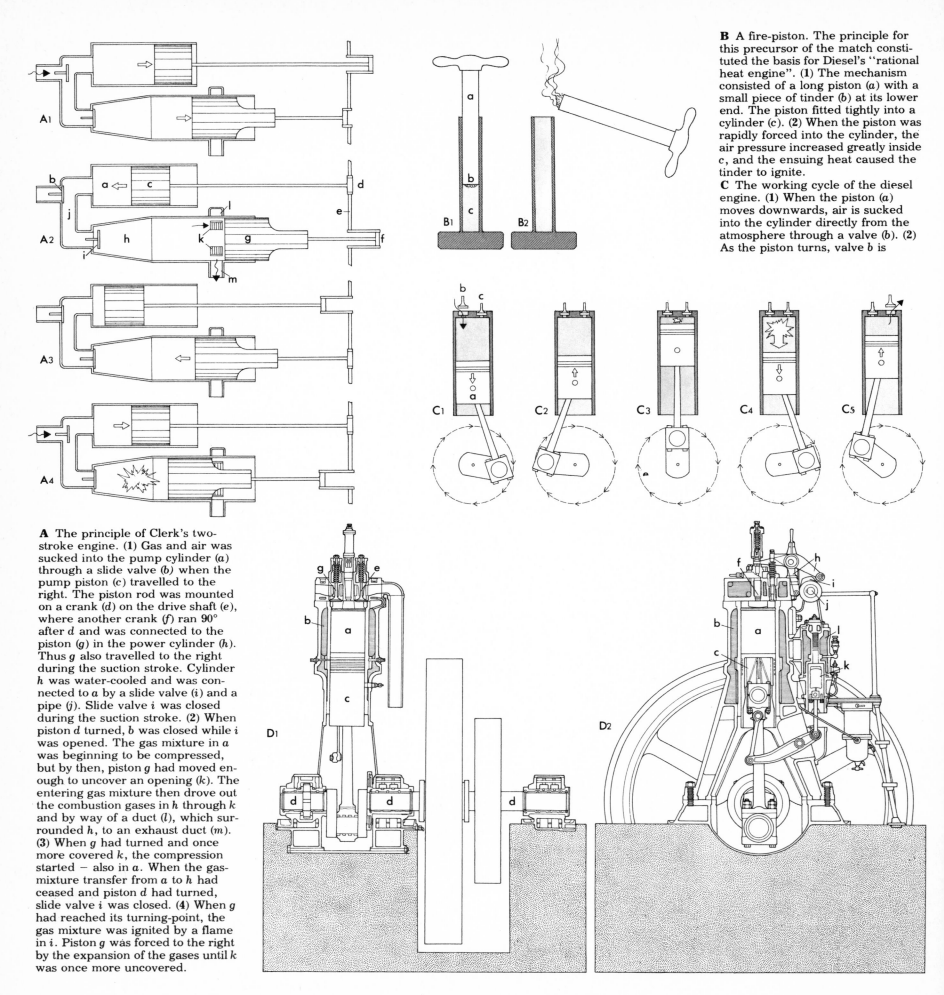

B A fire-piston. The principle for this precursor of the match constituted the basis for Diesel's "rational heat engine". (**1**) The mechanism consisted of a long piston (*a*) with a small piece of tinder (*b*) at its lower end. The piston fitted tightly into a cylinder (*c*). (**2**) When the piston was rapidly forced into the cylinder, the air pressure increased greatly inside *c*, and the ensuing heat caused the tinder to ignite.

C The working cycle of the diesel engine. (**1**) When the piston (*a*) moves downwards, air is sucked into the cylinder directly from the atmosphere through a valve (*b*). (**2**) As the piston turns, valve *b* is

A The principle of Clerk's two-stroke engine. (**1**) Gas and air was sucked into the pump cylinder (*a*) through a slide valve (*b*) when the pump piston (*c*) travelled to the right. The piston rod was mounted on a crank (*d*) on the drive shaft (*e*), where another crank (*f*) ran 90° after *d* and was connected to the piston (*g*) in the power cylinder (*h*). Thus *g* also travelled to the right during the suction stroke. Cylinder *h* was water-cooled and was connected to *a* by a slide valve (*i*) and a pipe (*j*). Slide valve *i* was closed during the suction stroke. (**2**) When piston *d* turned, *b* was closed while *i* was opened. The gas mixture in *a* was beginning to be compressed, but by then, piston *g* had moved enough to uncover an opening (*k*). The entering gas mixture then drove out the combustion gases in *h* through *k* and by way of a duct (*l*), which surrounded *h*, to an exhaust duct (*m*). (**3**) When *g* had turned and once more covered *k*, the compression started – also in *a*. When the gas-mixture transfer from *a* to *h* had ceased and piston *d* had turned, slide valve *i* was closed. (**4**) When *g* had reached its turning-point, the gas mixture was ignited by a flame in *i*. Piston *g* was forced to the right by the expansion of the gases until *k* was once more uncovered.

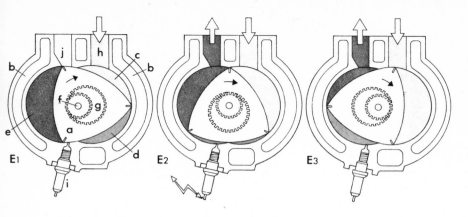

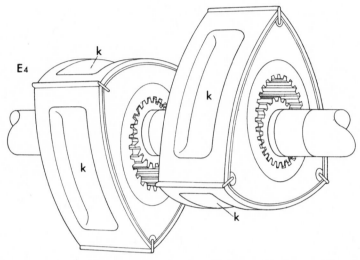

closed, and the air inside the cylinder is compressed to about 35 atmospheres. Its temperature rapidly increases. (3) Oil is injected under high pressure when the compression has reached its maximum. The oil mist immediately ignites and quietly burns at an almost constant pressure. A governor decides how large an amount of fuel should be injected, so that the charge matches the engine's work load. (4) During the combustion, the piston is forced downwards, and during the last phase (5) of the working cycle, the combustion gases are forced out of the cylinder through a valve (c).
D An early diesel engine; (1) longitudinal-section, (2) cross-section. (a) Cylinder. (b) Cooling-water jacket. (c) Piston. (d) Crankshaft. (e) Air-intake valve. (f) Fuel-injection valve. (g) Exhaust valve. These valves were opened and closed by levers (h), whose movements were controlled by cams (i) on the camshaft (j). A two-stage air compressor (k) with a cooling-water jacket (l) supplied air compressed to 55−60 atmospheres for the fuel injection.
E The Wankel engine consists of an equilateral rotor (a), which turns inside a chamber equipped with a cooling duct (b). The rotor's points run in trochoidal paths along the inside wall of the chamber, where

they form gas-tight seals for three sub-chambers (c, d, e). (f) Drive shaft. (g) Planetary gearing. (1) During the first phase of the working cycle in sub-chamber c, a fuel-and-air mixture is sucked in through a duct (h). At the same time, the fuel mixture in d is compressed, while the combustion gases in e have just reached maximal expansion. (2) The volume of c gets larger and larger because of the rotor's eccentric motion, and fuel mixture is still being sucked into e. The volume of d is decreasing, and when the fuel mixture in it has reached maximal compression, it is ignited by a spark from a spark-plug (i). The combustion gases in e start leaving through the now uncovered exhaust duct (j). (3) The volume of sub-chamber e is now at its largest. The combustion gases in d expand and force the rotor in a clockwise direction; meanwhile, e has almost been emptied of combustion gases. When the rotor has turned a little further, e will start sucking in fuel and air anew. (4) A Wankel engine is often equipped with two rotors to achieve greater efficiency. One is then turned 180° in relation to the other, so that the engine will run as smoothly as possible. In practice, the combustion chambers (k) are partly sunk into the rotors.

and also partook in the further development of the engine. In the United States the Diesel Motor Co. of America was founded in St. Louis, Missouri, in 1896, at the instigation of the master brewer Adolphus Busch; the first unit made in the United States was delivered in 1898 and generated 60 horsepower. It was used to power an electric generator. The patent rights for the Swedish market were acquired by the financier Knut Wallenberg, who, in 1899, founded AB Diesels Motorer in Sickla outside Stockholm. Jonas Hesselman was employed there as a designer, and he improved the diesel engine considerably; he also designed the first marine diesel engine, which was ready in 1905.

The Wankel Engine

In the last hundred years, many inventors and technicians have tried to find new ways of developing the combustion engine, but both the four-stroke principle and its technical application in the piston engine have proved extremely long-lasting. The only real newcomer in this area is the Wankel engine, invented by the German engineer Felix Wankel (1902−   ). This is a four-stroke engine in which the piston and cylinder have been replaced by a rotor, rotating inside a housing. The cross-section of the rotor is shaped like an equilateral triangle with convex sides, and the inside of the rotor housing in cross-section looks like an oval, slightly constricted in the middle. The rotor runs eccentrically on the axle shaft, and the power is transmitted by a sun-and-planet gear. One of the greatest problems in developing this engine was to achieve both a totally tight seal and a minimum of friction between the rotor and the housing. The solution was a sealing strip designed in a way similar to that for the piston rings in a conventional engine. The rotor is oil-cooled, and the housing is normally water-cooled, but air-cooling has also been tried out. After many years of experimental work, Wankel was able to test-drive his first working engine at New Year, 1957. A production prototype was ready as early as 1963, at NSU i Neckarsulm, and the Wankel engine began to be mass produced during the following year. The prototype can now be seen in the Deutsches Museum in Munich.

The advantages of the Wankel engine over the piston engine are its compact structure and the small number of its parts. Vibration is much less due to the fact that it has a rotary motion and not, like the piston engine, a reciprocating motion.

The Gas Turbine

In its design, the gas turbine is the simplest of the combustion engines, but laymen sometimes have difficulty in understanding how it works. In 1897, Nils Gustaf Dalén (1869−1937), a Swedish engineer who won the Nobel prize in physics, wrote a letter to a friend to persuade him to become his partner in the development of a gas turbine engine; he described its principle as follows:

> Imagine a stove! If you blow through the grate, the hot smoke goes out through the chimney. But the clever thing is, if you blow in one cubic metre, two or three will go out. A pump up there, in other words, could drive another pump down there to suck in the air. Now, if we substitute these pumps with turbines. . . .

In his letter, Dalén also made a simple drawing of the process as he imagined it, and the principles expressed in this drawing of his more or less apply also to a modern gas turbine. From the end of the eighteenth century, many designers had devoted themselves to finding a practical application for this simple principle, thus obtaining a heat engine with a technical application. The first to try was, in fact, Leonardo da Vinci, who invented a roasting spit driven by smoke

A The drawing sent by Gustaf Dalén to a friend to whom he wanted to explain how a gas turbine works. B The principle of the gas turbine. Air is sucked into a compressor (a) and is compressed before travelling on to a combustion chamber (b), into which fuel is sprayed and ignited. The hot combustion gases expand in the vanes of a turbine (c), where the heat energy is converted into mechanical energy. Part of this energy is employed to drive a, which is mounted in the same shaft as c. C Holzwarth's turbine of 1903. (a) Fuel valve. (b) Air valve. (c) An electrical ignition device. (d) Combustion chamber. (e) Nozzle. (f) Valve for e. (g) Turbine wheel. (h) Turboshaft. (1) Combustion gases in d expand and travel towards g until the pressure in d has sunk to atmospheric pressure. Valve f is open; a and b are closed. (2) Valve b is opened, and air from a compressor flows in. The remaining combustion gases are driven out by the air, which also cools the vanes on g. (3) Then f is closed and a is opened, so

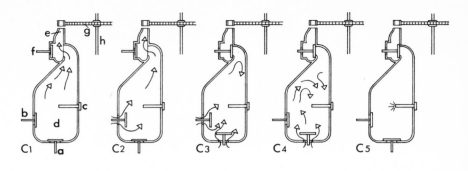

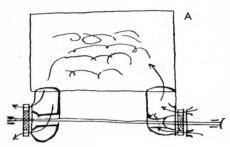

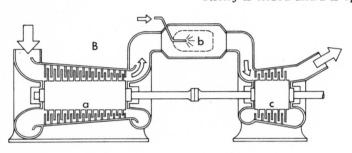

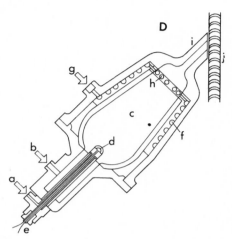

that fuel, too, enters d. (4) A little later, b is closed while a remains open. (5) Soon, a is closed as well, and the fuel mixture in d is ignited by c.

D The combustion chamber of Lemale's and Armengaud's turbine engine. The fuel was sprayed in at a under a pressure of five atmospheres. At the same time, compressed air entered through b and swept the fuel, now split into very tiny droplets, along to the chamber (c). The mixture was electrically ignited by a glowing metal wire (d), which had been inserted through an insulator (e). A tube (f) was coiled round the chamber in a double cooling jacket. Water under a pressure

gas. The device worked all right, but it hardly deserves to be called a gas turbine.

The problems in constructing a gas turbine are many and extremely difficult to solve. The speed of rotation must be very high to give adequate efficiency, something that Watt stated when von Kempelen claimed, in 1784, that he had invented a steam turbine; and if this speed should be achieved, the temperature inside the turbine, and especially of the turbine blades, would be extremely high so that a heat-resistant material must be used. Moreover, a gas turbine must have high efficiency, since no less than two-thirds of the power of the working turbine are consumed by the compressor that forces air into the combustion chamber; its total efficiency must exceed fifty-four per cent if it is to keep going by itself! Not until the end of the nineteenth century did a constructor of a gas turbine manage to achieve an efficiency exceeding this magic figure. One of the first was Egidius Elling (1861–1949), a distinguished Norwegian engineer and a methodical researcher. He had patented his first gas turbine as early as 1884, the year Charles A. Parsons was granted a patent for his steam turbine. But Elling needed another twenty years to modify this sufficiently to make it efficient; it did not generate surplus energy until 27 June, 1903, and Elling achieved this by cooling the very hot exhaust fumes from the combustion chamber before they came in contact with the blades of the working turbine. They were cooled in the coiled tube of an exhaust-gas boiler, designed like a steam boiler, and gave off their heat by causing the surrounding water to boil. The volume of the cooled exhaust gases was augmented by this steam, and the whole acted on the turbine blades, thus improving the efficiency of the gas turbine.

Let us return for a moment to Gustaf Dalén, who had had his idea for a gas turbine while enrolled at the Eidgenössische Technische Hochschule in Zürich, where he studied under Aurel Stodola. Dalén

managed to persuade a fellow-student, Arthur Hultqvist, to join him in an attempt to find a practical application for his idea; they rented some primitive premises in Gothenburg, Sweden, and with the enthusiasm of youth, began their experiments. Just at that time, at the end of the 1890s, various inventors were attempting to build somewhat fanciful flying machines, and so Dalén and his partner aimed at producing a light and compact motor to propel these. Their first experimental engine gave promising results to begin with. Its efficiency was fifty per cent and its turbine wheel achieved 25,000 rpm but lasted only a short time. They tested another motor with a redesigned turbine wheel at New Year, 1899; its efficiency was fifty-eight per cent but even this new turbine wheel could not withstand the high temperatures. Dalén continued his development work at AB de Lavals Ångturbin for another couple of years but did not succeed in solving the problem of materials. The experiments were abandoned in 1902 and Dalén applied himself to other projects. As chief engineer at AB Gasaccumulator, he had the illuminating idea, to coin a phrase, of using acetylene gas in the lamps of lighthouses, among other things. In 1912, he was awarded the Nobel prize in physics for a number of inventions in this area.

These attempts by Elling and Dalén, at the turn of the century, to solve the problems of constructing a gas turbine engine illustrate development up to about 1930. Dalén gave up in the face of the problem of finding suitable materials. Elling was undoubtedly the first man to produce a viable gas turbine, elegantly solving the problem of materials by side-stepping it. But industry in early-twentieth-century Norway was not highly enough developed to enable any mass production of Elling's turbine.

The Frenchmen Marcel Armengaud and Charles Lemale also experimented with gas turbines in the early twentieth century. Their first experimental engine, an old rebuilt de Laval turbine, was comof five atmospheres entered the coil at *g* and was let into *c* at *h* after the end of the combustion. (*i*) Nozzle for the combustion gases and the steam. (*j*) Turbine vanes.

E The first jet plane to leave the ground, a Heinkel He 178, is here shown from the side (**1**) and from above (**2**). (*a*) The reaction motor's air channel. (*b*) Fuel tank. (*c*) Turbomotor.

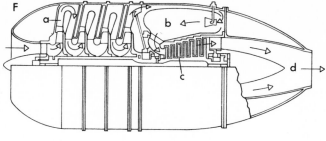

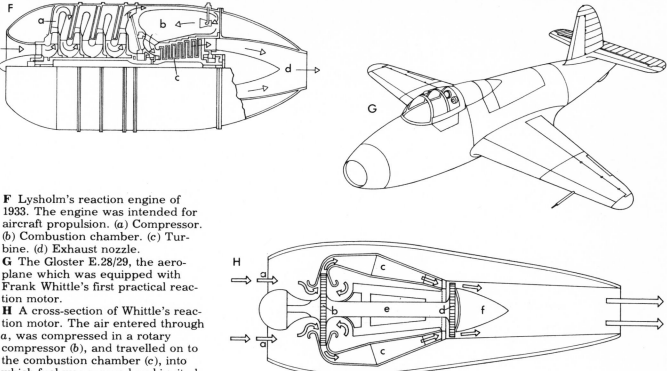

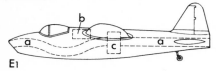

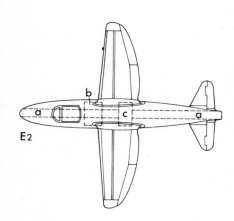

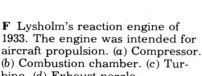

F Lysholm's reaction engine of 1933. The engine was intended for aircraft propulsion. (*a*) Compressor. (*b*) Combustion chamber. (*c*) Turbine. (*d*) Exhaust nozzle.

G The Gloster E.28/29, the aeroplane which was equipped with Frank Whittle's first practical reaction motor.

H A cross-section of Whittle's reaction motor. The air entered through *a*, was compressed in a rotary compressor (*b*), and travelled on to the combustion chamber (*c*), into which fuel was sprayed and ignited. The combustion gases expanded in a gas turbine (*d*), mounted on the same shaft (*e*) as the compressor. (*f*) Exhaust nozzle.

pleted in 1905; it was fuelled with paraffin injected into the combustion chamber, into which water was also injected and vaporized, thus cooling the exhaust fumes and so protecting the turbine blades. Its surplus output was only some few per cent, but experiments with it proved the principle to be correct. Armengaud and Lamale founded the Société Anonyme de Turbomoteurs in Paris, and in 1908, they built a larger gas turbine of about 80 horsepower, which, however, also had low efficiency.

In 1903, in Germany, Hans Holzwarth patented a design for a gas turbine based on a partly new principle. This "explosion turbine", as Holzwarth called it, had a combustion chamber with guided admission and exhaust valves, and a spark plug. The first turbine based on this patent was built in Hanover, being completed by 1908. Holzwarth then cooperated with the Mannheim subsidary of the Swiss company Brown Boveri and there designed a gas turbine to generate 1,000 horsepower, although the 1913 prototype managed only 200 horsepower. Brown Boveri continued the development work, however, and the initially simple design became increasingly complicated. Not until 1933, after a 2,000-horsepower gas turbine had been built in 1930, did the company stop development work on the Holzwarth turbine.

So far we have considered only stationary gas turbines, mainly intended for driving generators and producing electrical energy, but it was as a propulsion motor for aeroplanes that the gas turbine came into its own.

In 1929, the Swedish company Bofors decided to develop a gas turbine engine for aeroplanes. The research and development team operated under the direction of Alf Lysholm (1893–1973), a professor of steam technology at Tekniska Högskolan in Stockholm. Bofors had in mind an "aeroplane without a propeller", where the propeller's powerful air stream would be replaced by the gas jet from a

steam turbine. After four years of development, Lysholm had an experimental model ready, and, in 1934, he presented two different versions of the propeller-jet turbine (the term "turboprop" had not been invented then), one of them having an output of 1,200 horsepower. Bofors tried to interest the Royal Swedish Air Force in the project, but this happened at a time when the defence budget had been greatly cut, so the scheme was abandoned in 1935.

Many designers in the German aviation industry had been trying since about 1930 to produce a gas turbine which could be used in aeroplanes. A team led by Ernst Heinkel (1888–1958), with Pabst von Ohain as its chief designer, was the first to reach a solution. A few days before the outbreak of the Second World War in 1939, the world's first jet plane, the Heinkel He 178, flew for the first time, at Warnemünde. The air channel ran through the whole body of the jet plane, the exhaust being at the tail. The Junkers works started to develop another gas turbine engine around the New Year of 1940, and the first flights took place two years later with the Jumo 004 engine, designed by Anselm Franz. This later became the first jet engine to be mass produced. A slightly modified version of the Jumo 004 engine was installed in the German twin-engine fighter-bomber aircraft, Messerschmidt Me 262, which began to be produced in 1943.

In England, Frank Whittle (1907–) was the chief protagonist for aeroplanes propelled by gas turbine motors. While still a cadet of twenty at the Royal Air Force College in Cranwell, Whittle had been fascinated by the idea of jet propulsion, and he patented a gas turbine in 1930. His superiors in the RAF showed little sympathy for his ideas at first, but in 1936, he was given permission to devote part of his time to experimental work and, together with R. D. Williams, he founded the company Power Jets Ltd. to develop his invention. The following year, Whittle began to test his gas turbine, and at the outbreak of the Second World War, he received an order for one

A In 1950, the British Rover Co. of Birmingham introduced this gas-turbine-powered car. The engine had continuous combustion and was the result of ten years of research work, in which Frank Whittle had also taken part.

such motor—given the name W1—while, at the same time, the aeroplane manufacturers Gloster Aircraft Co. Ltd. were given the job of building an experimental aeroplane to fit the motor. This aircraft, the Gloster E.28/39 made its first flight in May, 1941. Further development of Whittle's engine was carried out mainly by British Thomson-Houston Co. Ltd. and by Rolls-Royce.

These startling breakthroughs of gas turbines in aviation opened car manufacturers' eyes to this new power source. In England more than elsewhere, attempts were made to transfer experience of wartime aviation to the car industry. In 1947, Rover began to work intensely on development and started to get results in the early 1950s, when Jet 1, the turbine-driven Rover, became one of the world's most talked-about cars; but, for various reasons, it never went into mass production. In the late 1950s, the French company Renault put a lot of effort into gas turbine propulsion, but the project was abandoned after a few years. In the United States, the Chrysler Corporation was interested early on in jet motors for cars; their first gas-turbine-driven car was completed in 1950, and in 1963, after thoroughgoing improvements, the company took its Chrysler turbine on a European tour which aroused a great deal of interest. Despite the optimism, this motor was never put in production. The turbine motor was too expensive to operate and more expensive to build than a conventional car motor. In the 1970s, trucks and buses with turbine motors have been built, for example, by British Leyland, General Motors, and Ford, but these companies have not had any great success with them. Still, it is not unlikely that various cars in the 1980s will have gas turbine engines. The engines will initially be "hybrids", such as that installed in the Saab Turbo, first mass produced in 1978. Experience based on these designs should make it possible, at a later stage, to go the whole way.

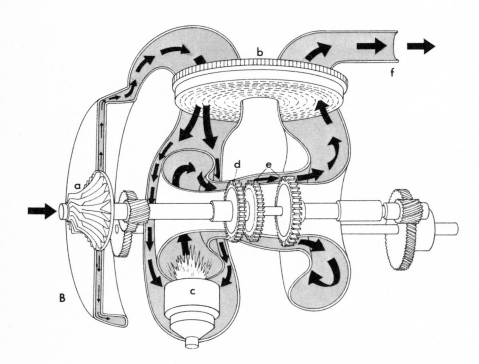

B At the end of the 1970s, this advanced gas turbine engine intended for propulsion of road vehicles was built in Sweden under the guidance of Professor Sven-Olof Kronogård. Air is sucked through a dust-collecting filter into the compressor (a), then passes a rotating heat exchanger (b), from which it absorbs heat. The compressed and heated air is then led into the combustion chamber (c), into which fuel is continually sprayed and combusted. The resulting gases first pass through a turbine (d), which drives the compressor, and then through two power turbines (e), one of which powers only the vehicle while the other helps drive the compressor as well. Because of this arrangement, an automatic gearbox can be dispensed with, and the turbine wheels can be given relatively small dimensions. Finally, the combustion gases pass the heat exchanger (b), to which they give off heat before leaving the engine through the exhaust pipe (f). Almost any liquid or gaseous fuel can be utilized to drive the engine.

CHAPTER 6
PRIME MOVERS III
Electricity

A

Electric phenomena of various kinds were already known in antiquity. The word "electricity" derives from the Greek word *elektron*, meaning amber, one of many substances which become electrically charged when rubbed. Over the centuries, many natural scientists had tried to trace the secret of this remarkable natural power, but litte became known until the 1790s, when an Italian physicist, Luigi Aloisio Galvani (1737–98), made his famous experiments on the legs of frogs, after he–or possibly his wife–had noticed that a pair of freshly prepared frogs' legs twitched whenever there was a spark from the conductor of an electric machine, close to which the frogs' legs were suspended on a copper wire. Galvani made a number of experiments and found that the frogs' legs twitched whenever the nerves and muscles were touched at the same time by two different metals which were in contact with each other. His compatriot Allessandro Volta (1745–1827) repeated these experiments and then discovered that electricity was generated when two different metals were in contact with each other. The frogs' legs served merely as evidence of the electrical charge. Later, Volta proved that electricity also appears when a metal is in contact with a fluid. His experiments resulted in the production of the first electric power source, the voltaic pile, which he made public in 1800. The first version consisted of a series of pairs of copper and zinc discs piled one on top of each other (sometimes, silver was used instead of copper). Each disc was separated from the next by a layer of felt or porous board moistened with a solution of sodium chloride. In a later version, the felt or the board was replaced by cups containing sodium chloride solution, in which the zinc and copper discs were immersed (cup elements, or *couronnes de tasses* cells).

Within only a few months of the public showing of the voltaic pile, physicists all over Europe had built their own voltaic piles and attacked this new area of research with great zest. Electricity became the fashion and different colleges competed to build the highest voltaic pile–a competition bringing to mind nuclear research during the 1950s and 1960s, when larger and larger accelerators were built. The largest, most famous voltaic pile was the one installed at the Royal Society in London. With its help, the famous chemist Sir Humphry Davy (1778–1829) made many discoveries and, by electrolysis, isolated several elements that were then unknown, including the metals potassium and sodium. Davy was also able to demonstrate the first electric arc. At the Royal Institution in London the first voltaic pile was successively extended, and in 1819, what was known as the "Great Battery" was put into operation. It consisted of 400 porcelain cups containing 4,000 copper and zinc discs, each with a surface of about 15.5 sq in (c. 100 sq cm), and the most popular demonstration of this power source was to cause it to produce its magnificent electric arcs. Even so, in 1819, no one knew

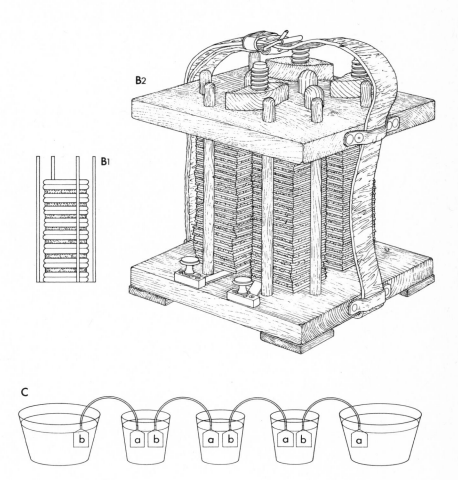

A Galvani's experiments with frogs' legs are shown here in a contemporary illustration. Little hands, wearing neat cuffs and hanging in the air on their own, demonstrate how a metal bar was charged by being held against an electric machine. The bar was then brought into contact with the frogs' legs, which had been arranged in various ways.
B In 1796, Volta constructed the first source of electricity, the voltaic pile (**1**). It consisted of pairs of zinc and silver discs, and between each pair, there was a layer of felt or porous pasteboard, soaked in brine. The pile was supported by four glass bars. If the top disc (which was of zinc) was connected to the bottom disc (which was of silver) by means of a metal wire, an electric current ran through the wire. (**2**) An early voltaic battery.
C In Volta's crown cups, the felt or pasteboard discs had been replaced by cups which contained brine or diluted acid. The zinc (*a*) and silver (*b*) discs were coupled in pairs by metal wires.

A

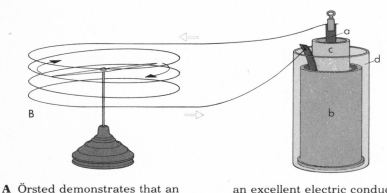
B

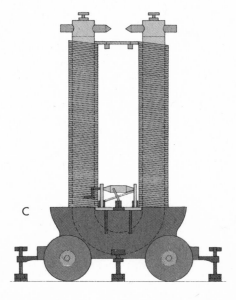
C

A Örsted demonstrates that an electric current generates a magnetic field, and that a compass needle is thus influenced by a live wire.
B An early galvanic element constructed by the German chemist and physicist Robert W. Bunsen (1811–99). The element consisted of a piece of carbon (*a*), which was immersed in nitric acid, and a zinc cylinder (*b*), which was surrounded by diluted sulphuric acid. The liquids were separated by a porous earthen vessel (*c*), and the element was contained in a glass vessel (*d*).
C Örsted's great electromagnet consists of a horseshoe magnet which has been wound with insulated wire. He found that if current from eight Bunsen elements, connected in series, was led through the wire, a 32-lb (14.5 kg) iron object, which had been placed between the ends of the magnet, would be held there with a force of about 3,000 lb.
D A model of Ampère's apparatus to demonstrate how electric currents influence each other. It consisted of one fixed (*a*) and one movable (*b*) bar; the latter was suspended from pivots hanging in small mercury-filled hollows (mercury is

an excellent electric conductor). If the two bars were connected so that the current flowing through *a* had the same direction as that in *b*, the bars attracted one another (**1**), whereas they repelled each other if the current flowing through one of them was reversed (**2**).

very much more of the nature of electricity than had Galvani and Volta, and while the first electric power source was indeed a great step forward, its secret still lay concealed.

In 1820, however, hectic activity in the field of electrics was sparked off when the Danish physicist Hans Christian Örsted (1777–1851) discovered, after some simple, methodical experiments, that an electric current can cause a compass needle to change direction. It had long been known that some materials, such as certain ores, had magnetic properties, but the "galvanic" current, on the other hand, was a relatively new discovery. That the two had something to do with each other was a scientific sensation. In July, 1820, Örsted sent a report of his discovery of electromagnetism to European scientists, and later the same year, he published an account of some complementary observations, but after that he left the field open for others. He had unlocked the door to electrical engineering, and all at once, there were many helping to open it. Before the end of 1820, several fundamental components of electrical technology had been arrived at. First, the German physicist Johann Salomo Christoph Schweigger (1779–1857), who was professor at Halle, designed the first electric coil, the solenoid, after observing that a magnetic field was more powerful if the magnetic needle was encircled with more than one turn of wire. Second, the French physicist Dominique François Jean Arago (1786–1853) built a primitive electromagnet, and third, his compatriot Ampère made an important discovery—that electric currents have an effect on each other.

Michael Faraday (1791–1867), Experimentalist at the Royal Institution in London, repeated Örsted's experiments but made up his mind to demonstrate by their means that magnetism could produce electricity, and he succeeded in this in 1831, with the help of his "Faraday's disc". This was a disc of copper, made to rotate between the poles of a horseshoe magnet; on its axis and at its periphery were rubbing contacts, from which electric current could be drawn. Thus, Faraday's disc was the first electric generator!

These discoveries of Faraday's, of electrodynamic and electromagnetic induction, were a great theoretical breakthrough and meant much for the continued practical development of electrical engineering. Faraday realized this but, being primarily a researcher, he left the task of technical application to others. From 1831 until his death, Faraday devoted himself only to experiments and lectures at the Royal Institution, where he had become director in 1825. His discovery was, however, immediately taken up by Ampère in Paris. On Ampère's instructions, Hippolyte Pixii, an instrument maker, built a number of electric machines for experiments and demonstrations, and the first of them was shown in Paris in 1832. This was a hand-driven electromagnetic generator, where the induction affected a number of windings connected in series and gave a higher voltage than Faraday's disc, which had only one induced conductor. Pixii's generator, moreover, was later equipped with a commutator designed by Ampère. This commutator was the first device that could cause the direction of a current in an electric cable to reverse itself, and so, yet another component was added to electromagnetic technology.

The ice was broken as far as electromechanical engineering was concerned, and various engineers all over Europe now entered this new and promising field. They received some quite unexpected assistance. To the public, electricity was something mysterious and exciting which stimulated the imagination. A lot could be read in the papers about its possible uses. Could not this magic "fluid", as the papers called electric current, also have a miraculous effect on man? As early as 1804, the famous Swedish chemist Jac Berzelius (1779–1848) had received a doctor's degree in medicine for his dissertation on the use of galvanic current to cure illnesses. In the 1830s, several

E A drawing by Faraday of his discovery of electromagnetic induction. He had wound five long copper wires, insulated with string and calico, round a ring of soft iron – three on one half, *A*, and two on the other, *B*. The wires on *A* were not in contact with those on *B*. Thereupon, he connected the ends of the wires on *B* two and two with a copper wire and let its coil run over a compass needle, which had been placed about 3 ft (1 m) from the ring. When the ends of the wires on *A* were connected three and three to the poles of a battery, the compass needle flickered – but the deflection did not last, although the wires remained in contact with the battery. However, when the battery was disconnected, the needle flickered again. Thus, it was the

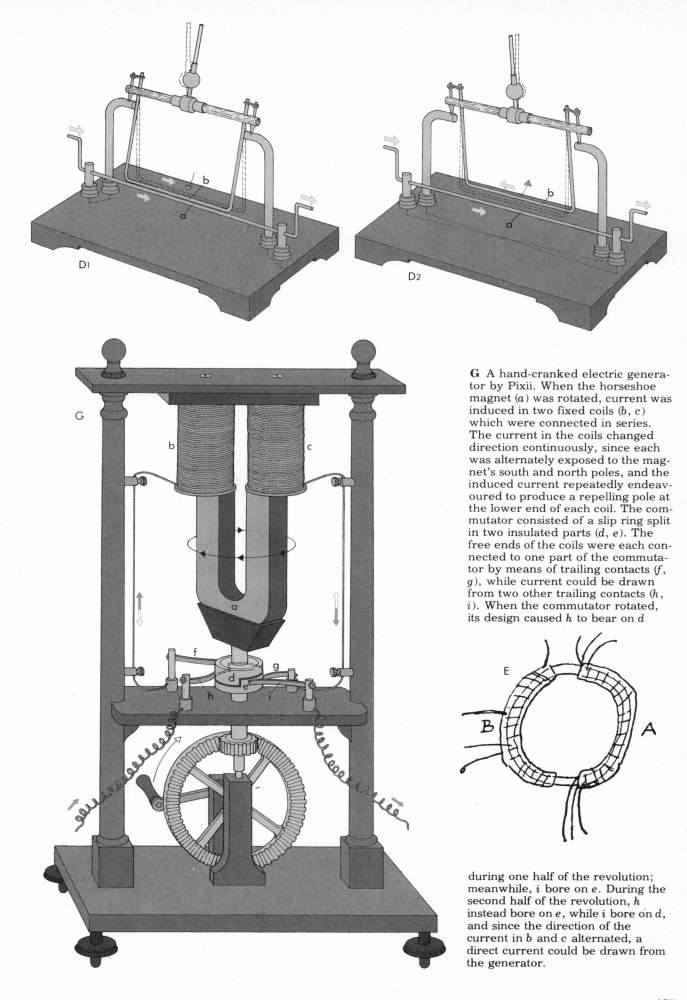

variation of the flux in *B*'s magnetic field which caused the induced current impulse.

F Faraday's disc was a copper disc (*a*) on whose shaft there was a crank (*b*). The disc was rotated between the poles of a horseshoe magnet, and a trailing contact (*c*) bore on the shaft of the disc while another (*d*) bore on the disc's periphery between the poles of the magnet. When the disc was rotated, voltage was induced in it at right angles to the flux of the magnetic field and the disc's direction of rotation, and a current could be drawn from the trailing contacts. In the later version of the generator, shown here, Faraday let the disc rotate between the poles of an electromagnet.

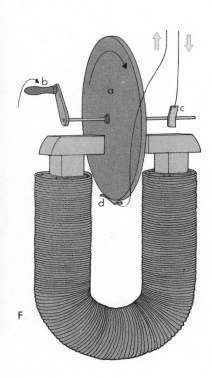

G A hand-cranked electric generator by Pixii. When the horseshoe magnet (*a*) was rotated, current was induced in two fixed coils (*b*, *c*) which were connected in series. The current in the coils changed direction continuously, since each was alternately exposed to the magnet's south and north poles, and the induced current repeatedly endeavoured to produce a repelling pole at the lower end of each coil. The commutator consisted of a slip ring split in two insulated parts (*d*, *e*). The free ends of the coils were each connected to one part of the commutator by means of trailing contacts (*f*, *g*), while current could be drawn from two other trailing contacts (*h*, *i*). When the commutator rotated, its design caused *h* to bear on *d*

during one half of the revolution; meanwhile, *i* bore on *e*. During the second half of the revolution, *h* instead bore on *e*, while *i* bore on *d*, and since the direction of the current in *b* and *c* alternated, a direct current could be drawn from the generator.

A In the 1850s, several inventors tried to construct electrical engines whose operation corresponded to that of the steam-engine. The American Charles Grafton Page proposed such a "piston" engine, which is shown here at two different stages of its work cycle. Two soft-iron cylinders (*a*, *b*) were, in turn, pulled into solenoids (*c*, *d*) when these, each during one-half of the flywheel's (*e*) revolution, were fed with electric current.

B The steam-engine-powered Alliance generator (**1**) was primarily used for lighthouse illumination. (**2**) Explanatory sketch. The machine consisted of a great number (here, twenty-four) of horseshoe magnets (*a*), which were arranged regularly in rows round a drum (*b*). On the drum, twice as many solenoids (*c*) as magnets were symmetrically mounted. (*d*) Belt pulley. The ma-

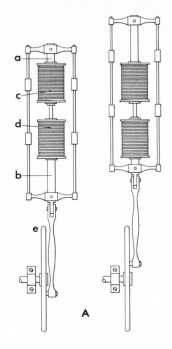

A

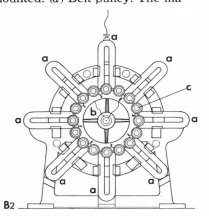

B2

B1

chine was large and heavy, and supplied alternating current; because of the many solenoids, it was difficult to make a useful commutator.

C A generator which was considerably less bulky and heavy than the Alliance generator was constructed in 1866 by Henry Wilde. He had discovered the possibility of replacing the large horseshoe magnets with electromagnets (*a*), which were fed with current from a small generator (*b*). The latter was equipped with an

instrument makers, including E. M. Clarke in London, supplied small hand-driven electric generators, in which the current was conducted to two handles, which the patient grasped firmly to get rid of his ailments. The higher the voltage generated by the device, the better the patient could feel the miraculous effect of the electric current. The manufacturers, consequently, experimented with methods of varying the voltage, their attempts including different ways of winding the coils and a way to short-circuit the magnetic field to a higher or lower degree with a magnetic shunt. The manufacture of these "medicinal" devices was the first large-scale production—although by craftsmen—of electromachines, and as such, had some effect on development. Many such generators also made their way to scientific laboratories. Being simple and straightforward, they certainly contributed to making electricity less dramatic. From 1830 onwards, it attracted the interest of leading physicists. The theories of electricity moved in the high, cool spheres of science, beyond the intellectual reach of the average man. That was at least the common view of electricity in those days, and one can understand the public's attitude by a comparison between electromechanical engineering and steam technology, which was, at this stage, more down-to-earth and accessible. It was typical for the time that Georg Simon Ohm (1787–1854) was excluded from scientific circles and actually had to go underground—he grew a full beard and worked as a livery-man—after propounding his well-known law in 1827, that the current flowing in a metal wire is directly proportional to the voltage between its ends. The relations between current, voltage, and electrical resistance really *could not* be as simple as that! But, before long, Ohm was vindicated.

The first full-scale electromachines were built in the 1840s and 1850s. The magnetic fields of these magneto-electric generators were produced by powerful permanent magnets. The pioneers in this field were principally F. Nollet in France and Frederick Hale Holmes in England. Nollet developed a magnetic-electric generator specially intended for the lamps of lighthouses; it used limelight, with the lime being heated in an electric arc. Nollet, however, died in 1853, but his partner then founded the Compagnie de l'Alliance and summoned Holmes, asking him to continue Nollet's research. Holmes made some important contributions but returned to England after only a few years. The successively improved Alliance generator, with its characteristic appearance, was fairly widespread in the 1860s; it was probably the first commercially viable electromachine.

One disadvantage was, however, the dependence on permanent magnets. In generators such as the Alliance, a large array of horseshoe magnets was required to give a reasonably acceptable magnetic field. In the 1850s, many designers tried the logical solution of replacing the permanent magnets by electromagnets. In Britain, Henry Wilde (1833–1919) built a generator in which the magnetic field was created by electromagnets whose current was supplied by an exciter—a smaller magneto-electric generator, connected to the large generator. Several other designers were working on similar solutions, and the next stage of development was not far away—"stealing" part of the generator's working current and feeding it into the field windings. In this way, a self-generating magnetic field could be obtained. This type of machine is called a dynamo, and the dynamo-electric principle was formulated in 1866 by the German industrialist and electrical engineer Werner Siemens (1816–92), who was later ennobled in his home country. At New Year, 1867, Werner's brother William (later Sir William) Siemens showed a demonstration model of the dynamo to the Royal Institution in London. One of the people present was the great electrical engineer Charles Wheatstone (1802–75), who claimed he had reached the same solution. On the same occasion he, too, displayed a similar model!

There was a fierce battle over who was first with the dynamo-electric principle, which was fundamental to all further developments in electrical engineering. Several designers had, no doubt, been pursuing the same idea, but it is quite clear that Siemens was the first to implement it; a dynamo-electric generator made by Siemens was shown at the Paris exhibition in 1867. In his autobiography, *Lebenserinnerungen*, Werner von Siemens refers to this controversy and states—without really taking a stand—firstly that he clearly realized that the dynamo-electric principle immediately made it possible to build generators for practically any voltage and amperage, and secondly that it was he who coined the word dynamo, derived from the Greek word meaning power. Colloquially, it soon became synonymous with "electric generator".

Electric Lighting

During the 1870s, better and better arc-lamps were introduced for lighting, which increased the demand for electric generators. The dynamo underwent considerable improvement, and many companies in both Europe and the United States began manufacturing electromachines. The big breakthrough for electric lighting came, however, when the electric light bulb was introduced. Many people believe that Thomas Alva Edison (1847–1931), "The Wizard of Menlo Park", invented the light bulb. As a matter of fact, he did not—it had been "invented" in different versions before Edison presented his, although his *was* the first practicable light bulb. Edison's great contribution was his creation of a whole system for electric lighting, consisting of a steam-engine-driven electric generator with cables, conductor joints, and other devices for transmitting the current to the consumer. Further, the system included domestic wiring, electric meters, fuses, switches, and fittings for his light bulb, things that, earlier, had not existed. Most components in this system were devised and tested by Edison himself.

Edison's light bulb, the carbon filament lamp, was ready for production in 1879, and in the same year, 115 lamps were installed on board the luxury paddle-steamer *Columbia*, where they lit the velvet-upholstered saloons. The European début of the Edison lamp was at the world exhibition in Paris in 1881, where part of Edison's package solution for electric lighting was also shown. In professional circles Edison's generator attracted a great deal of attention. He himself called it Jumbo (it weighed 27 tons), and it was a further development of European designs. The following year, Edison installed three Jumbo generators, each of 125 horsepower, in Pearl Street, New York, where, in other words, the world's first electric power-station was situated. Via a distribution system, current for 5,000 lamps in 225 houses was delivered. Electricity had become consumer goods, with "free delivery" to the place it was required.

Edison's power-station received full press coverage on both sides of the Atlantic, and soon there were power-stations in other countries. In Sweden the first light bulbs were mounted in Strömparterren at Norrbro in Stockholm. They were lit together with a number of arc-light lamps at the royal palace when, on 16 September, 1881, King Oscar II left Stockholm for Karlsruhe to celebrate the engagement of Crown Prince Gustaf and Princess Victoria of Baden. These light bulbs were not, however, made by Edison but by the Englishman St. George Lane-Fox. In the 1880s, there was a sharp increase in the use of electricity for lighting and other purposes. Electric household appliances soon came into use—cookers, fans, immersion heaters, irons, etc. Electric motors were also taken into operation in workshops and factories. This made great demands on the distribution networks, where Ohm's law quite simply demonstrated that their capacity was limited. Heat losses and voltage drops in cables

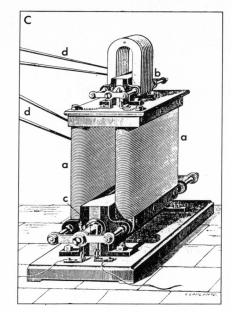

iron magnet and was driven by the same steam-engine as was the main engine. (c) Commutator. (d) Belt drive.
D The electrodynamic principle. For the sake of perspicuity, the rotor in this illustration has been

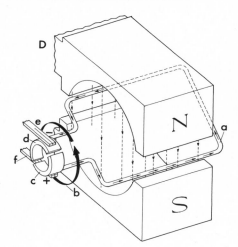

drawn as a single wire coil (a), placed in a magnetic field. When the rotor turns in the direction of the arrow (b), the coil's upper and lower halves cross the magnetic lines of force, and a voltage is induced in the coil. The voltage is proportional to the number of magnetic lines of force passed by the coil per unit of time. Thus, the voltage is at its maximum when the coil is vertical and is equal to zero when the coil is horizontal. As soon as the coil passes the horizontal position, that half of it which was earlier the upper becomes the lower, and vice versa, which means that the polarity of the voltage is reversed. At the same time, however, the two commutator segments (c, d) change places in relation to the brushes (e, f), which means that the segments will keep their polarity. If a light bulb, for instance, is connected to the brushes, an electric current starts passing through the coil because of the voltage. The current generates a magnetic field whose direction is opposite that of the field in which the current moves. This means that the coil now resists being turned round, and the energy needed to turn it is the energy consumed in the connected light bulb (plus the friction loss in the generator).

E Siemens's generator with a drum-wound armature is shown here in section; note how well-enclosed the armature (a) lies in the magnetic field produced by the pole shoes (b, c). This magnetic field is generated by the two "field windings" (d, e), which are fed with current by the generator's armature (self-excitation). This is possible because, in the soft iron, there is from the start a weak, remaining magnetism, which is why the generator always has "something to start with" when it must build up its own magnetic field. In principle, Siemens's construction is still used today.

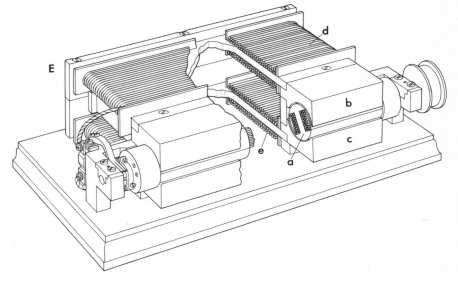

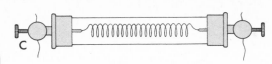

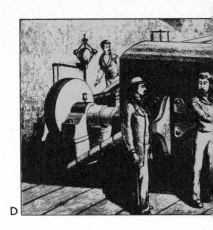

B The Englishman W. E. Staite (1809–54) experimented with incandescent filaments of platino-iridium alloy, but he did not succeed in making his lamps burn for very long. One reason was that the wire oxidized rather rapidly, since Staite failed to attain a good enough vacuum inside the bulbs; another was that the temperature at which pla-

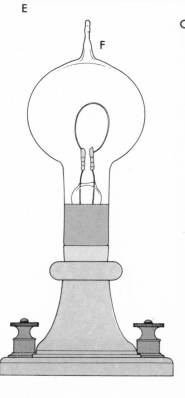

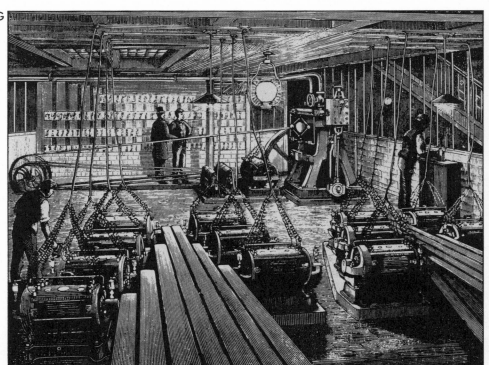

A A richly ornamented arc lamp for outdoor use. Arc lamps gave an intensive light, whose colour could be varied by impregnating the carbons with certain salts.

tinum becomes incandescent and that at which the metal starts to melt are too near each other. The light bulb shown here was constructed by Staite in the 1840s.

C The Englishman Warren de la Rue (1815–89), too, had realized the necessity of attaining a vacuum inside the lamps to stop the incandescent wire from oxidizing, but his lamp, which is shown here, did not burn for very long, either.

D An interior of Edison's power-station at Pearl Street. Two years after the power-station had started delivering electric cur-

rent, the number of dynamos had been increased to six, and the current powered over ten thousand light bulbs at 508 subscribers' houses.

E It took two years to lay the 14 miles (22.5 km) of cable needed for Edison's power-station. The cables consisted of double copper wires which had been insulated with impregnated hemp string and had been enclosed in iron tubes. A section of the cable can be seen at the top right of the picture.

F After a great number of experiments, Edison found that the most

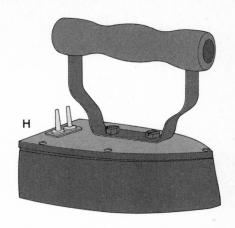

made it impossible to extend the distribution networks further than a few miles and limited the power to a few dozen kW. It was suggested that the voltage be increased, so as proportionately to reduce the amperage; the transmitted power would then remain the same, while heat losses and voltage drops would be lessened. But even the voltage employed by Edison at the Pearl Street power station (110 V) was considered by many to be lethal. The distribution systems of those days employed direct current, a property of which is an inability to be transformed to a higher voltage. The solution to this really complicated technical problem came around 1890, from several directions simultaneously. The only choice was obviously—as we may say now—to change over to alternating current, which can easily be transformed. The idea was that if the generator gives a low voltage, this can be stepped up to tens of thoausands of volts for transmission and then be stepped down to a normal consumption voltage. Alternating current as such was already known. Nikola Tesla (1856–1943) in the United States had worked on a polyphase alternating-current system and, in 1888, had patented a polyphase motor. For high voltage transmission, however, an entirely new system was required.

The breakthrough came in 1891, when an international electrical engineering exhibition was held in Frankfurt-on-Main in Germany. The preparations for this were supervised by Oskar von Miller, in many respects a pioneer in electrical engineering: He took the bold step of providing the exhibition with electric power from the waterfalls at Neckar on the river Lauffen, which was over 100 miles (c. 175 km) from the exhibition site. Von Miller put his faith in two inventions made by Michael von Dolovi-Dobrowolsky, chief designer at the Allgemeine Elektrizitäts-Gesellschaft (AEG). These were an alternating-current engine and a system for three-phase alternating current; they had been patented in 1888 and in 1889, respectively. AEG cooperated on the development of transformers and equipment for high-voltage lines with Oerlikon in Switzerland, where Charles Brown was now employed. The power transmission from Lauffen to Frankfurt was energized in August, 1891, and—naturally—became the great sensation of the exhibition. The transmission voltage was 30,000 volts and the output about 175 kW. With this breakthrough, electric power technology came of age. Ever since, there has been rapid and impressive progress, but it is disputable whether we have yet seen the real blossoming of electric power technology.

The question of who was first with the three-phase system has been vehemently debated over the years. In the mid-1950s, the Verein Deutsche Elektrotechniker (VDE) charged an unbiased committee with the task of finding out who was the first to introduce such a system. In 1959, the VDE published an extensive report which stated that von Dolivo-Dobrowolsky and Brown were the first. The report also gave a detailed analysis of the contributions made by a number of other people who had presented similar ideas at the same time.

suitable material for incandescent wire was carbon. His first carbon filament lamp, which is shown here, burnt for forty-five hours; the incandescent filament consisted of a piece of carbonized cotton thread which had been fixed between two platinum screw vices. The air inside the bulb was evacuated – this problem had been solved in 1868, when a practicable vacuum pump had been invented in Germany – and the lamp was screwed into a socket. The wires were connected to pole screws on the socket.

G In c. 1880, a Paris department store had these direct-current machines installed. They were used for lighting.

H An electric iron of 1888. In principle, the iron functioned in the same manner as did the light bulb; the current passed through a thread-shaped rheostat, heating it.

I As early as the last decades of the nineteenth century, a great many electrically powered articles, such as these various pots and pans, were manufactured.

Alternative Energy Sources

In 1973, the abstract physical concept of "energy" suddenly hit the headlines all over the world. There was talk of an energy crisis. The reasons for this so-called crisis which, in reality, existed only in the news headlines, will not be enlarged upon here. We shall merely state that it had one important consequence: the public at large became aware of the international energy situation. People began to question if, from a global point of view, we could afford the present intense consumption of energy. The most usual raw materials used for producing energy – coal, oil, natural gas, and uranium – will run out one day. The debate provoked a keen interest in what are called alternative energy sources, such as the wind, the sun, the waves, and the tide.

Before looking more closely at some of these sources of energy, it may be useful to make clear what is meant by the term "energy". First, though, "mechanical work": in physics this is defined as the force multiplied by the distance travelled in the direction in which the motive force is applied, while "power" is "mechanical work" per unit of time. The now obsolescent unit "horsepower" was defined as 550 foot-pounds (75 kilogram metres) per second. By "energy" is meant the capacity to perform "mechanical work", a capacity that is related to some source of energy. "Energy" and "mechanical work" are expressed in the same units, while a principle called in physics "the mechanical heat equivalent" is also relevant here: it states that a given quantity of work or "energy" is the same as a given quantity of heat, meaning that while energy can take different forms, it cannot be created or destroyed.

Let us take a simple example: a tower clock driven by a weight of 8 kg is wound up 1.5 m at the beginning of each week. As the weight slowly sinks, it performs mechanical work. The amount of energy is 8 kg multiplied by 1.5 m, that is 12 kilogram metres (kgm). If this is divided by the number of seconds in one week, 604,800, the result is 0.00002 kilogram metres per second (kgm/s). By winding up the clock, what is called potential energy is transferred to the raised weight, and as it sinks, this potential energy is converted into kinetic energy which, in moving the cog-wheels of the clock, is not consumed except in the sense of once more being converted, this time into heat caused by the friction of the clockwork.

This indestructible quality of energy gave rise to many philosophical speculations when the concept of energy was first being explored, mainly through the thermodynamic studies made in the 1850s by Lord Kelvin. Kelvin talked of the "decadence of energy", meaning that the heat energy comprised in the universe strives towards an equilibrium by becoming more and more uniformly spread.

Generally, energy has to be converted or refined through several stages before it can be used. Electric energy can be seen as a highly refined form of energy. Oil cannot be converted directly into electric energy, but an oil-fired steam boiler can deliver steam to a turbine, which then provides mechanical kinetic energy. This energy can be finally converted in a generator into electric energy.

Wind-Power – in its Second Wind

The keen interest taken today in wind power is widely believed to have originated during the "energy crisis" of 1973. The truth is that this was merely the occasion on which politicians became aware of the energy problem generally and of the potential of wind power in particular. In fact, over the past hundred years or so, very much research and development has gone into attempts to produce better designs than those of the old windmills for exploiting the kinetic energy inherent in the wind.

In the late 1870s in the United States, Stuart Perry designed a

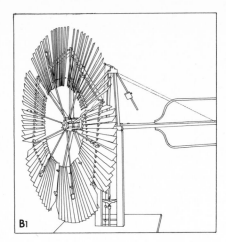

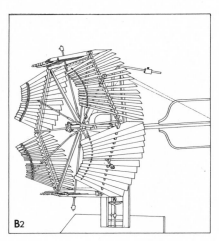

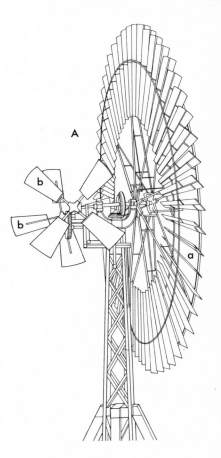

B The prototype of all self-regulating wind wheels was the Halladay wheel, seen here in its unfolded (**1**) and folded (**2**) states. The vanes were rotatable and mounted on crossbars, and since their surfaces were greater towards the wheel's periphery than towards its centre in relation to the turning-point, the vanes, under wind pressure, tilted backwards. This movement was opposed by a weight at the back of the wheel. As the wind pressure increased, it outbalanced the weight,

A The vanes of the Reinsch wheel were pivoted round their longitudinal axes. Each vane was attached to a rotatable ring (*a*), whose movements were determined by the influence of the centrifugal force on a weight. Propellers (*b*) automatically turned the wheel to face the wind.

wind turbine of steel, which was based on Daniel Halladay's wooden rotor of 1854 and which later became known as the American fan mill. It immediately became very popular in agricultural areas, where it was used to drive pumps for drainage and irrigation. Unlike the windmills with, typically, four sails, Perry's wind turbine had 100 to 150 small sails on the wind wheel, which had a diameter of 3 to 9 ft (1 to 3 m). These fan mills became quite common also in Europe and, in places, are still a typical feature of the landscape. In the beginning of the 1880s, the market in the United States was supplied with such mills connected to electric generators which, via buffer batteries, delivered power for electric lighting, the great novelty of the time.

During the 1890s, the American fan mill was developed in several countries, mainly Germany, where mills were built with wind wheels measuring up to 30 ft (c 10 m) in diameter. These were equipped with smaller wind wheels, called rosettes, which caused the apparatus automatically to face squarely into the wind. This was an invention taken from the windmills of old. These mills were able to drive many of the machines which were then used in agriculture, such as and the vanes tilted backwards. When only a low output was needed in hard winds, the wheel was kept at a safe speed through the centrifugal force of weights on its periphery causing the vanes to tilt backwards. **C** Sörensen's conical wind wheel is shown here in longitudinal-section (*1*); (*2*) front view. The vanes consisted of small tin plates, each of which was carried on a shaft and could be given a crosswise position when the wheel was to be stopped. The wind wheel's comparatively

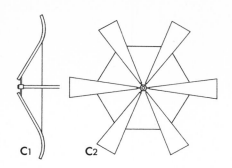

high efficiency was maintained because the vanes were designed to change the direction of the wind which hit them.
D On large farms, wind engines used to be used to power, for example, the chaff cutter (*a*), the grinding machine (*b*), the thresher (*c*), the groats mill (*d*), and the circular saw (*e*). Pumping, irrigation, and draining were other tasks for which wind engines were used.

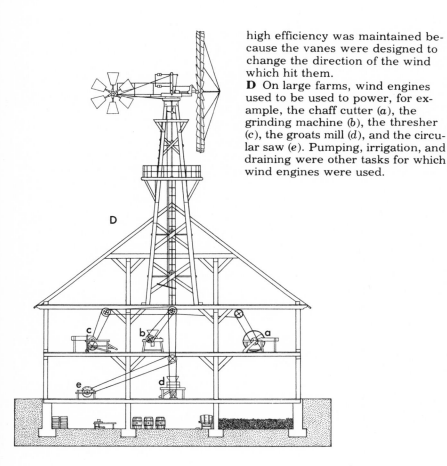

threshing machines, roller-mills, hacking machines, and even circular saws.

During the first decade of the twentieth century, the electrics industry in the United States and Europe spent large amounts of money trying to adapt the American fan mill for the generation of electric power, especially to suit agricultural requirements. In 1900, a Dane, Christian Sörensen, designed a conical wind wheel which had an effect exceeding that of the flat wind wheel by over fifty per cent. Electric power-stations with Sörensen's wind wheel were built by ASEA and others, and the construction had a certain amount of success. Various remedies were tried out in attempts to solve the problem of power regulation. This problem arises from the variation of the wind force and the fact that the power of a fan mill is in proportion to the cube of the wind velocity. In other words, if the wind force is doubled, the capacity will increase by $2^3 = 8$ times. This development work was interrupted when hydroelectric power began to solve the problem of rural electrification.

The first actual research project in the field of wind power was

started in Denmark in 1894. It continued for about ten years and was headed by Poul La Cour (1846–1908), a professor of physics. In an experimental mill built at Askov, La Cour's theoretical calculations were tried out in practice. The main aim of these experiments was to achieve a high output even if the wind velocity was low. The Danish government supported this ambitious project with large sums of money, in the hope that the result would enable them to bring electricity to the countryside. This was of vital importance to the agricultural nation of Denmark, which has no waterfalls of its own; in most other countries, waterfalls provided the power which, in those early days, supplied the farming areas with electricity.

While the admirable experiments carried out by La Cour did not solve the problem of rural electrification, they did set an example for many later Danish experiments with wind power. One of La Cour's successors was Jakob Juul, who, in the mid-1950s, designed a wind turbine with a capacity of 200 kilowatts (kW). It was built at Gedser and began operation in 1957.

During the years between the two world wars, many original wind-power projects were tried out in Europe and the United States. One example is the wind rotor wheel with a vertical axle, which was patented in 1927 by the Frenchman G. J. M. Darrieus. The rotor wheel was about 66 ft (20 m) high and had two blades and a capacity of 10 kW. An experimental model was taken into operation in 1929 and gave very promising results. One advantage of the Darrieus, or arc, rotor wheel is the fact that it works independently of wind direction.

In the 1930s, various German engineers devoted themselves to designing gigantic projects to exploit wind power. Although none of these ever left the drawing-board, they can be said to have paved the way for the designs which are being developed in many places today. Two examples are those suggested by Herman Honeff. One included 1,300-ft (400 m) high towers of framework construction, each having five wind turbines with vertical axles. The towers were to be built in groups of four and give an average power of 50 megawatts (MW). The other project planned by Honeff was to consist of power-stations on pontoons anchored in the turbulent North Sea. The electric power was then to be transferred to land via a sea cable. In the 1950s, Honeff was succeeded by the very able Ulrich Hüttner, who designed a wind power-station of 100 kW. It was completed in 1957 in Stötten in southern Germany and was in operation until 1966.

In the 1930s, the Soviet Union, too, had a wind power-station built near Yalta on the Black Sea. Its output was 100 kW, and it had a rotor wheel with two blades and a diameter of almost 100 ft (30 m).

The largest wind-power project in this period was, however, carried out in the United States. Its originator was a Boston geologist, Palmer C. Putnam. In the late 1930s, a friend of his asked him if he had any idea how to construct a wind generator which could supply electric power to a remote farm. Putnam quickly solved the problem—to his friend's delight—and became fascinated by the potential of wind energy. He attacked the task of designing a wind power-station of 1 megawatt (MW) and, when his project was completed, he showed his plans to Vannevar Bush (1890–1974), the then principal of the Massachusetts Institute of Technology. Bush was impressed by the bold project, managed to find a patron to finance the building of a full-scale prototype, and brought in a number of eminent engineers to solve the various problems involved. In the autumn of 1941, the prototype was put into operation on Grandpa's Knob, a 2,130-ft (650 m) high mountain near Rutland in Vermont. The company financing the wind power-station was S. Morgan Smith & Co., and the power lines were built by the Vermont Public Service Co.

In the past, similar constructions had employed direct-current gen-

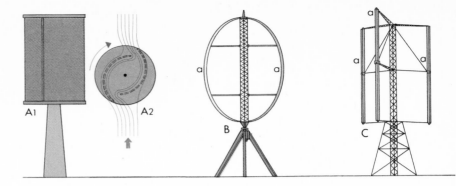

A In the 1920s, the Finnish engineer S.J. Savonius constructed this rotor (1) with its vertical shaft. (2) A cross-section of the rotor. The vanes are semi-circular and mounted so that the wind can pass between them, giving the rotor increased torsion.
B Like the Savonius rotor, the Darrieus, or arc, rotor works independently of the wind direction. It consists of two or more vanes (*a*), which are mounted on a vertical shaft.

C This rotor, Giromill, also works independently of the wind's direction. It consists of straight vanes (*a*), whose angle is continually varied during rotation.
D A modern, rapidly rotating two-vane rotor with horizontal shaft. With a rotor like this, up to eighty per cent of the theoretically available wind energy can be transformed into kinetic energy.
E The peripheral speed of a two-vane rotor is high, while the

erators and buffer batteries, but this project, which is now often referred to as the Smith-Putnam project, employed an alternating-current generator. Such a generator can only feed power into an existing distribution network provided it runs synchronously with the grid frequency, and the designers here managed to do this, thus solving the regulation problem of the fan mills. The rotor wheel had two stainless steel blades, about 95 ft (29 m) long, and was mounted on top of a 120-ft (36 m) high tower. The rotor-wheel axle was at an elevation angle of 12.5° and the blades rotated at 28.5 rpm. The rotor wheel drove a synchronous generator via a hydraulic connection, and the generator turned at 600 rpm. The speed was controlled by a centrifugal governor connected to hydraulic servo-motors which affected the rotor blades. In the first three-week period that the power-station was in operation, it supplied 82,000 kW hours (kWh), which considerably exceeded calculations. But after the rotor wheel broke in 1946, the project was abandoned.

During the latter part of the 1970s, many countries initiated sizable projects for exploiting wind energy, most of them based on old ideas and designs which are now being tried again in conjunction with modern technology. In Canada, for example, the Darrieus rotor wheel has been taken up again in a large-scale project. In 1975, the Canadian National Aeronautical Establishment (NAE) gave notice of a competition to design a 1-kW wind generator primarily intended for lighthouses and remote Indian reservations. The competition was won by Dominion Aluminum Ltd. with a 15-ft (4.5 m) high updated version of the Darrieus rotor wheel. This company's next project was a 200-kW wind generator which was 120 ft (36 m) high and had a Darrieus rotor wheel with a diameter of 80 ft (24 m); this power-station was commissioned by the government and built on the windy Magdalen Islands off Nova Scotia. The wind researchers of the NAE are at present at an advanced stage in planning a gigantic 980-ft (300 m) high wind generator with a Darrieus rotor wheel.

In 1974, a then recently formed energy body in the United States, the Energy Research and Development Agency (ERDA), started a research programme to investigate the possibilities of making the nation independent of imported energy by the year 2000. Much of ERDA's programme concentrates on wind energy, and one of the original aims was to have wind power-stations with a total capacity of 100 MW in operation from 1981, with wind power supplying twenty-five per cent of the nation's total energy consumption by the year 2000. As early as the summer of 1975, a 100-kW wind power-station was put into operation at the NASA–Lewis Research Centre in Ohio. The rotor wheel has two blades and a diameter of 123-ft (37.5 m) and is mounted on top of a 100-ft (30 m) high tower. In general terms, this wind power-station has been developed from the previously mentioned construction built by Hütter in Stötten. After a running-in period of about two years and with the necessary modifications made during this period, a small series of similar units were manufactured. These were then offered to the different power companies of the country for further development.

In 1974, in Holland, the promised land of windmills, a development programme for wind energy was initiated. The first project was simply a redesign of a traditional windmill, which was equipped with metal sails and an electric generator of 80 kW. It was built on the island of Texel. But it had an unexpected side effect: the metal sails interfered with the television transmission and gave rise to flickering ghost images on the TV screens. The considerate wind researchers therefore operated the mill only during the day.

The Dutch, incidentally, have always remained faithful to wind power. The traditional windmills are still in operation, and so are thousands of little wind engines which pump water for drainage. At least three Dutch factories currently manufacture wind engines for this purpose. A wind engine is more expensive than an electrically driven pump, but the extra cost is compensated by the fact that no cables have to be drawn across the fields and also by the free supply of energy.

The development work which has been carried out in recent years

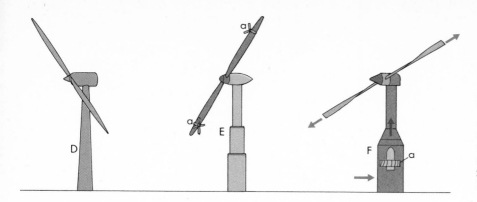

number of revolutions per minute is relatively low. The use of a large speed gear is then necessary if the rotor is to drive a generator directly. Another solution is to equip the rotor with brake turbines (a), which will achieve a sufficient number of revolutions per minute to drive a generator directly. However, if brake turbines are used, the kinetic energy produced is cut by about one-fourth.

F When the Enfield-Andreau rotor

is rotated by the wind, centrifugal force pushes air out through holes in the vane tips. A negative pressure then occurs inside the stand, and air which is sucked in from the outside drives the turbine (a).

G Honeff's suggestion for a gigantic wind power-station: 1,300-ft (400 m) high towers, each equipped with five wind turbines, were to be erected in groups of four. According to Honeff, these would produce extremely cheap energy.

in the area of wind power has been directed mainly towards the problems of control technology, whereas the basic design ideas have been taken from the past. Several new rotor-wheel designs have been introduced, but the early designs have proved the most reliable.

Solar Energy

Several of the ancient religions worshipped the sun as their supreme god, the god who gave light and heat, life to all that lived. And the sun is in truth a most generous source of energy: it transforms literally astronomical amounts of nuclear energy into radiation. The earth is hit by only about half of one billionth of the total radiation of the sun, but in spite of that, the surface of the earth absorbs an average of 1 kW per 10 sq ft (1 sq m) in clear weather. Some of the incident radiation is consumed in heating the atmosphere—which is one reason why the wind blows, as solar energy is converted into wind power. In the same way, the solar radiation heats oceans and lakes. When heated, these give off vapour which then falls as rain, snow, or hail. In other words, hydroelectric power-stations are ultimately driven by solar energy, as, indeed, are windmills.

The idea of using solar energy has appealed to scientists and engineers ever since antiquity. Euclid, for example, in his work on optics, described the ability of the burning-mirror to concentrate the radiation of the sun and thus achieve a high temperature. Archimedes' feat of using burning-mirrors to set ablaze the rigs of the attacking Roman ships has been mentioned in a previous chapter, although it is unknown whether this is myth or reality. Philo of Byzantium exploited the thermal power of solar energy in a thermoscope, a forerunner of the thermometer: a tube filled with air and sealed at the top had its lower end immersed in water in a container. When the tube was exposed to radiation, the air expanded, and the water in the container rose. The Renaissance engineer Salomon de Caus took up this idea and in his art book of 1615 described two devices in which solar energy was exploited in a similar manner. In one, solar radiation was concentrated through lenses into a sealed container connected to a water tank which was joined to a fountain. As the sun heated the water of the tank, the fountain began to play. The other "sun machine" consisted of the hollow statue of a shepherd. The air inside the statue expanded due to the heat of the sun and was conducted to two organ-pipes which then sounded. These flippant ideas fired the imagination of many natural scientists. Athanasius Kircher, for example, described the "sun machines" in his comprehensive work on light and optics, *Ars magna lucis et umbrae* (1646), without mentioning, however, either Philo or de Caus, as was the custom of the time.

During the seventeenth and eighteenth centuries, various burning-glasses and parabolic burning-mirrors were manufactured in science laboratories. Around 1690, a famous burning-mirror was produced in Dresden by E. W. von Tschirnhausen (1651–1708). It had a diameter of 5 ft 3 in (1.6 m) and was used in experiments with pottery kilns.

But it was not until the latter part of the nineteenth century that any realistic ideas for exploiting solar energy appeared. In the 1860s, the originator of the *Monitor*, John Ericsson, became fascinated by the potential of solar energy, after the crew of the *Monitor* had complained that the sun made the flat deck of the ship so hot that it became almost unbearable in the forecastle. Ericsson enthusiastically attacked the task of designing instruments to measure the energy content of solar radiation—in those days, this was a practically unknown field of research.

Ericsson lived on Beach Street in New York and built a solar research laboratory there on the top floor and the roof. He equipped one of his small caloric engines with a parabolic solar reflector, so that the fuel was replaced by solar energy. The engine drove a meat spit, which was inserted in the focus of another parabolic mirror. Both mirrors were adjusted to start the machinery in time to broil a chicken or steak for lunch. This *rôtissoire solaire* is probably the first example of how solar energy can be applied outside a laboratory.

Ericsson designed in all about fifty measuring instruments for his research in solar energy. In 1868, when he was awarded an honorary doctorate by Lund university in Sweden, he wrote a paper entitled "On the Use of Solar Energy as a Mechanical Driving Power", which was published in the university's periodical, *Acta*. In this paper, Ericsson described his efforts to trace the physical nature of solar radiation. The basic connection between radiation and temperature was, however, not defined until 1884, when an Austrian scientist, Ludwig Boltzmann (1844–1906) managed to deduce theoretically the law which his compatriot Joseph Stefan (1835–93) had stated empirically some years before and which is now called the Stefan-Boltzmann radiation law.

In 1883, when Ericsson was eighty, he designed what was perhaps his most famous solar machine. The mirror was a rectangular trough, 11 ft 6 in (3.5 m) long and 6 ft 6 in (2 m) wide, with a parabolic section. A longitudinal tube with a diameter of 6 in (15 cm) was mounted along the focal line of the mirror and could be used as a boiler for a steam-engine, while the "solar engine", as Ericsson called it, could also drive a caloric engine, if the tube contained air.

At the time when John Ericsson began to take an interest in solar energy, two French engineers, Augustin Mouchot and Abel Pifre, were busy building a solar machine which they demonstrated first in Algeria around 1879 and then in the Tuileries in Paris. The solar collector was a conical mirror with a diameter of 7 ft 3 in (2.2 m) at its base, with a tubular steam boiler at its point. It fed a steam-engine which drove a water pump. Mouchot was something of a missionary for solar energy and often demonstrated his sun machine connected to a small printing press which printed pamphlets about the excellence of solar energy in general and about Mouchot's exploitation of it in particular.

At the beginning of the twentieth century, an Anglo-American consortium took up Ericsson's designs and built a machine which was very much like the one built by Ericsson in 1883, although its dimensions were larger. Experiments were made with this machine at Meadi, near Cairo in Egypt. Once enough experience had been gained, a solar collector was built with a total surface area of 12,900 sq ft (1,200 sq m) which drove a steam-engine of 100 horsepower. The five mirrors, 200 ft (60 m) long and 13 ft (4 m) wide, followed the course of the sun via a system of jointed levers, and the full power of the steam-engine could be achieved for nine hours of the twenty-four. The construction was situated at the edge of the Sahara desert, and the aim of the project was to use an irrigation plant driven by the steam-engine to "make the desert bloom". The mirrors, however, required a lot of space—a surface area of 38,000 sq ft (3,500 sq m)—so that they would not shade each other. Besides, the customers found construction costs too high, and so, the much larger plant planned was never built.

During the first half of the twentieth century, there was little activity in the field of solar energy, one reason for this probably being the fact that the technical applications of solar energy had become closely connected with steam-engines and heat engines generally. When electric power started to triumph, at the beginning of our century, engineers were so much attracted by it that any technology related to steam-engines was considered hopelessly antiquated. When the petrol engine appeared, it meant access to yet another power source which could be moved to where it was needed. It was not until the 1950s that the wind changed for solar power. Several controversial books written then, one of them by the American physicist Harrison Brown, pointed out the limited resources of fuel and minerals on our planet and called for a halt to the ever accelerating increase of energy consumption.

In the United States the Association for Applied Solar Energy was formed in 1954, with its solar research centre situated at Phoenix, Arizona. The association is very active, its activities including the publication of the periodical *The Sun at Work*. During its first decade,

A John Ericsson's solar engine consisted of narrow glass strips which had been silvered on their outer sides and mounted on a stand, bent like a parabolic cylinder. In the focus of the mirror cylinder, a tubular boiler (a) was mounted.
B Ericsson's solar engine could also be used to drive a caloric engine.

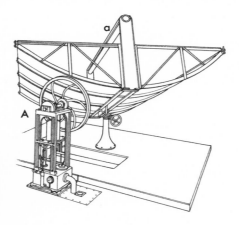

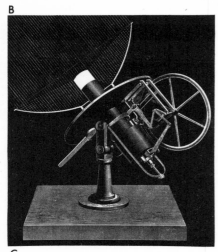

C Mouchot's and Pifre's solar engine consisted of a wide cone with a 7 ft 3 in (2.2 m) diameter. It was built of copper plates which had been silver-plated on the inside. The tubular boiler was placed in the centre of the mirror and was blackened, to absorb the sun's radiation better. A glass casing prevents heat loss. The steam drove a small, 0.4-horsepower steam-engine which, in turn, drove a printing press.

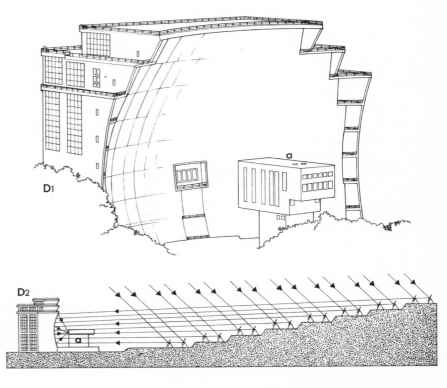

D The solar furnace at Odeillo. (1) The northern facade of an eleven-storey building faced with a parabolic mirror, which consists of nine thousand smaller mirrors. (2) In the slope in front of the building, eleven thousand movable, flat mirrors (heliostats) are scattered, and these reflect solar radiation towards the parabolic mirror. The solar furnace (a) is situated within the parabolic mirror's focus.
E Glaser's suggestion for a solar power-station in space. The power station was to be geostationary, which means that its speed in space would equal the speed of the earth's rotation and it would always appear to be in the same spot in the sky. Since the problems of overcast skies, seasonal variations, and fluctuations between night and day which we have on earth with regard to solar power-stations do not exist in space, a solar power-station of this type would give a practically constant production of electric current. The conversion from solar radiation to electric direct-current power would take place in photocells on the surface of the solar radiation catcher.
F A solar cell has the ability to transform radiation energy into electric energy and consists of semiconductors such as silicon or germanium crystals. These crystals have the ability either to be conductors of electricity or not, depending on the "pollutions" added to them. An atom in a semiconductor crystal easily loses one of its electrons, and the "hole" created will then be filled by an electron from another atom in the crystal. This exchange of electrons goes on continuously, but the crystal still does not become electrically charged, since

the association concentrated on the development of devices which would make it possible to exploit the abundant solar energy available in many developing nations, where there is a shortage of wood; an information campaign was organized to instruct the people in these countries to exploit the heat of the sun, mainly for cooking. One item introduced by the association for this purpose was a handy solar collector, called the "Umbroiler", a compound of "*um*brella" and "*broiler*", the name revealing all about the construction of the device.

In the 1950s, two large solar furnaces were built, one in the United States and one in France; this began a new stage of development. The American solar furnace is situated in Natick in Massachusetts, and its gigantic mirror produces at its focus a temperature of 4,400°C, enough to gasify steel! The large French solar research centre is now at Odeillo in the Pyrenees. The French research board, Centre National de la Récherche Scientifique, initiated research in solar

E

energy as early as 1946, and the first solar furnace in the Pyrennees was built in 1949 at Mont-Louis near Odeillo. It had a capacity of 50 kW and was built under the guidance of Felix Trombe. In the 1960s, a parabolic mirror was built in Odeillo, covering the whole façade of an eleven-storey building. This huge solar collector concentrates solar radiation which is reflected from a large number of small mirrors on the hills in front of the building. The temperature at the point of focus of the solar collector is about 4,000°C, and its effect is 1,000 kW. Extensive development and research work is also carried out at Odeillo to find methods of using solar energy to heat houses and the like.

In the 1950s, the Soviet Union also began to take solar energy seriously, and a trial plant was erected in a desert area in Armenia. Its dimensions were huge—1,300 large mirrors, moving on concentric rails to follow the course of the sun, concentrated the solar radiation towards a steam generator on a 180-ft (55 m) high tower. An electric generator driven by steam turbines then supplied electric power for irrigation, domestic requirements, and other purposes.

Yet another breakthrough in the development of solar energy came during the latter part of the 1950s with the advent of the solar cell, which converts solar radiation directly into electric energy. The first solar cells were built in the United States to supply electric power to space probes and satellites. In very simple terms, one can say that a solar cell works like an inverted transistor; it, too, consists of a coated silicon crystal from which radiation energy displaces electrons which are caught by the coatings. A very large number of such cells are connected in series and in parallel to give the voltage and power required for the electrically powered devices. Solar cells have hitherto been very expensive to produce, but considerable progress has been made in recent years. In the long run, and with a certain optimism, one can look forward to a competitive supply of electricity from solar cells.

In the 1950s, scientists in many parts of the world—for instance in the United States and in Israel—began to take an interest in the use of solar energy for heating houses. The preferred form of solar heater was one for water-borne heat, often connected to a heat pump; this system heated both the central-heating and the hot-water systems. The Royal Swedish Academy of Sciences has a solar research station in Capri, where astrophysical studies of the sun have been carried out for a long time, and in 1960, it installed a solar heating plant there under the supervision of Yngve Öhman. In 1974, the International Energy Agency (IEA) was formed as a sub-division of OECD, the European body for economic cooperation, and this has resulted in widespread international cooperation in the development of possible methods of heating houses by solar energy. At present, domestic heating accounts for more than half of our total energy consumption. Many forecasters believe that, by the turn of the century, solar energy may be responsible for at least fifty per cent of all heating—with variations in both directions, depending on the latitude.

In the 1970s, several projects have been started both in the United States and in Europe for large-scale solar power-stations. In 1975, the American energy body ERDA commissioned plans for a 10-MW solar power-station from the Sandia Laboratories in California. They in turn commissioned four industries to develop the different solutions. All four companies decided to place a steam boiler on top of a tower and arrange thousands of mirrors, or heliostats, to concentrate the solar radiation toward the steam boiler. However, their solutions differ widely when it comes to the construction and control of the heliostats, and the storing of energy, which must be stored so that the power-station can operate continuously, even when the sky is cloudy or after the sun has set. The steam produced by solar energy

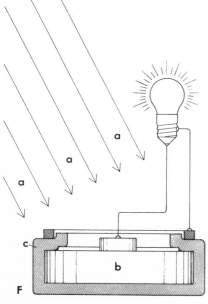

F

the total number of electrons in it does not vary. If a small amount of an element whose atoms each have fewer electrons than those of the semiconductor is added to the semiconductor crystal, "holes" are left in the crystal, which will then become positively charged (p-crystal). In the same manner, a semiconductor crystal can become negatively charged (n-crystal) if one adds a small amount of an element whose atoms each have more electrons than have those of the semiconductor. When the sun's rays (a) hit the joint between the solar cell's n-crystal (b) and the surrounding p-crystal, electrons are ejected from the n-crystal, and an electric voltage occurs between the two layers. The conversion efficiency of a solar cell is, however, only about eleven per cent, and such cells are still very expensive to manufacture.

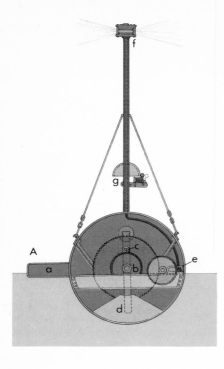

A A wave-powered electric whistle and light buoy from the first decades of the twentieth century. The wave motion was transferred by a jib (*a*) to the cylindrical buoy, which was then rotated round its longitudinal axis (*b*). The motion was transmitted to a gear train, which was stopped from turning the wrong way by a pawl (*c*). As the gearwheels turned, they brought a weight (*d*) upwards, and when the latter had reached its uppermost position, gravity caused it to fall down on the other side. Since the speed of the gearwheels was then increased, the rotor (*e*) of a small, electromagnetic engine was rotated fast enough to generate an electric current, which lit up a light bulb (*f*) and caused a bell (*g*) to sound.
B A proposal for a wave power-station (**1**) by Stephen Salter. The floats consist of cams (**2**) whose front edges are shaped to utilize the available wave energy as much as possible.

C A Swedish proposal for a wave power-station (**1**). Each buoy (*a*) is, by way of a spring-loaded hinged rod (*b*), connected to a float (*c*) anchored to the sea bed. (*d*) Electric cable. The transformer (**2**) contains a bar magnet (*e*) and an inductor (*f*) with a spring-loaded suspension (*g*). (*h*) Concrete float. (*i*) Plastic walls. (*j*) Diode bridge.

is estimated to have a temperature of 500°C and a pressure of about 10 megapascal. In other words, the turbine and the generator part of the solar power-station will be conventional. However, the constructional problems connected with the other parts are rather difficult to solve. One major problem is to build heliostats which can resist strong gusts of wind and yet be easy to orientate towards the sun. ERDA aims to begin operating the first pilot plant in 1980 in Barstow, California.

In Europe, IEA and ERDA are together planning to build a solar power-station of 0.5 MW in the early 1980s, probably in Almeria, Spain. A working party within the European Economic Community also plans a solar power-station, to be built in Italy, but any further details about the plant are, unfortunately, being kept secret.

In the 1970s, moreover, very ambitious plans for solar power-stations have been introduced by American scientists. They want to place solar collectors in space and to transmit the effect to receivers on the earth via microwaves. The first outline for such a power-station was published in 1973, and a more detailed plan was presented in 1977 by Peter E. Glaser, head of the Arthur D. Little Institute in Boston. Glaser suggests that a geo-stationary satellite, at a distance of about 22,500 miles (*c*. 36,000 km) from the earth, be equipped with a solar collector of about 40 sq miles (*c*. 100 sq km) (there's plenty of room out there!) which is constantly orientated towards the radiation of the sun. A direct-current power of about 15 GW (gigawatt = 10^9 watt) would be achieved and converted into radio waves for transmittal to earth, where a receiving station with an area of about 20 sq miles (*c*. 50 sq km) was to be built, consisting of a very large number of dipole antennas, each fitted with a crystal diode to rectify the radio waves. After the whole chain of energy conversions had been completed, about 10 GW would remain of the original 15 GW, which is equal to the estimated total energy demand in Sweden for 1979! The whole development programme for this project has been estimated to cost 60 billion US dollars. In the United States they expect to have some kind of a pilot plant in operation before the turn of the century.

Wave Energy

The energy found in the waves of the oceans and larger lakes is also a form of solar energy. A 10-ft (3 m) high wave contains more than 6 kW per ft (20 kW per metre)! The first patents of devices to exploit the energy of waves did not appear until the 1890s, and they had no practical significance. Not until the 1920s was a device invented which exploited wave energy on a small scale. It has since been used for sound buoys. Such a buoy is anchored to the seabed and contains an air dome where air flows in and out through a turbine driving a generator. Such pneumatic energy converters on a larger scale would be suitable for installation on, for example, oil platforms. A large number of energy converters are at present being studied in different places in the world, and some extensive research and development work is being carried out in Britain, France, the United States, and Scandinavia, with the aim of having wave power-stations in the megawatt class ready for experimental operation in the mid-1980s. Each wave power-station will probably include ten thousand or more converters and will, in other words, take up large areas at sea. Scientists are aware of the negative effect this will have on shipping and fishing, but they believe a positive effect will be a reduction of tidal movement. A wave power-station under favourable conditions could make traffic easier in channels which are normally difficult to navigate, since it would act as a primary breakwater. Cautious forecasters, however, do not expect wave power-stations to make any significant contributions to our energy supply until the year 2000 or so.

CHAPTER 7
THE GENESIS OF CONTROL SYSTEMS

The previous chapters of this book have dealt with some aspects of the technical developments that have led to the multitude of machines and devices which surround us today. If they are to be used as intended, it is often of vital importance that they be properly governed and controlled. The more complicated a machine, the more advanced must be the technique required to govern and control it. It is ultimately a question of man's ability to master technology.

Let us illustrate this with an example: when the bicycle was introduced in the 1860s, it became immediately popular in many places. At last a simple and handy means of transportation! But the first version of the bicycle could be quite lethal in certain situations: it had neither free wheel—that is, the pedals were fixed to the driving wheel—nor braking device. Going downhill, the rider had to keep his feet on the pedals and control his speed as best he could, and were he unsuccessful, he would very likely end up on a wild trip through the scenery. A modern bicycle, however, is equipped with a "control system", i.e., a free-wheel hub and, often, both hand and foot brakes, which together enable it to be controlled fully.

Some Elementary Terms

Modern control systems form one of the most advanced branches of engineering and aim at finding methods of controlling even the most intricate piece of machinery as easily and effectively as one can steer and brake a modern bicycle. A control engineer sees a machine as a system—a word of very general application: it comprehends a bicycle, a washing-machine, a spacecraft, the traffic flowing through a junction, a microwave oven, a nuclear reactor—briefly, any coherent unit which is controllable.

We talk about control *systems*, since the technical devices required nowadays to control plant or machinery have become complicated enough to justify this designation. They may be divided into two groups, those with *open-loop control* and those with *closed-loop*, or *feedback*, *control*. An example of a simple form of an open-loop control system is a light switch, which switches a lamp on and off. Control, or governing, can also be effected in an open system by a programming device which turns the light on or off at certain predetermined times. Such open-loop control systems are to be seen at street junctions, where traffic lights have been programmed for decided, regular intervals, but motorists do not much like such systems for controlling traffic, because queues easily build up on the busier of two roads at a junction. This problem can be solved by implanting vehicle detectors into the road and letting them report to the program device how many cars are approaching the junction. The program device in this case must be equipped with a counter, adjusted to let the traffic lights turn green for the busier road when, say, five cars are reported from one direction and none, or perhaps only one, from the other. Such a control system for traffic surveillance is, to a

A A road junction with an open control system. The automatic controller (*a*) keeps changing the lights so that they are green for the cars on road *b* for as long and as frequently as they are green for the cars on road *c*.

B A road junction with a closed control system. Vehicle detectors (*a*) sunk into the road surfaces report all cars approaching the junction to the automatic controller (*b*). If a single car is reported and the lights are red for traffic on the road in question, the lights will change before the car has reached the junction. However, if the lights are green, the signals will remain unchanged. If a car is approaching on each road, the car first actuating a vehicle detector will be the first to get green, and the lights will change as soon as it has crossed the junction. If a continuous stream of cars is reported from one road (*c*) whereas only one or two cars are reported from the other (*d*), the continuous stream of cars is allowed to cross until a gap occurs; then the signals are changed. If there is heavy, continuous traffic on both roads at the same time, the lights keep changing at regular intervals until a gap occurs in the traffic on either of the roads.

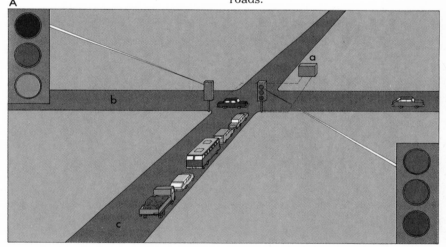

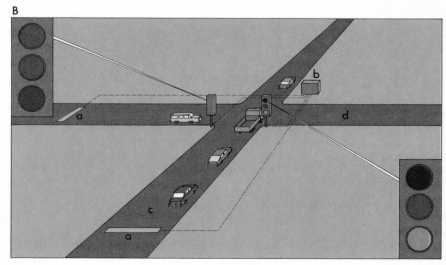

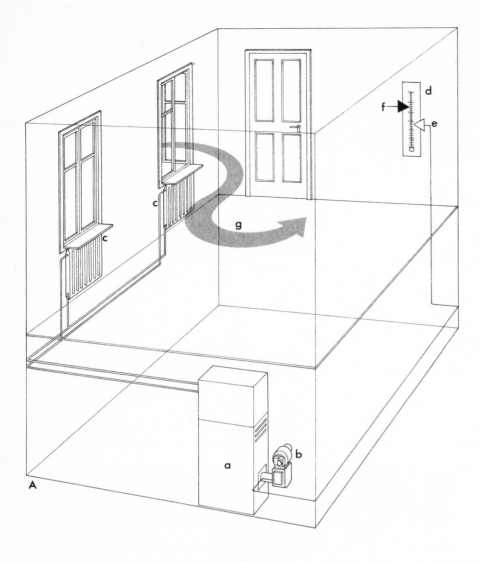

certain extent, responsible for its own actions, due to the feedback given via the vehicle detectors in the road. Consequently, this is called a *closed-loop control* system. An example of a purer feedback control system is the temperature regulation which is used in many buildings, mainly in houses with oil-fired central heating. The terminology used in control technology describes the system like this:

1 The *controlled system* consists of the boiler with its oil burner and the radiators heating the rooms.

2 The thermostat, which is in principle a thermometer, has the function of delivering a continuous *control signal* – a report of the room temperature – to the controlled system.

3 The *desired value* of the control signal is set on the thermostat in each room, indicating the temperature desired in the room.

4 If the desired value for the temperature is 68°F (20°C) and the control signal reports that the room temperature, the actual value, is only 60°F (16°C) an *error signal* is introduced, and the oil burner starts. It remains in operation until the room temperature has gone up to the desired value and eliminated the error. Then it is turned off automatically.

5 A *disturbance* to the system occurs, when, for example, a window is opened and cold air flows into a room.

The distinguishing factor in open-loop as well as closed-loop control systems is that they are automatic. They are therefore called *automatic control systems*.

Simulacra and Automata

Automatic devices appeared at a very early stage in human history. The hunting people of the early Stone Age, for example, probably knew the art of catching or killing wild animals with gin traps. There are many different types of animal trap; one of them, fitted with a "gin", a releasing mechanism, was probably the first automatic device.

An animal trap of interest in this context is the Scandinavian moose spear, an ancient trapping device that was quite common in parts of the region until well into this century. When the moose broke a line with its chest, a spear was released, being propelled by a "spring" formed by a young tree-trunk under tension. This animal trap, and also others of the same sort, in which the gin releases some kind of missile (we do not include things like pitfalls) can be seen as an arrangement whereby man has tried technically to simulate or imitate the way a hunter brings down his quarry, so that these animal traps can be called simulacra. Constructions with the idea of technically imitating human behaviour have been of great importance in the appearance of many tools and aids. The connected levers of a pair of tongs, for example, can be seen as a simulation or imitation of a human hand and its gripping function. This manner of description relates closely to the principle by which a sledge hammer is regarded as an extension of the human arm. We have referred to this principle, called organ projection, earlier; it has made an important contribution to, among other things, ergonomics, or work science, which aims at a better understanding of man's function in different working situations.

The attempt to imitate the behaviour of man or animals in a technical construction has often been the first step of a development in which the next has been an attempt to make this simulation an automatic mechanism – an automaton. When this automaton has achieved a certain degree of technical perfection, the desire has often arisen to try to simulate still more complicated functions. In such a step-by-step chain of development the tension between simulacra and automata emerges as a powerful driving force in furthering technical development in many areas. We shall later give other examples of such chains of development, but let us mention here just

A An example of a feedback control system: thermostat-controlled heating of a house. The controlled system consists of the central-heating boiler (a) with its oil burner (b) and the radiators (c). A thermostat (d), which continually delivers information of the prevailing indoor temperature (e) is connected to the system. The required value of the control signal (the temperature de-sired – f – in the room) is set on the thermostat. If the actual room temperature sinks below the desired temperature, the oil burner is automatically started and remains in operation until the room temperature is again at the desired level, when b is turned off. A disturbance to the system occurs if, for instance, a window is opened and cold air (g) flows in.

one, the chain which led to the modern computer. The first mechanical adding machines appeared in the seventeenth century and, in a way, simulated man's habit of counting on his fingers. Then, automatic calculating machines, automata, were produced successively, and after another few development stages, refined electronics managed to simulate man's way of making more complicated calculations. Simply put, this is done by giving the computer a program for calculating. During the course of operation, it can, among other things, store information in and retrieve it from a memory. This is all done automatically, acording to the program it has been fed. In other words, the computer is an automaton. However, methods are at present being developed to make the computer imitate man's ability to receive and interpret verbal instructions. This goal will, most probably, be achieved, and the computer will acquire these simulative functions while also being able to function automatically, that is, it will become a simulacrum as well as an automaton.

Some Early Control Systems

We have suggested that the gin of an animal trap is the earliest automatic mechanism. It is impossible to give the date for its appearance, but it is likely that it occurred while the hunting and gathering people were still nomadic, i.e., perhaps more than ten thousand years ago. The function of the gin has many modern equivalents, such as the limit switch, which releases or interrupts a movement in manufacturing automats, packing machines, etc.

A gin trap can be regarded as an open control system with program control, in which the quarry, in a random manner, supplies the "program". Many of the earliest control systems can be referred to as open systems, and it was not unusual for them to be equipped with some primitive form of programming. One such system is a method of cooking used by the hunting peoples in several of the earliest cultures. The cooking vessel was a leather bag; and heat was obtained from a stone heated in a fire. The stone was selected or brought along because it was just large enough to give the right cooking time for the food to be prepared. The "choice of program", in this case, was the size of the stone. It can be seen, with a little bit of imagination, as an early predecessor of today's electric time-controlled cookers. Almost nine thousand years separate these technically related methods for rationalizing domestic duties. Werner zur Megede, a German historian of technology, reports that North African finds of such cooking equipment have been dated to about 6650 BC.

Continuing our historical review of control systems, we find magnificent examples of programmed control in the huge irrigation systems of the river cultures. When the rivers rose during the rain periods, the water was led off via canals that started a long way upriver from the area that needed irrigation. The water was gathered in large basins well above the high-water level of the river in the area to be irrigated, thus making it possible to irrigate large areas untouched by the flooding. In Mesopotamia, the Land of the Twin Rivers, such irrigation systems, albeit local ones, were built as early as the fourth millennium BC. After the powerful ruler Hammurabi had united the many small kingdoms along the Euphrates and the Tigris in the 1780s BC, he proclaimed a law which aimed at co-ordinating the operation of the many networks of basins and canals which were then in use. Hammurabi's famous law was mainly a handbook for the organization and administration of the irrigation systems. The law laid down the obligation of each citizen to contribute to the maintenance, operation, and extension of the systems. Also, there were detailed paragraphs about the punishment for any neglect of these obligations. The slightest disobedience or negligence in fulfilling the state's severe requirements was seen as a cardinal

B A moose spear is shown here from above (**1**) and from the side (**2**). When the moose moved against a line (*a*), a catch (*b*) was released. The spear (*c*), which was mounted on a young tree-trunk under tension, was then flung forwards and buried itself in the moose.

B1

B2

C The ancient Egyptians irrigated areas normally untouched by the Nile's floods by digging feeder canals (*a*), which started far upstream of the area in question. The water was then allowed to trickle down-wards, from basin to basin (*b*), when dams in the walls between them were opened. Thus, the soil in the basins was thoroughly soaked. Similar irrigation systems occurred in other early river cultures.

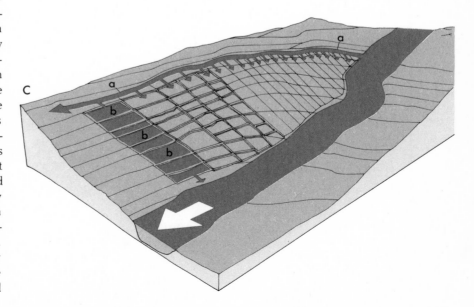

crime. It was vital for the whole of society that the irrigation system worked. An enormous labour force was needed to control this huge system during the critical period when the "program device" was released, i.e., when the rivers started to overflow. This did not happen with the precision one should expect from a program device, since both the Euphrates and the Tigris were fairly unpredictable. The very able Sumerian civil engineers were really hard tried, but eventually, they developed an admirably accurate technique for controlling the life-giving water—there was often a difference of only half an inch or so between the successive levels of the irrigation systems. But in the eleventh century BC, when the Euphrates changed course, the surrounding part of the irrigation system became hopelessly confused. This contributed to the disintegration of the society and to the decline of the Sumerian culture.

Irrigation systems similar to the Sumerian were built by other early river cultures—on the Yellow River in China, in the Indus valley, and along the Nile. In ancient Egypt impressive irrigation works were constructed. The Egyptians started somewhat later than the neighbouring Sumerians, but their problem with regulation was much simpler, for the Nile flooded with an unfailing precision that has earned it the epithet, "the gentleman river". Because the program for controlling the irrigation worked perfectly, it was easier to manage the regulation of the water flow, with the result that the long, narrow strips of arable land along the Nile valley could be made wider and wider, thus strengthening the economic foundation of this remarkable, advanced culture.

Early Automata and Closed Systems

The simple water clock, the clepsydra, became common in ancient Greece some time during the sixth or fifth century BC, but had probably come into being in Egypt long before. The oldest document to mention a clepsydra is a record of judicial proceedings where it is named as an aid to ensure that both the prosecutor and the defendant are given the same time for their final pleadings. The simplest form of the clepsydra was a basin with a spillway. Since water was added to the basin continuously, it ran with a reasonably constant flow out of a lower opening and into another, graded vessel. This primitive chronometer was improved and more or less perfected by the engineers of the Alexandrian school, primarily by Ctesibius (see page 33). The clepsydra, in its most refined version, can be regarded as a simulacrum by means of which an imitation is sought of the unfaltering, constant movement of the heavenly bodies, which is the basis of our measuring of time.

The idea of giving the clepsydra an automatic function, however, had already been thought of when this mechanism existed only in its simplest form. No less a person than the great philosopher Plato (427–347 BC) designed such an automaton. The pupils of the academy founded by Plato in Athens in 378 BC had difficulty in waking up in the morning, and it was a problem to gather them for the day's discussions, so Plato built a magnificent "alarm clock", which was placed in the olive grove of the academy. It was a simple clepsydra, in which the usual graded vessel had inside it a bowl which was hinged across its width and contained a number of lead balls. During the night, the vessel filled with water which, as it rose, lifted the bowl, causing, in due time, the lead balls to roll out and fall on a copper plate. The noise ought to have awakened at least the lighter sleepers, who probably then aroused their friends.

Plato's alarm clock, like his academy, attracted a great deal of contemporary attention, and in the following century, many clepsydras with signal devices were designed. One of them used compressed air to achieve a loud, whistling noise. The water of the clepsydra was fed into a container divided into an upper and a lower compartment; between these ran a pipe which was open at both ends and almost long enough to reach the upper edge of the upper compartment, but not going too far into the lower compartment. A thicker pipe was arched over the first pipe and fixed a small distance above its top. This thicker pipe was closed at the top, and its open end almost reached the dividing wall between the upper and the lower compartments. When the water of the clepsydra had reached the upper edge of the inner pipe, the upper compartment emptied itself relatively quickly, and the water ran into the lower compartment, due to the two pipes working together as a hydrometer. The air in the lower compartment was compressed and pressed out through another pipe in its upper part. This was fitted with a whistle or a flute, which then sounded.

The Alexandrian School

Technology and the natural sciences flourished at that famous seat of learning of antiquity, the Museum of Alexandria, to which we have referred already. A large number of brilliant talents, such as Pythagoras, Ctesibius, Euclid, Hero, and Philo of Byzantium, made their contributions to science there. Archimedes, too, may be reckoned as of the Alexandrian school, although he was active in Syracuse, an important administrative centre within the same cultural sphere. The engineers of the Alexandrian school constructed various simulacra and automata, which have been variously discussed already. One may wonder why these advanced engineers designed things such as singing birds, moving figures for the stage, self-propelled carriages, and automatic devices, some of which, to be sure, had a practical purpose, such as the holy-water dispenser and the odometer-taximeter; but most of them were intended to simulate pure magic, such as the heat machine which automatically opened the doors of the temple's inner sanctum. Why did not the engineers of the Alexandrian school do something useful instead?

The reason is that they regarded themselves as natural philosophers, whose only objective was to explore the laws of nature. This they did by theoretical speculation, calling logics and mathematics to their assistance, when needed. In cases where the theories were suited to experimental trials, devices for practical experiments were built. It is apparent that the natural philosophers had skilful instrument makers and craftsmen available for this work, and that they had a supply of refined equipment and tools. These instrument makers must have had their own internal training system, for which a selected number of apprentices were recruited. The professional skill of the instrument makers was really put to the test when the "professors" ordered the devices they needed to test their theories. Usually, it was a question of designs never tried before, something that must have stimulated thinking along new lines. Many flippant constructions, today attributed to the engineers of the Alexandrian school, were no doubt the result of teamwork between the natural philosophers and their skilful instrument makers.

A rich source of inspiration for the school's ingenious simulacra and automata was the mythology and the whole imaginary world of ancient Greece, which included a comprehensive fauna of artificial birds, walking and talking statues, and skilfully made imitations of divinities as well as servants. Homer's *Iliad* tells about the crafty god Hephaestus, "the engineer of Olympus", who had designed self-propelled carriages. The engineers of the Alexandrian school made this mythological achievement a practical reality (see page 36). Hephaestus surrounded himself with servant girls made of pure gold. According to Homer, these golden girls were both strong and intelligent. They could talk and were assiduous in learning the handicrafts the gods taught them. This is one of the first mentions of artificial human beings, or androids. From the Renaissance onwards, many attempts were made to produce such creatures. We shall come back to this later.

The story about Daedalus, his son Icarus, and their flying adventure is commonly known and, without doubt, belongs to the world of myth. The hellenic fables say that Daedalus served King Minos in Crete and amused himself, and possibly also the king, by designing moving animals, among them a cow. Quite contrary to the story of the flying adventure, there may be a grain of truth in the tradition that Daedalus built moving, walking statues. He is said to have used mercury to change the centre of gravity and so get the arms, legs, and even the eyes of the statues to move. The manner of depicting an "arrested action" in Greek sculpture is attributed to Daedalus (a famous example of arrested action is the discobolus by Myro). The technique of depicting eyes with a hole in the pupil is also attributed to Daedalus.

Many historians and writers of ancient Greece and Rome, including Herodotus of Halicarnassus, Lucian, and Diodorus Siculus, give detailed descriptions of self-propelled mechanisms and androids, and similar accounts occur in other early cultures, especially that of China. What is myth and what reality is often very difficult to determine exactly, but this sphere of thought seems to have excited the imagination everywhere. There is, without doubt, an extremely rich tradition in the history of ideas for the theories of control systems.

The story of Archytas of Tarentum (400?–365? BC) and his famous flying wooden pigeon lies on the borderline between myth and reality. As Archytas was a contemporary and friend of Plato's, and was also a pupil of Pythagoras', he can be considered to belong to the Alexandrian school. Of his work, only fragments remain, among them dissertations on acoustics and musical theory, but there is enough to demonstrate that he was an advanced natural philosopher. What has afforded him his greatest renown is the story about the pigeon; however, this story was first written down several hundred years after his death. In the story, the pigeon has inside its body a magic container, which keeps it soaring in the air. This container was probably no more than a hot-air balloon or kite. The Alexandrian school knew these toys, and the fact that Archytas worked with acoustics makes it likely that he also studied the properties of air. The story about Archytas' flying pigeon has been related by many different chroniclers down the centuries, and each time, it has been expanded in the telling, but the reality behind it may very well be what we have suggested.

One example of the many unsuccessful attempts to solve the problem of flying by simulating the flight of birds occurred in Rome in the middle of the seventeenth century. Members of the learned Roman society, *Accademia dell'Esperienze*, were inspired by the story about Archytas' pigeon to construct a mechanical version driven by springs, but this academic pigeon did not fly. The myth about Daedalus and Icarus, the legend about Archytas' pigeon, and several other stories from antiquity about mechanical birds are probably partly responsible for many inventors, even in the twentieth century, trying to build their flying-machines according to what is called the ornithopter, or flapping, principle, despite Sir George Cayley's statement as early as 1799 that this was not possible.

Back to the Alexandrian school, whose natural philosophers and engineers were certainly unaware of how important their various programmed simulacra and automata would be in the future, or that their devices with feedback, which can now be called the first closed control systems, would be even more important, if that were possible. One of the first was Hero's design for the control of the level of a liquid by means of a floating body which affected the discharge valve, a design whose principle is still used, both in industry and in our immediate surroundings: one variant is to be found in the car

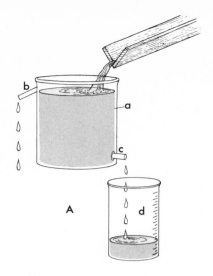

A The simplest type of water clock consisted of a vessel (*a*) with an overflow (*b*). From the lower part of this vessel, water dripped through a tube (*c*) and into another, graded vessel (*d*). Since the water constantly supplied to *a* amounted to a little more than the amount of water dripping out through *c*, the water pressure in *a* was approximately constant.

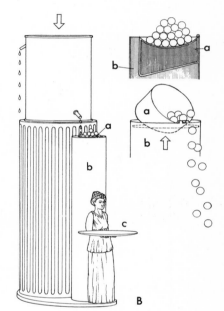

B Plato's alarm clock was a simple clepsydra, in which a bowl (*a*) containing lead balls had been hinged to the brim of a (usually) graded vessel (*b*). When the water level in *b* had risen enough, the bowl was lifted, and the lead balls were tipped out and fell onto a copper plate (*c*).

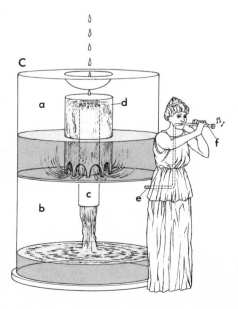

C This clepsydra with its signalling device has also been attributed to Plato. The water from the clepsydra was collected in a vessel which was divided into an upper (*a*) and a lower (*b*) compartment. Between these ran a pipe (*c*) which was open at both ends. Vaulted over pipe *c* was a wider pipe (*d*) whose closed upper end was situated a short distance above the top of the inner pipe, whereas its open, lower end had been designed so that water could enter between the two pipes. When the water in *a* had risen above the upper edge of the inner tube (*c*), *a* was fairly rapidly emptied of water, which ran into *b*, since the two pipes together worked as a siphon. The air in *b* was then compressed and forced out through a pipe (*e*), to whose outer end a flute (*f*) was attached.

A In 1863, a Frenchman, J.-J. Bourcart, constructed this pedal-propelled craft with which, in his opinion, one ought to be able to fly. One advantage which he emphasized was that the "pilot" had both hands free.
B This ornithopter model, built in 1870 by the Frenchman Gustave Trouvé, was propelled by gunpowder and could be made to fly all of 77 yds (70 m).
C Accademia dell'Esperienze's clockwork-powered, mechanical pigeon was one of many unsuccessful attempts to simulate the flight of birds.

carburettor and another in the water closet. Several other engineers of the Alexandrian school described different versions of the level control. One of these, a fine example of constructive thinking and usually attributed to Ctesibius, combines the floating body with the valve to form an integral unit, a solution which eliminates the play that can occur in the joints of the levers in Hero's version. Ctesibius's device was intended to meet a demand for precision, namely to achieve a uniform flow of water in a water clock.

Philo of Byzantium, another great thinker of the Alexandrian school, designed a control device adapted to the special requirements of an oil lamp, which does not necessarily need a constant oil level, but whose level must be neither too high nor too low, if the wick is to burn well. Philo's design consisted of a closed oil container with an ascending pipe, open at both ends. The lower end was immersed in the oil bath supplying fuel to the wick. When the level of the oil fell below the lower end of the pipe, air bubbled up through it, allowing oil to run out of two thin pipes at the bottom of the oil container until the level of the oil in the oil bath once again covered the lower end of the ascending pipe, whereupon no more oil ran out of the container because no more air was entering it through the ascending pipe. Philo's control ensured that the level of the oil stayed between a minimum and a maximum level. This closed control system, too, has many successors in modern technology, although it is usual that separate devices assess the upper and lower limits.

Arabic Interlude

We have mentioned briefly that the works of the Alexandrian school became widely spread in the Eastern Roman Empire and in the Arabic cultural sphere after the decline and fall of the Western Empire. A great deal of the literature of antiquity had certainly been lost by the senseless plunderings of the wars of conquest, but a number of classical books had been preserved by scholars and in monasteries. The rapid Islamic conquests in the seventh and eighth centuries AD were followed by a period in which Arabic culture had a magnificent flowering, its main inspiration being the Hellenic heritage, especially as regards the natural sciences. Representative of this cultural revival is the systematic search for the classical works of antiquity, which was instigated by the khalif of Bagdhad, Abdullah-al-Manun (786–833) in the early ninth century. He commissioned three men, the *Banu Musa*, the three sons of his court astrologer, Musa, to go out and buy whatever they could lay their hands on in the way of works by the Greek natural philosophers. One of them travelled extensively in Asia Minor and Greece and tracked down numerous works by the philosophers of the Alexandrian school and by earlier equally distinguished Hellenes. This search laid the foundations of the Bagdhad library, later so renowned. Similar searches resulted in libraries of equivalent standing in Cairo and Cordoba, the other two capitals of the realms of Islam.

Musa's sons translated first and foremost Hero's and Philo's works and also revised them. They described a number of their own designs in the large work *Kitab al-Hiyal* ("The Book of Ingenious Devices"), which became almost a standard work in Arabic culture, judging, at least, by the large number of hand-written copies to be found in libraries and archives in the extensive Islamic dominion. The prototypes of the designs in this work can, however, easily be traced to the Alexandrian school.

The engineers of the Arabic world were no less fascinated by self-propelled devices than their predecessors, but within the Arabic world practical applications were sought for their designs. Many of the Greek prototypes had come about only to illustrate a natural law or a physical principle. In *Kitab al-Hiyal*, the Musa brothers de-

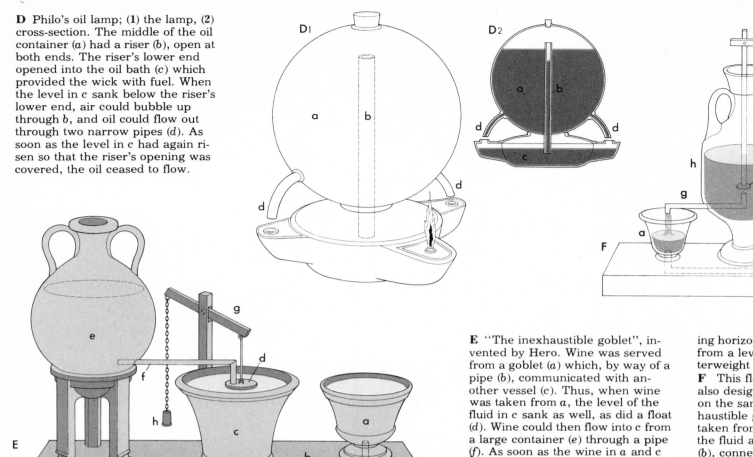

D Philo's oil lamp; (1) the lamp, (2) cross-section. The middle of the oil container (*a*) had a riser (*b*), open at both ends. The riser's lower end opened into the oil bath (*c*) which provided the wick with fuel. When the level in *c* sank below the riser's lower end, air could bubble up through *b*, and oil could flow out through two narrow pipes (*d*). As soon as the level in *c* had again risen so that the riser's opening was covered, the oil ceased to flow.

E "The inexhaustible goblet", invented by Hero. Wine was served from a goblet (*a*) which, by way of a pipe (*b*), communicated with another vessel (*c*). Thus, when wine was taken from *a*, the level of the fluid in *c* sank as well, as did a float (*d*). Wine could then flow into *c* from a large container (*e*) through a pipe (*f*). As soon as the wine in *a* and *c* was again at its original level, the float once more covered the opening of pipe *f*, and the wine ceased to flow. The float was kept from moving horizontally by being suspended from a lever (*g*) with a small counterweight (*h*).

F This flow-controlling valve was also designed by Hero. It is based on the same principle as "the inexhaustible goblet"—when wine was taken from a goblet (*a*), the level of the fluid also sank in another vessel (*b*), connected to *a* by a pipe (*c*). A float (*d*) then pulled a lever (*e*) downwards, so that the valve (*f*) of an outlet pipe (*g*) in a large wine container (*h*) was opened.

scribed a round one hundred designs and made great efforts to indicate different ways of putting them to practical use. From a modern point of view, many of these constructions may seem slightly far-fetched, but in those days, it may have been enough that on beholding them, "the spectator was petrified", as the writers on a few occasions remarked.

Those who came after the Musa brothers, however, discovered a large and fruitful area in which the designs could be applied, namely clockmaking. From the early Middle Ages onwards, magnificent ornamental clocks were built to adorn the princely houses of the Arabic world. The famous ornamental clock in Ghaza has already been named (see page 47) as an example of advanced manufacturing technology; it had appeared before the spread of Islam and is interesting proof that the heritage of the Alexandrian school was kept alive in this part of the world. Although the details of the design of the clock are unknown, it can be assumed that it was based mainly on the ideas of the Alexandrian engineers.

One of the first important books on clockmaking in the Arabic world is entitled *Work of Archimedes on the Building of Clocks*. The text claims that the book is based on works by Archimedes of Syracuse; in other words, it was a translation and revision of his works, similar to the translations made by the Arabs of Hero, Philo, and other writers. Still, no work on the building of clocks has been found among Archimedes' books, although contemporary writers suggest that he actually did study this branch of technology. It is certainly not unlikely that the great genius of the natural sciences in the ancient

world should have been fascinated by the automata of time-measuring. The Arabic translator may possibly have had a book by Archimedes, which has later been lost. The American historian of technology Otto Mayr cautiously calls the writer of this detailed description of the making of water clocks "Pseudo-Archimedes". It is apparent that the man who wrote the book must have known a great deal about clockmaking and also must have had plenty of practical experience of the existing machine elements. The book, which is thought to have been written in the tenth century AD, was translated into German by Friedrich Hauser and Eilhard Wiedemann in the 1910s. On the basis of the very comprehensive text, they could make a complete reconstruction of this remarkable water clock. It had a square base of 1 ft 8 in (0.5 m) and was more than 19 ft (4 m) high. After each "winding", i.e., filling with water, the clock ran for twelve hours, and the time was marked on a clock face. On the hour, a number of mechanisms were set in motion. A bird's beak dropped stone balls onto a metal gong—as many balls as there were hours to indicate. A snake attacked some birds and the eyes rolled in a representation of a woman's head.

Pseudo-Archimedes' book spread and was widely accepted as a handbook on clockmaking. Several later writers often refer to it, one of them being Ridwan al-Khurasani, the son of a clockmaker who became very famous at the end of the twelfth century for building an intricate ornamental clock at the "Gate of Hours" in the Great Mosque in Damascus. This clock showed the hours of the day with effects rather like those described by Pseudo-Archimedes, but more-

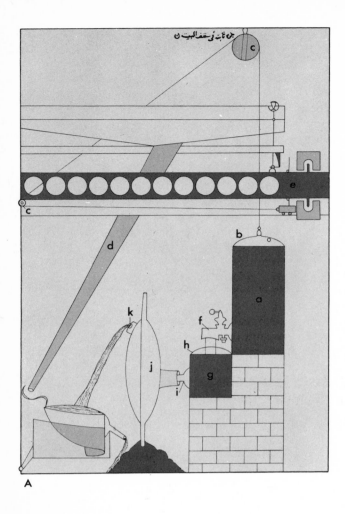

A A water clock, described and illustrated by al-Jazari. The clock was "wound up" when a tank (*a*) was filled with water. In the tank was a float (*b*), to which a string was attached. The string ran over pulleys (*c*), and, as *b* sank at an even pace, a pointer (*d*) was pulled by the string along a board (*e*) with twelve holes, one for each hour. From *a*, the water ran through a tap (*f*) into another, smaller vessel (*g*). The float (*h*) in this vessel carried on its top a carefully ground stopper, which fitted into the opening of the tap and turned off the flow of water when the float reached its upper level. As soon as it sank again, the water started to run anew. Thus, the water in *g* flowed under constant pressure through a pipe (*i*) which was placed near the bottom of *g*, and into a round vessel (*j*). In this vessel, there was an overflow (*k*) through which the water finally left. When *k* was in its highest position, it was level with the top of vessel *g* (the proportions in al-Jazari's illustration do not correspond to reality). By turning vessel *j*, the position of the overflow in relation to vessel *g* could be altered; thus, the length of the hours could be varied.

B Pseudo-Archimedes described

his water clock in such detail that Wiedemann and Hauser, who translated his work to German in the 1910s, could reconstruct practically the whole clock. It is shown here from the front (**1**), in cross-section from one side (**2**), and in semi-cross-section from the rear (**3**). Enough water for twelve hours was poured into a vessel (*a*) through a funnel (*b*). Just like al-Jazari's 300-years-earlier construction, Pseudo-Archimedes' clock was driven by a float (*c*) which sank at an even pace in this vessel, since the outflow of water was governed by a float (*d*) in a smaller vessel (*e*), to which a pipe (*f*) ran. From *e*, the water flowed through a pipe (*g*) and out through an overflow (*h*) whose position could be altered in a vertical direction, since pipe *g* could be rotated along a scale (*i*). The length of the hours could thus be varied in this clock as well, since the water's flow could be altered. From *h*, the water ran into a dipper (*j*) and on to another, pivoted dipper (*k*) with a counterweight (*l*) at one end. When *k* had been filled, it tipped over and activated the mechanism (*m*) which made a snake attack birds. Finally, the water was collected in the lower part of the clock, from where it

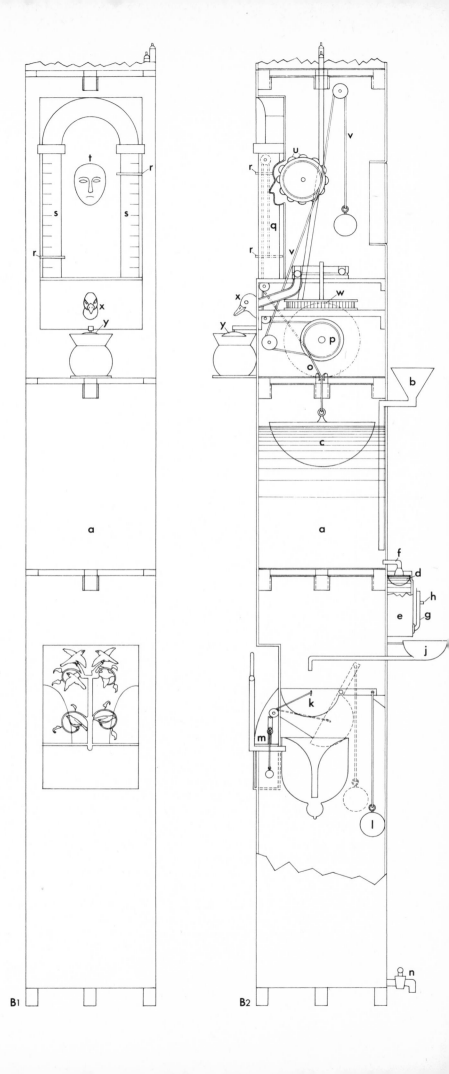

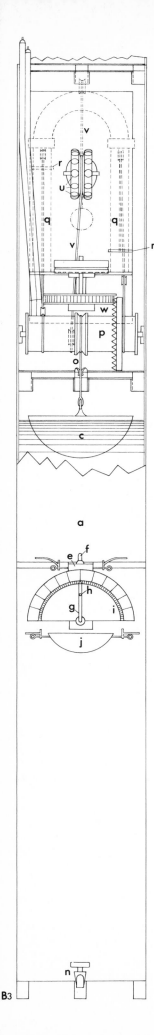

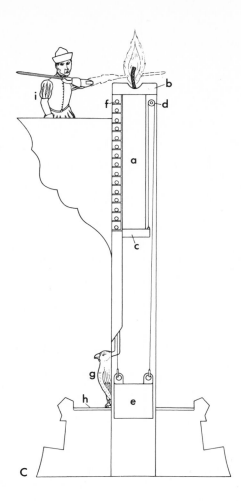

over, it had a special mechanism to show the time at night. A flame appeared in one after another of the twelve windows. Ridwan al-Khurasani, who is also known in literature as Ibn al-Saati ("the son of the clockmaker"), restored this ornamental clock, which had fallen into decay after the death of his father, and wrote a comprehensive instruction book for its future maintenance.

At the beginning of the thirteenth century, another renowned clockmaker, Ismaeel al-Jazari (1150?–1220?), was active in Amid on the upper reaches of the Tigris. He wrote a large book, *The Science of Ingenious Mechanisms*, in which he described some ten ornamental clocks. His first description is almost identical to Pseudo-Archimedes' design from three hundred years earlier. Apart from different versions of water-clocks, al-Jazari also described a highly original chronometer, which consisted of a wax candle with metal balls held individually in a vertical container. As the candle burnt down, the balls were released and fell onto a metal disc. This was not the first candle with a time-measuring function, but the striking mechanism was probably al-Jazari's invention.

This clockmaker's great fame is evidenced by the fact that he was called to Ghaza to put into working order the renowned ornamental clock, which had by then fallen into almost total decay. He managed to restore it to its past splendour, but the clock only existed for another fifty years or so. Most manifestations of this culture were eradicated when the Mongols attacked the eastern parts of the Arab dominion, Bagdhad falling in 1258.

The Automata of the Renaissance

We have already touched upon the important technical developments which took place in the West during the last few centuries of the Middle Ages. Water and wind power were exploited to a greater and greater extent and for more and more varied purposes. The supply of metals increased and the guilds appeared; one result of this was organized professional training. Many necessities, such as bricks and needles, were manufactured on a semi-industrial scale. Spiritual life also blossomed, with the foundation of universities and the growth of monastic orders. From the end of the thirteenth century onwards, inspiration in all areas was sought in the works of Greek and Roman writers. The culture of classical antiquity was to be reborn! This important phase in the history of technology has been called earlier in this book the "technical revolution of the Renaissance", and this concept is certainly richly emphasized in the field of automata.

Interest in natural science began to stir among the scholars of the time—mainly monks and theologians. It is not surprising that they were particularly interested in the ingenious devices and automata of the Alexandrian school. There is a story, typical for the time, about Thomas Aquinas (1225–74) and his teacher Albertus Magnus (1193?–1280), who was a Dominican friar, Bishop of Regensburg, and one of the great mediaeval polymaths, with extensive scientific interests. Albertus Magnus is said to have constructed a door-keeper of metal, wood, wax, and leather, who greeted visitors by uttering "*Salve*"! and by asking them their business, before admitting them to the great scholar. The young Thomas once became so annoyed with the impertinent questions of the android that he smashed it into pieces. Naturally, Albertus was incensed and admonished his student: "Thomas, Thomas, what have you done? You have smashed the work of thirty years to smithereens!"

This story is obviously a myth, although several versions of it have been repeated in various contexts through the centuries. But it is indicative of its time. People experienced one great change after another, and the technical revolution of the Renaissance often gave them an exaggerated belief in the possibilities of technology to pro-

could be discharged through a cock (*n*). When float *c* sank, it pulled on a string (*o*), which ran round a drum (*p*). Other strings (*q*) on the same drum drove the pointers (*r*) indicating the time on a dial (*s*). The gorgon's (*t*) rolling eyes (*u*) were also driven by a string (*v*) from this drum. Via a gear train (*w*), the drum also drove the mechanism which made a bird's head (*x*) release stone balls onto a metal gong (*y*).

C Al-Jazari's timekeeper in the form of a wax taper with a "striking apparatus". The taper (*a*) was inserted under a bronze disc (*b*) in which there was a hole for the wick. A holder (*c*) underneath the taper was suspended from a string, which ran over a pulley (*d*) and had a lead weight (*e*) at its other end. Thus, the taper was continually pushed upwards as it burned, releasing a metal ball from a small compartment (*f*) once an hour. The ball fell through a tube and out through the beak of a hollow falcon (*g*), landing on a metal plate (*h*). On its way down, the ball hit a mechanism which made the figure of a man swing a sharp sword at the wick, thus snuffing the taper.

A At a very early stage in the history of mechanical clocks, striking devices were constructed. These often took the form of jacquemarts, mechanical watchmen who struck bells with hammers.

B All that remains today of the fourteenth-century clock in the cathedral of Strasbourg is the bellows-powered mechanical cock (**1**), which flapped its wings and crowed at noon. When the mechanism was working, all the lower feathers in the cock's plumage were slanted. The cock, shown in cross-section at **2**, is today exhibited in the museum of Strasbourg.

A

B1   B2

duce "miracles" such as Albertus Magnus's ill-fated talkative doorkeeper.

According to certain historians, the invention of the mechanical clock was a way of solving an irritating problem from which the water clock suffered, namely, that it could work only in temperatures above freezing-point. There is, however, a very obvious common denominator between the more advanced water clocks and the first mechanical clocks. Weights, suspended from a rope over a roller, set various mechanisms working in Pseudo-Archimedes' water clock, and these important components were also used in its many successors. The advanced knowledge and experience of the Arab engineers in the field of self-moving mechanisms could certainly have enabled them to invent a mechanical clock which can be seen as a further development of the weight mechanisms of the water clocks. However, as has already been mentioned, the Mongols prevented this. What the Arab engineers lacked was an efficient "checking mechanism", which could reduce the movement driven by the weight—or rather, by gravity—to a rotation that was constant and slow enough. The escapement in mechanical clocks has this very function. In the mid-thirteenth century, an Arab clockmaker, Taqi al-Din, introduced a device which is extremely interesting in this context, being something of the missing link between the water clock and the mechanical clock. To moderate the movement of a weight-driven mechanism in a water clock, Taqi al-Din built an annular container, partly filled with mercury and contained in the drum round which the rope of the weight was wound. The mercury container was divided radially into sections by walls that had small holes in them; the movement of the drum was regulated by the arrested movement of the mercury through these holes. This device seems to have been unknown in the West at the time of the appearance there of the first mechanical clocks. Taqi al-Din's checking mechanism would probably have been able to provide a more even movement than that given by the first primitive escapements.

During the early Renaissance, the newly awakened interest in the writings of antiquity was undoubtedly a strong force in the development of mechanical clocks. When, in the fourteenth century, the mechanical timekeeper acquired the form of a simulacrum—the constant movement of the universe being simulated by the uniform movement of an axle—its design began to be developed so as to acquire another form of imitation. In the first mechanical clocks, the passage of the hours was indicated on a cylindrical or circular clockface, so that a watchman would know when to sound a horn or ring a bell. The automatic mechanism of the timekeeper was complemented with other mechanisms which copied the tasks of the watchman. These simulacra were the striking mechanisms, and many were built in different versions quite early in the history of mechanical clocks. The most logical thing to do was to make a mechanical copy of a watchman strike a bell. There are many examples of such functional decorations, called clock jacks, on tower clocks from the fourteenth century onwards. (The origin of the word "jack" is unclear, but it is believed that the word comes from the French *jacquemarts*, the *mart* being a corruption of the Latin *martellus*, a hammer.) The striking mechanisms were made as separate devices driven by the clockwork, and this was certainly nothing new. The skilfully made Arabic water clocks often had several separate devices whose functions were released in different ways by the time-measuring escapement. The simplest form of striking mechanism for mechanical clocks was a rudimentary wheel with cams, which enabled the jack to strike a hammer against a bell. The striking mechanism in this context can be seen as an early form of mechanical memory.

In the use of jacks we can trace the strong influence of the theatre automata of the Alexandrian school and of the advanced Arabic art of clockmaking, with its moving figures of gods, people, birds, and other animals. One of the first jacks was not a man with a hammer, but a mechanical cock attached to the tower of the cathedral of Strasbourg about 1350. At twelve o'clock, the cock flapped its wings and crowed. The cock was the symbol of vigilance and, therefore, often appeared—although not usually in its mechanized version—on many European church spires. The mechanical cock in Strasbourg may be regarded as a symbol of the rapid development which was to follow. With water clocks and other designs from antiquity as prototypes, numbers of intricate ornamental clocks were produced which showed the passage of the sun through the zodiac, the phases of the moon, and the movements of the planets. Often, these clocks were additionally equipped with moving figures representing kings, emperors, apostles, warriors, or clowns; these not only marked the passage of time but also performed elegant scenes containing both religious and profane symbolism. The automatic mechanisms must have been made with the same precision and have had the same certainty of motion as the clockwork; this instigated many instances of impressive precision mechanics, which demanded much of the material and of the principles of design, as well as of the craftsmanship. Ornamental clocks have been described from these points of view in Chapter Two.

Life-size Automata

The rapid technical progress that occurred during the Renaissance made it possible for designers to construct life-size automata in a wholly different manner than before—the engineers of the Alexandrian school had built their automatic devices on a scale suitable for playthings. Several revisions of the ancient classics of technology, as well as translations of both Greek and Arabic originals, were published in Europe in the sixteenth and seventeenth centuries. One of these is the extensive work, *Les raisons des forces mouvantes . . .* ("About Violent Forces. A Description of Some Useful and Amusing Devices") by the French engineer Salomon de Caus. This lavishly illustrated artbook was first published in 1615. De Caus was active for a large part of his life in Heidelberg, in the service of the elector, Fredrik V of Pfalz. His book describes many of Hero's automata but develops these construction ideas further, converting them for use in the technology of his own time, a technology embellished with all the colour and panache of the seventeenth century. Unlike many contemporary art books, however, de Caus's work was not merely theoretical: in the garden of the Heidelberg palace, he had built a number of scenes with moving figures, romantically framed by caves. The whole thing was driven by water wheels, and the movements of the figures were released by "programs" consisting of drums with cams. De Caus later built something of the same sort, but on a larger scale, at the Duke of Burgundy's palace, Saint-Germain, outside Paris, which became, because of this, one of the greatest attractions in Europe. Construction of a similar installation began in 1613 at the Hellbrunn Palace at Salzburg, and this also gained a great reputation. It originally consisted of a number of caves with moving mythological figures, dragons, and birds. The installation was enlarged between 1748 and 1752 to comprehend in total 256 figures. The Hellbrunn installation was water-driven, too, and had several gear mechanisms, connected to cylinders with cams, which shifted levers that pulled copper wires to set the figures moving according to a programmed sequence. A hydraulic organ provided effective background music and, moreover, smothered the noise of the driving mechanisms. Salomon de Caus had many successors who copied—as well as they could—his automatic theatre scenes, and for centuries, it remained fashionable to provide stately gardens with caves and moving figures.

Salomon de Caus was the great pioneer of life-size automata construction, an art which flowered at this time. The many royal, imperial, and ducal courts started to employ their own art masters, who made androids and other automata that more or less literally wandered about in the stately salons, showing off their skills. At about the same time, another art emerged and has continued to flourish until our time—the art of producing toy-scale automata, as had been done in classical antiquity. One of the great originators of this art was Juanelo Turriano, the brilliant designer of the "ballet-dancing machine" (see p. 103). This extremely talented engineer served Emperor Charles V, who, forced to abdicate in 1556, retired to the monastery of Geronimo de San Yuste in Estremadura, where he declined in sad meditation of his fate. Turriano tried in every way to cheer up his master by making amusing automata: wooden birds flying round the room, a shepherdess playing the lute, horn blowers and drummers, soldiers fencing with swords, and many other things. Some European museums, including the Kunsthistorisches Museum in Vienna, now have exhibitions of automata attributed to Turriano, but evidently, none of them can be proved to have been made by the clever Cremonese.

Turriano's automata became renowned, as had his great engineering feat of arranging the water supply to the city of Toledo, and the abbot of the monastery of San Yuste contributed a great deal to the fame of the former, although quite unintentionally. He happened to witness a performance of some of Turriano's automata, and the sight of this frivolous spectacle totally convinced the abbot that Turriano was in league with the devil himself. In those days, such an opinion, especially when held by such an important churchman, rapidly spread among the hierarchy and the faithful.

Whether the remarkable Turriano was in league with the devil or not, he certainly became the basis of a large number of myths, and something of a folk hero, especially after providing Toledo with water in such an elegant fashion. A chronicle from the mid-1600s tells how Turriano had designed an android in the form of a valet, who would go out in the streets every day to do the shopping for the household. One might remark that technology seems to have been more advanced at this time than it was when Albertus Magnus was said to have designed a door-keeper! But the myth of Turriano's valet is in the same spirit as that of the door-keeper. Firm belief in the achievements of a recognizedly eminent man formed, in both cases, the basis of the myth. As regards Turriano, the power of legend over thought became so strong that the alley where he lived in Toledo was later given the name *Calle del Hombre del Palo* ("The Alley of the Wooden Man").

There were, however, real equivalents of Turriano's "wooden man". They certainly could not move freely, but they still had an impressive range of skills. A number of goldsmiths and precision mechanics in Nürnberg led the field within this genre, one of the first being the father-in-law of Albrecht Dürer, Hanns Frey, a merchant whose hobby was precision mechanics. Frey built many automata, especially drinking automata, based on Hero's and the Arab masters' designs. His successor, Hanns Bullmann, was more important; he was a goldsmith and a contemporary of Peter Henlein, the locksmith and precision mechanic who designed one of the first spring-driven pocket watches (see page 52). Bullmann was possibly the first designer of automata to use spring-driven clockwork to move his figures; quite probably he was familiar with Henlein's work. A guild chronicle of 1547, *Nachrichten von Künstlern und Werkleute in Nürnberg*, gives a fairly comprehensive description of Bullmann's automata. They consisted of a large number of spring-driven figures of men and women, which could walk back and forth and play different instruments. As a designer of automata, Bullmann later had many automata from this pioneering era. A closer look at the programs and other control devices of the designs reveals that the extremely skilful craftsmen who manufactured them applied many sophisticated techniques which have been reinvented many times since.

When interest in automata became really widespread in the seventeenth century, not only precision engineers but also the great humanists and philosophers began to interest themselves in this technical art. The French philosopher René Descartes (1596–1650), in his pioneering work, *Discourse de la méthode*, published in 1637, deals with, among other things, the relationship between man and animals. They have all been made by God, he writes, but only man has an immortal soul. The animals, however, must be seen as intricate machines, as automata. Descartes goes on to expound his views on *la bête machine* ("the animal as a machine") and maintains that it is quite likely that, one day, man will succeed in designing "soulless machinery", shaped and behaving like animals. He makes his ideas more concrete by comparing the inner organs of man and animals and their hydraulic systems. The heart could be likened to a hydraulic engine (in modern terms), the brain corresponds to a reservoir and the blood system, tendons, and muscles are like the escapement which achieves movement in a clock. It is obvious that Descartes had been inspired both by the automatic devices which were becoming more and more common at this time, and by William Harvey's discovery that the circulation of the blood was like a mechanical pumping procedure. Harvey gave an account of this discovery in a pamphlet published in 1628, which attracted a lot of attention.

Descartes is said to have built a true-to-nature android in the shape of a girl, which he called Francine. He was certainly as advanced a physicist as a religious philosopher, but it is not likely that he would have been able to achieve such a feat in practice. The background of this legend—because it must be considered a legend—is, maybe, the fact that Descartes had a daughter called Francine on the wrong side of the blanket, so that the legendary android Francine could have been a substitute for the girl. The more serious biographers of Descartes neglect this legend, which in one version has a drastic climax: in 1649, Descartes was summoned to the court of Queen Christina of Sweden and set out by boat from Amsterdam to Stockholm, bringing Francine well packed in a seaman's trunk. The captain, however, had heard that this remarkable creation was on board, and when the ship ran into a storm on the North Sea, he blamed Descartes for their troubles, for a man with an android must be in league with the devil! The captain ordered that Francine be thrown overboard, but whether the North Sea grew calmer after that is not revealed.

One might add, by the way, that Descartes's stay in Stockholm had an unfortunate ending. The queen, who was thirsty for knowledge but also very eccentric, received Descartes at five o'clock every morning, in the middle of winter, for lessons in philosophy. The warm-blooded southerner began to teach in the ice-cold halls of the badly heated royal palace but in January, 1650, contracted a heavy cold, and died about a week later.

Descartes's ideas about *la bête machine* were a source of inspiration to future philosophers and theologians. For example, the talented and learned German Jesuit Athanasius Kircher (1602–80), worked with automata, building among other things a talking head, singing birds, and figures playing musical instruments. Kircher also followed Salomon de Caus's line in adopting automatic theatres for gardens. In 1650, he and another Jesuit, Kaspar Schott (1608–66), published a book which describes a number of these.

False Prophets

The great public interest in automata in the eighteenth century also

A One of Salomon de Caus's theatrical sets at Hellbrunn Castle, in which movable figures were placed in mountain caves. Via a gear transmission, a water-wheel (*a*) drove a shaft (*b*) to which both ends of a rope (*c*) were attached. The rope ran over pulleys (*d*) and round a wheel (*e*) at the bottom of a pillar, which carried a mythological figure. Thereupon, the rope ran over more pulleys (*f*) and back to the shaft.

resulted in the appearance of various humbugs. One of the best-known was the Hungarian baron, Wolfgang von Kempelen, who invented the "chess-playing Turk". We have met the imaginative baron before: it was he who introduced a steam turbine which, he claimed, would immediately outdo the existing steam-engine, but on that occasion, James Watt taught the good baron a lesson.

Towards the end of the 1760s, von Kempelen had built an automaton in the form of a male in Turkish dress, which sat beside a sturdy chest, on which was a chessboard. The designer challenged famous chess players to play against the Turk and, for years, he toured Europe and the United States with his show. The android could talk as well, although its vocabulary was limited to "Check!" and "Gardez!". The baron claimed, moreover, that in this android he had managed to copy man's intelligence and ability to combine thoughts. In that case, it would have been a question of a simulacrum rather than an automaton.

After attending a much publicized demonstration of the chess-playing Turk in London, Edgar Allan Poe wrote an essay in which he denounced with sharp logic any suggestion that the device had an ability to think. As a result, the humbug was revealed—von Kempelen had hidden a dwarf, a skilful chess-player, in the chest, and the machinery consisted of mechanisms for moving the chessmen on the board.

Other designers have "succeeded" with different forms of simulacra and automata by hiding individuals within them in one way or another, and in the seventeenth and eighteenth centuries, many news items were written about "self-propelled carriages", based on

B Vaucanson's famous duck (1) had a weight-powered mechanism which consisted of over a thousand movable parts. These were hidden inside the duck and in the foundation upon which the bird stood.

Unfortunately, the duck has now been lost. Some illustrations depicting it survive, however, among them this one (2), showing its innards.

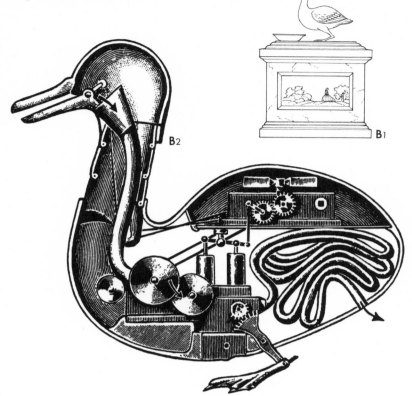

the same secret—sometimes revealed, sometimes not. One example will suffice. In 1793, the French balloon pioneer Jean-Pierre François Blanchard demonstrated a remarkable carriage at an exhibition in Philadelphia, where he also made the first ascent in a balloon in the New World. The balloonist's brother has left an enraptured description of the self-propelled carriage, which could travel faster than a stage-coach and could drive across unbroken ground where no other vehicles could make their way. But nothing is said about the machinery, and there are no accounts of it ever having been disclosed. A modern reader, however, would pity the obviously muscular fellows, who were hard at work inside the carriage . . .

The false prophets with their wishful thinking, however, portended a development which has resulted in the realization of both automotive carriages and chess-playing machines.

A Zenith

The constructions made by the highly talented French engineer Jacques de Vaucanson (1709–82) undoubtedly represent the zenith of the technical genre which produced automata. Even in his youth, in Grenoble, de Vaucanson had worked on various inventions and modifications for machines. In the mid-1730s, he decided to move to Paris and to involve himself with automata, which were all the rage at the time. He approached the subject systematically, beginning with a thorough study of anatomy, as he wanted to use mechanical aids to illustrate an *anatomie mouvante* ("moving anatomy"), which was to present human and animal organs in a three-dimensional atlas, no easy task! Here were Descartes's philosophical ideas, about

to be turned into a technical reality at the hands of the clever de Vaucanson.

After much painstaking work and many failures, de Vaucanson managed to build a life-size flute-playing shepherd. It was not life-like, the "moving anatomy" being reproduced in the lips, jaws, and tongue. The whole arrangement was controlled by a programming device with a range of twelve tunes, and the air was supplied by three clockwork-driven bellows. The features of the shepherd were copied from a statue by the French sculptor Antoine Coyzevox. De Vaucanson is said to have fallen in love with this statue, which was exhibited in the Tuileries, and he nursed secret hopes of giving it movement and life . . . But even as it was, the flute-player caused a sensation when de Vaucanson showed it to the *Académie des Sciences* in 1738, and this spurred him on to build another automaton, also a shepherd playing the flute, but this time accompanying himself on a tambourine. The flute in this case was a very special instrument, in French called a *galoubet*, which is particularly high-pitched. De Vaucanson was to try out almost three hundred different versions of the design before he was completely satisfied. The musical performances of this automaton have been compared to those of a virtuoso—nothing human could ever have achieved the like.

In pursuit of his ideas about the "moving anatomy", de Vaucanson built yet another automaton, a mechanical duck which could move in the typical, wagging way of a duck, eat and digest fish, and excrete the remains in a "natural" way. The mechanism was driven by a weight and had more than a thousand moving parts, which were concealed, some inside the duck, and some in the base on which the bird stood. The feats performed by the duck were of a similar order to those performed by other automata of the time, but during the course of de Vaucanson's work, his genius for designing gave birth to new ideas, which represent important progress in the development of technology. To produce his mechanisms, which demanded great exactitude, he designed among other things a precision lathe to cut threads. He was also the first to use a rubber hose. In his search for a suitable material for the duck's digestive canal, de Vaucanson came across the reports left by his compatriot Charles Marie de la Condamine about the remarkable material *cautchouc*, which he had discovered on the Amazon River during his expedition to South America in 1731. Vaucanson made hoses of this material and also invented a machine for that purpose.

De Vaucanson became a rich man from exhibiting his automata, and for several years, his mechanical duck was the most talked-about bird in Europe! He was also given public recognition for his work and was elected to the esteemed *Académie des Sciences*. But after touring for only a couple of years, he abandoned the building of automata, which was primarily a hobby, and became the director of the state-owned silk-mills. In his later years, he spent his time collecting interesting machines and pieces of apparatus. These eventually amounted to an impressive collection, which he bequeathed to the *Conservatoire National des Arts et Métiers*, then an institute for technical education, and today a highly thought-of museum.

De Vaucanson's three automata met different fates. The flute- and tambourine-playing shepherd was destroyed in the revolution, while the others were bought by a German collector, Gottfried Christoph Beireis, a judge in Hemstedt. The social circle of this eccentric included Johann Wolfgang Goethe, who in his diary for 1805 described a meeting with de Vaucanson's automata. "They were in the most deplorable condition," the great poet wrote. "The duck was like a skeleton and had digestive problems . . ."

Jacques de Vaucanson initiated a whole new era in the field of self-propelled mechanisms. His automata had an ancient heritage in the history of scientific ideas, but he broke new ground as regards both theory and practice. Much of what he discovered soon found a direct application within the then growing manufacturing industry. It is significant that de Vaucanson, as the director of the silk-mills, renewed their machinery and made considerable improvements to a semi-mechanical loom designed by Basile Bouchon. These improvements later made possible Joseph Marie Jacquard's punch-card programmed, fully automatic loom (see page 195).

Automata had been a technical hobby for a couple of thousand years, but de Vaucanson made it possible to go beyond this and to apply different forms of automata in industry. It was only then that the ideas of the Alexandrian school had matured to a point where an automatic control system could become a reality.

A A description of Bonnemain's temperature governor was published in 1824 by the Société d'encouragement. The governor was then shown mounted in a geyser. (**1**) The temperature sensor (*a*) was sunk into the water jacket of the furnace. (**2**) A detail, showing the governor. The temperature sensor (*a*) consisted of a circular iron rod (*b*) whose top end was screwed into a casing (*c*) and which was surrounded by a zinc or lead pipe (*d*). The pipe's lower end ended in a copper plug (*e*) into which *b* had been screwed. At the top of *d* was a copper ring (*f*). Since lead—as well as zinc—expands when heated, more than twice as much as iron, *f* was pushed upwards when the temperature sensor was heated. At a certain temperature, *f* acted on a lever (*g*) which, in its turn, acted on another lever (*h*), equipped with a

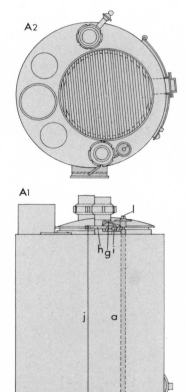

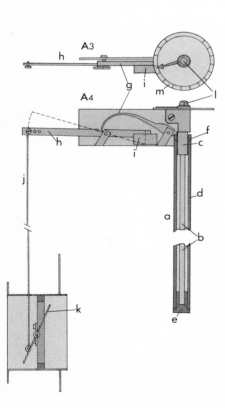

counterweight (*i*). The intention behind this arrangement was to multiply *f*'s movement. By way of a rod (*j*), lever *h* was connected to the furnace's damper (*k*), and when the water's temperature sank, the damper's opening was reduced so that there was less draught in the furnace. When the water's temperature sank, the damper's opening was increased. (**3**) The temperature governor was set at different temperatures when a screw (*l*) was turned. Rod *b* was then raised or lowered, so that the temperature at which ring *f* started to act on the levers was increased or reduced. The desired temperature could be set on a scale (*m*).

Automatic Controls before the Industrial Era

The mythical and real androids and other automata in the sixteenth, seventeenth, and eighteenth centuries were spectacular expressions of the technical heritage of antiquity. But the classical writings also inspired many of the great natural scientists of this era to apply and develop many of the ideas of the Alexandrian school. One of these was the principle of Hero's level control, the first closed control system, which more or less directly became the prototype of early designs of controls for temperature, pressure, and reaction speed, and some examples of these follow.

Temperature Regulators
An obvious similarity can be traced between the ancient level control, as shown in a sixteenth-century translation of Hero's *Pneumatica*, and the first thermostat. Around 1610, the Dutch physicist and chemist Cornelis Drebbel (1572–1634) designed a temperature regulator in two different versions. One was to control the temperature of an oven for chemical experiments, the other to keep the temperature of an incubator constant. Drebbel was a learned natural scientist and had spent most of his working life at the royal court in London. Between 1610 and 1612, however, he visited the court in Prague, where he met, among others, the German astronomer Johannes Kepler. Very little work by Drebbel exists in a published form, but his thermostats have been described in several books by scientists and others who visited him in his laboratory. Drebbel also had active contacts with the scholars of the time, Francis Bacon and Salomon de Caus, for example, and this contributed to the widespread circulation of the knowledge of both the thermostat and of Drebbel's other inventions.

One physicist to develop Drebbel's regulator was the Frenchman René Antoine Ferchault de Réamur (1683–1757), who has lent his name to the temperature scale common in southern Europe. In his old age, Réamur worked on methods to rationalize agriculture, and among other things devoted himself to improving an egg incubator; he equipped this with a simplified version of Drebbel's thermostat. The works published by Réamur about this device came to the attention of a successful poultry breeder in Paris, Bonnemain, a practical man who developed the thermostat into an efficient regulator for incubators. Bonnemain patented his thermostat in 1783, but the details of his construction were not published until 1824.

Pressure Regulators
The first pressure regulator has already been mentioned: the safety valve invented by Denis Papin for his pressure cooker and used for his high-pressure steam-engine (see page 115). When Newcomen's atmospheric steam-engine began to come into more common use, Papin's safety valve was fitted as standard equipment on the boilers. It seems that this simple device worked very satisfactorily, for nothing new in the way of pressure regulators appeared until the end of the eighteenth century, although improvements were made to some of the safety valve's construction details. One factor contributing to the lack of new inventions in this area may, however, have been the fact that the steam pressure used hardly exceeded atmospheric pressure, and it was not until James Watt's patent expired, in 1800, that the field was left free for designers of high-pressure steam-engines.

In 1799, however, two regulator patents came almost simultaneously. One was granted to the Irishman Robert Delap and was for a device in which the supply of steam to a steam-engine was controlled by a cock. The other, invented by the Englishman Matthew Murray, was for a device which worked on a similar principle, but instead controlled the draught in the boiler flue. Four years later, Boulton & Watt patented a pressure regulator which came to be used for several decades, even with high-pressure steam-engines.

A quite different type of pressure regulator became necessary when larger transmission networks for the distribution of town gas came to be built at the beginning of the nineteenth century. The gas pressure was either too low in the outer parts of the network, or too high in the central branches. Samuel Clegg, who had been trained in the workshops of Boulton & Watt, then designed a gas-pressure regulator which was placed at strategic points of the network to give a reasonably uniform pressure in the different branches. He patented his first design in 1815.

Similar problems with pressure were also encountered when the first modern water conduits were extended in the cities. Before it was realized that the pressure could be moderated by reducing the dimensions of the pipes step-by-step, different kinds of pressure-reducing valves were tried out, including a valve basically like Papin's safety valve. However, by the middle of the nineteenth century, the lever which had been used in the original version was replaced in most cases by a coil spring.

Regulating Windmills
The increasingly advanced technology developed during the Renaissance for improving the exploitation of wind and water has already been discussed, although we would like to repeat for the sake of emphasis that the engineering profession has its roots, to a large

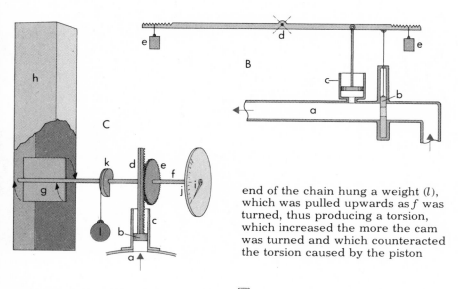

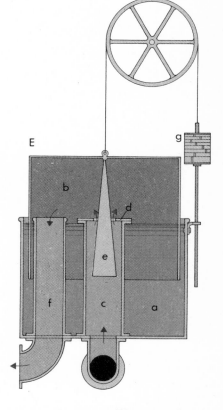

rod's action on *e* and, thus, *f*. This arrangement caused *f* to be turned in proportion to the pressure increase in *a*.

D Boulton & Watt's pressure regulator of 1803; (**1**) from the side, (**2**) cross-section. Sunk into the boiler (*a*) was a pipe (*b*), which was open at both ends and contained a float (*c*). The float was suspended from a chain which ran over a pulley on a shaft (*d*). The damper (*e*) of the furnace also hung on a chain, which ran over another pulley on the same shaft. As soon as the pressure of the steam rose above that of the atmosphere, water was forced into pipe *b*, and the opening of the damper (*e*) was reduced in proportion to the

end of the chain hung a weight (*l*), which was pulled upwards as *f* was turned, thus producing a torsion, which increased the more the cam was turned and which counteracted the torsion caused by the piston

B Robert Delap's pressure regulator, patented in 1799. Steam from the boiler passed through a pipe (*a*), in which there was a slide valve (*b*). As long as the slide valve was sunk into the pipe, steam could pass freely. On the pipe there was also a cylinder (*c*), open at the top, whose piston was suspended, as was the slide valve, from a pivoted balance beam (*d*). As soon as the pressure of the steam exceeded that of the atmosphere, the piston was forced upwards, the balance beam was turned, and the slide valve turned off the supply of steam. If steam of a higher or lower pressure than atmospheric was desired, the balance beam was loaded with weights (*e*) on either side of *b*'s fulcrum.

C In the same year as Delap, Matthew Murray, too, patented a pressure regulator. When the steam pressure in the boiler (*a*) became too high, a piston (*b*) was pressed upwards in a cylinder (*c*). The toothed piston rod (*d*) then turned a cog-wheel (*e*) on a shaft (*f*) on which the damper (*g*) inside the smoke stack (*h*) was also mounted. A pointer (*i*) on *f* indicated the size of the pressure increase on a scale (*j*). On shaft *f*, there was also a cam (*k*), over which a chain ran. At the other

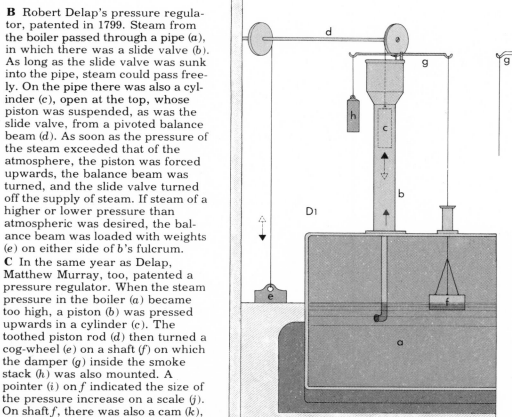

pressure increase. The water level inside the boiler was controlled by a float (*f*) suspended from a balance beam (*g*) at whose other end a counterweight (*h*) hung. When the water level sank too much, a valve (*i*) was opened, and more water entered.

E Clegg's pressure regulator consisted of a partly water-filled, cast-iron tank (*a*), into which a dome (*b*) was sunk. Gas entered through a pipe (*c*), which carried a pierced disc (*d*) on its top. Through the hole in the disc hung a cone (*e*), the top of which was attached to *b*. When gas of too high a pressure entered, *b* was raised, so was *e*, and the size of the gas inlet was reduced. (*f*) Gas exit pipe. The size of the inlet could be varied by altering the height of the dome above the water's surface. (*g*) Counterweight.

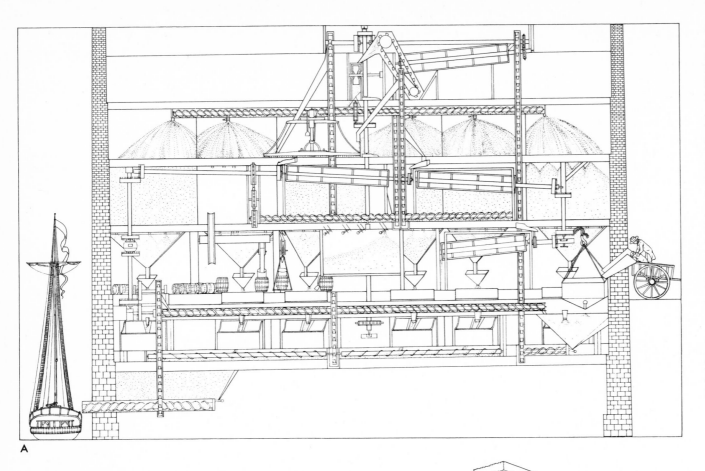

A

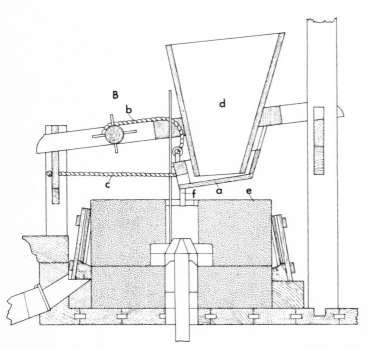

B

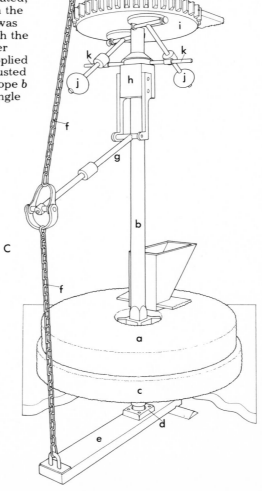

C

C Mead's lift-tenter of 1787. The runner stone (a) is attached to a shaft (b) which runs through the fixed millstone (c), the bedder, and rests in a lower bearing (d) on a lever (e). Between e and a roof beam, a chain (f) runs and is kept taut like a bow-string by a strut (g) because of the weight of a casing (h), which can move freely on b. The result is that the weight of the runner stone is kept off the bedder for as long as the mill is not in operation. When it is started and the wallower (i) begins to rotate, the pendulums (j), which are suspended from the wallower, are flung outwards, lifting a bar (k) to which they are attached. Since k's central part is ring-shaped, rotatable, and is attached to h, the latter is lifted and brings g's end upwards, so that the tension in f is reduced. The lever (e), the shaft (b), and the runner stone (a) are then lowered, and the distance between the millstones becomes the correct one for grinding.

D A cutaway of a nineteenth-century windmill which carries the patent sails invented by Cubitt; each

A Oliver Evans's mill at Philadelphia. Since both grain and flour were transported by means of worm conveyors, very few employees were needed to run the mill.

B At an early stage, grain was fed to the millstones by means of a vibrating board (a), which was suspended in ropes (b, c) beneath the feed hopper (d) into which the grain was poured. When the upper millstone (e), the runner stone, rotated, a shoulder on it hit a bar (f) on the vibrating board, so that grain was moved forward and fell through the hole in the middle of the runner stone. The amount of grain supplied for each vibration could be adjusted by lengthening or shortening rope b to vary the vibrating board's angle of inclination.

wooden shutter on the sails has one edge attached to a long rod pivoted to a cog-wheel, and the rack is in turn mounted on a bell crank whose other end is attached to a rod which runs through the centre of the windshaft (a). Cogs at the other end of this rod mesh with a cog-wheel, on whose shaft there is another wheel (b), which carries a counterweight (c) on a rope. By means of (c), it was also possible to control the angle of the shutters manually. The drive wheel (d) on a could be braked by means of a long rod which was used to bring a semi-circular, wooden brake (e) to bear against d's periphery. The wallower (f), which meshed with d, was fixed to the main vertical shaft (g) and employed a gear transmission (h) to drive two upper stones, which, together with their fixed under stones, were enclosed in cases (i) in which the flour was collected. A centrifugal governor (j) controlled the gap between the upper and lower millstones. (k) Grain bin. A fantail (l) worked via a gear transmission (m) against a toothed ring (n) on the curb. A wind-shift caused the fan to rotate, and the cap to turn until the fan's plane of rotation was again in line with the wind. The cap also could be turned manually by the chain wheel (o). The sack hoist (p) was driven by g via another gear transmission.

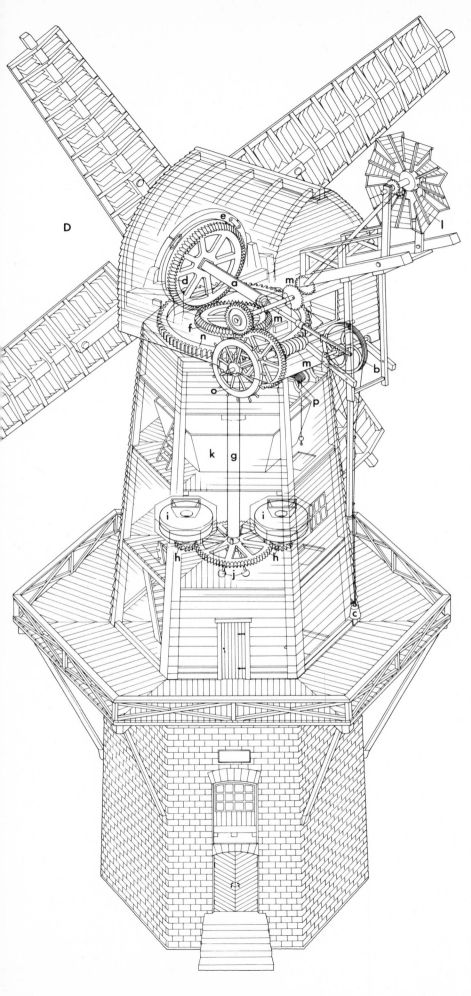

extent, in mill technology. One plant of great interest in this context was built in Philadelphia in the 1780s by Oliver Evans, a man we have already mentioned as a steam-engine pioneer in the United States. The plant, a flour mill requiring a minimum of manpower, can be seen as an early predecessor of the fully-automated factory. It was driven by three water-wheels and had six automatically controlled millstones. Both the grain and the flour were transported by worm conveyors, a word not then invented, the contemporary name being ''Archimedean screw''. The flour was weighed automatically and moved by an endless-chain conveyor to a worm conveyor, which delivered it directly down into the hold of a ship.

The eighteenth century saw the invention of a number of control devices for windmills, that later became very important to industry; some examples follow.

One problem when grinding is to feed in the grain at the right speed, so as to keep the mill—whether a water- or windmill—from grinding empty; in other words, a flow regulator is required. A primitive version, a hopper of rudimentary design, appeared as early as the Renaissance, and Ramelli describes several versions in his art book. In the first part of the eighteenth century, this regulator acquired the form it was to retain until the end of the windmill era. The grain was fed into a wide funnel, at the bottom of which was a shaking conveyor, vibrated by being struck by projections mounted on one of the millstones. The faster the millstone turned, the more grain was fed to the stones.

Windmills were generally built in places where the wind usually blew from a certain direction, for as soon as the wind shifted, the mill had to be turned so that its sails faced the wind squarely; during the eighteenth century, there were many ideas about how to achieve this automatically. In the 1740s, the Englishman Edmund Lee patented a ''Self-Regulating Wind Machine'', especially intended for tower mills, that is, windmills with a fixed millhouse and a rotatable upper part, or top cap. Lee arranged a propeller, called a rosette, on a boom so that its plane of rotation was at right angles to that of the sails of the mill; it worked via a gear against a gear rim on the periphery of the top cap. A side wind would cause the propeller, and the top cap, to rotate until the rotation plane of the propeller was once again parallel to, and the windmill's sails were at right angles to, the direction of the wind. Lee's device became very common in England and northern Germany.

Edmund Lee also built a device to control the speed of a mill by varying the size of the surfaces of the sails. This regulator was patented in 1745 but was never tried out, for it soon showed itself to be unworkable. Several inventors attacked the same problem, but a serviceable solution was arrived at only in 1807, when the Englishman William Cubitt patented his method for vaning the hinged, spring-loaded plates, which by now had replaced canvas on the sails of larger mills. Cubitt's ''patent sails'' became standard for such mills for the remainder of the nineteenth century.

When grain is ground between millstones, the quality of the flour depends largely on two factors: the distance between the fixed and the rotating stone, and the speed of rotation. In the latter part of the eighteenth century, several inventors tried to find ways of varying these factors. In 1787, the Englishman Thomas Mead patented a design which combined the solution of the two problems: the millstones were kept apart when the mill was not working, but when it started, a regulator caused them to press against each other with a force proportional to the speed of rotation. Mead then combined this regulator with another that varied the setting of the sail surfaces, so that the millstone rotated at a controllable speed.

This construction is particularly interesting because Mead used as a sensing device a rotating pendulum, something that later would be

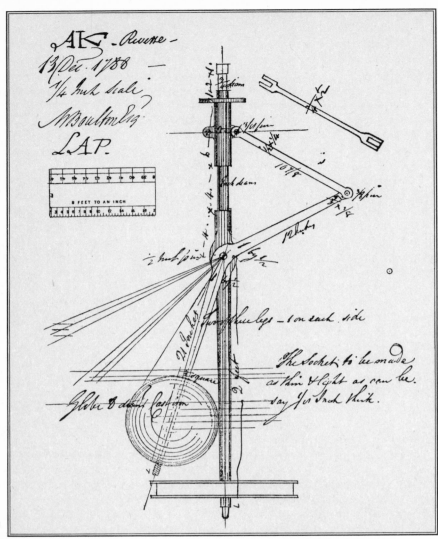

A1

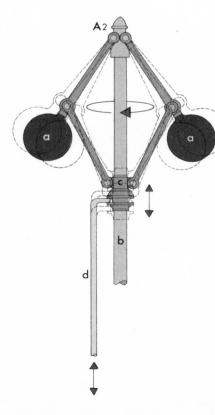

A2

A Watt did not invent the centrifugal governor, but he was the first to use such a construction to automatically regulate a steam-engine. This occurred in 1788, and in November of that year, a drawing (1) of such a governor was entered into Boulton & Watt's "Drawing Day Book", where a running account of the work done in the company's drawing office was kept. Watt's centrifugal governor (2) consisted of two pendulums, equipped with weights (a) and mounted on the output shaft (b) of the steam-engine. The governor's function was based on the fact that the speed of the steam-engine tended to increase when its work load was decreased, whereas the speed decreased when the work load increased. Because of the action of the centrifugal force, the weights swung further and further outwards the faster the regulator revolved. A sliding collar (c) was then brought upwards and pulled with it a rod which, directly or indirectly, regulated the steam supply to the engine.

called a centrifugal regulator. The rotating pendulum was, in fact, not a new machine element, for rotating weights fixed to chains or bars are mentioned in documents dating from the fifteenth century onwards, even if these had the form of a balance wheel or a flywheel mass. Before Mead made his invention, rotating pendulums had been used also in more rudimentary types of regulators, intended to modify the distance between the millstones.

Regulators in Industry

If industrial regulators were to be dealt with here in anything like a comprehensive manner, the result would be a volume of considerably greater bulk than this book, even if we limited ourselves to a mere survey. Therefore, we shall describe here only some of the most important regulators.

The Centrifugal Governor

The first large steam-engine with a rotary motion was installed by Boulton & Watt in 1786 at the Albion Mill in London. The mill machinery had been built by the Scotsman Andrew Meikle (1719–1811), who later installed centrifugal governors for the millstones; it should be noted that the invention of the centrifugal governor is often attributed to Meikle, who was a leading designer of mills, but it is likely that Meikle had based his centrifugal governors on the device that had been patented by Mead in 1787. Be that as it may, in 1788, Boulton reported by letter to Watt that he had visited the Albion Mill and seen the millstone regulators in operation, and also described how they worked. Watt immediately realized the possibility of applying the same principle to controlling the speed of steam-engines, and it is probable that they had tried out such a governor before the end of that year.

Strange as it may seem, Boulton & Watt tried to keep the design of the centrifugal governor secret for as long as possible. However, when Watt's steam-engine patent expired in 1800, centrifugal governors instantly became standard equipment in practically all the steam-engines which then appeared on the market. Few devices in machine technology have taken on so many different shapes as the centrifugal governor during its almost two-hundred-year history. Its heyday as regards the number of varieties in which it existed was, naturally, the era of steam-engines and turbines, but the principle of the centrifugal governor is still applied in a number of different areas.

The theory of the function of the centrifugal governor, the way it reacts to the varying load of the steam-engine and to different kinds of external disturbance, was not worked out fully until the latter part of the nineteenth century, when, in 1868 and 1876 respectively, two great mathematicians, the Scotsman James Clerk Maxwell and the Russian Ivan Vyshnegradsky, presented the general theories of the function of the centrifugal governor. They provided a mathematical basis for the general calculation of automatic control in closed systems. This pattern of development is, by the way, characteristic of all control technology, in that the theoretical analysis usually comes long after the practical introduction of a device.

Electrical Controls

Electric governors of different kinds—and they are now innumerable—are mostly of the same age as that part of electrotechnology to which their function is applied.

The electric relay is a component of control technology, without which today's automatic control systems would be hard put to function. An electric relay usually consists of an electromagnet which breaks or closes another circuit when the circuit of the magnet changes in a certain way. Samuel F. B. Morse (1791–1872) invented the electric telegraph, which is often considered the first technical and commercial application of the electromagnetic principle, which is the basis of the relay. The Englishman Sir Charles Wheatstone, however, had been experimenting with electromagnetic couplings few years prior to this, and it was probably he who introduced the concept of a relay (1839). Wheatstone, too, designed a telegraph, the so-called indicator telegraph, which came into use from the middle of the 1830s in the rapidly expanding British railway network. But his name is better known for Wheatstone's bridge, his design to measure electrical resistance—an electrotechnical equivalent of the balance scale—which he introduced in 1843.

Wheatstone fully realized the potential of using the relay as an electric amplifier. The relatively weak "control current" required by the electromagnet of the relay could be used to close a circuit with a very much more powerful current. This principle found a number of applications during the breakthrough of electric power, some fifty years after Wheatstone had presented his ideas.

However, telecommunications are, without doubt, the largest area of application for the electric relay. Relays have been used in this field from about 1890 onwards, not as amplifiers but as coupling components, particularly in telephone switchboards. The high standards of reliability and safety of operation required by telecommunications have compelled the development of increasingly efficient relays, with important consequences for the application of relays in automatic governing and control of, first and foremost, industrial processes.

Regulating Arc Lamps

The electric arc began to be used for lighting purposes in the 1840s. It gave a very strong light compared to the other light sources of the time: the recently introduced stearin, or tallow, candle and the gas lamp. But the problem was that the arc lamp needed continuous attention, for its carbon rods constantly had to be brought closer together as they burned, lest the arc go out. Even the first arc lamps introduced for general use featured an attempt at controlling automatically the distance between the carbon points. In 1847, the Englishman W. E. Staite (1809–54) designed one of the first devices for this purpose; in it, one carbon rod was moved forward by a clockwork device that was controlled by a copper rod placed close enough to the arc to be affected by its heat. As the distance between the carbon rods increased, the arc became hotter and expanded the copper rod, causing it to lift a catch, thus setting in motion the clockwork which moved the carbon rod far enough forward to reduce the heat, so that the copper rod contracted, lowering the catch and arresting the movement of the carbon rod. More refined versions of this were applied by many arc-lamp manufacturers, among them Edison, as late as the 1870s.

When the arc lamp became more common in the 1860s and 1870s, however, new control methods were invented, which caused the current of the arc and the voltage across it to control the feeding of the carbon rods. Many of the great names of the time in electrical engineering devoted themselves to designing more and more sophisticated governors based on these principles. They included J. B. L. Foucault and V. L. M. Serrin in France, R. E. B. Crompton in England, Werner von Siemens and F. von Hefner-Alteneck in Germany, and C. F. Brush in the United States. Many control principles and couplings that were invented and tried out at this time came to acquire a fundamental importance in controlling current and voltage during the further development of electric power systems.

Synchro Systems

The electric three-phase system came into common use in the 1890s,

B Two connected Morse telegraphs. (**1, 2**) The Morse telegraph consisted of a key (a), which was pressed by a spring (b) against a metal head (c) on the so-called connection block (d). The key handle (e) was made of an insulating material. (**3**) As the telegraphist pushed the handle downwards, the key came into contact with the anvil (f), and an electric circuit was closed from one terminal of the battery (g) to the key anvil and lever (h) and out onto the connecting line (i). The other battery terminal was grounded. (**4**) In the receiving telegraph, the current passed the key's lever (h) and head (c) and continued through the winding of the electromagnet (j) and to the ground. When this occurred, the iron core of the electromagnet became magnetic and attracted a metal armature (k) on a lever, at whose other end was a peg (l), which marked a paper strip (m).

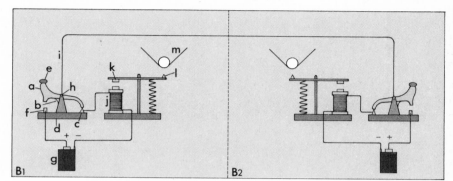

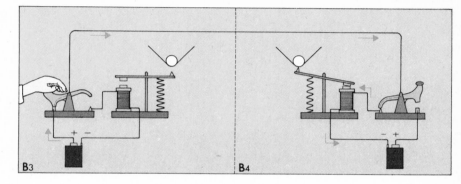

C In Serrin's arc lamp, the upper carbon holder (a) hung from an arm (b), attached to a rod. This ran inside a casing (c) and had at its lower end a weight-loaded rack (d), which meshed with a cog-wheel (e). On e's shaft was a roll (f) to which a chain (g) was attached; this ran over a cylinder (h) and had its other end attached to the lower carbon holder (i). When d sank, g was wound onto f, and the carbons approached. Current entered through the winding of an electromagnet (j), whose core then attracted an armature (k) which pulled a rod (l), attached to (i), downwards with it. Thereupon, e was turned to the right by g, and the carbons were separated to the correct distance for the arc to form. A catch (m) then engaged a cogwheel (n), connected by other cogwheels with e. When part of the carbons had been consumed, the resistance increased in the circuit, and the amperage dropped so that j no longer attracted k. The armature was then lifted by a spring (o), and when l and m were lifted at the same time, n was released, so that a and i could again approach each other.

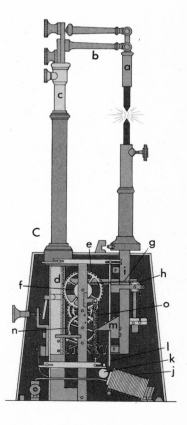

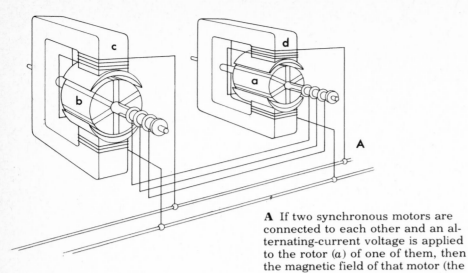

A If two synchronous motors are connected to each other and an alternating-current voltage is applied to the rotor (*a*) of one of them, then the magnetic field of that motor (the transmitter) will be reproduced in the other motor (the receiver). The receiver's rotor (*b*) will then adopt the same angle to stator (*c*) as the transmitter's rotor has to its stator (*d*).

B Farcot's mechanical power amplifier. When the double piston (*a*) in the open control cylinder (*b*) was moved, steam could enter at one or the other side of the piston (*c*) in the working cylinder (*d*) through one of two ducts (*e*), which had earlier been blocked by *c*. At the same time, the space on the other side of *c* was connected to the atmosphere through the other duct. The power amplifier's way of working was based on the principle that if a liquid (or a gas) in a closed vessel is exposed to pressure, then this pres-

not least because of the synchronous motor's great use as a source of motive power. The properties of this motor also resulted in the development of an important component in modern control systems, the torque element. Carl Michalke of Siemens in Germany realized that synchronous motors can be used as transmitters and receivers of position information, that is, the transfer of information primarily about angular torsion. If two synchronous motors be connected and an alternating voltage applied to the rotor of the first, the magnetic field of the first motor will be reproduced in the second, causing its rotor to adopt the same angle to its stator as that between the rotor and the stator of the first. If one rotor be turned, the other will follow it exactly.

To start with, Michalke saw the phenomenon as a curiosity, but nevertheless, he patented his discovery in 1896. Practical application came only after 1910, when torque elements were first used in gunnery control devices in the German navy. The development took off again in the 1930s, when a whole family of governing components, based on Michalke's discovery, was put into use in both military and civil control systems.

Power Amplified Mechanically
The mechanical power amplifier, which in control contexts is usually called the servomotor, is today as indispensable a component in automatic control systems as the electric relay. The servomotor is one of the first examples of a control device invented intrinsically, or within control technology itself, to fulfil one of that technology's own requirements. In the 1860s, the Frenchman M. J. Farcot designed a very sensitive centrifugal governor whose output signal was too weak, however, to affect the steam valve. To make his design work, Farcot had to find a method of amplifying the signal, or, in other words, the controlling power of the rotating pendulum. His solution was a small-diameter control cylinder with a twin piston that directed steam to one or other of the two sides of a piston in a power cylinder of considerably larger diameter. The amplifying factor provided by the device then became proportional to the ratio between the areas of cross-section of the control cylinder and the working cylinder. In his patent specification of 1868, Farcot makes a comparison between his servomotor and the rider of a horse: "The rider can direct the muscular horse with very light movements of his hands; it follows his slightest intention with great force. Only a Frenchman could be so poetic in a patent application; Farcot's was entitled "*Servomoteur, ou moteur asservi*" and is the origin of the word "servomotor".

The Autopilot
One of the first automatic control systems was the autopilot, which came into being comporatively early in aviation. The reason is largely that Orville and Wilbur Wright designed an intentionally unstable aeroplane (the first being completed in 1903) in the firm belief that this would make it easier to manoeuvre. While their first flights confirmed this belief, they showed also that the pilot had to work the controls all the time in order to keep the aeroplane on course and on an even keel. Already at this early stage, they discussed the possibility of transferring at least some of the pilot's work to some kind of automatic device, and about 1910, Elmer Ambrose Sperry (1860–1930), an American engineer, applied himself to this problem. He designed what was later to be called an autopilot; it consisted essentially of gyroscopes functioning as sensing elements, and of servomotors that altered the control surfaces of the aeroplane. A version of this first autopilot was successfully tried out in 1912 in a Curtiss flying-boat.

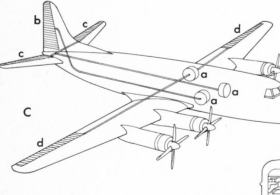

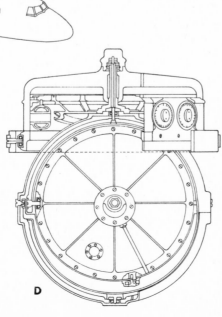

sure is propagated equally to all parts of the vessel. Thus, the pressure per square inch was as great on *a* as it was on *c*.
C In aeroplanes, gyroscopes (*a*) were used at an early stage to supervise the yaw (*b*), pitch (*c*), and roll (*d*) controls.
D The gyroscope is based on the principle that a rotating body tends to preserve its plane of rotation. Here, one of Sperry's gyrostatic compasses is shown in vertical section.

CHAPTER 8
COMPUTERS

A s already mentioned, the interaction of simulacra and automata has been the basis upon which was built the development that has resulted in the computer. In the history of ideas we may locate the roots of the computer's richly branched family tree in the "self-moving" mechanisms of classical antiquity, with its tap root going back to the gin of the late Stone Age animal trap. Other roots show a junction of several development chains, one of which consists of the mechanization of arithmetic and the mathematical principles that have emerged alongside it, mainly in the theory of numbers. Another important root is the continued development that started with the electric relay, whose power-amplifying and connecting functions were soon taken over by electronic components.

Arithmetic Mechanized

Counting on one's fingers can be seen as the imitation of the series of numbers from one to ten, thus making it extremely easy to add or subtract; looked at like this, the use of the fingers as a method of counting can be called a mathematical simulacrum, so that one can continue this line of logic and describe the abacus as a mechanization of counting on the fingers. The abacus can also be seen as a proto- or pre-automaton, that is, the first step towards making arithmetical operations automatic.

The abacus was known in ancient Greece and Rome and was called in some places "Pythagoras' slate". This name gives us a hint of what the original construction was like; stone balls were used and moved on a tablet of stone or marble. The Latin word for a ball of limestone, *calculus*, has given us words like calculate, calculator, etc. The Greeks did not use a tablet but a tray with sand in it, where calculations were made by marking the positions of the balls and notingthe result. "Tray of sand" is called *abax* in Greek; hence the word *abacus*, which in this cultural sphere was the name commonly given to the device. The use of the abacus spread via the Arabic culture to India, the Far East, and Russia. It arrived in China in the twelfth century and was there called a *suan-pan*. About a hundred years later, it was introduced in Japan, where it was called a *soroban*. These countries, mainly Japan and Russia, have developed the art of using this arithmetic instrument to perfection. A skilful person using this technique can achieve a speed of calculation quite on a par with modern desk calculators.

The numbers used in the West are called Arabic numbers and originated in India. It was the Indians who introduced the concept "nought" for an "empty" space on the abacus. This very important step in the development of arithmetic did not reach Europe until the ninth century.

The scientific discoveries of the seventeenth and eighteenth centuries, flourishing trade, and particularly the complications brought about by taxation and its collection were some of the factors which made it necessary to simplify and automate the increasingly time-

A thirteenth-century Chinese *suan-pan*. On an abacus, one indicates a given number by pushing the balls towards the cross-bar. On this abacus, the value of each ball in the various rows underneath the cross-bar is 1 (*a*), 10 (*b*), 100 (*c*), 1,000 (*d*), 10,000 (*e*), and so on, while each ball above the cross-bar corresponds to five balls in the row underneath it. The number indicated on this abacus is thus 965,831.

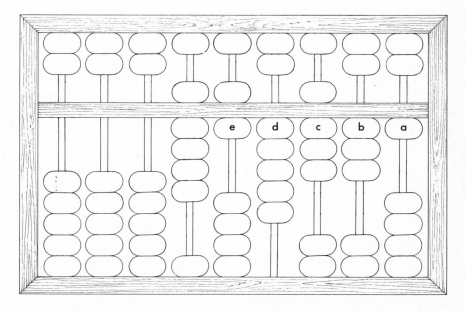

A The young Blaise Pascal seated at the mechanical adding-machine "Pascaline", an invention which brought him great fame. The illustration is based on an engraving in Jean-Gauffin Gallon's *Machines et inventions approuvées par l'Académie Royale des Sciences*, published in Paris in 1735.

B Pascal's machine (**1**) measured only 14.2 × 5.1 × 3.5 in (36 × 13 × 9 cm) and could really only be used for addition and subtraction. It had eight dials, set with a metal stylus. The French monetary unit used in those days, the *livre*, was divided into 12 *deniers*, each subdivided into 20 *sols*; there were dials for *sols*, *deniers*, and up to 999,999 *livres*. The essential part of Pascal's machine was its decimal transfer, that

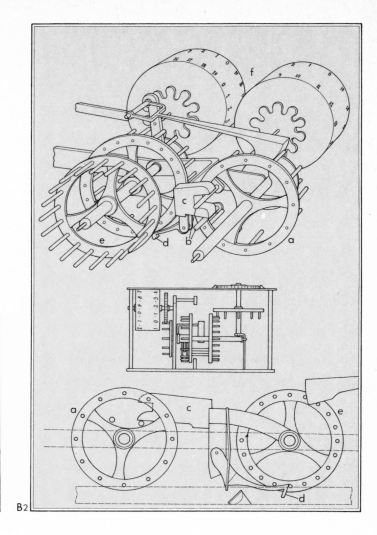

B1

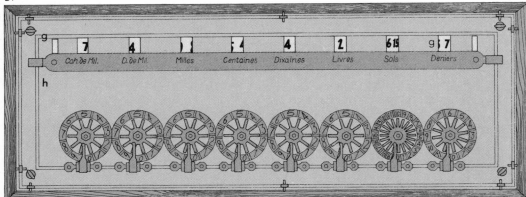

B2

is, that each toothed wheel was moved on one unit (one-tenth of a revolution on each wheel except those for *deniers* and *sols*) when the previous wheel had completed one revolution. (**2**) Explanatory sketch of the adding-machine's construction. When one wheel (*a*) was moved from 9 to 0, a lever (*c*), which had been lifted by pins (*b*), fell downwards. The lever was coupled to a pawl (*d*) which then brought the next wheel (*e*) one step forward. The numbers on the drums (*f*) could be seen in windows (*g*) on the face of the machine, and by moving a strip (*h*), the complementary number of each number could be seen instead.

C Leibniz realized that a multiplication is really a series of repeated additions. He thus constructed a machine (**1**) in which a set number was automatically repeated each time a crank was turned a full 360°. Leibniz's machine, too, had decimal transfer, but instead of toothed wheels, it had stepped rolls (**2**), that is, cylinders with nine cogs of varying length for the digits 1–9.

D A type of multiplying machine with stepped rolls, shown here with

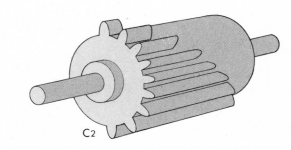

C2

its lid partly removed. The calculating capacity depended on the number of stepped rolls (here: six). Above each stepped roll (*a*) was a cog-wheel (*b*) moving to and fro on a square shaft (*c*) by means of a setting device (*d*). The latter ran along a scale on which each number corresponded to the number of cogs on the roll with which the cog-wheel (*b*) was going to mesh. The factor to be multiplied (the multiplicand) was set on the scale by means of the setting

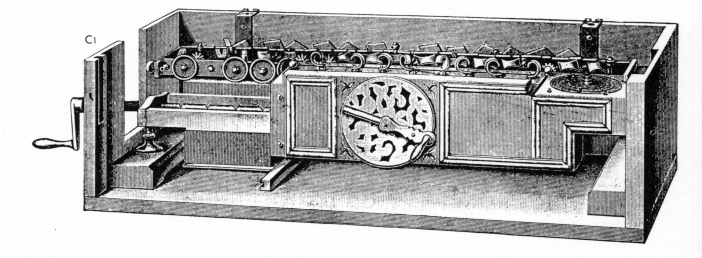

C1

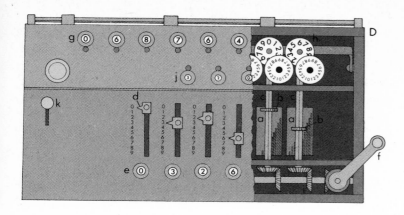

devices (*d*) and could then be seen in the windows of the control register (*e*). When a crank (*f*) was turned clockwise once, the set number could be read in the windows of the product register (*g*) at the top of the machine, since dials (*h*) were connected to the crank axle by means of bevel gears (*i*). Each time the crank was turned, the multiplicand was then added to the numeral which could be read in *g*; after seven revolutions, the product of the set number multiplied by seven could be read in the windows of the quotient register (*j*). The machine could be set for division by pushing a lever (*k*) downwards. The stepped rolls then changed their direction of rotation.
E What characterized the Odhner machines (**1**) was that they worked by means of stud wheels (**2**), an

eighteenth-century invention which had been considerably improved by, among others, Odhner. (**3**) Explanatory sketch of an Odhner machine. The stud wheel consisted of a disc (*a*) fixed to a crankshaft (*b*), and of a rotatable part (*c*). When one turned *c* by pushing a protrusion (*d*) on it along a scale (*e*) on the top of the machine, cogs ("studs", *f*) protruded along the periphery of the stud wheel. The number of cogs corresponded to the number set on the scale. When a crank (*g*) was then rotated, the cogs meshed with the cogs of a counting apparatus, and the set number could be read in the product register (*h*). (*i*) Quotient register. The calculating capacity of the machine depended on the number of stud wheels, and the crank was turned anti-clockwise when a division was to be made.

consuming calculations required. The first mechanical adding-machine, in the true sense of the word, was designed by the French physicist and mathematician Blaise Pascal (1623–62). His father was a senior inspector of taxes, and even as a young man, Blaise Pascal sought ways to facilitate the hard work involved in tax calculation. In 1645, Pascal's first machine was completed; later, it was improved successively, and a number were made. Descartes brought one with him when he left for the royal court in Stockholm in 1649, and he presented it, and an elevated dedication by Pascal, to Queen Christina. Its fate is unfortunately unknown, although several of Pascal's machines have been preserved, for instance, in the Conservatoire National des Arts et Métiers in Paris, the Science Museum in London, and the Mathematisch-physikalische Salon in Dresden.

Pascal's machine won him great renown throughout Europe, and this inspired several seventeenth-century mathematicians to attempt to produce similar devices. One of them was the polymath Gottfried Wilhelm von Leibniz. In the 1670s, he built a machine which can be called the prototype of our modern mechanical desk calculators, that is, those which have not yet been displaced by electronic ones. The new component introduced by Leibniz was a ratchet wheel for units, tens, hundreds, and so on. The balance wheel of the original version was like a roller with a cam that moved the next roller one step, when number nine on the first had been passed. This principle was developed further by Leibniz, who, in the 1690s, completed a machine which could add, subtract, and multiply by repeated additions. Leibniz also worked out on paper a machine for division and the calculation of square and cube roots, but the precision mechanics of the time were not sophisticated enough to let him realize this in practice. The ratchet wheel has been used as a component in desk calculators far into this century and is still used in simple counters, such as electric kWh meters and milometers.

In the eighteenth century, several attempts were made to produce a handy adding-machine by using the principle of the ratchet wheel, and several variations were developed, the first workable machines coming on the market only at the beginning of the nineteenth century. In 1820, mass production started of the "*Arithomètre*" machine, designed by the Frenchman Charles Xavier Thomas and considered the first commercial adding-machine. Later on, some Swedish designers made pioneering contributions in the area of mechanical adding-machines. They included Willgodt Teophil Odhner, with his well-known whirligig, and Carl Fridén, who designed a number of desk-top calculators and also founded a company in the United States, which is today active in the computer field.

The Computing Machine

The mechanical calculator is a more or less automatic aid in arithmetical calculation, and it relieves the operator of much time-consuming work. Still, the operator has to keep the order of the calculations in mind and constantly provide data for the machine, receive partial results, and generally organize the work. The next link to be forged in the chain of development we have referred to, with its interaction of simulacra and automata should be, logically, the use of a fully developed mechanical calculator to try to simulate the interventions of the operator in the calculation procedure. In this context such a machine could be called a computing machine, a term which implies that the machine takes over even the organization of the mathematical program of the calculations. It might be added that the first computers were actually called "computing machines".

The great pioneer in the area of computing machines was the British mathematician Charles Babbage (1791–1871), a very talented and most eccentric person. Even as a young student in Cambridge, where he studied, among other things, astronomy, Babbage became

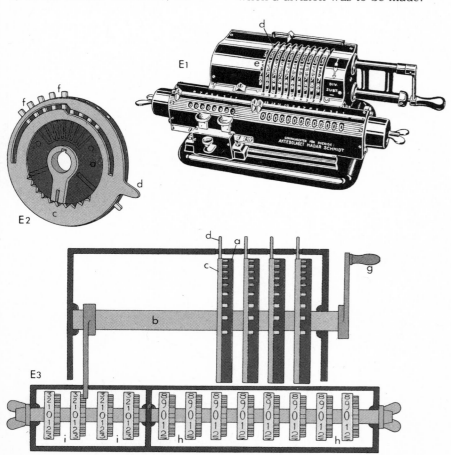

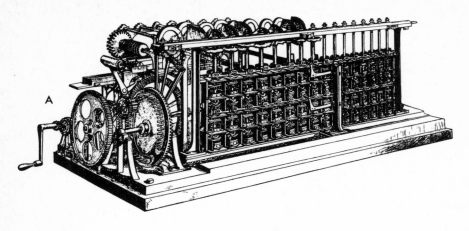

A The difference engine for the calculation of logarithmic tables built by Georg and Edvard Scheutz was a simplified version of Babbage's construction.

B Babbage's difference engine had already cost him over £17,000 when work on it was interrupted in 1834. The reasons why the machine was never completed were partly economical difficulties and partly that Babbage's chief instrument maker had resigned after an argument.

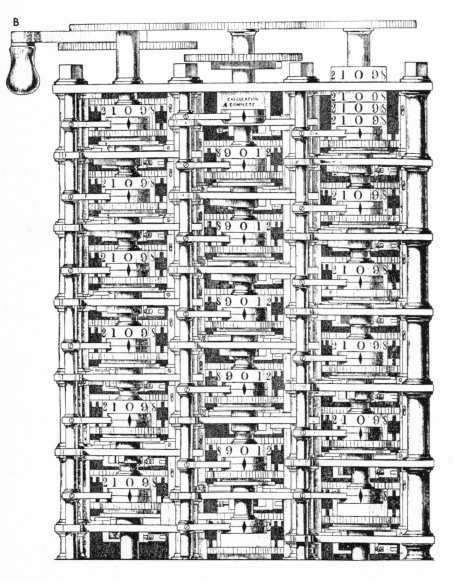

obsessed with the great idea of his life: to automate arithmetical calculations completely. He and John F. W. Herschel (1792–1871), the son of the great astronomer Sir F. William Herschel, were together assigned the task of compiling astronomical tables and checking existing tables which had been produced by mechanical calculators. After painstaking figure-work, Herschel and Babbage found many mistakes, due to what is called the human factor. Babbage is said to have remarked that this kind of work ought to be relegated to a "soul-less steam engine".

These were not heedless words spoken by a temperamental twenty-year-old student; they marked the beginning of a remarkable life-long contribution to the task of automating arithmetical calculations. Babbage was wholly familiar with the adding-machines available in 1812, when his idea came to him, but they had not yet achieved the standards he demanded of them. To accomplish this, Babbage was obliged to find new mathematical principles for the function of the machine, for he saw quite clearly that it would not be sufficient merely to improve the design of an existing type. He succeeded in solving this problem by using a principle which meant a considerable short cut in calculation, being moreover particularly suitable for compiling tables. Put very simply, his idea was to base the function of the machine on the constant differences that are obtained between different series of numbers, in contradistinction to counting one by one, as mechanical adding-machines did, and still do. In 1822, Babbage presented these new design principles for a rapid calculating machine in his paper, "On the Theoretical Principles of the Machinery for Calculating Tables", and during the same year, he began to build a machine based on his ideas, calling his creation "Difference Engine No. 1". Here the difficulties cropped up: actually making the machine demanded a degree of precision that no mechanical workshop of the time could provide, not even a clockmaker's. Babbage devoted all his indefatigable energy to solving the technical problems of construction and production, being obliged to invent new tools, no less, to produce the intricate parts for the machine.

Fortunately, Babbage was a man of private means, being the son of a banker who had left him a large fortune. But his work on his difference engine devoured large sums, and in 1829, he applied to the government for financial assistance to complete the project. The Royal Society then appointed a committee to judge Babbage's application, and although the eminent scientists on it reached a very favourable conclusion, no money was forthcoming. By this time, Babbage had been appointed Lucasian Professor of Mathematics at Cambridge University, an honorary title held earlier by Isaac Newton, among others. "The only honour I ever received in my own country", Babbage bitterly remarked in his autobiography.

By the early 1830s, after intensive work, Babbage had completed such parts of the difference engine as could verify the practicability of his principles. By then, he had also compiled over two hundred drawings of the complete machine. A very comprehensive description of it was published in July, 1834, in the *Edinburgh Review* and happened to be seen by an eminent Swedish engineer, Per Georg Scheutz (1785–1873), in Stockholm. Scheutz was, besides, an editor of the *Periodical of the Swedish Association of Industry* and was a well-known journalist who covered technical matters and culture in general. Scheutz, with his all-round technical knowledge and his nose for news, immediately understood the importance of the difference engine, but he realized also, according to his autobiographical notes, "that in spite of all the technical skills in England, no further development can ever be made, as long as these plans are followed". Scheutz, too, tried to build an adding-machine according to Babbage's principles, but he chose a different mechanical construction. His son, Edvard Scheutz (1821–81), who had just commenced his studies at the Teknologiska Institut at the time his father was working on the new version, set about the task of building this simplified difference engine. After much labour and sacrifice, this machine stood ready in 1843 and was demonstrated to the Royal Academy of Sciences. The Scheutzes had plans to go further with the design, thinking to equip it with, among other things, the "output device", to use the modern term for what Babbage had in mind. This was an arrangement whereby the results of the calculation were engraved on a copper plate which was ready to be used to print the calculated tables as soon as the plate was fed out from the machine. But their resources were exhausted, and they turned to the government for financial help. Only after parliamentary bills and extremely favourable statements from the Royal Academy of Sciences, were they granted, in 1854, a small sum to realize their ideas. The following year, the machine was exhibited at the world exhibition in Paris, where it was awarded a Gold Medal. On their way to Paris, Georg and Edvard Scheutz visited London, where they called on Charles Babbage and his son Henry, who gave their Swedish colleagues a very friendly reception. The Scheutz difference engine was also demonstrated to the Royal Society, which treated the two Swedes with distinction.

After the Paris exhibition, the difference engine was sold to the Dudley observatory in Albany, in the state of New York, for the tidy sum of five thousand dollars. The machine was in use there for some decades for astronomical calculations. In the 1930s, it was bought by a private collector in Chicago, and in the early 1960s, the difference engine was acquired by the Smithsonian Institution, being now on display there in the Museum of History and Technology.

The Babbage-Scheutz difference engine represents an advanced automation of arithmetic: it is a automaton, albeit one limited to a single program. But as early as the 1830s, Babbage understood the possibility of going one step further and designing a machine which could make any kind of calculation; in other words, it could organize its own calculations according to given instructions. Consequently, this "analytical engine", as Babbage called it, would be a simulacrum, a technical imitation of a mathematician's way of calculating. Babbage had the idea of grouping auxiliary functions around the difference engine, which would then form an arithmetic unit; one auxiliary unit would then be a mechanical device for feeding calculating instructions, another a unit for storing partial results (a memory), and another a device which could compare the partial results with one another and on that basis make "decisions" regarding the continued course of calculations. A block diagram of these functions would be practically identical to a block diagram of the equivalent functions in a modern computer. For the input and output of data, Babbage thought of using punched cards of the kind that were then being used in Jacquard-type pattern-weaving looms.

Babbage's understanding of the possibilities of the analytical engine was brilliant, even visionary. But this project was even more difficult to realize than his earlier project for the difference engine. Even a simplified version of the analytical engine would have contained over fifty thousand moving parts! Babbage thought of training mechanics to build the machine and employed the most skilful he could find, including Joseph Whitworth, who later became famous for his standardization of thread systems. And for years, Babbage laid seige to the Treasury, pleading for money. The only result of this was that the government caused a fire-proof building to be erected in which Babbage could safely deposit his drawings and calculations.

In 1840, Babbage presented his plans for the analytical engine to a scientific congress in Turin. A good account of it was later published in a Swiss periodical by the Italian military engineer L. F. Mena-

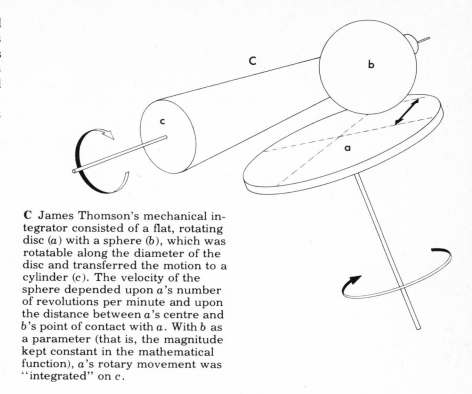

C James Thomson's mechanical integrator consisted of a flat, rotating disc (a) with a sphere (b), which was rotatable along the diameter of the disc and transferred the motion to a cylinder (c). The velocity of the sphere depended upon a's number of revolutions per minute and upon the distance between a's centre and b's point of contact with a. With b as a parameter (that is, the magnitude kept constant in the mathematical function), a's rotary movement was "integrated" on c.

brea; the account was translated into English and commented on by Ada Augusta, Lady Lovelace, Byron's daughter and a mathematician. Both the original account and her comments suggest possible uses for the analytical engine as a scientific instrument, and outline applications which computer technology did not manage to approach until the 1950s. In 1888, Babbage's son Henry published a description of his father's machine, that was mathematically and technically comprehensive. Charles Babbage was far ahead of his time, so much so that there was then no chance of realizing his brilliant ideas for systems to solve the problems of automating mathematical calculations. These ideas had to wait for technical development to catch up.

The Analog Computer

The attention aroused by Babbage's ideas led many mathematicians and physicists in the latter part of the nineteenth century to interest themselves in arithmetic machines. One was William Thomson, later Lord Kelvin, who tried to find a way round the difficulties Babbage had come up against, seeking a solution by abandoning the series of numbers in favour of a machine based on the mechanical analogy to a mathematical function, in this case an integral. In 1876, his brother, James Thomson, had designed a mechanical integrator which consisted of a level, rotating disc along the diameter of which a sphere moved, transferring its motion to a cylinder. Using a system of integrators of this sort, Kelvin built a machine to calculate the motion of the tides, the first analog computer. He designed similar machines for calculations concerning a series of different physical problems, including those leading to differential equations. But Kelvin, too, ran into the problem of insufficiently precise mechanics and did not succeed in achieving the accuracy he desired for his calculations. He was, however, convinced that the analog computer would afford a considerable relief to mathematicians and scientists in their research work, or as he himself put it: "The objective of this machine is to substitute brass for brain in the great mechanical labour of calculating."

During the First World War, some progress in mechanical analog computers was made, and in the late 1920s, Lord Kelvin's ideas were revived, when the American Vannevar Bush (1890–1974), of the Massachusetts Institute of Technology, designed a mechanical differential analysator, based on the principle of integrators. The analysator could carry out a number of different calculating programs. In the 1930s, this analysis engine developed into a quick and reliable computer, its use coming to include the calculation of artillery firing tables.

The Breakthrough

The work of Vannevar Bush, mainly during the 1930s, in developing calculating machines with increased flexibility and capacity has been compared to that of an ice-breaker. In the English-speaking world, great efforts were now devoted to both the physical and theoretical sides of designing calculating machines. In England Alan M. Turing made contributions of lasting value in the theoretical area.

But a technical breakthrough was about to occur, for while purely mechanical components had, in the main, been used in calculating machines, the rapid development of telecommunications in the 1920s had produced a component of great interest in this context–the telephone relay. This had proved its operating reliability in the telephone networks which were becoming more and more automatic. The German Konrad Zuse (1910–   ) was the first to exploit systematically the relay in a calculating machine. In his autobiography, published in 1970, Zuse states that, even as a young student, around 1932, he had thought of building a "universal adding machine . . . so that people with creative talents need not waste their precious time on boring calculations". After graduating as a construction engineer in Berlin in 1935, Zuse worked for about a year with calculations of structural strength, but from 1936 onwards, he worked full-time with his adding machine. An experimental model with mainly mechanical components was complete by 1938, but after that, Zuse designed an arithmetic unit built entirely of electromagnetic relays, and the machine was almost complete at the outbreak of war in 1939. During his military service, Zuse managed to arouse the interest of the German Air Force, which caused the machine to be completed in 1941; it was called Z3 but was, however, destroyed in an air raid. During the final stages of the war, Zuse was active in Göttingen, where he built a full-scale relay machine, Z4, which was put into operation in 1945. It is to be seen today in the Eidgenössische Technische Hochschule in Zürich.

The honour of having designed the first electric arithmetic machine, that is, the first computer in the modern sense of the word, must undoubtedly go to Konrad Zuse, even if his work remained unknown outside the close circle around him, being unpublished until the late 1960s. Therefore, his contributions, although pioneering, never influenced the development of the modern computer.

On the other side of the Atlantic, at Harvard University, work had begun in 1939 on a large relay machine, the Automatic Sequence Controlled Calculator, later called Mark I. The design and construction of the machine was supervised by Professor Howard H. Aiken, and it was built with the assistance of the International Business Machine Corporation (IBM), being completed in 1944. Standard versions of relays had been used for its arithmetic units, but the memory was mechanical, consisting of calculating wheels, whose principle was that of an advanced contemporary office machine. The capacity of its memory was seventy-two "words" of twenty-three figures each–in other words, numbers–and the machine could complete the multiplication of two such numbers in four and a half seconds. A few more machines of the same sort were built, including the Mark II, which was also designed by Aiken. It was ready in 1948 and was used to calculate artillery firing tables.

The great resources devoted to research and technical development in the United States during the Second World War stimulated a demand for larger and quicker computers. Once the theoretical principles of the relay machines had been proved correct, appetites grew for more complicated projects. What people really wanted from computers was higher speeds of calculation and greater memory capacities; relays were soon replaced by electronic tubes, which have the same function as relays but work much faster.

Work on the first electronic computer commenced in 1942 under the supervision of J. G. Brainerd, J. Presper Eckert, and John W. Mauchly at the University of Pennsylvania in Philadelphia. This machine, later to become famous as ENIAC–Electronic Numeral Integrator and Calculator–marks the beginning of the modern computer era. ENIAC was first taken into service at New Year, 1946, and remained in use up to 1955. It was in many ways "first and best". The machine contained eighteen thousand electronic tubes, consumed about 175 kW, and took up a floor space of about 2,150 sq ft (c. 200 sq m). Its calculation speed was a thousand times greater than that of contemporary relay machines. The capacity of the memory was twenty words of ten figure each, and, moreover, the machine could store three hundred words of program instructions.

ENIAC was the definite breakthrough for the automation of arithmetic, and it attracted enormous attention both in scientific circles and among the general public. The press christened ENIAC the "electronic brain", and the British scientific periodical *Nature* introduced it under the headline, "Babbage's Dream Comes True".

The relay and electron-tube computers of the pioneering era of the 1940s and 1950s are usually called first generation computers. Seen from today's point of view, these one-off machines are characterized by a low memory capacity and long access time (the time it takes to gain access to the memory and retrieve data from it).

$1 + 1 = 10$. True or False?

As the designers of the first computers very likely would not have seen the point of the question: "Is the statement $1 + 1 = 10$ true or false?", any reader who feels confused need not worry. However, this question implies the two main principles of computer theory, both of which were developed intensely from the late 1940s onwards and exemplify once more how control technology has stimulated theoretical considerations. If the apparently simple equation in the question is taken to read "one plus one equals ten", it is, of course, nonsense, but if "ten" is taken as "one-zero", in other words, the binary "ten", then the equation makes complete sense. The binary system of figures, ("binary" deriving from the Latin *bini*, two together), has a base of two and employs two figures only–0 and 1. It was first described by Leibniz in the late seventeenth century. Its properties are simply excellent and fit the components of computer technology like a glove. We shall not enlarge upon the mathematical theories of computers, which belong to the more advanced chapters of modern technology, but the basic principles are surprisingly clear and easy to understand.

What is most unusual about the binary numerical system is the fact that it has a base of two. We have been accustomed since childhood to counting with the decimal system, which has a base of ten, but the two systems are formed in exactly the same way. In the decimal system, the number 365 is equivalent to $3 \times 10 \times 10$ ($3 \times 10^2 = 300$) plus 6×10 ($6 \times 10^1 = 60$) plus 5×1 ($5 \times 10^0 = 5$). If any number is raised to the power of zero, the result is 1. In the binary system, however, the number 365 is equivalent to 1×2^8 ($= 256$) plus 1×2^6 ($= 64$) plus 1×2^5 ($= 32$) plus 1×2^3 ($= 8$) plus 1×2^2 ($= 4$) plus 1×2^0 ($= 1$). Since the series of powers from 2^8 to 2^0 are 2^8, 2^7, 2^6, 2^5, 2^4, 2^3, 2^2, 2^1, and 2^0, the powers 2^7, 2^4, and 2^1 are missing in the number 365. In the binary system, a figure 1 is inserted for the powers included, and a figure 0 for the powers excluded. The number 365 is thus written as 101101101, and the number 2 is written as 10, that is $1 \times 2^1 + 0 \times 2^0$. Therefore, we can say that $1 + 1$ is indeed equal to 10!

If the number of days in a year is thus expressed, the year certainly seems exceptionally long! The binary numbers are altogether unmanageable by people, for whom the decimal system is far superior, but a computer's fundamental components understand the two binary figures 0 and 1 as "yes"–"no", or "either–or", so the computer and the binary system seem made for each other. The mathematicians call these components "bistable elements", meaning that they have only two positions; a current is passed either through the circuit (1, or "yes") or not (0, or "no"), and there is no third choice. Popular scientific books about computers, however, often liken bistable elements to water taps, which can be either off or on. But who does not know that, even in the most costly bathroom or kitchen, a tap has its third position: it drips!

If we recall the title of this section, we can claim to have established that one plus one equals one-zero is "true". The terminology is taken from the other theoretical foundation for computer technology, logical algebra, which was formulated as early as the 1840s by the English logician and mathematician George Boole (1815–64), although it found no practical or theoretical application until the late 1940s, when it was discovered that the Boole algebra's simple means of counting was just what computer technology needed. Its advantage is that it can express in the simplest possible mathematical form, whether combinations "yes–no" and "either–or" are true or false. It is, in other words, very well suited for the binary numerical system: yes = 1, no = 0, either 0 or 1. In its simplest form, Boole's algebra consists of two arithmetic rules. We do not need to go further than this to show the principles.

1 The conjunctive law, $C = A \wedge B$ ($\wedge$ is read as "and"), which says that C is true if A *and* B are true.

2 The disjunctive law, $C = A \vee B$ ($\vee$ is read as "or"), which says that C is true if *either* A or B is true.

Even those who are intimidated by mathematics are bound to agree that Boole's algebra illustrates the logical concepts in a clear and easily understood way.

In 1847, when Boole published his *Mathematical Analysis of Logic*, he was probably totally unaware of the enormous impact his work would have in the future, for at the time, this little book attracted only some casual attention in the world of science, being anyway greatly overshadowed by a more extensive work, *Formal Logic*, published the same year by the English mathematician and philosopher Augustus de Morgan (1806–71). One hundred years later, however, it was discovered that Boole's logical algebra could be extremely useful to computer technology. Those who designed the first computing machines had more or less followed their instincts rather than a particular theory, but in the late 1940s, when several great mathematicians and physicists were devoting themselves to the theoretical principles of the design and function of computers, Boole's little book was rediscovered, reprinted, and discussed. It contained the arithmetic rules that computer technology required!

This was discovered in 1948, the same year that the professor of mathematics at the Massachusetts Institute of Technology, Norbert Wiener, published his pioneering work, *Cybernetics, or Control and Communication in the Animal and the Machine*, in which he presented a general theory for all kinds of automatic control, including the control of computers. This was to be the foundation of a new science, cybernetics, which we shall discuss further on. Although the mathematical descriptions in the book were very complicated, even

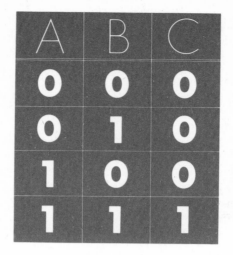

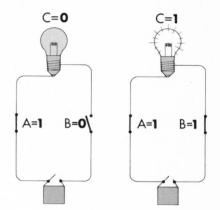

The conjunctive law in Boole's algebra can be illustrated in the following manner: two electric switches, A and B, are connected in series with a light bulb, C, and a battery. If the bulb is to be lit, the circuit must be closed. If A and B are both open (= 0), C will not burn (= 0). If A is open (= 0) and B is closed (= 1), just as if A is closed (= 1) and B is open (= 0), C will still not burn (= 0), but if both A and B are closed (= 1), C will be lit (= 1). The results are entered in a so-called truth table (*left*), from which one can deduce that C is true (= 1) only if A *and* B are true (= 1).

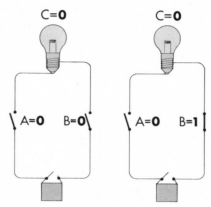

The disjunctive law can be explained in a similar manner. The two switches, A and B, are here connected in parallel to the light-bulb, C, and the battery, which means that the bulb will be lit if either switch is closed. If both A and B are open, C will not burn. If A is open and B is closed, just as if A is closed and B is open, C will burn. If both A and B are closed, C will still burn. From the truth table (*right*) one can deduce that C is true if either A *or* B is true.

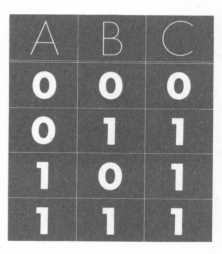

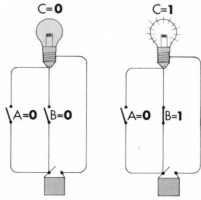

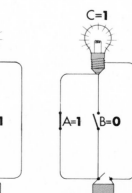

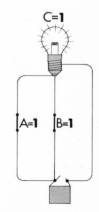

for a mathematician, cybernetics became something of a general topic of conversation in wider circles, far beyond those of natural science and technology, for its theory could be applied to practically anything capable of being governed and controlled, from autopilots and computers to socio-economic developments. The debate gained even more momentum the following year when Wiener published a masterly summary of his ideas, which was completely free of reference to mathematics and entitled *The Human Use of Human Beings*.

The same eventful year of 1948 saw further important progress when Claude E. Shannon (1916–   ) published *The Mathematical Theory of Communication*, a work which attracted if possible even more attention than Wiener's book on cybernetics. Shannon was one of Wiener's students and followed in the footsteps of his teacher, giving a mathematical description of his theories. The similarity extended further: Shannon's book, too, became the basis of a new science: information theory. This theory of the transfer of information, which is very general and mathematically very precise, was at first misunderstood and misinterpreted, just as cybernetics was. Several scientists, above all the American mathematician Warren

Weaver, helped, however, to make the ideas accessible to a wider circle. During the Second World War, Weaver had made some pioneering contributions to the automatic control of anti-aircraft guns, and he was well acquainted with the problems of control technology. It was, by the way, Weaver who first thought of using a computer for translating from one language into another.

Further on, we shall give a brief explanation of the practical implications of information theory. But since we are at present discussing the basic technical principles of computers, we shall explain another word, "bit", meaning a unit of information. The word is a contraction of *bi*nary dig*it* and can be seen as a pun: a bit of information. The term was suggested in 1948 by the mathematician John W. Tukey, one of Shannon's colleagues, and was soon accepted internationally. A "bit" is the amount of information represented by a "yes/ no" or an "either/or" decision.

Nineteen forty-eight also saw the publication of yet another discovery of great importance to computer technology, one that was to have a fundamental impact on the future of computers. This was the transistor, introduced by the trio John Bardeen, Walter Houser Brattain, and William Shockley of the Bell Telephone Laboratories in the United States. They produced this entirely new electronic component after several years of research. The transistor has been seen, quite rightly, as one of the greatest technological breakthroughs of the twentieth century. The research team shared the 1956 Nobel prize in physics for their discovery.

We shall not enlarge upon the details of the construction and function of the transistor but simply state that it has two important properties: it is a bistable element, and it changes extremely quickly from one state to the other, from conducting to non conducting. The word transistor is a contraction of "*transfer*" and "*resistor*". From the start, the first transistors had very small dimensions, not larger than the head of a match, so that the electrons, that is the electric current, had to move only a very short distance to react. The speed of electric current is about 200,000 miles (300,000 km) per second, in other words, 1 ft (0.3 m) in one thousand millionth of a second (a nano second). One talks about the speed of lightning to describe very quick reactions, but the lightning bolt lasts for at least a few thousandths of a second. So the speed of lightning, compared to the reaction speed of a transistor, is extremely slow: over one million times slower!

The small dimensions and extremely quick reactions of the transistor rekindled the imaginations of mathematicians and researchers. When the sensation surrounding the first computers, and principally ENIAC, had subsided, many mathematicians and others had become sceptical, seeing that the admittedly promising possibilities of the computer were severely restricted by the low capacity of its memory. Should capacity be increased a thousandfold, and this was desirable, the external dimensions of the computer would be extremely unmanageable! ENIAC already required the same amount of floor space as a large ballroom, and besides, it devoured large amounts of energy. With the appearance of the transistor, the limitations of the early computers were suddenly removed, for both memory and computing capacities could now be increased considerably, without making the computer larger than a piece of furniture of any more energy-consuming than a deep freeze!

Many mathematicians all over the world were fascinated by these prospects; one who made essential contributions to the theory and design of the computer was the Hungarian-born American mathematician John von Neumann (1903–57). Very largely, it was he who developed the ideas of Turing and others, while he also adapted Shannon's information theory to the practical reality of the computer. Apart from this, von Neumann's abiding contribution is the

A transistor consists of semi-conductor crystals and is, in its original form (1), built like a hamburger in a roll. The hamburger (a) is a p-crystal, whereas the roll (b, c) consists of n-crystals. (2) A transistor circuit. If a battery (d) is connected to the transistor's base (a) and to its emitter (c), so that a positive voltage is applied to the base, electrons are brought from the lower n-crystal (c) through the p-crystal (a) and over to the upper n-crystal (b), the collector. A current then flows through the left-hand circuit. However, if a negative voltage is applied to a, the current in the outer circuit is stopped.

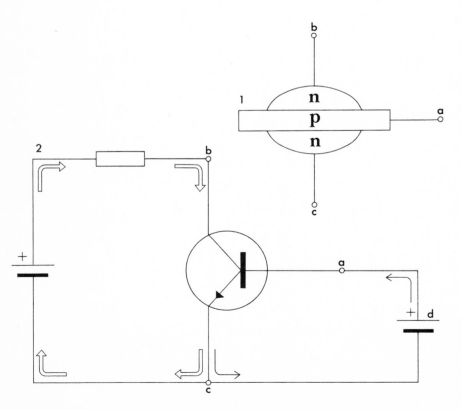

division of the functions of the electronic memory into several specialized units. He introduced a whole hierarchy—this use of the word was coined by him—of memories, each of which had a different task in the handling of data and in making calculations. Von Neumann's principles have guided the internal grouping of the various computer units—the grouping which, later, was to be called the system organization. The first large computer in which von Neumann's ideas were applied was the American UNIVAC (*Universal Automatic Computer*), which came into service in 1951.

The Punched Card and the Punched Tape

The technique used for communicating with UNIVAC was that which Charles Babbage had planned to use for his machine a hundred years earlier, namely the technique of punched cards and punched tape. It had, however, not been invented by Babbage—it is much older than that. We have already come across the talented designer Jacques de Vaucanson, who, after success with his automata, settled in the textile city of Lyons, where he improved the semi-automatic devices for controlling fancy-weaving looms which had been designed by Basile Bouchon (1725) and M. Falcon (1728). In both of these devices, the index fingers (the hooks lifting and lowering the warp threads) were controlled by holes punched in cardboard or an endless paper tape. Each time a new card or a new piece of paper tape was to be fed forward, a manual operation was necessary. Vaucanson then designed such a device which was fully automatic. But since he had plenty of other interests, his device was never commonly known. After his death in 1782, Vaucanson's whole technical estate, including the fancy-weaving device, was transferred to the Conservatoire National des Arts et Métiers, an educational institution in Paris and now a museum of technology.

Joseph Marie Jacquard (1752–1834), who also lived in Lyons, started at an early stage to ponder over a method to mechanize fancy weaving. Both his parents worked in a silk mill, as did Jacquard himself from a very early age. It was quite common that children worked in mills at that time, and the young Jacquard hated this. The children had to sit on top of the looms, looking after the harnesses which made the pattern shafts rise. The work was heavy and monotonous. At the end of the 1790s, Jacquard had completed a design for an automatic harness controlled by punched cards connected in an endless tape. This machine was shown at an industrial exhibition in Paris in 1801, and the following year, Jacquard was granted a patent for his invention. In 1804, Jacquard, thanks to his various designs, which then included a netting machine, was employed by the Conservatoire National in Paris so that he could further develop fully automatic devices for fancy-weaving looms.

In this institution, Jacquard came across Vaucanson's automatic loom, which he had not seen before, although he was familiar with the designs of Bouchon and Falcon. Bouchon was, no doubt, the first to think of using the punched card as a carrier of information. Vaucanson perfected the idea and used it for the automatic control of fancy-weaving looms, and Jacquard combined and developed the previous ideas into an industrially useful design. Jacquard's weaving loom with an automatic harness was completed in 1805 and, as early as 1812, ten thousand Jacquard machines were in operation in France alone.

When Jacquard died, his portrait, about 57 in (1.5 m) square, was woven on a fancy-weaving loom with the aid of twenty-four thousand punched cards. When Charles Babbage saw this extremely detailed portrait, he was convinced that punched cards offered the possibility, as he said, of "weaving algebraic patterns of the same beauty as a Jacquard fabric".

But Babbage was ahead of his time. Not until the end of the

nineteenth century was the idea of using punched cards tried again, when the German-American Hermann Hollerith (1860–1929) was working as a statistician at the United States Census Bureau. According to the American Constitution, a census has to be taken every ten years: the census of 1880 had taken seven years to complete, the population then numbering over 50 million and obviously increasing rapidly. Could the census of 1890 be completed before the next was due? Hollerith's solution was to introduce a rectangular card divided into 240 squares, in each of which a hole could be punched according to a code. Each square corresponded to a question; a punched square represented the answer "yes", an unpunched square a "no". In that way one card could contain information about a person's age, sex, and so on. The punching was done manually, one card per person, but cards were read by a machine; the card was placed on small containers holding mercury, one container for each row of holes, and then a die with electrically conducting pins was brought down upon the card. The holes permitted contact between the pins and the mercury containers, and the coded information was registered by a comptometer. While the population turned out to have grown since 1880 by twenty-five per cent, to 63 million, the result of the 1890 census could be presented after only a little more than two years.

Hollerith developed his methods further and started a company which, in the following decades, was to provide the business world with a whole family of punched-card machines for book-keeping and statistics. It produced punching machines for punching data into the cards, sorting machines, and tabulators for computing operations and for writing out the computed data. Hollerith's company flourished and became one of the corner stones of the International Business Machines Corporation, IBM, which was founded in 1912.

When the computer appeared, there was, in other words, a well-developed technology of information-carrying punched cards and punched tapes. This was very well suited to the "language" of the computer, the binary system of figures, the absence of a hole in a certain place representing 0, and a hole representing 1. In a punched tape with five channels there are $2^5 = 32$ possible combinations in a line, making it possible to include the whole alphabet plus some punctuation marks. With seven channels, $2^7 = 128$ combinations are obtained, which holds the whole alphabet plus all the numbers from 0 to 99.

A magnetic tape stores data similarly, the hole in the punched card becoming a magnetic pulse in a given place in the channels of the tape, and no hole becoming the absence of a magnetic pulse.

Second Generation Computers

In the general enthusiasm following the remarkable breakthroughs in the world of computers in 1948, many people predicted a development at breakneck speed. That never came about for several reasons, but especially because of the extreme difficulty in mastering the mass production of transistors. It took almost ten years from the time when the first laboratory products were tested in 1948 until transistors in large quantities were available on the market. Initially, prices were also relatively high—contrary to early predictions. The first wholly transistorized computer, "Leprechaun", was built at Bell Laboratories and was finished in 1956. A *leprechaun*, one of the little people in Irish mythology, can produce gold and fame with a wave of his hand. The name referred mainly to the speed of the computer—pioneering contributions usually give more fame than gold. Leprechaun soon had successors in both the United States and in Europe, for instance the American IBM 7090 (1958), the British Elliott 803 (1959), and the German ER56 (1959, built by SEL).

During the early 1950s, the large computer companies had been

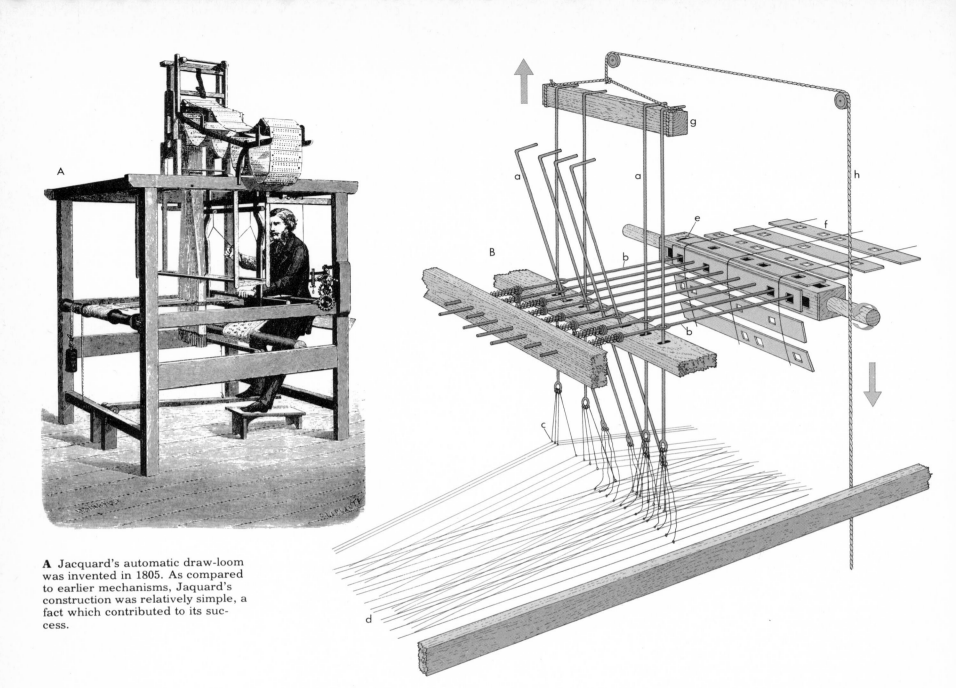

A Jacquard's automatic draw-loom was invented in 1805. As compared to earlier mechanisms, Jaquard's construction was relatively simple, a fact which contributed to its success.

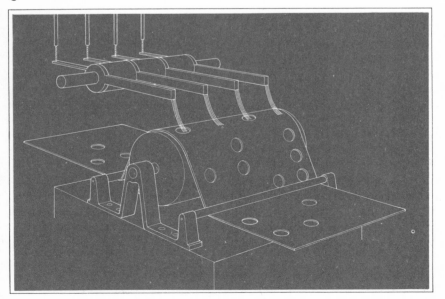

B A simplified explanatory sketch of Jacquard's automatic draw-loom. The vertical hooks (*a*) ran through eyes in spring-loaded needles (*b*). At the bottom end of the hooks were bunches of strings, which carried the healds (*c*). Through these ran the warp threads (*d*), which were distributed among the needles according to the pattern. The needles bore on a hollowed-out, square-section roller (*e*), over which an endless chain of punched cards (*f*) ran. Every time the weaver pushed a foot-pedal downwards, the roller was rotated one-fourth of a revolution, and a new punched card was pulled forward. At the same time, the griff (*g*) was raised, pulling with it the hooks whose needles had beeen able to enter the roller through the holes in the punched card. All other needles were pulled backwards. (*h*) Pedal rope. The Jacquard looms could have very large numbers of hooks, and at the end of the nineteenth century, looms with four hundred and six hundred hooks were the commonest.

C Hollerith's reading machine for punched cards was originally battery-powered. The cards were hand-fed into the machine, where brush contacts were run across them. Inside the roller were mercury containers, one for each row of holes, and when contact was made, an electric circuit was closed. The circuit either sent impulses to a tabulator's counting device or decided which way the card was to take in order to land in the correct box in a sorting machine. This illustration is based on a drawing in Hollerith's patent application of 1889.

concentrating strongly on computers with miniaturized electron tubes, having more or less given up in the face of the great technical difficulties involved in mass producing transistors, and also of the vast investments required. It was not until the early 1960s that the grand visions of 1948 could be gradually realized. The transistorized computer soon assumed the shape of an acceptable item of furniture and was put into practical use, being used both for scientific calculations and as an aid in administration and management.

The Super Computer which never Arrived

Around 1960, there was a lot of talk in computer circles about a "super computer", a gigantic central computer that was to be the spider in a network of hundreds or thousands of terminals. Large companies as well as small, and even members of the general public, would be able to subscribe to the services of this central computer, which would work as a public utility. The computer intelligence, in other words, like gas, water, and electricity, would be distributed to its consumers.

A series of technical breakthroughs in the latter part of the 1950s had given rise to this idea. The transistor and a number of other technical solutions indicated the possibility of an unlimited extension of the memory capacity of the computer. By greatly increasing speeds of calculation and by organizing systems in a better way, it seemed possible to process several problems simultaneously. On top of all this, drastically simplified methods of instructing and programming were available in the programming languages, principally AL-GOL, which appeared in 1958. Instructions about the course of computations, and also other instructions and data, could now be "translated" into a programming language which the computer understood. The word ALGOL is a contraction of *Algo*rithmic *L*anguage, an algorithm being, in computer technology, any partial operation in the computation of a problem. With ALGOL, anyone with a little training could present a problem and then instruct the central computer to solve it. If the central computer had enormous amounts of data stored in its memory, it would not only be capable of working as a calculating machine for research laboratories and of dealing with data processing for companies, but also would be able to help mother to plan next week's menu and father to do the kids' maths homework.

Several companies, such as General Electric in the United States and J. Lyons & Co. in Great Britain, had already installed computers by the beginning of the 1950s to calculate wages and salaries, and these computers had gradually taken over additional tasks, such as inventory control, the issuing of invoices, cost calculations, general book-keeping, and the like. As soon as data could be transferred over great distances, a central computer would be able to serve a whole industrial or business concern, even if offices and other units were geographically far apart. Various such computers, with huge networks of terminals, were actually built in the early 1960s. But all of a sudden, the plans for a gigantic central computer as a public utility were scrapped, the reason being the introduction of a new type of electronic component, and that was the *integrated circuit*.

The second generation computers usually had their electronic circuits built on what were called circuit cards, sheets of insulating material on which were mounted the transistors, resistors, condensors, and other components which formed a connected group of circuits. The connections between the components ended in flat pin plugs which made it easy to extract or exchange the card. In the more advanced integrated circuit, abbreviated here and in computer language to IC, the transistors and other components have been placed on and in a semi-conductor crystal, usually made of silicon. The first mass-produced ICs appeared in 1964 and contained only a few transistors and their associated components. But even at this early stage, it could be seen that development would consist of a drastic miniaturization, and that this would open up entirely new perspectives in computer technology. The transistors with their circuit components on a small silicon chip occupied a surface of only a few square millimetres. As the first computers with ICs became available on the market, only about a year after the introduction of the first ICs, it became clear that the central computer had been technically surpassed.

IC computers are generally called third generation computers, and with them a new era began. The revolution in computer technology can be compared to the revolution that took place in engineering workshops in the early 1900s. Up to then, all machine tools, such as lathes, drills, etc., had been driven by a central steam-engine, with power transmitted by belts, but at the beginning of the century, electric motors were introduced, allowing each machine to be worked individually. In much the same way, the central "steam computers" with their large network of terminals were gradually replaced by smaller computers placed where they were needed, a development that accelerated during the 1970s. It has been made technically possible because of the rapid development of the IC technique. While the first ICs were less than a hundredth the size of the earlier circuit cards, most of their volume consisted of connecting wires; and the solution of this volume problem was found when as many circuits as possible were integrated on one single silicon crystal. *L*arge *S*cale *I*ntegration, LSI, became the motto, but the design and construction of such circuits required a refined technique, a process called *M*etal *O*xide *S*emi-Conductor Technique, MOS, which requires, among other things, that a silicon crystal be oxidized in an oxygen atmosphere and coated with metal in a vacuum. This very sophisticated manufacturing process was introduced in 1967 and, since then, has been refined further. As the properties of a MOS transistor differ slightly from those of the "ordinary" transistor, once-but-now-no-longer common, it became necessary to modify the principles of construction for computer circuits. "If the computer had not been invented by then, we would have found ourselves in a blind alley!" is a remark made by one of the researchers behind the MOS project, and a computer was indeed programmed to design LSI circuits, being fed with the characteristics of the MOS transistors and the properties desired of the circuits. It was programmed further to calculate the shortest possible connections between the components. It produced its results in the form of a neat large-scale constructional drawing of an IC. Through a photographic method, this drawing could be directly used as the basis of production.

A computer designing a computer . . . The popular and daily press made some frightening comments on this in the late 1960s. Was there not a risk that the old legend of the sorcerer's apprentice would become a reality? On the other hand, there is the soothing anecdote of Queen Christina's learned talks with Descartes. When he had made his point about animals being automata, the queen pointed at a clock on the wall and said, "Monsieur Descartes, would you please arrange for that object to have offspring".

In the 1970s, the LSI and MOS techniques with computer-designed computer circuits spectacularly reduced not only the volume of the circuits, but also their price and energy consumption, while at the same time making them more reliable in operation. They have done this to a far greater extent than anyone dared even to suggest during the era of electron tubes, when, after all, the great possibilities of the computer were first suggested.

A Computer in a Nutshell

Larger and larger circuit units were soon produced with the MOS

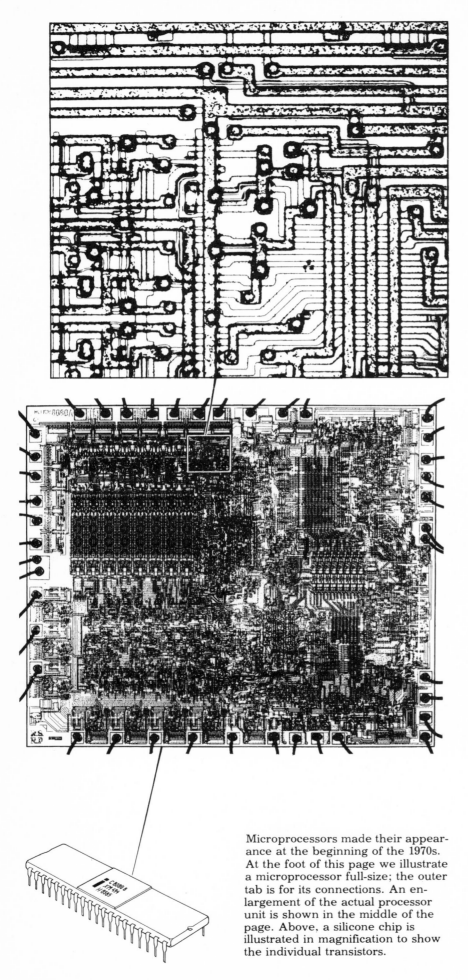

technique, and in 1971, this resulted in an important breakthrough, when the microprocessor was invented, a simplified computer consisting of a small semi-conductor plate, called a chip. The name LSI was now inadequate, so the new term was VLSI (*Very Large Scale Integration*). The microprocessor soon found many areas of application in industrial governing and control systems, being used in industrial robots, among other things. The public at large first met the microprocessor in 1973, when the pocket calculator was introduced and immediately started to spread like wildfire.

The first pocket calculators could calculate the four modes, roots, powers, logarithms, and possibly trigonometric functions. More and more sophisticated calculators followed, however, in rapid succession. These could be programmed over a relatively wide range and had several thousand times the memory capacity that ENIAC once had. One model was able to talk, although with a limited vocabulary. The electronic wrist watch, the quartz watch, became the next triumph for microcircuit technology. The watch was introduced in 1975 and also met with immediate success. Two years later, a quartz watch with a built-in calculator was on sale, and in 1978, an American manufacturer announced the *speaking* quartz clock. The impulses to the figures in this clock—as in the pocket calculator—are transformed to analog speech currents which tell the time via a miniature loudspeaker. A daily paper made this remark: "Let's hope the microelectronics people don't fall asleep now—we're waiting for Dick Tracy's bracelet viewphone." It will probably appear. In 1976, various kinds of television games started to gain popularity, and these entertainment machines are also based on microcircuit technology.

Our closest surroundings will soon see a number of versions of the microprocessor, performing functions which we cannot even imagine today. For example, several automobile manufacturers have equipped their latest models with trip computers which compute information such as the average speed during a certain distance and the distance to, and time of arrival at, the destination. Another gadget also made possible by microprocessors is the talking "traveller's dictionary" of the size of a pocket calculator, which translates some hundred simple phrases and reads them aloud. So far, the translation is word by word, but in most situations, this is sufficient to make oneself understood.

One of the great philosophers has said that all comparisons limp, and the most picturesque fall and break their necks. To get an idea of how quickly computers have changed from ENIAC up to the microprocessor, one can make a comparison with a car, for example, a Volkswagen, the civil version of which appeared in the same year as ENIAC. Had the Volkswagen undergone the same degree of development as computers, it would have a fuel consumption of a few cubic millimetres per mile, cost perhaps a dollar, have a trouble-free working life of about ten thousand years, and have a top speed of over 600,000 mph (c. 1 million km/h). Its fuel consumption is appealing, even if its speed might be a health hazard.

This is merely a somewhat fanciful way of linking the computer and the car in a comparison that, sure enough, stumbles and breaks its neck: our putative Volkswagen would be so small that it would be lost in the dust on the desk at which it has been dreamt up!

Machines Controlling Machines

The technology of the automatic control of industrial procedures emerged from the 1920s onwards, alongside the development described in the previous pages. More and more demands arose for the automatic control of procedures that could no longer be managed manually, since human reactions were insufficient. An example is procedures in the chemical industry, such as the oil refineries which

Microprocessors made their appearance at the beginning of the 1970s. At the foot of this page we illustrate a microprocessor full-size; the outer tab is for its connections. An enlargement of the actual processor unit is shown in the middle of the page. Above, a silicone chip is illustrated in magnification to show the individual transistors.

began to be built in ever-increasing numbers to meet the growing demand for fuel, brought about by the expanding number of motorists.

It was, more than anything else, electrical engineering, with its urgent need for automatic control, that hastened the discovery of new components and principles. Initially, electric power was distributed in relatively small networks with moderate voltages, the current being supplied by a generator driven by a steam-engine or a water turbine. The dominant control component in the driving engine was the centrifugal governor, and the operator had no great difficulty in manually making fine adjustments to the speed—that is, to the frequency in alternating-current networks—or in adjusting the power with a starter rheostat. As the power and load of the networks increased, however, it soon became impossible to intervene only manually, especially when several networks were linked in a grid. It became technically unavoidable that automatic controls would replace man; at first, electromechanical methods were tried out, but it soon became necessary to boost the relatively small output signals which these gave. During the first decades of the twentieth century, Farcot's servomotor was applied in many different ways by those attempting to solve the various problems of electric-power control, and the servomotor was developed along several different lines. Farcot had considered steam to be the most logical driving power, but now, compressed air and oil at pressure—in other words, pneumatics and hydraulics—were tried instead. In due course, several variations on these two themes appeared.

The servomotor, the muscle of control engineering, also turned out to be very useful in other branches of technology, such as the processing industry and the metal-working industry. In the 1920s and 1930s, servomechanics developed into a new branch of engineering, and an industry emerged which manufactured more and more specialized components for automatic control. The "classic" problem of servomechanics is the control of vessels, while in the period between the wars, there was also the problem of aligning anti-aircraft guns. The armaments industries in both Europe and the United States made great efforts to solve the latter, and this work also resulted in the production of a number of control systems which could be applied to civilian industry. At the outbreak of the Second World War, the Massachusetts Institute of Technology set up the Servomechanism Laboratory for research and development in development in control engineering. Pioneering theoretical and practical work was done here by Gordon S. Brown, Donald P. Campbell, N. B. Nichols, and others. They have become famous for their text books, published immediately after the War, which became standard works in this field for a long time afterwards.

Long-Distance Telephones

Let us look now at telecommunications, another branch of electrical engineering which has made some extremely important contributions to modern control technology. We who use the telephone every day sometimes forget that there was a time during the first decades of the telephone age when conversations were limited to an area with a relatively small radius. This was due to the damping of the current on the line. If a normal bare wire was used, this radius was approximately 30 miles (50 km). At the beginning of the century, the damping could be reduced by artificial means—inserting a series of self-induction coils, called coil loading—which extended the radius of the telephone area to about 120 miles (c. 200 km). Experiments were made with a "high-tension microphone", one which could take a very high voltage. The radius could then be extended to about 250 miles (c. 400 km), or the distance between Paris and Berlin. One kilowatt was fed into this monstrous microphone, a normal telephone

microphone needing only about one milliwatt. On top of everything else, as damping is exponential, nearly three hundred gigawatt (300×10^9 W) would be needed to make audible a telephone call through uninsulated wire 620 miles (1,000 km) long, an impossible demand, for this amount of electrical effect was then—about 1910—not even available. Today, this would amount to about half of the total installed capacity in Europe!

Telecommunications had a difficult problem. To make long-distance connections possible, it was necessary to amplify the speech currents at regular intervals along the line and so counteract the damping. The only feasible solution was to use the electron tube, which at that time, however, had hardly left the laboratory stage. The triode, the electronic tube with three electrodes, had been invented in 1906, independently by the German R. von Lieben and by the American Lee de Forest; now, it was a matter of developing it into a safe component in repeaters, and it took over ten years to do this, the First World War both hampering and stimulating the work. Development work was led in the United States by the Western Electric company, and in Europe by several German engineers. One of them, H. Barkhausen, was one of the first people to make use of the word "electronics". The first long-distance cable in Europe was taken into service in 1923: it connected Stockholm and Gothenburg (a distance of about 300 miles, or 500 km) and had been made by Western Electric with triode repeaters.

Long-distance telephony spread very rapidly. Long-distance calls became as easy to make as local calls, and the quality of sound was at least comparable. In a short time, hundreds of thousands of triode repeaters were in operation in the telephone networks—and that was when the deficiencies of this type of repeater were revealed. Slight individual variations in the properties of the triodes, uneven current supply, differences of temperature, and other things could cause a severe disturbance in operation when hundreds of triode repeaters were linked together in a long-distance cable. As so many times before in the history of technology, the solution to one problem had created another.

The attempts to solve this new problem, however, led to a completely new design principle for electron-tube repeaters, namely *negative feedback*, and this had a revolutionary impact, not only on telecommunications. H. S. Black of the Bell Laboratories in the United States first described the negative-feedback repeater in 1923. It played a fundamental role in all telecommunications, which, at the time, was expanding rapidly due to the emergence of broadcasting, and also due to an electrical method, invented in 1925, of recording gramophone records. Feedback gave the repeater or amplifier high stability and made it quite insensitive to external disturbances—properties very well suited to various types of control systems. The word "feedback" became something of a catchword among engineers of the time, and while the feedback repeater was being applied in various control systems, it was also triumphing in the sphere of telecommunications. Still, what had been achieved was merely a technical solution. A more complete description of the theory of the feedback repeater did not appear until the mid-1930s, and then largely thanks to the contributions made by J. Bode and Harry Nyqvist, both of Bell Laboratories. A generalization of this theory also formed the basis of a better understanding of the feedback or closed-control system.

Cybernetics and Information Theory

Very simply put, it may be said that both cybernetics and the information theory are logical extensions of the work done by Black, Bode, Nyqvist, and others in the 1920s and 1930s, for these sciences each include a mathematical and physical extension of the concept of

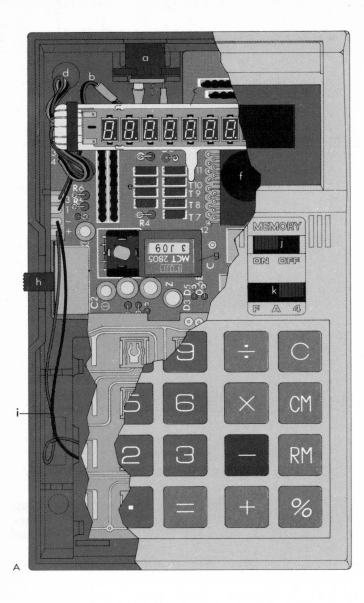

feedback. In the early 1940s, Norbert Wiener became interested as a mathematician in the obvious similarities between technical closed-control systems and various processes in living organisms, especially the transfer of signals in nervous systems. By applying the theories and calculation methods of servomechanisms to experiments on animals, Wiener and his assistant, the neurologist Arturó Rosenbleuth, could predict the contraction and relaxation of a muscle with different loads. These and other experiments gave Wiener the idea of applying the theory of the closed-loop servosystem not only in physiology but also in the behavioural sciences, political economy, and many other areas. Wiener noticed, however, that his "technical" theories and his terminology were accepted only with difficulty within other branches of science, so he then reshaped the whole complex of theories into a new, generalized form. Moreover—and this was, perhaps, the most important thing—he found a new, exciting name for it all: "cybernetics". The name derives from the Greek word for helmsman and, freely translated, means "the science of steerability"; it is interesting to note that Ampère used the same concept in his catalogue of all human knowledge. One of Wiener's colleagues pointed this out to him, and Wiener replied: "Well, that was the only word I came to think of!"

With this new designation, Wiener wanted above all to stress the interdisciplinary character of cybernetics, and he succeeded. Many widely different scientific circles received Wiener's ideas with great enthusiasm—and misunderstood much of them. Even so, he would surely have encountered great resistance, not least among behavioural scientists, had he tried instead to deliver his message as "the theory of the negative-feedback electron tube repeater". Nevertheless, this is the theory on which cybernetics is based, although the form is refined and developed. In economics, for example, a number of feedback processes had been identified as such by the British economist John Maynard Keynes (1883–1946) and others long before Wiener had presented his theory. The ratio between supply and demand is one such process, and another is the increase or decrease in the total consumption of a certain commodity following inversely on a change in its price. A servomechanic block diagram can be drawn up to illustrate such processes, something that can make the concepts clearer and easier to understand. But it is only possible to make a mathematical calculation of a feedback process in economics and to express the results in precise economical terminology, if all the quantities involved are described in the language of mathematical formulae, so that they can be inserted in the equations that express the concept. And this is where the difficulties begin. If the economists could describe the national and global economical processes mathematically with the precision of the astronomers' definitions of the motion of the planets, cybernetics would enable them to calculate very accurately the effects of, say, a devaluation. Today, this is possible neither theoretically nor practically, but the science of cybernetics has to a large extent stimulated economists to try to design mathematical models of economic feedback processes. This has resulted in a new branch of economic sciences, *econometrics*, which has developed methods to define and measure economical changes. The possibility of "simulating" economical reality has also been tried out with the help of computers programmed with econometric mathematical models.

Recently, some historians have launched the term "cliometry" to describe feedback processes in historical studies, Clio being the Greek muse of history. This may for the time being be taken as a joke, for the difficulties of defining the parameters in such a process, with even the slightest mathematical precision, are altogether too great.

The whole technique of cybernetics, however, is still in an early

A Compared to the latest products, early calculators were both uncomplicated and costly. All they could cope with were the four modes: addition, subtraction, division, and multiplication. The model shown here worked off batteries placed in a recess at the back, but it could also be plugged into the mains. (*a*) Plugs for mains connection and for disconnecting the batteries. (*b*) Lead for *a*. (*c*) Diode display of figures, each formed by a number of the seven segments. (*d*) Lead to *c*. (*e*) Transistors activating *c*. (*f*) The calculator unit, which also contains the memory, the whole consisting of many transistors. (*g*) Voltage regulator for mains connection. (*h*) Switch. (*i*) Leads to batteries. (*j*) Button to switch the memory on and off. (*k*) Button for the desired number of decimals.

stage of development, but very likely, the methods will be successively refined, and in the future, cybernetics will be of great practical importance. It will also have a great impact on a number of other sciences, where it has given rise to a fruitful cooperation between different disciplines. One example is the physiological analysis of the human brain, made for the purpose of studying the process of learning, this being one of many cases where cybernetics can be complemented with models of thought from the theory of information.

The scientific theory of information was introduced, as we have mentioned, by Claude E. Shannon, in the eventful year of 1948. It deals with the transfer of information from a "transmitter" via a "channel" to a "receiver", and with what can happen to the information on the way. The transmitter can be a radio transmitter; the information is then telegraphic signals, speech, or music. Those who listen to the short-wave band on the wireless know that there are many sources of interference in the channel—nearby transmitters, electric storms in the atmosphere, the neighbour's electric razor, and so on. Shannon himself has likened the transfer of information to a conveyor belt, loaded at one end with various kinds of wooden goods which are received and sorted at the other end of the belt. During the journey, the pieces of wood (or "bits" of information) can be shaken off, chipped, or in some other way deformed, so that it becomes difficult for the receiver to sort them out. These things happen by chance, just like disturbances to the transfer of information, but statistical methods can give an idea of the damage they cause. Shannon also showed how statistics can help calculate, in "bits", the content of information in a message. The theory of information can thus be seen as an advanced branch of mathematical statistics.

The importance of the information theory for all types of telecommunication is quite clear, but only when it has been applied on an interdisciplinary, general level has the theory of information advanced the frontiers of human knowledge, and this has occurred in many branches of science. For example, when the transmitter is a brain cell of an organism and the receiver a nerve cell in a muscle, the information transmitted can be exposed to interference, caused by disease in the organism. The theory of information has also been successfully applied to everything connected with verbal and other forms of communication between human beings.

The Return of the Androids!

Earlier in this chapter we have come across numbers of actual and imaginary artificial beings. Having been absent from the scene for almost a hundred years, the androids returned in the 1920s. In 1923, the Czech playwright Karel Čapek presented his play *R. U. R.* (Rossum's Universal Robots), and so gave a new name to these walking mechanical monsters. The word robot is derived from the Czech *robota*, compulsory labour, while the word means "to work" in other Slavic languages.

As a contribution to the European social debate, Čapek's play caused a lively discussion, which soon subsided, however. The comic strips, on the other hand, warmly welcomed the robot, but it was mainly films which gave it its great vitality. The first film showing robots was the now classic German *Metropolis*, which was released in 1926, and since then, robots have appeared in a number of different shapes on the screen. In the 1930s, every self-respecting fair or exhibition had its own robot. At the world exhibition in New York in 1939 and 1940, the walking and talking robot "Electro" appeared together with its dog "Sparko", which could run, bark, and sit up and beg at the order of its master.

But the game became serious. It is understandable that many members of the scientific world took it as a bad joke when Norbert

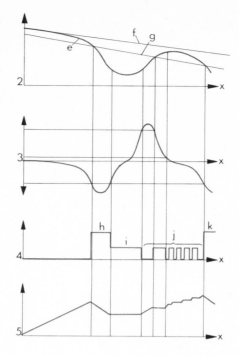

B An anti-locking braking system could not be built until the LSI and MOS techniques had been developed. The German company Bosch launched its ABS anti-locking system in 1978 and made it available at first only in Germany and only to order on the more expensive Mercedes and BMWs.

In a car equipped with ABS (**1**) an electromagnetic transmitter (*a*) is mounted in the hub of each front wheel. The transmitter's coil is fitted beside a cog-wheel which rotates with the car's wheel. A similar arrangement (*b*) is mounted on the

back axle. The transmitters send continuous electric impulses to a governing device (*c*) as the car's wheels rotate, and if one of them starts to lock, the impulses from it rapidly increase in frequency. The hydraulic unit (*d*), with its electromagnetically controlled valves and pump, then stops the flow of brake fluid to that wheel. If this does not stop the tendency to lock, the pump begins to extract fluid from the relevant braking circuit, so that retardation is reduced. If the electronic governor senses that the transmitter has stopped functioning correctly, it activates the reserve system, and if that fails, the governor cuts out the system's valves and the braking system reverts to a normal, foot-controlled one. (**2**) Diagrams of one wheel's speed (*e*) in relation to the car's speed (*f*) during sharp braking. The x-coordinate gives the time in each diagram. The bump in *e* indicates that the wheel is about to lock. (*g*) The speed calculated by *c* at which maximum lock-free braking can be achieved. (**3**) The wheel's change of speed. When the wheel is about to lock—at the bump on the curve—retardation is reduced and the wheel's speed rapidly increases. (**4**) The governor's instructions upon calculating the changes of speed in **2** and **3**. (*h*) Instructions to the hydraulic valve and pump to reduce pressure in the brake circuit. (*i*) The hydraulic valve is instructed to close, so that the wheel's speed may increase. (*j*) As soon as the wheel has regained enough grip on the road to permit braking, instructions are sent to increase pressure in the brake circuit. (*k*) If the wheel again nearly locks, the instructions in *h* are repeated in a new cycle. (**5**) The vehicle's changes of speed during braking.

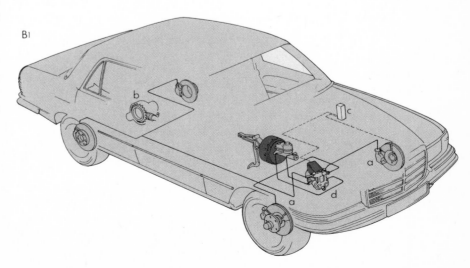

Wiener and his asistant Jerome Wiesner published, in 1950, details of a robot that they called "the moth and the light", an artificial being that could either be attracted by a source of light or, by turning a simple switch, be repelled by it. It was simply a visual demonstration of a cybernetic process. Claude E. Shannon also joined in the serious game and designed a similar robot, which he called "the mouse in the maze". Soon, there was a whole cybernetic menagery in scientific laboratories all over the world. It was mainly physicists, neurologists, and behavioural scientists who used this "laboratory cybernetics" to enlighten and enrich their sciences, and to study, among other things, the resistance of physiological systems to external disturbances: the automatic maintenance of the stability of such a system is called homeostatis. In the early 1950s, the British neurologist W. Ross Ashby built a very sophisticated robot which he called "homeostat" and which attracted a great deal of attention. Unlike other robots, it consisted of two apparatus boxes with connected magnetic circuits which could internally assume a large number of positions of equilibrium. The system reacted to external disturbance by feeling its way towards a new position of equilibrium. Sometimes, it could be some time before the new position of equilibrium was achieved. Too frequent or too powerful disturbances could bring on a "nervous breakdown" of the homeostat. Several experts in behavioural sciences, among them the Austrian Heinz Zemanek, built similar robots, which they used as aids in the work of exploring the behaviour of man.

In the last years of his life, John von Neumann worked on the theoretical possibilities of constructing an automaton which, unlike Queen Christina's clock, could reproduce itself. It remained a mathematical picture, a blueprint, as von Neumann himself put it. Von Neumann's idea is not totally absurd from a technical point of view, but as far as practice goes, we can relax. Someone must supply such an automation with "food", that is, transistors, connecting wires, and other things, and there must also be someone to program and control it. During the last ten years, various robots have been put to practical use in both industry and research. A number of different types have been produced for handling radioactive material; some are intended for regular work in nuclear power-stations, whereas others are kept prepared for possible emergencies. In the United States the robot "Beetle" has been built for emergencies: it will automatically go to the source of radiation, i.e., the dangerous material, take it, and leave it to be destroyed in the place to which it has been directed.

It is, however, the space researchers who have taken into their service the most sophisticated robots, ranging from moon-vehicles like the unmanned Soviet Lunochod to various kinds of probes which can soft-land on other planets and do as much work as a whole research team on earth, yet another example of a development chain in which automata and simulacra succeed one another.

Automation

Let us return to 1948, that year which was so eventful in terms of the contents of this chapter, when automation, another phenomenon which, a few years later, was to set off a violent debate throughout the western world, lay latent. The word "automation" had been coined in 1947 by Delmar S. Harder of the Ford Motor Co. in Detroit. Harder thought that "automation" ought to be a coordinating concept embracing all designs and devices that attempted to achieve fully automated production. Initially, Harder conducted a campaign for automation within Ford, but rumour of this spread rapidly all over American industry, and a vehement debate was joined about automation. It was felt that its ultimate aim was to rationalize man out of production, and mass unemployment was predicted. There

A

A This modern American robot, Beetle, automatically locates radioactive material and is programmed to bring it out of the danger area and deposit it where it can be neutralized.
B Sabor IV, built in 1938 by the Frenchman Auguste Huber. The robot could both move and speak, its lips moving synchronously with what it said. The legs were moved forwards by little wheels, which were mounted under the soles and were, in turn, rotated and braked.

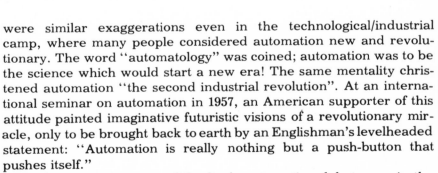

were similar exaggerations even in the technological/industrial camp, where many people considered automation new and revolutionary. The word "automatology" was coined; automation was to be the science which would start a new era! The same mentality christened automation "the second industrial revolution". At an international seminar on automation in 1957, an American supporter of this attitude painted imaginative futuristic visions of a revolutionary miracle, only to be brought back to earth by an Englishman's levelheaded statement: "Automation is really nothing but a push-button that pushes itself."

The lasting importance of the lively automation debate was in the incipient awareness that all procedures and processes, even those which had previously been reserved for the crafts, could in principle be mechanized and automated. One example of this, which has often been mentioned, is a machine which forms dough into pretzels far faster than the most skilful baker. Another is the "mechanical hand" which rolls cigars more quickly and evenly than any Carmen. The automation debate and the vivid exchange of thoughts between specialists within different branches of industry also resulted in insights about the possibility of generalizing—a system for the automation of a certain procedure can often be modified slightly and used for a different procedure, even though the product may be totally different. For example, automatic systems for making crisp-bread can also be used for producing steam-hardened concrete slabs.

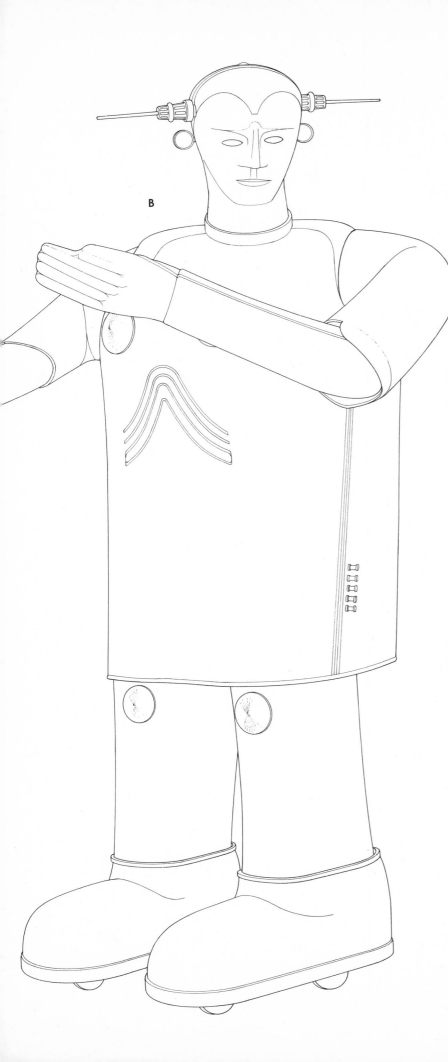

B

Computer Process Control

It has been mentioned already, but bears repeating, that technical solutions in automatic control technology often have preceded theoretical insights. In the wake of the automation debate, bold attempts were made to automate procedures which it had not been possible to master before. Many times, these attempts resulted in bad failures, especially in chemical process technology. In the 1950s, the market began to be offered good-quality components, such as measuring devices, servomotors, and regulators for temperature, pressure, flow, etc. But there was often a lack of knowledge of the dynamic properties of the chemical processes, that is, of how they reacted in operation to various kinds of control intervention. The work of dimensioning the process often resulted in very complicated mathematical expressions. At an early stage, computers had to be used for such computations, and thence it was a short step to letting the computers take over the governing and control of whole processes.

The first computer for process control was designed by the American Ramo-Woolridge Corporation and was called the RW-300. It was first available in 1957 and was soon followed by others. Ten years later, about sixteen hundred process computers were installed in the West and in 1977, the number had risen to about twelve thousand. There are, however, many who believe that this figure will now remain static or at least rise more slowly. Instead, the microprocessor will take over various functions which so far have been directed by the central process computer.

By Rocket to the Planets

By far the most complicated of contemporary processes controlled by computers are space flights—without access to automatic control systems and computers, it would be totally impossible for man to travel into space. The first space pioneers—the Russian Constantin E. Tsiolkovsky (1857—1935), the German Hermann Ganswindt (1856—1934), and others—were criticized by astronomers and mathematicians who believed that it was beyond human ability to correct course and speed with the precision required for space navigation. One of the first to realize the extent of this problem was the German Hermann Oberth (1894—   ), who stressed in his now classical work *Die Rakete zu den Planetenräumen* ("Rockets into Interplanetary Space"), published in 1923, that one precondition for flight in space was access to techniques for automatic governing and control that would have to be far more sophisticated than those then available. In the much extended 1929 edition, *Wege zur Raumschiffahrt* ("Methods for Space Travel"), Oberth quite rightly predicted that the development of rockets with sufficient propulsive force (another essential precondition), would take time and stated that control technology also would have to be improved in that time. The vital necessity for precision in manoeuvring a spaceship is due to the fact that the speeds and distances involved are literally astronomical. On top of this are the complications caused by such phenomena as the motion of the planet systems, and so on.

If the carrier rocket is to place a satellite—a word meaning a companion, and here, a companion to the earth—in an orbit round the earth, it has to achieve a speed of at least 4.911 miles (7.904 km) per second, a velocity called circular, or the first cosmic velocity: it can be rounded off to 5 miles (8 km) per second. Here on earth it is difficult to try to imagine how high this velocity really is. A car driven at 60 mph (100 km/h) needs some five minutes to cover this distance of 5 miles (8 km), so in other words, the rocket must move at a speed three hundred times faster than that of the car! If the velocity of the carrier rocket is increased beyond the first cosmic velocity, the elliptic orbit of the satellite will be larger, since the apogee (the point of orbit furthest removed from the surface of the earth) is then removed

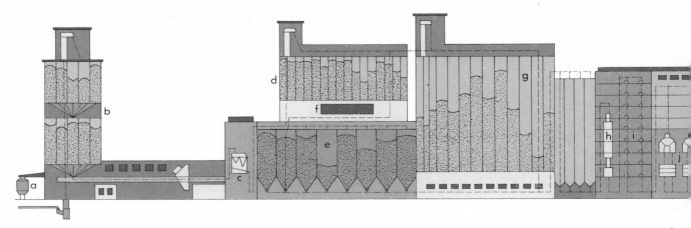

In the early 1960s, AB Wasa Spisbrödsfabrik at Filipstad, Sweden, erected this highly automatized combined mill and bakery for the production of crispbread. (a) At one end of the factory, the raw material, grain, is unloaded from lorries and railway cars. The grain is stored in silos (b) while it is analyzed for, among other things, protein content. When the tests are finished, the grain undergoes preliminary screening (cleaning) (c) and is brought to one of several classification silos (d), depending on its quality. The correct amounts of grain of different qualities for each

even further from the earth. By correcting the velocity of the satellite at suitable points on the orbit, the perigee (the point of orbit closest to the surface of the earth) can be changed until, for example, the orbit alters and becomes more or less circular. If the velocity of the carrier rocket exceeds a certain limit, the satellite will, however, become a spacecraft and travel out into the planetary system. This magic limit is 6.946 miles (11.178 km) per second (about 25,000 mph, or 40,240 km/h), a velocity usually called the velocity of escape, or the second cosmic velocity. It is about forty per cent higher than the first cosmic velocity.

The overriding problem which the early space travel enthusiasts had to combat was how to construct a rocket engine with sufficient propellant force to accelerate a spacecraft to this "astronomical" velocity, which is about twenty times that of a rifle bullet leaving the muzzle. And the only rockets of the 1920s and 1930s were fireworks and the life-saving rockets for shooting lines to ships in distress. If a rocket is to reach out into space, its motor must be able to lift not only its own fuel at the start, but also the oxygen which, later, is needed for combustion. In space, gunpowder rockets are not enough. Pioneering contributions in the area of rocket engines were made primarily by the American Robert H. Goddard (1882–1945), who published his now classic work, *A Method of Reaching Extreme Altitudes*, as early as 1919. In it he describes different liquid-fuelled rockets, and in 1926, he managed to get the first liquid-fuelled rocket to take off, the fuel being hydrocarbons and liquid oxygen.

In 1927, a handful of enthusiasts in Breslau, inspired by Oberth's book mentioned earlier, formed the *Verein für Raumschiffahrt* ("The Society for Space Travel"), and within a year, the society had over five hundred members. The register of members contained not only Germans but also other Europeans and Americans who had been swept up by the huge wave of interest in space travel which was then flooding the world. The leading Soviet rocket experts Nikolaí A. Rynin and Jakov J. Perelman were members, as were the Frenchman Robert Esnault-Pelterie and the Austrian Count Guido von Pirquet. A year after the foundation of the society, Oberth was chairman and Willy Ley vice-chairman. In 1928, the latter presented a masterly book of popular science, *Die Möglichkeit der Weltraumfahrt* ("The Possibility of Space Travel"), to which many theoreticians and scientists had contributed. Space travel now became the object of headlines on the front pages of the daily press, largely helped by the German film of the same year, *Frau im Mond* ("The Girl in the Moon"), directed by the famous Fritz Lang, with Hermann Oberth as scientific advisor.

The time was now ripe—as Willy Ley put it in his book—to transfer the ideas of the theorists to the laboratory and from there to the workshop, where would be made the rocket motors to make space travel possible. The members of the Society for Space Travel put

this into practice in 1930 when, after much hardship, they managed to establish a laboratory for the development of liquid-fuelled rockets in a remote place outside Berlin. The zealots behind this project were Hermann Oberth and his assistants from the work on the film, Rudolph Nebel and Klaus Riedel, together with Willy Ley. They called their eventually well-equipped laboratory *Raketen Flugplatz* ("Rocket Aerodrome"). About a year later, this circle of pioneers was joined by a young engineer called Wernher von Braun (1912–76).

As an eye witness, and to a large extent the stimulus behind the spectacular development of the projects started at the Rocket Aerodrome, Willy Ley wrote a book in which he gives a personal, charming account of the labour pains of modern space adventure. The title of the book is *Raketen und Raumschiffahrt* ("Rockets, Missiles & Space Travel") of which the first edition was published in 1944, in the midst of a raging world war, and since then, over a dozen revised editions and translations have followed.

Robert H. Goddard's contributions in the field of rocket engines should in no way be underrated, but the basic technical progress leading up to the realization, in 1969, of man's immemorial dream to land on the moon was made at the German rocket base Peenemünde on the island of Usedom in the Baltic. Peenemünde was built between 1936 and 1940 and was the joint rocket-base of the army and the air force, rocket research being by this time no longer a private affair. The research and development done at Peenemünde, led mainly by the men who had earlier worked at the Rocket Aerodrome, is one of the most exciting chapters in the history of modern technology. We shall not go into detail here but return to the subject of automatic governing and control.

Willy Ley, like Oberth before him, stressed the fundamental importance of the automatic control of spacecraft. The first units built by the German Air Force, Al and A2, were mainly intended for testing rocket engines, but it was soon realized that the most serious problem, once a practicable engine had been produced, was to achieve stability. "What was then known about rocket stability could have been written on a postcard, leaving some blank space", Willy Ley wrote in the book we have mentioned. For the third unit, therefore, the A3, the German navy provided an expert who had plenty of experience in stabilizing and aligning gun turrets, the classical problem of servomechanics. But this unit, the A3, was not successful either, because the control mechanism turned out to be inadequate, and after that, in 1942, another, then very advanced, control system was designed, with gyroscopes and accelerometers as the sensor organs and with electric servomotors to move fins which were made of the heat resistant metal molybdenum and placed in the gas jet from the rocket engine. To study the dynamic properties of this system, a mechanical simulator was built, its design being

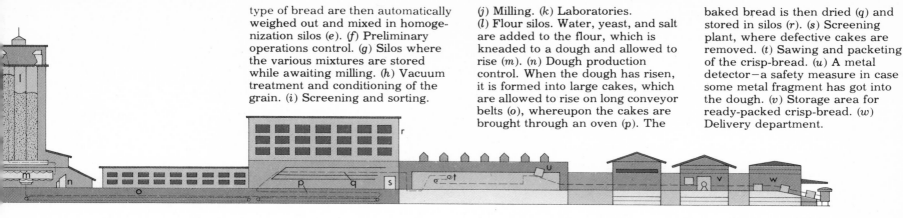

type of bread are then automatically weighed out and mixed in homogenization silos (*e*). (*f*) Preliminary operations control. (*g*) Silos where the various mixtures are stored while awaiting milling. (*h*) Vacuum treatment and conditioning of the grain. (*i*) Screening and sorting.

(*j*) Milling. (*k*) Laboratories. (*l*) Flour silos. Water, yeast, and salt are added to the flour, which is kneaded to a dough and allowed to rise (*m*). (*n*) Dough production control. When the dough has risen, it is formed into large cakes, which are allowed to rise on long conveyor belts (*o*), whereupon the cakes are brought through an oven (*p*). The

baked bread is then dried (*q*) and stored in silos (*r*). (*s*) Screening plant, where defective cakes are removed. (*t*) Sawing and packeting of the crisp-bread. (*u*) A metal detector—a safety measure in case some metal fragment has got into the dough. (*v*) Storage area for ready-packed crisp-bread. (*w*) Delivery department.

based on measurements obtained from a system for radio telemetering from rockets—another pioneering work. By that time, Willy Ley would have needed at least twelve dozen postcards.

This concentration of effort on solving the problems of control and stabilization was to produce A4, the unit which Herr Goebbels later called V2—V for *Vergeltungswaffe* ("retribution weapon"). When the first trial launchings were made with this weapon, it had been provided with extensive radio equipment for telemetering as well as for an attempt at radio control. One such A4 crashed in 1943 on Bornholm, where it was retrieved by Danish intelligence agents who sent photographs and drawings to England via Stockholm. Another went off course and crashed in southern Sweden at midsummer, 1944, and was passed on to the Allies, who in this way were given another warning of what was to come. But it was wrongly concluded that all these rockets were radio controlled. The tests had shown the German researchers that it was impossible to control the rockets with any great accuracy. They were aligned towards the area of destination, first Paris and then London, but once the rocket had been launched, its course could not be affected. The V2 was a mere terror weapon.

During the closing stages of the Second World War, work had been done at Peenemünde on other rocket projects, and engines with greater and greater propulsive power had been designed: the A9 was to be transatlantic. . . Wernher von Braun was arrested by the Gestapo because he talked openly about the possibility of sending objects into space. He was, however, released after the director of the Peenemünde base, General Walter Dornberger, had intervened and explained to the high officials that von Braun's ideas were useful for even more powerful retribution weapons. On the collapse of Germany, in May, 1945, Peenemünde and its whole arsenal of manufactured rockets fell into the hands of the Allies, and by July that year, three hundred freight cars of A4 rockets had arrived at the White Sands Proving Ground in New Mexico. Development work continued here, and the core of the research team was the same as that at the Rocket Aerodrome and Peenemünde.

The difficult of problems of stability and control had already been solved in Peenemünde, and these solutions are still fundamentally valid. Still, the control systems have become more and more sophisticated as further progress has been made in instrument and component technology, and in telecommunications. The simple but useful mechanical simulator built for the A4 has been replaced by computers which handle the navigation and check the function of all systems onboard the rocket.

The demands on course accuracy and velocity control of the first satellites, the Soviet Sputniks 1 and 2 (1957) and the American Explorer (1958), were not as high as they were to become twenty years later. The velocity of their carrier rockets had to exceed the circular

velocity enough to place the perigee at a safe distance from the earth. At this stage, there was no risk that the velocity of escape would be attained, because the rocket engine did not yet have the power necessary for this.

The take-off itself and the first ten seconds of flight are the most critical period when launching a rocket. At the moment of take-off, the stability of the rocket is about that of a pencil balanced on a finger-tip. But after only a few seconds, the rocket reaches a speed at which it can be steered, and its upward course then almost invariably follows that described by Oberth as early as 1929, which he called the synergic (energy saving) curve. Having held a vertical course for about ten seconds, the rocket changes its course gradually, moving on a slight incline towards the horizontal plane. If the rocket is moving east, its speed is accelerated by the rotation of the earth, which gives a certain fuel saving. The rotation speed of the earth at the equator is 1,525 ft (465 m) per second. On the latitudes where the two "satellite states", the Soviet Union and the United States, have their launching sites, this help amounts to about 1,148 ft (350 m) per second.

A rocket flying freely in space has course control and navigation problems of a totally different order. A correction wrong by only a fraction of a degree or one hundredth of a second can have fatal consequences, for all navigation in space must follow the laws of planetary motion which the German astronomer Johannes Kepler established in the seventeenth century. For a rocket, the least energy-consuming course from one planet to another, such as from the earth to Mars, is elliptic. These orbits are called Hohmann ellipses after the German Walter Hohmann, the city architect of Essen, who published calculations of cosmic orbits in Willy Ley's book of 1929.

The real trial of strength concerning the precision of control systems took place in 1964, when the American space probe Mariner 4 was launched to explore the planet Mars. The probe passed Mars at the predetermined distance of about 7,450 miles (c. 12,000 km) and took a great many television pictures of the surface of the planet. A more sophisticated Mariner probe was launched in 1977 to travel round the solar system and, after two years, it passed Jupiter and Saturn. The Americans, within the framework of their Gemini project, have worked to test a system for determining the speed and position of craft in space. By means of what is called the Doppler effect, it was possible, in 1979, to determine the position of a probe far out in interstellar space to within 10 ft (3 m) and its speed to an accuracy of one tenth of a millimetre per second. And remember, the velocity of escape is almost 7 miles (c. 11 km) per second! By choosing this measuring system, the Apollo project could be carried out with the great precision that many of us followed on our television screens.

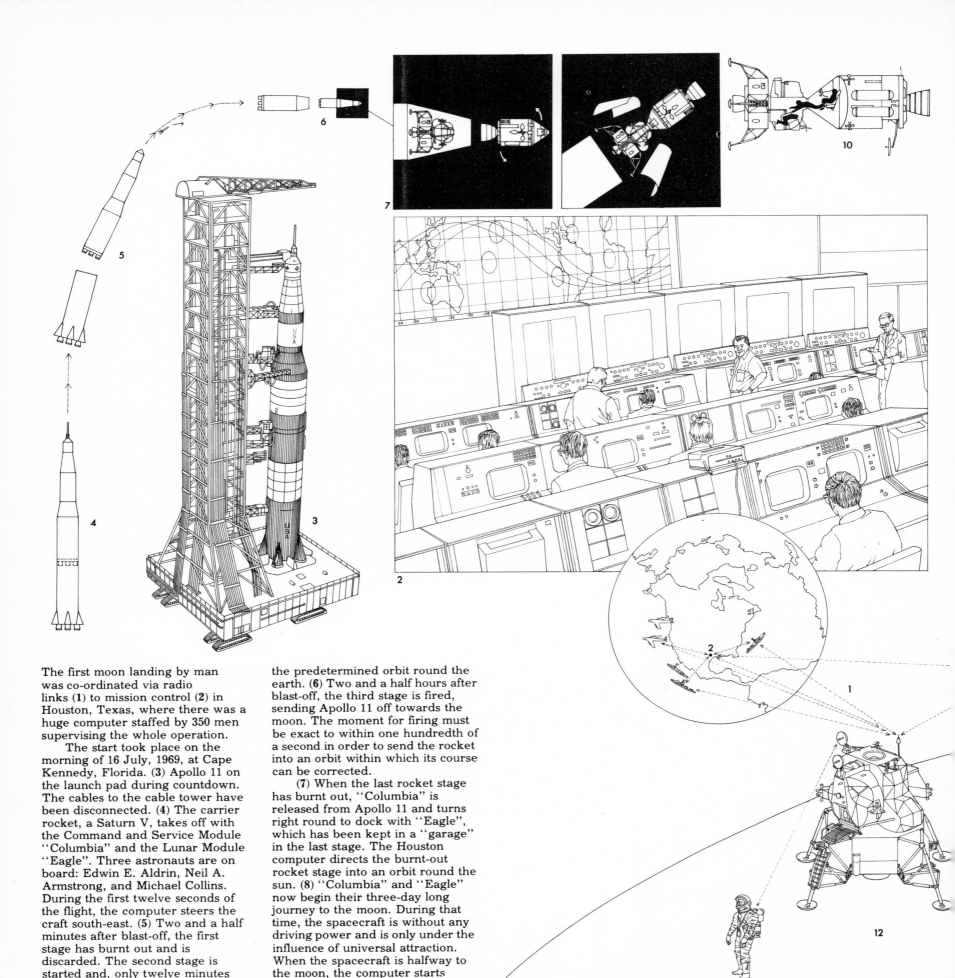

The first moon landing by man was co-ordinated via radio links (1) to mission control (2) in Houston, Texas, where there was a huge computer staffed by 350 men supervising the whole operation.

The start took place on the morning of 16 July, 1969, at Cape Kennedy, Florida. (3) Apollo 11 on the launch pad during countdown. The cables to the cable tower have been disconnected. (4) The carrier rocket, a Saturn V, takes off with the Command and Service Module "Columbia" and the Lunar Module "Eagle". Three astronauts are on board: Edwin E. Aldrin, Neil A. Armstrong, and Michael Collins. During the first twelve seconds of the flight, the computer steers the craft south-east. (5) Two and a half minutes after blast-off, the first stage has burnt out and is discarded. The second stage is started and, only twelve minutes after takeoff, the craft has entered

the predetermined orbit round the earth. (6) Two and a half hours after blast-off, the third stage is fired, sending Apollo 11 off towards the moon. The moment for firing must be exact to within one hundredth of a second in order to send the rocket into an orbit within which its course can be corrected.

(7) When the last rocket stage has burnt out, "Columbia" is released from Apollo 11 and turns right round to dock with "Eagle", which has been kept in a "garage" in the last stage. The Houston computer directs the burnt-out rocket stage into an orbit round the sun. (8) "Columbia" and "Eagle" now begin their three-day long journey to the moon. During that time, the spacecraft is without any driving power and is only under the influence of universal attraction. When the spacecraft is halfway to the moon, the computer starts "Columbia's" rocket for a few

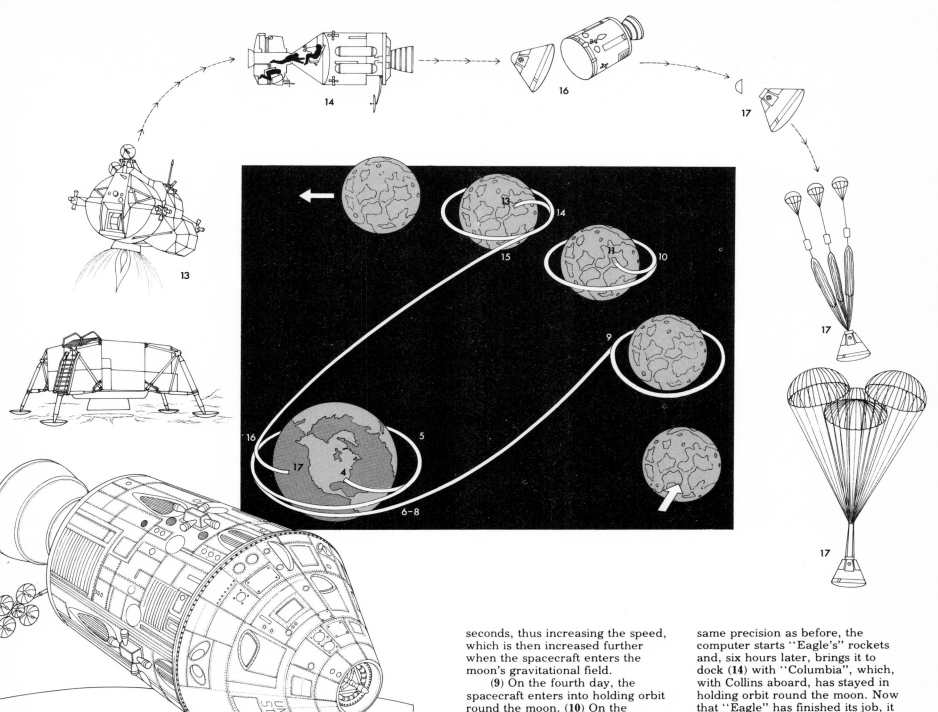

seconds, thus increasing the speed, which is then increased further when the spacecraft enters the moon's gravitational field. (9) On the fourth day, the spacecraft enters into holding orbit round the moon. (10) On the thirteenth orbit, it is time for "Eagle", manned by Armstrong and Aldrin, to descend and land on the moon. The moment when "Eagle" is to fly on its own is carefully determined by the Houston computer. (11) On Sunday, 20 July, "Eagle" lands on the moon. The last twenty seconds of the descent are very dramatic, and despite the fact that the action is totally directed by Houston, Armstrong's pulse reaches 156 beats per minute. (12) The same day, Armstrong becomes the first man to set foot on the surface of the moon; Aldrin follows right behind him. In all, "Eagle" spends twenty-four hours on the moon. (13) With the

same precision as before, the computer starts "Eagle's" rockets and, six hours later, brings it to dock (14) with "Columbia", which, with Collins aboard, has stayed in holding orbit round the moon. Now that "Eagle" has finished its job, it is sent by Houston into an orbit round the moon and crashes onto its surface after several orbits. (15) The rockets start and are driven for a few minutes, this time to send Apollo 11 back towards earth. (16) The Command and Service Module is fired off by its steering rockets a few minutes before the capsule, with the astronauts on board, re-enters the atmosphere. The conic capsule turns so as to be protected by the heat shield during the rapid descent. (17) After releasing a stabilizing parachute, the capsule is slowed down during the last part of its fall by three main parachutes.

A A Hohmann ellipse touches the orbits of both the start (*a*) and the target planet (*b*) and is the least energy-demanding path between two planets. However, it takes a missile longer to follow a Hohmann ellipse than any other ellipse between two planets. (*c*) The sun.

B The initial part of a space missile's synergic orbit. (*a*) During the first few seconds, the missile climbs vertically in order to reach sufficient dynamic stability. (*b*) The missile is then briefly guided in a somewhat smaller angle to the surface of the earth. (*c*) During the next phase, the missile's path is

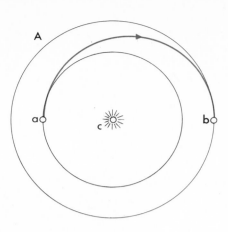

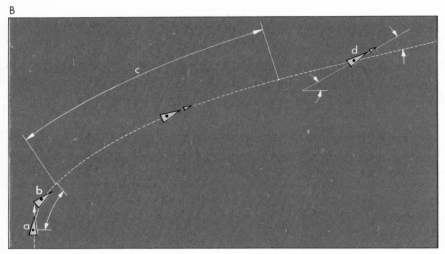

levelled out, due to gravity. (*d*) Before the second stage takes over, the missile is aimed upwards to increase the height of orbit.

C In 1842, the Austrian C.J. Doppler (1803–53) discovered that the frequency of a wave motion seems to vary if the wave motion is emitted from a moving object while the observer is stationary. The radio transmitter of a missile continually emits electromagnetic waves in all directions, but since the missile is moving forwards, the waves do not expand concentrically but are "crowded" in front of it.

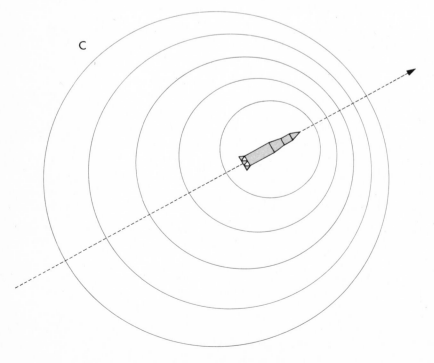

CHAPTER 9
THE MACHINE—
OUR DAILY COMPANION

In daily life, we constantly come across machines, although perhaps indirectly or in shapes we do not recognize; without machines and mechanical aids, we would not have, for example, our daily bread.

Were manual labour, without machines, to take over the whole chain of different procedures preceding the actual baking of the bread—preparation of the land, sowing, harvesting, threshing, and milling—and were the labourers to be paid what is considered a normal wage, the price of bread would far exceed the price of gold. In our industrialized world, such a procedure would be absurd. But that is how it used to be. The exhortation from the Bible, "In the sweat of thy face shalt thou eat bread" was, for many thousands of years, a hard, severe reality for mankind.

Let us look back in time to see what machines have been invented to facilitate the production of our daily bread. For at least the past ten thousand years, bread has been man's staple food, and while its taste and appearance have varied, the difference between the bread we have today and the bread baked by the Sumerians, for example, is not considered very great. Experience taught early man that bread became porous and tastier, if the dough was left to rise before being baked. It was discovered that flour, mixed with tepid water and then left in a warm place for a day, turned into leaven, which could be used to make the bread rise. The fermentation process could also be employed in producing beer from grain, and this art is probably as old as the art of baking bread. Most of the oldest river cultures have closely related words for bread, beer, and fermentation.

During antiquity, enormous numbers of people were required to ensure the supply of daily bread. It was heavy work to till the fields with primitive tools. A simple sickle was used for harvesting, being first made of flint and later of metal. Threshing was done with a flail or some other implement and was also very exhausting, and flour was ground by hand in mortars rather than querns. This process alone kept the women of each household busy for most of the working day. Most cultures seem to have considered it beneath male dignity to undertake this main household chore. In the Odyssey, there is a vivid description of the household at the court of Penelope, Odysseus' beautiful wife, who was considered to be more or less a widow, as her roving husband had been away for so long. She was besieged by suitors who had to be fed and housed while they were courting her! In order to have a sufficient supply of flour for her guests' bread, Penelope had to send messengers to summon all the women in the vicinity.

This was in the eighth century BC, but bread had been made in the same way for many thousands of years and was to continue like that for yet another few hundred years. For the common man—in other words, for nine-tenths of the population—it was hard work just to survive. The biography of one of these people might be summarized briefly like this: "He was born. He worked. He died."

A

A A late nineteenth-century threshing-machine, powered by a traction engine.
B In this double-screening threshing-machine from the start of the twentieth century, the hand-opened sheaves were fed in at a. The stalks were pulled onwards and beaten by a threshing drum (b) against a concave plate (c). Some of the grain and chaff then fell straight down to the riddle plates (d), while the straw and the rest of the grain were brought forward to the straw shaker (e), through which grain and chaff fell onto a plate (f) and slid down to d, while the straw was carried forward and was expelled at g. The riddle plates (d) had a slow, reciprocating movement, and the remaining short pieces of straw (cavings) were expelled at h. Grain, chaff, and dust were detached and fell onto plate i, whence they were brought into the main riddle (j), where air from a fan (k) blew away the light chaff and expelled it at l, while the heavier, unthreshed ears fell out of the threshing-machine at m. The dust was separated and expelled at n, while the grain was brought to the elevator (o) to be raised to the winnower (p). In the winnower, bristle and cusps were rubbed off the ears. The grain then entered another, though smaller, fan-equipped riddle (q), where more dust and other foreign particles were separated from it. Finally, small and imperfect grain, weed seeds, etc., were removed by the rotary screen (r), whereupon the clean grain fell into a sack (s).

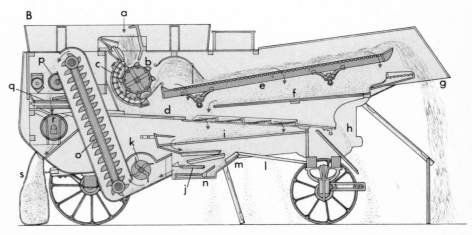

As we saw in Chapter Four, milling was not mechanized until the first century BC, when the water-mill appeared and rapidly came into use throughout the Mediterranean world, spreading thence to the rest of Europe. The windmill appeared a little more than a thousand years later, and the first steam-driven mill—the Albion Mill in London—was put into operation in 1786. The women's task had now become big business.

Threshing was originally done by hand, or rather, in the hand, by rubbing the ears to loosen the corn. The first mechanization came with the introduction of the flail, an implement developed many thousands of years ago by several different cultures, which were geographically totally separated, and its form has changed only inessentially since then. Threshing by flail claimed most of the effort of the agricultural labour force, from harvest almost until Christmas. During the eighteenth century, several proposals were made for machines which would make threshing simpler, most of them being mechanical imitations of the flail. One of the many who interested

A A harvester, built by McCormick in *c*. 1880. The cut stalks were bound into sheaves by hand.
B A nineteenth-century mechanical harvester; (**1**) the mechanism as seen from the side, (**2**) the harvester as seen from above, (**3**) detail of the finger-knife. The harvester was pulled by two horses. The fingers (a) on a protruding girder (b) split the stalks into bunches, which were cut by a reciprocating, toothed knife (c). The knife was moved by a crank (d) on a wheel (e), which was driven through two bevel gears (f, g) by a small, toothed wheel engaging the inside of the central wheel (h), which was driven by being in contact with the ground. A lever (i) could be used to disengage the bevel gears and stop the knife (c). If another lever (j) was depressed, a pawl engaged a ratchet-wheel (k) on g's shaft, and the whole machine came to a standstill. (l) Lever for raising and lowering the cutting mechanism.
C A mechanical harvester at work.
D In this modern Massey Ferguson combine harvester, the cut stalks are pulled towards the cutting table (a) with its knives by a rotating pick-up reel (b). Both a and b are vertically adjustable, as is a rotating

themselves in this was Christopher Polhem, whose threshing-machine was introduced in the 1720s and consisted of a number of vertical thresher bars which were raised and released alternately by a roller with cams. The thresher bars beat the grains out of the ears just like the flail, and some labour was thus saved. In the 1780s, the Scotsman Andrew Meikle introduced an entirely new principle for threshing-machines; in his invention, the corn sheaves were fed, ears first, between two rollers, the grain being extracted from the ear by the action of four thresher bars attached to a rotating horizontal cylinder, called the thresher drum, which worked inside a concave iron covering. The chaff was separated from the grain in a reciprocating shaker, which was placed underneath the cylinder. This design of Meikle's has remained basically unchanged to the present day, although some improvements have been introduced.

Mechanizing the work of harvesting was more difficult, and here as well, attempts were made to design imitative machines. In the 1790s, an Englishman built a harvester employing scythes which

rotated beneath a two-wheel carriage and were activated, via a gearing, by the carriage wheels. As a solution, it was, however, rather impractical, if not lethal, and the machine is of little importance in the development of the mechanical harvester. The technical breakthrough did not come until the 1830s, when the young American Cyrus Hall McCormick designed a harvester with finger bars running level with the ground next to a horse-drawn, two-wheel carriage. The use of the machine soon spread in the United States, and in 1851, at the world exhibition in London, it was introduced in Europe. In England, the mowing-machine became common during the following few decades, and it soon spread throughout the rest of Europe as well.

As early as the 1860s, the first so-called distributors were introduced in the United States. These harvesters gathered the cut stalks into suitable bundles, which were then bound into sheaves by hand. But those who bound the sheaves were soon rationalized away, when the first automatic binder, another American invention, was

auger (c) that brings the stalks onto an elevator (d) leading to the threshing unit. Immediately in front of this unit, there is a stone bin (e). The grain is worked by the threshing cylinder (f) with its flails against

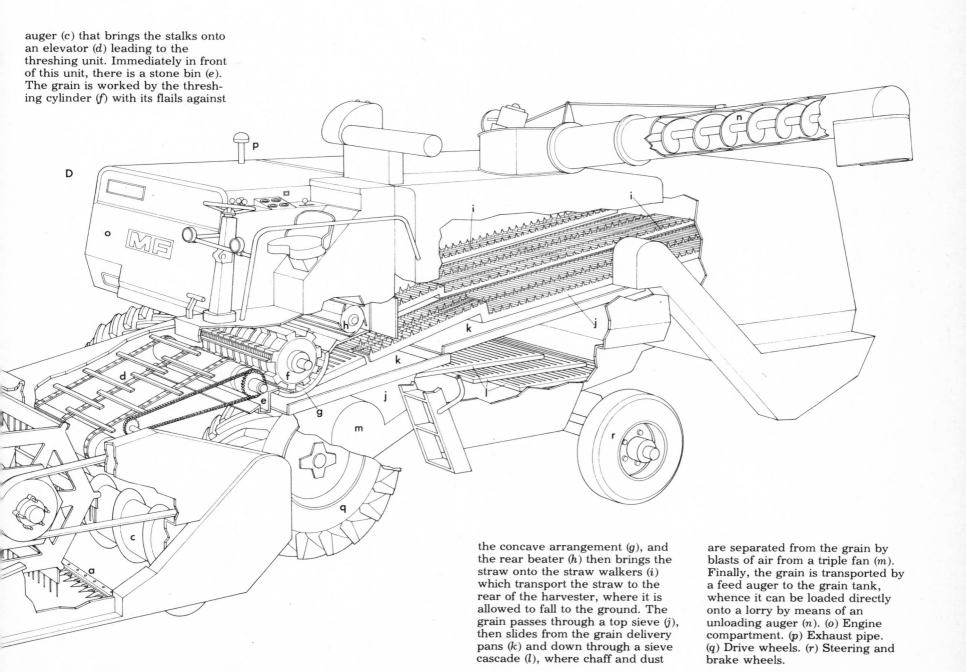

the concave arrangement (g), and the rear beater (h) then brings the straw onto the straw walkers (i) which transport the straw to the rear of the harvester, where it is allowed to fall to the ground. The grain passes through a top sieve (j), then slides from the grain delivery pans (k) and down through a sieve cascade (l), where chaff and dust

are separated from the grain by blasts of air from a triple fan (m). Finally, the grain is transported by a feed auger to the grain tank, whence it can be loaded directly onto a lorry by means of an unloading auger (n). (o) Engine compartment. (p) Exhaust pipe. (q) Drive wheels. (r) Steering and brake wheels.

introduced in 1875. These developing stages of the harvester, the distributor, and the automatic binder, however, did not achieve very widespread use in Europe until after the First World War.

But what about the combine harvester? The first tentative attempts to design such a device were made in the United States only about ten years after McCormick invented his harvester, but the first machines for combined harvesting and threshing appeared in California in the 1870s. These were veritable technical monsters, drawn by eighteen pairs of horses and operated by a team of five men. These extraordinary combines were gradually improved, and by the 1920s, they had developed into automatic machines which could be operated by one or two men. In Europe, the combine first began to gain ground after the Second World War, but it was not in common use until the 1960s.

The last stage of the long process of obtaining our daily bread is

A A copperplate engraving from an edition of Frontinus's work on the aqueducts of Rome, published in Padua in 1722. The illustration shows the cross-section of an aqueduct with two conduits, and of another with three.
B In the English town of Canterbury, a vast system of water-works and sewers was built in the area around the cathedral in the twelfth century. The water came from a source some 1,300 yds (1,200 m) from the cathedral and passed through several settling-tanks before flowing, in leaden pipes, through the north town wall (a) and into the cathedral area. (b) Reservoirs. Part of the water entering the fish-pond (c) was used to flush the latrines in the grandly dimensioned *necessarium* (d), which had been erected for the employees

in this ecclesiastical centre. The sewer system also drained rainwater from the area. It emptied into the town ditch. The illustration is based on a contemporary drawing, from probably just after the completion of the system in 1153.

today executed in highly automated bakeries which are becoming more and more like chemical process industries, even to the extent of being computer controlled. Still, many people find pleasure and satisfaction in baking their own bread. And this becomes much easier, if they have labour-saving domestic appliances for kneading and thermostat-controlled electric ovens for baking.

Bread production is only one of many examples of the rôle of machines in modern society or—if you will—in the rationalization and automation of agriculture. A hundred years ago, about four-fifths of the population in most of the now industrial countries were employed in agriculture, which was then quite rightly called a "principal occupation", while only one-fifth lived in towns, being employed in trade, administration, and industry. Today, the ratio is the reverse, but the production per capita of those working in agriculture is considerably higher than a hundred years ago.

Another example of the rôle machines play in our daily life is in the production of butter and cheese, which like that of bread, has always played a key rôle in the agricultural household and has its origins in the earliest farming cultures. For thousands of years, butter was made by briskly beating cream in a container until the globules of fat in the cream stuck together to produce lumps which were then kneaded by hand into a mass of butter. The very large quantities of cream required for butter production were obtained by skimming milk which had been left to stand for a day or so in shallow troughs. On larger farms, a lot of people were needed merely to do this, and it was a task which required both routine and skill. Even when the first agricultural machines were introduced, followed by a wave of enthusiasm for the rationalization of agriculture, it was considered impossible to mechanize the skimming of milk. It has been mentioned briefly in Chapter Five that Gustaf de Laval managed to solve this problem. At the time, de Laval was working at the Kloster Iron Foundry Works in Sweden, one of the few small iron works to survive the rationalization which, during some ten years, had reduced the number of iron works from about seven hundred to barely three hundred. The Kloster iron works had managed to survive this painful period by merging with several other small works, each of which had considerable farming and forest lands. The forests supplied the raw materials for the charcoal used in the blast furnaces. After the merger, things went well for the iron works, but the question arose as to how the farms with their great labour forces could be rationalized. The enterprising owner of the works, J. F. Lagergren, presented Gustaf de Laval with this problem, and they decided to see if anything could be done about the skimming of milk, since some new ideas pertaining to this had been circulated recently in the trade journals.

After a long period of extensive experimentation, de Laval had his continuous-process cream separator ready. It exploited centrifugal force to separate the lighter cream from the heavier skimmed milk. In 1878, he took out a patent for the separator, and large-scale manufacture began in the early 1880s. The demand was immediately considerable, not only in Sweden, but also internationally. With the invention of the separator, yet another task of the country household had been taken over by a machine.

For more than fifty years, the separator was indispensable on both large and small farms all over the world. Even after the production of butter and cheese had been taken over by central dairies in the 1920s and 1930s, many farms kept a manual or electric separator for domestic use.

The Invisible Product

The vitally necessary machines which have just been described give highly tangible products. However, like all other industrialized processes in our society, they also produce something else. This product is invisible, or rather, immaterial, although it is indeed noticeable to everyone today: increased leisure time.

Most of us would reject indignantly the statement that we all have slaves who labour and drudge for us. Still, it is true. We have already come across quite a few of these "slaves"—in the shape of machines which, today, do a lot of the work that was really hard labour some generations ago. Most of these machines are electrically powered. In Sweden, each person consumes about 3 kW of electric power daily. A human slave develops a maximum of 100 W, if he works continuously. In other words, each one of us has at his disposal thirty "slaves" working round the clock, performing a number of different tasks. Most of them work, however, behind the scenes. We do not meet them eye to eye, but they are there. For example, when we turn a water tap, several "slaves" are responsible for the cleanliness of the water. Others take care of the waste water.

It might be appropriate to take a brief look at the development of the different techniques for supplying cities with water. The most famous installations of this kind are the Roman aqueducts. During the fourth century BC, Rome developed into a large, unhygienic city; infant mortality was high, and the average life expectancy was only a little over twenty. The eminent statesman Appius Claudius Caecus realized that, first of all, the problem of improving living conditions in Rome had to be solved through an assured supply of food and water; what we would today call the infrastructure. First of all, he caused a road to be built, running south through the agricultural districts to Capua near Naples. This—the *Via Appia*—was finished in 312 BC, and agricultural goods began to flow into the still growing city. A few years later, work was begun on the first large aqueduct, the *Aqua Appia*, which was finished in 305 BC. It was over 10 miles (c. 17 km) long and ran to a large extent underground. The growth of the admirable technology developed by the Romans for building aqueducts dates from this time. The *Aqua Appia* supplied central Rome with water, but as the city kept growing, it became necessary to build another aqueduct some decades later. This was called the *Anio Vetus*, was 41 miles (66 km) long, and diverted water from the river Anio. It was finished about 265 BC, and since its capacity greatly exceeded that of the *Aqua Appia*, the supply of water to the city was assured for the next hundred years. The next aqueduct, the *Aqua Marcia*, was built about 145 BC and was no less than 57 miles (91.7 km) long.

In ancient Rome, arrangements were also made to dispose of sewage. As early as the sixth century BC, work was begun on the large sewer, the *Cloaca Maxima*; it is in part still in use. It had initially been built to drain the marshes where the Forum was later built. The *Cloaca Maxima* was extended bit by bit and given a superstructure of solid stone vaults.

From the beginning of the Christian era, the water supply of the Eternal City was supervised by a water department under the direction of the *curator aquarum*. One holder of this office was an eminent engineer called Sextus Julius Frontinus (30?–104) who devoted much energy to improving and extending the whole system of aqueducts. He summarized his experience in a thick volume, *De aquis urbis Romae*, ("On the Waters of the City of Rome"), completed in 97. This work set the standards for water supply in other cities throughout the Roman Empire. Magnificent ruins of Roman aqueducts are still in existence, for example in Segovia and Tarragona in Spain, and near Nîmes in France. Frontinus's work, however, eventually fell into oblivion but was rediscovered in the eighteenth century, when several annotated editions were published. As late as 1858, a German translation of the book appeared.

The Roman Empire and Roman technology deteriorated together,

and in several places the Church took over responsibility for the water supply and for maintaining the aqueducts. The task was more than it could handle, and after a few hundred years, the aqueducts could no longer serve their purpose. By that time, however, a guild of specialists in water supply had been created under the protection of the Church, and when the monastic orders began to spread over Europe, they took their technique with them. There are many examples of monasteries which had extensive installations for the supply of water. The pipe lines from the source of supply were usually made from hollowed-out logs, connected with cast-iron collars. Indoors, pipes of lead or bronze were used. In ancient Rome, incidentally, all pipes for the detailed distribution of water were of lead (there were about twenty different standard dimensions). But lead is a poisonous metal, and it is to be feared that a common cause of death in Rome was lead poisoning.

C

C Part of the Croton aqueduct.
D The shock siphon for raising water was invented in the eighteenth century. It was mounted so that it was situated a couple of yards below the surface of the water about to be raised. When the shock valve (*a*) was open, water flowed in through the pipe (*b*) and ran out at *a* until its speed had increased enough for *a* to be lifted by it. Then the water's rapid progress suddenly came to a halt. Because of the ensuing pressure increase, the valves (*c*) of a partly air-filled dome (*d*) were opened, and water was forced through them. The air pressure in *d* then increased, the valves (*c*) were closed once more, and water was forced up through an ascending pipe (*e*). When the rapid flow of water was abruptly stopped, its direction was reversed, and a negative pressure occurred in *b*. A valve (*f*) then opened, and a little air entered. Valve *a*, too, was opened by the pressure decrease, and water could again enter *b*, when *f* was closed.

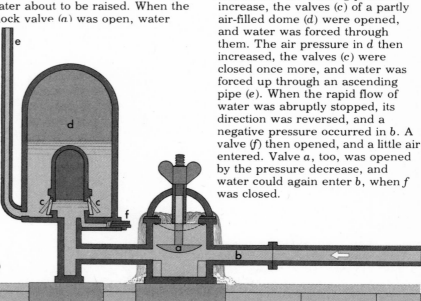

The monastic methods for providing a water supply were applied in various European cities in the Middle Ages, but the system was difficult to maintain: the wooden pipes rotted easily, and systems often fell into decay. The inhabitants of the cities had then to return to getting their household water from public or private wells.

Whatever arrangements were made for water supply in mediaeval cities, drainage was not too well provided for. The streets were flanked by ditches, only rarely dressed with stone, and people threw rubbish of all sorts into them. It is easy to imagine the situation. Hygienic conditions were appalling, and the population was afflicted with disease and epidemics. The ravages of the Black Death in the 1340s opened the eyes of the surviving administrators in many cities to the sanitary situation. The prosperous trading towns of Flanders were, relatively speaking, spared from the plague, because, in the early fourteenth century, rigorous laws had been introduced prohibiting any kind of contamination of streets and water courses. This legislation set the pattern for an Urban Sanitary Act which came into force in England in 1388 and which prohibited contamination of ditches and water courses under pain of severe penalty.

During the technical revolution of the fifteenth and sixteenth centuries, piston pumps came into use for the draining of mines. This pump technology (hydraulics) developed mainly in southern Germany, whence came the use of pumps to provide cities with water. The water pump is, in fact, the first machine we have come across so far in this short review of water and drainage technology. The Roman aqueducts did not need pumps—gravity did the work.

In the eighteenth century, the development of hydraulics and the rediscovery of Frontinus's work on the Roman aqueducts led to renewed attempts to supply cities with water, steam being used at an early stage to power the pumps. As a rule, however, hollowed-out logs were used for pipes, for at this time, metal pipes were made manually and, anyway, could withstand only very limited pressure. These limitations greatly hampered early attempts to pump water by steam and held back water supply technology in general.

In the nineteenth century, the water systems of most large cities were expanded; new techniques and methods were gradually introduced, steam power came into increasing use, cast-iron and steel pipes came onto the market, and purification plants began to be built. An example of this development is the extension of New York's water-supply system. During the eighteenth century, when New York was becoming more important as a city, its inhabitants had to get water, which was often foul, from public wells, although one of them, the "Tea Water Pump", was famous for its fine, clear water. It was situated on today's Park Row, and water from there was distributed in horse-drawn tank wagons to households, where it was almost a luxury item.

In 1799, the private Manhattan Company was founded, and it built a waterworks system with pipes of hollowed-out logs, establishing wells and reservoirs so that, after some ten years, two thousand households in New York were thus supplied with water. Two 18-horsepower steam-engines were installed to pump water up to reservoirs. In 1800, New York had a population of about sixty thousand, and the city was growing rapidly.

The city authorities of the time realized that they, too, had to contribute, and in 1829, they started to build a waterworks system which was supplied with water from a reservoir of over 175,000 gallons (180,000 US gallons or 800,000 l) situated near Union Square, which was then considered far uptown of lower Manhattan. The main pipes were now of cast iron and had a diameter of 12 in (30 cm), and the water was pumped up from a nearby well to the reservoir by a 12-horsepower steam-engine.

By 1832, the population had increased to two hundred thousand,

and only a few years later, the city fathers realized that they had to look for new sources to ensure an adequate water supply. Their choice fell upon the Croton River, a tributary of the Hudson, which is 42 miles (about 70 km) from New York; a dam was built on the Croton, and from it ran an aqueduct, in places as architecturally resplendent as its Roman predecessors. It took five years to build the aqueduct, which was completed in 1842, and there was a stately inaugural ceremony, also based on the ancient Roman model. During the following decades, new and larger dams were built to increase the supply of water to the Croton aqueduct. The population in New York, however, was soon two million, and by the 1880s, it had become necessary to build yet another Croton aqueduct. This was completed in 1893 after eight years' work and was a mountain tunnel, cut with pneumatic drills and dynamite, and lit by electricity.

By the turn of the century, it once more became obvious that even greater water resources were required, for the population had risen to 3.5 million. Discussion began of a very bold project to supply New York with water from the rivers and lakes of the Catskill Mountains, which lie about 90 miles (150 km) from the city. While many engineers considered this wholly unrealistic, construction work nevertheless began in 1907, after careful planning. Up to seventeen thousand workers were employed on this project, which featured several new construction methods. The aqueduct was taken into service in 1917, and since then the Catskill system has been extended in several stages. Today, New York has aqueducts and water tunnels which in length and capacity greatly surpass their ancient Roman prototypes.

Waterworks in large modern cities are huge plants with technically sophisticated equipment for filtering the water, and treating and controlling it in other ways. In the past few decades, these plants have become more and more like large-scale chemical-process industries. They have been automated to a large extent and, in many cases, are controlled by process computers.

Waste Disposal over the Centuries

We have today a comprehensive technology for the disposal of all the waste our society produces. However, it is instructive to consider how *Homo sapiens* has rid himself of his rubbish throughout the ages, for the modern ecological debate seems often to doubt whether man is rational in this respect.

On excavation, neolithic refuse heaps, or what are called kitchen middens, have yielded much interesting information about, for example, the food that was then eaten. The people of the Stone Age gathered their refuse in one place, not to please archaeologists, but to keep their living quarters tidy, an instinct that, in the early towns, became a necessity. The oldest town-building cultures disposed of their refuse in ways which indicate as highly developed a technology as that required to build *quanaats*, for instance. In the towns of Harappa and Mohenjo-Daro, which came into being during the early culture of the Indus valley in the fourth millennium BC, houses were usually three storeys high and were equipped with chutes, flushed with water supplied through pipes leading from the kitchen and the lavatory. The chutes were used for the immediate disposal of solid and liquid refuse and ran out into an underground tunnel where the refuse was collected in a container, one for each chute. These containers were then transported on ox carts to a place where the refuse was regularly burnt. Most of the transport routes were underground. The first excavation in this part of the Indus valley took place in the 1920s under the supervision of the eminent British archeologist Sir R. E. Mortimer Wheeler, whose work revealed, among other things, this technically very sophisticated refuse-disposal method. Since the mid-1970s, an American research team has been engaged in further excavations that, it is hoped, can answer the question of how the refuse was burnt. It is probable that they used furnaces designed to achieve temperatures high enough to reduce to ashes even the most moist form of refuse. Experience may have taught the engineers of the Indus culture that the temperature is considerably increased if the smoke is allowed to preheat the combustion air, a principle applied in modern reverberatory furnaces.

The technique of refuse combustion spread from the Indus valley via the Sumerian culture of Mesopotamia to the Mediterranean, where it was obviously commonly known and applied during the last millennium BC. We have evidence of this in the biblical simile about the burning Gehenna, which was nothing more than the refuse-disposal unit of Jerusalem. It was equipped with a "reverberatory furnace", in which everything was burnt to ashes at a consuming temperature. If that technique had not been commonly known in this cultural sphere, the Gehenna simile would have been meaningless.

The total combustion of refuse was an important technical advance that, together with many other factors, permitted the formation and continued existence of the early town cultures. When these cultures declined, this form of disposal fell into oblivion. Not until our own century has refuse again been incinerated on a large scale, now in technologically efficients units, in many of which metal can be extracted from the refuse before it is burnt.

Only in the more prosperous parts of medieval Europe were efforts made to solve the problems of refuse disposal. During the Renaissance, sewers were built on the Roman model in the larger cities, and by the middle of the seventeenth century, the system in Paris had grown to comprise over 10 miles (16 km) of sewers. The population of the city was then about 500,000, and it expanded very slowly; about 1800, the population was around 550,000 and the length of the sewers was slightly more than 12 miles (20 km). During the following decades, however, Paris expanded rapidly, and by the early 1830s, the population was nearly 800,000. Neither the water supply nor the sewage system could cope with such a large population, and the city authorities were forced to draw up plans for a large-scale expansion of the system in anticipation of an even more rapid increase of population. Work began in 1833, and several of the most eminent French engineers were employed. The result would show the way for future sewer development. When the project began, Paris had about 24 miles (40 km) of sewers. By 1850, the population exceeded one million, and in the early 1860s, it had increased to 1.7 million. By then, however, the sewage system comprised over 215 miles (350 km) of pipelines and was arranged along radically different principles, being built to cope with the needs of a future population of 2.5 million. In 1951, when Paris celebrated its 2,000th anniversary as a city, its inhabitants numbered 2.8 million.

It was not until the twelfth century that London took on the character of a political capital. In the following centuries, it grew into a typical mediaeval town. To begin with, the river Fleet provided a natural outlet, a "Cloaca Maxima", but it became totally silted up in the fourteenth century and was no longer navigable. A drainage system was then gradually built, with the Fleet as the "main pipe". Mediaeval conditions obtained in London until the Great Fire of 1666, when the whole town centre was reduced to ashes and ruins. This devastating catastrophe, however, had one positive effect: the city fathers were entirely free to create a new town plan. When the enormous projects following the fire were being realized, several of London's famous monumental edifices were erected, and the city acquired a completely new and modern look. An organization was set up to dispose of household refuse, which was gathered up in laystalls on the street corners and then transported away. Legislation enjoined house owners to keep clean the street in front of their houses, a law that was also applied in many other places.

A cross-section of a street in Paris at the end of the nineteenth century. Directly beneath the paving is the sewage-disposal system with its tunnels and waste pipes. The catacombs are situated considerably further down.

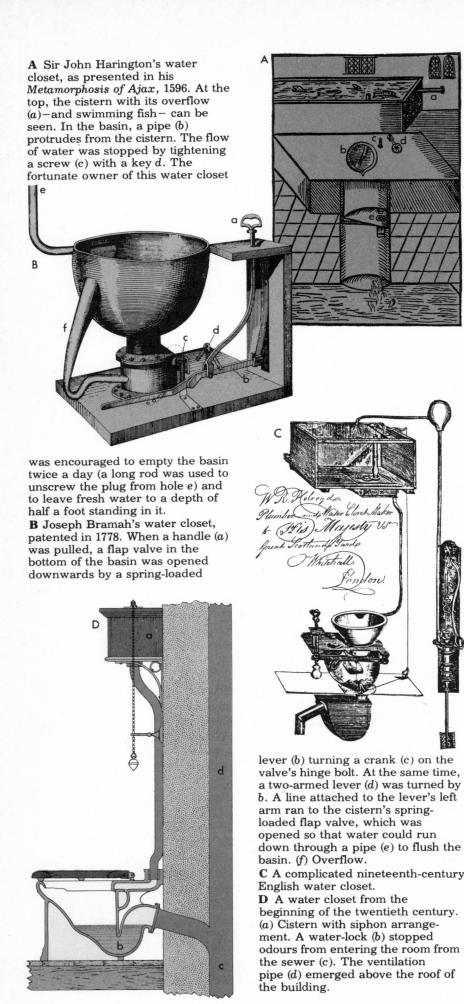

A Sir John Harington's water closet, as presented in his *Metamorphosis of Ajax*, 1596. At the top, the cistern with its overflow (*a*)—and swimming fish— can be seen. In the basin, a pipe (*b*) protrudes from the cistern. The flow of water was stopped by tightening a screw (*c*) with a key *d*. The fortunate owner of this water closet was encouraged to empty the basin twice a day (a long rod was used to unscrew the plug from hole *e*) and to leave fresh water to a depth of half a foot standing in it.

B Joseph Bramah's water closet, patented in 1778. When a handle (*a*) was pulled, a flap valve in the bottom of the basin was opened downwards by a spring-loaded lever (*b*) turning a crank (*c*) on the valve's hinge bolt. At the same time, a two-armed lever (*d*) was turned by *b*. A line attached to the lever's left arm ran to the cistern's spring-loaded flap valve, which was opened so that water could run down through a pipe (*e*) to flush the basin. (*f*) Overflow.

C A complicated nineteenth-century English water closet.

D A water closet from the beginning of the twentieth century. (*a*) Cistern with siphon arrangement. A water-lock (*b*) stopped odours from entering the room from the sewer (*c*). The ventilation pipe (*d*) emerged above the roof of the building.

For centuries, the river Fleet remained the main drain of much of the London sewage system. It had, finally, to be built over, for it stank, and flowed through the most densely populated areas. In the 1830s and 1840s, the riverbed was made into a revetted sewer on top of which a road was built.

This London version of the *Cloaca Maxima*, however, was by no means even an adequate method of disposing all the waste, and the excess—in a mediaeval fashion that persisted into the seventeenth and eighteenth centuries—was thrown into the ditches along the streets or, at best, into the gutters. The turning point for London was the "rediscovery" of the water-closet, a primitive version of which had been designed as early as 1596 by Sir John Harington, although it was not until the end of the eighteenth century that, as the water-supply system was extended, improved versions were actually installed. However, the water-closets could not be connected to the sewage system; instead, each house had a cesspool. The idea was to empty the pools regularly, but this rarely happened, and overflows with the most devastating consequences were quite common. Moreover, the early water-closets had no water seal, which meant that an abominable stench would fill the whole house. In 1782, the water seal was invented by John Gaillait, but not until the first decades of the nineteenth century did it come into common use.

The population in London, and the number of water-closets, increased sharply during the first half of the nineteenth century. The closets were now connected to the sewage system, which became, consequently, greatly overloaded. A number of water courses like the Fleet had been rebuilt into sewage systems, and as they all flowed into the Thames, the river became seriously contaminated. Most of London's supposedly fresh water was taken from the Thames, and the inevitable consequence was serious cholera epidemics, mainly in 1849 and 1853, when almost twenty thousand people died. This prompted the formation of a commission to plan the restructure of the whole drainage system, extending it sufficiently to dispose of the sewage of three to four million inhabitants. Under the guidance of Sir Joseph William Bazalgette (1819–91), a gigantic project was planned and, in 1856, presented. It was to take almost twenty years to complete. The main idea was to build intercepting sewers parallel to the Thames and to let them gather up the contents of the numerous sewers, which up to then had run out into the river. The sewage was then to be conducted to a place about 12 miles (20 km) downstream from London Bridge before being let out there into the Thames.

Work on this project commenced towards the end of the 1850s. The intercepting sewers were built as tunnels whose cross-sections in many cases were larger than the tunnels of the later underground railway. Over 90 miles (150 km) of tunnels were built, and by 1875, Bazalgette's magnificent project was finished. The sewage flowed by gravity through most of the tunnels, but in a couple of places it was necessary to pump, and the machines required to take care of the huge amounts of sewage were gigantic. Each pump station was equipped with eight 140-horsepower steam-engines, each driving two double-acting piston pumps, with cylinders of a diameter of 43.5 in (115 cm). The first of four such pump stations was completed in 1865 and was then described by a London magazine as "perhaps the finest specimen of engineering work in the country".

Towards the end of the nineteenth century, people realized that sewage had to be purified before being released into lakes and rivers. At a very early stage, attempts were made to precipitate the contamination chemically with such precipitants as lime, alum, compounds of iron and aluminium, and iron sulphate. Chemical precipitation is what we today call the "third stage" of sewage treatment. It means that one retrieves the nutritive salts which would otherwise fertilize a choking vegetation in the watercourse into which the purified water is let out. Above all, it is the modern synthetic detergents which are responsible for the high content of nutritive salts in sewage, and in the 1880s, that problem did not exist.

The basis of modern sewage technology must be considered to have been laid in 1895, when the Englishman Cameron took out a patent for the sedimentation, or septic, tank in which the sewage is collected and the organic substances break down as they decompose, a relatively slow process. The sludge has to be removed about once a year—the interval depends on the relative size of the tank. The septic tank soon became very popular and was manufactured in all sizes, from those large enough for a family house to installations adequate for large cities. Over the years, several different versions of Cameron's original design have been invented, but the principle is unchanged in the septic tanks manufactured today.

The disadvantage of the septic tank is that it must be emptied at regular intervals. In the United States, however, a similar but continuous method was tried out in the 1910s, the idea being to lead the sewage relatively slowly through a long, narrow pool, at the bottom of which the sludge gathered. Then the sludge was "activated" by air blown into the pool, thus causing the micro-organisms in the sludge to reproduce themselves rapidly under the stimulation of the increased oxygen supply. They fed on the organic substances in the sewage. The activated sludge was then taken back upstream and mixed with the incoming sewage which, surprisingly soon, became decontaminated. A full-scale plant for the treatment of sewage by the activated-sludge process was built in Milwaukee, Wisconsin, in 1915.

Thereafter, the process was developed mainly in Great Britain, where, since the last decades of the nineteenth century, methods of biological treatment had been tried out under the guidance of the energetic Sir Edward Frankland, who would today be called an ecologist. "Biological beds" of coke or cinders were used to filter the sewage, but the oxygen supply in them was insufficient, however, for the growth of micro-organisms, a problem that was solved by blowing in large quantities of air. From the 1920s onwards, the activated-sludge process became the most important method of sewage treatment, and it has since been improved, mainly in recent times, due to the stimulus derived from the increasing general awareness of the importance of the environment.

The Environment and Technology

The main purpose of the "reverberatory furnace" in Gehenna, of the *Cloaca Maxima*, and of the other installations described here, has been to remove refuse from man's immediate environment. It is true that, in many cases, the more distant environment has suffered because of this. It is easy to imagine the ancient refuse-disposal units, like Gehenna, spreading clouds of belching, stinking smoke. Towards the middle of the last century, however, as refuse disposal became sanitation technology, its goal was the protection of the immediate environment, one example being Sir Joseph Bazalgette's ambitious project to divert London sewage into that part of the Thames that did not flow through the city itself. At the outflow of the intercepting sewers, however, about 12 miles (20 km) downstream from London Bridge, the effect of a rising tide was to prevent the dispersal of the outflowing sewage. Treatment plants were built here after a catastrophe in 1878, when an excursion boat capsized and sank in front of a sewer outlet. Over six hundred people died, and it was found that most of them were not drowned but poisoned.

The treatment plants were enlarged successively during the twentieth century, but many of them were destroyed by bombing during the Second World War. The situation again became precarious, and by the early 1950s, precise continuous analysis of the water in the Thames was begun to determine the measures that should be taken against contamination. It was immediately established that the Thames was a dead river, devoid of fish and all other living creatures. A plan for the total decontamination of the Thames was presented in 1961, an admirable plan with the direct purpose of protecting the environment by technical means.

The cleaning of the Thames took sixteen years and entailed, among other things, the building of several large treatment plants, of which the two largest, at Beckton and Crossness, now take care of sixty per cent of London's sewage and are considered the most sophisticated and automated in Europe. At strategic points along the river, air pumps have been installed to aerate the water, thus helping to increase the chances of survival for living organisms. The whole project cost about £125 million ($250 million) and was completed in 1977. The Thames now supports a rich variety of life and is a fine example of how technology can remedy even the worst environmental problems.

What Can Be Done About Air Pollution?

It is unlikely that anything was done about the belching smoke from Gehenna, but measures to combat air pollution were taken surprisingly early in history. In the thirteenth century, coal was first used for heating in England, but it was bituminous—really more like bitumen than coal—and was gathered on the shores of eastern England, whence it was transported by sea to London. When this sea-coal burnt, it gave off an acrid, thick smoke, especially in rainy and foggy weather, and the contaminated air became difficult to breathe. A decree of 1306 prohibited the use of such coal in London—but only when parliament was in session! The decree was not respected, and capital punishment was introduced for the offence, the first offender being hanged in 1308. It is interesting to note that similar events took place at about the same time in Mexico, where bituminous coal was also used as fuel, and a ban on it was declared and backed up by capital punishment. However, the Mexican authorities were more refined than the British. Their offenders were locked up in a cage—and smoked to death.

In England, and especially in London, frequent measures were taken against air pollution in the fifteenth and sixteenth centuries. In 1661, that chronicler of many talents, John Evelyn (1620–1706), published a thundering polemical pamphlet against the bad air of the capital. It had the title *Fumifugium*, which can be freely translated as, "Get Rid of the Smoke". The measures Evelyn suggested included the planting of trees along all of London's streets. The trees should be "fragrant", although he did not say how he thought that could be arranged. The pamphlet was printed in several editions, one of which was widely read in the last years of the eighteenth century, when the steam-engine was coming into common use, and when many people realized that this was a new source of air pollution. During the first decades of the nineteenth century, when steam had gained considerable ground, the problem became apparent. The growing industrial cities became more and more polluted, and in 1819, parliament felt obliged to appoint a commission to investigate both the damaging effect coal smoke could have on health and the technical means that could be used to reduce or prevent the discharge of smoke. High chimneys and soot traps were suggested, but no legislation was passed on this occasion. When the railway began to spread in Great Britain, however, new commissions were appointed, and these pushed through laws about the control of the discharge of smoke from both locomotives and industry.

When the great breakthrough of industrialism in the United States came in the 1850s, laws were introduced in several states regulating, among other things, the lowest acceptable height of factory smokestacks. In 1864, the first offender against these laws, a factory owner in St. Louis, Missouri, was convicted. In general, a lively and remarkably "modern" ecological debate was carried on in the United States in the latter part of the 1860s. Immigration was on the increase, and many engineers and politicians realized that, even in that vast country, densely populated areas would become established in due course.

By the 1970s, the whole of the industrialized world had become sharply aware of the necessity of protecting the environment against the consequences of industrialization. An entirely new technology began to develop to reduce the pollution of air and water from, for example, the steel and pulp industries. Forced on by increasingly stringent legislation, research and development work in this area managed to find technical solutions to problems which had long been regarded as insoluble. Today, a steelworks can be incomparably cleaner than it was only ten years ago, for the discharge of smoke can be reduced to a fraction of its earlier volume.

From the point of view of the environment, the pulp industry is traditionally the arch-villain. The pulp production process requires large volumes of water which are then badly polluted, and the smoke discharged is both harmful and stinking. At an early stage, the Swedish forestry industry became involved in a large joint research project, the result of legislation—and managed to achieve purification methods which are now being applied in pulp factories in many parts of the world.

But What About the Car?

In most countries, the 1970s have been a turning-point as regards the control of industrial pollution, but much still remains to be done. Ecological technology is advancing rapidly, and the public has been made aware of the values which are at stake. But although the engineers have managed to reduce industrial effluent considerably, there remains one bad source of pollution: the sharply increasing number of cars. The exhaust fumes from cars contain carbon monoxide and poisonous lead compounds. The rubber worn off the tyres of cars is washed away by rain water into natural water-courses and eventually ends up in the water table.

The situation has changed markedly since the first cars appeared in city streets around the turn of the century. "Horseless carriages" were then greeted as liberators from an almost chaotic situation. In New York, for example, the horse-drawn traffic was very lively, and the accident rate was high, due to the human (and also the animal!) factor. Moreover, working horses contributed to the contamination of the streets with large amounts of waste—over 1,000 tons of solid and 60,000 gallons (c. 200 cubic metres) of liquid waste every day! An army of tens of thousands of refuse collectors with horse-drawn carriages was needed to dispose of all this.

The car gave no waste at all, wasn't it wonderful? The little puffs from the exhaust were surely nothing to worry about? Anyway, there were so few cars.

But we know what has happened since. In many cities today, the exhaust fumes from cars are a real plague. There are three ways of reducing the harmful constituents of the exhaust fumes: the level of lead can be reduced, the engine can be equipped with an exhaust emission device, or the petrol engine can be abandoned completely. Some success has been achieved with the first two methods, and in many places, intensive research is going on into entirely new principles of propulsion, both regarding engines and fuels. It is not totally impossible that the steam car may return, perhaps propelled by hydrogen. A wonderful vision—a car running practically without noise, and with exhaust fumes consisting of pure steam!

There is, of course, a fourth way to reduce the damaging effects of motoring on the environment, and that is to use *bicycles* to a larger extent. In this book we have met many impressive examples of engineering prowess, but the question is whether the bicycle is not the most perfect of all machines, from both the human and the technical point of view. It is also healthy, both for the environment and for the person using it. This wonderful machine has had a great impact on both industrial and cultural development. For this reason, we shall give the bicycle its own section.

The Bicycle—a Technical Beauty

The wheel has existed for at least five thousand years, and it is really quite remarkable that it took so long for someone to think of combining two wheels to make a steerable vehicle. The eminent Roman engineers, for example, had the technical ability to design a bicycle. And the inventive Italian and French engineers of the Renaissance built monstrous versions of four-wheel carriages but never designed a handy two-wheeler! From this point of view alone, the invention of the bicycle must be considered. extremely important. This occurred about 1816, when a German superintendent of forests, Freiherr Karl Friedrich Drais von Sauerbronn (1785—1851) designed his famous "running machine", a steerable bicycle propelled by kicking. The inventive forester became known all over Baden for his wild trips on

A Horse-drawn street-sweepers of this type were used in London and other places during the second half of the nineteenth century. The garbage container was secured with heavy chains (a), and the endless belt with its brushes (b) was driven by the wheel shaft by way of a gear transmission (c). By means of a worm gear (d) to which a chain (e) was attached, the driver could adjust the brush unit's angle to the ground. The gearwheel in d meshed with another gearwheel (f) on a shaft, from which a chain with a counterweight (g) hung over a wheel (h). The brushes brought the garbage up a chute (i) and into the container.
B A horse-drawn street-sprinkler from the end of the nineteenth century; (**1**) side view, (**2**) rear view.

Chains (a) ran from two levers (b) at the driver's seat over two blocks (c) each and down to a valve inside the water tank (d). When the driver lowered the levers, the valve was opened, and water could run out through the rear strainer plate.

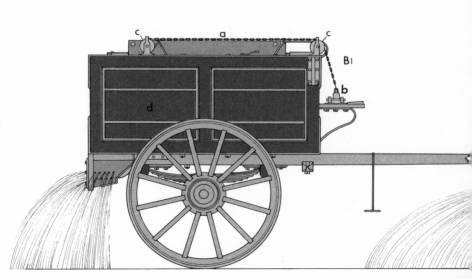

the running machine, and he is said to have covered the distance between Mannheim and Schwetzingen in only one hour in 1817. It took the mail coach four hours to travel the same distance! It seems that the originator of the steerable bicycle must have had the stamina of a star athlete. Drais was complacently satisfied with his invention, taking out a patent for it in 1818. He would have nothing to do with the various improvements made in the following decades, for instance, the addition of pedals to the front wheel.

However, the first bicycle in the true sense of the word was made in France. Pierre Michaux (1813−83) and his son Ernest (1849−89) built a *vélocipède* for the 1867 world exhibition in Paris. It was modern in appearance. The wooden wheels were iron shod, and it was propelled by pedals which directly drove the front wheel.

In spite of being nicknamed "bone-shaker"−due to the iron-shod wooden wheels−this velocipede soon became popular, and, to meet the demand, the Michauxs were forced to find subcontractors. In 1869, an order for five hundred velocipedes went to a British sewing-machine manufacturer in Coventry, Josiah Turner, who thereupon re-formed his firm, naming it Coventry Machinists Co. But the Franco-Prussian war broke out just as the bicycles were ready for delivery, so Turner had to try to sell the vehicles on the home market. He was successful beyond expectation. The bicycle ap-

peared exactly at the right moment, just as a wave of enthusiasm for physical exercise was sweeping over England.

This was the beginning of an unusual development that resulted not only in the technical perfection of the bicycle, but also in a great boost to the progress of mechanical industry. Moreover, the bicycle literally paved the way for motoring, both from the technical point of view and because of the better roads demanded by cyclists.

In the 1870s, a new bicycle-manufacturing company was founded in Coventry by James Starley (1801−81), formerly a foreman at the Coventry Machinists Co. Together with his partners, William Hillman and B. Smith, Starley made a number of pioneering designs, beginning with the first penny-farthing, which had a large driving wheel with a diameter of 60 in (150 cm) and a smaller rear wheel with a diameter of 20 in (50 cm). The idea of this most extraordinary design had originally come from the Michauxs. The aim was to achieve higher efficiency. For each turn of the pedals, a large driving wheel will take you further than a small one.

It might be added that the penny-farthing, which has many bruised and broken limbs on its metallic conscience, was a mistake in the development of the bicycle. The penny-farthing is sometimes called the "ordinary" bicycle, which is a euphemism, since it is certainly far from ordinary. Still, in spite of its shortcomings, this design persisted for almost twenty years, and it, too, brought development further along, as the radially mounted spokes of the front wheel could not take the great strain, and to remedy this, Starley invented the tangentially spoked wheel, a design he patented in 1874 and still almost invariably applied to bicycle wheels.

The friction in the hubs and handlebars of the bicycles was high, but it could be lessened by the use of ball bearings. The ancient Romans used both ball- and roller-bearings, and the ball-bearing has been rediscovered several times in recent centuries, by, for example, the Englishmen Philip Vaughan (1794) and Louis Thirion (1862) and the Frenchman Jean Suriray (1869). From 1877 onwards, Thirion's bearing was used by Starley, in tricycles, but their price was disproportionately high compared to the price of the other parts. The balls were hand-ground, and this was a slow, laborious method. In 1883, the German Friedrich Fischer designed the first grinding machine for steel balls, and this made the mass production of ball-bearings possible. Friedrich Fischer was the son of Philipp Moritz Fischer, who was a manufacturer of sewing-machines and bicycles, both of which required large numbers of ball-bearings. The factory Friedrich Fischer founded in Schweinfurt for the manufacture of ball-bearings has grown today into a worldwide company.

In 1877, Starley's Coventry factory introduced frames made of steel tubes; this made it possible to produce a light, durable machine, well suited to its purpose. Since then, steel tube designs have found a very wide application in various areas of technology. For one thing, they were used in the first aeroplanes.

In 1879, power transmission by a gear and chain from the bicycle pedals to the rear wheel was introduced. This was a great step forward. The principle of the bicycle chain is included in Leonardo da Vinci's sketch books and had been rediscovered in France in the 1860s. In 1874, an improved version was patented by the Englishman Harry J. Lawson, and he began then to manufacture bicycles with such transmissions. However, the manufacturers found the chain to be a great headache. It may be a very simple construction, but it makes extremely high demands on manufacturing precision and on the durability of the material. Up to about 1900, broken chains were the most common fault with bicycles. The bicycle manufacturers' search for a remedy led them to cooperate with metallurgists in an attempt to produce new materials, new methods for hardening, and so on. They also had to develop machines for the mass production of

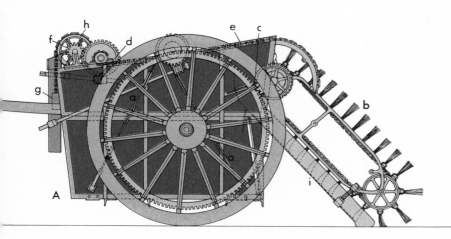

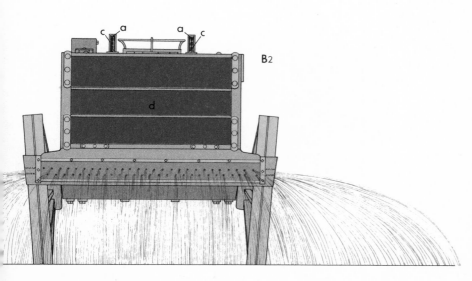

bicycle chains. By the time mass production of automobiles began, technology had reached a point where the "bicycle" chain could be used in the power transmission of the car, which made even higher demands on the chain than did the bicycle.

From this point of view, the bicycle was the forerunner of the car. Chain drive for cars was, it is true, abandoned after about ten years and replaced by shaft drive, but even today, some car engines have chain drive, for example, to drive the cam shaft from the crank shaft. The "bicycle" chain has become a very useful component in all areas of mechanical engineering and now comes in all dimensions.

The main milestone in the development of the bicycle is the appearance of the Rover Safety Bicycle, manufactured by James Starley's nephew John K. Starley (1854–1901) and introduced on the market in 1885. Both its wheels were the same size, and it had a tubular frame of steel, and pedals with chain drive. The name "sa-

fety bicycle" was, of course, a criticism aimed at the penny-farthing, which was now becoming outdated. The Rover bicycle was an enormous success, and cycling soon had great numbers of devotees in various parts of the world. One important detail, which—if possible—increased the popularity of the bicycle even further, was introduced in 1888. That was the pneumatic rubber tyre, invented by the Scottish veterinary surgeon John B. Dunlop (1840–1921). His son had complained because his fine children's bicycle was so shaky and difficult to ride on uneven surfaces. It occurred to Dunlop that the wheels could be equipped with air-filled inner tubes covered by rubber tyres. The production of tyres and inner tubes soon got under way and greatly contributed to a standardization of bicycle wheels. Also, cycling became more comfortable. Once the safety bicycle with rubber tyres appeared, the modern bicycle had found its form.

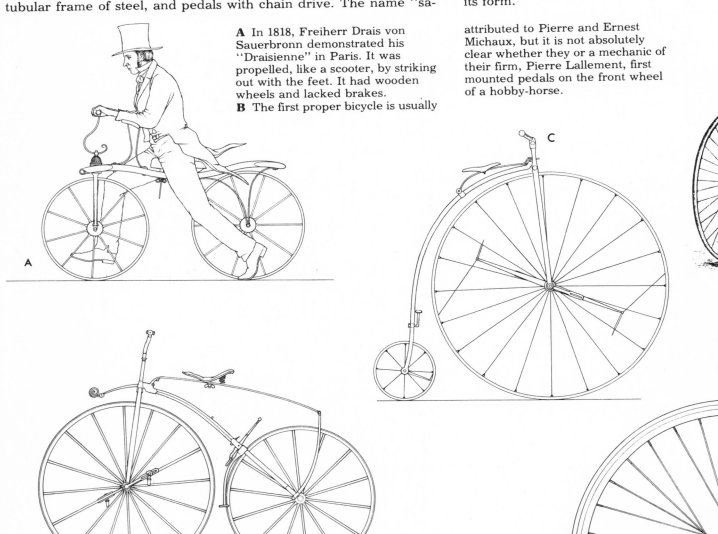

A In 1818, Freiherr Drais von Sauerbronn demonstrated his "Draisienne" in Paris. It was propelled, like a scooter, by striking out with the feet. It had wooden wheels and lacked brakes.
B The first proper bicycle is usually attributed to Pierre and Ernest Michaux, but it is not absolutely clear whether they or a mechanic of their firm, Pierre Lallement, first mounted pedals on the front wheel of a hobby-horse.

C Starley's and Hillman's Ariel bicycle of 1870 was manufactured under licence by Haynes and Jefferies at Coventry. On the front wheel hub was a cross-bar which was connected to the rim by two short, adjustable tie-rods. When the tie-rods were stretched, the rim was turned in relation to the hub, and the spokes were tightened.
D The British Facile bicycle of 1879 had a vertical pedal movement, and the pedals were mounted on levers to bring them closer to the ground.
E John Starley's Rover Safety Bicycle is considered to be the prototype of the modern bicycle. It had pedals with chain transmission, direct steering of the front wheel, an adjustable seat, and tangential spokes.

The bicycle as a machine was perfected in the 1890s, when some important details, such as the free wheel, the brake, and gears were introduced. In 1892, one of the first free wheels was patented by the Swedish inventor Birger Ljungström, who later used it in a bicycle design, the *Svea* velocipede, which he and his brother Fredrik had developed. The project was supported by the "dynamite king", Alfred Nobel. Instead of the normal rotary pedalling movement, the *Svea* bicycle had a vertical pedalling movement. The power was transmitted by a chain from each pedal to eccentric gear wheels on the free wheel of the rear hub. This device made it possible to change gears while the bicycle was moving. Also, the brake could be applied simply by pushing both pedals down at the same time.

In 1896, the *Svea* bicycle was introduced in England, where it gained many supporters, among them the well-known engineer and firearms designer Hiram S. Maxim. The New Cycle Company was

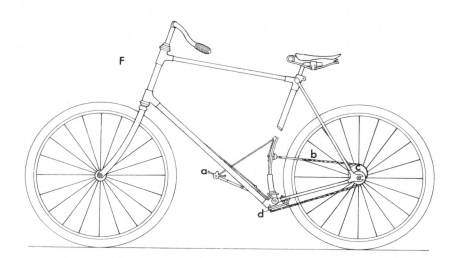

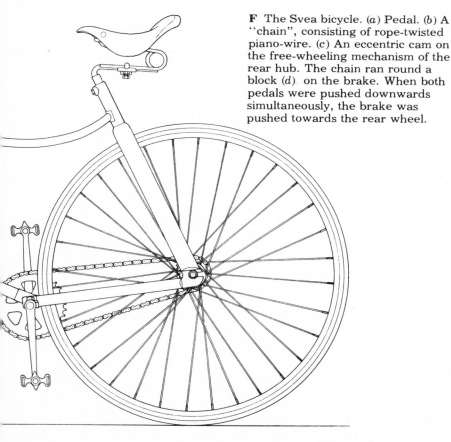

F The Svea bicycle. (*a*) Pedal. (*b*) A "chain", consisting of rope-twisted piano-wire. (*c*) An eccentric cam on the free-wheeling mechanism of the rear hub. The chain ran round a block (*d*) on the brake. When both pedals were pushed downwards simultaneously, the brake was pushed towards the rear wheel.

formed, and the bicycle was made in several different versions, including a bicycle rickshaw. However, in 1898, the English bicycle industry went through a recession, and the company was wound up. Only about a hundred bicycles were made, and these are now much sought-after collectors' pieces. In other words, the Ljungström hub was not the first free-wheel hub to be widely used. This honour instead befell one invented in 1898 by the German Ernst Sachs. He started to manufacture his "Torpedo" hub in Schweinfurt in 1900.

The attentive reader is sure to have noticed that the names of two well-established motor-cars have been mentioned above: Hillman and Rover. The bicycle manufacturer William Hillman went over in due course to manufacturing cars, and the great success Starley had with the Rover bicycle led to a change of the name of the company to The Rover Company. This company produced an electrically driven tricycle in 1889, motor bikes from 1902, and cars from 1904.

The list of bicycle manufacturers who have turned to the motor industry is very long. The many other British car manufacturers who started their careers building bicycles include William Morris and Henry Leyland. In the United States, the first car was built in 1892 by the bicycle manufacturers Charles E. and Frank Duryea. The first petrol-driven "cars" indicate the close relationship with the bicycle: Gottlieb Daimler attached an engine to a Michaux-type velocipede in 1885, and the same year, Karl Benz motorized a tricycle.

The Biggest Industry in the Country

If one speaks of the biggest industry in the country, most people visualize an enormous concern with rows of factories and office blocks. But this industry does not look like that – on the contrary, it is extremely decentralized – for, as regards both production volume and number of employees, domestic households form the biggest industry.

Yet for a long time, this enormous "industry" resisted the mechanization of production that has characterized the industrial unit. The tools and implements used in the home remained largely unchanged until the middle of the nineteenth century, and in many areas until even more recently. Kitchen equipment more than anything else had had the same appearance for generations – in many cases for hundreds or even thousands of years. This applies to the fireplace, for example, which had remained fundamentally unchanged since the early Stone Age. The primitive Stone Age houses probably had a fireplace in the middle, an open hearth bordered by a ring of stones. In the ceiling over the hearth was a hole for the smoke. In ancient Rome, houses were built according to the same principle. The room with the fireplace was placed in the centre of the house; the roof above the fireplace rose in the shape of a pyramid towards a hole through which the smoke escaped. These houses were called *atrium*-houses – atrium is derived from the latin word for "black", for the ceiling and walls of the room with the fireplace were probably covered in soot.

Roman technology and architecture spread all over the Empire, that is, southern Central Europe and England. The design of kitchens assumed many different shapes, as Roman construction technology mingled with local tradition and local culinary customs. In the early Middle Ages, the chimney was added, and the kitchen got the form it then retained almost up until this century.

In large kitchens, the fireplace with its chimney had several different functions. It was formed into a large dome at the point where it joined the chimney, and this became a bearing construction taking the weight of the roof. From the actual hearth, where the food was cooked, one or more vents led to flues which heated up the rooms closest to the kitchen. It was a simple and different type of central heating. In the same way, water could be heated in a large boiler adjoining the hearth. And along the wall above the hearth was often a long, narrow trough for drying malt to brew beer.

A separate oven for baking was usually attached to this central heating plant. The baking oven was often constructed so that it was possible to light a fire inside it, being made of natural stone or brick to enable the maximum amount of heat to be retained. When the temperature of the oven was high enough, the fire was left to burn out, and then the ashes were removed, the oven was brushed clean, and the risen dough was put in. In some places the oven door was sealed or blocked to preserve the heat better. This kind of functional kitchen was mainly found on large farms and estates. The kitchens of the common people had the simplest type of fireplace, even if many of them also had a flue and a boiler.

The first improvement since the Middle Ages to the standard of the kitchen occurred in the eighteenth century with the introduction, in the United States, of the cast-iron stove. Its design was inspired by Benjamin Franklin, and it was consequently called the "Franklin stove". It arrived in Europe some decades later and in places acquired the name "cannon stove", which referred to the large cylindrical mantle characteristic of the design. One practical detail was the round top, which had a small lid and several rings to enable the cook to adapt the size of the hole to the pan in use. This idea turned up later in the kitchen range, which was first manufactured in Central Europe in the 1820s. The practical, efficient kitchen range had been developed gradually. The first version was just a top of cast iron, equipped with legs or built into the open hearth. On the top there were holes for pans and, often, a grate for grilling. Then the top was given sides, and after that it was a short step to a separate enclosed fire. The first kitchen ranges often had gridirons.

The kitchen range was one of the first products of mechanical engineering to find its way into the kitchen, and in most countries this took place in the middle of the nineteenth century. A few decades earlier, in some places even earlier than that, mass-produced cutlery had become widely available. The most successful products of Christopher Polhem's manufacturing works at Stjernsund in the early eighteenth century were plates and cutlery of tin-plated iron. In France knives and forks were made on a semi-industrial scale around the middle of the same century.

When town gas was introduced around 1800 in France and Great Britain this source of energy was tried both for heating and cooking. Gas networks were developed, mainly in the larger British cities, although gas was mainly intended for lighting large, commercial premises for, in an ordinary home, the dangerous, stinking products of combustion were unbearable. Efficient burners did not come until the 1840s, and it was some time before these were accepted, since people were very sceptical about gas light. It is indicative of the time that the Crystal Palace in London, built for the world exhibition in 1851, did not have gas light. The exhibition, a spectacular monument of contemporary technical progress, closed every day at sunset!

In 1855, the German chemist R. W. Bunsen (1811–99) presented a new burner design, in which the gas was mixed with air before being ignited. This made the flame hotter and burnt the gas completely. The Bunsen burner was originally intended for chemical laboratories (where, ever since its invention, it has formed part of the standard equipment), and it was a long time before the principle of the burner was applied to gas cookers. In Britain, the gas cooker had its breakthrough in the 1870s, and this resulted in a great boom both for the gasworks industry and for the industry that manufactured cookers, lamps, and other equipment. During the following decades, gas technology became one of the most important of British exports. But it did not last very long; gas light was soon overtaken by electric lighting.

The first real machine to enter the home was the sewing-machine. It appeared around 1850 in Britain and the United States, and a few years later in other countries. Wherever it was introduced it was hailed as a sensation, with huge headlines in the newspapers. In the textile industry, a high degree of mechanization had been achieved, while the budding clothing industry occupied large numbers of seamstresses, mainly employed in workshops where large quantities of shirts, blouses, and other garments were made manually.

The first working sewing-machine was patented in 1846 by a Boston instrument maker, Elias Howe (1819–67). In the early 1840s, when Howe was young and newly married, he, like so many other men in the same situation, had problems making ends meet. His pretty young wife had to work at home making dresses to order; this was monotonous, tiring work. In his workshop, Howe heard of sewing-machines and was told that they did not work. He then resolved to build a machine which could sew better and faster than the most skilful seamstress. After a lot of hard work, he finished his machine in 1846 and proudly invited potential manufacturers and financiers to a public showing of the miracle. But those who came were the tailors of Boston, who feared that the sewing-machine would take the bread from their mouths! Howe had to run for safety, and the tailors demolished both his machine and the contents of the room.

In other words, the climate in Boston was not too favourable for sewing-machine manufacture. Howe had the good sense to launch the machine in England instead. His success was beyond his expectations and was the result of some skilful marketing which included competitions to determine whether a whole team of dressmakers or one single person using a sewing-machine could get results faster. This was the right approach in the country which gave the world the concept of "sportsmanship". There was no rebellion, either among tailors or seamstresses. The swift triumph of the sewing-machine in Great Britain was repeated in the United States, as Howe had reckoned, and manufacture soon started on both sides of the Atlantic.

Let us not delve too deeply into the continued development of the sewing-machine for the time being and just state that the sewing-machines of today, with their transistorized automation, are little wonders of technology. Instead, let us refer to the enormous impact the sewing-machine has had on the progress of the light engineering industry. Once the original patents had expired, many people started to manufacture sewing-machines. Competition was extremely sharp, and the manufacturers who survived were those who managed to design and manufacture reliable and durable machines. The sewing-machine, with all its moving parts, could not have come at a better time from the point of view of kinematics, which was the current fashion in design technology, and many eminent engineers were attracted by it. Only a few decades after Howe's breakthrough, the market was able to offer machines that were surprisingly reliable for the time, due mainly to the contribution of the German-American Isaac M. Singer (1811–76).

During the last decades of the nineteenth century, as has been mentioned above, bicycle and sewing-machine manufacturers became by far the largest consumers of ball-bearings, something which meant a lot to the development of the ball-bearing industry. Several leading sewing-machine manufacturers also contributed to the technical development of precision-made interchangeable parts—an area in which the armaments industry is generally considered to have been pioneering. Over the years, several arms companies branched out into sewing-machine manufacture. The sewing-machine industry has also encouraged the production of very durable materials with high resistance to wear and tear; for example, powder metallurgical materials and methods to a large extent have been developed within this industry.

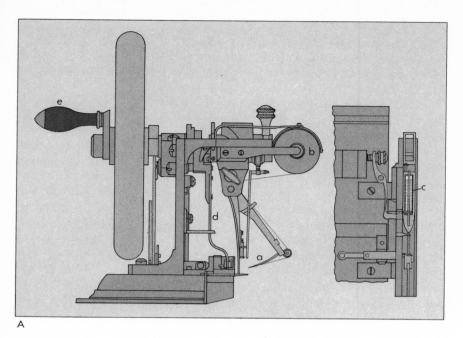

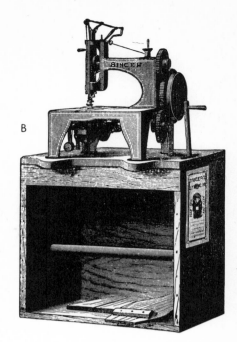

A Elias Howe's lock-stitch sewing-machine. The cloth was fixed on needles mounted along the edge of the baster plate, a thin metal strip. The plate had a row of holes in which a cog-wheel engaged and moved it forward as each stitch was completed. When a seam as long as the plate had been sewn, the plate had to be moved back to its original position and a new length of cloth attached to it. The machine used a bent needle (a) with the eye at the pointed end. (b) Thread reel. The shuttle (c) was given a reciprocating movement by a picker (d), which—like the needle on its lever and the baster plate—had its movements controlled by cams on a shaft which was rotated manually by means of a crank (e).

B In Singer's first sewing-machine, the cloth was fed by an inter-mittently rotating, serrated wheel.

The presser foot was spring-loaded, and the needle had a rectilinear movement.

C Chain-stitch machine by the American James Perry in 1858.

D A modern sewing-machine; explanatory sketch. (a) Wheel for the belt from the engine. (b) Belt,

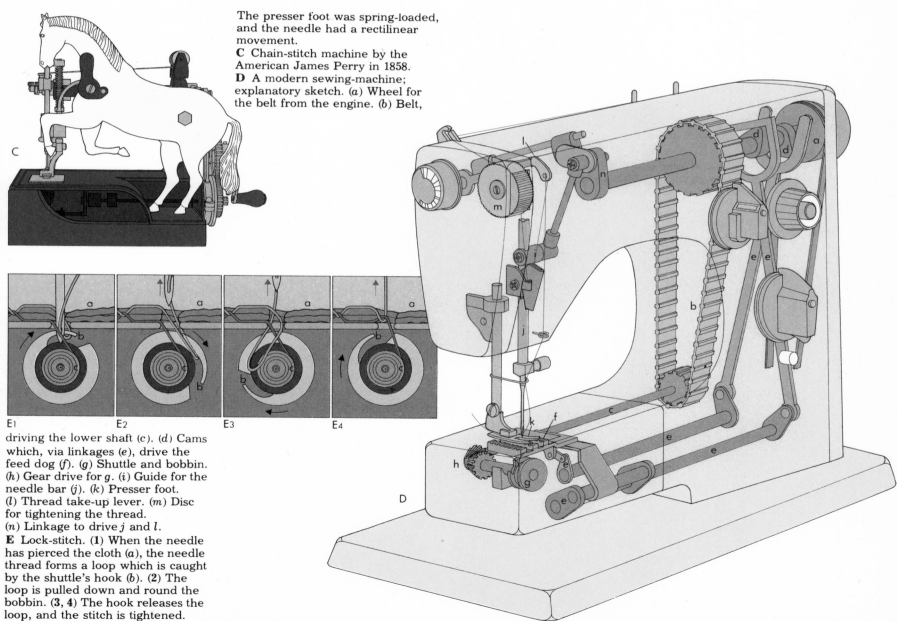

driving the lower shaft (c). (d) Cams which, via linkages (e), drive the feed dog (f). (g) Shuttle and bobbin. (h) Gear drive for g. (i) Guide for the needle bar (j). (k) Presser foot. (l) Thread take-up lever. (m) Disc for tightening the thread. (n) Linkage to drive j and l.

E Lock-stitch. **(1)** When the needle has pierced the cloth (a), the needle thread forms a loop which is caught by the shuttle's hook (b). **(2)** The loop is pulled down and round the bobbin. **(3, 4)** The hook releases the loop, and the stitch is tightened.

A

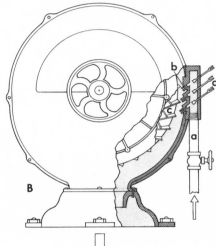

B

C

A In this American printing-works, the machines were driven by a central water engine, built by Backus Bros. & Co.
B A cutaway drawing of a water engine. Water entered through a pipe (*a*), was forced through nozzles (*b*) towards the buckets (*c*) of the rotating wheel, and finally left through the bottom of the motor. The motor's effect could be varied by closing one or two of the nozzles by means of plungers (*d*).
C According to the advertisements, water engines, or motors, were excellent power sources for all sorts of household machinery.

The Water Engine

The 1870s saw the introduction of a power source which, today, is entirely forgotten, namely, the water engine. It was connected to the water mains and became widespread, especially in cities and areas with favourable water rates.

At the Centennial Exposition in Philadelphia in 1876, different water engines for powering sewing-machines were shown. Most of these engines were designed basically like the Pelton turbine, but there were other types, too. The manufacturers' catalogues describe how more and more domestic machines driven by water engines appeared during the following decades. Fans were introduced at an early stage, as were cream whippers; washing-machines, clothes wringers, ice-cream machines, and many other machines then followed in rapid succession. Water engines were also used in other areas, for instance, for driving bellows for church organs. Larger models with turbine wheels of diameters up to 50 in (125 cm), were used for driving machines in mechanical workshops, printing works, bakeries, and so on. They were also used for driving hand-rope elevators of a type common in the United States around the turn of the century.

The manufacture of water engines ceased during the First World War. New water rates and the competition provided by small electrical engines contributed to the demise of this episode in the history of power engines—an episode which, nevertheless, lasted for about half a century!

The Electric Era

''Epoch'' or ''epoch-making'' are often abused words, but once the public had gained access to electricity, their living conditions changed radically, and one can really talk about the beginning of a new epoch which saw the transformation of the home and, especially, of the kitchen.

It has often been said that domestic electrical appliances appeared at the same time as the first electric power-station, Edison's ''package solution'', which came into operation in 1882. But the first patent on an electric cooking utensil was, in fact, taken out as early as 1874 by the Englishman St. George Lane-Fox, who is also one of the many inventors of the light bulb. This might suggest that all kinds of cooking and heating apparatuses got off to a flying start when electric power distribution was introduced. This, however, was not the case, mainly because there were no suitable materials available for the resistor elements which were needed to convert the electric current into heat. In 1890, the Carpenter Company in America introduced an element consisting of fine silver-plated threads embedded in an enamel element, which was at first used in domestic irons, the first electric appliance to break through on a large scale. In 1891, the same company introduced a whole range of electric saucepans, coffee makers, and so on; they were put on display under the slogan ''the electric kitchen'' at the world exhibition in London the same year. The British firm Crompton & Company became licensees of Carpenter's appliances but then, after about a year, started their own development programme, which made them pioneers in this area.

In 1894, a restaurant with a kitchen that was fully electric opened in New York. It was shown to the guests, which is indicative of the great enthusiasm at this time for electricity as a source of heat: it was clean, hygienic, and efficient. Electricity made it possible to apply heat exactly where it was required and where it would be most useful. And there was no soot.

Enthusiasm was, however, considerably subdued by the fact that, initially, electricity was rather expensive, Edison's first customers having to pay as much as 28 cents per kWh, even if their consumption was low. They had only two kinds of light bulbs to choose between—giving 8 or 16 candlepower—and, so far, there were no electrical appliances to connect. When the first municipal electric power-station was put into operation in Stockholm in 1888, the price of energy was about 18 cents per kWh. In those days, people learnt to have the light on in a room when they were actually in it!

In spite of the price of electrical energy, all the "electric heat appliances" (which was the official term) which we have today existed as early as the mid-1890s. But the resistor elements of the early appliances had several shortcomings. After they had been used for some time, the enamel in them became brittle and broke easily. Some important progress was made in 1907, when a new resistor material was patented in the United States. It was a nickel-chrome alloy, which could be heated up to 1,000°C without oxidizing or deforming, and it opened the possibility of producing all kinds of durable cooking appliances, including good electric toasters. The first one consisted of a horizontal open tray with nickel-chrome wire stretched zigzag under a grille. Around 1910, electric cookers appeared in the United States; the first models could be described as connected hot plates. After the First World War, the electric cooker was introduced in Europe. It had a baking oven and often a warming compartment, too. The first electric baking ovens were not much appreciated, since they needed constant watching. Not until 1930 were the ovens equipped with thermostats, so that the desired temperature could be set beforehand and the oven left to look after itself.

In the early 1930s, yet another resistor material came onto the market. It was called Kanthal and had been developed by the Swedish metallurgist Hans von Kanzow, who patented it in 1926. It consisted of an alloy of iron, chromium, and aluminium and could withstand temperatures of at least 1,400°C. The material soon found a wide application as a resistor material in domestic heat appliances, as did the material which came later, Kanthal Super, which consists of molybdenum silicon compounds and can withstand temperatures of up to 1,700°C. Kanthal Super has also been used for industrial electric furnaces and other industrial heat appliances.

Domestic Appliances of the Electric Era

The sewing-machine was the first domestic appliance of the electric era to be electrified. Singer introduced the first electrically powered sewing-machine in 1889, but it was another twenty years or so before electric power took over completely. Around 1890, the first electrically driven fans appeared on the market. Devices for air conditioning, that is, air cooling, were not produced until the end of the 1930s in the United States.

The vacuum cleaner, one of our most common domestic appliances, took so to speak the long way round before it entered the home. The first practicable vacuum cleaner was designed and patented by the Englishman Hubert Cecil Booth in 1901, but various patents of similar machines had already been granted in, for example, Great Britain, the United States, and France. At the turn of the century, some very bizarre designs appeared for machines which, intended to make house-cleaning easier, could be operated by one person only. The inventors very likely found their inspiration for these in the *fin de siècle* style of interior decoration then so popular among the upper classes, a style that was a dreadful dust-collector. At the time, a reception room was more of a textile-hung cave than a room!

The main problem for the vacuum-cleaner designers was the motor. Electric motors for devices with small energy consumption were still both heavy and bulky, and therefore, it was easier to go the whole way and concentrate on large-scale devices. During the first

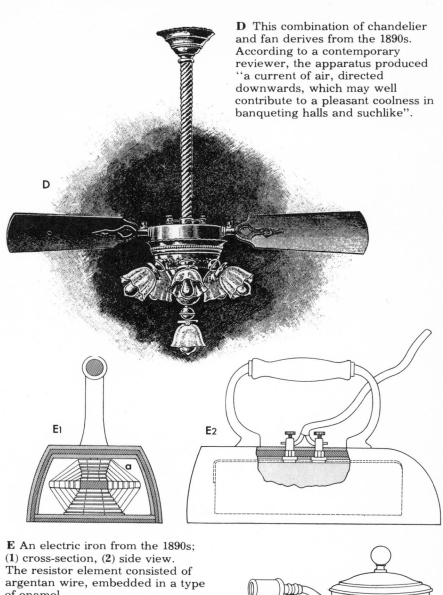

D This combination of chandelier and fan derives from the 1890s. According to a contemporary reviewer, the apparatus produced "a current of air, directed downwards, which may well contribute to a pleasant coolness in banqueting halls and suchlike".

E An electric iron from the 1890s; (1) cross-section, (2) side view. The resistor element consisted of argentan wire, embedded in a type of enamel.
F "Electric tea-urns" of this type were manufactured by AEG in Berlin in the 1890s. The resistor element was situated round and beneath the inner water-container.
G Even electric frying-pans were sold in the 1890s to those lucky few who were able to make use of the newfangled source of power.

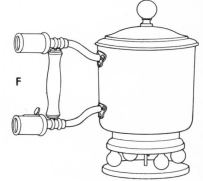

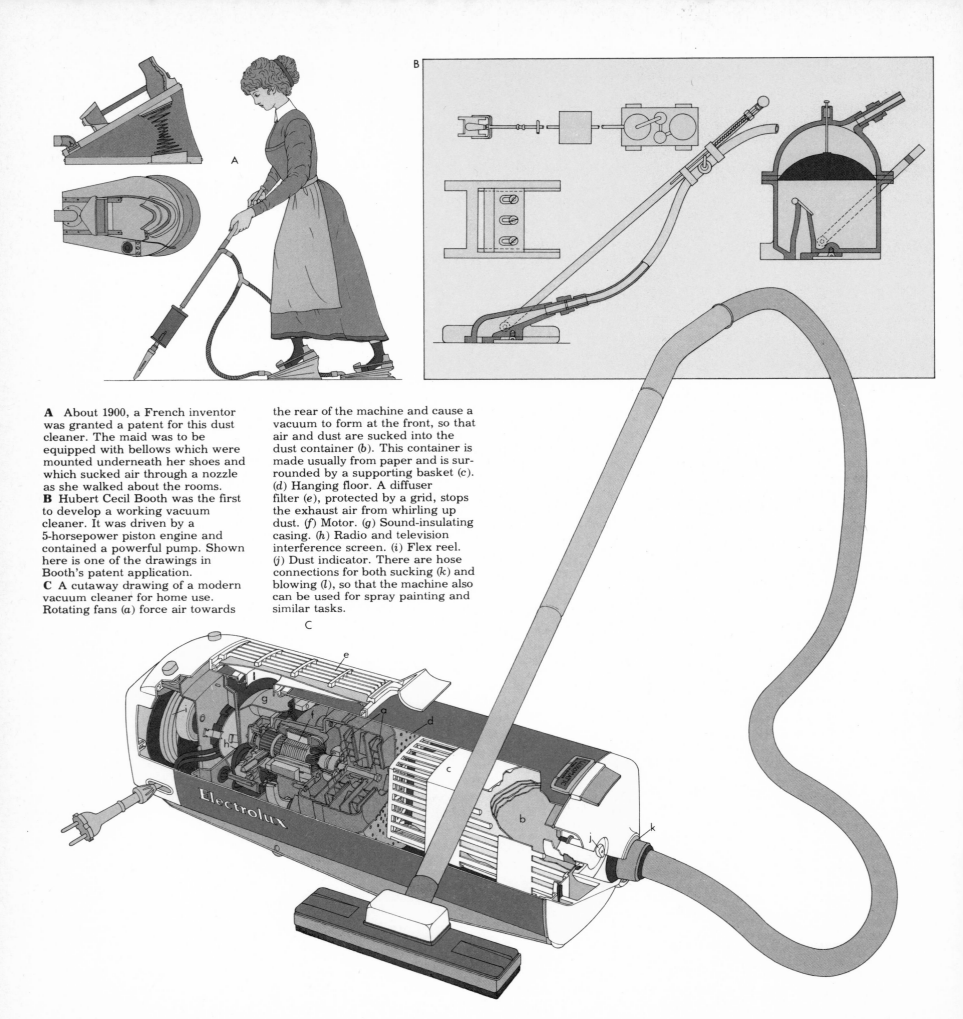

A About 1900, a French inventor was granted a patent for this dust cleaner. The maid was to be equipped with bellows which were mounted underneath her shoes and which sucked air through a nozzle as she walked about the rooms.
B Hubert Cecil Booth was the first to develop a working vacuum cleaner. It was driven by a 5-horsepower piston engine and contained a powerful pump. Shown here is one of the drawings in Booth's patent application.
C A cutaway drawing of a modern vacuum cleaner for home use. Rotating fans (*a*) force air towards

the rear of the machine and cause a vacuum to form at the front, so that air and dust are sucked into the dust container (*b*). This container is made usually from paper and is surrounded by a supporting basket (*c*). (*d*) Hanging floor. A diffuser filter (*e*), protected by a grid, stops the exhaust air from whirling up dust. (*f*) Motor. (*g*) Sound-insulating casing. (*h*) Radio and television interference screen. (*i*) Flex reel. (*j*) Dust indicator. There are hose connections for both sucking (*k*) and blowing (*l*), so that the machine also can be used for spray painting and similar tasks.

years of the twentieth century, several companies in Great Britain and Central Europe made some large machines for installation in the basements of blocks of flats and public buildings. The suction was caused by a piston pump, and there were suction hoses built into the walls. Each apartment or group of rooms had one or more connections to the suction system, and the extracted dust was filtered through water-flushed filters at the suction pump.

The first vacuum cleaners designed by Booth were rather heavy and expensive. But Booth was as good at selling as he was at designing, and he gained some royal support. One of his first jobs was to vacuum-clean the carpet used in Westminster Abbey for the coronation of Edward VII. Booth went on to vacuum-clean Buckingham Palace—to the great satisfaction of Queen Alexandra—and continued his triumphant course to Kaiser Wilhelm in Berlin, to Czar Nicolas in St. Petersburg, and to the Turkish Sultan Abdul Hamid II.

Just as the vacuum cleaner had ceased to be a curious novelty and had become a luxury item instead, a young Swedish businessman out walking in Vienna came across one. The year was 1908, the man's name was Axel Wenner-Gren (1881–1961). He bought the vacuum cleaner, which cost £55 ($275) and weighed 88 lb (40 kg), and took it with him back to Stockholm, determined to produce a machine that could be handled easily and marketed at a reasonable price. A few years later, Wenner-Gren and his designers introduced the new vacuum cleaner. It weighed only 13 lb (6 kg), cost £15 ($75), and appeared on the market in 1913. Wenner-Gren was certainly not alone in having this business idea, but his vacuum cleaner had a technically new component, the closed fan, which gave the machine a very powerful suction. Such fans are now used in practically all types of vacuum cleaner.

The problem of storing foodstuffs in such a way that they keep longer has been with mankind ever since the early Stone Age. It was discovered in some of the ancient cultures that food keeps longer in a cool than in a warm place, and a means of making ice was also known. When the cities of the Indus culture were excavated, "ice factories" were found—thousands of moulds with covers, made of unglazed porous stoneware. These moulds were filled with water and covered, sprinkled with water, and fanned by a whole bevy of slaves. The evaporation thus brought about caused the temperature in the moulds to fall below freezing point. Unglazed earthen vessels are still in use in Africa and India to cool drinking water. Alexander the Great had huge ice cellars built to safeguard the food for his troops during the long siege of Petra in 329 BC. In ancient Rome, ice was used to cool both food and drink. The ice was taken in the winter from lakes in the Alps, was packed in straw, and transported to the Eternal City. The Romans also knew the art of making freezing mixtures. If, for example, one portion of salt is mixed with ten portions of crushed ice, the temperature of the mixture will be about −10°C.

During the seventeenth and eighteenth centuries, when the natural sciences had begun to flourish, there were many who attempted to construct freezing machines. Various experiments were made with air pumps, after Otto von Guericke had built a workable pump in about 1650. A bowl of water was placed in a vessel, from which the air was pumped out. The temperature of the water then sank so much that it would even freeze. But no one succeeded in explaining the phenomenon. The theoretical basis of thermodynamics was not formulated in an intelligible manner until the nineteenth century (see page 160).

What the scientists dreamed about was a machine that could make ice, demand for which was constantly increasing. But the only source of ice was in nature, and from the middle of the nineteenth century onwards, and well into the twentieth, ice was an important item of trade. Great Britain imported ice from Norway at an early stage, and by the 1850s, an ice company in London had bought a spring lake with clear and pure water near Dröbak on Oslo Fjord. The trade name of the company's product was "Norwegian Crystal Ice", and it was sold in large quantities for several decades.

The Swedes also exported ice to Great Britain, but their main customers were in the United States, especially in New York and the other East Coast cities. It was mainly fishermen on Lake Väner and Lake Vätter who cut up ice in the winter and transported it down the Göta Canal to Gothenburg, whence it was shipped to New York, where it dominated the market. There were, to be sure, several methods known at the end of the nineteenth century for making ice artificially, but this product was never commercially competitive. However, the winter of 1890–91 was an unusually mild one in Sweden, and the following summer in the United States was unusually long and hot. The outcome was a severe shortage of ice in New York, the artificial-ice manufacturers did good business, and the development of freezing machines was stimulated. After this, the export of ice from Sweden to New York declined to nothing after a few years.

The foundations of modern cooling technology were laid in the 1870s in the brewing industry. In Munich, the Bavarian beer capital, they had great problems keeping the beer from spoiling during the summer months. In 1870, a young professor at the Polytechnicum in Munich, Karl von Linde (1842–1920), started experiments on a cooling process which was based on the main principles of thermodynamics. After three years, he had completed an experimental plant which was installed in the Sedlmayr brewery and gave very promising results. After having added further improvements to the plant, von Linde founded a company for making cooling units, on an industrial scale, based on the compression and expansion of a cooling agent, ammonia.

The 1870s saw the introduction of another important novelty in cooling technology, the first refrigerator ship, the *Frigorifique*, which, in 1877, sailed between Buenos Aires in the Argentine and Rouen in France, loaded with meat. The cooling unit on board had been designed by the French engineer Charles Tellier (1828–1913) and was based on the other main principle for the mechanical production of cold, that is, the absorption principle.

Von Linde's and Tellier's cooling devices were both primarily designed to cool large quantities, and the size of the plants reflected this. Not until well into the twentieth century was it realized that it was possible to build cooling devices on a smaller scale. The first refrigerator with a compressor device was made in Chicago in 1913 and was marketed under the name of Domelse. The cabinet was made of wood and had a compressor unit mounted on top, but it did not find any wide application. Iceboxes were well established, and the distribution of household ice was efficiently organized. Only in the 1920s did the manufacture of refrigerators start on a large scale, first in the United States and then in Europe.

Mild winters in Sweden in the early 1920s led to a severe lack of ice and inspired two engineers at the Tekniska Högskolan in Stockholm to develop a new cooling process based on the absorption principle but working without any moving parts. In simplified terms, when the cooling agent, ammonia, was heated, it evaporated and started to circulate. The next step was to let the ammonia condense and then vaporize again in a hydrogen atmosphere. This drew heat from the air in the refrigerator. The whole unit was hermetically sealed and heated by gas or electricity.

The two designers, Baltzar von Platen and Carl Munters, turned to the then well-established vacuum-cleaner manufacturer Axel Wenner-Gren, who bought the invention. Von Platen and Munters

A

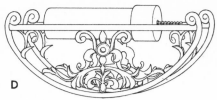

D

E Von Platen's and Munters's absorption refrigerator; (1) explanatory sketch, (2) the unit as mounted in a cupboard. The machine consisted of a closed tube system without movable parts and worked in the following way: a coiled tube (*a*) was heated electrically or by a gas flame. Ammonia water in the tube then started to boil, and the ammonia evaporated. Water and gaseous ammonia left through the top end of the pipe, and whereas the water dripped into the boiler (*b*), the gaseous ammonia escaped through a pipe (*c*) and into the water-cooled condenser (*d*), where it was condensed to liquid ammonia, which ran into a generator (*e*) inside the cupboard (*f*). Hydrogen, too, was introduced into *e*, and the ammonia thus vaporized at a low temperature. For this process, heat was needed, and it was taken from the inside of the cupboard. The

B1

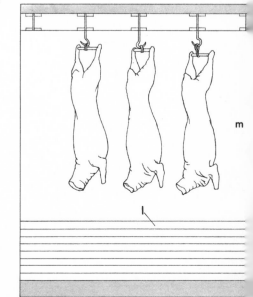

C

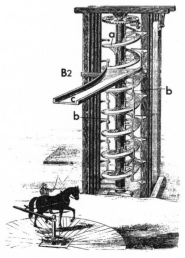

B2

A This ice-sawing machine, driven by a steam-engine, was constructed in the early 1880s by an American named Sauncry A. Sager.
B In the nineteenth century, ice was stored in large store-houses (1), where the blocks were placed a couple of inches apart (to give room for drainage and ventilation) and were covered with hay. The ice was sometimes brought up to the correct level by horse-powered screw elevators (2) The ice blocks were then placed at the bottom of the screw (*a*) behind vertical rods (*b*). When the screw rotated to the left, the blocks slid upwards until they reached a vertically adjustable slide

(*c*), on which they slid into the storehouse.
C An ice machine from the middle of the 1870s. It was a compressortype machine, and it worked according to the same principle as the refrigerating plant shown at F.
D An early ice machine for home use. In the container were chemical solutions, and the water to be frozen was poured into a small container which was inserted into the larger one. When the machine was set rocking, a chemical reaction which consumed heat was started, and the necessary heat was taken from the water in the inner container.

mixture of hydrogen and gaseous ammonia then sank, because of its weight, and passed on through a pipe (g) to the absorber (h), in which the ammonia was dissolved in water while the hydrogen passed on through a pipe (i) and back to the generator to be mixed again with ammonia. Since heat was released when the ammonia was absorbed by the water, the absorber was surrounded by a water jacket (j) so that the process would not come to a halt. The ammonia water then passed through a pipe (k), which ran partly inside another pipe (l). The hot water which had given off ammonia in the boiler (b) ran through the latter pipe, and gave off its heat to the ammonia water in k while running towards h to reabsorb ammonia. The ammonia water in k was thus already preheated before entering the coiled tube (a) to be heated. (m) Coolant supply and drainage. Ammonia was used as a cooling medium because it is readily absorbed by water. At average room temperature and normal air pressure, one litre of water can absorb about 660 litres of gaseous ammonia. It is also easy to free the ammonia from the water again by heating the solution. Hydrogen, on the other hand, is not water soluble.

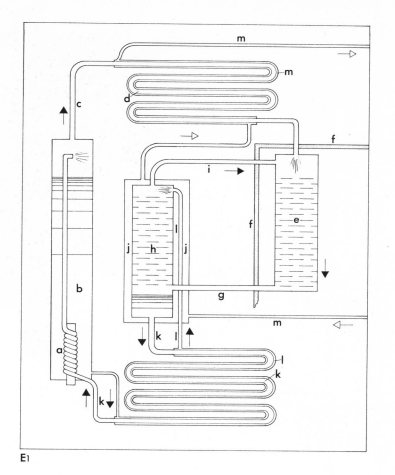

E1

E2

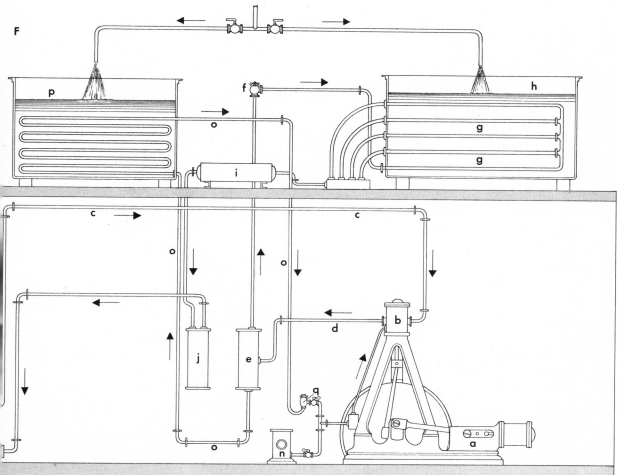

F

F It is possible to produce refrigeration by evaporating liquid ammonia at low pressure. This is the principle of the compressor refrigerator. Here is one from the end of the nineteenth century. A steam-engine (a) drives a pump (b) which sucks in gaseous ammonia from one pipe (c) and delivers it in compressed form into another (d). Via a container (e), the gas is led through a check valve (f) and into pipes (g) in a water chest (h). There, the compressed gas is transformed to a liquid and runs via two containers (i, j) down through a check valve (k) and into the generator (l), where the pressure is low and the liquid ammonia evaporates once more. The heat needed for this process is taken from the chamber (m) which is to be kept cold. The gaseous ammonia then flows through a pipe (c) back to the pump (b), which is lubricated by oil from a tank (n). The oil extracted from the pump by the passing compressed gas is again separated from it in e and runs through a pipe (o) which passes through a water chest (p). Finally, the oil passes through a sieve (q) before returning to the pump.

finished an experimental version of their cooling machine in 1923, but the invention was not announced until New Year, 1925. One Stockholm newspaper headlined: "No lack of ice this summer".

In the 1930s, different brands of refrigerator became common in most industrial countries. As a rule, the temperature in a refrigerator is 4–8°C, but as early as the 1920s, several manufacturers started to equip their refrigerators with smaller freezing compartments with a temperature of some degrees below freezing point. These were mainly intended for freezing ice-cubes. Attempts were also made to see whether it was possible to store food for any length of time by cooling it to a temperature which was considerably lower than that of the refrigerator. This freezing technique was developed mainly in the United States during the Second World War. It was discovered that most types of food, after quick freezing to −18° or lower, would keep for at least six months.

Deep-freezing technology had a rapid breakthrough in the United States during the years after the War, and in Europe in the 1950s. It caused major changes within the food industry: modes of production, packing techniques, and distribution systems had to be reorganized, the retail trade had to get deep freezes, and so on. And to domestic households the new technique brought considerable changes. Before the appearance of the deep freeze, most countries had had very few vegetables available all year round. Today, fruit and vegetables are frozen in southern Europe, for example, and transported to the north; or are frozen in Florida and southern California and supplied to the rest of North America and even to Europe. Frozen vegetables are available all year round, often as semi-finished products, so that the cooking takes very little time.

Handling the household laundry used to be a labour consuming task, and attempts to mechanize it were made at an early stage. In Christopher Polhem's model chamber there are a couple of different "mechanical" washing-machines, promoted by Polhem but not too successful on the market. In the middle of the nineteenth century, several models of washing-machine were introduced both in Great Britain and the United States. Large steam-driven laundries also started to appear in Great Britain at that time. These became common in the United States in the early twentieth century, and the technology developed for these became the basis of the domestic washing-machine. As early as the 1920s, the large American laundries were highly automated. The first domestic washing-machines appeared around 1930 and were equipped with a programmer for what is today called semi-automatic drive. Considerable improvements of the programmer were made in the early 1930s by Seeburg & Co. in Chicago, a company which was one of the leading juke-box manufacturers in the United States. The juke box, of course, is also a highly automated machine! The basic product of Seeburg & Co., however, sold badly during the depression of the 1930s, and the company then concentrated on programmers for automatic washing-machines. But it was not until the late 1940s that the washing-machine came into common use.

Along with the new electrically powered domestic machines which became popular in the 1930s and 1940s, a new concept was also created: domestic appliances. Many more of these have appeared since then: different kinds of electric mixers, percolators, liquidizers, dish washers, and can openers, to name but a few. Even the electric coffee-mill made a brief guest appearance on the market.

We have frequently mentioned the increased leisure time which is a result of the appearance of machines. But do we really need machines in our leisure time? It seems like the anticlimax of mechanization, but many people want to use their spare time to produce things, and why should they not take advantage of modern labour-saving equipment—electric drills, hobby lathes, etc.?

A A wool-washing machine constructed by Polhem in the early eighteenth century. The drum is covered with a net of canvas yarn, so that the wool is pulled from the tub and worked between the drum and the upper roll, which was hand-cranked. It is possible to vary the roll's pressure against the drum by putting weights on the board at the bottom.

B An electric washing-machine of the 1920s, made in Germany. The laundry was placed in a perforated drum (*a*), and water and detergent were added. Then the lid (*b*) was put on, and a fire was lit in the furnace (*c*) underneath the machine. An electric motor (*d*) was switched on and rotated the drum alternately in one direction or the other. (*e*) Drainage pump.

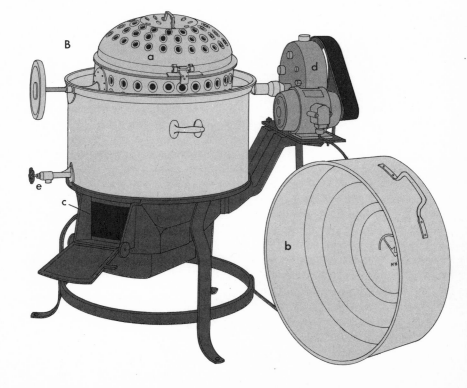

C

D1   D2

C A steam-powered washing-machine which was used in the middle of the nineteenth century at St. Pancras Workhouse in London.

D Around the middle of the nineteenth century, this washing-machine (1) was constructed in Germany. It was intended for home use and was—as can be seen—manually operated. On the turnable disc was a number of spring-loaded pegs (2) which worked the laundry mechanically when the disc was repeatedly thrust down into the tub.

E Cutaway view of a modern, front-loading, cylinder-type washing-machine. It has a rotating inner drum (*a*), which is perforated so that the detergent solution can pass through it, and a fixed drum (*b*). The inner drum regularly changes its direction of rotation, so that the laundry will not become entangled. The machine can be programmed for different types of washing by means of two controls (*c*). (*d*) Dispensers for detergent and conditioner. The door (*e*) is automatically locked by an electro-magnet when the machine is started. When a button (*f*) is pressed, the electricity is cut off and the lock is released. (*g*) Counterweight to balance (*b*). (*h*) Controls. (*i*) Suspension springs for *b*. (*j*) Support for *a*'s shaft. (*k*) Ball bearings. (*l*) Belt pulley for driving *a*. (*m*) Drive belt. (*n*) Heater. (*o*) Drainage pump. (*p*) Shock absorber. (*q*) Filter. (*r*) Access panel for *q*. (*s*) Thermostat sensor. (*t*) Motor.

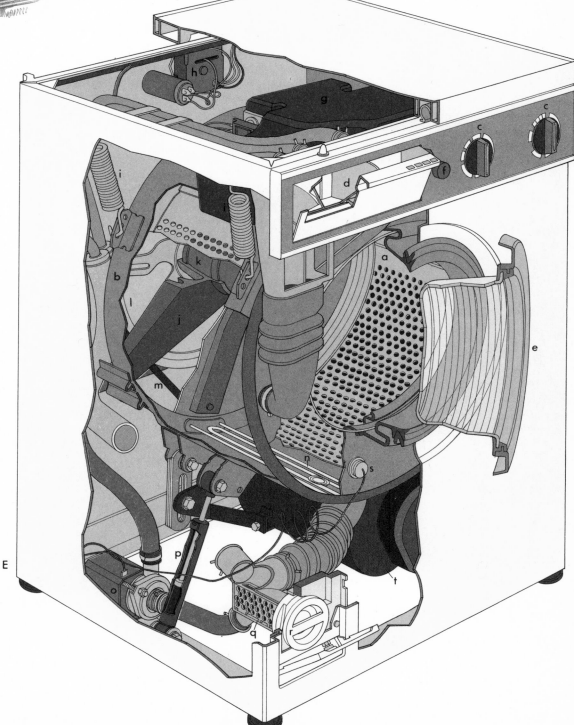

E

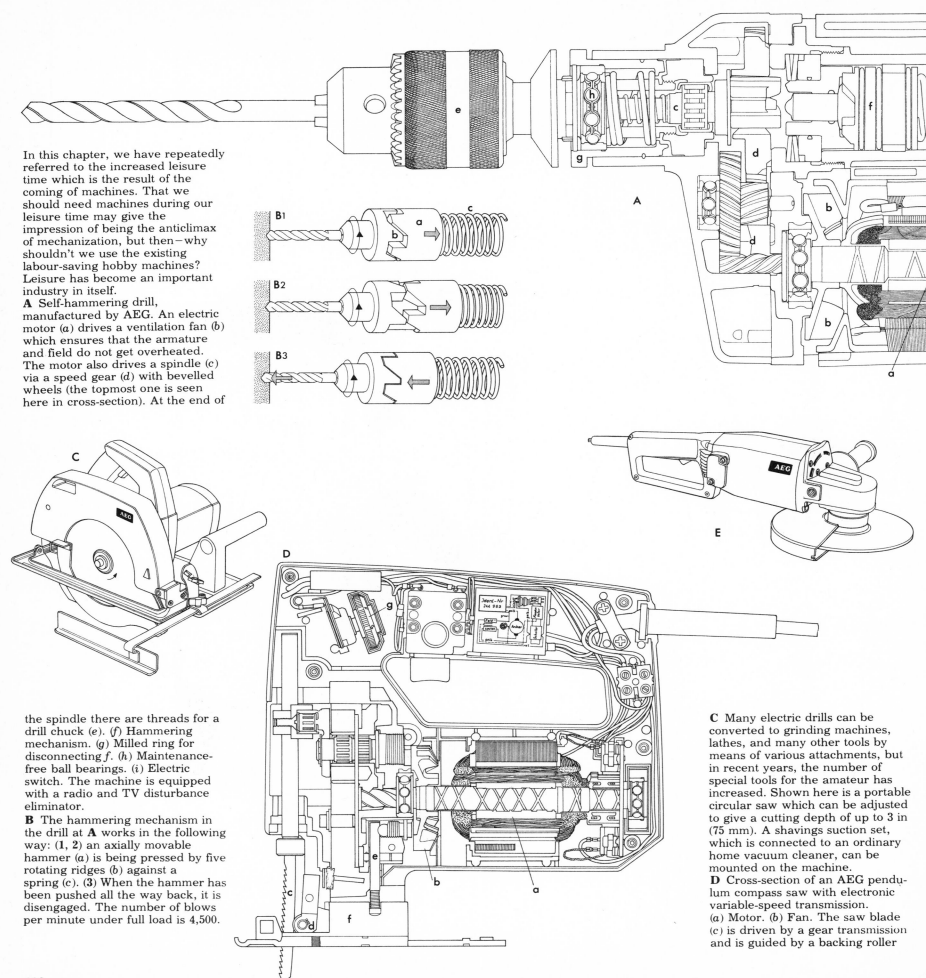

In this chapter, we have repeatedly referred to the increased leisure time which is the result of the coming of machines. That we should need machines during our leisure time may give the impression of being the anticlimax of mechanization, but then—why shouldn't we use the existing labour-saving hobby machines? Leisure has become an important industry in itself.

A Self-hammering drill, manufactured by AEG. An electric motor (a) drives a ventilation fan (b) which ensures that the armature and field do not get overheated. The motor also drives a spindle (c) via a speed gear (d) with bevelled wheels (the topmost one is seen here in cross-section). At the end of

the spindle there are threads for a drill chuck (e). (f) Hammering mechanism. (g) Milled ring for disconnecting f. (h) Maintenance-free ball bearings. (i) Electric switch. The machine is equipped with a radio and TV disturbance eliminator.

B The hammering mechanism in the drill at **A** works in the following way: (**1, 2**) an axially movable hammer (a) is being pressed by five rotating ridges (b) against a spring (c). (**3**) When the hammer has been pushed all the way back, it is disengaged. The number of blows per minute under full load is 4,500.

C Many electric drills can be converted to grinding machines, lathes, and many other tools by means of various attachments, but in recent years, the number of special tools for the amateur has increased. Shown here is a portable circular saw which can be adjusted to give a cutting depth of up to 3 in (75 mm). A shavings suction set, which is connected to an ordinary home vacuum cleaner, can be mounted on the machine.

D Cross-section of an AEG pendulum compass saw with electronic variable-speed transmission. (a) Motor. (b) Fan. The saw blade (c) is driven by a gear transmission and is guided by a backing roller

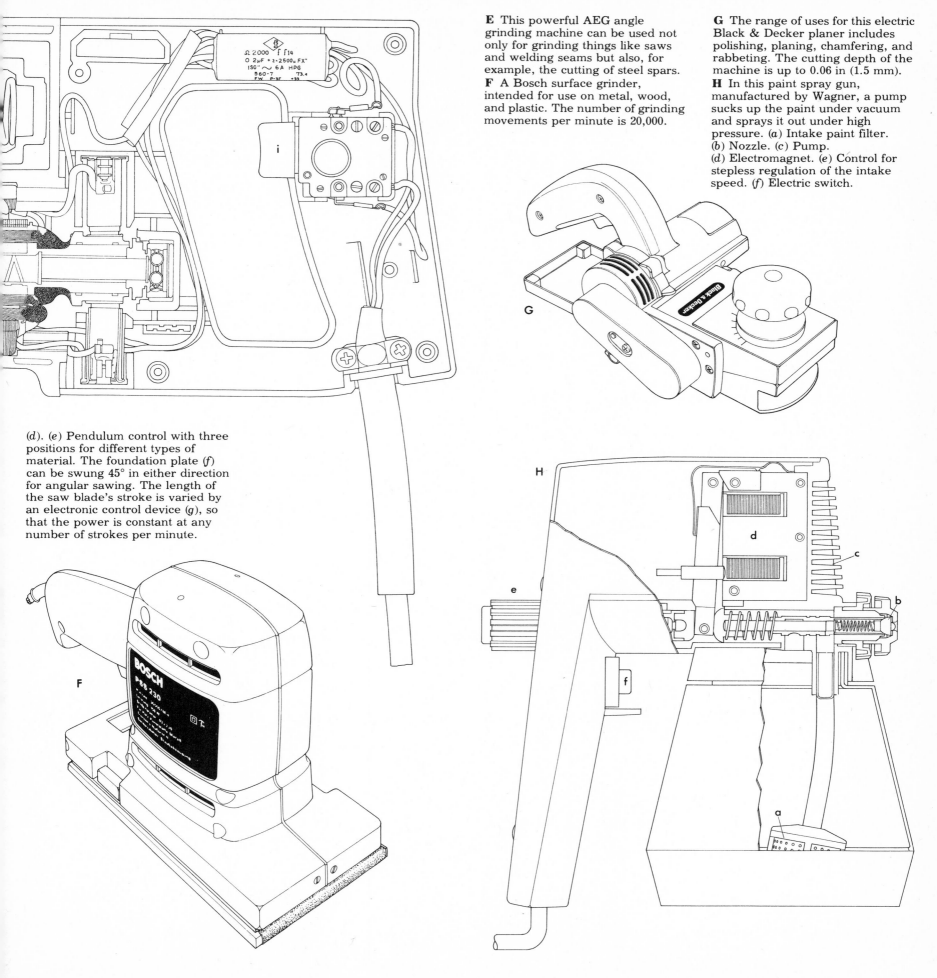

E This powerful AEG angle grinding machine can be used not only for grinding things like saws and welding seams but also, for example, the cutting of steel spars.
F A Bosch surface grinder, intended for use on metal, wood, and plastic. The number of grinding movements per minute is 20,000.

G The range of uses for this electric Black & Decker planer includes polishing, planing, chamfering, and rabbeting. The cutting depth of the machine is up to 0.06 in (1.5 mm).
H In this paint spray gun, manufactured by Wagner, a pump sucks up the paint under vacuum and sprays it out under high pressure. (*a*) Intake paint filter. (*b*) Nozzle. (*c*) Pump. (*d*) Electromagnet. (*e*) Control for stepless regulation of the intake speed. (*f*) Electric switch.

(*d*). (*e*) Pendulum control with three positions for different types of material. The foundation plate (*f*) can be swung 45° in either direction for angular sawing. The length of the saw blade's stroke is varied by an electronic control device (*g*), so that the power is constant at any number of strokes per minute.

233

BIBLIOGRAPHY

General

CHARLES SINGER, (ed.) et al., *A History of Technology*, Vol. I–V. New York, London 1954 ff.

M. DAUMAS, (ed.), *Histoire Générale des Techniques*, Vol. I–IV. Paris 1962 ff.

ARTUR FÜRST, *Das Weltreich der Technik*, Vol. I–V. Berlin 1927 ff.

M. KRANZBERG, C. W. PURSELL JR, *Technology in Western Civilization*, Vol. I–II. New York 1967.

W. STEIN, *Kulturfahrplan*. Munich 1974.

Chapter 1

R. J. FORBES, *Man the Maker*. London 1958.

ALBERT NEUBURGER, *Die Technik des Altertums*. Leipzig 1919.

FRANZ MARIA FELDHAUS, *Die Technik der Antike und des Mittelalters*. Leipzig 1931.

W. FLINDERS PETRIE, *The Arts and Crafts of Ancient Egypt*. London 1910.

AHMED FAKHRY, *The Pyramids*. Chicago 1961.

CURT MERCKEL, *Die Ingenieurtechnik im Alterthum*. Berlin 1899 (facsimile edition: Hildesheim 1969).

A. VARAGNAC, *La Conquête des Energies*. Paris 1972.

KENNETH P. OAKLEY, *Man the Toolmaker*. London 1972.

HENRY KJELLSON, *Forntidens teknik*. Third edition: Uppsala 1973. – *Försvunnen teknik*. Third edition: Uppsala 1973.

Chapter 2

GEORGE SARTON, *A History of Science*, Vol. I–II. Cambridge, Mass., 1959.

ABBOT PAYSON USHER, *A History of Mechanical Inventions*. Fourth edition: London 1970.

A. G. DRACHMANN, *Antikkens teknik*. Copenhagen 1950.

DEREK DE SOLLA PRICE, *Gears from the Greeks; The Antikythera Mechanism – A Calendar Computer from c. 80 B. C.* Philadelphia 1974.

JOSEPH NEEDHAM, *Science and Civilization in China*, Vol. I–IV. Cambridge 1965 ff.

MARSHALL CLAGGETT, *The Science of Mechanics in the Middle Ages*. Madison, Wisc., 1961.

WILLIAM A. JOHNSSON, *Christopher Polhem, The Father of Swedish Technology*. Hartford, Conn., 1963.

SAMUEL BUTLER, *Erewhon, or Over the Range*. London 1872.

JACQUES POLIERI, *Scénographie Nouvelle*. Boulogne 1963.

Chapter 3

LEWIS MUMFORD, *Technics and Civilization*. New York 1934.

FRANZ REULEAUX, *Theoretische Kinematik. Grundzüge einer Theorie des Maschinenwesens*. Braunschweig 1895.

EUGENE S. FERGUSON, *Kinematics since the Time of Watt*. Washington 1962.

WALTHER RATHENAU, *Von kommenden Dingen*. Berlin 1917.

GEORG and PAUL AMBER, *Anatomy of Automation*. Englewood Cliffs 1962.

JOHN DIEBOLD, *Automation. The Advent of the Automatic Factory*. New York 1952.

BERTRAND GILLE, *Les Ingénieurs de la Renaissance*. Paris 1964.

HERMANN HALLENDORFF, *Slagsten och automat*. Stockholm 1967.

Chapter 4

R. S. KIRBY et al, *Engineering in History*. New York 1956.

FRANZ MARIA FELDHAUS, *Die Maschine im Leben der Völker*. Basel 1954.

GÖSTA E. SANDSTRÖM, *Byggarna*. Stockholm 1964.
 – *Sextusen år under jorden*. Stockholm 1964.
 – *The History of Tunneling*. London 1963.

R. KELLERMAN, W. TREUE, *Die Kulturgeschichte der Schraube*. Munich 1962.

Chapter 5

WALTER KIAULEHN, *Die eisernen Engel*. Berlin 1935.

H. W. DICKINSON, *A Short History of the Steam Engine*. Second edition: London 1963.

E. J. HOBSBAWM, *Industry and Empire*. London 1969.

TORSTEN ALTHIN, *Gustaf de Laval – de höga hastigheternas man*. Stockholm 1953.

Chapter 6

JOHN AMBROSE FLEMING, *Fifty Years of Electricity*. London 1921.

P. DUNSHEATH, *A History of Electrical Engineering*. London 1961.

Chapter 7

A. CHAPUIS, E. DROZ, *Les Automates*. Zürich 1949.

HELMUT SVOBODA, *Der künstliche Mensch*. Munich 1967.

WERNER ZUR MEGEDE, *Am Wege zur Automation*. Berlin 1974.

OTTO MAYR, *The Origins of Feedback Control*. London 1970.

Chapter 8

PH. and E. MORRISON (ed.), *Charles Babbage and his Calculating Engines*. New York 1961.

WALTER R. FUCHS, *Knaurs Buch der Denkmaschinen*. 1968.

THOMAS P. HUGHES, *Elmer Ambrose Sperry, Inventor and Engineer*. New York 1970.

WILLY LEY, *Rakete und Raumschiffahrt*. Berlin 1944. (Revised edition: *Vorstoss im Weltall, Rakete und Raumschiffahrt*. Wien 1949.)

Chapter 9

W. H. G. ARMYTAGE, *A Social History of Engineering*. London 1961.

M. KRANZBERG, J. GIES, *By the Sweat of Thy Brow*. New York 1974.

W. T. O'DEA, *The Meaning of Engineering*. London 1961.

VICTOR J. DANILOV (ed.), *The Future of Science and Technology*. Chicago 1976.

STUART CHASE, *Men and Machines*. London 1929.

NIGEL CALDER, *Technopolis*. London 1929.

JACQUES ELLUL, *La Technique ou l'Enjeu du Siècle*. Paris 1954.

INDEX

235

237

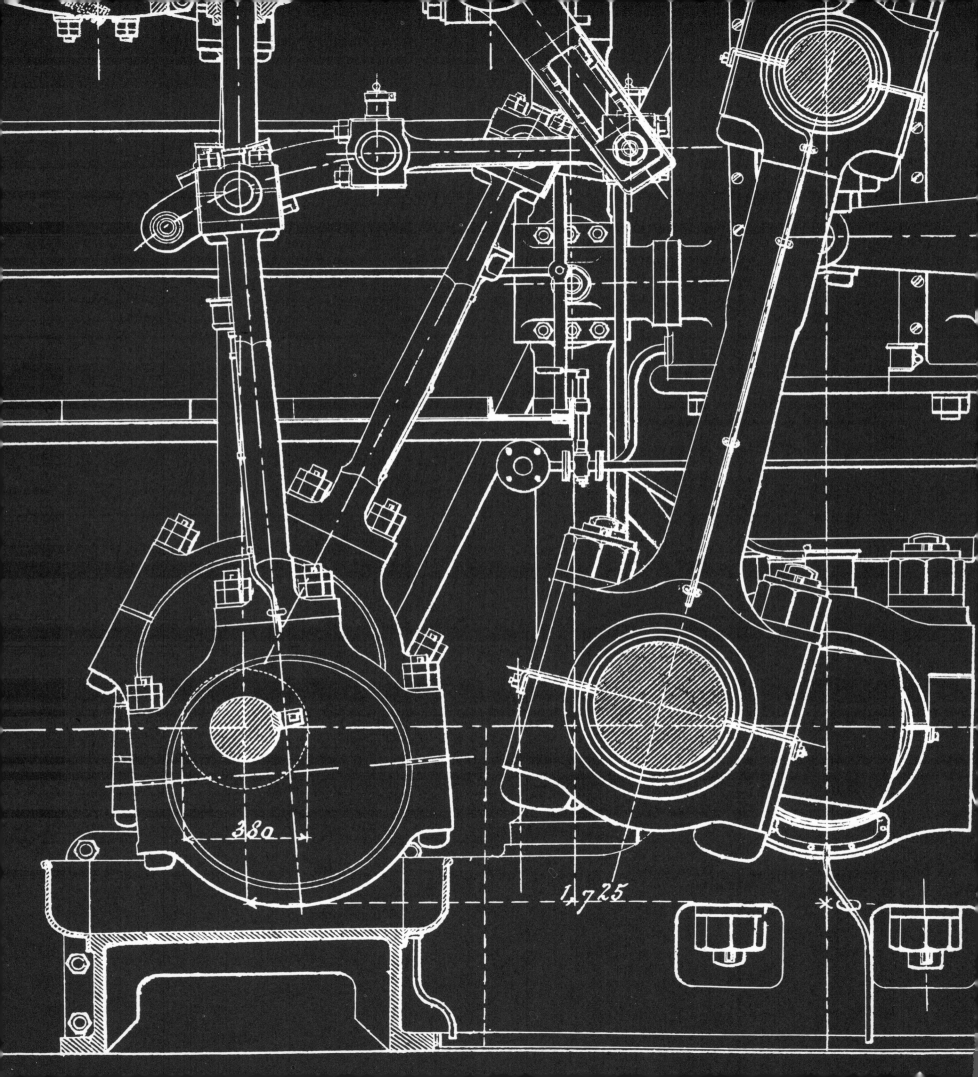